Scott Foresman · Addison Wesley

enVisionMATH™ Texas

Scott Foresman • Addison Wesley

enVisionMATH™

Texas

Authors

Randall I. Charles
Professor Emeritus
Department of Mathematics
San Jose State University
San Jose, California

Janet H. Caldwell
Professor of Mathematics
Rowan University
Glassboro, New Jersey

Mary Cavanagh
Mathematics Consultant
San Diego County Office of Education
San Diego, California

Dinah Chancellor
Mathematics Consultant with Carroll ISD
Southlake, Texas
Mathematics Specialist with Venus ISD
Venus, Texas

Juanita V. Copley
Professor
College of Education
University of Houston
Houston, Texas

Warren D. Crown
Associate Dean for Academic Affairs
Graduate School of Education
Rutgers University
New Brunswick, New Jersey

Francis (Skip) Fennell
Professor of Education
McDaniel College
Westminster, Maryland

Kay B. Sammons
Coordinator of Elementary Mathematics
Howard County Public Schools
Ellicott City, Maryland

Jane F. Schielack
Professor of Mathematics
Associate Dean for Assessment and
Pre K-12 Education, College of Science
Texas A&M University
College Station, Texas

William Tate
Edward Mallinckrodt Distinguished
University Professor in Arts & Sciences
Washington University
St. Louis, Missouri

John A. Van de Walle
Professor Emeritus, Mathematics Education
Virginia Commonwealth University
Richmond, Virginia

Consulting Mathematicians

Edward J. Barbeau
Professor of Mathematics
University of Toronto
Toronto, Canada

Sybilla Beckmann
Professor of Mathematics
Department of Mathematics
University of Georgia
Athens, Georgia

David Bressoud
DeWitt Wallace Professor of Mathematics
Macalester College
Saint Paul, Minnesota

Gary Lippman
Professor of Mathematics and Computer Science
California State University East Bay
Hayward, California

Editorial Offices: Glenview, Illinois • Parsippany, New Jersey • New York, New York
Sales Offices: Boston, Massachusetts • Duluth, Georgia • Glenview, Illinois
Coppell, Texas • Sacramento, California • Mesa, Arizona

Consulting Authors

Stuart J. Murphy
Visual Learning Specialist
Boston, Massachusetts

Jeanne Ramos
Secondary Mathematics Coordinator
Los Angeles Unified School District
Los Angeles, California

Verónica Galván Carlan
Private Consultant Mathematics
Harlingen, Texas

ELL Consultants/Reviewers

Jim Cummins
Professor
The University of Toronto
Toronto, Canada

Alma B. Ramirez
Sr. Research Associate
Math Pathways and Pitfalls WestEd
Oakland, California

Texas Reviewers

Norma Dorado Armijo
Math Coach
El Paso Independent School District

José Rafael Cantú
Teacher
Jose Antonio Navarro Elementary
McAllen ISD

Aimee M. Delaney
Teacher
Aldine ISD

Cassandra R. Fulton
Teacher
Lancaster ISD

Debra Gibson
Math Specialist
Lubbock ISD

Sherry M. Johnson
Teacher
Round Rock ISD

Nelda R. Lujan
Teacher
Frisco ISD

Kim Mayo
Math Specialist
Houston ISD

Kristine Quisenberry
Teacher
McKinney ISD

Courtney J. Ridlehuber
Teacher
Mansfield ISD

Paulette Savoie-Speyrer
Campus Lead Teacher
Katy ISD

Tricia Shaughnessy
Teacher
San Antonio ISD

Nancy Shock
Teacher
Conroe ISD

Rebecca Spikes
Teacher
Fort Worth ISD

Anne Turner
Teacher
Klein ISD

Christe Warner
Math Specialist
Alief ISD

Debbie Wells
Math Facilitator
Victoria ISD

Elba Armandina Williams –Alejandro
Mathematics Curriculum Coach
Austin ISD

Scott Foresman • Addison Wesley

ISBN-13: 978-0-328-27276-1
ISBN-10: 0-328-27276-0

3 4 5 6 7 8 9 10 V042 12 11 10 09 08

Scott Foresman • Addison Wesley

enVisionMATH Texas

Topic Titles

Table of Contents

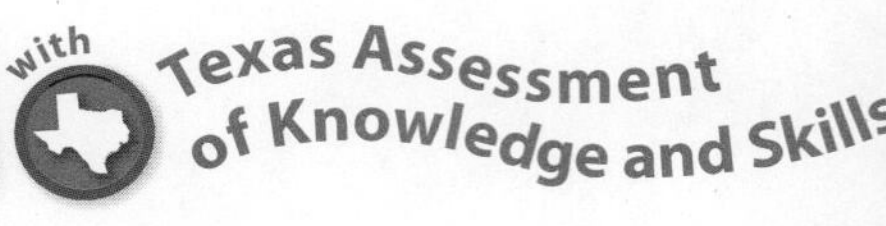

TAKS OBJECTIVE COLORS

TAKS Objective 1	Number and Operations
TAKS Objective 2	Algebraic Thinking
TAKS Objective 3	Geometry
TAKS Objective 4	Measurement
TAKS Objective 5	Probability and Statistics
TAKS Objective 6	Problem Solving

Underlying Processes and Mathematical Tools, which includes problem solving, are infused throughout all lessons.

TAKS Objective 1

Topic 1 Numeration (TEKS 3.1A, 3.1B, 3.1C)

TAKS Objective 1

Topic 2 Addition Number Sense

(TEKS 3.3A, 3.3B, 3.5A, 3.5B)

TAKS Objective 1

Topic 3 Adding Whole Numbers to Solve Problems

(TEKS 3.3A, 3.5A, 3.5B)

TAKS Objective 1

Topic 4 Subtraction Number Sense (TEKS 3.3A, 3.3B, 3.5A, 3.5B)

TAKS Objective 1

Topic 5 Subtracting Whole Numbers to Solve Problems (TEKS 3.3A, 3.3B, 3.5A, 3.5B)

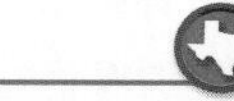

TAKS Objective 1

Topic 6 Multiplication Meanings (TEKS 3.4A)

TAKS Objectives 1 & 2

Topic 7 Multiplication Fact Strategies: Use Patterns (TEKS 3.4A, 3.4B, 3.6B)

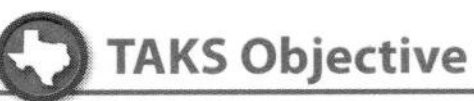

TAKS Objective 1

Topic 8 Multiplication Fact Strategies: Use Known Facts (TEKS 3.4A, 3.4B)

TAKS Objectives 1 & 2

Topic 9 Multiplication Patterns and Number Sense (TEKS 3.4B, 3.5A, 3.6B)

TAKS Objectives 1 & 2

Topic 10 Division Meanings and Facts (TEKS 3.4C, 3.6C)

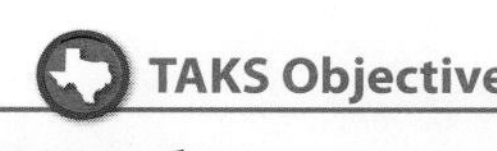

TAKS Objective 1

Topic 11 Fraction Concepts
(TEKS 3.2A, 3.2B, 3.2C, 3.2D)

TAKS Objective 2

Topic 12 Patterns and Relationships
(TEKS 3.6A, 3.7A, 3.7B)

TAKS Objective 3

Topic 13 Whole Numbers and Fractions on the Number Line
(TEKS 3.2B, 3.10)

TAKS Objective 3

Topic 14 Solids and Shapes
(TEKS 3.8)

TAKS Objective 3

Topic 15 Congruence and Symmetry (TEKS 3.9A, 3.9B, 3.9C)

TAKS Objective 4

Topic 16 Estimating and Measuring Length (TEKS 3.11A)

TAKS Objective 4

Topic 17 Perimeter and Area (TEKS 3.11B, 3.11C)

TAKS Objective 4

Topic 18 Volume, Capacity, Weight, and Mass (TEKS 3.11D, 3.11E, 3.11F)

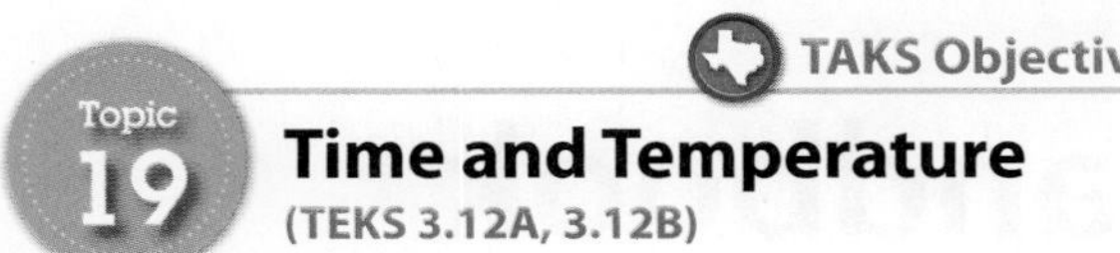

Topic 19 Time and Temperature

TAKS Objective 4

(TEKS 3.12A, 3.12B)

Topic 20 Data, Graphs, and Probability

TAKS Objective 5

(TEKS 3.13A, 3.13B, 3.13C)

Student Resources

Problem-Solving Handbook

Use this Problem-Solving Handbook throughout the year to help you solve problems.

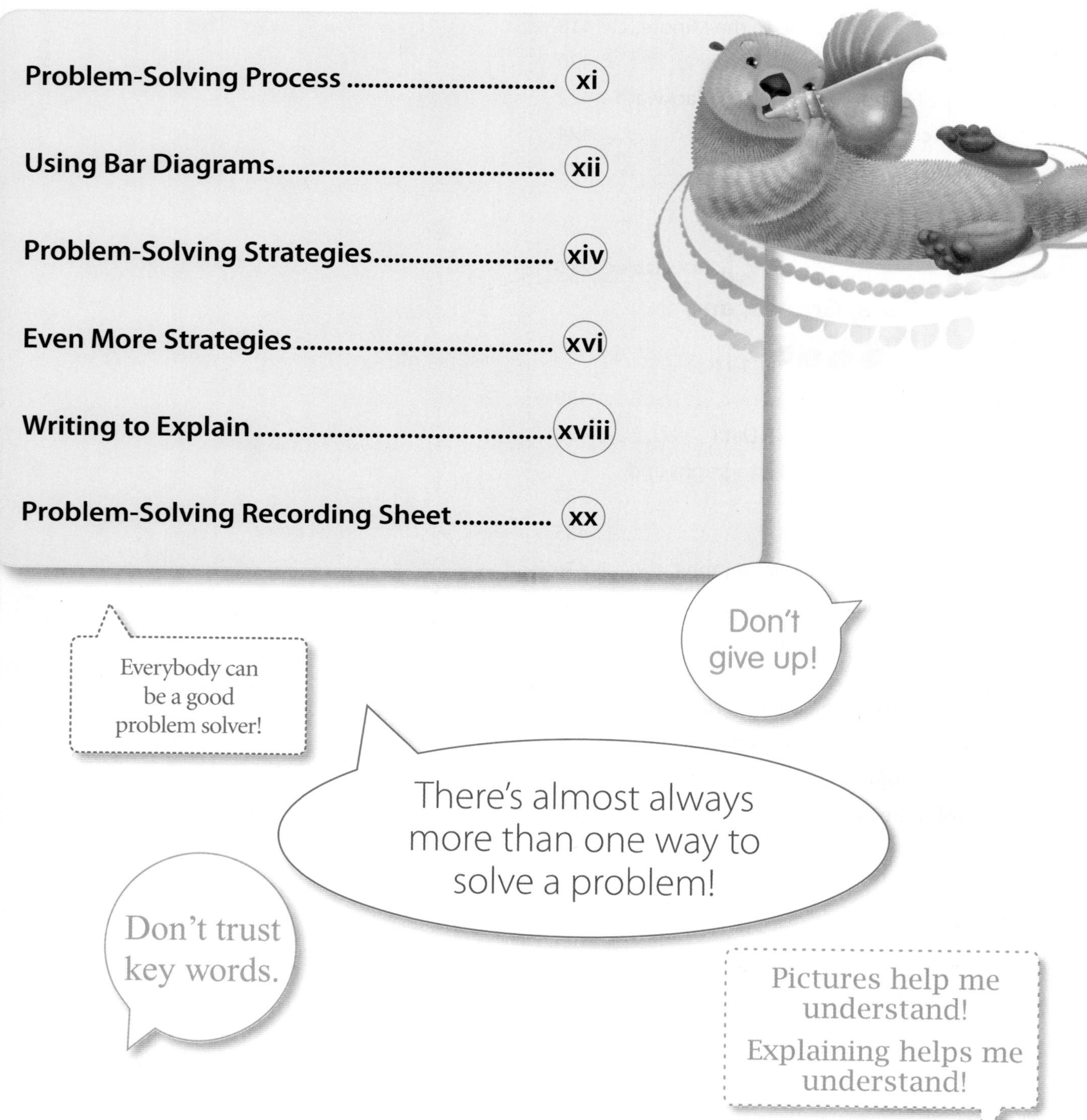

Problem-Solving Process

Read and Understand

What am I trying to find?
- Tell what the question is asking.

What do I know?
- Tell the problem in my own words.
- Identify key facts and details.

Plan and Solve

What strategy or strategies should I try?

Can I show the problem?
- Try drawing a picture.
- Try making a list, table, or graph.
- Try acting it out or using objects.

How will I solve the problem?

What is the answer?
- Tell the answer in a complete sentence.

Strategies

- Show What You Know
  - Draw a Picture
  - Make an Organized List
  - Make a Table
  - Make a Graph
  - Act It Out/ Use Objects
- Look for a Pattern
- Try, Check, Revise
- Write a Number Sentence
- Use Reasoning
- Work Backward
- Solve a Simpler Problem

Look Back and Check

Did I check my work?
- Compare my work to the information in the problem.
- Be sure all calculations are correct.

Is my answer reasonable?
- Estimate to see if my answer makes sense.
- Make sure the question was answered.

Using Bar Diagrams

Use a bar diagram to show how what you know and what you want to find are related. Then choose an operation to solve the problem.

Problem 1

Carrie helps at the family flower store in the summer. She keeps a record of how many hours she works. How many hours did she work on Monday and Wednesday?

Carrie's Work Hours

Data

Days	Hours
Monday	5
Tuesday	3
Wednesday	6
Thursday	5
Friday	5

Bar Diagram

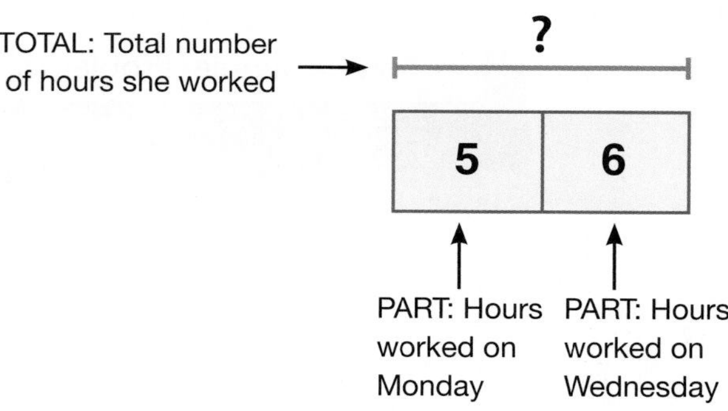

5 + 6 = ?

I can add to find the total.

Problem 2

Kim is saving to buy a sweatshirt for the college her brother attends. She has $9. How much more money does she need to buy the sweatshirt?

Bar Diagram

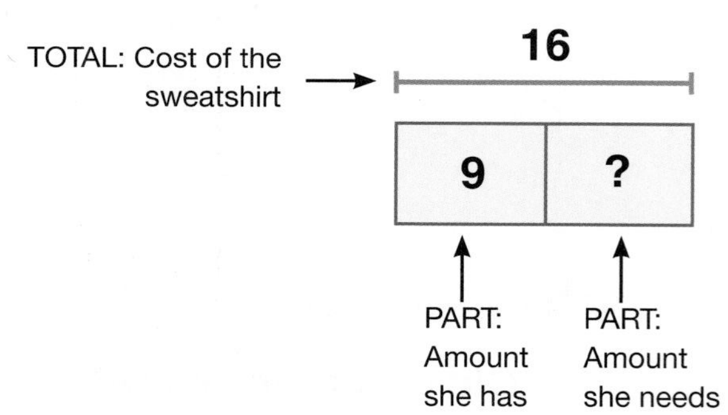

16 − 9 = ?

I can subtract to find the missing part.

Pictures help me understand!

Don't trust key words!

Problem 3

Tickets to a movie on Saturday cost only $5 each no matter what age you are. What is the cost of tickets for a family of four?

Bar Diagram

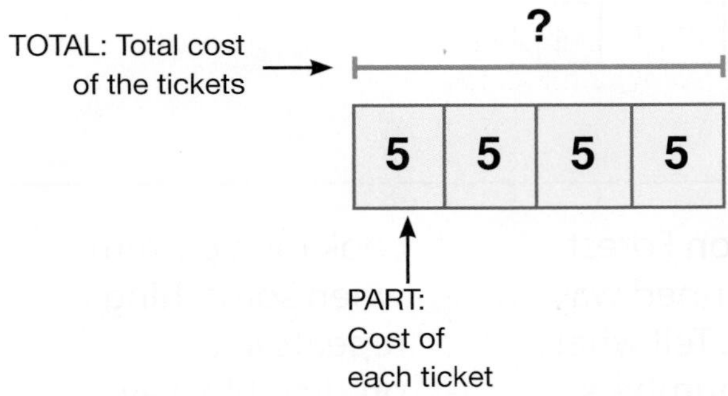

$$4 \times 5 = ?$$

I can multiply because the parts are equal.

Problem 4

Twelve students traveled in 3 vans to the zoo. The same numbers of students were in each van. How many students were in each van?

Bar Diagram

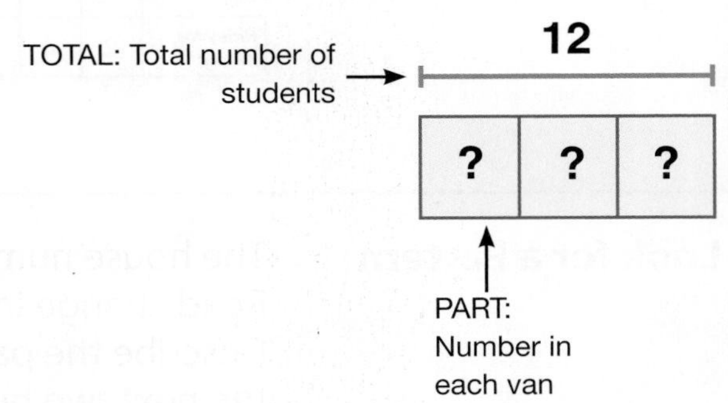

$$12 \div 3 = ?$$

I can divide to find how many are in each part.

Problem-Solving Strategies

Strategy	Example	When I Use It
Draw a Picture	The race was 5 kilometers. Markers were at the starting line and the finish line. Markers showed each kilometer of the race. Find the number of markers used. Start Line — Finish Line Start Line, 1 km, 2 km, 3 km, 4 km, Finish Line	Try drawing a picture when it helps you visualize the problem or when the relationships such as joining or separating are involved.
Make a Table	Phil and Marcy spent all day Saturday at the fair. Phil rode 3 rides each half hour and Marcy rode 2 rides each half hour. How many rides had Marcy ridden when Phil rode 24 rides?	Try making a table when: • there are 2 or more quantities, • amounts change using a pattern.
Look for a Pattern	The house numbers on Forest Road change in a planned way. Describe the pattern. Tell what the next two house numbers should be. 3, 6, 10, 15, ?, ?	Look for a pattern when something repeats in a predictable way.

Rides for Phil	3	6	9	12	15	18	21	24
Rides for Marcy	2	4	6	8	10	12	14	16

Everybody can be a good problem solver!

Strategy	Example	When I Use It
Make an Organized List	How many ways can you make change for a quarter using dimes and nickels? 1 quarter = 1 dime + 1 dime + 1 nickel 1 dime + 1 nickel + 1 nickel + 1 nickel 1 nickel + 1 nickel + 1 nickel + 1 nickel + 1 nickel	Make an organized list when asked to find combinations of two or more items.
Try, Check, Revise	Suzanne spent \$27, not including tax, on dog supplies. She bought two of one item and one of another item. What did she buy? \$8 + \$8 + \$15 = \$31 \$7 + \$7 + \$12 = \$26 \$6 + \$6 + \$15 = \$27	Use Try, Check, Revise when quantities are being combined to find a total, but you don't know which quantities. Dog Supplies Sale! Leash .... \$8 Collar .... \$6 Bowls .... \$7 Medium Beds .... \$15 Toys \$12
Write a Number Sentence	Maria's new CD player can hold 6 discs at a time. If she has 54 CDs, how many times can the player be filled without repeating a CD? Find 54 ÷ 6 = ■.	Write a number sentence when the story describes a situation that uses an operation or operations.

Even More Strategies

Strategy	Example	When I Use It
Act It Out	How many ways can 3 students shake each other's hand?	Think about acting out a problem when the numbers are small and there is action in the problem you can do.
Use Reasoning	Beth collected some shells, rocks, and beach glass. **Beth's Collection** 2 rocks 3 times as many shells as rocks 12 objects in all How many of each object are in the collection?	Use reasoning when you can use known information to reason out unknown information.
Work Backward	Tracy has band practice at 10:15 A.M. It takes her 20 minutes to get from home to practice and 5 minutes to warm up. What time should she leave home to get to practice on time? Time Tracy leaves home ? ← 20 minutes ← Time warm up starts ← 5 minutes ← Time practice starts **10:15**	Try working backward when: • you know the end result of a series of steps, • you want to know what happened at the beginning.

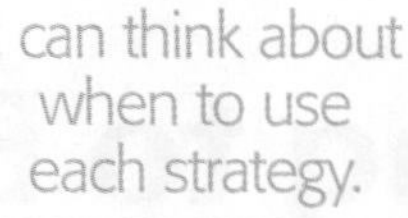

Strategy	Example	When I Use It
Solve a Simpler Problem 	Each side of each triangle in the figure at the left is one centimeter. If there are 12 triangles in a row, what is the perimeter of the figure? I can look at 1 triangle, then 2 triangles, then 3 triangles.  perimeter = 3 cm 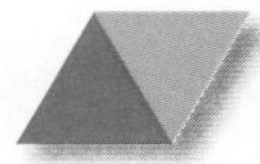 perimeter = 4 cm  perimeter = 5 cm	Try solving a simpler problem when you can create a simpler case that is easier to solve.
Make a Graph	Mary was in a jump rope contest. How did her number of jumps change over the five days of the contest? 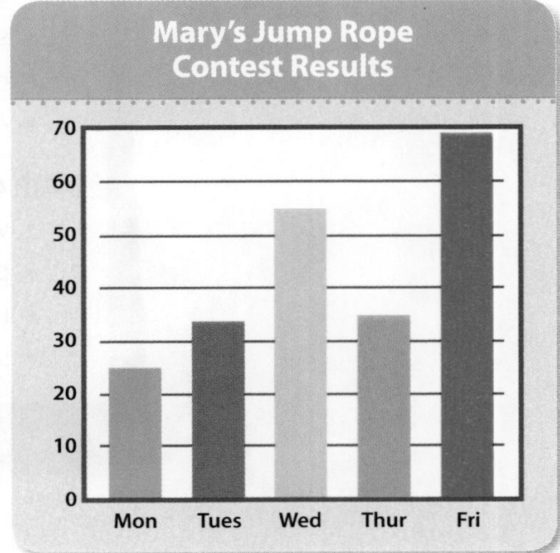	Make a graph when: • data for an event are given, • the question can be answered by reading the graph.

Writing to Explain

Here is a good math explanation.

Writing to Explain What happens to the area of the rectangle if the lengths of its sides are doubled?

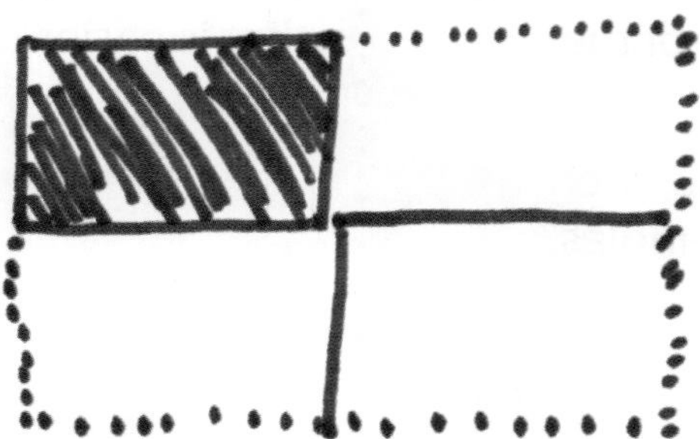

▨ = $\frac{1}{4}$ of the whole rectangle

The area of the new rectangle is 4 times the area of the original rectangle.

Tips for Writing Good Math Explanations....

A good explanation should be:

- correct
- simple
- complete
- easy to understand

Math explanations can use:

- words
- pictures
- numbers
- symbols

This is another good math explanation.

Writing to Explain Use blocks to show 3 × 24. Draw a picture of what you did with the blocks.

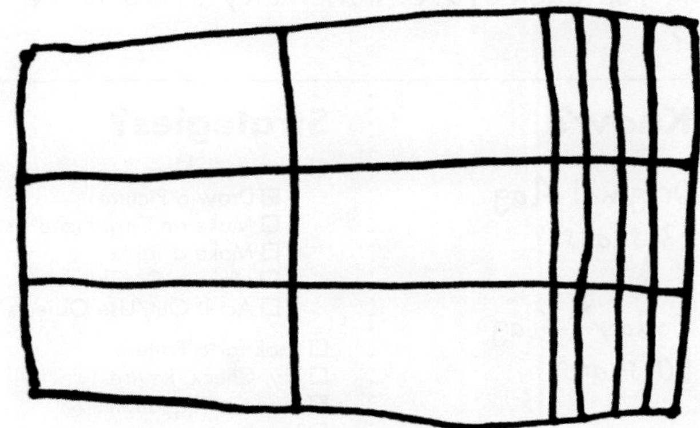

First we made a row of 24 using 2 tens and 4 ones. Then we made 2 more rows. Then we said 3 rows of 2 tens is 3 × 2 tens = 6 tens or 60. Then we said 3 rows of 4 ones is 3 × 4 = 12. Then we added the parts. 60 + 12 = 72 So, 3 × 24 = 72.

Problem-Solving Recording Sheet

Name Jane

Teaching Tool 1

Problem-Solving Recording Sheet

Problem:
On June 14, 1777, the Continental Congress approved the design of a national flag. The 1777 flag had 13 stars, one for each colony. Today's flag has 50 stars, one for each state. How many stars were added to the flag since 1777?

Find?
Number of stars added to the flag

Know?
Original flag
13 stars

Today's flag
50 stars

Strategies?
Show the Problem
- ☑ Draw a Picture
- ☐ Make an Organized List
- ☐ Make a Table
- ☐ Make a Graph
- ☐ Act It Out/Use Objects

- ☐ Look for a Pattern
- ☐ Try, Check, Revise
- ☑ Write an Equation
- ☐ Use Reasoning
- ☐ Work Backwards
- ☐ Solve a Simpler Problem

Show the Problem?

50	
13	?

Solution?
I am comparing the two quantities.
I could add up from 13 to 50. I can also subtract 13 from 50. I'll subtract.

$$\begin{array}{r} 50 \\ -\ 13 \\ \hline 37 \end{array}$$

Answer?
There were 37 stars added to the flag from 1777 to today.

Check? Reasonable?
37 + 13 = 50 so I subtracted correctly.

50 − 13 is about 50 − 10 = 40
40 is close to 37. 37 is reasonable.

Here's a way to organize my problem-solving work

Name Benton

Teaching Tool 1

Problem-Solving Recording Sheet

Problem:

Suppose your teacher told you to open your math book to the facing pages whose pages numbers add to 85. To which two pages would you open your book?

Find?

Two facing page numbers

Know?

Two pages.
Facing each other.
Sum is 85.

Strategies?

Show the Problem

- ☑ Draw a Picture
- ☐ Make an Organized List
- ☐ Make a Table
- ☐ Make a Graph
- ☐ Act It Out/Use Objects

- ☐ Look for a Pattern
- ☑ Try, Check, Revise
- ☑ Write an Equation
- ☐ Use Reasoning
- ☐ Work Backwards
- ☐ Solve a Simpler Problem

Show the Problem?

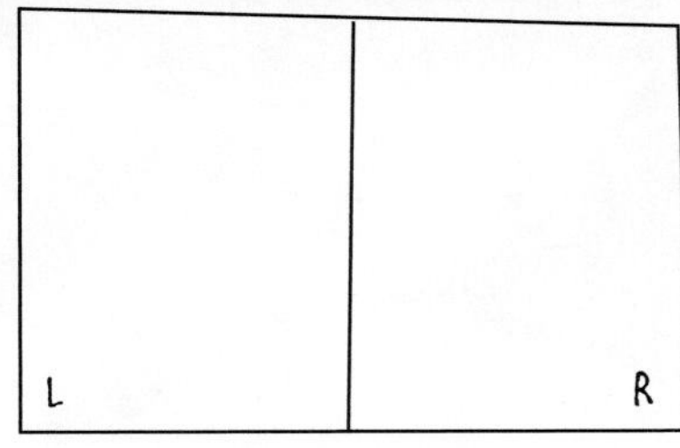

L + R = 85
L is 1 less than R

Solution?

I'll try some numbers in the middle.
40 + 41 = 81, too low
How about 46 and 47?
46 + 47 = 93, too high
Ok, now try 42 and 43.
42 + 43 = 85.

Answer?

The page numbers are 42 and 43.

Check? Reasonable?

I added correctly.
42 + 43 is about 40 + 40 = 80
80 is close to 85.
42 and 43 is reasonable.

Topic 1 Numeration

1 How tall is the San Jacinto Monument in La Porte, Texas? You will find out in Lesson 1-4.

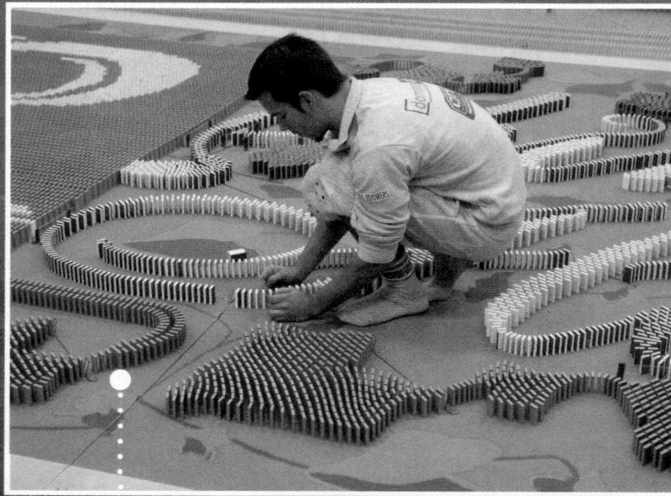

2 How many dominos were used to set the world record for domino-toppling? You will find out in Lesson 1-3.

3 How much did the world's largest pumpkin weigh? You will find out in Lesson 1-2.

4 In one minute, does the United States Treasury Department produce more coins or more bills? You will find out in Lesson 1-6.

Review What You Know!

Vocabulary

Choose the best term from the box.

- hundreds
- numbers
- ones
- tens

1. The number 49 has 4 ? .
2. The number 490 has 4 ? .
3. The number 54 has 4 ? .

Place Value

Write each number.

4. 3 tens 5 ones
5. 9 tens
6. forty-six
7. ninety-eight

Money

Write the value of each coin.

8. 9. 10. 

Compare Numbers

11. **Writing to Explain** Which is greater, 95 or 59? How do you know?
12. Write these numbers in order from least to greatest:
 14 54 41

Lesson

1-1

TEKS 3.1A: Use place value to read, write (in symbols and words), and describe the value of whole numbers through 999,999.

Hundreds

Hands-On
place-value blocks

How can you read and write a number in the hundreds?

All numbers are made from the digits, 0, 1, 2, 3, 4, 5, 6, 7, 8, and 9.

Place value is the value of the place a digit has in a number.

Bicycles with chains have been used for more than 125 years.

Another Example

How can you show 850 on a place-value chart?

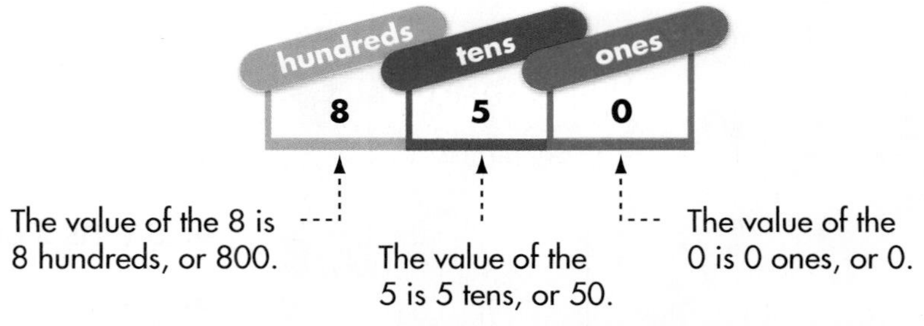

Guided Practice*

Do you know HOW?

For **1–3**, write each number in standard form.

1.

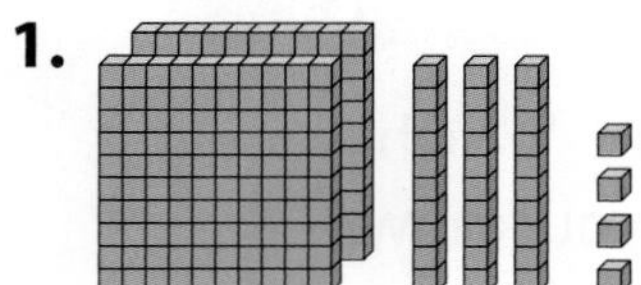

2. 600 + 50 + 3

3. eight hundred seventy-nine

4. Write 156 in expanded form.

Do you UNDERSTAND?

5. How does a place-value chart show the value of a number?

6. When 850 is written in expanded form, why are there only two addends?

7. How do you know that 37 and 307 do not name the same number?

*For another example, see Set A on page 24.

You can show 125 in different ways.

place-value blocks:

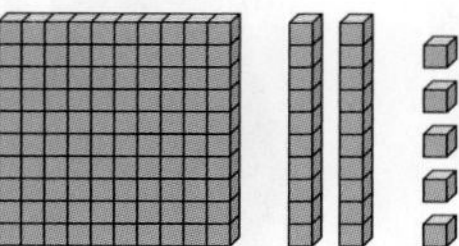

A number written in a way that shows only its digits is in standard form.

125

A number written as the sum of the values of its digits is in expanded form.

100 + 20 + 5

A number written in words is in word form:

one hundred twenty-five

Independent Practice

Write each number in standard form.

8.

9. 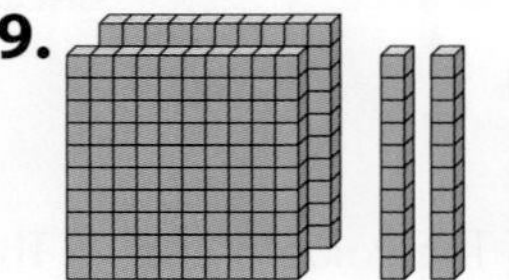

10. 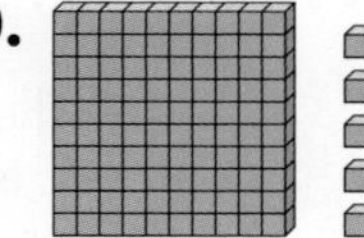

11. 900 + 80 + 5

12. 400 + 70 + 8

13. three hundred four

Write each number in expanded form and word form.

14. 707

15. 683

16. 894

17. 520

18. 251

19. 402

TAKS Problem Solving

20. Reasoning The sum of the digits in a three-digit number is 4. The ones digit is 3. What is the number?

21. Algebra Find the value of the missing number.
389 = ▢ + 80 + 9

22. Writing to Explain Which digit has the greatest value in 589?

23. Which is the standard form of 700 + 50?

A 570

B 1,200

C 750

D 705

Lesson

1-2

TEKS 3.1A: Use place value to read, write (in symbols and words), and describe the value of whole numbers through 999,999.

Thousands

Hands-On
place-value blocks

How can you read and write 4-digit numbers?

Ten hundreds equal one thousand.

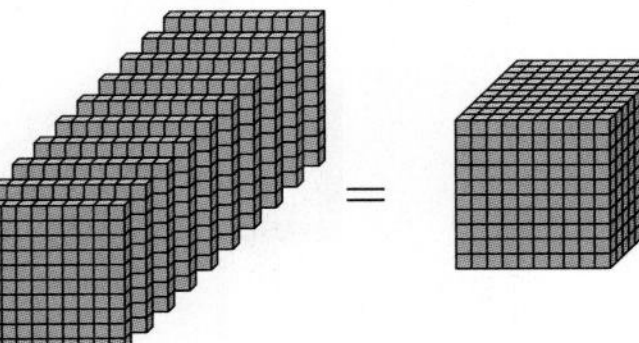

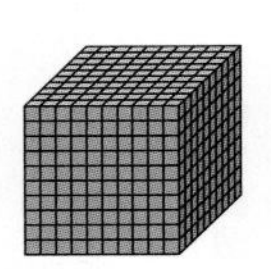

Did you know that a two-humped camel weighs between 1,000 and 1,450 pounds?

This camel weighs 1,350 pounds.

Another Example

You can also show 1,350 on a place-value chart.

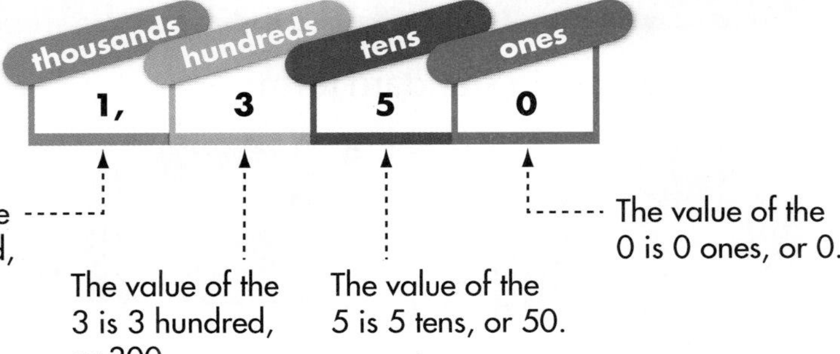

Guided Practice*

Do you know HOW?

Write each number in standard form.

1. 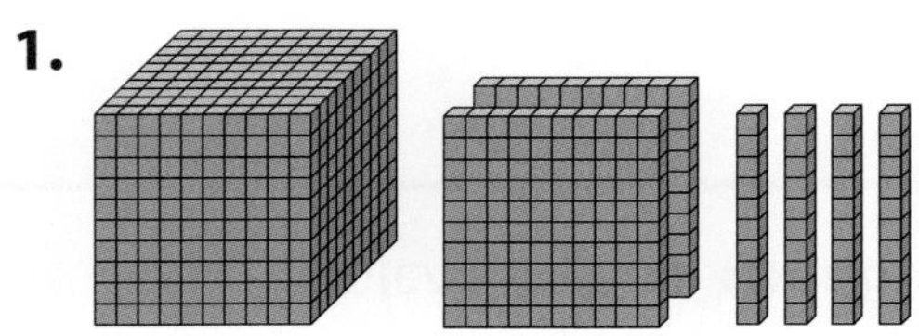

2. 8,000 + 500 + 30 + 9

3. two thousand, four hundred sixty-one

Do you UNDERSTAND?

4. Explain the value of each digit in 6,802.

5. Write a 4-digit number that has a tens digit of 5, a hundreds digit of 2, and 6 for each of the other digits.

6. Suppose another animal is three hundred pounds heavier than the camel in the photo. How would you write that weight in expanded form?

7. How could you show 1,350 with place value blocks if you don't have a thousand block?

*For another example, see Set B on page 24.

You can show 1,350 in different ways.

place-value blocks:

1 thousand 3 hundreds 5 tens 0 ones

expanded form: 1,000 + 300 + 50

standard form: 1,350

Write a comma between the thousands and the hundreds.

word form: one thousand, three hundred fifty

Write a comma between the thousands and the hundreds.

Independent Practice

For **8–10**, write each number in standard form.

8.

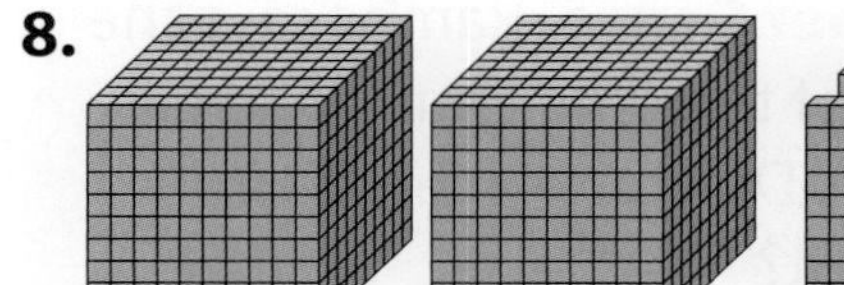

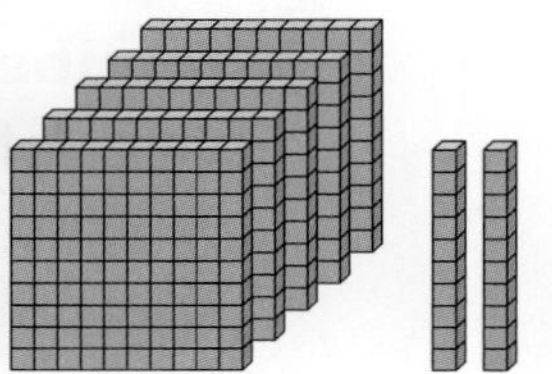

9. 4,000 + 600 + 50 + 8

10. 7,000 + 200 + 1

For **11** and **12**, write each number in expanded form.

11. six thousand, two hundred four

12. 5,033

For **13–17**, write the place of the underlined digit. Then write its value.

13. 4,865 **14.** 3,245 **15.** 9,716 **16.** 5,309 **17.** 7,240

TAKS Problem Solving

18. **Writing to Explain** Is one thousand, four hundred the same as fourteen hundred? Explain why or why not.

19. In 2005, the world's largest pumpkin weighed 1,469 pounds. Write that number in word form.

20. Which is the word form of 2,406?

A twenty four thousand, six

B two thousand, four hundred six

C two thousand, forty-six

D two hundred forty-six

21. **Number Sense** Write the greatest possible number and the least possible number using the four digits 5, 2, 8, and 1.

Lesson
1-3

TEKS 3.1A: Use place value to read, write (in symbols and words), and describe the value of whole numbers through 999,999.

Greater Numbers

How can you read and write greater numbers?

Capitol Reef National Park in Utah covers 241,904 acres of land.

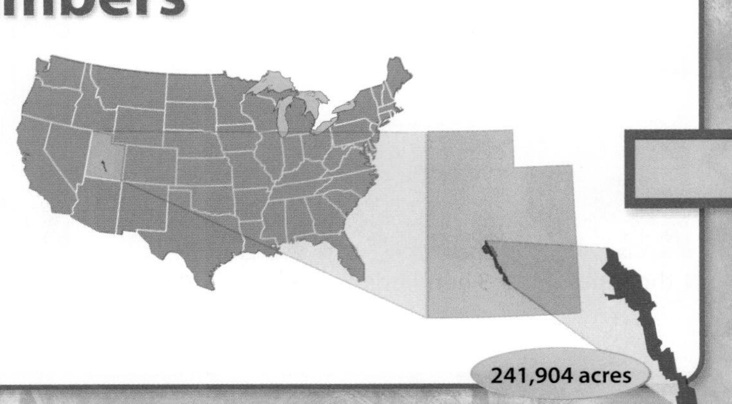

Guided Practice*

Do you know HOW?

Write each number in standard form.

1. three hundred forty-two thousand, six hundred seven

2. ninety-eight thousand, three hundred twenty

3. 500,000 + 40,000 + 600 + 90 + 3

4. What is the value of the 9 in the number 379,050?

Do you UNDERSTAND?

5. **Number Sense** Ramos says the value of the digit 7 in 765,450 is 70,000. Do you agree? Why or why not?

6. **Writing to Explain** Describe how 130,434 and 434,130 are alike and how they are different.

Independent Practice

Write each number in standard form.

7. twenty-seven thousand, five hundred fifty

8. 800,000 + 20,000 + 6,000 + 300 + 50

Write each number in expanded form.

9. 46,354

10. 395,980

Write the place of the underlined digit. Then write its value.

11. $40\underline{4},705$ **12.** $\underline{1}63,254$ **13.** $\underline{4}5,391$ **14.** $983,\underline{9}71$ **15.** $6\underline{5}7,240$

*For another example, see Set C on page 24.

How can you show 241,904 in different ways?

place-value chart:

hundred thousands	ten thousands	thousands	hundreds	tens	ones
2	4	1,	9	0	4

thousands period — ones period

A period is a group of 3 digits in a number, starting from the right. Two periods are separated by a comma.

standard form:
241, 904

expanded form:
200,000 + 40,000 + 1,000 + 900 + 4

word form: two hundred forty-one thousand, nine hundred four

Algebra Find each missing number.

16. 26,305 = 20,000 + ▢ + 300 + 5

17. 801,960 = 800,000 + 1,000 + ▢ + 60

18. 400,000 + ▢ + 30 + 2 = 470,032

19. 618,005 = ▢ + 10,000 + 8,000 + 5

20. 300,000 + ▢ + 600 + 3 = 304,603

21. 200,000 + 4,000 + 60 + 3 = ▢

TAKS Problem Solving

For **22–24**, use the table.

City Populations

City	Number of People
Austin, TX	681,804
Jacksonville, FL	777,704
Columbus, OH	730,008

22. Write the population of each city in the table in expanded form.

23. Write the population of Columbus, OH in word form.

24. Which cities listed have more than seven hundred thousand people?

25. A new world record was set when 303,628 dominos fell. Write 303,628 in expanded form.

26. Which is the word form of 805,920?

A eighty-five thousand, ninety-two

B eight hundred five thousand, ninety-two

C eight thousand, five hundred ninety-two

D eight hundred five thousand, nine hundred twenty

Lesson
1-4

TEKS 3.1B: Use place value to compare and order whole numbers through 9,999.

Comparing Numbers

How do you compare numbers?

When you compare two numbers you find out which number is greater and which number is less.

Which is taller, the Statue of Liberty or its base?

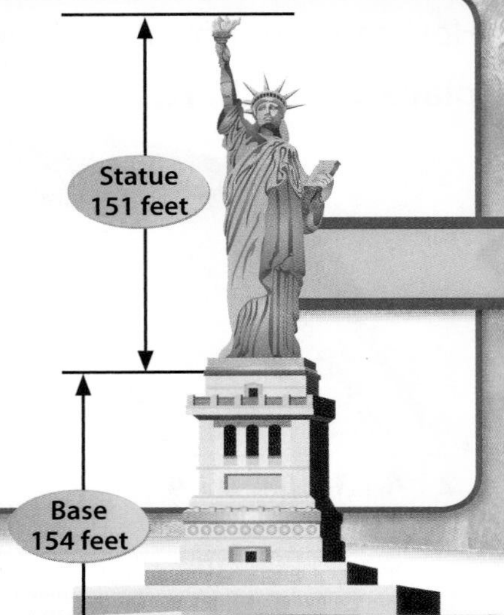

Another Example How can you use place value to compare numbers?

Compare 3,456 and 3,482 using a place-value chart.

Line up the digits by place value.
Compare the digits starting from the left.

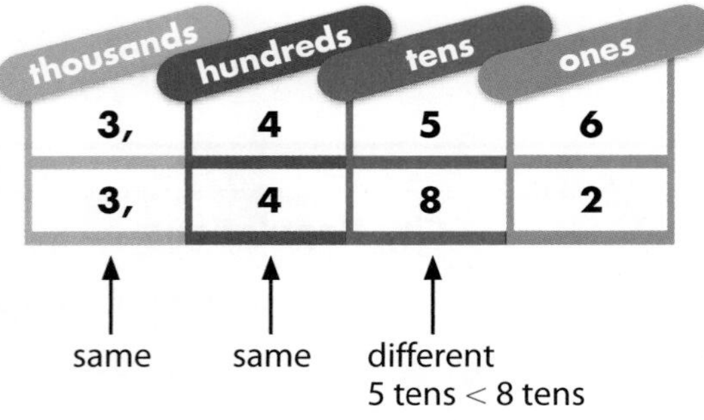

thousands	hundreds	tens	ones
3,	4	5	6
3,	4	8	2
same	same	different $5 \text{ tens} < 8 \text{ tens}$	

So 3,456 **is less than** 3,482.

$3{,}456 < 3{,}482$

Explain It

1. In this example, why don't you need to compare the digit in the ones place?
2. Why can't you tell which number is greater by just comparing the first digit in each number?

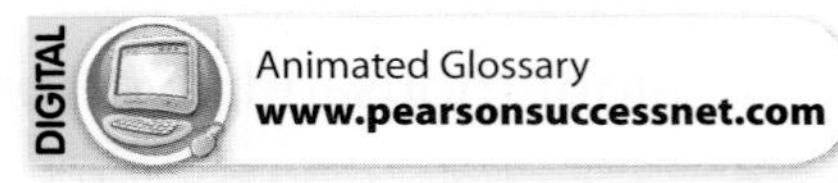

You can use symbols.

Symbol	Meaning
$<$	is less than
$>$	is greater than
$=$	is equal to

You can compare 151 and 154 with place value.

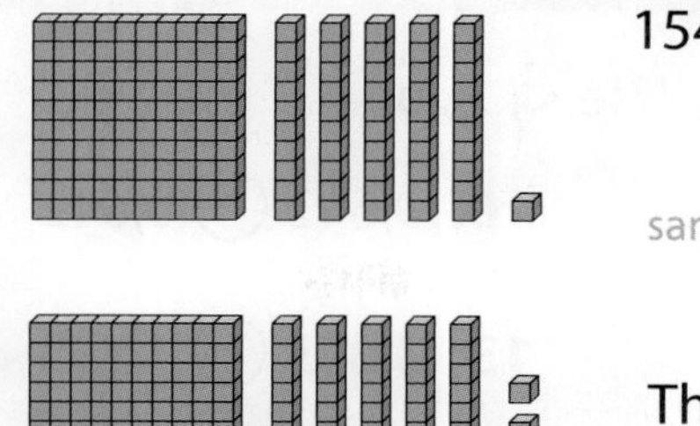

154 is greater than 151.

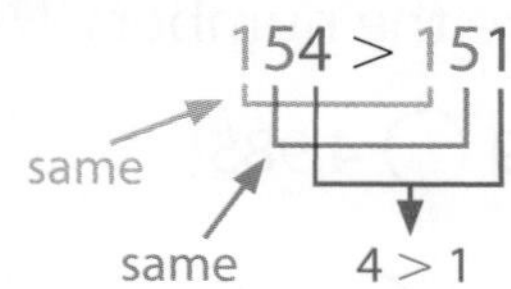

The place-value blocks also show that 151 is less than 154.

$151 < 154$

So, the base is taller than the statue.

Guided Practice*

Do you know HOW?

Compare the numbers. Use $<$, $>$, or $=$.

1. 141 ◯ 64

2.

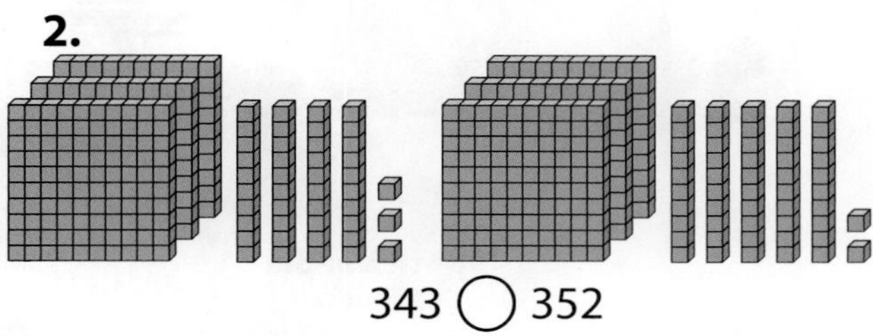

343 ◯ 352

3. 2,561 ◯ 2,261

4. 6,807 ◯ 6,807

Do you UNDERSTAND?

5. Number Sense Cara says that since 4 is greater than 1, the number 496 is greater than 1,230. Do you agree? Why or why not?

6. Writing to Explain The total height of the Statue of Liberty is 305 feet. The height of the Washington Monument is 555 feet. Which is taller? Explain how you know.

Independent Practice

Compare the numbers. Use $<$, $>$, or $=$.

7. 93 ◯ 120

8. 243 ◯ 234

For another example, see Set D on page 25.

Independent Practice

Compare the numbers. Use <, >, or =.

9. 679 ◯ 4,985 **10.** 9,642 ◯ 9,642 **11.** 5,136 ◯ 5,163

12. 8,204 ◯ 8,402 **13.** 3,823 ◯ 3,853 **14.** 2,424 ◯ 2,242

Number Sense Write the missing digits to make each number sentence true.

15. ☐24 > 896 **16.** 6☐7 < 617 **17.** 29☐ = 2☐0

18. ☐,000 < 1,542 **19.** 3,☐12 > 3,812 **20.** 2,185 > 2,☐85

TAKS Problem Solving

Use the pictures for **21** and **22**.

21. **Writing to Explain** Which is taller, the Washington Monument or the San Jacinto Monument? How do you know?

22. Which is taller, the Gateway Arch or the Space Needle?

23. **Reasoning** Mark is thinking of a 3-digit number. Rory is thinking of a 4-digit number. Whose number is greater? How do you know?

24. **Number Sense** Suppose you are comparing 1,272 and 1,269. Do you need to compare the ones digits? Explain.

25. Which number sentence is true if the number 537 replaces the box?

A 456 > ☐

B ☐ = 256

C 598 < ☐

D ☐ > 357

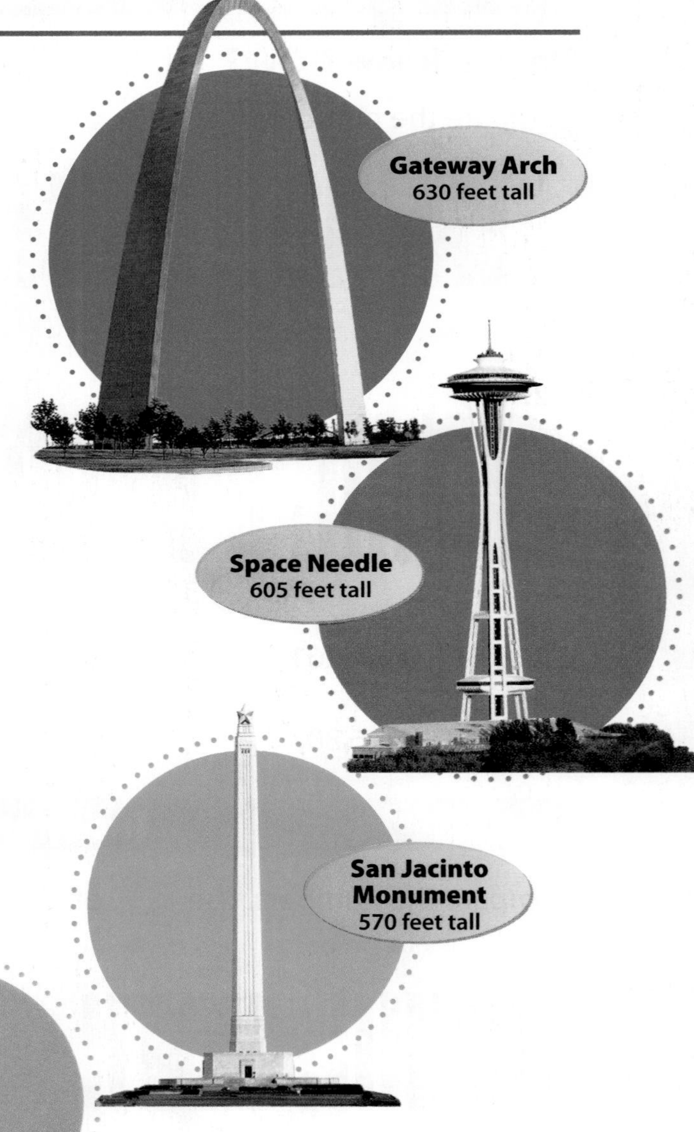

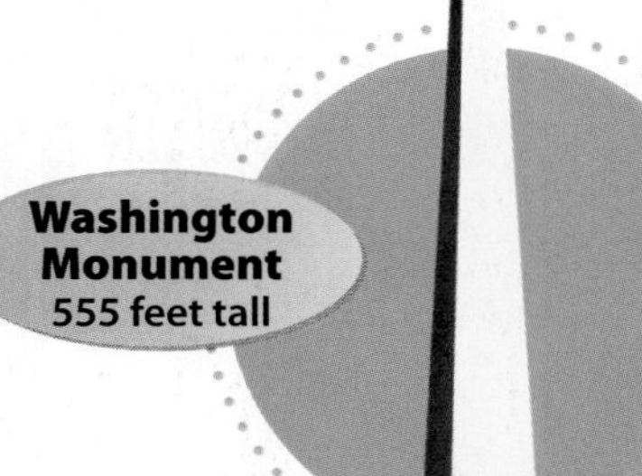

Algebra Connections

Number Patterns

Remember that skip counting can be used to make a number pattern. Skip counting can also be used to find missing numbers in a given pattern.

Copy and complete. Write the number that completes each pattern.

Examples: 2, 4, 6, 8, ___, 12

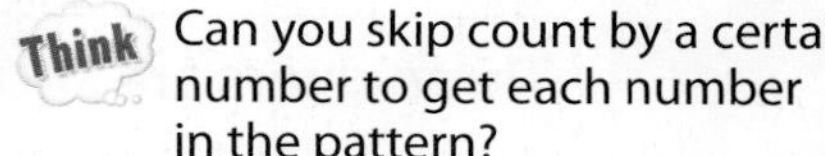

Can you skip count by a certain number to get each number in the pattern?

Skip count by 2s for this pattern.

2, 4, 6, 8, 10, 12

1. 5, 10, 15, 20, ___, 30

2. 14, ___, 18, 20, 22, 24

3. 20, 30, ___, 50, 60, 70

4. 25, 50, 75, 100, 125, ___

5. 3, 8, 13, 18, 23, ___

6. 9, 19, 29, ___, 49, 59

7. 7, 9, 11, ___, 15, 17

8. 12, ___, 20, 24, 28

9. 90, 80, 70, ___, 50, 40

10. 22, 20, 18, 16, ___, 12

11. 86, 81, ___, 71, 66, 61

12. 150, ___, 100, 75, 50, 25

For **13** and **14**, copy and complete each pattern. Use the pattern to help solve the problem.

13. Rusty saw that the house numbers on a street were in a pattern. First he saw the number 101. Then he saw the numbers 103, 105, and 107. There was a missing number, and then the number 111. What was the missing number?

101, 103, 105, 107, ___, 111

14. Alani was skip counting the pasta shapes she made. The numbers she said were 90, 95, 100, 105, 110, 115. She needed to say one more number in the count to finish counting the pasta. How many pasta shapes did Alani make?

90, 95, 100, 105, 110, 115, ___

15. Write a Problem Copy and complete the number pattern below. Write a real-world problem to match the number pattern.

2, 4, 6, 8, 10, 12, ___

Lesson
1-5

TEKS 3.1B: Use place value to compare and order whole numbers through 9,999.

Ordering Numbers

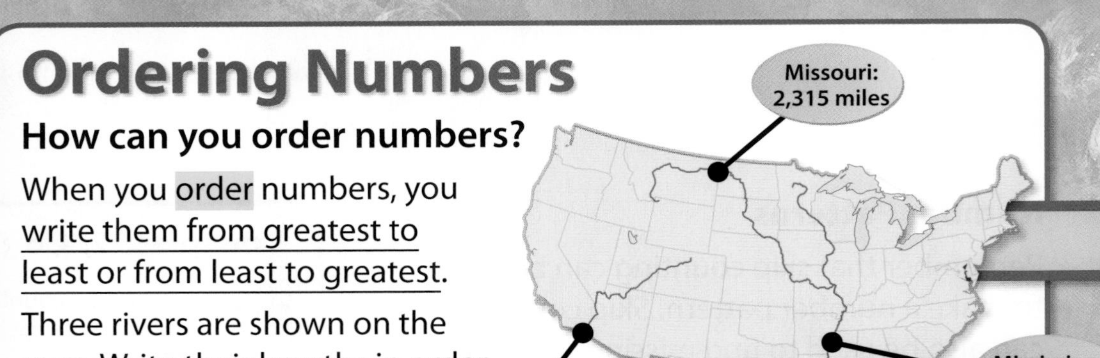

How can you order numbers?

When you order numbers, you write them from greatest to least or from least to greatest.

Three rivers are shown on the map. Write their lengths in order from greatest to least.

Guided Practice*

Do you know HOW?

For **1** and **2**, order the numbers from least to greatest.

1. 769 679 697

2. 359 368 45

For **3** and **4**, order the numbers from greatest to least.

3. 4,334 809 4,350

4. 1,137 1,573 1,457

Do you UNDERSTAND?

5. Writing to Explain The length of another river has a 2 in the hundreds place. Can this river be longer than the Colorado? Why or why not?

6. Draw a place-value chart showing hundreds, tens, and ones. Write the numbers 315, 305, and 319 in the place-value chart. Use the place-value chart to write the numbers in order from greatest to least.

Independent Practice

Order the numbers from least to greatest.

7. 6,743 6,930 6,395 **8.** 995 1,293 1,932 **9.** 8,754 8,700 8,792

Order the numbers from greatest to least.

10. 2,601 967 2,365 **11.** 3,554 3,454 3,459 **12.** 5,304 5,430 5,403

DIGITAL Animated Glossary **www.pearsonsuccessnet.com**

*For another example, see Set D on page 25.

You can use a place-value chart to help you.

thousands	hundreds	tens	ones
1,	4	5	0
2,	3	4	8
2,	3	1	5

1 < 2
So 1,450 is the least number.

3 = 3

4 > 1
So 2,348 is the greatest number.

The lengths of the rivers in order from greatest to least are:

Mississippi: 2,348 miles;
Missouri: 2,315 miles;
Colorado: 1,450 miles.

TAKS Problem Solving

Use the pictures for **13–16**.

13. Which animal weighs 100 pounds more than a moose?

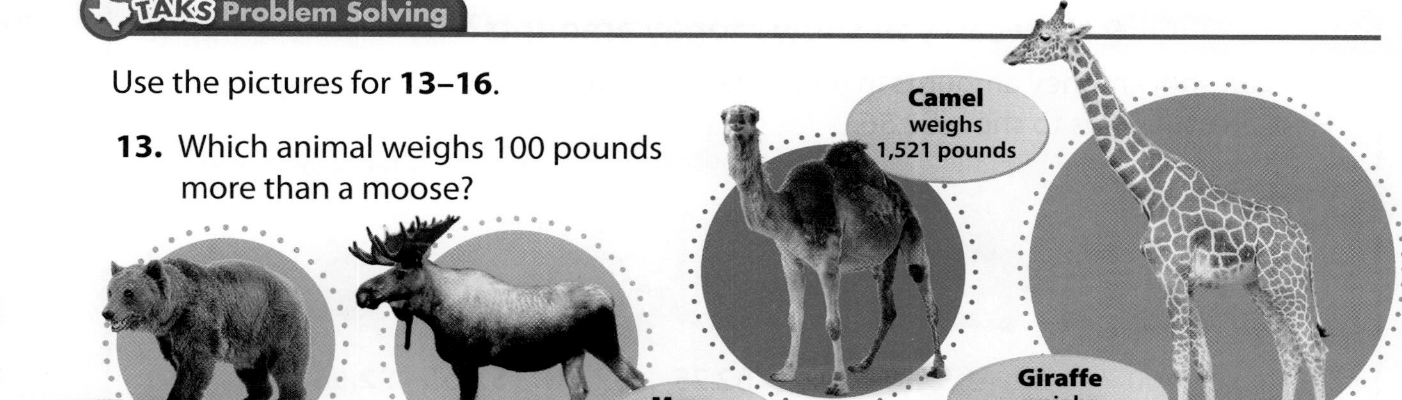

14. Number Sense A ton is equal to 2,000 pounds. Which animals weigh less than 1 ton?

15. Write the names of the animals in the order of their weights from least to greatest.

16. Reasonableness Margo says the camel weighs about fifteen hundred pounds. Do you agree or disagree?

17. Writing to Explain Describe how you would write the numbers below from least to greatest.

3,456 3,654 2,375

18. The table shows the population of four towns. Which town has a population that is more than 2,550 but less than 2,570?

A Hopeville **C** Mudville

B Smithville **D** Pleasantville

Data

Town	Population
Hopeville	2,542
Smithville	2,586
Mudville	2,356
Pleasantville	2,568

19. Which number is between 5,695 and 6,725?

F 5,659 **G** 6,735 **H** 6,632 **J** 6,728

5,695		6,725

Lesson
1-6

TEKS 3.1C: Determine the value of a collection of coins and bills.

Counting Money

play money

How do you count money?

Here are some familiar bills and coins.

5 dollars
$5 or $5.00

1 dollar
$1 or $1.00

half dollar
50¢ or $0.50

quarter
25¢ or $0.25

dime
10¢ or $0.10

nickel
5¢ or $0.05

penny
1¢ or $0.01

Another Example How can you show money amounts?

You can show money amounts in more than one way. Here are two ways to show $2.56.

One Way

$1.00 $2.00 $2.25 $2.50 $2.55 **$2.56**

Another Way

$1.00 $1.50 $2.00 $2.25 $2.35 $2.45 $2.55 **$2.56**

Explain It

1. Could you show $2.56 without using pennies? Explain.
2. How could you show $2.56, using the least number of bills and coins?
3. How do you use skip counting when you count money?

This toy costs one dollar and ninety-five cents.

A dollar sign shows money amounts.

A decimal point separates dollars and cents.

Greg has the money shown below. Can he buy the toy?

To count money, start with the bill or coin of greatest value. Then count on to find the total value.

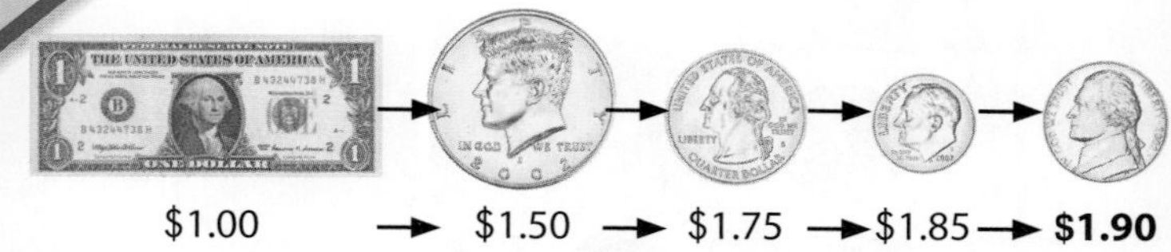

$1.00 → $1.50 → $1.75 → $1.85 → **$1.90**

Write: $1.90

Say: one dollar and ninety cents

No, Greg doesn't have enough money.

Guided Practice*

Do you know HOW?

Write the total value in dollars and cents.

1. 

2. 

3. 

Do you UNDERSTAND?

4. How could you show $7.95 using the least number of bills and coins?

5. What coins and bills could you use to show $2.65 two ways?

6. **Number Sense** If you have 195 pennies, do you have enough money to buy the toy above?

Independent Practice

Write the total value in dollars and cents.

7.

8. 

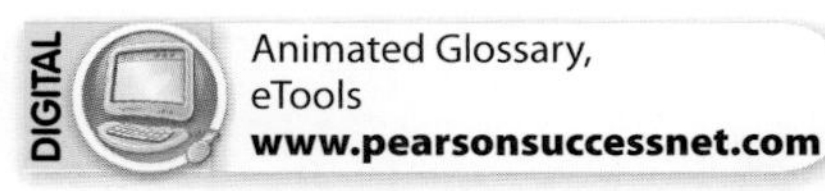

For another example, see Set E on page 25.

Independent Practice

Write the total value in dollars and cents.

9. 

  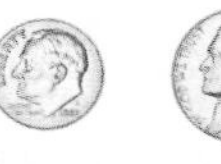 

10.  

11. 1 one-dollar bill, 1 half dollar, 3 nickels

12. 1 one-dollar bill, 2 half dollars, 1 quarter, 4 dimes, 4 nickels

13. 1 five-dollar bill, 1 one-dollar bill, 2 quarters, 3 dimes, 4 pennies

14. 1 five-dollar bill, 3 quarters, 2 dimes, 2 nickels

Compare the amounts. Write <, >, or =.

15. $1.01 ◯ 1 one-dollar bill

16. $0.83 ◯ 3 quarters, 1 dime

17. 9 dimes, 2 nickels ◯ $0.95

18. $1.60 ◯ 2 half dollars, 3 quarters

19. 10 quarters ◯ $2.50

20. $3.15 ◯ 4 half dollars, 4 quarters

TAKS Problem Solving

21. Look at the top of page 17. Keisha says Greg needs 5 more coins to have enough to buy the toy. Reni says he needs only 1 more coin. Explain who is correct.

22. **Reasoning** Bob has 3 quarters, 1 dime, and 1 nickel. What coin does he need to make $1.00?

23. **Draw a Picture** Show two ways to make $3.62. Draw rectangles to represent bills. Draw circles with letters to represent coins.

24. Tyler has 5 coins worth $0.65. He only has quarters and dimes. How many of each coin does he have?

25. Each minute, the U.S. Treasury Department produces 30,000 coins. Are more coins or bills produced in 1 minute?

Each minute about 24,300 bills are printed.

Use the table for **26–28**.

Ticket Prices for Gateway Arch

Attraction	Adults (17 and up)	Youth (13–16)	Child (3–12)
Tram Ride	$10.00	$7.00	$3.00
Movie	$7.00	$4.00	$2.50

26. Suppose you had only half dollars and quarters. How many half dollars would you need to buy a child's ticket for the tram ride? How many quarters do you need?

27. Suppose you had only quarters and dimes. How many quarters would you need to buy a child's movie ticket? How many dimes do you need?

28. **Reasoning** The total cost for 2 adult tram tickets and 1 child's tram ticket when the Gateway Arch opened in July 1967 was $2.50. What can you buy for that amount now?

29. What is the total value of the 6 coins below?

A $0.81

B $0.96

C $1.21

D $1.06

30. What is the total value of the 8 coins below?

F $1.02

G $1.20

H $1.07

J $ 0.92

Lesson

1-7

TEKS 3.14B Solve problems that incorporate understanding the problem, making a plan, carrying out the plan, and evaluating the solution for reasonableness.

Problem Solving

Make an Organized List

Randy is playing a game called *Guess the Number*. What are all the possible numbers that fit the clues shown at the right?

You can make an organized list to find all the possible numbers.

Clues

- It is a 3-digit even number.
- The digit in the hundreds place is greater than 8.
- The digit in the tens place is less than 2.

Guided Practice*

Do you know HOW?

Make an organized list to solve.

1. Rachel has a quarter, a dime, a nickel, and a penny. She told her brother he could take two coins. List all the different pairs of coins her brother can take.

Do you UNDERSTAND?

2. Writing to Explain How did making an organized list help you solve Problem 1?

3. Write a Problem Write and solve a real-world problem by making an organized list.

Independent Practice

For **4** and **5**, make an organized list to solve.

4. List all the 4-digit numbers that fit these clues.

- The thousands digit is less than 2.
- The hundreds digit is greater than 5.
- The tens digit and ones digit both equal 10 − 5.

5. Jen, Meg, and Emily are standing in line at the movies. How many different ways can they line up? List the ways.

Stuck? Try this....

- What do I know?
- What am I asked to find?
- What diagram can I use to help understand the problem?
- Can I use addition, subtraction, multiplication, or division?
- Is all of my work correct?
- Did I answer the right question?
- Is my answer reasonable?

*For another example, see Set F on page 25.

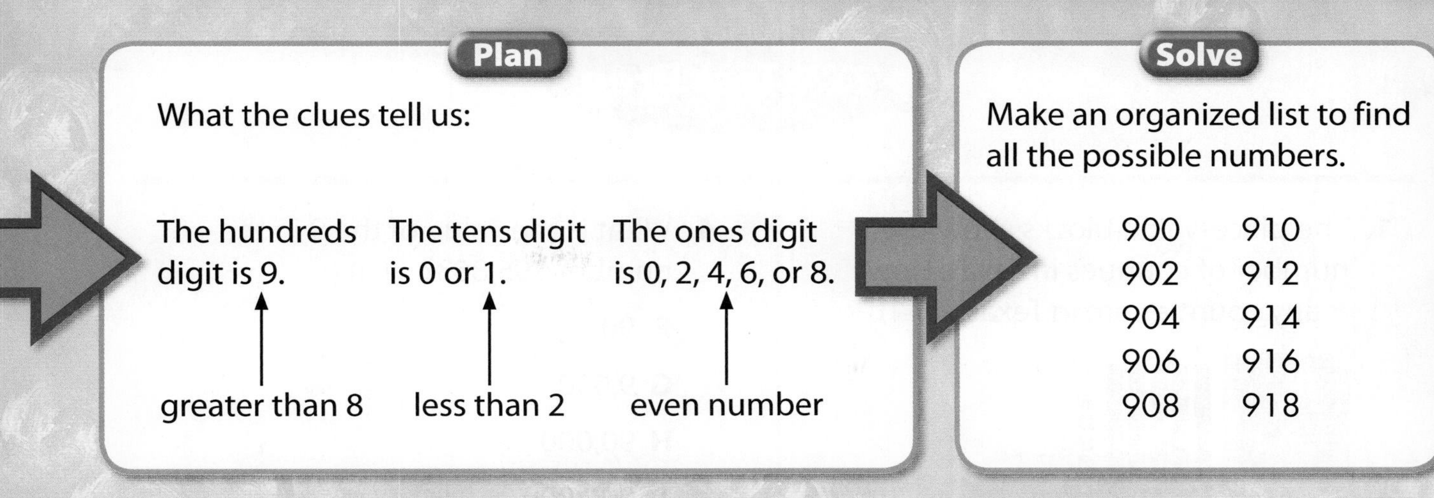

For **6–8**, use the table.

Sandwich Choices	
Bread Choices	**Filling Choices**
White	Ham
Rye	Tuna
	Turkey

6. How many different kinds of sandwiches can you choose if you want white bread?

7. How many different kinds of sandwiches can you choose if you don't want turkey?

8. Suppose wheat bread was added as a bread choice. How many different kinds of sandwiches could you choose then?

9. Jeremy has tan pants and black pants. He also has three shirts: blue, green, and red. List all the different outfits that Jeremy can wear.

10. Dennis bought a 3-pound bag of apples for $3. He also bought some grapes for $4. How much did Dennis spend?

11. How many different ways can you make 15 cents using dimes, nickels, or pennies?

A 15 ways **C** 6 ways

B 9 ways **D** 3 ways

12. Carla bought 4 sheets of poster board. Each sheet cost $2. She paid with a $10 bill. Carla cut each sheet into 2 pieces. How many pieces does Carla have?

13. Reasoning What is this 3-digit number?

- The hundreds digit is 3 less than 5.
- The tens digit is greater than 8.
- The ones digit is 1 less than the tens digit.

1. The place-value blocks show the number of counties in Texas. How many counties are in Texas? (1-1)

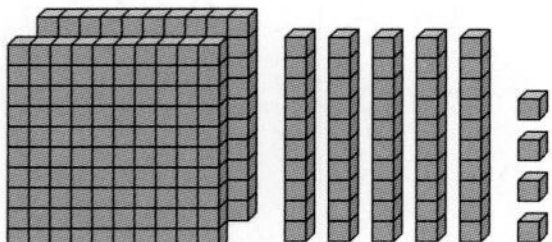

A 2,054

B 254

C 250

D 245

2. On Friday, 1,593 people watched the play *Cinderella*. On Saturday, 1,595 people watched, and on Sunday, 1,586 people watched. Which lists these numbers in order from least to greatest? (1-5)

F 1,586 1,593 1,595

G 1,586 1,595 1,593

H 1,593 1,595 1,586

J 1,595 1,593 1,586

3. The cashier gave Hector the money shown below as change. How much change did he receive? (1-6)

A \$3.82

B \$7.67

C \$7.82

D \$7.87

4. What is the value of the 9 in the number 295,863? (1-3)

F 90

G 9,000

H 90,000

J 900,000

5. The place-value chart shows the height, in feet, of the highest point in Texas. Which is another way to write this number? (1-2)

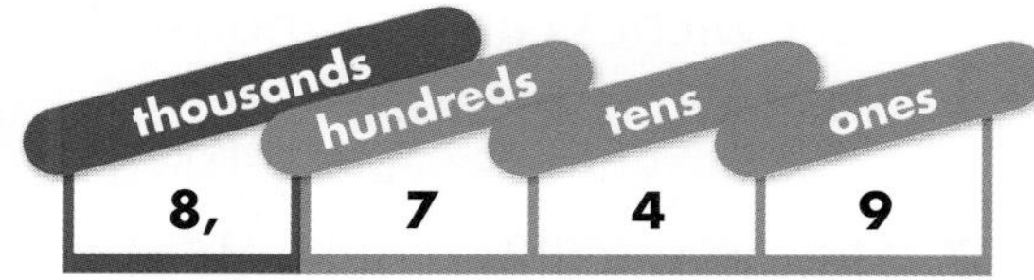

thousands	hundreds	tens	ones
8,	7	4	9

A 800 + 700 + 40 + 9

B 8,000 + 70 + 40 + 9

C 8,000 + 700 + 40

D 8,000 + 700 + 40 + 9

6. Which is the word form of the number 530,450? (1-3)

F Five hundred thirty thousand, forty-five

G Five hundred thirty thousand, four hundred fifty

H Five hundred thirty, four fifty

J Fifty-three thousand, four hundred fifty

7. Which is greater than 4,324? (1-4)

A 4,342

B 4,322

C 4,314

D 3,424

8. Which is another way to write the number 34,003? (1-3)

F 30,000 + 400 + 3

G 30,000 + 4,000 + 30

H Thirty-four thousand, three

J Thirty-four and three

9. Which number is between 3,674 and 5,628? (1-5)

3,674		5,628

A 5,629

B 3,673

C 3,629

D 5,575

10. Which of the following has a 7 in the thousands place? (1-2)

F 7,403

G 6,937

H 5,743

J 5,271

11. Which is the standard form of 700 + 8? (1-1)

A 78

B 708

C 780

D 7,008

12. Which group of coins shows 67¢? (1-6)

F

G

H

J

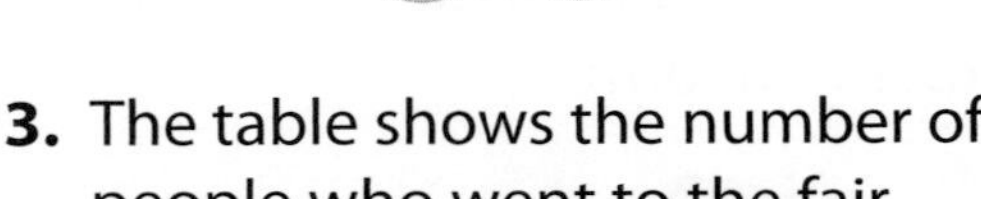

13. The table shows the number of people who went to the fair.

Data

Night	People
Wednesday	346
Thursday	326
Friday	354
Saturday	349

On which night did more than 347 people, but fewer than 352 people, go to the fair? (1-4)

A Wednesday

B Thursday

C Friday

D Saturday

14. **Griddable Response** Alex, Eric, Josh, and Tony are playing tennis. How many different pairs can they make? (1-7)

Set A, pages 4–5

Write the number in expanded form, standard form, and word form.

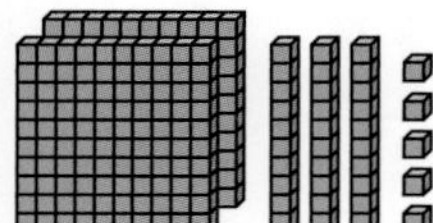

Standard form: 236

Expanded form: 200 + 30 + 6

Word form: two hundred thirty-six

Remember that, in some numbers, the digit 0 is needed to hold a place.

Write each number in standard form.

1. 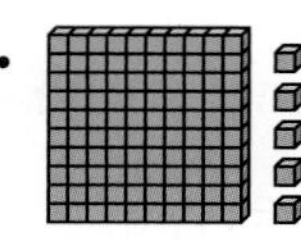
2. 300 + 20 + 7

Write each number in expanded form and word form.

3. 456
4. 620

Set B, pages 6–7

Write four thousand, sixteen in standard form and expanded form.

Standard form: 4,016

Expanded form: 4,000 + 10 + 6

Remember to use a comma to separate thousands from hundreds.

Write each number in standard form and expanded form.

1. Two thousand, one hundred four
2. Six thousand, seven hundred twenty-two

Set C, pages 8–9

Find the value of 4 in 847,193.

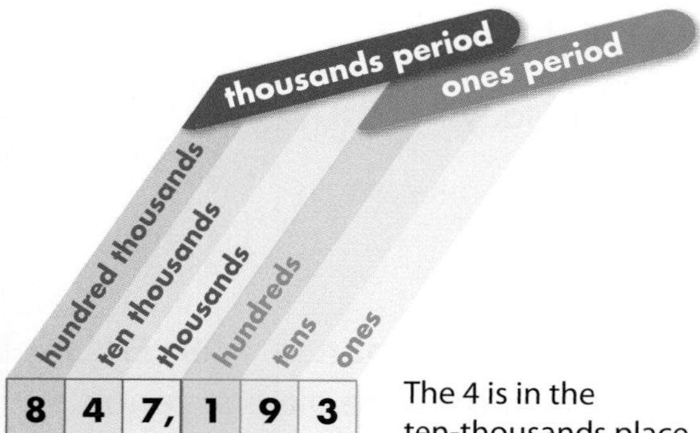

The 4 is in the ten-thousands place.

The value is 40,000.

Remember that 10 thousands equal 1 ten thousand.

Write the place of each underlined digit. Then write its value.

1. $\underline{3}41{,}791$
2. $82\underline{9}{,}526$
3. $570{,}\underline{8}90$
4. $2\underline{1}5{,}003$

Set D, pages 10–15

Compare 7,982 and 7,682.
Line up the digits by place value.
Compare the digits starting from the left.

7,	9	8	2
7,	6	8	2
↑ same	↑ different: 9 hundreds > 6 hundreds		

7,982 > 7,682

Remember when ordering numbers, compare one place at a time.

Compare the numbers.
Use <, >, or =.

1. 479 ◯ 912

2. 1,156 ◯ 156

Write the numbers in order from greatest to least.

3. 393 182 229

4. 1,289 2,983 1,760

Set E, pages 16–19

Write the total value in dollars and cents.

$5.00, $5.25, $5.35, $5.40, $5.45, $5.46

The total is $5.46.

Remember to count on from the bill or coin with the greatest value.

Write the total value in dollars and cents.

1. 

2.   

Set F, pages 20–21

When you make an organized list to solve problems, follow these steps.

Step 1
Carefully read the clues or information from the problem.

Step 2
Choose one clue or piece of information and use it to start your list.

Step 3
Repeat step 2 as often as needed until you have used all of the clues or information to make an organized list.

Remember to make sure each item on your organized list matches all of the clues from the problem.

1. Pedro has a red marble, a blue marble, a yellow marble, and a green marble. He told Frank to take two marbles. How many different pairs of marbles can Frank take? List the pairs.

Topic 2 Addition Number Sense

1 The Texas horned lizard is the state reptile of Texas. How many eggs can it lay in one place? You will find out in Lesson 2-2.

2 How many spines does a lionfish have? You will find out in Lesson 2-1.

3 How many days do students in Japan attend school each year? You will find out in Lesson 2-5.

4

How many steps lead to the top of the Leaning Tower of Pisa? You will find out in Lesson 2-4.

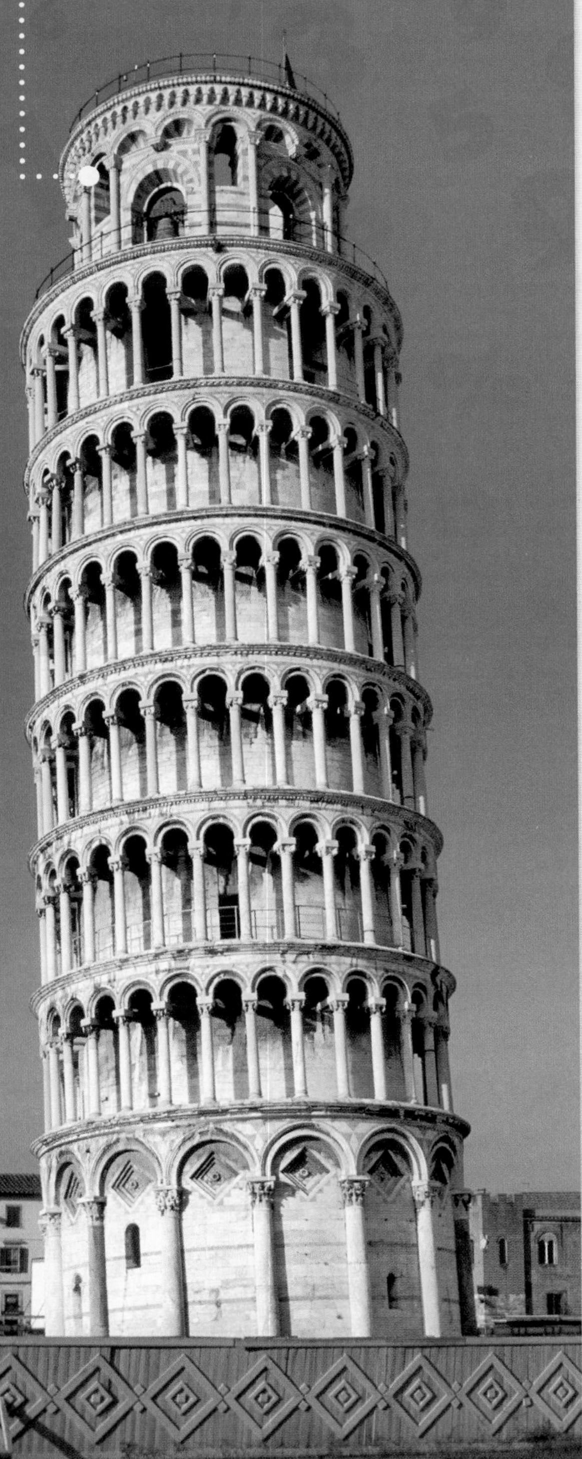

Review What You Know!

Vocabulary

Choose the best term from the box.

- hundreds
- sum
- ones
- tens

1. In 259, the 2 is in the _?_ place.
2. In 259, the 9 is in the _?_ place.
3. The answer in addition is the _?_.

Place Value

Copy and complete.

4. 35 = ▢ tens ▢ ones
5. 264 = ▢ hundreds ▢ tens ▢ ones
6. 302 = ▢ hundreds ▢ tens ▢ ones

Addition Facts

Write each sum.

7. 3 + 5	**8.** 1 + 8	**9.** 6 + 4
10. 4 + 3	**11.** 8 + 2	**12.** 6 + 6
13. 7 + 6	**14.** 8 + 6	**15.** 9 + 9

16. Janika bought 3 books on Monday and 6 books on Tuesday. How many books did she buy in all?
17. **Writing to Explain** Derrick has 4 red, 2 blue, 2 green, 2 yellow, and 2 orange balloons. Explain how to skip count to find how many balloons he has in all.

Lesson

2-1

TEKS 3.3A: Model addition and subtraction using pictures, words, and numbers.

Addition Meaning and Properties

What are some ways to think about addition?

You can use addition to join groups.

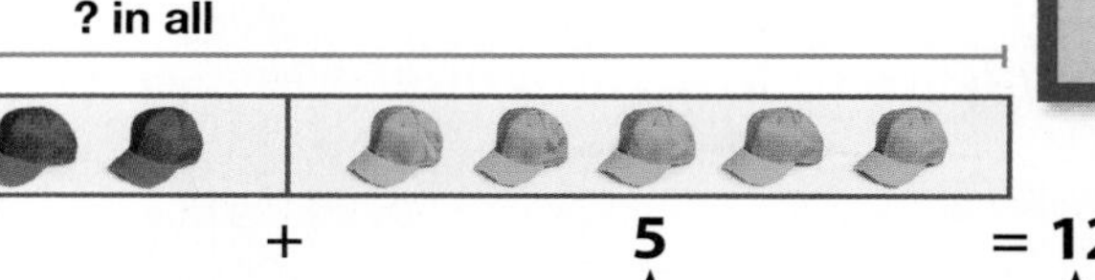

7 + 5 = 12

Addends: Numbers being added together

Sum: Answer when adding

Another Example What is another way to think about addition?

Marda has two pieces of ribbon. One is 4 inches long and the other is 3 inches long. How many inches of ribbon does Marda have all together?

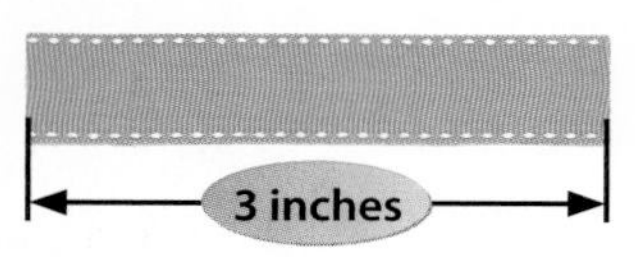

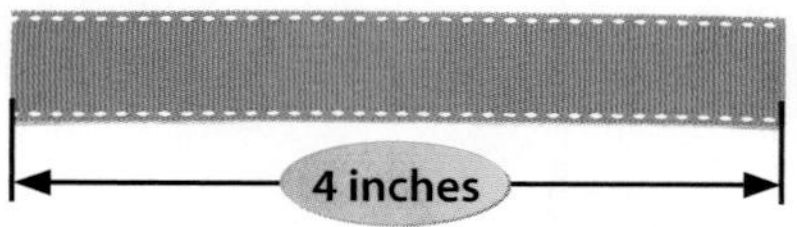

You can use a number line to think about addition.

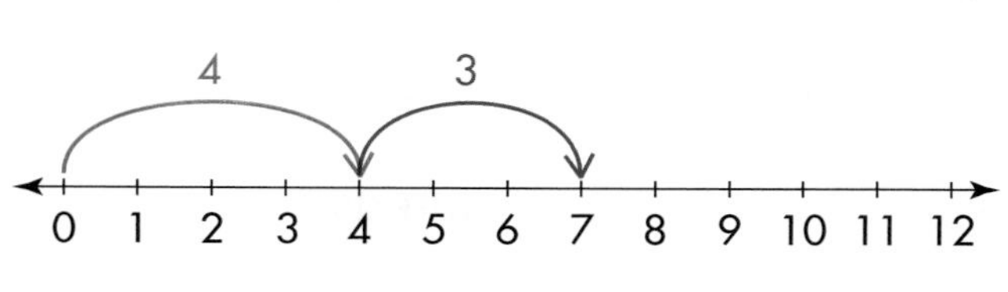

4 + 3 = 7

All together, Marda has 7 inches of ribbon.

Guided Practice*

Do you know HOW?

Write each missing number.

1. ☐ + 9 = 9
2. 4 + 6 = 6 + ☐
3. (2 + ☐) + 6 = 2 + (3 + 6)

Do you UNDERSTAND?

4. Why does it make sense that the Commutative Property is also called the order property?
5. **Writing to Explain** Ralph says you can rewrite (4 + 5) + 2 as 9 + 2. Do you agree? Why or why not?

*For another example, see Set A on page 48.

Commutative (Order) Property of Addition: You can add numbers in any order and the sum will be the same.

$7 + 5 = 5 + 7$

Identity (Zero) Property of Addition: The sum of zero and any number is that same number.

$5 + 0 = 5$

Associative (Grouping) Property of Addition: You can group addends in any way and the sum will be the same.

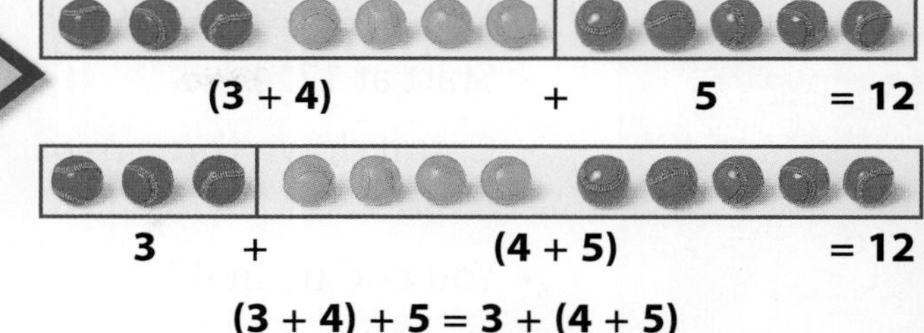

$(3 + 4) + 5 = 3 + (4 + 5)$

Parentheses, (), show what to add first.

Independent Practice

Write each missing number.

6. ▢ + 8 = 8 + 2

7. 19 + ▢ = 19

8. (3 + ▢) + 2 = 2 + 8

9. 4 + (2 + 3) = 4 + ▢

10. 7 + 3 = ▢ + 7

11. ▢ + 25 = 25

12. (3 + ▢) + 6 = 3 + (4 + 6)

13. (6 + 2) + ▢ = 8 + 7

TAKS Problem Solving

14. Reasoning What property of addition is shown in the number sentence 3 + (6 + 5) = (6 + 5) + 3? Explain.

15. Draw a Picture Draw objects of 2 different colors to show that 4 + 3 = 3 + 4.

16. A lionfish has 13 spines on its back, 2 near the middle of its underside, and 3 on its underside near its tail. Write two different number sentences to find how many spines a lionfish has in all. What property did you use?

17. Which number sentence matches the picture?

A 3 + 8 = 11

B 11 + 0 = 11

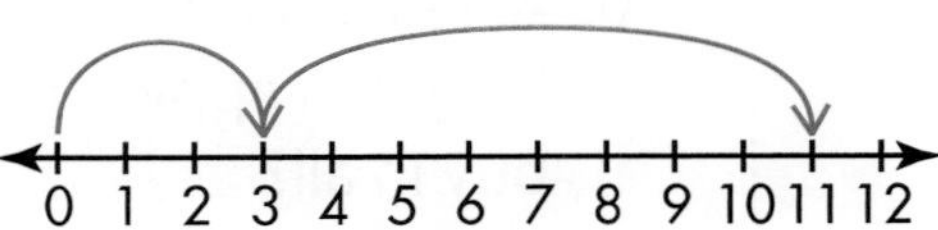

C 11 − 8 = 3

D 11 − 3 = 8

Lesson

2-2

TEKS 3.3A: Model addition and subtraction using pictures, words, and numbers.

Adding on a Hundred Chart

How can you add on a hundred chart?

Follow these steps to add 17 + 30.

- Start at 17.
- Count down three rows to add 30.
- You end up at 47.

So, 17 + 30 = 47.

1	2	3	4	5	6	7	8	9	10
11	12	13	14	15	16	17	18	19	20
21	22	23	24	25	26	27	28	29	30
31	32	33	34	35	36	37	38	39	40
41	42	43	44	45	46	47	48	49	50

Another Example How can you add on a hundred chart by counting backward?

Follow these steps to add 44 + 29:

- Start at 44.
- Move down 3 rows to add 30. You added 30 to 44. But you only needed to add 29, so you need to subtract 1.
- Move left 1 space.
- You end up at 73.

So, 44 + 29 = 73.

1	2	3	4	5	6	7	8	9	10
11	12	13	14	15	16	17	18	19	20
21	22	23	24	25	26	27	28	29	30
31	32	33	34	35	36	37	38	39	40
41	42	43	44	45	46	47	48	49	50
51	52	53	54	55	56	57	58	59	60
61	62	63	64	65	66	67	68	69	70
71	72	73	74	75	76	77	78	79	80
81	82	83	84	85	86	87	88	89	90
91	92	93	94	95	96	97	98	99	100

Guided Practice*

Do you know HOW?

Use a hundred chart to add.

1. 34 + 20

2. 78 + 19

3. 53 + 26

4. 68 + 18

5. 37 + 16

6. 44 + 29

7. 26 + 38

8. 57 + 35

Do you UNDERSTAND?

9. Reasoning Look at the examples at the top of pages 30 and 31. Compare the steps used to find each sum. How are they the same? How are they different?

10. Allie's mom bought 21 red apples and 18 green apples. How many apples did she buy in all?

For another example, see Set B on page 48.

Follow these steps to add 56 + 35.

- Start at 56.
- Move down 3 rows to add 30.
- Move right 4 spaces to add 4 more. You have added 30 + 4 so far.
- Go down to the next row and move right 1 space to add 1 more.

51	52	53	54	55	56	57	58	59	60
61	62	63	64	65	66	67	68	69	70
71	72	73	74	75	76	77	78	79	80
81	82	83	84	85	86	87	88	89	90
91	92	93	94	95	96	97	98	99	100

You end up at 91.

56 + 35 = 91

Independent Practice

Use a hundred chart to add.

11. 48 + 50 **12.** 75 + 15 **13.** 73 + 20 **14.** 55 + 34

15. 38 + 15 **16.** 22 + 17 **17.** 68 + 16 **18.** 55 + 29

Number Sense Compare. Use <, >, or =.

19. 23 + 50 ◯ 23 + 65 **20.** 37 + 40 ◯ 47 + 30 **21.** 65 + 34 ◯ 65 + 43

22. 25 + 35 ◯ 35 + 45 **23.** 71 + 20 ◯ 61 + 20 **24.** 82 + 16 ◯ 72 + 26

TAKS Problem Solving

25. A Texas horned lizard laid 37 eggs in one place. To the nearest ten, about how many eggs did the lizard lay?

26. **Reasoning** You have learned to add 9 to a number by first adding 10 and then subtracting 1. How could you add 99 to a number using mental math? Try using your method to find 24 + 99.

27. Which number is missing in the pattern below?

0, 50, 100, ▢, 200

A 190 **C** 175

B 180 **D** 150

Lesson

2-3

TEKS 3.3: Add and subtract to solve meaningful problems involving whole numbers.

Using Mental Math to Add

How can you add with mental math?

Dr. Gomez recorded how many whales, dolphins, and seals she saw. How many whales did she see during the two weeks?

Find 25 + 14.

Data

Marine Animals Seen

Animal	Week 1	Week 2
Whales	25	14
Dolphins	28	17
Seals	34	18

Another Example **How can you make tens to add mentally?**

How many dolphins did Dr. Gomez see during the two weeks?

You can make a ten to help you find 28 + 17.

Think

- Break apart 17.
  17 = 2 + 15
- Add 2 to 28.
  2 + 28 = 30
- Add 15 to 30.
  30 + 15 = 45

? dolphins in all

28	17

So, 28 + 17 = 45.

Forty-five dolphins were seen.

Explain It

1. How does knowing that 17 = 2 + 15 help you find 28 + 17 mentally?
2. Can you find another way to make a 10 to add 28 + 17?
3. How many whales and seals did Dr. Gomez see during the second week?

One Way

Break apart one of the addends.

Think
- Break apart 14.
  14 = 10 + 4
- Add 10 to 25.
  25 + 10 = 35
- Add 4 to 35.
  35 + 4 = 39

So, 25 + 14 = 39.

Dr. Gomez saw 39 whales.

Another Way

Break apart both addends.

Think
- Break apart both addends.
  25 = 20 + 5   14 = 10 + 4
- Add the tens. Then add the ones.
  20 + 10 = 30   5 + 4 = 9
- Add the tens and ones together.
  30 + 9 = 39

So, 25 + 14 = 39.

Dr. Gomez saw 39 whales.

Guided Practice*

Do you know HOW?

1. Make a ten to add 38 + 26.

38 + 26
26 = 2 + 24
38 + ☐ = 40
40 + ☐ = 64
So, 38 + 26 = ☐.

2. Use breaking apart to add 25 + 12.

25 + 12
12 = 10 + 2
25 + 10 = ☐
☐ + 2 = 37
So, 25 + 12 = ☐.

Do you UNDERSTAND?

3. Reasoning Compare the two examples at the top of the page. How are they the same? How are they different?

4. Number Sense To find 37 + 28 you could add 37 + 30 = 67. Then what should you do next?

5. Use breaking apart or making tens to find how many seals Dr. Gomez saw during the two weeks. Explain which method you used.

Independent Practice

Leveled Practice Make a ten to add mentally.

6. 72 + 18
18 = 10 + ☐
72 + ☐ = 82
82 + ☐ = 90
So, 72 + 18 = ☐.

7. 34 + 25
25 = 20 + ☐
34 + ☐ = 54
☐ + 5 = 59
So, 34 + 25 = ☐.

8. 53 + 36
36 = ☐ + 6
53 + ☐ = 83
☐ + 6 = 89
So, 53 + 36 = ☐.

For another example, see Set C on page 48.

Independent Practice

Leveled Practice Use breaking apart to add mentally.

9. 47 + 9
9 = ▢ + 6
47 + ▢ = 50
▢ + 6 = 56
So, 47 + 9 = ▢.

10. 55 + 37
37 = 5 + ▢
▢ + 5 = 60
60 + ▢ = 92
So, 55 + 37 = ▢.

11. 49 + 29
29 = ▢ + 28
49 + ▢ = 50
50 + ▢ = 78
So, 49 + 29 = ▢.

Find each sum using mental math.

12. 35 + 26 **13.** 50 + 42 **14.** 43 + 4 **15.** 71 + 13

16. 52 + 44 **17.** 7 + 54 **18.** 63 + 12 **19.** 62 + 34

20. 37 + 9 **21.** 5 + 38 **22.** 65 + 15 **23.** 33 + 23

TAKS Problem Solving

24. How long can a python be?

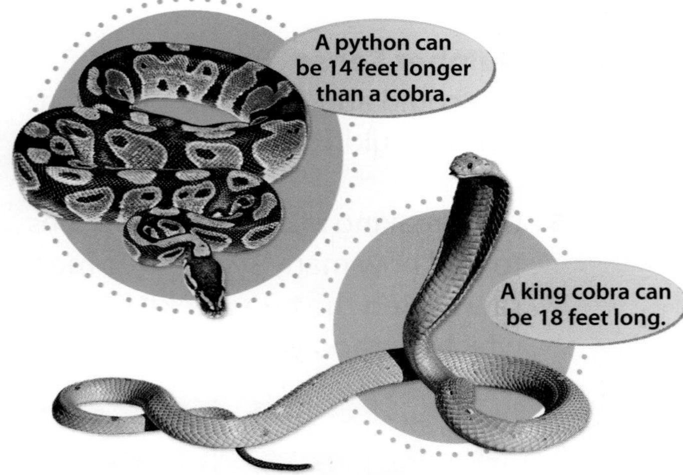

25. What is the total length of the iguana?

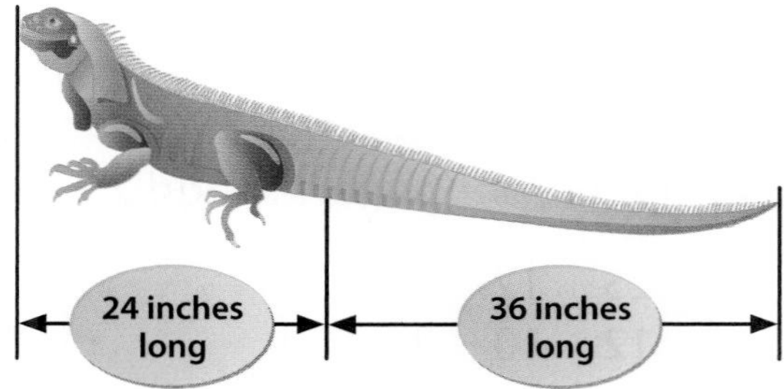

26. Writing to Explain Is Bill's work right? If not, tell why and write a correct answer.

Find 38 + 7.
I'll think of 7 as 2 + 5.
38 + 2 = 40
40 + 7 = 47
So, 38 + 7 is 47.

27. How is the number 4,038 written in word form?

A four hundred thirty-eight

B four thousand, three hundred eight

C four thousand, thirty-eight

D forty thousand, thirty-eight

Adding with Mental Math

Use eTools

Place-Value Blocks

Show two ways to make a ten to add 27 + 38.

Step 1 Go to the Place-Value Blocks eTool. Click on the Two-part workspace icon. In the top space, show 27 with place-value blocks. Show 38 in the bottom space.

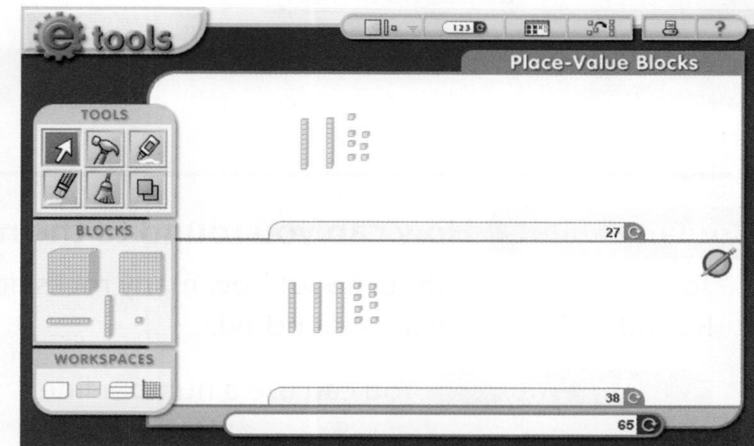

Step 2 Use the arrow tool to select ones from the bottom space and drag them to the top space. Do this until you make a ten on top. The odometers show that you have 30 + 35 = 65. So, 27 + 38 = 65, and 30 + 35 = 65.

Step 3 Use the arrow tool to move the blocks back to show 27 + 38. Then select ones from the top space and drag them to the bottom space until you make a ten on the bottom. The odometers show that you have 25 + 40 = 65. So 27 + 38 = 65, and 25 + 40 = 65.

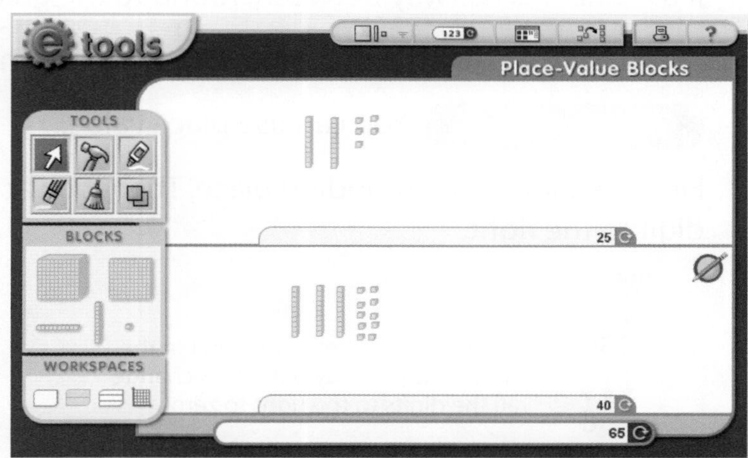

Practice

Use the Place-Value Blocks eTool to find two ways to make a ten to add.

1. 47 + 29 = ☐ + ☐ = 76
47 + 29 = ☐ + ☐ = 76

2. 58 + 36 = ☐ + ☐ = 94
58 + 36 = ☐ + ☐ = 94

Lesson

2-4

TEKS 3.5A: Round whole numbers to the nearest ten or hundred to approximate reasonable results in problem situations.

Rounding

How can you round numbers?

To the nearest 10, about how many rocks does Tito have?

Round 394 to the nearest ten. To round, replace a number with a number that tells about how many.

Another Example How can you round to the nearest hundred?

To the nearest hundred, about how many rocks does Donna have? Round 350 to the nearest hundred.

One Way You can use a number line.

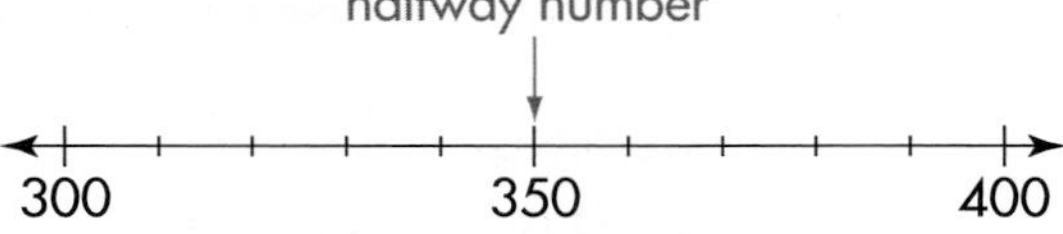

If a number is halfway between, round to the greater number.

350 is halfway between 300 and 400, so 350 rounds to 400.

Another Way You can use place value.

Find the digit in the rounding place. Then look at the next digit to the right.

hundreds place

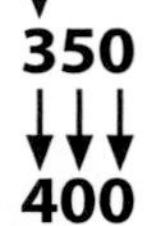

Since 5 = 5, increase the digit in the hundreds place by one. Then change all the digits to the right to zero.

So, 350 rounds to 400. Donna has about 400 rocks.

Explain It

1. If you round 350 to the nearest ten, would you still say that Donna has about 400 rocks? Why or why not?
2. Explain why 350 is the least number that rounds to 400.

One Way

You can use a number line.

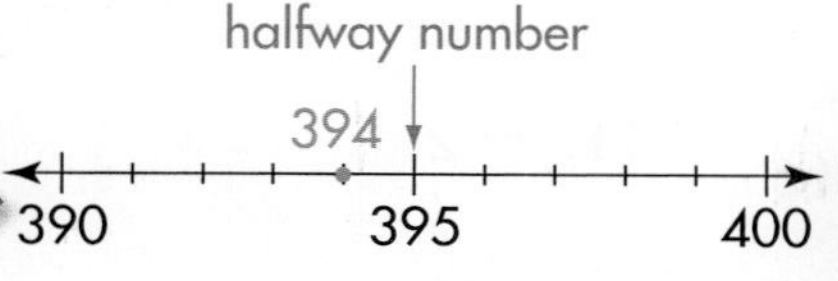

394 is closer to 390 than 400, so 394 rounds to 390.

Tito has about 390 rocks.

Another Way

You can use place value.

- Find the digit in the rounding place.
- Look at the next digit to the right. If it is 5 or greater, add 1 to the rounding digit. If it is less than 5, leave the rounding digit alone.
- Change all digits to the right of the rounding place to 0.

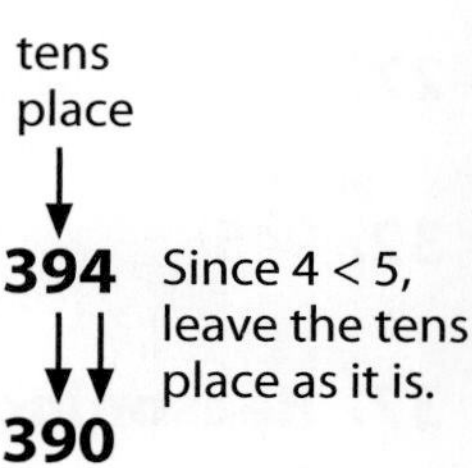

So, 394 rounds to 390.

Tito has about 390 rocks.

Guided Practice*

Do you know HOW?

Round to the nearest ten.

1. 37 **2.** 63 **3.** 85

4. 654 **5.** 305 **6.** 752

Round to the nearest hundred.

7. 557 **8.** 149 **9.** 552

10. 207 **11.** 888 **12.** 835

Do you UNDERSTAND?

13. Number Sense What number is halfway between 250 and 260?

14. Reasoning Tito adds one more rock to his collection. Now about how many rocks does he have, rounded to the nearest ten? rounded to the nearest hundred? Explain your answer.

15. Writing to Explain Tell what you would do to round 46 to the nearest ten.

Independent Practice

Round to the nearest ten.

16. 45 **17.** 68 **18.** 98 **19.** 24 **20.** 55

21. 249 **22.** 732 **23.** 235 **24.** 805 **25.** 703

26. Reasoning Round 996 to the nearest ten. Explain your answer.

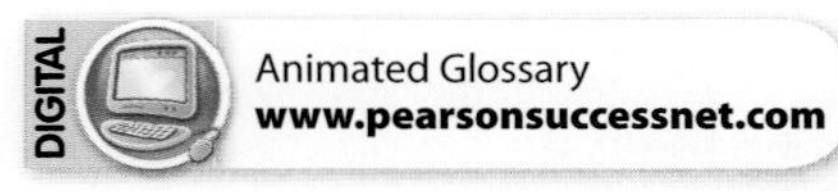

For another example, see Set D on page 49.

Independent Practice

Round to the nearest hundred.

27. 354 **28.** 504 **29.** 470 **30.** 439 **31.** 682

32. 945 **33.** 585 **34.** 850 **35.** 702 **36.** 870

37. **Reasoning** Round 954 to the nearest hundred. Explain your answer.

TAKS Problem Solving

38. **Number Sense** Give a number that rounds to 200 when it is rounded to the nearest hundred.

39. **Writing to Explain** Describe the steps you would follow to round 439 to the nearest ten.

40. **Number Sense** If you are rounding to the nearest hundred, what is the greatest number that rounds to 600? What is the least number that rounds to 600?

41. **Number Sense** A 3-digit number has the digits 2, 5, and 7. To the nearest hundred, it rounds to 800. What is the number?

42. To the nearest hundred dollars, a computer game costs \$100. Which could **NOT** be the actual cost of the game?

A \$89 **C** \$95

B \$91 **D** \$150

43. What is the standard form of 700 + 40?

F 740 **H** 470

G 704 **J** 407

44. There are 293 steps to the top of the Leaning Tower of Pisa in Italy. To the nearest hundred, about how many steps are there?

Algebra Connections

Greater, Less, or Equal

Remember that the two sides of a number sentence can be equal or unequal. A symbol $>$, $<$, or $=$ tells how the sides compare. Estimation or reasoning can help you tell if one side is greater.

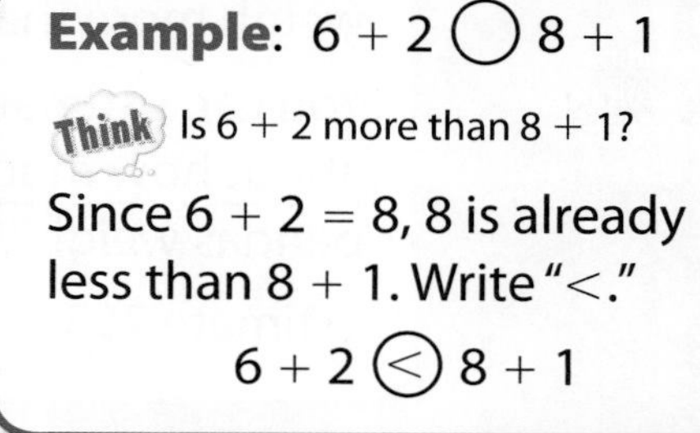

$>$	$<$	$=$
is greater than	*is less than*	*is equal to*

Copy and complete. Replace the circle with $<$, $>$, or $=$. Check your answers.

1. 3 + 4 ◯ 2 + 7 **2.** 9 + 1 ◯ 5 + 4 **3.** 5 + 3 ◯ 6 + 3

4. 2 + 9 ◯ 1 + 8 **5.** 4 + 6 ◯ 4 + 7 **6.** 8 + 6 ◯ 9 + 5

7. 18 + 2 ◯ 16 + 4 **8.** 15 + 5 ◯ 10 + 8 **9.** 14 + 4 ◯ 12 + 4

10. 17 + 3 ◯ 20 + 1 **11.** 21 + 2 ◯ 19 + 2 **12.** 27 + 3 ◯ 26 + 4

For **13** and **14**, copy and complete each number sentence. Use it to help solve the problem.

13. Al and Jiro had some toy animals. Al had 8 lizards and 3 frogs. Jiro had 11 lizards and 2 frogs. Who had more toy animals?

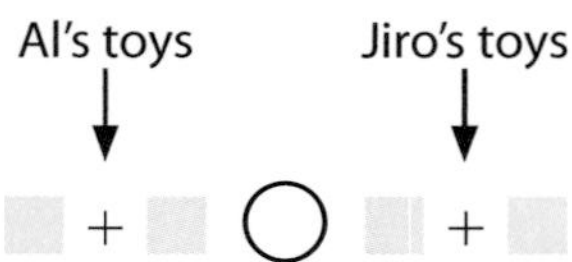

14. Look at the number of blocks that come in a set below. Val used all of the small and large cylinders. Jen used all of the small and large cubes. Who used more blocks?

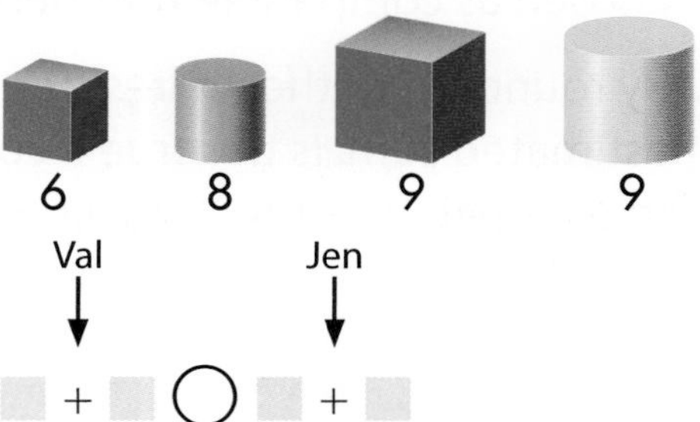

15. Write a Problem Write a real-world problem using this number sentence: $9 + 2 > 4 + 5$.

TEKS 3.5B: Use strategies including rounding and compatible numbers to estimate solutions to addition and subtraction problems.

Estimating Sums

How can you estimate sums?

Do the two pandas together weigh more than 500 pounds?

You can estimate to find out about how much the two pandas weigh.

Estimate 255 + 322.

Another Example What is another way to estimate sums?

You can use compatible numbers to estimate.

Compatible numbers are numbers that are close to the addends, but easy to add mentally.

Use compatible numbers to decide if the pandas together weigh more than 500 pounds.

$$\begin{array}{r} 255 \\ +\ 322 \\ \hline \end{array} \longrightarrow \begin{array}{r} 250 \\ +\ 325 \\ \hline 575 \end{array}$$

250 + 325 is about 575.
575 > 500

The pandas together weigh more than 500 pounds.

Explain It

1. **Number Sense** Why were the numbers 250 and 325 chosen as compatible numbers in the example above?
2. By rounding to the nearest ten, everyone gets the same estimated sum. Is this true if compatible numbers are used to estimate the sum? Explain.

One Way

Round to the nearest hundred.

$$\begin{array}{r} 255 \\ +\ 322 \\ \hline \end{array} \longrightarrow \begin{array}{r} 300 \\ +\ 300 \\ \hline 600 \end{array}$$

255 + 322 is about 600.
600 > 500

The pandas together weigh more than 500 pounds.

Another Way

Round to the nearest ten.

$$\begin{array}{r} 255 \\ +\ 322 \\ \hline \end{array} \longrightarrow \begin{array}{r} 260 \\ +\ 320 \\ \hline 580 \end{array}$$

255 + 322 is about 580.
580 > 500

The pandas together weigh more than 500 pounds.

Guided Practice*

Do you know HOW?

Round to the nearest ten to estimate.

1. 28 + 46 **2.** 75 + 17

Round to the nearest hundred to estimate.

3. 114 + 58 **4.** 198 + 426

Use compatible numbers to estimate.

5. 136 + 437 **6.** 654 + 253

Do you UNDERSTAND?

7. Writing to Explain Which estimate in the example above is closer to the actual sum? Explain your thinking.

8. How could you use rounding to estimate 487 + 354?

9. Number Sense If both addends are rounded down, will the estimate be greater or less than the actual sum?

Independent Practice

In **10–13**, round to the nearest ten to estimate.

10. 18 + 43 **11.** 75 + 72 **12.** 39 + 102 **13.** 376 + 295

In **14–17**, round to the nearest hundred to estimate.

14. 403 + 179 **15.** 462 + 251 **16.** 64 + 403 **17.** 539 + 399

In **18–21**, use compatible numbers to estimate.

18. 75 + 26 **19.** 167 + 27 **20.** 108 + 379 **21.** 145 + 394

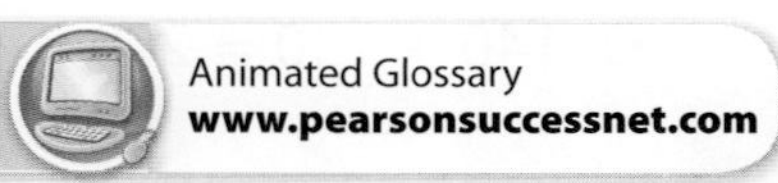

*For another example, see Set E on page 49.

Independent Practice

Reasonableness Estimate to decide if each answer is reasonable. Write *yes* or *no*. Then explain your thinking.

22. 32 + 58 = 70

23. 83 + 46 = 129

24. 55 + 64 = 99

25. 105 + 23 = 308

26. 713 + 118 = 830

27. 328 + 365 = 693

In **28–30**, use the table at the right.

28. Which city is farthest from Austin?

29. Mr. Tyson drove from Austin to Houston and back again. To the nearest ten miles, about how many miles did he drive?

30. Mr. Tyson drove from San Antonio to Austin to Fort Worth. To the nearest 10 miles, about how many miles in all did he drive?

Data

Distance from Austin, TX

City	Miles Away
Houston	162 miles
Dallas	192 miles
Fort Worth	187 miles
San Antonio	79 miles

31. In the United States, students go to school about 180 days per year. Students in Japan go to school about 60 days more per year than students in the United States. About how many days per year do students in Japan attend school?

32. How could you use rounding to estimate 268 + 354?

33. **Number Sense** Why might you round to the nearest ten instead of the nearest hundred when you estimate a sum?

34. How could you use compatible numbers to estimate 229 + 672?

35. **Think About the Process** Jared has 138 marbles. Manny has 132 marbles. Which number sentence is best to estimate how many marbles they have in all?

A 38 + 32 = 70

B 100 + 100 = 200

C 108 + 102 = 210

D 140 + 130 = 270

Mixed Problem-Solving

Read the story and then answer the questions.

We Can't Wait!

Jamie and her sisters stared out of the front window of their home. They were talking about all the good stories their grandmother always tells them when she visits. About 10 minutes ago, their dad had called home from the airport. He said that he was exactly 26 blocks away. He needed to make one more stop 12 blocks farther away. Then he would come home.

When Dad finally came around the street corner, the sisters jumped off the sofa and ran to the door. Dad arrived at the door with some grocery bags, a suitcase, and a special visitor. Soon the family would be hearing many good stories.

1. What conclusion can you draw?

2. When the sisters were staring out of the window, their dad had called about 10 minutes ago. Write a number of minutes that rounds to 10 minutes.

3. To the nearest 10 blocks, about how many blocks away from home was Dad when he called home?

4. To the nearest 10 blocks, about how many blocks did Dad travel from his last stop to home?

5. Look at the table below.

   Write the distances in order from least to greatest.

Data

Place	Distance from Home
Bakery	38 blocks
Bank	12 blocks
Grocery Store	21 blocks
Toy Store	26 blocks

6. **Strategy Focus** Solve the problem. Use the strategy Make an Organized List.

   Jamie earned some money doing chores. She wants to put 70 cents in her bank. What are two different ways she could use coins to make 70 cents?

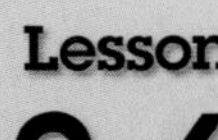

Lesson
2-6

TEKS 3.14C Select or develop an appropriate problem-solving plan or strategy including drawing a picture, looking for a pattern, systematic guessing and checking, acting it out, making a table, working a simpler problem, or working backwards to solve a problem.

Problem Solving
Draw a Picture

David wants to buy some soccer souvenirs. How much money does David need to buy shorts and a shirt?

Guided Practice*

Do you know HOW?

1. Suppose David's brother bought a poster and a pennant as souvenirs. Copy and complete the diagram to find how much money he spent.

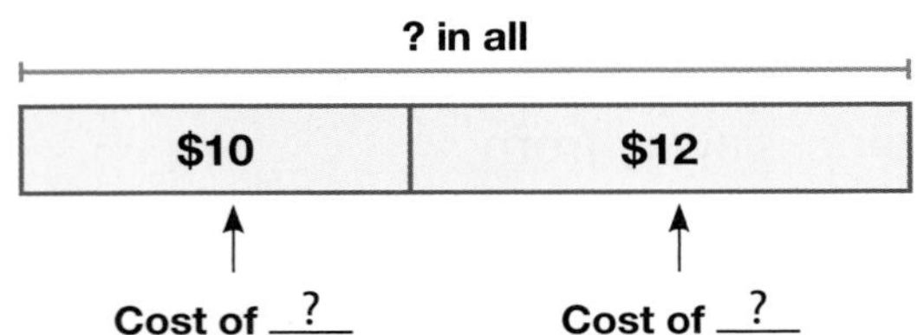

Do you UNDERSTAND?

2. Look at the diagram for Problem 1.
   - **a** What does each box show?
   - **b** What does the line above the whole rectangle show?

3. **Write a Problem** Write and solve a problem that can be solved by drawing a picture.

Independent Practice

4. David's dad spent $27 for tickets to the baseball game. He also spent $24 on food. **About** how much did he spend?

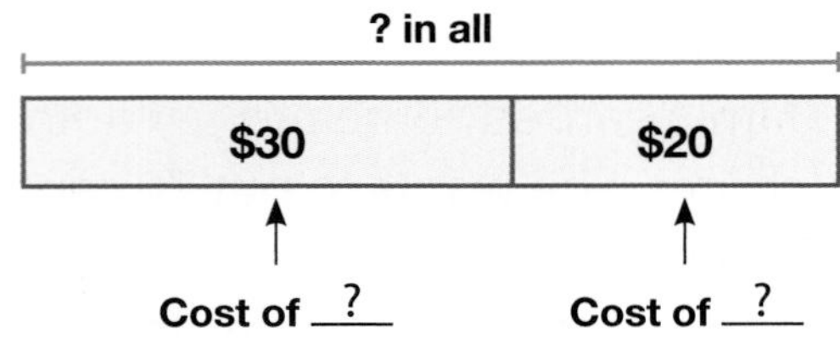

5. **Writing to Explain** Look back at the diagram for Problem 4. Why are the numbers in the diagram $30 and $20 instead of $27 and $24?

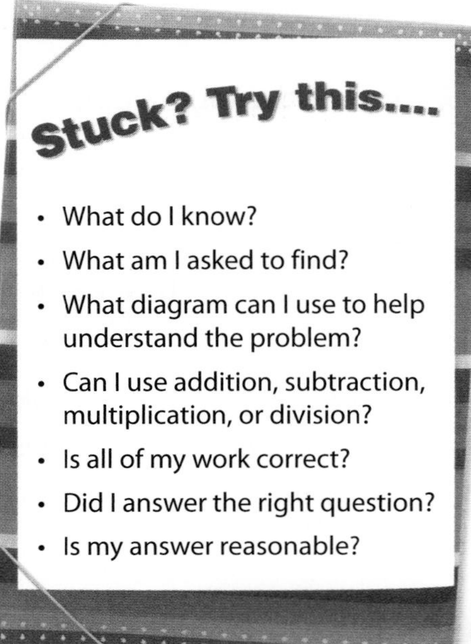

*For another example, see Set F on page 49.

Plan and Solve

Use a diagram to show what you know.

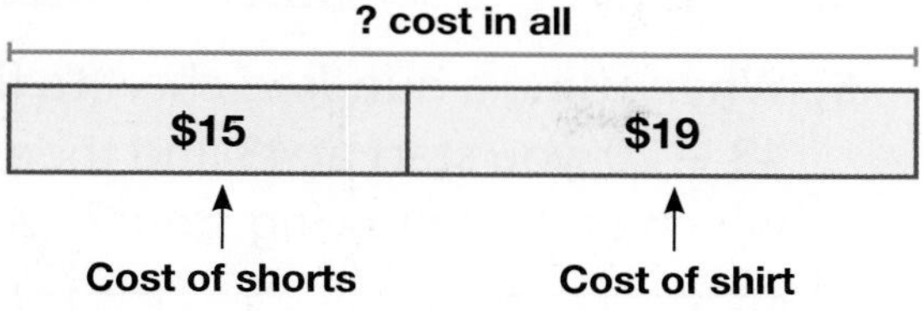

You know the parts. So add to find the total.

$15 + $19 = ▢

$15 + $19 = $34

Think: $15 + $20 = $35
$20 is $1 more than $19.

David needs $34 to buy shorts and a shirt.

Check

Make sure the answer is reasonable.

Estimate.

$15 + $19 is about $20 + $20, or $40.

The answer is reasonable because $34 is close to $40.

The table at the right shows the pets owned by third graders at Smith School. Use the table for **6–8**. For **6** and **7**, copy and complete the diagram. Answer the question.

Data

Student Pets

Pets	Number of Students
Cats	18
Dogs	22
Fish	9
Hamsters	7
Snakes	2

6. How many students have fish or hamsters?

? students in all

?	?
Students with ?	Students with ?

7. How many students have cats, dogs, or snakes?

? students in all

?	?	?
Students with ?	Students with ?	Students with ?

8. Draw a diagram to find about how many students have cats or dogs.

9. Estimation At the aquarium, Janika counted 12 sand sharks, 9 zebra sharks, and 11 nurse sharks. About how many sharks did Janika count?

A 50 sharks **B** 30 sharks **C** 20 sharks **D** 15 sharks

TAKS Test Prep

1. To the nearest ten pounds, Riley weighs 90 pounds. Which could be her weight? (2-4)

A 84 pounds

B 86 pounds

C 95 pounds

D 98 pounds

2. Juan took 48 pictures at the Alamo and 22 pictures on the River Walk. How many pictures did he take in all? Use mental math to solve. (2-3)

F 80

G 70

H 68

J 26

3. Rex has 252 football cards and 596 baseball cards. Which number sentence shows the best estimate of how many cards Rex has in all, using compatible numbers? (2-5)

A $300 + 550 = 850$

B $300 + 500 = 800$

C $250 + 550 = 800$

D $250 + 600 = 850$

4. Which number makes the number sentence true? (2-1)

$\square + 6 = 6 + 3$

F 9

G 4

H 3

J 0

5. When using a hundred chart to find $43 + 20$, you start at 43 and then do which of the following steps? (2-2)

21	22	23	24	25	26	27	28	29	30
31	32	33	34	35	36	37	38	39	40
41	42	43	44	45	46	47	48	49	50
51	52	53	54	55	56	57	58	59	60
61	62	63	64	65	66	67	68	69	70

A Count down 2 rows.

B Count to the right 2 squares.

C Count to the left 2 squares.

D Count up 2 rows.

6. Zoe saw a 268-pound ostrich at the zoo. What is 268 rounded to the nearest ten? (2-4)

F 200

G 260

H 270

J 300

7. Which number sentence can be used to find how many erasers in all? (2-1)

A $8 + 6 = 14$

B $9 + 6 = 15$

C $9 + 5 = 14$

D $3 + 6 = 9$

8. Mr. Kipper's class collected $453 for the local animal shelter. What is $453 rounded to the nearest hundred? (2-4)

F $500

G $460

H $450

J $400

9. Ava swam for 39 minutes on Saturday and 49 minutes on Sunday. To find 39 + 49, Ava made a ten, as shown below. What is the missing number? (2-3)

$39 + 49 = 40 + \square = 88$

A 29

B 30

C 47

D 48

10. Frank had 5 yards of rope. He bought 3 more yards. Which number line shows how many yards of rope Frank has now? (2-1)

F
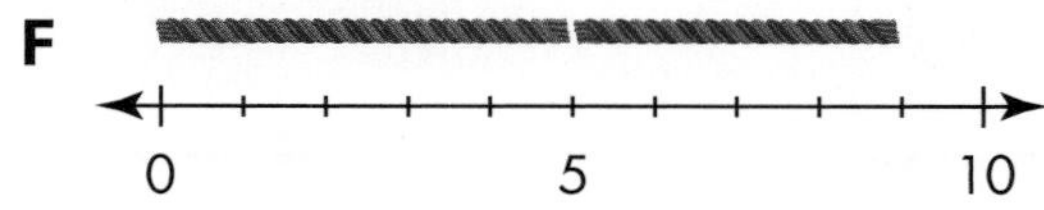

G
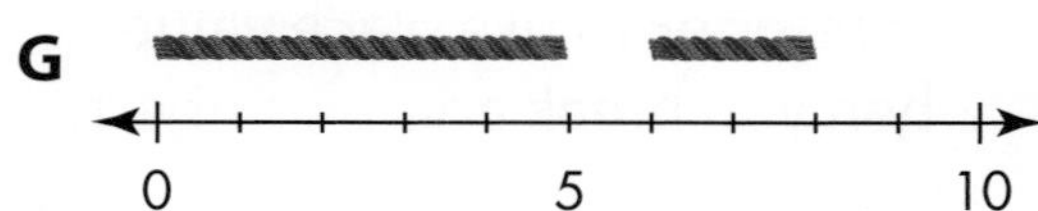

H
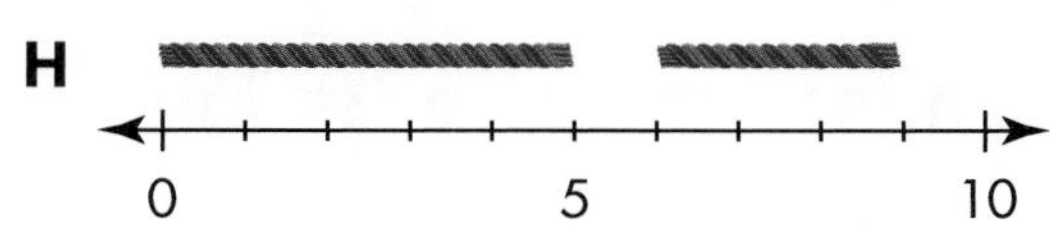

J
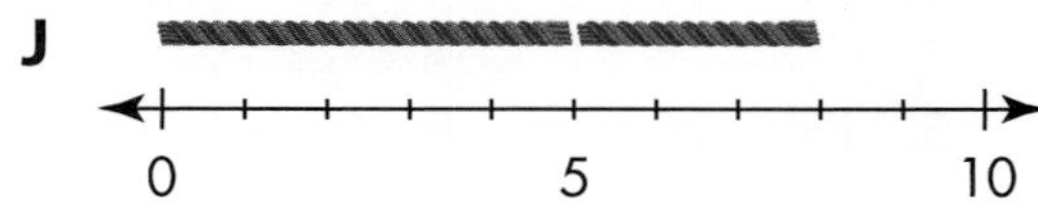

11. Walker threw a 19-yard pass and then a 22-yard pass. Which is the best estimate for the total number of yards for these two passes? (2-5)

A 20

B 30

C 40

D 50

12. Cindy drew 1 rose and then 3 daisies. She repeated the pattern of 4 flowers until she drew a total of 18 daisies. How many roses did she draw? (2-6)

F 5

G 6

H 7

J 54

13. Kaitlyn read a 48-page book. Her sister read a 104-page book. Which is the best estimate for the total number of pages the sisters read? (2-5)

A 150

B 140

C 120

D 100

14. **Griddable Response** Mary brought 23 bananas and 13 oranges for the third-grade picnic. How many pieces of fruit did she bring? Use mental math to solve. (2-3)

Reteaching

Set A, pages 28–29

Write the missing number.

(2 + ▢) + 1 = 2 + (5 + 1)
The Associative Property of Addition states that you can group addends in any way and the sum will be the same.
(2 + 5) + 1 = 2 + (5 + 1)

7 + ▢ = 6 + 7
The Commutative Property of Addition states that you can add numbers in any order and the sum will be the same.
7 + 6 = 6 + 7

Remember the Identity Property of Addition states that the sum of any number and zero is that same number.

Write each missing number.

1. 8 + 4 = 4 + ▢
2. (2 + 3) + 5 = 2 + (3 + ▢)
3. ▢ + 0 = 6
4. (1 + ▢) + 6 = 1 + (4 + 6)

Set B, pages 30–31

Use a hundred chart to add 14 + 19.

1	2	3	4	5	6	7	8	9	10
11	12	13	14	15	16	17	18	19	20
21	22	23	24	25	26	27	28	29	30
31	32	33	34	35	36	37	38	39	40

Start at 14. Count down 2 rows to add 20.
You need to add only 19 so go left 1 space.
14 + 19 = 33

Remember that to add on a hundred chart, first add the tens. Then move to the right or left if necessary to adjust the ones.

Use a hundred chart to add.

1. 37 + 20
2. 52 + 17
3. 18 + 45
4. 52 + 30
5. 24 + 32
6. 36 + 39

Set C, pages 32–34

Use mental math to find 38 + 21.

Break apart both numbers into tens and ones.
38 = 30 + 8 21 = 20 + 1

Add the tens.
30 + 20 = 50

Add the ones.
8 + 1 = 9

Add the tens and ones together.
50 + 9 = 59
So, 38 + 21 = 59.

Remember to use place value when you break apart numbers.

Find each sum using mental math.

1. 30 + 56
2. 45 + 19
3. 83 + 11
4. 39 + 31
5. 25 + 16
6. 66 + 33

Set D, pages 36–38

Round 867 to the nearest hundred.

hundreds place

Since 6 > 5, increase the digit in the hundreds place by one. Then change all the digits to the right to zero.

867 rounds to 900.

Remember to think of halfway.

Round to the nearest ten.

1. 65 **2.** 813 **3.** 489

Round to the nearest hundred.

4. 229 **5.** 349 **6.** 651

Set E, pages 40–42

Estimate 478 + 134.

One Way

Round each number to the nearest ten.

$$\begin{array}{r} 478 \\ +\ 134 \\ \hline \end{array} \longrightarrow \begin{array}{r} 480 \\ +\ 130 \\ \hline 610 \end{array}$$

Another Way

Use compatible numbers.

$$\begin{array}{r} 478 \\ +\ 134 \\ \hline \end{array} \longrightarrow \begin{array}{r} 470 \\ +\ 130 \\ \hline 600 \end{array}$$

Remember to check place value when rounding.

In **1–6**, estimate. Use the method described.

Round to the nearest hundred.

1. 367 + 319 **2.** 732 + 110

Round to the nearest ten.

3. 98 + 42 **4.** 459 + 213

Use compatible numbers.

5. 372 + 123 **6.** 211 + 164

Set F, pages 44–45

Sarah's dad spent $26 for tickets to a baseball game and $18 for food and drinks. How much did he spend in all?

? spent in all

$26	$18

cost of tickets — cost of food and drinks

$26 + $18 = ☐

$26 + $18 = $44

Remember to draw pictures to show the information you know.

Draw a picture and then solve.

1. Jason had 35 trading cards. Then he bought 27 more trading cards. How many does he have in all?

Spiral Review

Number and Operations

1. What number means the same as 4,000 + 300 + 5?

A 435

B 4,035

C 4,305

D 4,350

2. Sarah needs $2.35 to buy her lunch. Which group of money has a value of $2.35?

F  

G   

H   

J   

3. Round 2,583 to the nearest ten.

4. Write these numbers in order from least to greatest.

3,465   3,546   3,245

5. What number is missing?

$5 + (6 + 9) = (5 + \square) + 9$

6. **Writing to Explain** Explain how you can use mental math to find the sum of 68 + 33.

Geometry and Measurement

7. Julie played basketball with her friends. Which figure does a basketball best represent?

A Cylinder

B Cone

C Pyramid

D Sphere

8. Name a shape that has fewer than 4 sides.

9. Name two objects you could use to trace a rectangle.

10. Which is longer than 1 meter?

F Car

G Pencil

H Grasshopper

J Notebook

11. What time is shown on the clock?

A 5:30

B 6:00

C 6:30

D 7:30

12. **Writing to Explain** Would you go swimming outdoors or sledding when the temperature is 28°F? Explain your answer.

Topics 1–2

Spiral Review

Probability and Statistics

13. What color marble are you most likely to take without looking in the jar?

F Yellow

G Blue

H Red

J Green

14. There are 2 red balloons, 3 green balloons, 1 purple balloon, and 5 orange balloons in a bunch. If you took one without looking, which color are you least likely to pick?

A Green

B Purple

C Red

D Orange

Use the pictograph for **15** and **16**.

Science Fair Project	
Weather	4 flasks
Animals	2 flasks
Outer Space	3 flasks
Key: Each flask = 5 projects	

15. How many science fair projects were about weather?

16. How many projects were in the science fair all together?

17. **Writing to Explain** Explain how you found the answer to Exercise 15.

Algebraic Thinking

18. Which number completes the number sentence?

5 + ▢ = 8

F 3 **H** 5

G 4 **J** 11

19. Kara bought a can of juice. She paid with a $1 bill. This is the change she got. How much did the juice cost?

A $0.15 **C** $0.85

B $0.55 **D** $1.15

20. Which number sentence is in the same fact family as 7 + 3 = 10?

F 3 + 4 = 7

G 10 + 3 = 13

H 7 − 3 = 4

J 10 − 7 = 3

21. What number is missing in the pattern below?

3, 6, 9, ▢, 15

22. Julie scored 76 playing golf on Saturday. She scored 63 on Sunday. How much lower was her score on Sunday than on Saturday? Write a number sentence and solve.

23. **Writing to Explain** Continue the pattern. Explain how you got your answer.

100, 90, 80, 70, ▢, ▢, ▢

Topic 3

Adding Whole Numbers to Solve Problems

1 This statue of Abraham Lincoln is 19 feet tall. How tall would the statue be if President Lincoln were standing? You will find out in Lesson 3-1.

2 How many pecans are in each pound of nuts that a pecan tree produces? You will find out in Lesson 3-2.

Review What You Know!

Vocabulary

Choose the best term from the box.

- addends (2-1)
- hundreds (1-1)
- estimate (2-5)
- sum (2-1)

1. In the problem 56 + 42, 56 and 42 are called ___?___.
2. The answer in addition is the ___?___.
3. If you don't need an exact answer, you can ___?___.

Comparing

Compare. Write >, <, or =.

4. 24 ◯ 26
5. 81 ◯ 80
6. 156 ◯ 156
7. 654 ◯ 546
8. 478 ◯ 478
9. 639 ◯ 693

Estimating

Round to the nearest ten to estimate.

10. 13 + 25
11. 253 + 47
12. 129 + 482

Round to the nearest hundred to estimate.

13. 613 + 325
14. 253 + 347
15. 629 + 252

Addition Properties

16. **Writing to Explain** Is 24 + 16 the same as 16 + 24? How do you know?

Lesson

3-1

TEKS 3.3: Add . . . to solve meaningful problems involving whole numbers.
TEKS 3.5B: Use strategies including rounding and compatible numbers to estimate solutions to addition and subtraction problems.

Adding 2-Digit Numbers

Hands-On
place-value blocks

How can you use addition to solve problems?

How many ears of corn are there in all?

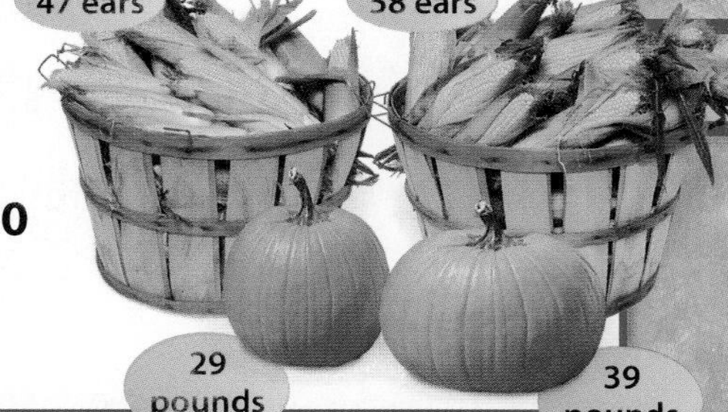

- Add to find the total. **58 + 47 = ▢**
- Estimate first. **60 + 50 = 110**
  58 + 47 is about 110.

Guided Practice*

Do you know HOW?

Estimate. Then find each sum. Place-value blocks may help.

1. 42 + 59

2. 64 + 22

3. 93 + 28

4. 57 + 52

5. 47 + 9

6. 84 + 28

Do you UNDERSTAND?

7. Look at the problem in the example above about ears of corn. Why is there a 1 above the 5 in the tens place?

8. Look at the pumpkins above.

a Estimate the total weight of the pumpkins.

b Write and solve a number sentence to find the actual total weight of the pumpkins.

Independent Practice

Estimate. Then find each sum.

9. 77 + 52

10. 19 + 24

11. 57 + 8

12. 72 + 26

13. 75 + 39

14. 33 + 45

15. 88 + 16

16. 24 + 54

17. 17 + 37

18. 59 + 13

19. 83 + 9

20. 71 + 19

21. 45 + 34

DIGITAL eTools www.pearsonsuccessnet.com

*For another example, see Set A on page 68.

What You Think

58 + 47 = ☐

- Add the ones.
  8 ones + 7 ones = 15 ones and 15 ones = 1 ten 5 ones.
- Add the tens.
  1 ten + 5 tens + 4 tens = 10 tens and 10 tens = 1 hundred.

What You Write

```
   1
   58
+  47
  105
```

105 is close to 110, so 105 is reasonable.

There are 105 ears of corn in all.

TAKS Problem Solving

In **22 and 23**, use the table at the right.

22. Follow the steps below to find how many points the Hoop Troop scored all together in Games 1 and 2.

a Write a number sentence to show how to solve the problem.

b Estimate the answer.

c Solve the problem.

d Is your answer reasonable? Explain.

The Hoop Troop

Games	Points Scored
Game 1	66
Game 2	57
Game 3	64

23. List the Hoop Troop's scores in order from the fewest to the most points.

24. **Reasonableness** Stan added 36 + 29 and got 515. Explain why his answer is not reasonable.

25. A statue of President Lincoln standing would be 9 feet taller than the statue in the picture. How tall would that statue be?

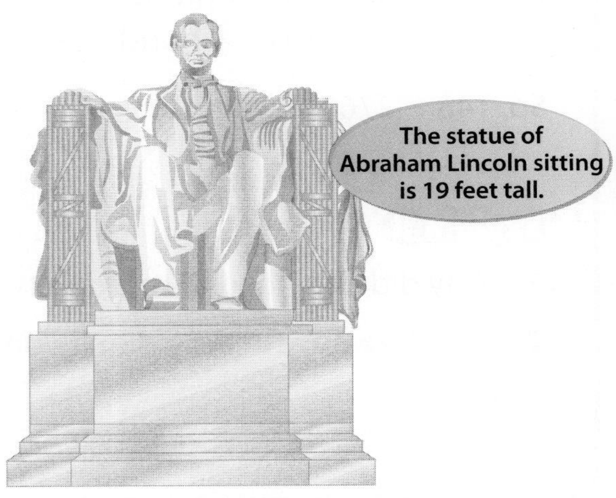

26. **Number Sense** What is the greatest possible sum of two 2-digit numbers? Explain.

27. Colleen ran 18 miles last week. She ran 26 miles this week. She plans to run 28 miles next week. Which number sentence shows how many miles she has run so far?

A 18 + 28 = ☐

B 18 + 26 = ☐

C 18 + 26 + 28 = ☐

D 28 − 18 = ☐

Lesson
3-2

TEKS 3.3A: Model addition and subtraction using pictures, words, and numbers.

Models for Adding 3-Digit Numbers

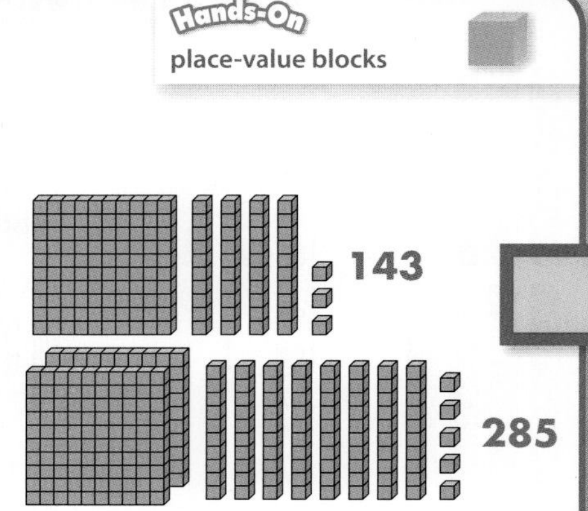

How can you add 3-digit numbers with place-value blocks?

You can add whole numbers by using place value to break them apart.

Find 143 + 285.

Another Example How do you add with two regroupings?

Find 148 + 276.

Step 1 Add the ones.
8 ones + 6 ones = 14 ones

Regroup.
14 ones = 1 ten 4 ones

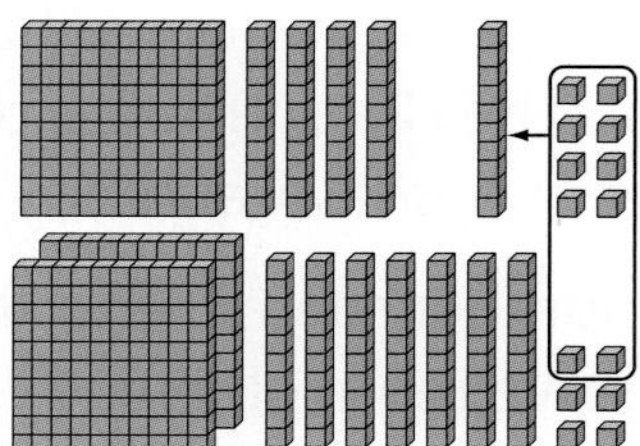

Step 2 Add the tens.
1 ten + 4 tens + 7 tens = 12 tens

Regroup.
12 tens = 1 hundred 2 tens

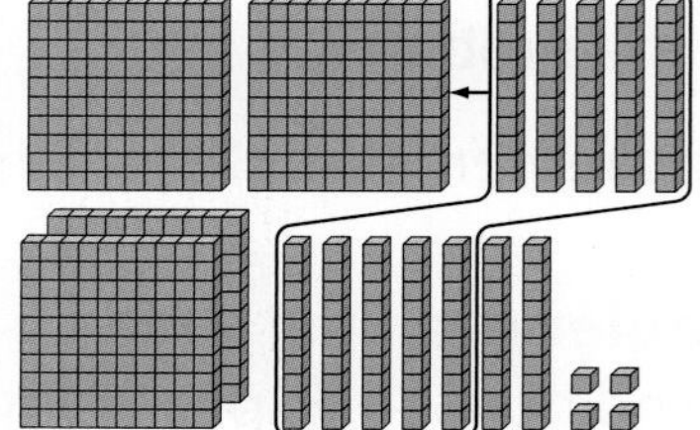

Step 3 Add the hundreds.
1 hundred + 1 hundred + 2 hundreds = 4 hundreds

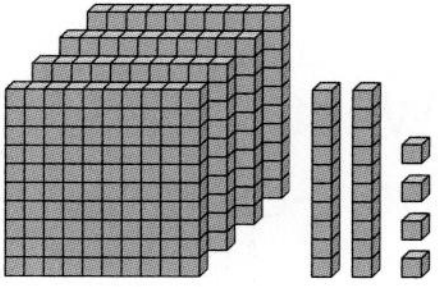

So, 148 + 276 = 424.

Explain It

1. Why did you need to regroup two times?
2. **Number Sense** Why didn't you regroup hundreds?

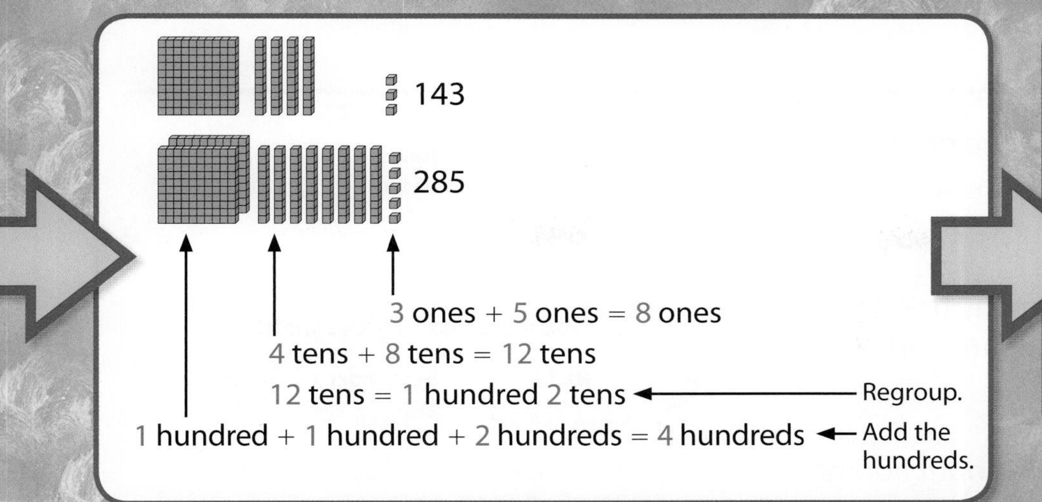

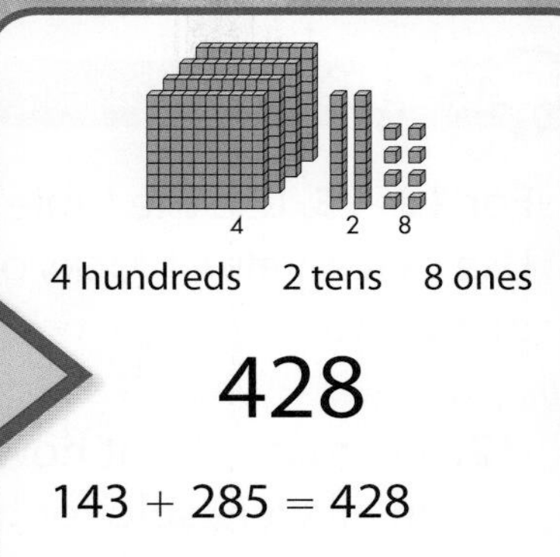

Guided Practice*

Do you know HOW?

1. Write the problem and find the sum.

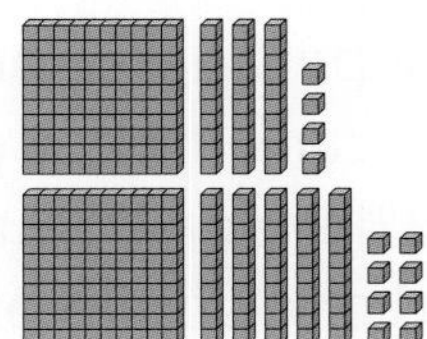

Use place-value blocks or draw pictures to find each sum.

2. 256 + 162
3. 138 + 29

Do you UNDERSTAND?

4. How do you know when you need to regroup?
5. Mr. Wu drove 224 miles yesterday. He drove 175 miles today. Use place-value blocks or draw pictures to find how many miles he drove in all.

Independent Practice

Write each problem and find the sum.

6. 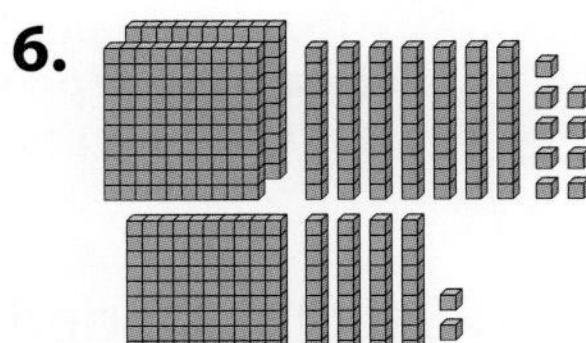

7. 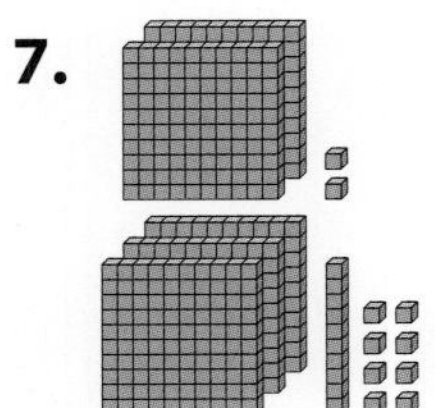

Find each sum. Use place-value blocks or draw pictures to help.

8. 635 + 222
9. 337 + 152
10. 359 + 211
11. 358 + 243

DIGITAL eTools **www.pearsonsuccessnet.com**

**For another example, see Set B on page 68.*

For **12–15**, use the table at the right. Use place-value blocks or draw a picture to help.

You can draw squares to show hundreds, lines to show tens, and ×s to show ones.

Number of Tickets Sold

Ride	Saturday	Sunday
Ferris Wheel	368	406
Roller Coaster	486	456
Swings	138	251

12. Estimate about how many tickets in all were sold for the three rides on Saturday.

13. **Writing to Explain** Without adding, how can you tell whether more tickets were sold in the two days for the Ferris wheel or the swings?

14. How many Ferris wheel tickets were sold in the two days?

15. How many roller coaster tickets were sold in the two days?

16. **Number Sense** Mike wants to use place-value blocks to show 237 + 153. He has 8 tens blocks. Is that enough to show the sum? Explain.

17. One kind of pecan tree produces about 45 pecans in each pound of nuts. If you have one pound of these pecans and one pound of the pecans shown below, how many pecans do you have?

18. **Writing to Explain** Is the sum of two 3-digit numbers always a 3-digit number? Explain how you know.

19. Which number sentence do these place-value blocks show?

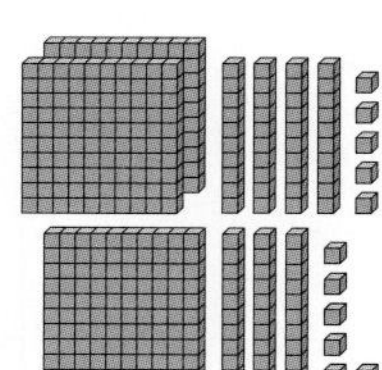

A 254 + 163 = 417

B 245 + 136 = 381

C 245 + 163 = 408

D 254 + 136 = 390

20. At a busy airport, 228 flights landed between noon and 3:00 P.M. On the same day 243 flights landed at that airport between 3 P.M. and 6 P.M. How many flights in all landed between noon and 6 P.M.?

? flights in all

228	243

Adding with Regrouping

Use eTools

Place-Value Blocks

Use the Place-Value Blocks eTool to add 367 + 175 by regrouping.

Step 1 Go to the Place-Value Blocks eTool. Click on the Two-part workspace icon. In the top space, show 367 with place-value blocks. Show 175 in the bottom space.

Step 2 Use the arrow tool to move the ones from 175 to the top space. Then use the glue tool to select 10 ones. Click on a group of ten ones to make one ten.

Use the arrow tool to move the tens from 175 to the top space. Use the glue tool to select 10 tens. Click on the group of ten tens to make one hundred.

Step 4 Use the arrow tool to move the hundred from 175 to the top space. Look at the blocks to find the sum, 367 + 175 = 542.

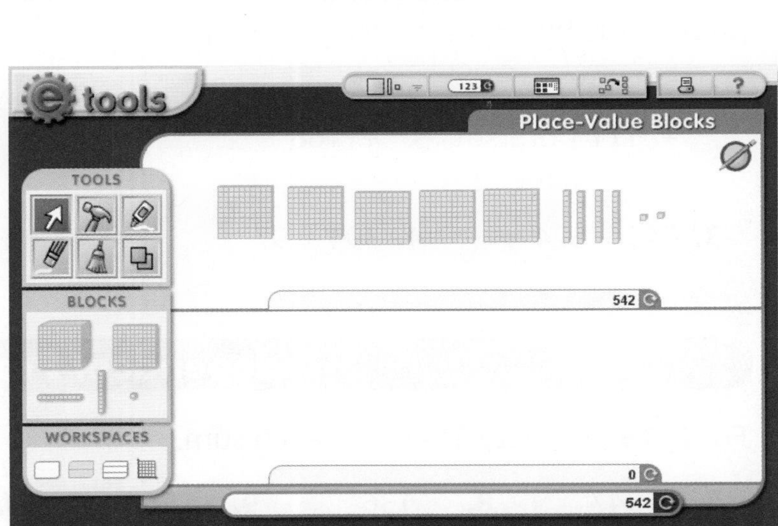

Practice

Use the Place-Value Blocks eTool to find the sums by regrouping.

1. 248 + 374 **2.** 459 + 178 **3.** 566 + 293 **4.** 675 + 189

Lesson

3-3

TEKS 3.3: Add . . . to solve meaningful problems involving whole numbers. TEKS 3.5A: Round whole numbers to the nearest ten or hundred to approximate reasonable results in problem situations.

Adding 3-Digit Numbers

How can you use addition to solve problems?

Jason's family drove from Albany to Niagara Falls. How far did they drive in all?

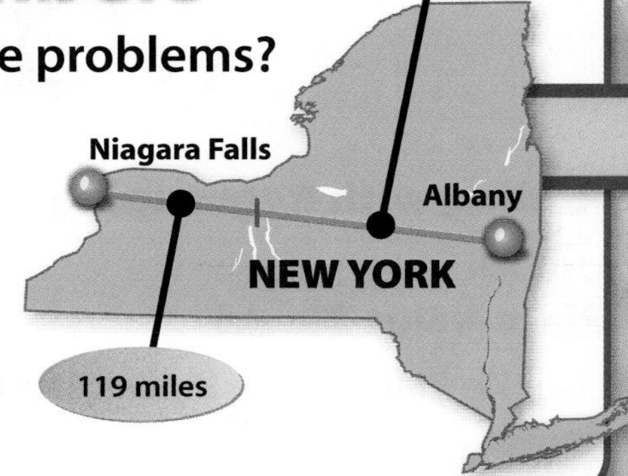

119 + 187 = ☐

Estimate by rounding: 100 + 200 = 300.
So, 119 + 187 is about 300.

Other Examples

4-Digit Sums

You can regroup 10 hundreds into 1 thousand 0 hundreds.

$$\begin{array}{r} 472 \\ +\ 625 \\ \hline 1{,}097 \end{array}$$

You can regroup ones, tens, and hundreds.

$$\begin{array}{r} {\scriptstyle 1\,1} \\ 568 \\ +\ 864 \\ \hline 1{,}432 \end{array}$$

Guided Practice*

Do you know HOW?

Estimate. Then find each sum. Use place-value blocks or drawings to help.

1. $\begin{array}{r} 126 \\ +\ 171 \\ \hline \end{array}$

2. $\begin{array}{r} 415 \\ +\ 168 \\ \hline \end{array}$

3. 645 + 524

4. 394 + 97

Do you UNDERSTAND?

5. **Reasonableness** In the example about Jason's family, is the answer 306 miles reasonable? Explain.

6. Ms. Lane drove 278 miles on Tuesday and 342 miles on Wednesday. Write and solve a number sentence to find how far she drove in all.

Independent Practice

For **7–15**, estimate. Then find each sum.

7. $\begin{array}{r} 347 \\ +\ 325 \\ \hline \end{array}$

8. $\begin{array}{r} 136 \\ +\ 252 \\ \hline \end{array}$

9. $\begin{array}{r} 564 \\ +\ 283 \\ \hline \end{array}$

10. $\begin{array}{r} 731 \\ +\ 344 \\ \hline \end{array}$

11. $\begin{array}{r} 324 \\ +\ 589 \\ \hline \end{array}$

12. 324 + 68

13. 709 + 94

14. 496 + 874

15. 526 + 307

*For another example, see Set C on page 69.

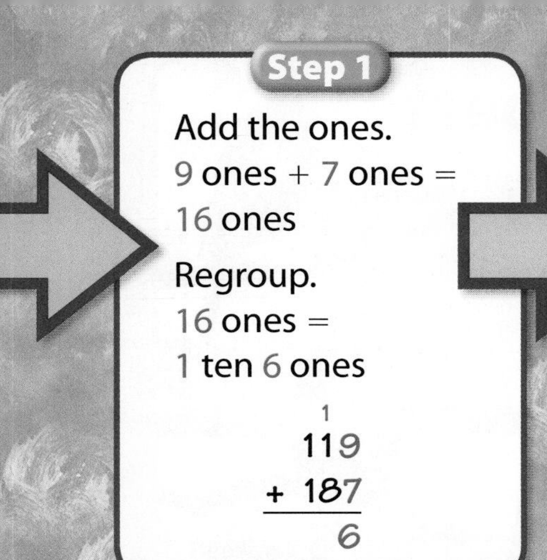

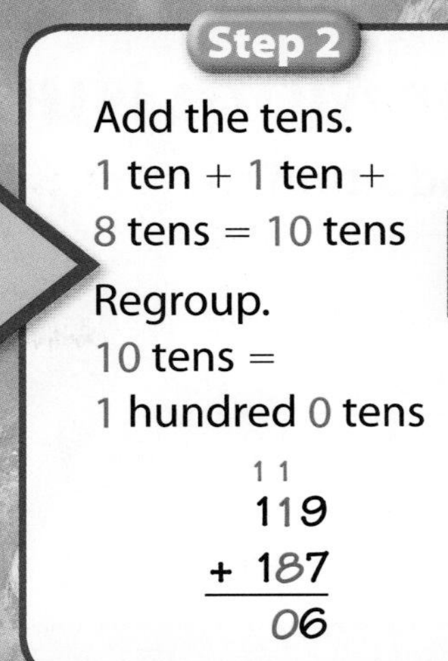

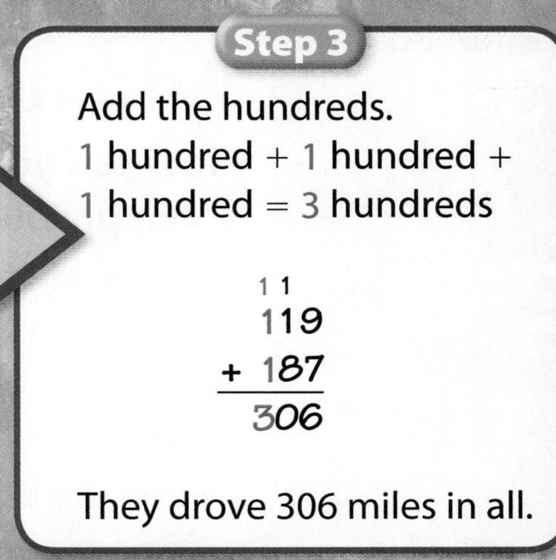

TAKS Problem Solving

For **16–19**, use the table at the right.

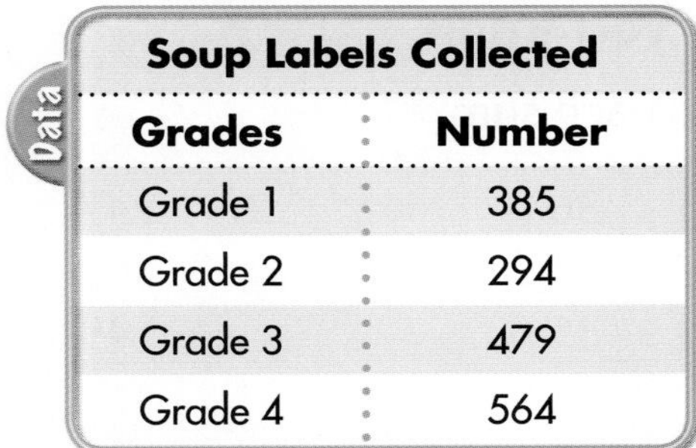

Soup Labels Collected

Grades	Number
Grade 1	385
Grade 2	294
Grade 3	479
Grade 4	564

16. **a** Write a number sentence to find how many labels the first and second grade collected in all.

b Estimate the answer.

c Solve the problem.

d Is your answer reasonable? Explain.

17. **Number Sense** Without finding the exact sum, how do you know that Grades 2 and 3 together collected more labels than Grade 4?

18. Write the number of labels collected from least to greatest.

19. Which number sentence shows how many labels Grades 1 and 4 collected in all?

A 385 + 479 = ▢

B 385 + 564 = ▢

C 294 + 479 + 564 = ▢

D 385 + 294 + 479 + 564 = ▢

20. The tallest roller coaster in the world is called Kingda Ka. It is 192 feet higher than the first Ferris wheel. How tall is Kingda Ka?

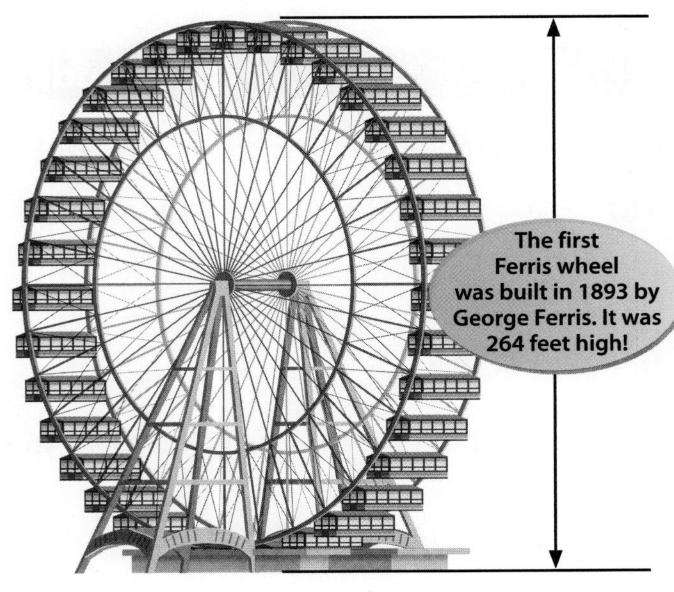

Lesson
3-4

TEKS 3.3: Add . . . to solve meaningful problems involving whole numbers.

Adding 3 or More Numbers

How can you use addition to solve problems?

Different kinds of birds are for sale at a pet store. How many birds are for sale in all?

- Find 137 + 155 + 18.
- Estimate: 140 + 160 + 20 = 320.

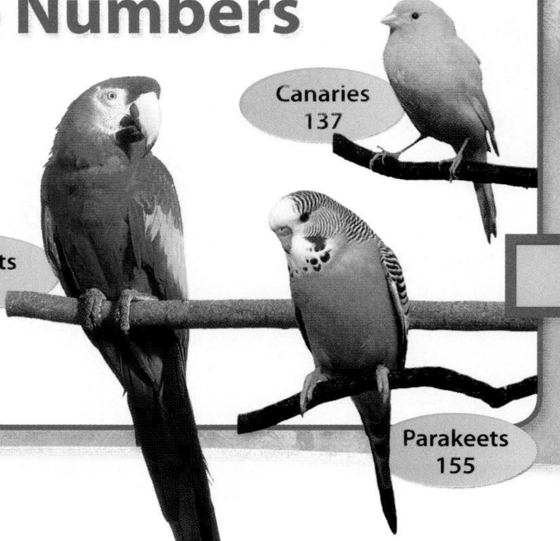

Guided Practice*

Do you know HOW?

Find each sum.

1. 36 + 47 + 35

2. 247 + 362 + 49

3. 273 + 82 + 124

4. 59 + 506 + 302 + 24

5. 9 + 46 + 24

6. 385 + 97 + 34

Do you UNDERSTAND?

For **7–9**, look at the example above.

7. Why is there a 2 above the tens place in Step 2?

8. **Reasonableness** How can you tell that 310 birds is a reasonable answer?

9. Suppose the pet store gets 46 love birds to sell. Write and solve a number sentence to show how many birds are for sale now.

Independent Practice

Find each sum.

10. 64 + 42 + 88

11. 307 + 37 + 234

12. 602 + 125 + 231

13. 246 + 54 + 233 + 205

14. 303 + 128 + 63 + 149

15. 164 + 68 + 35

16. 32 + 9 + 46 + 8

17. 125 + 36 + 124 + 239

*For another example, see Set D on page 69.

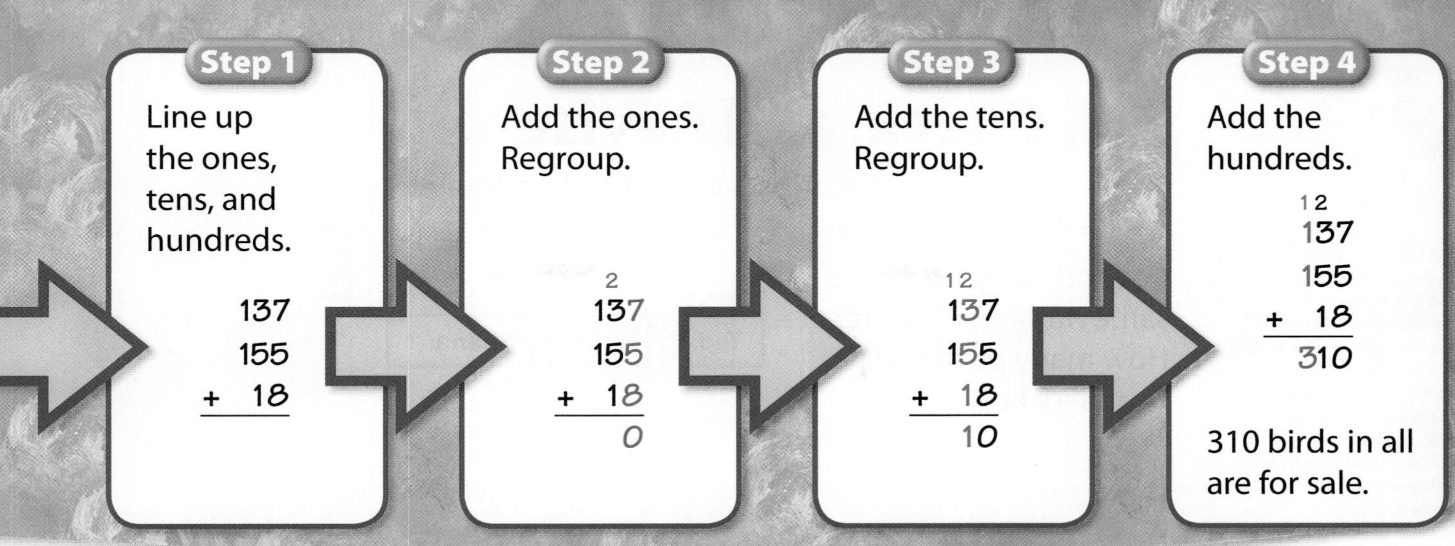

TAKS Problem Solving

Calories are used to measure the energy in food. Use the pictures for **18–20**.

18. Karin had cereal, a glass of milk, and a banana for breakfast. Follow these steps to find how many calories were in the food she ate.

- **a** Write a number sentence to show how to solve the problem.
- **b** Estimate the answer.
- **c** Solve the problem.
- **d** Use the estimate to explain why your answer is reasonable.

19. Stan put 2 tablespoons of maple syrup on the stack of two pancakes he ate for breakfast. Then he had an apple. How many calories were in the food he ate?

20. Compare the number of calories in an apple with the number of calories in a banana. Use $>$, $<$, or $=$.

21. **Reasonableness** Meg said that $95 + 76 + 86$ is greater than 300. Explain why her answer is not reasonable.

22. Ramos has 225 pennies, 105 nickels, and 65 dimes. How many coins does he have?

A 385 coins **C** 980 coins

B 395 coins **D** 3,815 coins

Lesson
3-5

TEKS 3.14C Select or develop an appropriate problem-solving plan or strategy including drawing a picture, looking for a pattern, systematic guessing and checking, acting it out, making a table, working a simpler problem, or working backwards to solve a problem.

Problem Solving

Try, Check, and Revise

Tad, Holly, and Shana made 36 posters all together. Shana made 3 more posters than Holly.

Tad and Holly made the same number of posters. How many posters did Shana make?

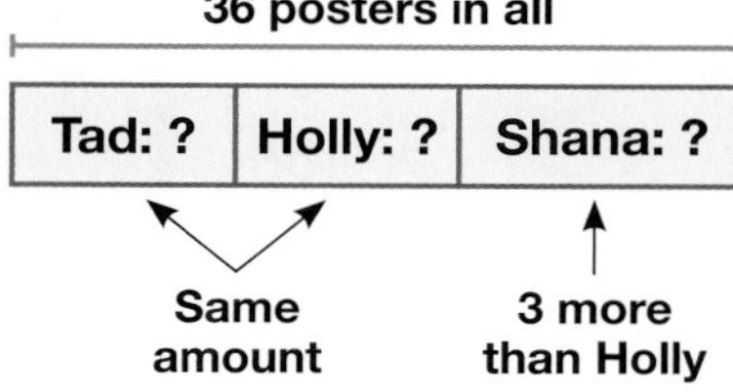

Guided Practice*

Do you know HOW?

1. Peg and Pat are sharing 64 crayons. Pat has 10 more crayons than Peg. How many crayons does each girl have?

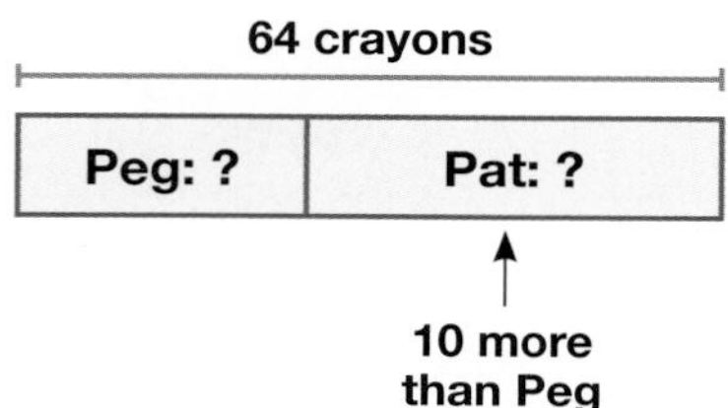

Do you UNDERSTAND?

2. Look at the diagram for Problem 1. Why aren't the two parts of the rectangle the same size?

3. **Write a Problem** Write a real-world problem that can be solved by using reasoning to make good tries.

Independent Practice

4. All together, Rod has 38 crayons, markers, and pencils. He has 5 more crayons than markers. He has the same number of markers and pencils. How many markers does he have?

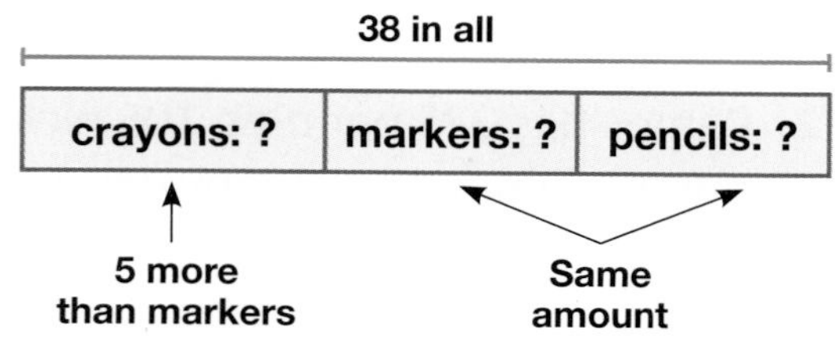

Stuck? Try this....

- What do I know?
- What am I asked to find?
- What diagram can I use to help understand the problem?
- Can I use addition, subtraction, multiplication, or division?
- Is all of my work correct?
- Did I answer the right question?
- Is my answer reasonable?

*For another example, see Set E on page 69.

Plan

Use reasoning to make good tries. Then check.

Try: 10 + 10 + 13 = 33

Check: 33 < 36

Too low, I need 3 more.

Try: 12 + 12 + 15 = 39

Check: 39 > 36

Too high, I need 3 less.

Solve

Revise, using what you know.

Try: 11 + 11 + 14 = 36

Check: 36 = 36

This is correct.

Shana made 14 posters.

Use the pictures at the right for **5** and **6**.

5. The clerk at the flower store puts all the roses into two vases. One vase has 2 more roses than the other vase. How many roses are in each vase?

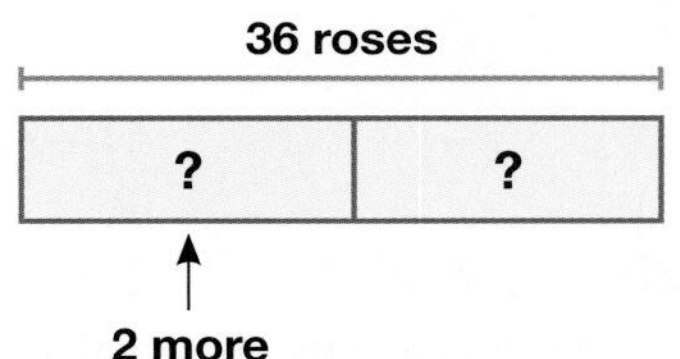

6. Edna, Jay, and Bob bought all of the carnations in the flower store. Edna bought 2 more than Jay. Bob and Jay bought the same number. How many carnations did Edna buy?

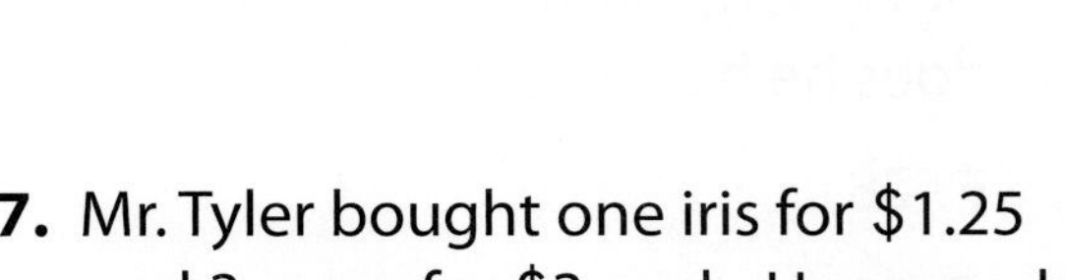

7. Mr. Tyler bought one iris for $1.25 and 3 roses for $3 each. How much did Mr. Tyler spend for the roses?

8. Cam bought an iris for $1.25. He paid with 6 coins. What coins did he use?

9. Jared is thinking of two numbers. They have a sum of 12 and a difference of 6. What are the two numbers?

A 11 and 1

B 10 and 2

C 9 and 3

D 8 and 4

10. Hanna has 6 coins worth 50¢ in all. Some of the coins are nickels and some are dimes. What coins does Hanna have?

F 5 dimes and 1 nickel

G 4 dimes and 2 nickels

H 3 dimes and 3 nickels

J 2 dimes and 4 nickels

TAKS Test Prep

1. The table shows the number of electoral votes for President of the United States, in 1789.

Data

First Election	
Vote For	**Number of Votes**
George Washington	69
John Adams	34
Others	35
Votes not cast	12

Which number sentence shows how many votes George Washington and John Adams got together? (3-1)

A 69 + 34 + 12 = ▢

B 34 + 35 = ▢

C 69 + 35 = ▢

D 69 + 34 = ▢

2. Between 6 A.M. and 10 A.M., 389 trucks and 599 cars crossed a bridge. How many vehicles is this in all? (3-3)

F 878

G 888

H 978

J 988

3. Tricia spent $35 on a toy bed, $48 on a toy dresser, and $24 on a table. How much did she spend in all? (3-4)

A $107

B $97

C $83

D $72

4. Dallas is 343 square miles and Fort Worth is 293 square miles. How many square miles is this in all? (3-3)

F 636

G 626

H 536

J 50

5. Which addition sentence is shown? (3-2)

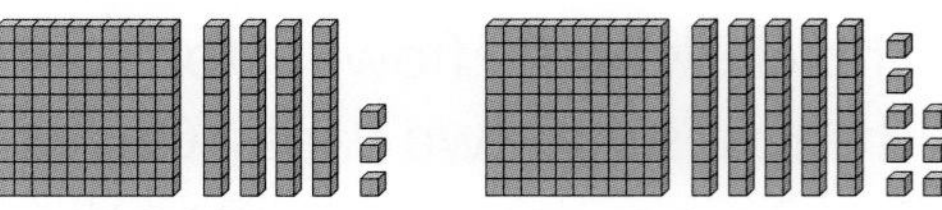

A 143 + 157 = ▢

B 143 + 158 = ▢

C 143 + 147 = ▢

D 8 + 14 = ▢

6. Kent has 28 butterflies, 16 beetles, and 12 grasshoppers in his collection. How many butterflies and beetles does he have? (3-1)

F 28

G 40

H 44

J 56

7. Two states have 64 counties each. Another state has 88 counties. Which number sentence shows how many counties these 3 states have in all? (3-4)

A 64 + 88 = ▢

B 64 + 88 + 3 = ▢

C 64 + 64 + 88 = ▢

D 64 + 88 + 88 = ▢

8. Each of the 26 students in Carrie's class chose either drums or horns to play during music class. If 4 more students chose drums than horns, how many chose each? (3-5)

F 16 chose drums, 10 chose horns

G 15 chose drums, 11 chose horns

H 14 chose drums, 12 chose horns

J 14 chose drums, 10 chose horns

9. Jupiter has 63 moons, Saturn has 47 moons, and Uranus has 27 moons. How many moons do these 3 planets have all together? (3-4)

A 110

B 127

C 137

D 140

10. The Aztec Ruins has about 318 acres. Capulin Volcano has about 793 acres. Which is a reasonable total size for these two national monuments in New Mexico? (3-3)

F 1,211 acres, because 318 + 793 is about 400 + 800 = 1,200

G 1,111 acres, because 318 + 793 is about 300 + 800 = 1,100

H 1,011 acres, because 318 + 793 is about 300 + 700 = 1,000

J 911 acres, because 318 + 793 is about 300 + 600 = 900

11. In a survey, 468 people said yes, a pet could make them happy, 293 said no, and 39 people did not know. Which number sentence shows how many people said yes or no? (3-3)

A 468 + 293 + 39 = ▢

B 468 + 39 = ▢

C 293 + 39 = ▢

D 468 + 293 = ▢

12. El Paso has 145 city parks and San Antonio has 193 city parks. How many city parks do the two cities have in all? (3-2)

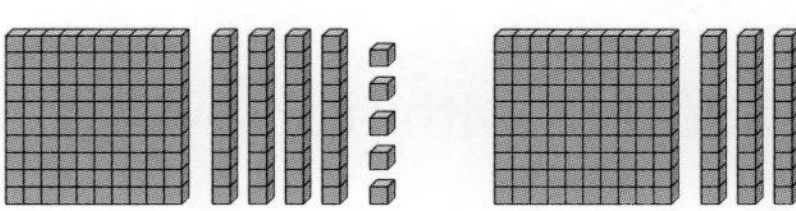

F 48

G 238

H 328

J 338

13. Party favors come in packages of 10, 20, or 25. Cristina bought 50 favors in 3 packages. Which sizes of packages could she have bought? (3-5)

A 20, 10, and 10

B 20, 20, and 10

C 25 and 25

D 25 and 20

14. **Griddable Response** Marty's Toy Store has 36 teddy bears and 28 stuffed horses. How many teddy bears and stuffed horses does it have in all? (3-1)

Reteaching

Set A, pages 54–55

Find 96 + 68.

First estimate: 96 + 68 =

100 + 70 = 170

Then, add.

```
   1
   9 6    6 + 8 = 14 ones
+  6 8    Regroup into 1 ten 4 ones.
 1 6 4    1 ten + 9 tens + 6 tens = 16 tens
```

164 is close to 170, so 164 is reasonable.

Remember to add ones first. Regroup if necessary. Then add tens.

Estimate. Then find each sum. Check that your sum is reasonable.

1. 38 + 47
2. 77 + 56
3. 62 + 9
4. 24 + 81
5. 55 + 89
6. 58 + 33

Set B, pages 56–58

Find 125 + 168.

Show 125 and 168 with place-value blocks.

5 ones + 8 ones = 13 ones
Regroup.
13 ones = 1 ten 3 ones

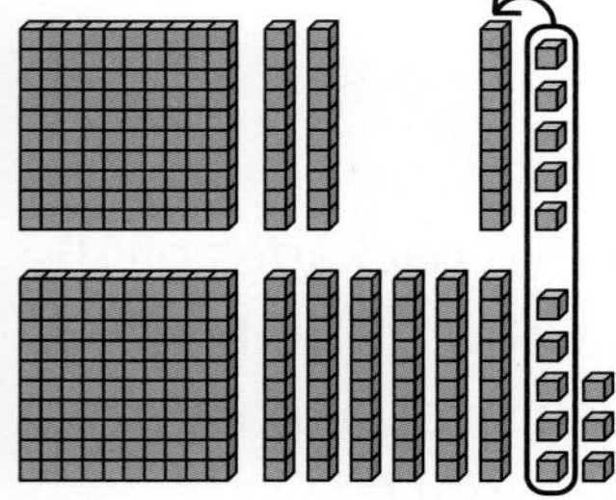

1 ten + 2 tens + 6 tens = 9 tens

Add the hundreds.
1 hundred + 1 hundred = 2 hundreds

So, 125 + 168 = 293.

Remember to add ones, then tens, then hundreds.

Find each sum. Use place-value blocks or draw a picture to help.

1. 265 + 116

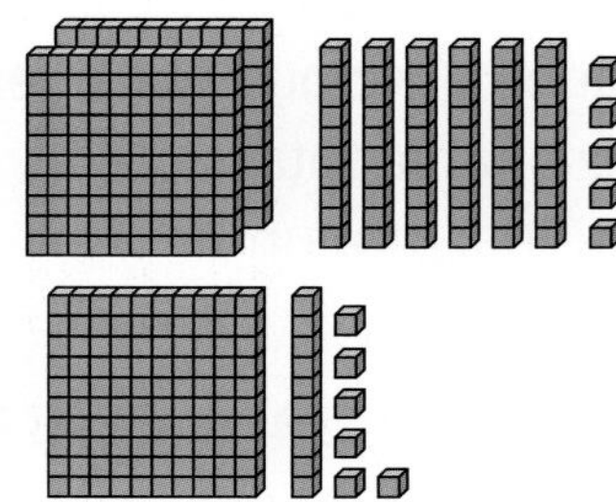

2. 113 + 37

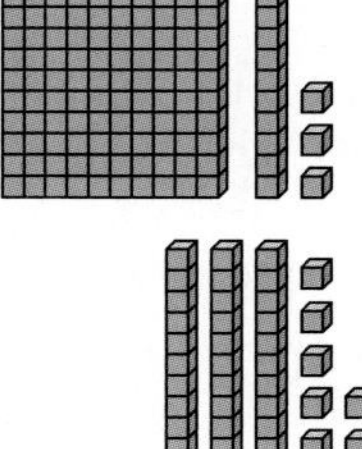

3. 318 + 188
4. 272 + 162

Set C, pages 60–61

Find 276 + 189.

Estimate: 300 + 200 = 500

Then, add.

```
  1 1
  2 7 6
+ 1 8 9
-------
  4 6 5
```

6 + 9 = 15 ones
Regroup into 1 ten 5 ones.

1 ten + 7 tens + 8 tens = 16 tens
Regroup into 1 hundred 6 tens.

1 hundred + 2 hundreds + 1 hundred = 4 hundreds

465 is close to 500, so 465 is reasonable.

Remember you can regroup 10 ones as 1 ten and 10 tens as 1 hundred.

Estimate. Then find each sum.

1. 718 + 156
2. 213 + 538
3. 652 + 184
4. 386 + 766
5. 311 + 289
6. 371 + 283

Set D, pages 62–63

Find 43 + 187 + 238.

Estimate: 40 + 190 + 240 = 470

```
  1 1
    4 3
  1 8 7
+ 2 3 8
-------
  4 6 8
```

Line up ones, tens, and hundreds. Then add each column. Regroup as needed.

468 is close to 470, so 468 is reasonable.

Remember to estimate so you can check if your answer is reasonable.

Find each sum.

1. 25 + 67 + 132
2. 139 + 209 + 55
3. 328 + 381 + 42
4. 56 + 167 + 35

Set E, pages 64–65

Follow these steps for using Try, Check, and Revise to solve problems.

Step 1 Think to make a reasonable first try.

Step 2 Check using information from the problem.

Step 3 Revise. Use your first try to make a reasonable second try. Check.

Step 4 Continue trying and checking until you find the correct answer.

Remember to check each try.

Use Try, Check, and Revise to solve.

1. Ray and Tony have 32 markers. Ray has 2 more markers than Tony. How many markers does each boy have?

2. The soccer club has 28 members. There are 4 more girls than boys. How many boys are in the soccer club?

Topic 4

Subtraction Number Sense

1 The Apollo astronauts talked with each other and with Mission Control at the Johnson Space Center in Houston, Texas. How many of the Apollo missions landed on the Moon? You will find out in Lesson 4-1.

2 How much longer was a *Brachiosaurus* than a *Tyrannosaurus rex*? You will find out in Lesson 4-4.

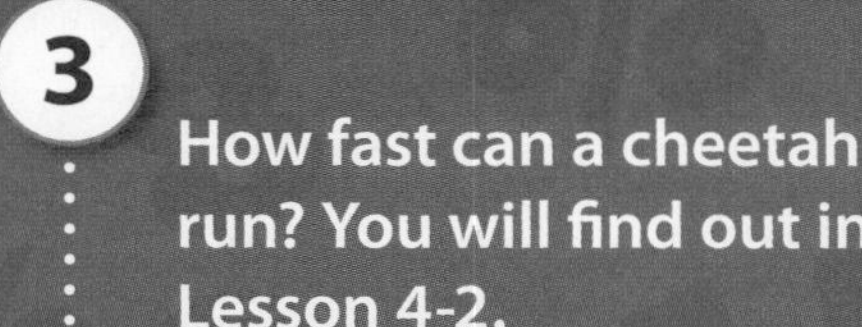

3 How fast can a cheetah run? You will find out in Lesson 4-2.

4 The giant Rafflesia plant has the largest flower in the world. How large is it? You will find out in Lesson 4-3.

Review What You Know!

Vocabulary

Choose the best term from the box.

- add
- round
- skip count
- subtract

1. To take away a part from a whole, you can __?__.
2. You can __?__ to find a number that is close to the actual number.
3. To join parts together, you can __?__.

Subtraction Facts

Find each difference.

4. 9 − 5 **5.** 11 − 3 **6.** 16 − 7

Addition Facts

Find each sum.

7. 4 + 8 **8.** 9 + 8 **9.** 6 + 7

Rounding

Writing to Explain

10. To what two numbers can you round 78? Explain why there is more than one way to round 78.
11. Is the sum of 5 + 8 the same as or different from the sum of 8 + 5? Explain.

Lesson

4-1

TEKS 3.3A: Model addition and subtraction using pictures, words, and numbers.

Subtraction Meanings

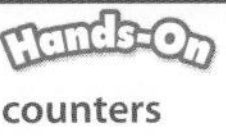

counters

When do you subtract?

Ms. Aydin's class is making school flags to sell at the school fair.

The table shows how many flags several students have made so far.

Data

Flags for School Fair	
Student	**Number Made**
Brent	12
Devon	9
Keisha	11
Ling	14
Pedro	7
Rick	8

Another Example **You subtract to find a missing addend.**

Rick plans on making 13 flags. How many more flags does he need?

The parts and the whole show how addition and subtraction are related.

13 flags in all	
8	?

$8 + \square = 13$

You can write a fact family when you know the parts and the whole.

A fact family is a group of related facts using the same numbers.

$5 + 8 = 13$ $\quad 13 - 8 = 5$

$8 + 5 = 13$ $\quad 13 - 5 = 8$

The missing part is 5. This means Rick needs to make 5 more flags.

Guided Practice*

Do you know HOW?

Use the table to write and solve a number sentence.

1. How many more flags has Ling made than Devon?

2. How many more flags must Pedro make to have 15 in all? to have the same number as Ling?

Do you UNDERSTAND?

3. Ling sold 8 of the flags she had made. Write a number sentence to find how many flags she has left. Then solve the problem.

4. **Write a Problem** Write and solve a word problem that can be solved by subtracting.

*For another example, see Set A on page 88.

Subtract to take some away and find how many are left.

Brent sold 5 of the flags he made. How many flags did he have left?

12 flags in all

5	?

$12 - 5 = 7$

Brent had 7 flags left.

Subtract to compare amounts.

How many more flags did Keisha make than Pedro?

Keisha	11	
Pedro	?	7

$11 - 7 = 4$

Keisha made 4 more flags than Pedro.

Independent Practice

Write a number sentence for each situation. Solve.

5. Pat has 15 pins. Chris has 9 pins. How many more pins does Pat have than Chris?

Pat	15	
Chris	9	?

6. How many more orange flags than green flags are there?

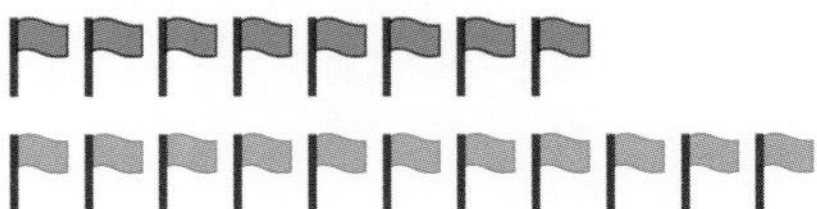

TAKS Problem Solving

7. Ching had 12 pies to sell. After she sold some of the pies, she had 4 pies left. How many pies had Ching sold?

8. A pole holding a state flag is 10 feet tall. The height of the flag is 4 feet. How many feet taller is the pole than the flag?

9. The space program had 12 manned *Apollo* missions. How many of these missions did not land on the Moon?

Six *Apollo* spacecraft landed on the Moon.

10. Rob had 17 pens. After he gave some of them to his friend, he had 8 pens. Which number sentence shows one way to find how many pens Rob gave to his friend?

A $17 + 8 = \square$

B $8 - 1 = \square$

C $17 - 1 = \square$

D $17 - \square = 8$

Lesson

4-2

TEKS 3.3A: Model addition and subtraction using pictures, words, and numbers.

Subtracting on a Hundred Chart

How can you subtract on a hundred chart?

Find 38 − 20 on a hundred chart.

Start at 38. To count back 2 tens, move up 2 rows.

38 − 20 = 18

1	2	3	4	5	6	7	8	9	10
11	12	13	14	15	16	17	18	19	20
21	22	23	24	25	26	27	28	29	30
31	32	33	34	35	36	37	38	39	40
41	42	43	44	45	46	47	48	49	50

Another Example How can you use counting on to find differences?

The difference is the answer when subtracting two numbers.

Find 43 − 19.

Think 19 + ☐ = 43.

Start at 19.
Move right one square to count on to the next ten.
20

Count on by tens by moving down two rows.
30, 40

Then count on by ones until you reach 43.
41, 42, 43

You counted on: 1 + 20 + 3 = 24.

So, 43 − 19 = 24.

1	2	3	4	5	6	7	8	9	10
11	12	13	14	15	16	17	18	19	20
21	22	23	24	25	26	27	28	29	30
31	32	33	34	35	36	37	38	39	40
41	42	43	44	45	46	47	48	49	50
51	52	53	54	55	56	57	58	59	60
61	62	63	64	65	66	67	68	69	70
71	72	73	74	75	76	77	78	79	80
81	82	83	84	85	86	87	88	89	90
91	92	93	94	95	96	97	98	99	100

Explain It

1. Why do you stop at 20 when you first count on from 19?
2. Why do you add 1 + 20 + 3?

Find 85 − 19.

Think 85 − 20 = ☐

Start at 85 on the hundred chart.

Count back 2 tens to subtract 20.
To do this, move up two rows.
75, 65

Since you subtracted 1 more than 19, add 1 by moving to the right one square.
65 + 1 = 66

51	52	53	54	55	56	57	58	59	60
61	62	63	64	65	66	67	68	69	70
71	72	73	74	75	76	77	78	79	80
81	82	83	84	85	86	87	88	89	90
91	92	93	94	95	96	97	98	99	100

So, 85 − 19 = 66.

Guided Practice*

Do you know HOW?

Use a hundred chart to subtract.

1. 72 − 40

2. 86 − 30

3. 54 − 29

4. 95 − 39

5. 37 − 18

Do you UNDERSTAND?

6. **Writing to Explain** When you move up 2 rows on a hundred chart, how many are you subtracting? Explain.

7. How is subtracting ten on a hundred chart different from adding ten on a hundred chart?

8. Janey has 75 cents. She wants to buy a sticker that costs 39 cents. How much money would she have left? Explain how to use a hundred chart to find the answer.

Independent Practice

Use a hundred chart to subtract.

9. 75 − 30 **10.** 53 − 20 **11.** 68 − 40 **12.** 27 − 10

13. 84 − 50 **14.** 96 − 60 **15.** 47 − 19 **16.** 53 − 28

17. 65 − 39 **18.** 81 − 58 **19.** 76 − 29 **20.** 94 − 38

21. 96 − 17 **22.** 79 − 15 **23.** 81 − 26 **24.** 77 − 48

DIGITAL Animated Glossary
www.pearsonsuccessnet.com

*For another example, see Set B on page 88.

TAKS Problem Solving

Use the table for **25–27**.

25. A cottonwood tree in Max's yard is 30 feet shorter than an average cottonwood tree. How tall is the tree in his yard?

26. Write the average heights of the trees from shortest to tallest.

Data

State Trees		
State	**Kind of Tree**	**Average Height**
Kansas	Cottonwood	75 feet
Michigan	Eastern White Pine	70 feet
New York	Sugar maple	80 feet

27. A sugar maple tree in the local park is 92 feet tall. How many feet taller is the tree in the park than an average sugar maple tree?

28. **Writing to Explain** A white pine tree is 52 feet tall. If it grows 10 feet in 7 years, how tall will it be in 7 years? Explain how you found your answer.

29. **Reasonableness** Liam used a hundred chart to find 92 − 62. He said the difference is 40. Is his answer reasonable? Why or why not?

Tip *What addition sentence can help?*

30. The workers in the lunchroom made 234 ham sandwiches and 165 tuna sandwiches. They also made 150 cheese pizzas and 125 veggie pizzas. How many sandwiches did they make in all?

31. For short distances, an elephant can run as fast as 15 miles per hour. How much faster can a cheetah run than an elephant?

A cheetah can run short distances as fast as 70 miles an hour.

32. John is 56 inches tall. John's father is 72 inches tall. How much taller is John's father than John? Explain how you found your answer.

33. Maya had 15 small rocks. She had 9 large rocks. Which number sentence shows one way to find how many more small rocks than large rocks Maya had?

A 15 − 9 = ☐

B 15 + 6 = ☐

C 15 + 9 = ☐

D 24 − 15 = ☐

Addition and Subtraction Number Sentences

The symbol = means "is equal to."
In a number sentence, the symbol = tells you that the value on the left is equal to the value on the right.

Examples: $29 = 20 + 9$

$6 = 11 - 5$

$9 + 4 = 13$

The value on the left side of the number sentence is equal to the value on the right side.

Copy and complete. Write the number that makes the number sentence true.

1. $9 + \square = 11$ **2.** $10 = 3 + \square$ **3.** $17 - \square = 9$

4. $5 + \square = 13$ **5.** $8 = 12 - \square$ **6.** $14 = 5 + \square$

7. $10 = 10 + \square$ **8.** $6 + \square = 26$ **9.** $19 + \square = 29$

10. $50 + \square = 60$ **11.** $30 = 40 - \square$ **12.** $25 = 5 + \square$

13. $10 + \square = 17$ **14.** $42 = 45 - \square$ **15.** $13 - \square = 0$

For **16** and **17**, copy and complete the number sentence below each problem. Use it to solve the problem.

16. Nate had 10 river stones. Chen had 26 river stones. How many more river stones did Chen have than Nate?

$10 + \square = 26$

17. Tania collected 10 more leaves than Gwen. Tania collected 37 leaves. How many leaves did Gwen collect?

$\square + 10 = 37$

18. **Write a Problem** Write and solve a real-world problem to match the number sentence on the right.

$48 = 20 + \square$

Lesson
4-3

TEKS 3.3B: Select addition or subtraction and use the operation to solve problems involving whole numbers through 999.

Using Mental Math to Subtract

How can you subtract with mental math?

The store is having a sale on jackets. A jacket is on sale for $17 less than the original price. What is the sale price?

You can use mental math to subtract and solve this problem.

Guided Practice*

Do you know HOW?

In **1–8**, find each difference using mental math.

1. 26 − 18 **2.** 34 − 19

3. 73 − 16 **4.** 45 − 27

5. 67 − 28 **6.** 83 − 39

7. 46 − 18 **8.** 49 − 19

Do you UNDERSTAND?

9. **Writing to Explain** In the One Way example above, why do you add 3 to 32 instead of subtract 3 from 32?

10. Suppose a coat has an original price of $74 and it is on sale for $18 less than the original price. What is the sale price of the coat? How can you use mental math to solve this problem?

Independent Practice

In **11–30**, find each difference using mental math.

11. 28 − 19 **12.** 46 − 18 **13.** 39 − 17 **14.** 68 − 11

15. 52 − 9 **16.** 75 − 12 **17.** 29 − 18 **18.** 49 − 18

19. 64 − 15 **20.** 43 − 16 **21.** 97 − 14 **22.** 86 − 13

23. 31 − 14 **24.** 98 − 17 **25.** 57 − 18 **26.** 72 − 19

27. 53 − 39 **28.** 27 − 19 **29.** 82 − 27 **30.** 73 − 39

*For another example, see Set C on page 89.

One Way

52 − 17 = ▢

It's easier to subtract 20.
52 − 20 = 32

If you subtract 20, you subtract 3 more than 17. You must add 3 to the answer.

32 + 3 = 35

52 − 17 = 35

The sale price is $35.

Another Way

52 − 17 = ▢

Make a simpler problem by changing each number in the same way.

You can change 17 to 20 because it's easy to subtract 20. So, add 3 to both 17 and 52.

52 − 17 = ▢
↓ +3   ↓ +3
55 − 20 = 35

52 − 17 = 35

TAKS Problem Solving

31. Number Sense The giant Rafflesia flower can be as wide as shown in the picture. One petal can be 18 inches wide. How can you use mental math to find how much wider the whole flower is than one petal?

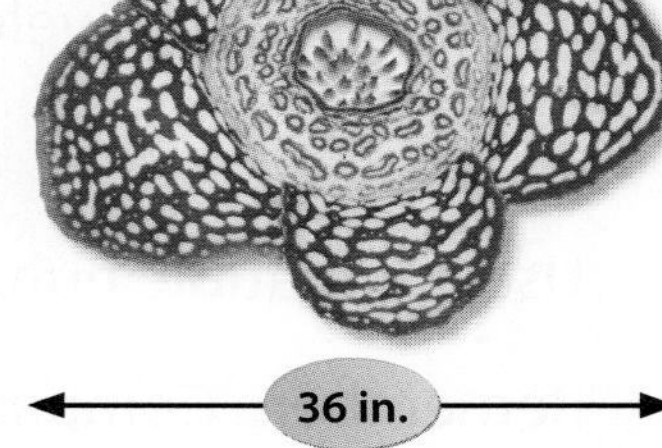

32. Writing to Explain To subtract 57 − 16, Tom added 4 to each number, while Saul added 3 to each number. Will both methods work to find the correct answer? Explain.

In **33** and **34**, use the photo below.

33. a What is the sale price of the jeans? Describe one way you can use mental math to find the answer.

b Maria bought two pairs of jeans. What was the total sale price of the jeans Maria bought?

34. Which number sentence shows the original price of two pairs of jeans?

A 46 + 46 = ▢

B 46 + 18 = ▢

C 18 + 18 = ▢

D 46 − 18 = ▢

35. Eva saved $38. She bought a book for $17. Which number sentence shows one way to find how much money Eva had left?

F 38 + 17 = ▢

G 38 − 17 = ▢

H ▢ − 38 = 17

J ▢ − 17 = 38

Lesson

4-4

TEKS 3.5A: Round whole numbers to the nearest ten or hundred to approximate reasonable results in problem situations.
TEKS 3.5B: Use strategies including rounding and compatible numbers to estimate solutions to addition and subtraction problems.

Estimating Differences

How can you estimate differences?

All of the tickets for a concert were sold. So far, 126 people have arrived at the concert. About how many people who have tickets have not arrived?

Since you need to find *about* how many, you can estimate.

Estimate 493 − 126 by rounding.

Another Example How can you use compatible numbers to estimate differences?

The Perry family is taking a car trip. The trip is 372 miles long. So far, the family has traveled 149 miles. About how many miles are left to travel?

Use compatible numbers to estimate 372 − 149.

Remember: Compatible numbers are numbers that are close and easy to work with.

$$\begin{array}{r} 372 \\ -\ 149 \\ \hline \end{array} \longrightarrow \begin{array}{r} 375 \\ -\ 150 \\ \hline 225 \end{array}$$

The Perry family still has about 225 miles to travel.

Explain It

1. How are the numbers 375 and 150 easy to work with?
2. Use a different pair of compatible numbers to estimate 372 − 149.
3. Is an estimate enough to solve this problem? Why or why not?

One Way

You can round each number to the nearest hundred.

$$\begin{array}{r} 493 \\ -\ 126 \\ \hline \end{array} \longrightarrow \begin{array}{r} 500 \\ -\ 100 \\ \hline 400 \end{array}$$

About 400 people have not yet arrived.

Another Way

You can round each number to the nearest ten.

$$\begin{array}{r} 493 \\ -\ 126 \\ \hline \end{array} \longrightarrow \begin{array}{r} 490 \\ -\ 130 \\ \hline 360 \end{array}$$

About 360 people have not yet arrived.

Guided Practice*

Do you know HOW?

In **1** and **2**, round to the nearest hundred to estimate each difference.

1. 321 − 112 **2.** 255 − 189

In **3** and **4**, round to the nearest ten to estimate each difference.

3. 579 − 214 **4.** 216 − 97

In **5** and **6**, use compatible numbers to estimate each difference.

5. 328 − 207 **6.** 472 − 148

Do you UNDERSTAND?

7. Writing to Explain In the problem above, which way of rounding gives an estimate that is closer to the actual difference? Explain why.

8. The theater sold 415 tickets to the comedy show. So far, 273 people have arrived at the show. About how many more people are expected to arrive? Tell which estimation method you used and how you found your answer.

Independent Practice

In **9–11**, round to the nearest hundred to estimate each difference.

9. 186 − 75 **10.** 704 − 369 **11.** 291 − 93

In **12–17**, round to the nearest ten to estimate each difference.

12. 88 − 32 **13.** 149 − 95 **14.** 361 − 117

15. 75 − 41 **16.** 86 − 38 **17.** 227 − 121

For another example, see Set D on page 89.

Independent Practice

In **18–23**, use compatible numbers to estimate each difference.

18. 77 − 28 **19.** 202 − 144 **20.** 611 − 168

21. 512 − 205 **22.** 342 − 153 **23.** 904 − 31

Use the table for **24–27**.

24. The concert hall sold 28 fewer tickets for the Sunday concert than for the Friday concert. About how many tickets were sold for the Sunday concert?

25. About how many tickets in all were sold for Thursday and for Friday?

Data

Grand Concert Hall	
Day of Concert	**Number of Tickets Sold**
Wednesday	506
Thursday	323
Friday	251
Saturday	427
Sunday	

26. Think About the Process About how many more tickets were sold for the Wednesday concert than for the Friday concert? Write a number sentence that uses numbers rounded to the nearest ten to estimate how many more. Explain your answer.

28. Writing to Explain About how many feet longer was a *Brachiosaurus* than a *T. rex*? Use compatible numbers to estimate. Explain why you chose the numbers you used.

27. Which number sentence shows the best way to estimate how many fewer tickets were sold for the Friday concert than the Thursday concert?

A 400 − 200 = 200

B 300 − 300 = 0

C 325 − 200 = 125

D 325 − 250 = 75

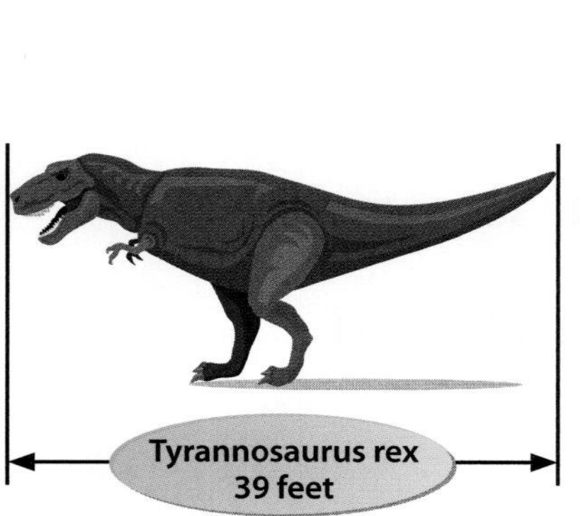

Mixed Problem Solving

The length of one year on a planet is the total time for the planet to make one complete trip around the Sun.

Planet	Length of Year (in Earth Days)
Mercury	88
Venus	225
Earth	365
Mars	687
Jupiter	4,330
Saturn	10,756
Uranus	30,687
Neptune	60,190

1. About how many fewer Earth days is a year on Mercury than a year on Earth?

2. About how many more Earth days is a year on Mars than a year on Earth?

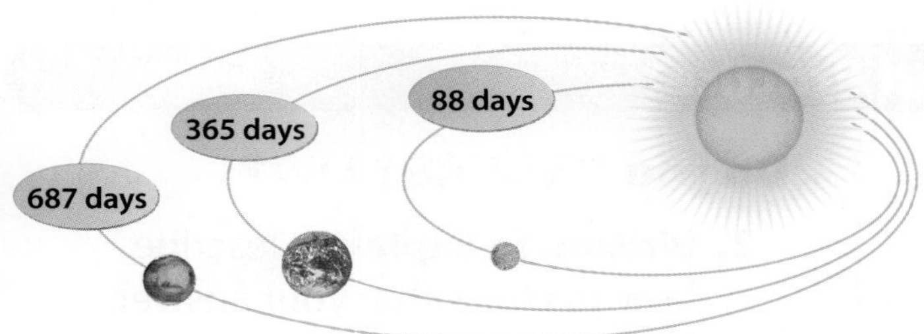

3. Which planet has a digit 6 with a value of sixty thousand in the length of its year?

4. Which planet has a year that is about six thousand Earth days more than Jupiter's?

5. Which space object listed in the table at the right has an average surface temperature closest to Mercury's?

6. Write the average surface temperatures in order from least to greatest.

Space Object	Average Surface Temperature
Mercury	332°F
Earth	59°F
Moon	225°F
Venus	854°F

7. Strategy Focus Solve. Use the strategy Make an Organized List.

Meg's favorite planet has at least 5 letters in its name. The length of its year is less than 10,000 Earth days. List all the planets that fit these clues.

Lesson

4-5

TEKS 3.16B Justify why an answer is reasonable and explain the solution process.

Problem Solving

Reasonableness

Al had the marbles shown at the right. He gave 18 marbles to his brother. How many marbles does Al have left?

After you solve a problem, ask yourself:

- Is the answer reasonable?
- Did I answer the right question?

53 marbles in all

18 marbles	?

Guided Practice*

Do you know HOW?

1. Rosita is reading a book that is 65 pages long. She has 27 pages left to read. How many pages has she already read?

65 pages in all

?	27

Do you UNDERSTAND?

2. **Writing to Explain** Describe how to check that your answer is reasonable and that you have answered the right question.

3. **Write a Problem** Write and solve a real-world problem. Check that your answer is reasonable.

Independent Practice

Solve. Then check that your answer is reasonable.

4. James is reading a book that is 85 pages long. He read 35 pages yesterday and 24 pages today. How many pages did James read in the two days?

? pages in all

35	24

5. Kyle had 56 model cars. He gave his brother 36 of them. How many model cars does Kyle have now?

- What do I know?
- What am I asked to find?
- What diagram can I use to help understand the problem?
- Can I use addition, subtraction, multiplication, or division?
- Is all of my work correct?
- Did I answer the right question?
- Is my answer reasonable?

*For another example, see Set E on page 89.

Jim's Answer

53 − 18 = 35
Al's brother has 35 marbles.

53 − 18 is about 50 − 20, or 30.

35 is close to 30, so 35 is reasonable.

The number 35 is reasonable, but Jim did not answer the right question.

Sally's Answer

53 − 18 = 45
Al has 45 marbles left.

53 − 18 is about 50 − 20, or 30.

45 is not close to 30, so 45 is not reasonable.

Sally answered the right question, but the number 45 is not reasonable.

Pablo's Answer

53 − 18 = 35
Al has 35 marbles left.

53 − 18 is about 50 − 20, or 30.

35 is close to 30, so 35 is reasonable.

The number 35 is reasonable, and Pablo did answer the right question.

Independent Practice

Use the table to solve **6–8**. Estimate, then check that your answer is reasonable.

Data

Total Points Scored	
Games	**Points**
Game 1	68
Game 2	74
Game 3	89

6. How many points were scored all together in Games 1 and 2?

? points in all

68	74

7. There were 39 points scored in the first half of Game 1. How many points were scored in the second half?

68 points in all

39	?

8. Estimation About how many points were scored all together in the three games?

? points in all

70	70	90

9. Carl practices the piano 45 minutes each day. Today, he practiced 15 minutes after school and 10 minutes before dinner. How much time does he still need to practice?

A 70 minutes
B 60 minutes
C 35 minutes
D 20 minutes

10. Carrie has 15 pennies. Her brother has 10 more pennies than Carrie. How many pennies do they have in all?

F 40 pennies
G 25 pennies
H 10 pennies
J 5 pennies

TAKS Test Prep

1. Mario wants to have 15 insects in his collection. He has 8 insects. Which number sentence shows a way to find how many more insects Mario needs to collect? (4-1)

   A 15 − 7 = ☐

   B 15 − ☐ = 7

   C 8 + 15 = ☐

   D 8 + ☐ = 15

2. Tom had $41. He spent $17. Which is the best estimate of how much he had left? (4-4)

   F $60

   G $30

   H $20

   J $10

3. To find 67 − 19 on a hundred chart, Casie started at 67 and then moved up 2 rows. What should she do next? (4-2)

31	32	33	34	35	36	37	38	39	40
41	42	43	44	45	46	47	48	49	50
51	52	53	54	55	56	57	58	59	60
61	62	63	64	65	66	67	68	69	70

   A Move right 1 square.

   B Move left 1 square.

   C Move right 9 squares.

   D Move left 9 squares.

4. Which number sentence is shown? (4-1)

   F 3 + 7 = 10

   G 17 − 7 = 10

   H 10 − 3 = 7

   J 10 − 7 = 3

5. There are 263 children at summer camp. There are 114 boys. Which is the best estimate for the number of girls? (4-4)

   A 250

   B 150

   C 120

   D 100

6. Rosa has 9 pens. Kim has 4 pens. Which number sentence shows how many more pens Rosa has than Kim? (4-1)

   F 9 + 4 = 13

   G 13 − 4 = 9

   H 9 − 5 = 4

   J 9 − 4 = 5

7. Which is the best estimate for 392 − 84? (4-4)

   A 500

   B 400

   C 300

   D 200

8. Tropical Fish Warehouse had 98 goldfish on Monday. By Friday, they had sold 76 of the goldfish. How many goldfish had not been sold? Use mental math to solve. (4-3)

F 22

G 32

H 38

J 174

9. Big Bend National Park has 32 kinds of snakes and 22 kinds of lizards. Which number sentence shows the best way to estimate how many more kinds of snakes than lizards are in the park? (4-4)

A $30 - 20 = 10$

B $30 + 20 = 50$

C $40 - 20 = 20$

D $40 - 30 = 10$

10. Stacy has 16 spelling words. She already knows how to spell 9 of the words. How many words does she still need to learn how to spell? (4-1)

16 words in all

9	?

F 25

G 9

H 7

J 6

11. Lee drove 348 miles on Monday and 135 miles on Tuesday. Which is the most reasonable answer for how much farther he drove on Monday than on Tuesday? (4-5)

A 113 miles

B 213 miles

C 313 miles

D 483 miles

12. To subtract $62 - 17$ mentally, Talia subtracted $62 - 20 = 42$ first. What should she do next? (4-3)

F Add $42 + 2$.

G Add $42 + 3$.

H Subtract $42 - 2$.

J Subtract $42 - 3$.

13. **Griddable Response** Mia had \$83. She spent \$49. To find how much money she has left, Mia used counting on.

$49 + 1 = 50$

$50 + 30 = 80$

$80 + 3 = 83$

How many dollars does Mia have left? (4-2)

14. **Griddable Response** Jorge and his grandfather have the same birthday. Jorge will be 8 on his next birthday. His grandfather will be 62. How many years older is Jorge's grandfather than Jorge? Use mental math to solve. (4-3)

Reteaching

Set A, pages 72–73

Write a number sentence for the situation. Solve.

Anthony has 10 flags. He gives 7 flags to his friends to wave during a parade on the 4th of July. How many flags does Anthony have left?

10 flags in all

7	?

10 − 7 = 3

Anthony has 3 flags left.

Remember that you can subtract to find how many are left, to compare, or to find a missing addend.

Write a number sentence for each situation. Solve.

1. There are 8 members in a band. 5 of the band members sing. How many do not sing?
2. Juanita had 13 flowers. She gave one flower to each of her friends. She had 4 flowers left. How many flowers did Juanita give to her friends?
3. The ceiling in a room is 12 feet high. A ladder is 8 feet tall. How much higher is the ceiling than the top of the ladder?

Set B, pages 74–76

Use a hundred chart to find 76 − 18.

51	52	53	54	55	56	57	58	59	60
61	62	63	64	65	66	67	68	69	70
71	72	73	74	75	76	77	78	79	80
81	82	83	84	85	86	87	88	89	90
91	92	93	94	95	96	97	98	99	100

Start at 76.

Count up 2 rows to subtract 20.

Go right 2 spaces because you only need to subtract 18.

76 − 18 = 58

Remember to first subtract the tens. Then move to the right or left if necessary to adjust the ones.

Use a hundred chart to subtract.

1. 88 − 20
2. 53 − 30
3. 52 − 14
4. 36 − 19
5. 66 − 43
6. 72 − 16

Set C, pages 78–79

Use mental math to find 83 − 16.

Change each number in the same way to make a simpler problem.

20 is easier to subtract than 16.
So, add 4 to each number and then subtract.

83 + 4 = 87 and 16 + 4 = 20

87 − 20 = 67 so 83 − 16 = 67

Remember to change each number in the same way.

Find each difference using mental math.

1. 56 − 14 **2.** 31 − 5

3. 74 − 12 **4.** 97 − 34

Set D, pages 80–82

Estimate 486 − 177.

One Way

486 →	500	Round each number to the nearest hundred.
− 177 →	− 200	
	300	

Another Way

486 →	500	Use compatible numbers.
− 177 →	− 175	
	325	

Remember to check place value when rounding.

For **1–6**, estimate each difference.

Round to the nearest hundred.

1. 367 − 319 **2.** 872 − 110

Round to the nearest ten.

3. 78 − 54 **4.** 952 − 227

Use compatible numbers.

5. 472 − 228 **6.** 911 − 347

Set E, pages 84–85

Carla is reading a book that has 87 pages. She has read 49 pages. How many pages does she have left to read?

Estimate: 87 − 49 is about 90 − 50, or 40.
87 − 49 = 38.

Carla has 38 pages left to read. The answer is reasonable because 38 is close to the estimate of 40.

Remember that you can use an estimate to check if your answer is reasonable.

1. Lucy has 45 tulips. There are 27 red tulips. The rest are yellow. How many yellow tulips does Lucy have?

2. Cody had 43 toys. He gave Ty 27 of them. How many toys does Cody have now?

Topics 1–4

Spiral Review

Number and Operations

1. What is the value of the underlined digit in 507,892?

   A 7

   B 70

   C 7,000

   D 70,000

2. Use the models to find 382 + 509.

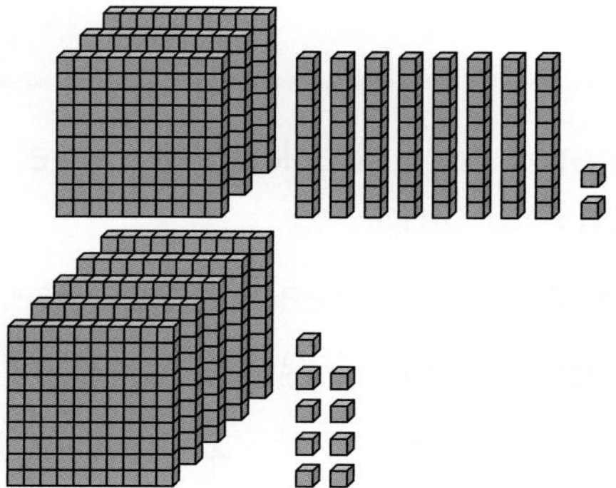

   F 871

   G 881

   H 891

   J 901

3. Estimate 88 + 73. Then find the actual sum.

4. Round to the nearest hundred to estimate 576 − 392.

5. Write and solve a number sentence for this situation: Hector has 15 markers in a box. He takes 9 markers out of the box to color a picture. How many markers are left in the box?

6. **Writing to Explain** Explain how you can use mental math to find the difference 83 − 17.

Geometry and Measurement

7. How many edges does the rectangular prism have?

   A 4 **B** 6 **C** 8 **D** 12

8. Ty traces around the flat surface of a cylinder. What shape will he make?

   F Square **H** Triangle

   G Circle **J** Rectangle

9. What is the area of the square?

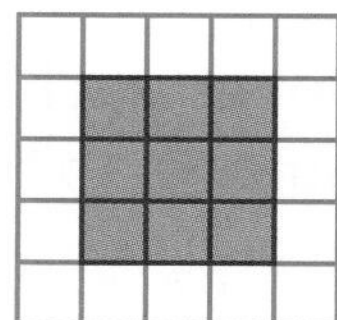

   A 3 square units **C** 8 square units

   B 6 square units **D** 9 square units

10. Which activity will you most likely be doing outside if the temperature is 30°F?

   F Ice skating **H** Raking leaves

   G Swimming **J** Roller blading

11. Devon left his house at 6 P.M. He returned home at 9 P.M. How long was Devon gone from his house?

12. **Writing to Explain** Suppose you want to fill a container with water. Will you need to use a greater number of quarts or gallons to fill the container? Explain.

Spiral Review

Probability and Statistics

Use the pictograph for **13–16**.

Lemonade Sold	
Saturday	◯ ◯ ◯
Sunday	◯ ◯ ◯ ◯ ◯
Monday	◯
Key: Each ◯ = 2 glasses	

13. How many glasses of lemonade were sold on Monday?

A 1 **C** 3

B 2 **D** 4

14. How many more glasses were sold on Sunday than on Saturday?

F 2 **H** 4

G 3 **J** 8

15. How many glasses were sold in all?

A 27 **C** 9

B 18 **D** 5

16. On this graph, how many symbols would be used to stand for 16 glasses?

17. Writing to Explain There are 10 red, 3 yellow, and 5 blue cubes in a bag. Which color are you more likely to pick than the others? Explain.

Algebraic Thinking

18. Continue the pattern.

3, 6, 9, ▢, ▢, ▢

F 12, 15, 18

G 10, 11, 12

H 11, 13, 15

J 10, 12, 14

19. What is the rule for this table?

Dan's age	6	13	11	19
Lina's age	13	20	18	26

A Add 6.

B Add 7.

C Subtract 9.

D Subtract 8.

20. Find the missing number:

$15 = \square + (4 + 5)$

F 23 **H** 9

G 15 **J** 6

21. Bill has 7 coins worth a total of $0.84. He has one half dollar and four pennies. Use the strategy Try, Check, and Revise to find what other coins Bill has.

22. Writing to Explain Write a whole number that makes the number sentence true. Explain how you found your answer.

$90 - \square < 50$

Topic 5

Subtracting Whole Numbers to Solve Problems

1 How much fresh and processed fruit does a person eat in a year? You will find out in Lesson 5-5.

2 The world's largest "basket" is really a building in Newark, Ohio. How big is this basket? You will find out in Lesson 5-4.

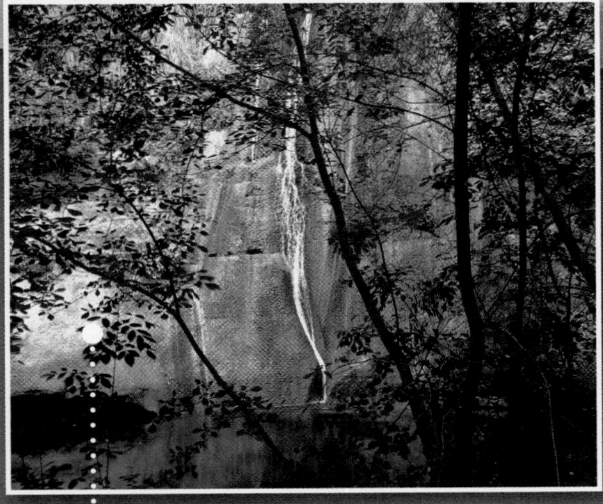

3 Madrid Falls is the second highest waterfall in Texas. How many feet less than the highest waterfall is it? Find out in Lesson 5-6.

4 How many musicians are in the largest accordion and trombone bands in the world? You will find out in Lesson 5-3.

Review What You Know!

Vocabulary

Choose the best term from the box.

- difference
- estimate
- order
- regroup

1. When you trade 1 ten for 10 ones, you ? .
2. The answer in subtraction is the ? .
3. When you find an answer that is close to the exact answer, you ? .

Estimating Facts

Round to the nearest ten to estimate each difference.

4. 255 − 104
5. 97 − 61
6. 302 − 38

Round to the nearest hundred to estimate each difference.

7. 673 − 250
8. 315 − 96
9. 789 − 713

Compatible Numbers

Writing to Explain

10. Use compatible numbers to estimate the difference 478 − 123. Explain why the numbers you chose are compatible.
11. How is rounding to estimate an answer different from using compatible numbers?

Lesson

5-1

TEKS 3.3A: Model addition and subtraction using pictures, words, and numbers.

Models for Subtracting 2-Digit Numbers

Hands-On
place-value blocks

How can you subtract with place-value blocks?

Whole numbers can be subtracted using place value. Subtract the ones first. Then subtract the tens. When needed, a ten can be traded for 10 ones.

Find 43 − 18.

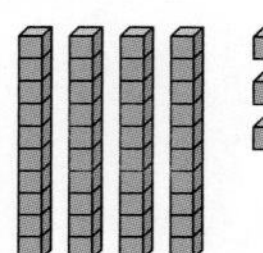

Show 43 with place-value blocks.

Guided Practice*

Do you know HOW?

In **1–6**, use place-value blocks or draw pictures to subtract.

1. 42 − 15

2. 34 − 18

3. 57 − 23

4. 25 − 16

5. 36 − 8

6. 50 − 18

Do you UNDERSTAND?

7. Why is a small 3 written above the 4 in the tens place in the example? Why is a small 13 written above the 3 in the ones place? What do you subtract to get 5 ones in the difference?

8. Nelson had 52 books in his bookcase. He gave away 38 of the books to the community center. How many books did Nelson still have in his bookcase?

Independent Practice

In **9–18**, use place-value blocks or draw pictures to subtract.

You can draw lines to show tens and Xs to show ones. This picture shows 27.

9. 21 − 17

10. 32 − 19

11. 28 − 17

12. 38 − 9

13. 43 − 24

14. 46 − 19

15. 54 − 42

16. 51 − 39

17. 63 − 37

18. 76 − 49

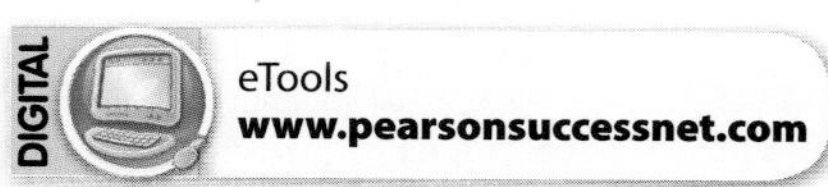

*For another example, see Set A on page 112.

Step 1

Subtract the ones.
3 ones < 8 ones
Regroup 1 ten
into 10 ones.

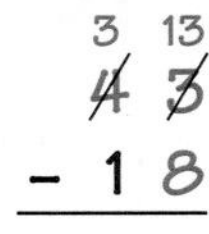

1 less ten 10 more ones

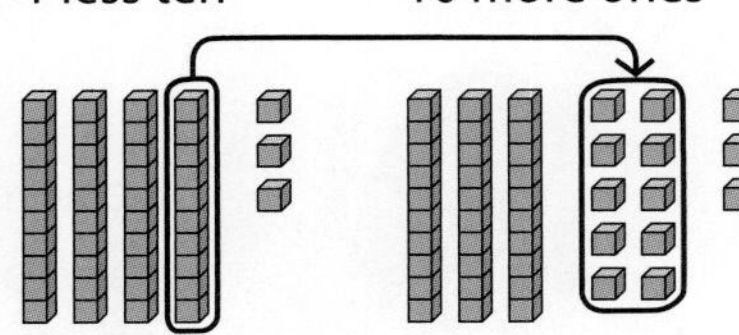

4 tens 3 ones = 3 tens 13 ones

Step 2

Subtract the ones.
13 − 8 = 5 ones

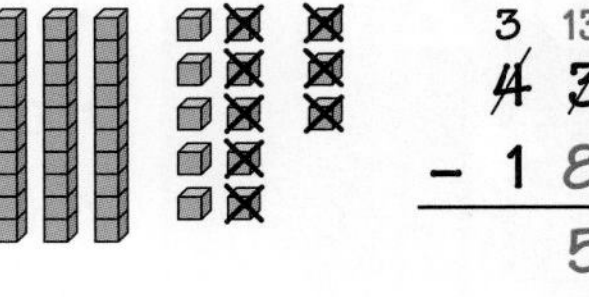

Subtract the tens.
3 tens − 1 ten = 2 tens

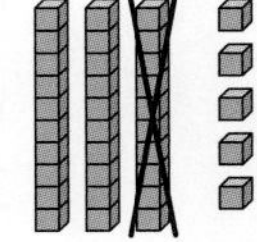

3 13
4 3
- 1 8
2 5

43 − 18 = 25

TAKS Problem Solving

For **19** and **20**, use the map at the right.

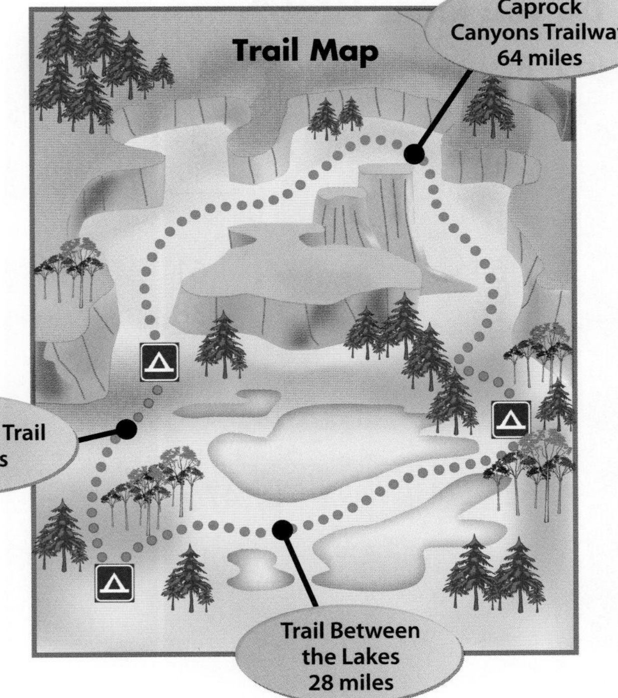

19. Hal wants to hike the Rancherias Trail and the Trail Between the Lakes. So far, he has hiked all of the Rancherias Trail and 19 miles of the Trail Between the Lakes.

a How many miles has Hal hiked so far?

b How many miles does Hal have left?

20. Tamara hiked the Trail Between the Lakes last month. She hiked the Caprock Canyons Trailway this month. How many miles did she hike in all?

21. Writing to Explain To subtract 34 − 18, Max said that 34 is equal to 2 tens and 14 ones. Is he correct? Explain how you know.

22. Ms Jones had 52 colored pencils in a package. She gave 25 of the pencils to her first art class and 18 of the pencils to her second art class. She put the rest of the pencils in a box. How many pencils are in the box?

A 95 **C** 19

B 27 **D** 9

Lesson

5-2

TEKS 3.3B: Select addition or subtraction and use the operation to solve problems involving whole numbers through 999.

Subtracting 2-Digit Numbers

How can you use subtraction?

Animal rescue workers have released 16 of the eagles they have cared for. How many eagles are left?

Find 34 − 16. Use compatible numbers to estimate.

35 − 15 = 20

Guided Practice*

Do you know HOW?

In **1–8**, subtract.

1. 35 − 19

2. 42 − 17

3. 54 − 26

4. 61 − 38

5. 47 − 9

6. 73 − 25

7. 62 − 34

8. 47 − 25

Do you UNDERSTAND?

9. In the example above, why is regrouping needed? What was regrouped?

10. Workers at the park have cared for 52 falcons. If 28 falcons are still at the park, how many of the falcons have left?

a Write a number sentence.

b Estimate the answer.

c Solve the problem.

d Use the estimate to explain why your answer is reasonable.

Independent Practice

In **11–20**, subtract.

11. 26 − 19

12. 45 − 17

13. 37 − 18

14. 56 − 38

15. 83 − 61

16. 75 − 48

17. 22 − 13

18. 31 − 14

19. 53 − 6

20. 48 − 29

*For another example, see Set B on page 112.

Subtract the ones.

6 ones > 4 ones
Regroup 1 ten 4 ones into 14 ones.

14 − 6 = 8 ones

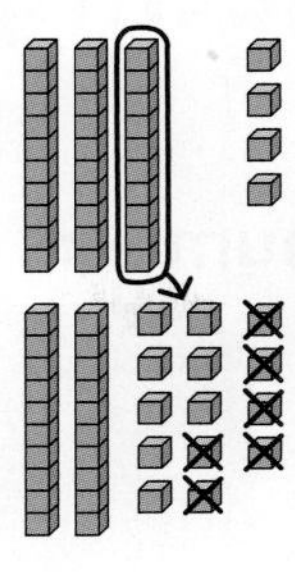

$$\begin{array}{r} \overset{2}{\cancel{3}}\,\overset{14}{\cancel{4}} \\ -\;1\;6 \\ \hline 8 \end{array}$$

Subtract the tens.

2 tens − 1 ten = 1 ten

34 − 16 = 18

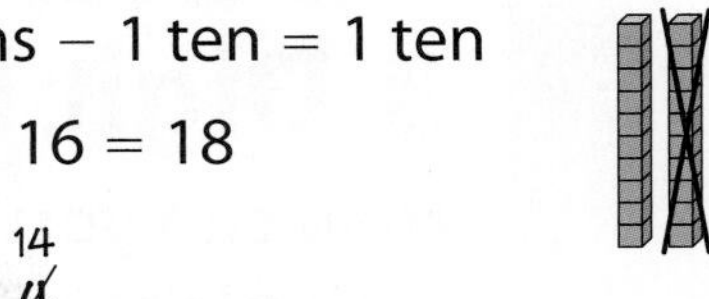

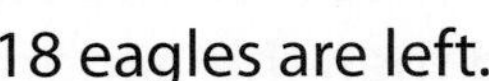

$$\begin{array}{r} \overset{2}{\cancel{3}}\,\overset{14}{\cancel{4}} \\ -\;1\;6 \\ \hline 1\;8 \end{array}$$

18 eagles are left.

The answer is reasonable because 18 is close to the estimate of 20.

TAKS Problem Solving

For **21** and **22**, use the table at the right.

21. Follow the steps below to find how many owls are left at the animal rescue park.

- **a** Write a number sentence that can be used to solve the problem.
- **b** Estimate the answer.
- **c** Solve the problem.
- **d** Use the estimate to explain why your answer is reasonable.

Animal Rescue Park (Data)

Kind of Bird	Number Taken In	Number Released
Hawk	51	34
Kite	32	19
Owl	43	27

22. How many fewer kites than hawks have been released from the animal rescue park?

23. Writing to Explain Do you need to regroup to find 64 − 37? Explain your answer.

24. Reasonableness Trista subtracted 75 − 48 and got 37. Explain why her answer is not reasonable.

25. Andy's family bought two pumpkins. One pumpkin weighed 17 pounds, and the other pumpkin weighed 26 pounds.

- **a** What was the total weight of the two pumpkins?
- **b** What was the difference of their weights?

26. A sweater costs $29. A shirt costs $18. Meg has $36. Which number sentence can be used to find how much money Meg would have left if she bought the sweater?

A 29 + 36 = ▢ **C** 36 − 29 = ▢

B 29 − 18 = ▢ **D** 36 − 18 = ▢

Lesson

5-3

TEKS 3.3A: Model addition and subtraction using pictures, words, and numbers.

Models for Subtracting 3-Digit Numbers

Hands-On
place-value blocks

How can you subtract 3-digit numbers with place-value blocks?

Use place value to subtract the ones first, the tens next, and then the hundreds.

Find 237 − 165.

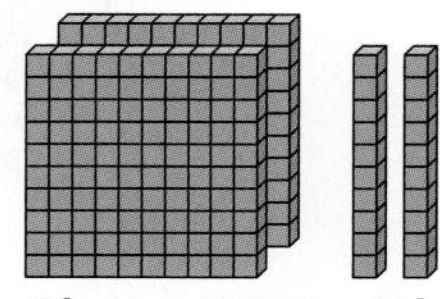

Show 237 with place-value blocks.

Guided Practice*

Do you know HOW?

In **1–6**, use place-value blocks or draw pictures to subtract.

1. 249 − 187

2. 261 − 134

3. 158 − 76

4. 384 − 182

5. 173 − 158

6. 325 − 213

Do you UNDERSTAND?

7. In the example above, why do you need to regroup 1 hundred into 10 tens?

8. Colby saved $256 doing jobs in the neighborhood. He bought a computer printer for $173. How much money did he have left? Draw a picture to help you subtract.

Independent Practice

In **9–18**, use place-value blocks or draw pictures to subtract.

You can draw squares to show hundreds, lines to show tens, and Xs to show ones. This picture shows 127.

9. 347 − 263

10. 196 − 149

11. 218 − 117

12. 251 − 132

13. 423 − 291

14. 123 − 81

15. 265 − 84

16. 539 − 275

17. 376 − 153

18. 417 − 308

*For another example, see Set C on page 112.

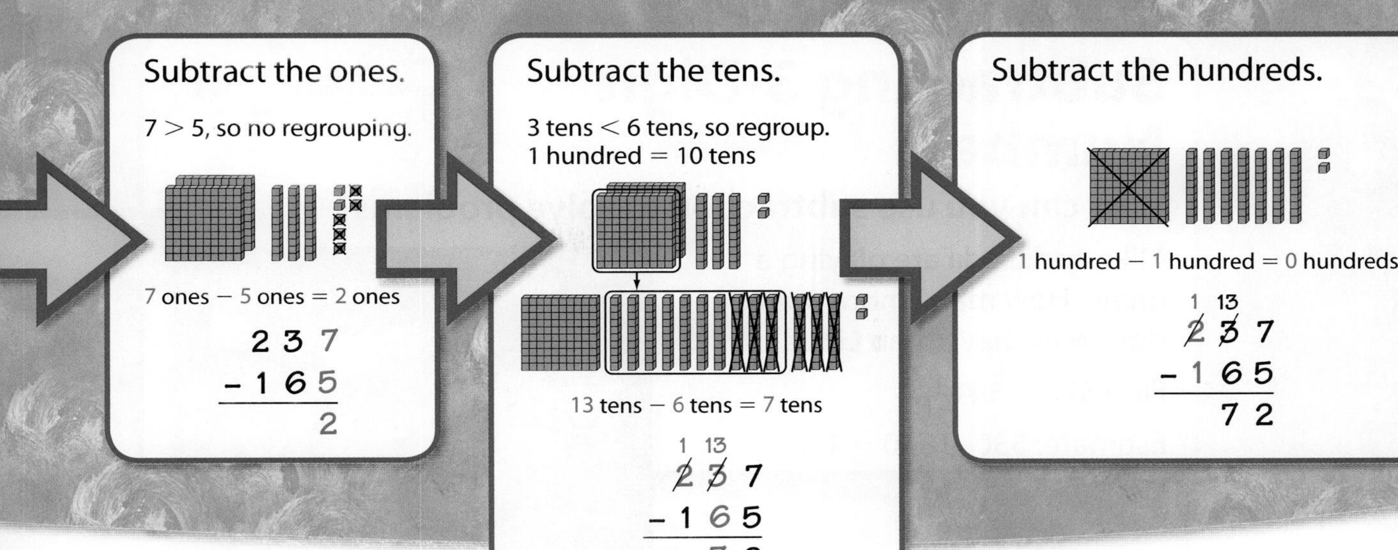

TAKS Problem Solving

For **19** and **20**, use the table at the right.

19. The Wen family drove from Cincinnati to Cleveland. Then the family drove to Chicago. How many miles did the family drive in all?

20. The Miller family is driving from Washington, D.C., to Cleveland and then to Cincinnati. So far the Millers have traveled 127 miles. How many miles are left in their trip?

Trip Distances

Trip	Miles
Cleveland to Chicago	346
Cincinnati to Cleveland	249
Washington, D.C., to Cleveland	372

21. **Estimation** Round to the nearest hundred to estimate how many more musicians are in the world's largest accordion band than in the world's largest trombone band.

World's Largest Bands

Trombone	289 musicians
Accordion	625 musicians

22. An amusement park ride can hold 120 people. There were 116 people on the ride and 95 people waiting in line. Which number sentence can be used to find how many people in all were on the ride or waiting in line?

A $116 - 95 = \square$

B $120 + 116 + 95 = \square$

C $116 + 95 = \square$

D $120 - 95 = \square$

Lesson
5-4

TEKS 3.3B: Select addition or subtraction and use the operation to solve problems involving whole numbers through 999.
Also TEKS 3.5A and TEKS 3.5B.

Subtracting 3-Digit Numbers

Hands-On
place-value blocks

How can you use subtraction to solve problems?

Mike and Linda are playing a game. How many more points does Mike have than Linda?

Find 528 − 341.

Estimate: 530 − 340 = 190

Another Example How do you subtract with two regroupings?

Find 356 − 189.
Estimate: 400 − 200 = 200

Step 1

Subtract the ones.
Regroup if needed.

6 ones < 9 ones. So, regroup 1 ten into 10 ones.

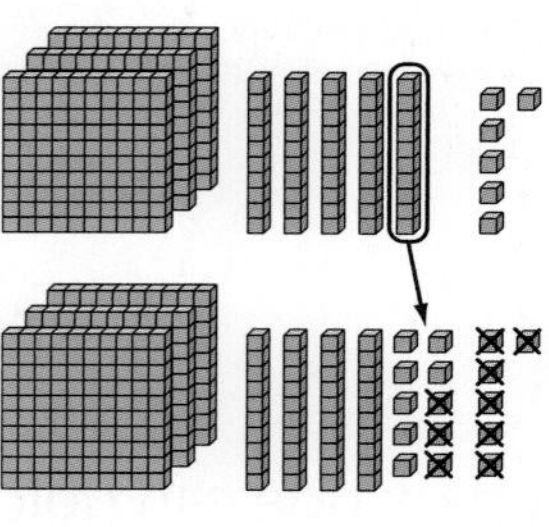

$$\begin{array}{r} \overset{4}{\not5}\overset{16}{\not6} \\ 3\,5\,6 \\ -\ 1\,8\,9 \\ \hline 7 \end{array}$$

Step 2

Subtract the tens.
Regroup if needed.

4 tens < 8 tens. So, regroup 1 hundred into 10 tens.

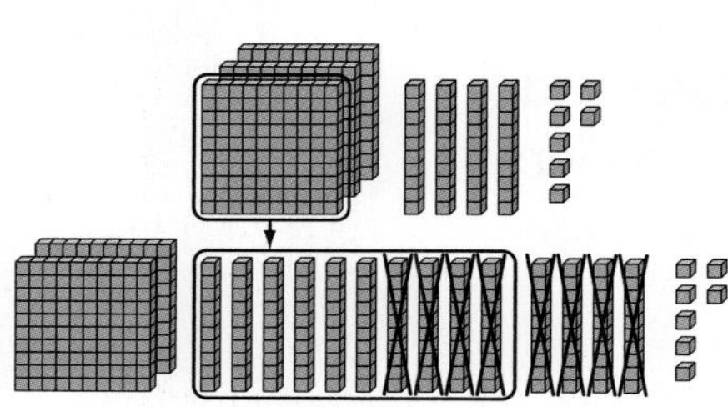

$$\begin{array}{r} 2\ \ 14\ \ 16 \\ 3\,5\,6 \\ -\ 1\,8\,9 \\ \hline 6\,7 \end{array}$$

Step 3

Subtract the hundreds.

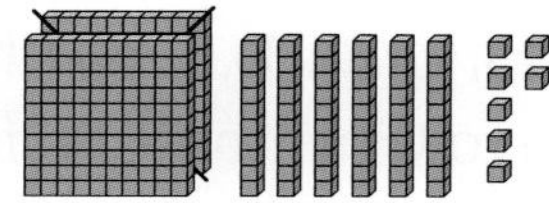

$$\begin{array}{r} 2\ \ 14\ \ 16 \\ 3\,5\,6 \\ -\ 1\,8\,9 \\ \hline 1\,6\,7 \end{array}$$

The answer 167 is reasonable because it is close to the estimate.

Explain It

1. Why do you need to regroup both a ten and a hundred?
2. How is 3 hundreds 5 tens 6 ones the same as 3 hundreds 4 tens 16 ones? How is 3 hundreds 4 tens 16 ones the same as 2 hundreds 14 tens 16 ones?

Subtract the ones.

8 ones > 1 one
You do not regroup.

8 ones − 1 one = 7 ones

$$\begin{array}{r} 528 \\ -\ 341 \\ \hline 7 \end{array}$$

Subtract the tens.

Since 2 tens < 4 tens, regroup 1 hundred into 10 tens.

12 tens − 4 tens = 8 tens

$$\begin{array}{r} \overset{4}{\cancel{5}}\,\overset{12}{\cancel{2}}\,8 \\ -\ 3\,4\,1 \\ \hline 8\,7 \end{array}$$

Subtract the hundreds.

4 hundreds − 3 hundreds = 1 hundred

$$\begin{array}{r} \overset{4}{\cancel{5}}\,\overset{12}{\cancel{2}}\,8 \\ -\ 3\,4\,1 \\ \hline 1\,8\,7 \end{array}$$

Mike has 187 more points.

187 is close to the estimate of 190. The answer is reasonable.

Guided Practice*

Do you know HOW?

In **1–6**, subtract. Use place-value blocks, if you wish.

1. $\begin{array}{r} 374 \\ -\ 176 \\ \hline \end{array}$

2. $\begin{array}{r} 431 \\ -\ 145 \\ \hline \end{array}$

3. $\begin{array}{r} 568 \\ -\ 269 \\ \hline \end{array}$

4. $\begin{array}{r} 327 \\ -\ 238 \\ \hline \end{array}$

5. 574 − 86

6. 410 − 257

Do you UNDERSTAND?

7. In the example above, explain how to decide if regrouping is needed.

8. At the end of their game, Lora had 426 points, and Lou had 158 points. How many more points did Lora have than Lou?

a Write a number sentence.

b Estimate the answer.

c Solve the problem.

d Explain why your answer is reasonable.

Independent Practice

Estimate then find each difference. Check answers for reasonableness.

9. $\begin{array}{r} 385 \\ -\ 296 \\ \hline \end{array}$

10. $\begin{array}{r} 276 \\ -\ 97 \\ \hline \end{array}$

11. $\begin{array}{r} 516 \\ -\ 238 \\ \hline \end{array}$

12. $\begin{array}{r} 629 \\ -\ 453 \\ \hline \end{array}$

13. $\begin{array}{r} 948 \\ -\ 569 \\ \hline \end{array}$

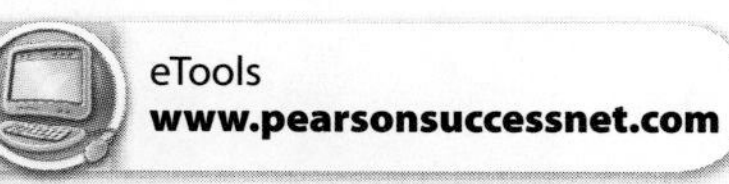

*For another example, see Set D on page 113.

Independent Practice

Subtract. Estimate and check answers for reasonableness.

14. 392 − 195

15. 754 − 476

16. 819 − 652

17. 123 − 84

18. 435 − 367

19. 236 − 78

20. 568 − 362

21. 147 − 58

22. 952 − 794

TAKS Problem Solving

For **23–25**, use the table at the right.

23. Follow the steps below to find how many more swimmers signed up for the first session at Oak Pool than for the first session at Park Pool.

a Write a number sentence that can be used to solve the problem.

b Estimate the answer.

c Solve the problem.

d Explain why your answer is reasonable.

Data

Swim Class Enrollment

Pool	Number of Swimmers	
	1st session	2nd session
Oak	763	586
Park	314	179
River	256	63

24. **Strategy Focus** At River Pool, late enrollments added 29 swimmers to the 2nd session. The total number of swimmers enrolled in the 2nd session is how many fewer than in the 1st?

Tip *What addition sentence can help?*

25. **Write a Problem** Write a real-world problem using the information in the table. Include too much information in your problem.

26. The world's largest basket is the building in the photo. It is 186 feet tall from the base to the top of the handles. What is the height of the handles?

27. Ana made 14 hats. After giving some hats to Ty's family and some to Liv's family, she had 3 hats left. If she gave Ty's family 6 hats, which of these shows one way to find how many hats Ana gave to Liv's family?

A $14 + 3 - 6 = \square$

B $14 - 3 - 6 = \square$

C $14 - 3 + 6 = \square$

D $14 + 3 + 6 = \square$

Algebra Connections

Using Properties to Complete Number Sentences

The properties of addition can help you find missing numbers.

Commutative (Order) Property You can add numbers in any order and the sum will be the same. Example: $4 + 3 = 3 + 4$

Identity (Zero) Property The sum of any number and zero is that same number. Example: $9 + 0 = 9$

Associative (Grouping) Property You can group addends in any way and the sum will be the same. Example: $(5 + 2) + 3 = 5 + (2 + 3)$

Example: $26 + \square = 26$

Think 26 plus what number is equal to 26?

You can use the Identity Property.

$26 + 0 = 26$

Example:

$36 + (14 + 12) = (36 + \square) + 12$

Think What number makes the two sides equal?

Use the Associative Property.

$36 + (14 + 12) = (36 + 14) + 12$

Copy and complete. Write the missing number.

1. $19 + \square = 19$

2. $15 + 32 = 32 + \square$

3. $28 + (17 + 32) = (28 + \square) + 32$

4. $\square + 27 = 27$

5. $\square + 8 = 8 + 49$

6. $(16 + 14) + \square = 16 + (14 + 53)$

7. $(\square + 9) + 72 = 96 + (9 + 72)$

8. $\square + 473 = 473$

For **9** and **10**, copy and complete the number sentence. Use it to help solve the problem.

9. Vin walked 9 blocks from home to the library. Then he walked 5 blocks farther to the store. Later he walked the same path back to the library. How many more blocks would he need to walk to his home?

$9 + 5 = 5 + \square$

$\square$ blocks

10. Bo scored 7 points in each of two tosses in a game. Then he made one more toss. He had the same total score as Ed. Ed scored 8 points in one toss and 7 points in each of two tosses. How many points did Bo score on his last toss?

$7 + 7 + \square = 8 + 7 + 7$

$\square$ points

Lesson

5-5

TEKS 3.3B: Select addition or subtraction and use the operation to solve problems involving whole numbers through 999.

Subtracting Across Zero

How do you subtract from a number with one or more zeros?

How much more does the club need?

Find: 305 − 178

305: 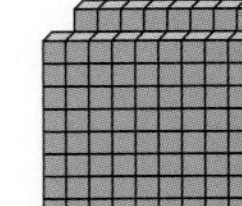

Another Example **How do you subtract from a number with two zeros?**

Find 600 − 164.

Subtract the ones.
0 ones < 4 ones
So, regroup.

```
 5 10
 6̸ 0̸ 0
-1  6 4
```

You can't regroup 0 tens.
So, regroup 1 hundred.
6 hundreds 0 tens =
5 hundreds 10 tens

```
    9
 5 1̸0̸ 10
 6̸  0̸  0̸
-1  6  4
```

Now regroup tens.
10 tens 0 ones = 9 tens 10 ones
Subtract the ones, the tens, and then the hundreds.

```
    9
 5 1̸0̸ 10
 6̸  0̸  0̸
-1  6  4
 4  3  6
```

Guided Practice*

Do you know HOW?

In **1–6**, find each difference.

1. 402 − 139

2. 300 − 157

3. 607 − 439

4. 820 − 167

5. 200 − 74

6. 501 −186

Do you UNDERSTAND?

7. In the examples above, why do you write 10 above the 0 in the tens place?

8. Lia says that she needs to regroup every time she subtracts from a number with a zero. Do you agree? Explain.

*For another example, see Set E on page 113.

Regroup to subtract the ones. There are no tens in 305 to regroup. Regroup 1 hundred.

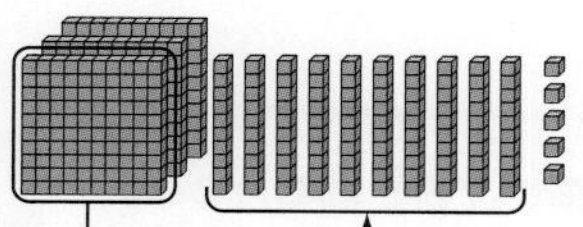

305 is the same as 2 hundreds 10 tens 5 ones.

$$\begin{array}{r} \scriptstyle 2\ \ 10\ \ \ \\ \not{3}\ \not{0}\ 5 \\ -\ 1\ 7\ 8 \\ \hline \end{array}$$

Regroup the tens.

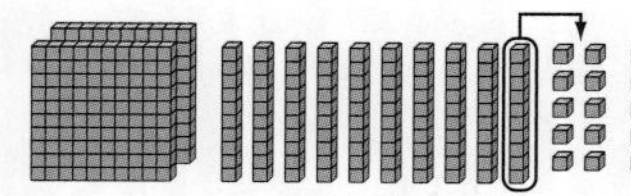

305 is the same as 2 hundreds 9 tens 15 ones.

$$\begin{array}{r} \scriptstyle 9\ \ \ \ \ \\ \scriptstyle 2\ \ \not{10}\ \ 15 \\ \not{3}\ \not{0}\ \not{5} \\ -\ 1\ 7\ 8 \\ \hline \end{array}$$

Subtract the ones, the tens, and then the hundreds.

$$\begin{array}{r} \scriptstyle 9\ \ \ \ \ \\ \scriptstyle 2\ \ \not{10}\ \ 15 \\ \not{3}\ \not{0}\ \not{5} \\ -\ 1\ 7\ 8 \\ \hline 1\ 2\ 7 \end{array}$$

The Art Club needs $127.

Independent Practice

In **9–18**, find each difference.

9. 203 − 157

10. 400 − 371

11. 304 − 95

12. 401 − 282

13. 500 − 64

14. 600 − 439

15. 306 − 248

16. 705 − 123

17. 800 − 74

18. 900 − 506

TAKS Problem Solving

19. The average person eats about 126 pounds of fresh fruit in a year. Write a number sentence to help you find how many more pounds of processed fruit you eat. Then solve.

An average person eats a total of about 280 pounds of fresh and processed fruit each year.

20. **Writing to Explain** The Art Club needs 605 beads. A large bag of beads has 285 beads. A small bag of beads has 130 beads. Will one large bag and one small bag be enough beads? Explain.

21. Dina counted 204 items on the library cart. There were 91 fiction books, 75 nonfiction books, and some magazines. Which number sentence shows one way to find the number of magazines?

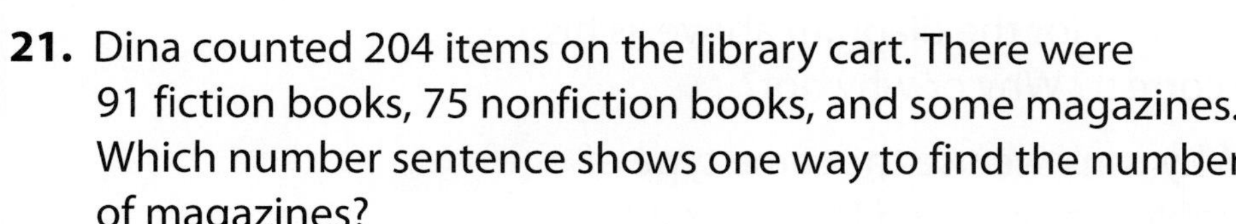

A 204 − 91 − 75 = ▢

B 204 + 91 + 75 = ▢

C 204 − 91 + 75 = ▢

D 204 + 91 − 75 = ▢

Lesson

5-6

TEKS 3.14C Select or develop an appropriate problem-solving plan or strategy including drawing a picture, looking for a pattern, systematic guessing and checking, acting it out, making a table, working a simpler problem, or working backwards to solve a problem.

Problem Solving

Draw a Picture and Write a Number Sentence

There are two lunch periods at Central School. If 221 students eat during the first lunch period, how many students eat during the second lunch period?

Central School
Grades K-6
458 Students

Another Example **Are there other types of subtraction situations?**

There are 85 students in Grade 2 at Central School. That is 17 more students than in Grade 3. How many students are in Grade 3?

Plan and Solve

Draw a diagram to show what you know.

Gr. 2	85	
Gr. 3	?	17

There are 17 more students in Grade 2 than in Grade 3. Subtract to find the number of students in Grade 3. Write a number sentence.

$$85 - 17 = \square$$

Answer

$$\begin{array}{r} 85 \\ -\ 17 \\ \hline 68 \end{array}$$

There are 68 students in Grade 3.

Check

Make sure the answer is reasonable.

85 − 17 is about 90 − 20, or 70.

68 is close to 70, so 68 is reasonable.

The number 68 is reasonable, and the question in the problem was answered.

Explain It

1. Harry wrote 17 + $\square$ = 85 for the diagram above. Is his number sentence correct? Why or why not?
2. **Number Sense** Why can't we use the same type of diagram for this problem as we used for the problem at the top of the page?

Plan and Solve

Draw a diagram to show what you know.

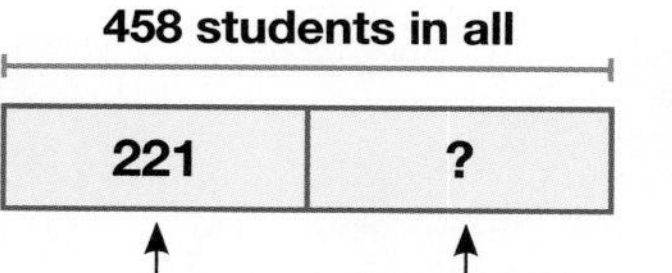

You know the total and one part. Subtract to find the other part. Write a number sentence.

$458 - 221 = \square$

Answer

$$\begin{array}{r} 458 \\ -\ 221 \\ \hline 237 \end{array}$$

There are 237 students who eat during the second lunch period.

Check

Make sure the answer is reasonable.

458 − 221 is about 460 − 220, or 240.

237 is close to 240, so 237 is reasonable.

The number 237 is reasonable and the right question was answered.

Guided Practice*

Do you know HOW?

1. A total of 254 people entered a bicycle race. So far 135 people have finished the race. How many people are still racing?

254 people in all

135	?

Do you UNDERSTAND?

2. **Writing to Explain** How do you know what operation to use to solve Problem 1?

3. **Write a Problem** Write a problem that can be solved by adding or subtracting. Then give your problem to a classmate to solve.

Independent Practice

4. The height of Capote Falls is 175 feet. The height of Madrid Falls is 120 feet. How much taller is Capote Falls than Madrid Falls?

Capote Falls	175	
Madrid Falls	120	?

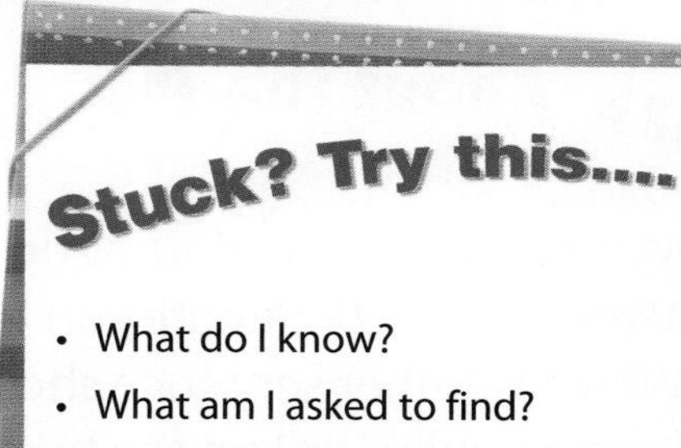

Stuck? Try this....

- What do I know?
- What am I asked to find?
- What diagram can I use to help understand the problem?
- Can I use addition, subtraction, multiplication, or division?
- Is all of my work correct?
- Did I answer the right question?
- Is my answer reasonable?

*For another example, see Set F on page 113.

Independent Practice

In the United States House of Representatives, the number of representatives each state has depends upon the number of people who live in the state.

Use the table at the right for **5–7**.

U.S. Representatives	
State	**Number**
California	53
Florida	25
Michigan	15
Texas	32

5. Copy and complete the diagram below. New York has 14 more representatives than Michigan. How many representatives does New York have?

? representatives in New York

15	14

6. Draw a diagram to find how many more representatives Texas has than Florida.

7. How many representatives are there all together from the four states listed in the chart?

8. When the House of Representatives started in 1789, there were 65 members. Now there are 435 members. How many more members are there now?

9. There are 50 states in the United States. Each state has 2 senators. Write a number sentence to find the total number of senators.

Think About the Process

10. Max exercised 38 minutes on Monday and 25 minutes on Tuesday. Which number sentence shows how long he exercised on the two days?

A 40 + 30 = ☐

B 40 − 30 = ☐

C 38 − 25 = ☐

D 38 + 25 = ☐

11. Nancy had $375 in the bank. She took $200 out to buy a scooter that cost $185. Which number sentence shows how much money is left in the bank?

F $375 + $185 = ☐

G $375 − $185 = ☐

H $375 − $200 = ☐

J $375 + $185 + $200 = ☐

Subtracting with Regrouping

Use eTools

Place-Value Blocks

Use the Place-Value Blocks eTool to subtract 324 − 168.

Step 1 Go to the Place-Value Blocks eTool. Click on the two-part workspace icon. In the top space, show 324 with place-value blocks.

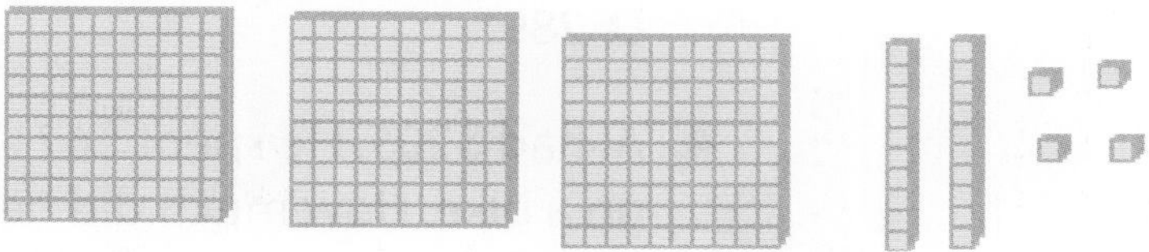

Step 2 Use the hammer tool to break one of the tens blocks into ten ones. Then use the arrow tool to take away 8 ones and move them to the bottom workspace.

Step 3 Use the hammer tool to break one of the hundreds blocks into 10 tens. Then take away the 6 tens in 168 and move them to the bottom workspace.

Step 4 Use the arrow tool to take away the hundred block in 168. To find the difference, look at all of the blocks that are left.

324 − 168 = 156

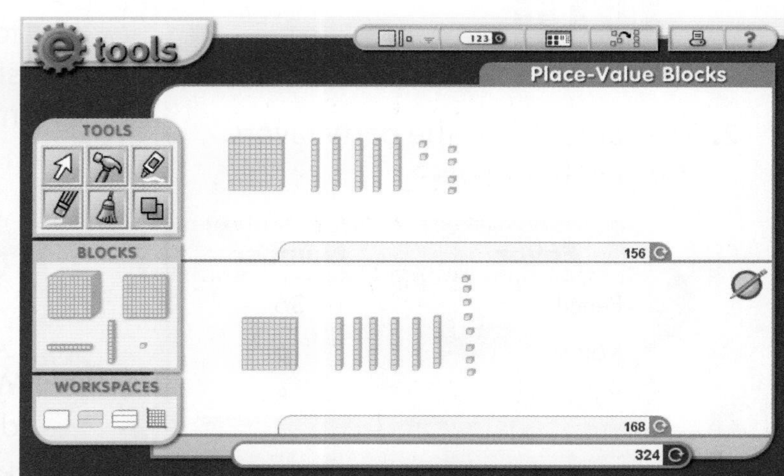

Practice

Use the Place-Value Blocks eTool to subtract.

1. 445 − 176 **2.** 318 − 142 **3.** 546 − 259 **4.** 600 − 473

TAKS Test Prep

1. Tracey knows that she will need to regroup to solve 52 − 18. Which picture shows how she should regroup 52? (5-1)

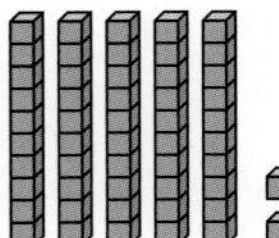

A 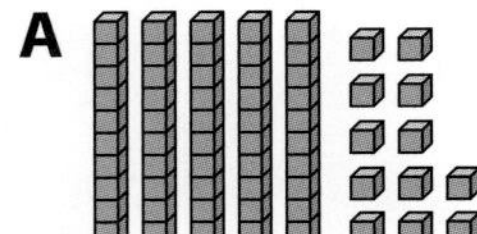

B 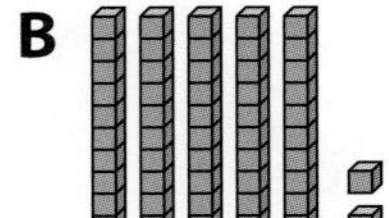

C 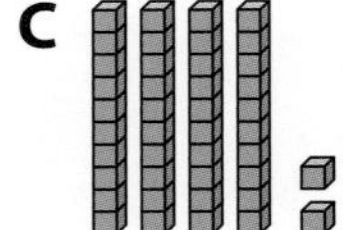

D

2. The table shows the party favors Zac purchased.

Favor	Number
Pencil	36
Kazoo	16
Yo-Yo	8

Which number sentence can be used to find how many more pencils than yo-yos were purchased? (5-2)

F 36 − 8 = ☐

G 36 + 8 = ☐

H 36 − 16 = ☐

J 36 + 16 = ☐

3. Cristina scored 485 points on a video game. Olivia scored 196 points. How many more points did Cristina score than Olivia? (5-4)

A 681

B 389

C 299

D 289

4. Al had $205. He spent $67 on a bike. How much did he have left? (5-5)

F $162

G $148

H $138

J $38

5. Mr. Chavez needs to order trophies for the band members. The table shows how many girls and how many boys are in the band.

Band Members	
Boys	32
Girls	28

Which of the following best describes the band members? (5-2)

A There are 4 more boys than girls in the band.

B There are 4 more girls than boys in the band.

C There are 32 more boys than girls in the band.

D There are 28 more girls than boys in the band.

6. Mrs. Wesley bought 325 drinks for a picnic. She bought 135 cartons of milk, 95 bottles of water, and some bottles of juice. Which number sentence shows one way to find how many bottles of juice she bought? (5-4)

F $325 - 135 + 95 = \square$

G $325 - 135 - 95 = \square$

H $325 + 135 - 95 = \square$

J $325 + 135 + 95 = \square$

7. What regrouping is shown? (5-3)

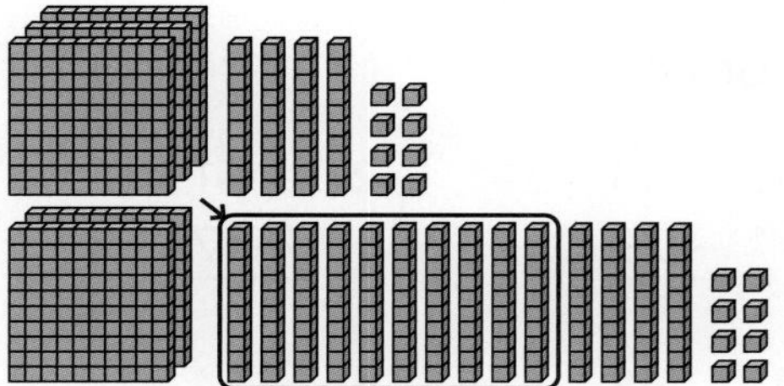

A 3 hundreds 4 tens 8 ones as 2 hundreds 3 tens 18 ones

B 3 hundreds 4 tens 8 ones as 2 hundreds 14 tens 8 ones

C 2 hundreds 4 tens 8 ones as 1 hundreds 14 tens 8 ones

D 2 hundreds 4 tens 8 ones as 2 hundreds 3 tens 18 ones

8. Texas has 254 counties. Georgia has 159 counties. How many more counties does Texas have than Georgia? (5-4)

F 195

G 145

H 105

J 95

9. Which picture represents the problem? While at Guadalupe National Park, Nessie saw 23 mule deer and 17 Texas antelope squirrels. How many more deer did she see than squirrels? (5-6)

A

?	
23	17

B

17	
23	?

C

23	
17	?

D

23
17

10. Ray had \$41. He spent \$14 for swim goggles and \$19 for admission to the water park. How much money did Ray have left for lunch? (5-2)

F \$27

G \$12

H \$8

J \$5

11. **Griddable Response** For an experiment, Trisha put 300 milliliters of water into a beaker. Then she poured 237 milliliters of the water from the beaker into a test tube. How many milliliters of water were left in the beaker? (5-5)

Reteaching

Set A, pages 94–95

Find 45 − 18.

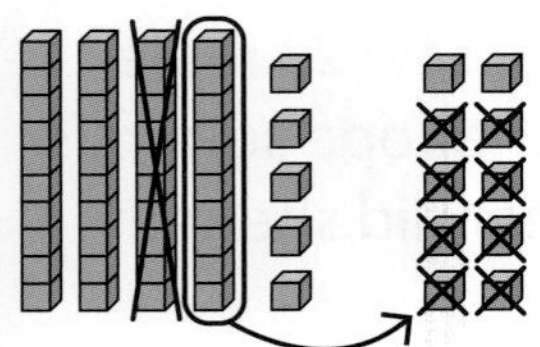

```
  3 15
  4̶ 5̶
- 1 8
-----
  2 7
```

Remember that you can regroup 1 ten as 10 ones.

Use place-value blocks or draw pictures to subtract.

1. 52 − 17

2. 38 − 25

3. 83 − 34

4. 75 − 53

Set B, pages 96–97

Find 31 − 17.

Estimate: 30 − 20 = 10

What You Think

31 = 3 tens 1 one

17 = 1 ten 7 ones

7 ones > 1 one, so regroup.

3 tens 1 one = 2 tens 11 ones

What You Write

```
  2 11
  3̶ 1̶
- 1 7
-----
  1 4
```

31 − 17 = 14
14 is close to 10, so the answer is reasonable.

Remember to check your answer by comparing it to your estimate.

Subtract.

1. 53 − 29

2. 41 − 17

3. 68 − 49

4. 34 − 28

5. 92 − 42

6. 70 − 54

Set C, pages 98–99

Find 236 − 127.

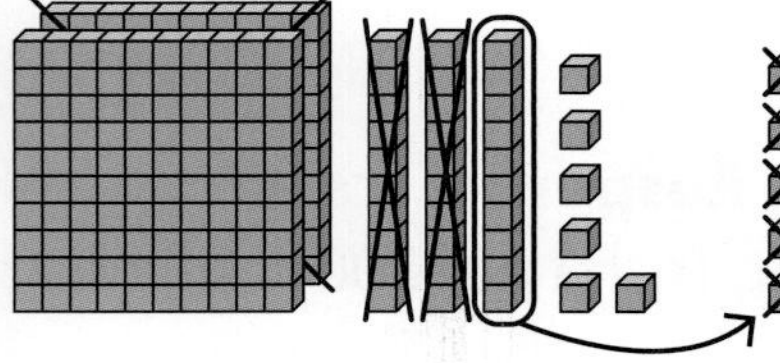

```
    2 16
  2 3̶ 6̶
- 1 2 7
-------
  1 0 9
```

Remember to subtract ones, then tens, and then hundreds.

Use place-value blocks or draw pictures to subtract.

1. 435 − 217

2. 255 − 161

3. 521 − 196

4. 332 − 108

Set D, pages 100–102

Find 312 − 186.

Estimate: 300 − 200 = 100

```
  0 12
3 1 2     Regroup
- 1 8 6   tens.
      6

   10
2  0  12
3  1  2   Regroup
- 1 8 6   hundreds.
  1 2 6
```

126 is close to 100, so the answer is reasonable.

Remember that sometimes you must regroup twice.

Estimate. Subtract and check answers for reasonableness.

1. 221 − 134
2. 397 − 138
3. 611 − 125
4. 854 − 296

Set E, pages 104–105

Find 306 − 129.

Estimate: 300 − 100 = 200

```
2 10
3 0 6     There are
- 1 2 9   no tens.
          Regroup
          hundreds.

   9
2  10 16
3  0  6   Regroup
- 1 2 9   tens.
  1 7 7
```

177 is close to 200, so the answer is reasonable.

Remember that when you need to regroup tens, but have 0 tens, regroup hundreds first.

Find each difference.

1. 308 − 125
2. 105 − 47
3. 200 − 136
4. 602 − 384

Set F, pages 106–108

At the school picnic, 234 students took part in the events. Of those students, 136 students were in the potato sack races. The other students were in the 3-legged races. How many students were in the 3-legged races?

234 students in all

136	?

Number of students in potato sack races (136) — **Number of students in 3-legged races** (?)

You know the total and one part, so you can subtract to find the other part: 234 − 136 = ▢.

234 − 136 = 98
98 students were in the 3-legged races.

Remember that drawing a picture of the problem can help you write a number sentence.

Draw a picture. Write a number sentence and solve.

1. A total of 293 people entered a running race. So far, 127 people have finished the race. How many people are still racing?

Topic 6 Multiplication Meanings

1 An armadillo needs more sleep than a horse. How many more hours of sleep does an armadillo need? You will find out in Lesson 6-3.

2

Monarch butterflies are best known for their bright orange wings. How many wings does a monarch butterfly have? You will find out in Lesson 6-4.

3

In 1999, the United States Mint began circulating new state quarters. How many states have new quarters every year? You will find out in Lesson 6-1.

Review What You Know!

Vocabulary

Choose the best term from the box.

- add
- equal groups
- skip count
- subtract

1. If you combine groups to find how many in all, you _?_.
2. _?_ have the same number of items.
3. When you say the numbers 2, 4, 6, 8, you _?_.

Equal Groups

Are the groups equal? Write *yes* or *no*.

4.  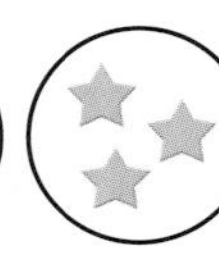 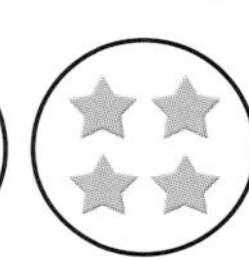

5.   

Adding

Find each sum.

6. $5 + 5 + 5$
7. $7 + 7$
8. $3 + 3 + 3$
9. $2 + 2 + 2 + 2$
10. $6 + 6 + 6$
11. $9 + 9 + 9$

Repeated Addition

12. **Writing to Explain** Draw a picture to show how to solve $8 + 8 + 8 = \square$. Then copy and complete the number sentence.

Lesson
6-1

TEKS 3.4A: Learn and apply multiplication facts through 12 by 12 using concrete models and objects.

Multiplication as Repeated Addition

Hands-On
counters

How can you find the total number of objects in equal groups?

Jessie used 3 bags to bring home the goldfish she won at a Fun Fair. She put the same number of goldfish in each bag. How many goldfish did she win?

Guided Practice*

Do you know HOW?

Copy and complete. Use counters.

1.

2 groups of ___
4 + 4 = ___
2 × ___ = ___

2. 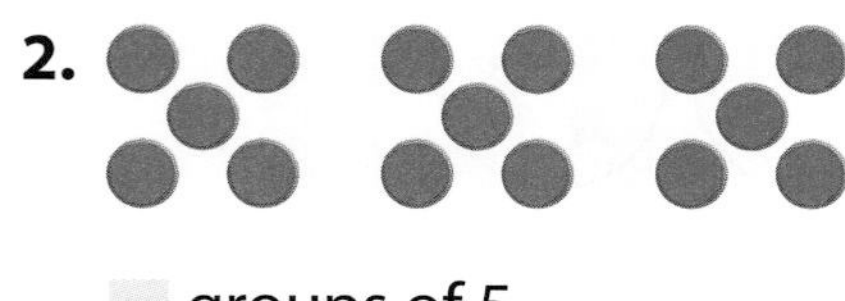

___ groups of 5
5 + ___ + ___ = ___
3 × ___ = ___

Do you UNDERSTAND?

3. Can you write 3 + 3 + 3 + 3 as a multiplication sentence? Explain.

4. Can you write 3 + 5 + 6 = 14 as a multiplication sentence? Explain.

5. Write an addition sentence and a multiplication sentence to solve this problem:

Jessie bought 4 packages of colorful stones to put in the fish bowl. There were 6 stones in each package. How many stones did Jessie buy?

Independent Practice

Copy and complete. Use counters or draw a picture to help.

6.

2 groups of ___
6 + ___ = ___
2 × ___ = ___

7. 

3 groups of ___
7 + ___ + ___ = ___
3 × ___ = ___

Animated Glossary, eTools
www.pearsonsuccessnet.com

*For another example, see Set A on page 132.

The counters show 3 groups of 8 goldfish.

You can use addition to join equal groups.

$8 + 8 + 8 = 24$

Multiplication is an operation that gives the total number when you join equal groups.

What You Say 3 times 8 equals 24

What You Write $3 \times 8 = 24$

3 ↑ factor, 8 ↑ factor, 24 ↑ product

Factors are the numbers that are being multiplied. The **product** is the answer to a multiplication problem.

Addition sentence:
$8 + 8 + 8 = 24$

Multiplication sentence:
$3 \times 8 = 24$

So, $8 + 8 + 8 = 3 \times 8$.

Jessie won 24 goldfish.

Copy and complete each number sentence. Use counters or draw a picture to help.

8. $2 + 2 + 2 + 2 = 4 \times$ ___

9. ___ + ___ + ___ $= 3 \times 7$

10. 9 + ___ + ___ = ___ $\times 9$

11. $6 + 6 + 6 + 6 + 6 =$ ___ $\times$ ___

Algebra Write +, −, or × for each □.

12. 4 □ 3 = 12

13. 3 □ 6 = 9

14. 4 □ 4 = 0

15. 6 □ 4 = 10

16. 5 □ 3 = 2

17. 2 □ 4 = 8

TAKS Problem Solving

18. What number sentence shows how to find the total number of erasers?

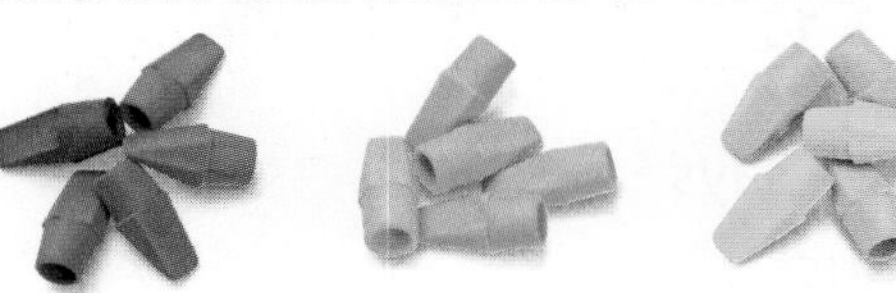

A $5 + 5 =$ ___

B $15 - 5 =$ ___

C $15 + 5 =$ ___

D $3 \times 5 =$ ___

19. Write an addition sentence and a multiplication sentence to solve this problem:

In 1999, the United States Mint began circulating state quarters. Every year, 5 new state quarters are released. After 10 years, how many state quarters will be released?

20. Writing to Explain Luka says that you can add or multiply to join groups. Is he correct? Explain.

21. Which picture shows 3 groups of 2?

F 

G  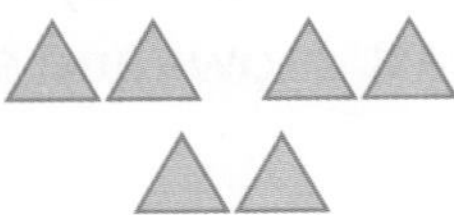

H 

J  

Lesson

6-2

TEKS 3.4A: Learn and apply multiplication facts through 12 by 12 using concrete models and objects.

Arrays and Multiplication

Hands-On

counters

How does an array show multiplication?

Dana keeps her entire CD collection in a holder on the wall. The holder has 4 rows. Each row holds 5 CDs. How many CDs are in Dana's collection?

The CDs are in an array. An array shows objects in equal rows.

Another Example **Does order matter when you multiply?**

Libby and Sydney both say their poster has more stickers. Who is correct?

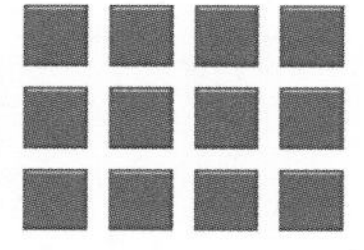

$4 + 4 + 4 = 12$
$3 \times 4 = 12$

Libby's poster has 12 stickers.

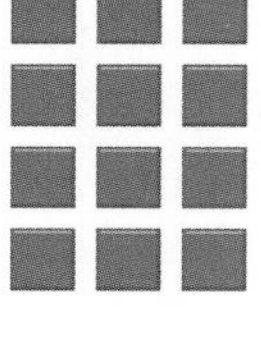

$3 + 3 + 3 + 3 = 12$
$4 \times 3 = 12$

Sydney's poster has 12 stickers.

Both poster boards have the same number of stickers.

$$\mathbf{3 \times 4 = 12} \text{ and } \mathbf{4 \times 3 = 12}$$

The Commutative (Order) Property of Multiplication says you can multiply numbers in any order and the product is the same. So, $3 \times 4 = 4 \times 3$.

Explain It

1. Miguel has 5 rows of stickers. There are 3 stickers in each row. Write an addition sentence and a multiplication sentence to show how many stickers he has.
2. Show the Commutative Property of Multiplication by drawing two arrays. Each array should have at least 2 rows and show a product of 6.

The counters show 4 rows of 5 CDs.

Each row is a group. You can use addition to find the total.

$5 + 5 + 5 + 5 = 20$

Multiplication can also be used to find the total in an array.

What You Say 4 times 5 equals 20

What You Write $4 \times 5 = 20$

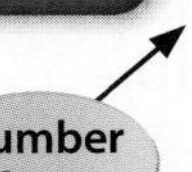

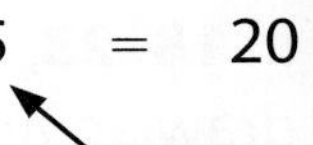

There are 20 CDs in Dana's collection.

Guided Practice*

Do you know HOW?

In **1** and **2**, write a multiplication sentence for each array.

1. 

2. 

In **3** and **4**, draw an array to show each multiplication fact. Write the product.

3. 3×6

4. 5×4

In **5** and **6**, copy and complete each multiplication sentence. Use counters or draw an array to help.

5. $5 \times \square = 10$
$2 \times \square = 10$

6. $4 \times 3 = \square$
$3 \times \square = 12$

Do you UNDERSTAND?

7. Look at the example above. What does the first factor in the multiplication sentence tell you about the array?

8. **Writing to Explain** Why is the Commutative Property of Multiplication sometimes called the *order property*?

9. Scott puts some sports stickers in rows. He makes 6 rows with 5 stickers in each row. If he put the same stickers in 5 equal rows, how many would be in each row?

Independent Practice

In **10–12**, write a multiplication sentence for each array.

10. 

11. 

12. 

*For another example, see Set B on page 132.

Independent Practice

In **13–17**, draw an array to show each multiplication fact. Write the product.

13. 3×3 **14.** 5×6 **15.** 1×8 **16.** 4×3 **17.** 2×9

In **18–23**, copy and complete each multiplication sentence. Use counters or draw an array to help.

18. $4 \times \square = 8$
$2 \times \square = 8$

19. $6 \times 4 = \square$
$4 \times \square = 24$

20. $5 \times \square = 40$
$\square \times 5 = 40$

21. $3 \times 9 = 27$
$9 \times 3 = \square$

22. $7 \times 6 = 42$
$6 \times 7 = \square$

23. $9 \times 8 = 72$
$8 \times 9 = \square$

TAKS Problem Solving

24. Writing to Explain How do the arrays at the right show the Commutative Property of Multiplication?

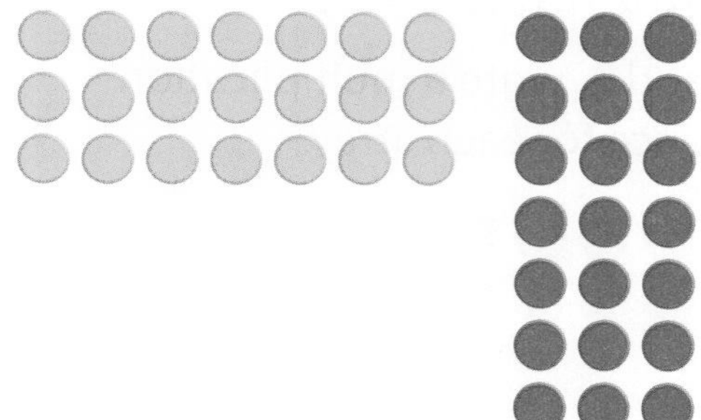

25. Number Sense How does an array show equal groups?

26. Taylor says that the product for 7×2 is the same as the product for 2×7. Is he correct? Explain.

27. Reasoning Margo has 23 pictures. Can she use all of the pictures to make an array with exactly two equal rows? Why or why not?

28. Dan bought the stamps shown at right. Which number sentence shows one way to find how many stamps Dan bought?

A $4 + 5 = \square$

B $5 \times 4 = \square$

C $5 + 4 = \square$

D $5 - 4 = \square$

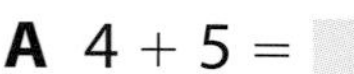

Mixed Problem Solving

Josie made the artwork on the right using stars and circles. Answer the questions about her artwork.

1. Explain the pattern shown in the artwork.
2. How many rows are in each array of stars?
3. Look at one array of circles. How many circles are in each row of the array?
4. Look at one array of stars. Write a number sentence for the array.
5. How many circles did Josie use in her artwork?
6. How many more stars than circles did Josie make?

7. Josie used the table below to plan how many of each shape she would need for different numbers of rows.

   Copy and complete the table.

Shapes Needed to Make Artwork

Total Number of Rows	Total Number of Stars	Total Number of Circles
2	42	15
4	84	30
6	126	45
8		

8. Mark made 56 stars. He made 18 circles. How many shapes did he make in all?
9. **Strategy Focus** Solve. Use the strategy Write a Number Sentence.

   Maggie made a pattern using a total of 92 shapes. Of the 92 shapes Maggie used, 44 were circles and the rest were stars. How many stars did Maggie use?

Lesson

6-3

TEKS 3.4A: Learn and apply multiplication facts through 12 by 12 using concrete models and objects.

Using Multiplication to Compare

Hands-On
counters

How can you use multiplication to compare?

Mike has 5 state quarters. Carl has two times as many, or twice as many as Mike. How many state quarters does Carl have?

Choose an Operation Multiply to find twice as many: $2 \times 5 =$ ▢

Mike's quarters

Guided Practice*

Do you know HOW?

Find each amount. You may use drawings or counters to help.

1. 3 times as many as 3
2. 2 times as many as 6
3. Twice as many as 3

Do you UNDERSTAND?

4. **Number Sense** Barry says you can add 5 + 5 to find how many state quarters Carl has. Is he correct? Why or why not?

5. Carl has 4 silver dollars. Mike has twice as many as Carl. How many silver dollars does Mike have?

Independent Practice

In **6–11**, find each amount. You may use drawings or counters to help.

6. 2 times as many as 7
7. 3 times as many as 8
8. Twice as many as 6
9. 4 times as many as 5
10. Twice as many as 9
11. 5 times as many as 4

In **12–15**, which coin or bill matches each value?

12. 2 times as much as 1 nickel
13. 10 times as much as 1 dime
14. 5 times as much as 1 nickel
15. 10 times as much as 1 nickel

dime

quarter

half dollar

one dollar

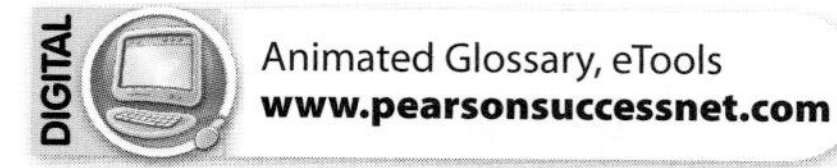

*For another example, see Set C on page 132.

What You Think

Mike has 5 state quarters.

Carl has 2 times as many.

2 times as many is 10.

What You Write

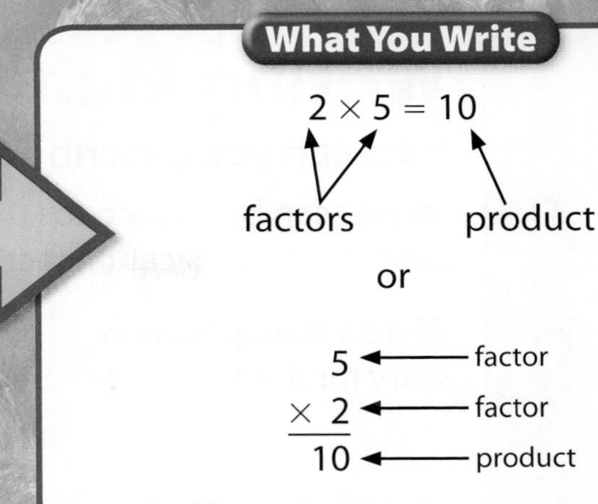

Carl has 10 state quarters.

TAKS Problem Solving

Number Sense For **16–17**, copy and complete.

16. 6 is twice as many as ▢.

17. 8 is eight times as many as ▢.

18. Reasoning Carol has 4 dolls. Her sister has twice as many. How many dolls do they have in all?

19. Writing to Explain How could this picture help you solve **Exercise 18**?

Carol's sister	4	4	twice as many
Carol	4		

20. What number sentence shows how to find twice as many marbles?

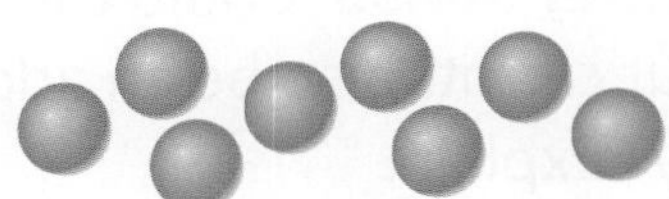

A $8 + 8 + 8 = $ ▢

B $1 \times 8 = $ ▢

C $2 \times 8 = $ ▢

D $3 \times 8 = $ ▢

21. Two of the U. S. coins that are worth one dollar are shown below. The Susan B. Anthony coin was first issued in 1979. The Sacagawea coin was issued 21 years later. When was the Sacagawea coin issued?

22. A horse needs about 3 hours of sleep each day. An armadillo needs 6 times as much sleep as a horse. About how many hours of sleep does an armadillo need each day?

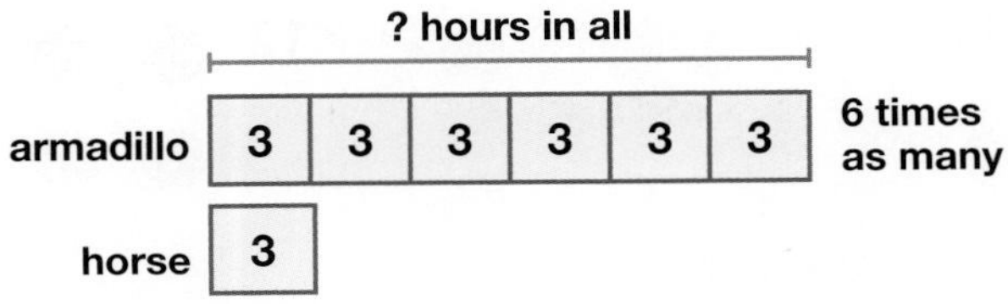

Lesson
6-4

TEKS 3.4A: Learn and apply multiplication facts through 12 by 12 using concrete models and objects.

Writing Multiplication Stories

How can you describe a multiplication fact?

Stories can be written to describe multiplication facts.

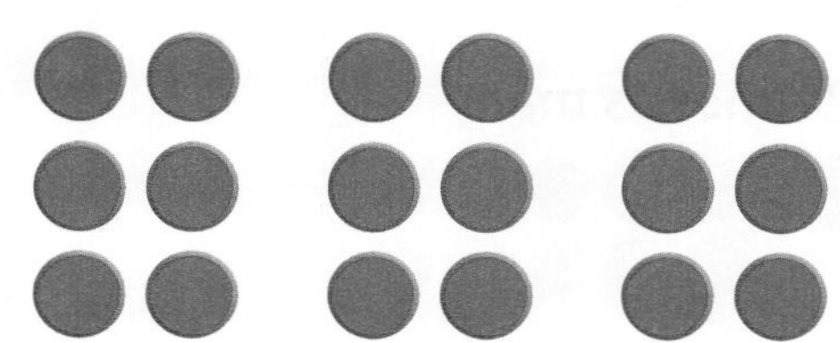

Write a multiplication story for $3 \times 6 = \square$.

Guided Practice*

Do you know HOW?

In **1–4**, write a multiplication story for each problem. Then draw a picture and find each product.

1. 2×6

2. 3×5

3. 4×2

4. 3×8

Do you UNDERSTAND?

5. How would the story about Randy change if the multiplication sentence was 2×6?

6. How would the story about Eliza change if the multiplication sentence was 3×5?

7. **Number Sense** Could the story about carrots also be an addition story? Explain.

Independent Practice

Write a multiplication story for each problem. Then, draw a picture to find each product.

8. 7×3

9. 2×9

10. 4×5

Write a multiplication story for each picture. Use the picture to find the product.

11. 

12.  

*For another example, see Set D on page 133.

Equal Groups

Randy has 3 packs of 6 buttons. How many buttons does he have?

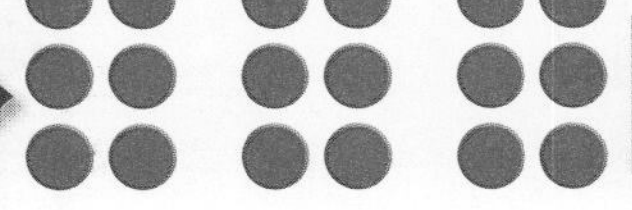

$3 \times 6 = 18$

Randy has 18 buttons.

An Array

Eliza planted 6 lilies in each of 3 rows. How many lilies did she plant?

$3 \times 6 = 18$

Eliza planted 18 lilies.

"Times as Many"

Kanisha has 6 carrots. Jack has 3 times as many. How many carrots does Jack have?

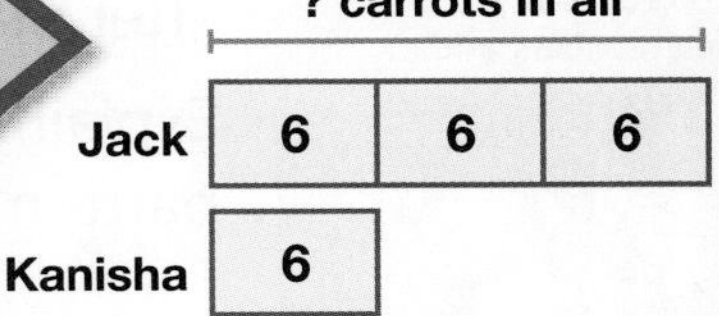

$3 \times 6 = 18$

Jack has 18 carrots.

TAKS Problem Solving

Number Sense For **13–15**, describe each story as an addition story, a subtraction story, or a multiplication story.

13. Kay has 6 pencils. She gave 4 of them to her friend. How many pencils does Kay have left?

14. Kay has 6 pencils. She bought 4 more pencils at the school store. How many pencils does Kay have now?

15. Kay has 6 bags of pencils. There are 2 pencils in each bag. How many pencils does Kay have?

16. A soccer team traveled to a soccer game in 4 vans. All four vans were full. Each van held 7 players. How many players went to the game?

A 47 **C** 24

B 28 **D** 11

17. Algebra Steve has some packages of balloons. There are 8 balloons in each package. He has 24 balloons in all. Draw a picture to find how many packages Steve has.

18. A group of 12 monarch butterflies is getting ready to migrate. How many wings will be moving when the group flies away?

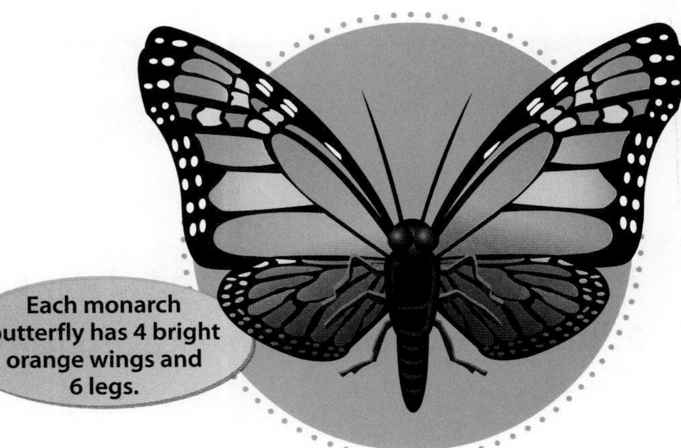

Each monarch butterfly has 4 bright orange wings and 6 legs.

Lesson
6-5

TEKS 3.15A: Explain and record observations using objects, words, pictures, numbers, and technology.

Problem Solving

Writing to Explain

Gina's dad gave her 2 pennies on Monday. He promised to double that number of pennies every day after that for one week.

Explain how you can use the pattern to complete the table.

Data

Day	Number of pennies
Monday	2
Tuesday	4
Wednesday	8
Thursday	16
Friday	32
Saturday	
Sunday	

Another Example

Jackie got on an elevator on the first floor. She went up 5 floors. Then she went down 2 floors. Then she went up 4 floors and got off the elevator. What floor is Jackie on?

Use *words, pictures, numbers,* or *symbols* to write a math explanation.

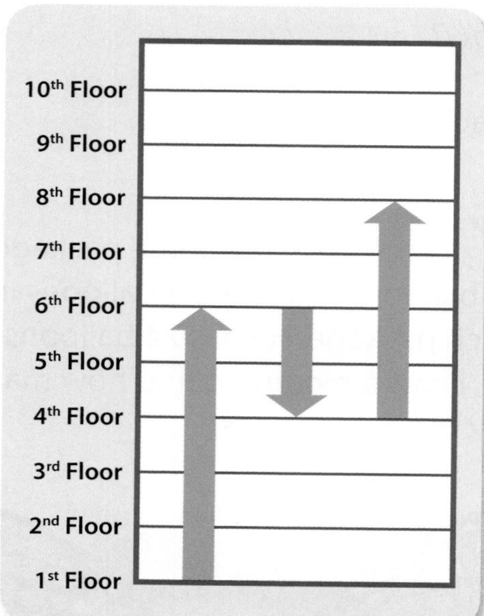

Jackie started on the first floor. Then she went up 5 floors.

$1 + 5 = 6$

Then she went down 2 floors.

$6 - 2 = 4$

Then she went up 4 floors and got off the elevator.

$4 + 4 = 8$

Jackie is on the eighth floor.

Explain It

1. Why is drawing a picture a good way to explain this problem?
2. How do the number sentences explain the problem?

Complete the table. Use *words, pictures, numbers,* or *symbols* to write a math explanation.

The number of pennies doubles each day. That means that Gina will get 2 times as many pennies as she got the day before.

So, I need to double 32.
32 + 32 = 64 pennies
Gina will get 64 pennies on Saturday.

Then, I need to double 64.
64 + 64 = 128 pennies
Gina will get 128 pennies on Sunday.

Data

Day	Number of Pennies
Monday	2
Tuesday	4
Wednesday	8
Thursday	16
Friday	32
Saturday	64
Sunday	128

Guided Practice*

Do you know HOW?

1. Brian bought 3 packs of baseball cards. There are 4 cards in each pack. How many baseball cards did he buy? Explain how you can solve this problem.

Do you UNDERSTAND?

2. If the pattern in the table above continued, how many pennies would Gina get next Monday?

3. **Write a Problem** Write a real-world problem. Explain how to solve it using words, pictures, numbers, or symbols.

Independent Practice

4. Pam is setting up tables and chairs. She puts 4 chairs at each table.

   a Explain how the number of chairs changes as the number of tables changes.

   b Copy and complete the table.

Number of Tables	1	2	3	4	5
Number of Chairs	4	8	12		

5. Aaron cut a log into 5 pieces. How many cuts did he make? Explain how you found the answer.

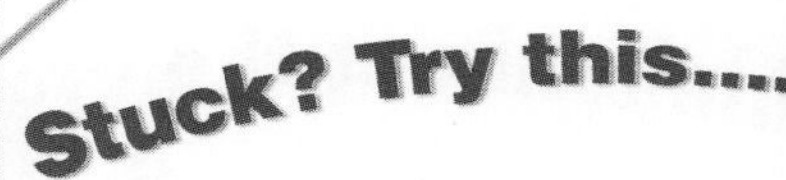

- What do I know?
- What am I asked to find?
- What diagram can I use to help understand the problem?
- Can I use addition, subtraction, multiplication, or division?
- Is all of my work correct?
- Did I answer the right question?
- Is my answer reasonable?

*For another example, see Set E on page 133.

Independent Practice

6. Copy and complete the table below. Then describe how the table helps you explain the pattern.

Cost of School Play Tickets

Number of Tickets	Cost
1	$5
2	$10
3	$15
4	▢
5	

7. If Margo continues the pattern in the table, what is the first day she will exercise for 1 hour? Explain how you know.

Margo's Exercise Schedule

Day	Minutes
Monday	20 minutes
Tuesday	30 minutes
Wednesday	40 minutes
Thursday	▢ minutes
Friday	▢ minutes

8. Hank earns $4 for raking lawns and $6 for mowing lawns. How much will Hank earn if he mows and rakes 2 lawns?

9. **a** Describe the pattern below.

   81, 82, 84, 87, 91

   b Write the next two numbers in the pattern and explain how you found them.

10. Jake is planting trees in a row that is 20 feet long. He plants a tree at the beginning of the row. Then he plants a tree every 5 feet. How many trees does he plant? Draw a picture to explain.

Think About the Process

11. Alexandra bought 5 bags of oranges. There were 6 oranges in each bag. Then she gave 4 oranges away. Which number sentence shows how many oranges Alexandra bought?

    A $5 + 6 = $ ▢

    B $5 \times 6 = $ ▢

    C $(5 \times 6) - 4 = $ ▢

    D $(5 + 6) - 4 = $ ▢

12. Tara ran 5 miles on Monday and 4 miles on Tuesday. Teresa ran 3 miles on Monday and 6 miles on Tuesday. Which number sentence shows how far Tara ran in all?

    F $3 + 6 = $ ▢

    G $5 + 4 = $ ▢

    H $5 - 4 = $ ▢

    J $5 + 4 + 3 + 6 = $ ▢

Meanings of Multiplication

Use eTools
Counters

Step 1 Go to the Counters eTool. Select a counter shape. Make 4 groups of counters with 3 counters in each group. The odometer tells how many counters in all. Write a number sentence: $4 \times 3 = 12$.

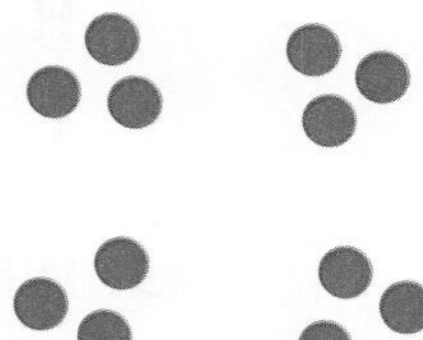

Step 2 Use the broom tool to clear the workspace. Show 3 groups with 8 counters in each and write a number sentence: $3 \times 8 = 24$.

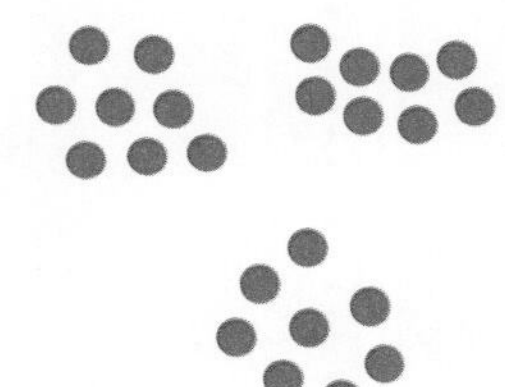

Step 3 Select the array workspace. Drag the button to show 7 rows with 6 counters in each row. Write a number sentence: $7 \times 6 = 42$.

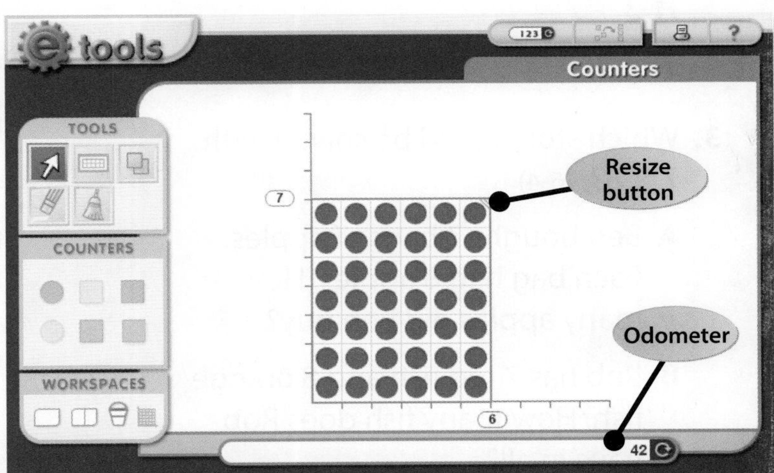

Practice

Use the Counters eTool to draw counters. Write a number sentence.

1. 5 groups with 3 counters in each
2. 7 groups with 4 counters in each
3. 8 rows with 6 counters in each
4. 9 rows with 5 counters in each

TAKS Test Prep

1. Which has the same value as 5×2? (6-1)

   A $5 + 2$

   B $2 + 2 + 2 + 2$

   C $2 + 2 + 2 + 5$

   D $2 + 2 + 2 + 2 + 2$

2. Mrs. Salinas planted her flowers in the pattern shown below. What operation best shows how she planted them? (6-2)

   F 3×7

   G 3×6

   H $3 + 7$

   J $7 + 3$

3. Which story could be solved with 7×8? (6-4)

   A Ben bought 7 bags of apples. Each bag had 8 apples. How many apples did Ben buy?

   B Rob has 7 red fish and 8 orange fish. How many fish does Rob have in all?

   C Tao had 8 math problems to solve. He has solved 7 of them. How many does he have left?

   D Max has 7 pages in his album. He has 8 pictures. How many pictures can he put on each page?

4. Maddie mailed 3 postcards during her vacation. Her sister mailed twice as many. How many postcards did Maddie's sister mail? (6-3)

   F 9

   G 6

   H 5

   J 2

5. Which number sentence shows how to find 4 times as many books as Trent read? (6-3)

   A $4 + 8 = 12$

   B $4 \times 8 = 32$

   C $4 \times 9 = 36$

   D $5 \times 8 = 40$

6. Tiffany bought the canisters of tennis balls shown below. How many tennis balls did she buy in all? (6-1)

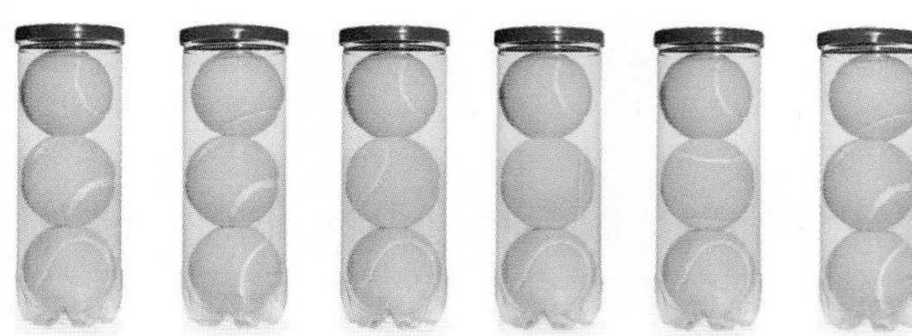

   F 6

   G 9

   H 12

   J 18

7. Which number makes the second number sentence true? (6-2)

$9 \times 7 = 63$
$7 \times \square = 63$

A 63

B 56

C 9

D 7

8. Ryan's pumpkin bread recipe calls for 2 cups of flour and 4 eggs to make 1 loaf. Ryan wants to make 3 loaves. Which can be used to find how many eggs Ryan needs? (6-1)

F 2×4

G 3×2

H 3×4

J 3×6

9. Which array shows 2×3? (6-2)

A 

B 

C 

D 

10. Alice is buying paper cups for the picnic. Each package has 8 cups. How does the number of cups change as the number of packages increases by 1? (6-5)

Packages	1	2	3	4	5
Cups	8	16	24	32	40

F There are 40 more cups for each additional package.

G There are 40 fewer cups for each additional package.

H There are 8 more cups for each additional package.

J There are 8 fewer cups for each additional package.

11. For the 4th of July, Ron put flags in his yard as shown below. Which number sentence would find how many flags Ron put in his yard? (6-2)

A $5 + 4 = \square$

B $4 \times 5 = \square$

C $4 + 5 = \square$

D $5 - 4 = \square$

12. **Griddable Response** Tony found 4 times as many seashells as Margo. If Margo found 6 seashells, how many seashells did Tony find? (6-3)

Reteaching

Set A, pages 116–117

Find the total number of counters.

●● ●● ●●

There are 3 groups of 2 counters.

You can use addition to join groups.

$2 + 2 + 2 = 6$

You can also multiply to join equal groups.

$3 \times 2 = 6$

So, $2 + 2 + 2 = 3 \times 2$.

Remember that multiplication is a quick way of joining equal groups.

Copy and complete.

1. 2 groups of ☐
   5 + ☐ = ☐
   2 × ☐ = ☐

2. 3 groups of ☐.
   6 + ☐ + ☐ = ☐
   3 × ☐ = ☐

Set B, pages 118–120

Draw an array to show 2×3.
Then write the product.

This array shows 2 rows of 3.

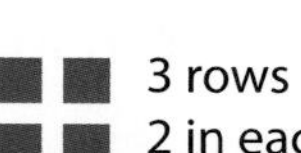

2 rows
3 in each row

$3 + 3 = 6$ or $2 \times 3 = 6$.

Draw an array to show 3×2.

This array shows 3 rows of 2.

3 rows
2 in each row

$2 + 2 + 2 = 6$ or $3 \times 2 = 6$.

Remember to use the Commutative (order) Property of Multiplication.

Draw an array to show each fact.
Write the product.

1. 2×4 2. 3×5 3. 4×4

Copy and complete each multiplication sentence.

4. 5 × ☐ = 10
   2 × ☐ = 10

5. 3 × ☐ = 21
   7 × ☐ = 21

Set C, pages 122–123

Find 2 times as many as 6.

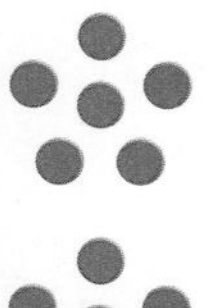

$2 \times 6 = 12$ or

$$\begin{array}{r} 2 \\ \times\ 6 \\ \hline 12 \end{array}$$

Remember that you multiply by 2 to find *twice as many*.

Find each amount. You may use drawings or counters to help.

1. 3 times as many as 5
2. 5 times as many as 4
3. Twice as many as 7

Set D, pages 124–125

Write a multiplication story for 3×5.

Draw a picture to find the product.

Jessica is putting pretzels into 3 bags. She will put 5 pretzels in each bag. How many pretzels does Jessica have in all?

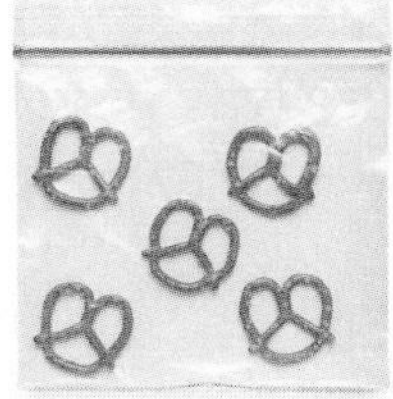

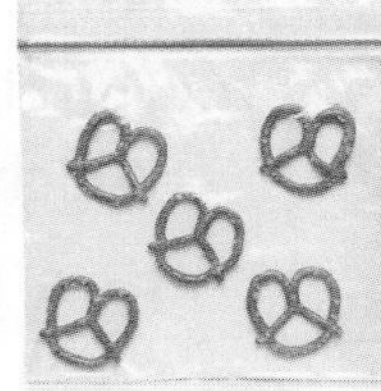

Jessica has 15 pretzels.

Remember that your multiplication story should always end with a question.

Write a multiplication story for each. Draw a picture to find each product.

1. 3×9 **2.** 5×6 **3.** 7×2

Write a multiplication story for each picture. Use the picture to find the product.

4. 

5.

Set E, pages 126–128

You can use words, pictures, numbers, or symbols to explain an answer. When you explain your answer to a problem, be sure that you:

- clearly show your explanation using words, pictures, numbers, or symbols.
- tell what the numbers mean in your explanation.
- tell why you took certain steps.

Remember that another person should be able to follow your explanation.

Solve. Explain how you found each answer.

1. Gina earns \$3 for making dinner and \$5 for changing the sheets on her bed. How much will Gina earn in one week if she makes dinner 3 times and changes the sheets one time?

2. Jack is setting up tables for a party. Each table has 6 chairs. How many chairs does he need for 10 tables?

Topics 1–6

Spiral Review

Number and Operations

1. Which number is between 2,583 and 3,125?

2,583		3,125

A 2,435

B 3,190

C 3,109

D 2,579

2. Jerome's parents spent $52 for dinner at a restaurant. Jerome's meal cost $13, and his sister Anna's meal cost $11. The rest of the money was spent on Jerome's parents' meals. How much was spent on Jerome's parents' meals?

F $24

G $28

H $34

J $38

3. What number makes this number sentence true?

$3 + (\square + 5) = (3 + 6) + 5$

4. Complete the multiplication sentences.

$3 \times \square = 15$
$5 \times \square = 15$

5. Write a multiplication story for 4×3. Draw a picture to find the product.

6. **Writing to Explain** Explain how you can use mental math to find the difference $83 - 17$.

Geometry and Measurement

7. What figure best describes the box of tissues?

A Cube

B Rectangular prism

C Sphere

D Cylinder

8. The classroom temperature was 72°F. Which thermometer shows 72°F?

F °F 90 80 70 60

H °F 90 80 70 60

G °F 90 80 70 60

J °F 90 80 70 60

9. Which measurement best describes the length of a student desk?

A 3 inches

B 3 centimeters

C 3 yards

D 3 feet

10. How long is the nail to the nearest inch?

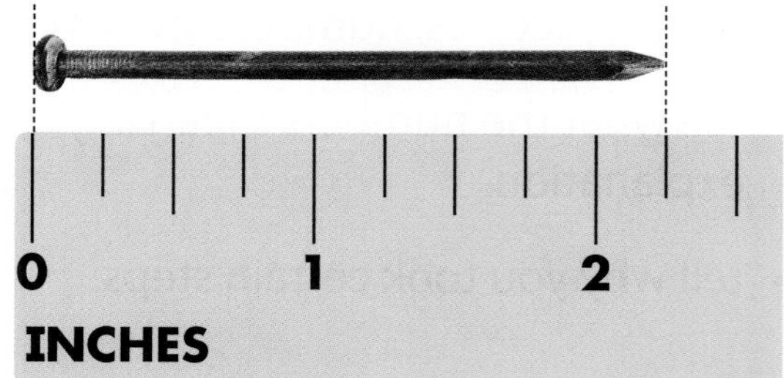

11. **Writing to Explain** Explain what the hands of a clock look like at 12:15.

Spiral Review

Probability and Statistics

12. Which color is the spinner more likely to land on?

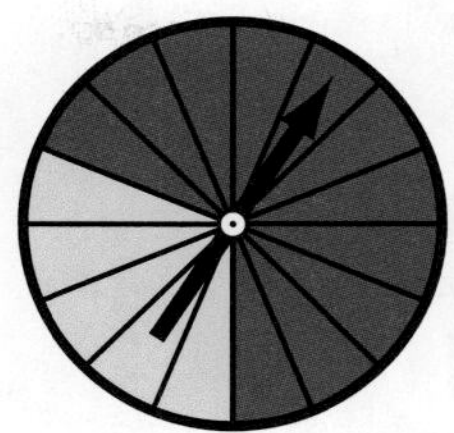

13. Draw a 2-part spinner on which it is less likely to spin letter A than the letter B.

Use the pictograph for **14–16**.

Children on Playground

Swings	☺ ☺ ☺
Slides	☺ ☺
Monkey Bars	☺ ☺ ☺ ☺

Key: Each ☺ = 2 children

14. How many children are playing on the monkey bars?

F 2 **H** 8

G 4 **J** 12

15. Suppose 4 more children join the children on the slides. How many more symbols would you add to show the total number of children on the slides?

A 1 **C** 3

B 2 **D** 4

16. **Writing to Explain** Explain how you can use multiplication or addition to find how many children are on the swings.

Algebraic Thinking

17. What number is missing in the pattern below?

3, 9, 15, ▭, 27

F 16 **H** 21

G 18 **J** 33

18. The table shows how many wings different numbers of dragonflies have.

Number of Dragonflies	3	4	5	6
Number of Wings	12	▭	20	24

How many wings will a group of 4 dragonflies have?

A 13 **C** 15

B 14 **D** 16

19. Which two factors could you multiply to get a product of 15?

F 3, 5 **H** 4, 4

G 2, 7 **J** 3, 6

20. Find three whole numbers that make the number sentence true.

$12 - \square > 8$

21. **Writing to Explain** Explain how the number of arms changes as the number of starfish changes.

Starfish	1	2	3	4	5
Arms	5	10	15	20	25

Topic 7

Multiplication Fact Strategies: Use Patterns

1 A dollhouse was made for Queen Mary of England. How do the objects in the dollhouse compare in size to the objects in her real-life castle? You will find out in Lesson 7-3.

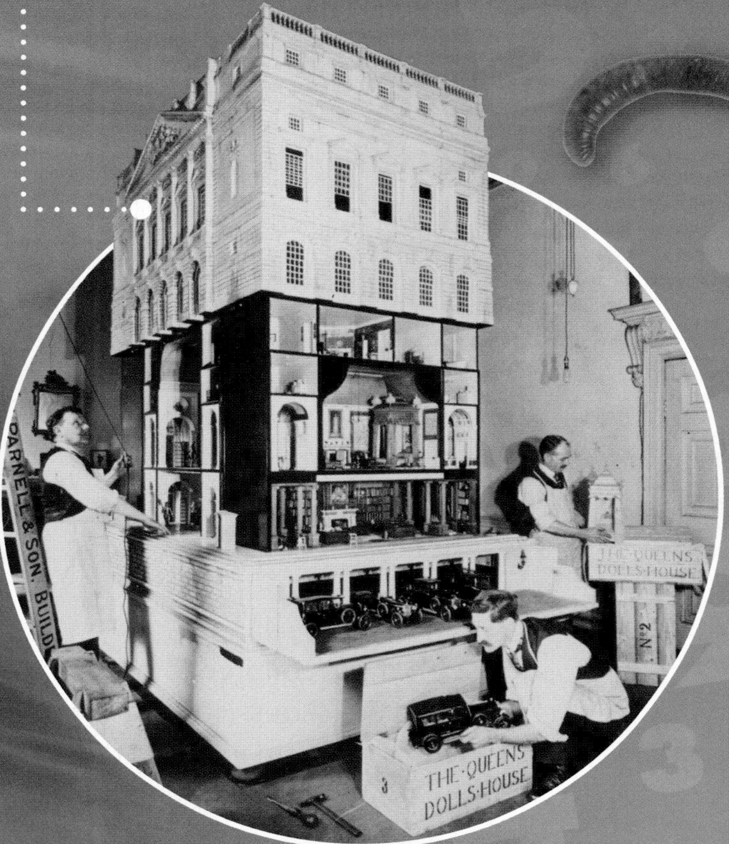

2 How many wheels are on the bikes of a unicycle relay team? You will find out in Lesson 7-3.

3

How many hearts does an earthworm have? You will find out in Lesson 7-1.

4

How many spikes did workers hammer into a railroad tie to hold it in place? You will find out in Lesson 7-4.

Review What You Know!

Vocabulary

Choose the best term from the box.

- addends
- factors
- product
- sum

1. The numbers you multiply are __?__.

2. The answer in an addition problem is the __?__.

3. The answer in a multiplication problem is the __?__.

Skip Counting

Write the missing numbers.

4. 10, 20, ▢, 40, 50, ▢

5. 10, 15, 20, ▢, ▢, 35

Repeated Addition

Find each sum.

6. 1 + 1 + 1 + 1 + 1 + 1 + 1

7. 2 + 2 + 2 + 2 + 2 + 2

Adding

Find each sum.

8. 80 + 16 **9.** 90 + 18 **10.** 70 + 14

11. 110 + 22 **12.** 110 + 11 **13.** 120 + 12

Multiplication

14. **Writing to Explain** Explain how to find how many items are in 3 groups if there are 4 items in each group. Draw a picture to help.

Lesson

7-1

TEKS 3.6B: Identify patterns in multiplication facts using concrete objects, pictorial models, or technology. Also **TEKS 3.4A** and **3.4B.**

2 and 5 as Factors

How can you use patterns to multiply by 2 and 5?

How many socks are in 7 pairs of socks? Find 7×2.

1 pair	2 pairs	3 pairs	4 pairs	5 pairs	6 pairs	7 pairs
1×2	2×2	3×2	4×2	5×2	6×2	7×2
2	4	6	8	10	12	14

There are 14 socks in 7 pairs.

Other Examples

What are the patterns in multiples of 2 and 5?

The products for the 2s facts are multiples of 2.
The products for the 5s facts are multiples of 5.
Multiples are the products of a number and other whole numbers.

Data

2s Facts	
$0 \times 2 = 0$	$5 \times 2 = 10$
$1 \times 2 = 2$	$6 \times 2 = 12$
$2 \times 2 = 4$	$7 \times 2 = 14$
$3 \times 2 = 6$	$8 \times 2 = 16$
$4 \times 2 = 8$	$9 \times 2 = 18$

Data

5s Facts	
$0 \times 5 = 0$	$5 \times 5 = 25$
$1 \times 5 = 5$	$6 \times 5 = 30$
$2 \times 5 = 10$	$7 \times 5 = 35$
$3 \times 5 = 15$	$8 \times 5 = 40$
$4 \times 5 = 20$	$9 \times 5 = 45$

Patterns for 2s Facts

- Multiples of 2 are even numbers. Multiples of 2 end in 0, 2, 4, 6, or 8.
- Each multiple of 2 is 2 more than the one before it.

Patterns for 5s Facts

- Each multiple of 5 ends in 0 or 5.
- Each multiple of 5 is 5 more than the one before it.

Explain It

1. Is 83 a multiple of 2 or a multiple of 5? How do you know?
2. **Reasoning** How can patterns help you find 10×2?

How many fingers are on 7 gloves?

Choose an Operation Find 7×5.

$1 \times 5 = 5$
$2 \times 5 = 10$
$3 \times 5 = 15$
$4 \times 5 = 20$
$5 \times 5 = 25$
$6 \times 5 = 30$
$7 \times 5 = 35$

There are 35 fingers on 7 gloves.

Guided Practice*

Do you know HOW?

Find each product.

1. 2×6 **2.** 2×3 **3.** 7×2

4. 5×3 **5.** 5×5 **6.** 6×5

7. 4×2 **8.** 5×2 **9.** 8×5

Do you UNDERSTAND?

10. How can you skip count to find the number of socks in 9 pairs? in 10 pairs?

11. How can you skip count to find how many fingers are on 9 gloves? on 10 gloves?

12. **Number Sense** Bert says that 2×8 is 15. How can you use patterns to know that his answer is wrong?

Independent Practice

For **13–22**, find each product.

13. 2×2 **14.** 5×2 **15.** 3×5 **16.** 8×2 **17.** 9×5

18. 3×5 **19.** 2×4 **20.** 4×5 **21.** 9×2 **22.** 5×7

23. Find 5 times 6.

24. Multiply 2 by 5.

25. Find the product of 7 and 5.

26. Find 6×2.

DIGITAL Animated Glossary **www.pearsonsuccessnet.com**

For another example, see Set A on page 154.

Independent Practice

Algebra Compare. Use <, >, or =.

27. $2 \times 5 \bigcirc 5 \times 2$

28. $4 \times 5 \bigcirc 4 \times 6$

29. $2 \times 5 \bigcirc 2 \times 4$

30. $6 \times 5 \bigcirc 5 \times 5$

31. $9 \times 5 \bigcirc 5 \times 9$

32. $7 \times 2 \bigcirc 2 \times 9$

TAKS Problem Solving

For **33–35**, use the table at the right.

33. How much does it cost to bowl three games without renting shoes?

34. Maru rented some bowling shoes. She also bowled two games. How much money did she spend?

35. Wendy paid for 2 games with a twenty-dollar bill. How much change did she get back?

Data

Bowling	
Cost per game	$5
Daily shoe rental	$2

36. **Writing to Explain** Eric has some nickels. He says they are worth exactly 34 cents. Can you tell if he is correct or not? Why or why not?

38. Use the picture below. How many hearts do 3 earthworms have?

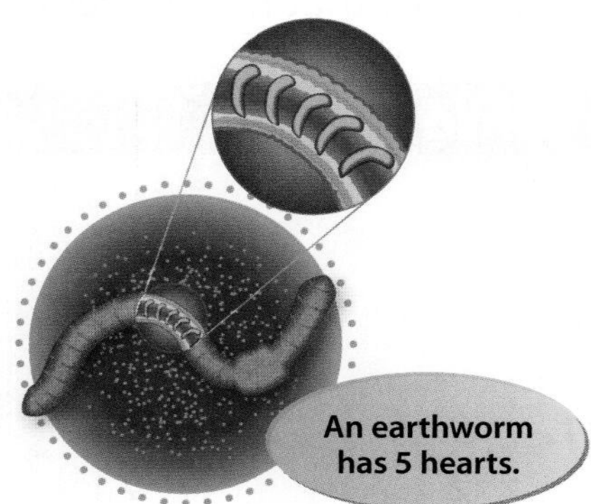

37. April has the coins shown below.

If April counted the value of these coins, which list shows numbers she could have named?

A 5, 10, 16, 20, 25

B 5, 10, 15, 22, 25

C 10, 15, 20, 25, 30

D 10, 15, 22, 25, 30

39. **Algebra** What two 1-digit factors could you multiply to get a product of 30?

40. Jake went bowling. On his first turn, he knocked down 2 pins. On his second turn, he knocked down twice that many. So far, how many pins in all has he knocked down?

Mixed Problem Solving

Animals get special features, called inherited traits, from their parents. Use the table on the right to answer the questions.

Some Traits of Animals

Kind of Animal	Inherited Trait
Birds	2 eyes, 2 legs, 2 wings
Fish	2 eyes
Insects	2 antennas, 6 legs, 3 body parts
Apes	2 hands, 5 fingers on each hand, 2 legs, 5 toes on each foot, 2 eyes

1. A mother and her two babies are on a tree branch. They have six wings in all. Which kind of animal from the table could these be?

2. Two adult apes and two baby apes are near the water. How many fingers do the apes have in all?

3. One of these animals is on a tree branch. It has six legs in all. Which kind of animal from the table could this be?

4. Which has more legs—two birds or one insect? How many more?

5. Look at the table below.

Kind of Animal	Number of Body Parts	Number of Legs
Insect	3	6
Spider	2	8

Danny saw three of the same kind of animal on the sidewalk. He counted six body parts in all. Did Danny see 3 spiders or 3 insects?

6. **Strategy Focus** Solve. Use the strategy Draw a Picture.

Trini had 31 baby fish and 5 adult fish in a fish tank. She put 18 of the baby fish in another tank, and all of the adult fish in a third tank. How many baby fish are left in the first tank? Check if your answer is reasonable.

Lesson

7-2

TEKS 3.6B: Identify patterns in multiplication facts using concrete objects, pictorial models, or technology. Also **TEKS 3.4A** and **3.4B**.

9 as a Factor

How can patterns be used to find 9s facts?

The owner of a flower shop puts 9 roses in each package. How many roses are in 8 packages?

Use patterns to find 8×9.

Data

9s Facts
$0 \times 9 = 0$
$1 \times 9 = 9$
$2 \times 9 = 18$
$3 \times 9 = 27$
$4 \times 9 = 36$
$5 \times 9 = 45$
$6 \times 9 = 54$
$7 \times 9 = 63$
$8 \times 9 =$
$9 \times 9 =$

Guided Practice*

Do you know HOW?

Find each product.

1. 9×2 **2.** 5×9 **3.** 7×9

4. 4×9 **5.** 2×8 **6.** 6×9

7. 3×9 **8.** 5×5 **9.** 8×9

Do you UNDERSTAND?

10. Writing to Explain Use the patterns above to find 9×9. Then explain how you found the product.

11. Number Sense Paul thinks that 3×9 is 24. Use a 9s pattern to show that he is wrong.

Independent Practice

Find each product.

12. 9×0 **13.** 5×8 **14.** 9×4 **15.** 8×9 **16.** 9×9

17. 1×9 **18.** 5×9 **19.** 9×2 **20.** 7×9 **21.** 5×2

22. 6×5 **23.** 9×1 **24.** 6×9 **25.** 9×5 **26.** 9×7

27. 9×2 **28.** 7×9 **29.** 8×2 **30.** 0×9 **31.** 2×3

*For another example, see Set B on page 154.

One Way

Use these patterns.

- The ones digit decreases by 1 each time. So the next ones digit is 2.
- The tens digit increases by 1 each time. So the next tens digit is 7.

$8 \times 9 = 72$

There are 72 roses in 8 packages.

Another Way

Use these patterns to find the product.

- The tens digit is 1 less than the factor being multiplied by 9.
- The digits of the product have a sum of 9.

$8 - 1 = 7$

$8 \times 9 = 72$

$7 + 2 = 9$

$8 \times 9 = 72$

There are 72 roses in 8 packages.

Algebra Copy and complete. Use $+$, $-$, or $\times$.

32. $2 \times 6 = 10 \square 2$ **33.** $5 \times 7 = 45 \square 10$ **34.** $9 \times 9 = 80 \square 1$

35. $20 - 2 = 2 \square 9$ **36.** $9 \square 3 = 30 - 3$ **37.** $9 \square 1 = 2 \square 5$

TAKS Problem Solving

The library is having a used book sale. For **38–41**, use the table at the right.

38. How much do 4 hardcover books cost?

Library Book Sale	
Paperback Books	$2
Hardcover Books	$5
Books on CDs	$9

39. How much more would Chico spend if he bought 3 books on CDs rather than 3 hardcover books?

40. Maggie bought only paperback books. The clerk told her she owed $15. How does Maggie know that the clerk made a mistake?

41. Writing to Explain Mr. Lee bought 2 books on CDs and 9 paperback books. Did he spend more on CDs or paperbacks? Tell how you know.

42. The owner of a flower shop counted the flowers in groups of 9. Which list shows the numbers he named?

A 9, 19, 29, 39, 49, 59

B 6, 12, 18, 24, 36, 42

C 18, 27, 36, 45, 56, 65

D 9, 18, 27, 36, 45, 54

Lesson

7-3

TEKS 3.6B: Identify patterns in multiplication facts using concrete objects, pictorial models, or technology. Also **TEKS 3.4A** and **3.4B**.

Multiplying with 0 and 1

What are the patterns in multiples of 1 and 0?

Kira has 8 plates with 1 orange on each plate. How many oranges does Kira have?

Find 8×1.

Guided Practice*

Do you know HOW?

Find each product.

1. 1×7 **2.** 5×0 **3.** 5×1

4. 0×0 **5.** 1×1 **6.** 8×1

7. 7×0 **8.** 1×9 **9.** 0×6

Do you UNDERSTAND?

10. Writing to Explain How can you use the properties above to find 375×1 and 0×754?

11. Draw an array to show that $1 \times 8 = 8$.

12. Chad has 6 plates. There is 1 apple and 0 grapes on each plate. How many apples are there? How many grapes are there?

Independent Practice

Find each product.

13. 0×4 **14.** 1×6 **15.** 1×3 **16.** 3×0 **17.** 4×1

18. 0×9 **19.** 1×3 **20.** 1×7 **21.** 0×7 **22.** 8×0

23. 8×1 **24.** 0×2 **25.** 1×2 **26.** 9×0 **27.** 0×1

DIGITAL Animated Glossary **www.pearsonsuccessnet.com**

*For another example, see Set C on page 155.

8 groups with 1 in each group equals 8 in all.

$8 \times 1 = 8$

Kira has 8 oranges.

1 plate with 8 oranges also equals 8 oranges.

$1 \times 8 = 8$

The Identity (One) Property of Multiplication: when you multiply a number and 1, the product is that number.

If Kira has 4 plates with 0 oranges on each plate, she has 0 oranges.

$4 \times 0 = 0$

If $4 \times 0 = 0$ then $0 \times 4 = 0$.

The Zero Property of Multiplication: when you multiply a number and 0, the product is 0.

Algebra Copy and complete. Write <, >, or = for each ◯.

28. 1×6 ◯ 8×0

29. 8×1 ◯ 1×9

30. 1×4 ◯ 4×1

31. 0×654 ◯ 346×0

32. 2×9 ◯ 9×1

33. 0×754 ◯ 5×1

TAKS Problem Solving

Algebra Copy and complete. Write ×, +, or − for each □.

34. 4 □ 1 = 4
4 □ 1 = 5
4 □ 1 = 3

35. 4 □ 0 = 4
4 □ 0 = 0

36. 6 □ 1 = 5
6 □ 1 = 6
6 □ 1 = 7

37. What is the missing factor?
548 × ▢ = 548

A 0 **B** 1 **C** 2 **D** 4

38. **Writing to Explain** The product of two factors is 0. One of the factors is 0. Can you tell what the other factor is? Explain your answer.

39. A unicycle relay team has 4 riders. Each rider has one unicycle. If each unicycle has 1 wheel, how many wheels does the team have?

40. **Reasoning** Why do you think the Identity Property of Multiplication is sometimes called the One Property of Multiplication?

41. Objects in Windsor Castle are 12 times the size of the miniature versions in Queen Mary's dollhouse. How tall is a real-life painting if it is 1 inch tall in the dollhouse?

Lesson

7-4

TEKS 3.6B: Identify patterns in multiplication facts using concrete objects, pictorial models, or technology. Also **TEKS 3.4A.**

10, 11, and 12 as Factors

What are the patterns in multiples of 10, 11, and 12?

Greg wants to train for a race that is 12 weeks away. The table shows his training schedule. How many miles will Greg swim to train for the race?

Weekly Schedule

Activity	Miles
Swimming	10 miles
Running	11 miles
Biking	12 miles

Choose an Operation
Find 12 × 10.

Other Examples

What are the multiples of 11 and 12?

11s Facts

Think	Write
0 × 11 = 0 + 0	0 × 11 = 0
1 × 11 = 10 + 1	1 × 11 = 11
2 × 11 = 20 + 2	2 × 11 = 22
3 × 11 = 30 + 3	3 × 11 = 33
4 × 11 = 40 + 4	4 × 11 = 44
5 × 11 = 50 + 5	5 × 11 = 55
6 × 11 = 60 + 6	6 × 11 = 66
7 × 11 = 70 + 7	7 × 11 = 77
8 × 11 = 80 + 8	8 × 11 = 88
9 × 11 = 90 + 9	9 × 11 = 99
10 × 11 = 100 + 10	10 × 11 = 110
11 × 11 = 110 + 11	11 × 11 = 121
12 × 11 = 120 + 12	12 × 11 = 132

Use patterns to multiply the factor that is not 11 by 10. Then add that factor to the product.

Example: Find 8 × 11.

8 × 10 = 80

80 + 8 = 88

So, 8 × 11 = 88.

12s Facts

Think	Write
0 × 12 = 0 + 0	0 × 12 = 0
1 × 12 = 10 + 2	1 × 12 = 12
2 × 12 = 20 + 4	2 × 12 = 24
3 × 12 = 30 + 6	3 × 12 = 36
4 × 12 = 40 + 8	4 × 12 = 48
5 × 12 = 50 + 10	5 × 12 = 60
6 × 12 = 60 + 12	6 × 12 = 72
7 × 12 = 70 + 14	7 × 12 = 84
8 × 12 = 80 + 16	8 × 12 = 96
9 × 12 = 90 + 18	9 × 12 = 108
10 × 12 = 100 + 20	10 × 12 = 120
11 × 12 = 110 + 22	11 × 12 = 132
12 × 12 = 120 + 24	12 × 12 = 144

Use patterns to multiply the factor that is not 12 by 10. Then multiply that factor by 2. Add the two products.

Example: Find 8 × 12.

8 × 10 = 80   8 × 2 = 16

80 + 16 = 96

So, 8 × 12 = 96.

Explain It

1. How can you use 9 × 10 to help you find 9 × 12?

Use patterns in the 10s facts to find the product.

10s Facts

Data

$0 \times 10 = 0$	$7 \times 10 = 70$
$1 \times 10 = 10$	$8 \times 10 = 80$
$2 \times 10 = 20$	$9 \times 10 = 90$
$3 \times 10 = 30$	$10 \times 10 =$
$4 \times 10 = 40$	$11 \times 10 =$
$5 \times 10 = 50$	$12 \times 10 =$
$6 \times 10 = 60$	

- Write the factor you are multiplying by 10.
- Write a zero to the right of that factor. A multiple of 10 will always have a zero in the ones place.

$10 \times 10 = 100$
$11 \times 10 = 110$
$12 \times 10 = 120$

Greg will swim 120 miles.

Guided Practice*

Do you know HOW?

Use patterns to find each product.

1. 10×3
11×3
12×3

2. 10×5
11×5
12×5

3. 10×7
11×7
12×7

4. 10×9
11×9
12×9

5. $\begin{array}{r} 10 \\ \times\ 11 \\ \hline \end{array}$

6. $\begin{array}{r} 11 \\ \times\ 11 \\ \hline \end{array}$

7. $\begin{array}{r} 12 \\ \times\ 11 \\ \hline \end{array}$

Do you UNDERSTAND?

8. **Writing to Explain** How can you use a pattern to find 12×10?

9. How many miles will Greg bike in 12 weeks?

10. **Number Sense** Greg multiplied 2×12 to find how many more miles he biked than swam in the 12 weeks. Does that make sense? Why or why not?

Independent Practice

Use patterns to find each product.

11. 10×2
11×2
12×2

12. 10×4
11×4
12×4

13. 10×6
11×6
12×6

14. 10×8
11×8
12×8

15.a $\begin{array}{r} 10 \\ \times\ 10 \\ \hline \end{array}$ **b** $\begin{array}{r} 11 \\ \times\ 10 \\ \hline \end{array}$ **c** $\begin{array}{r} 12 \\ \times\ 10 \\ \hline \end{array}$

16.a $\begin{array}{r} 10 \\ \times\ 12 \\ \hline \end{array}$ **b** $\begin{array}{r} 11 \\ \times\ 12 \\ \hline \end{array}$ **c** $\begin{array}{r} 12 \\ \times\ 12 \\ \hline \end{array}$

For another example, see Set D on page 155.

Independent Practice

Find each product.

17. 10×7 **18.** 8×2 **19.** 12×7 **20.** 9×9 **21.** 6×12

22. 11×11 **23.** 6×11 **24.** 5×9 **25.** 3×10 **26.** 12×8

27. $\begin{array}{r} 6 \\ \times \ 5 \\ \hline \end{array}$ **28.** $\begin{array}{r} 11 \\ \times \ 4 \\ \hline \end{array}$ **29.** $\begin{array}{r} 9 \\ \times \ 12 \\ \hline \end{array}$ **30.** $\begin{array}{r} 10 \\ \times \ 11 \\ \hline \end{array}$ **31.** $\begin{array}{r} 12 \\ \times \ 5 \\ \hline \end{array}$

TAKS Problem Solving

Use the table at the right for **32** and **33**. It shows the food that was bought for 120 third graders for a school picnic.

Data

Food Item	Number of Packages	Number in Each Package
Hot dogs	10	12
Rolls	12	10
Juice boxes	12	11

32. Find the total number of each item bought.

a Hot dogs

b Rolls

c Juice boxes

33. Each third grader got one juice box. How many extra juice boxes were bought?

34. **Algebra** How many dimes do you need to have $0.90?

35. **Number Sense** How can you tell that 64 is not a multiple of 11?

36. Sheila counted the value of the coins shown below. Which list is numbers she would have said?

A 10, 30, 50, 70, 80

B 10, 20, 25, 30, 40

C 50, 60, 70, 80, 90

D 40, 50, 60, 75, 90

37. A worker building one of the first railroads hammered several spikes into each railroad tie. How many spikes did he need for 7 ties?

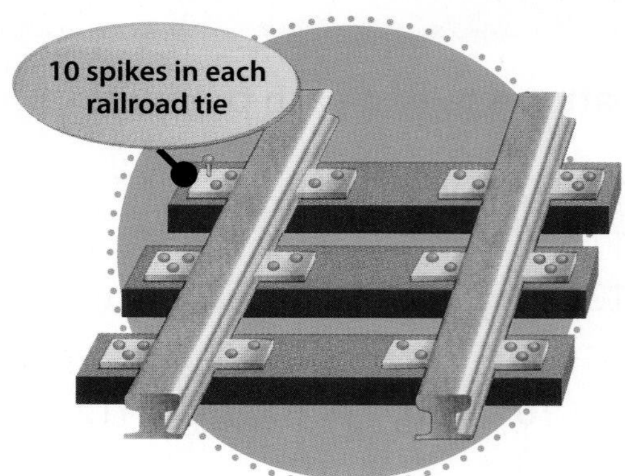

Algebra Connections

Missing Operations

Remember, the equal symbol means that two sides of a number sentence must have the same value. An operation symbol +, −, or × tells what to do with the numbers to find the value of the side. Reasoning can help you find a missing operation symbol.

Example: 72 = 8 ☐ 9

Think 72 is equal to 8 (plus, or minus, or multiplied by) 9?

Since 8 × 9 = 72. Write "×".

72 = 8 ☒ 9

Copy and complete. Replace the square with +, −, or ×. Check your answers.

+ add **− subtract** **× multiply**

1. 9 ☐ 36 = 45 **2.** 24 ☐ 17 = 7 **3.** 16 = 2 ☐ 8

4. 8 = 32 ☐ 24 **5.** 7 ☐ 5 = 35 **6.** 50 = 12 ☐ 38

7. 18 = 9 ☐ 2 **8.** 64 ☐ 36 = 28 **9.** 30 = 6 ☐ 5

10. 47 ☐ 37 = 84 **11.** 63 = 9 ☐ 7 **12.** 12 ☐ 1 = 12

For **13** and **14**, copy and complete the number sentence below each problem. Use it to help find your answer.

13. Lisa had some pens left after she gave 27 pens to her friends. She started with a package of 36 pens. What operation can you use to find the number of pens Lisa had left?

9 = 36 ☐ 27

14. The picture below shows the number of each kind of button in a package. What operation can you use to find the total number of buttons in one package?

60 = 5 ☐ 12

12 of each button

15. Write a Problem Write a real-world problem using this number sentence:

48 = 26 + 22

Lesson
7-5

TEKS 3.14B: Solve problems that incorporate understanding the problem, making a plan, carrying out the plan, and evaluating the solution for reasonableness.

Problem Solving

Two-Question Problems

Sometimes you must use the answer to one problem to solve another problem.

Problem 1: Four girls and five boys went to the movies. How many children went to the movies?

Problem 2: Children's movie tickets cost $5 each. What was the total cost of the tickets for these children?

Guided Practice*

Do you know HOW?

1a. A movie ticket for an adult costs $9. How much do 3 adult tickets cost?

? Total cost

$9	$9	$9

b. Mr. Jones paid for 3 adult tickets with $40. How much change will he get?

$40

$27	?

Do you UNDERSTAND?

2. What operations were used to solve Exercises 1a and 1b? Tell why.

3. Writing to Explain Why must you solve Exercise 1a before solving Exercise 1b?

4. Write a Problem Write 2 problems that use the answer from the first problem to solve the second one.

Independent Practice

5a. Jared bought a baseball cap for $12 and a T-shirt for $19. How much did the items cost all together?

?

$12	$19

b. Suppose Jared paid with a $50 bill. How much change should he get?

$50

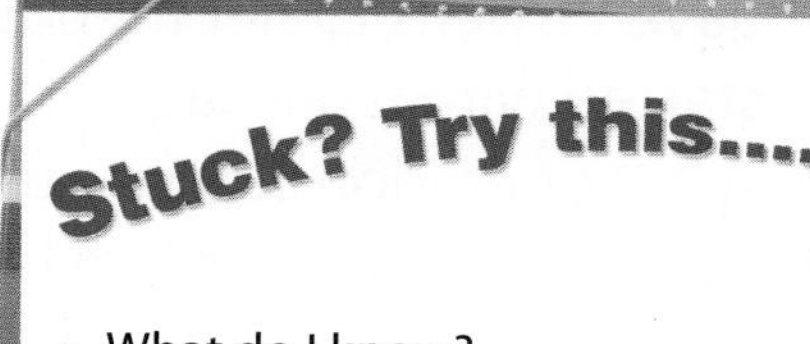

- What do I know?
- What am I asked to find?
- What diagram can I use to help understand the problem?
- Can I use addition, subtraction, multiplication, or division?
- Is all of my work correct?
- Did I answer the right question?
- Is my answer reasonable?

*For another example, see Set E on page 155.

Solve

Problem 1

Four girls and five boys went to the movies. How many children went to the movies?

? Children in all

4 girls	5 boys

$4 + 5 = 9$

Nine children went to the movies.

Solve

Problem 2

Children's movie tickets cost $5 each. What was the total cost of the tickets for these children?

? Total cost

\$5	\$5	\$5	\$5	\$5	\$5	\$5	\$5	\$5

$9 \times \$5 = \$45$

The total cost of the tickets was $45.

Independent Practice

Cara and some friends bought gifts in a museum shop. The gifts were from Hawaii. In **6–8**, use the answer from the first problem to solve the second problem.

6a. Cara bought a poster and a shirt. How much did her gifts cost?

b. Cara gave the clerk $30. How much change should she get?

7a. Dan bought 3 cups. How much did Dan spend on cups?

b. Dan also bought a CD. How much did Dan spend in all?

8a. Teri bought the most expensive and the least expensive gift. How much did she spend?

b. Teri's sister bought a CD. How much did the two girls spend in all?

9. On Monday, Roberta swam 10 laps. On Tuesday, she swam twice as many laps as on Monday. Which pair of number sentences can be used to find:

a how many laps Roberta swam on Tuesday?
b how many laps Roberta swam in all?

A $2 \times 10 = 20$
$20 + 10 = 30$

B $2 \times 10 = 20$
$20 - 10 = 10$

C $10 + 2 = 12$
$12 + 10 = 22$

D $10 + 2 = 12$
$12 - 10 = 2$

Topic 7

TAKS Test Prep

1. Which symbol makes the number sentence true? (7-3)

$5 \times 0 \bigcirc 2 \times 1$

A $>$

B $<$

C $=$

D $\times$

2. Salvador's family used 3 canoes at Caddo Lake State Park. Each canoe had 2 people. How many people went canoeing? (7-1)

F 5

G 6

H 8

J 9

3. Using the *sum of the digits* pattern, which number is a multiple of 9? (7-2)

A 55

B 26

C 43

D 36

4. Anita made 1 friendship bracelet for each of her 8 friends. How many friendship bracelets did Anita make? (7-3)

F 1

G 7

H 8

J 9

5. The scouts made scrambled eggs for breakfast. They used 7 cartons of eggs. Each carton had 12 eggs. Which shows a way to find 7×12? (7-4)

A $70 + 14$

B $70 + 7$

C $70 + 2$

D $70 + 12$

6. Sally bought 2 packages of balloons. Each package had 8 balloons. How many balloons did Sally buy? She gave 4 balloons to her brother. How many balloons did she have left? (7-5)

F Sally bought 18 balloons and had 14 left.

G Sally bought 10 balloons and had 6 left.

H Sally bought 16 balloons and had 10 left.

J Sally bought 16 balloons and had 12 left.

7. The 3rd graders at Willow School were put in 11 groups of 10 students. How many 3rd graders were there in all? (7-4)

A 111

B 110

C 101

D 100

8. Each starfish has 5 arms. If Shelly counted the arms in groups of 5, which list shows numbers she could have named? (7-1)

F 5, 10, 21, 40

G 10, 15, 21, 25

H 10, 15, 20, 25

J 15, 20, 26, 35

9. Which of these best describes all the snake lengths? (7-1)

Data

Snake	Length in Feet
Black Mamba	14
King Cobra	16
Taipan	10

A They are all greater than 12.

B They are all less than 15.

C They are all multiples of 5.

D They are all multiples of 2.

10. The Pet Store had 7 hamster cages. Each cage had 0 hamsters. How many hamsters did they have? (7-3)

F 0

G 1

H 7

J 10

11. Todd has 7 aquariums. Each aquarium has 9 fish and 3 plants. What is the total number of fish? (7-2)

A 63

B 62

C 27

D 21

12. Len has 3 rolls of quarters. Ryan has 8 rolls. How many more rolls does Ryan have than Len? Each roll has $10 worth of quarters. How much more money does Ryan have than Len? (7-5)

F Ryan has 11 more rolls, so he has $110 more than Len.

G Ryan has 5 more rolls, so he has $55 more than Len.

H Ryan has 5 more rolls, so he has $50 more than Len.

J Ryan has 6 more rolls, so he has $60 more than Len.

13. Griddable Response Rosa bought 3 spools of ribbon. Each spool has 5 yards of ribbon. How many yards of ribbon did Rosa buy? (7-1)

14. Griddable Response There are 12 inches in 1 foot. If Rodney is 4 feet tall, how many inches tall is he? (7-4)

Reteaching

Set A, pages 138–140

Find 8 × 5.

You can use a pattern to multiply by 5s.

- You can skip count to multiply by 5: 5, 10, 15, 20, and so on.
- Each multiple of 5 ends with a 0 or a 5.
- Each multiple of 5 is 5 more than the one before it.

8 × 5 = 40

Remember that making a table and using a pattern can help you to multiply by 2 or 5.

Find each product.

1. 2 × 4 **2.** 2 × 7 **3.** 3 × 2

4. 5 × 4 **5.** 5 × 9 **6.** 3 × 5

7. 6 × 2 **8.** 5 × 5 **9.** 8 × 5

Set B, pages 142–143

Find 7 × 9. Use a pattern.

The tens digit is 1 less than the factor being multiplied by 9.

Think 7 − 1 = 6 so 7 × 9 = 6▢

The digits of the product have a sum of 9.

Think 9 − 6 = 3 so 7 × 9 = 63

7 × 9 = 63

Remember you can use patterns and known facts to find products for facts involving 9s.

Draw an array for each multiplication fact. Write the product.

1. 9 × 5 **2.** 7 × 9 **3.** 10 × 9

4. 9 × 4 **5.** 5 × 9 **6.** 3 × 9

7. 9 × 1 **8.** 8 × 9 **9.** 9 × 9

Set C, pages 144–145

The **Identity Property of Multiplication** says that when you multiply a number and 1, the product is that number.

1 × 6 = 6 12 × 1 = 12

The **Zero Property of Multiplication** says when you multiply a number and 0, the product is 0.

0 × 6 = 0 12 × 0 = 0

Remember that you can think about an array with 1 row when you multiply by 1.

Find each product.

1. 7 × 0 **2.** 1 × 10 **3.** 0 × 9

4. 3 × 1 **5.** 7 × 0 **6.** 1 × 5

Set D, pages 146–148

Find 5×12.

- Use a pattern to multiply the factor that is not 12 by 10.
  $5 \times 10 = 50$
  Then multiply the same factor by 2.
  $5 \times 2 = 10$
- Then add the two products.
  $50 + 10 = 60$

$5 \times 12 = 60$

Remember that patterns can help you find multiples.

Use patterns to find each product.

1. 10×4
11×4
12×4

2. 10×7
11×7
12×7

3. $\begin{array}{r} 11 \\ \times \ \ 5 \\ \hline \end{array}$

4. $\begin{array}{r} 12 \\ \times \ \ 6 \\ \hline \end{array}$

5. $\begin{array}{r} 10 \\ \times \ \ 4 \\ \hline \end{array}$

Set E, pages 150–151

In two-question problems, you must solve one problem before you can solve the other.

Problem 1: A family of two adults and three children went to an air show. How many people in the family went to the air show?
$2 + 3 = 5$

Problem 2: Each pass to the air show cost \$10. How much did the family spend on passes for the air show?
$5 \times \$10 = \$50$

The family spent a total of \$50 on passes for the air show.

Remember to solve the first problem before you try to solve the second problem.

1. a For lunch, Julia bought a sandwich for \$8 and a glass of juice for \$3. How much did her lunch cost?

b Julia gave the clerk a \$20 bill. How much change should she get?

2. a A group of three girls and five boys went to the zoo. How many children are in the group?

b Each ticket to the zoo cost \$5. What was the total cost of tickets for these children?

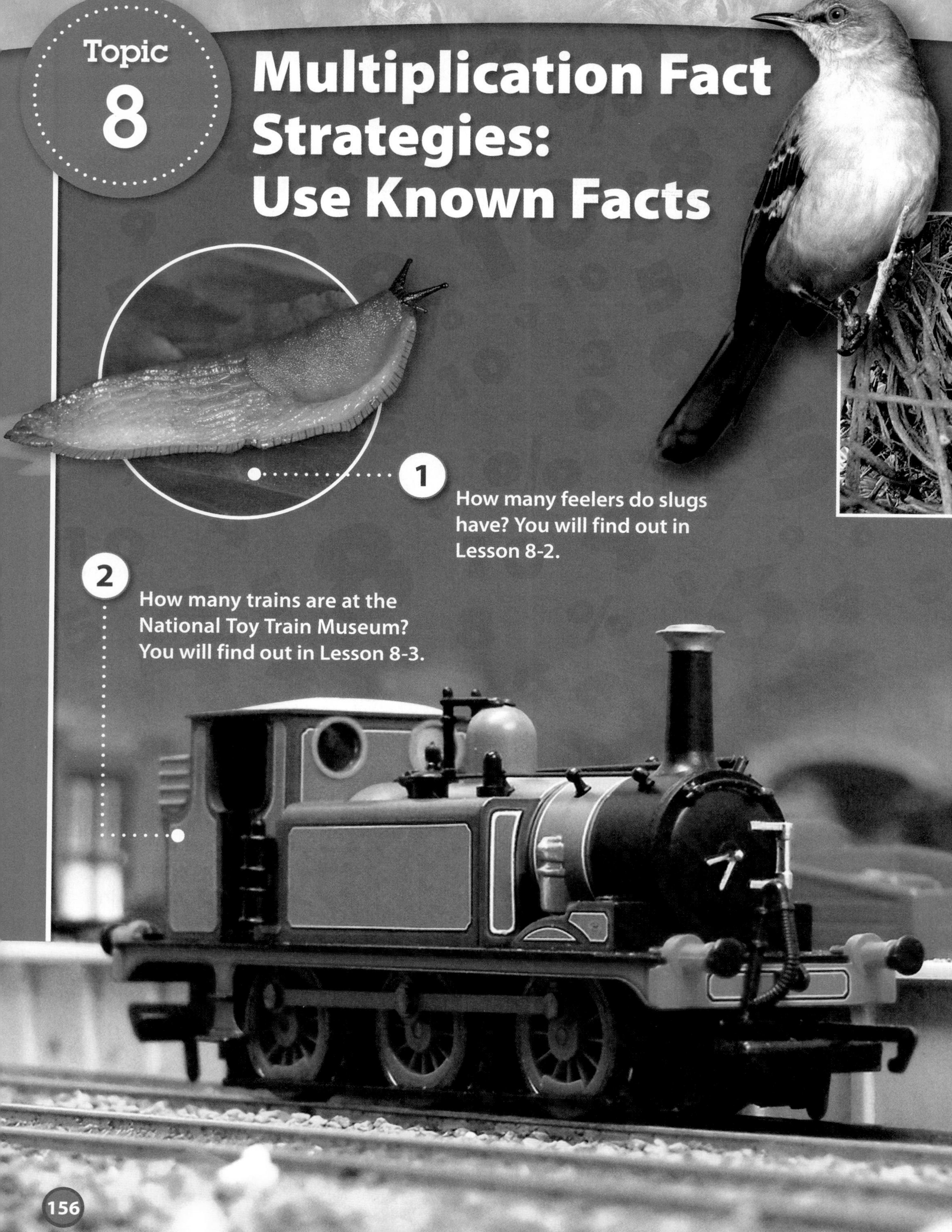

Topic 8 Multiplication Fact Strategies: Use Known Facts

1 How many feelers do slugs have? You will find out in Lesson 8-2.

2 How many trains are at the National Toy Train Museum? You will find out in Lesson 8-3.

3

Will you always find five eggs in a mockingbird's nest? You will find out in Lesson 8-5.

4

How long does Comet Encke take to orbit the Sun? You will find out in Lesson 8-1.

Review What You Know!

Vocabulary

Choose the best term from the box.

- addend
- array
- factor
- multiply

1. When you put together equal groups to get the total number, you ___?___.
2. When numbers are multiplied, each number is called a(n) ___?___.
3. When you display objects in rows and columns, you make a(n) ___?___.

Multiplication

Find each product.

4. 3×2
5. 4×5
6. 7×2
7. 6×1
8. 8×0
9. 5×9

Arrays

Draw an array for each multiplication fact.

10. 6×2
11. 4×9
12. Write a multiplication number sentence for the array shown at the right. Explain why you used the numbers you did.

13. **Writing to Explain** Is an array for 2×9 the same as or different from an array for 9×2? Draw a picture and explain your answer.

Lesson
8-1

TEKS 3.4A: Learn and apply multiplication facts through 12 by 12 using concrete models and objects.
Also TEKS 3.4B.

3 as a Factor

counters

How can you break apart arrays to multiply with 3?

The canoes are stored in 3 rows. There are 6 canoes in each row. What is the total number of canoes stored?

Find 3×6.

Choose an Operation Multiply to find the total for an array.

Guided Practice*

Do you know HOW?

In **1–6**, multiply. You may use counters or draw pictures to help.

1. 3×4

2. 3×11

3. 3×5

4. 3×9

5. $\begin{array}{r} 12 \\ \times\ 3 \\ \hline \end{array}$

6. $\begin{array}{r} 3 \\ \times\ 6 \\ \hline \end{array}$

Do you UNDERSTAND?

7. How can you use $2 \times 8 = 16$ to find 3×8?

8. Selena arranged plants in 3 rows at the community garden. She put 6 plants in each row. How many plants in all did Selena arrange into the rows?

Independent Practice

In **9–28**, find the product. You may draw pictures to help.

9. 3×2

10. 4×9

11. 3×10

12. 2×9

13. 11×3

14. 8×3

15. 4×7

16. 5×3

17. 0×3

18. 3×8

19. $\begin{array}{r} 7 \\ \times 3 \\ \hline \end{array}$

20. $\begin{array}{r} 12 \\ \times\ 8 \\ \hline \end{array}$

21. $\begin{array}{r} 3 \\ \times 3 \\ \hline \end{array}$

22. $\begin{array}{r} 5 \\ \times 4 \\ \hline \end{array}$

23. $\begin{array}{r} 3 \\ \times 9 \\ \hline \end{array}$

24. $\begin{array}{r} 1 \\ \times 3 \\ \hline \end{array}$

25. $\begin{array}{r} 6 \\ \times 3 \\ \hline \end{array}$

26. $\begin{array}{r} 9 \\ \times 5 \\ \hline \end{array}$

27. $\begin{array}{r} 3 \\ \times 4 \\ \hline \end{array}$

28. $\begin{array}{r} 3 \\ \times 7 \\ \hline \end{array}$

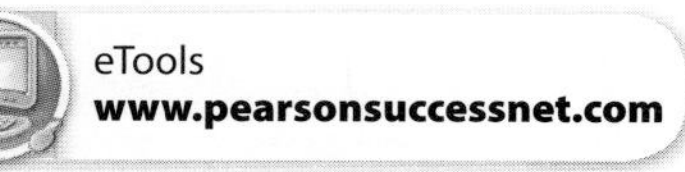

*For another example, see Set A on page 176.

What You Show

Find 3×6.

Use 1s facts and 2s facts to help multiply with 3.

Make an array for each multiplication sentence.

$2 \times 6 = 12$

$1 \times 6 = 6$

$12 + 6 = 18$

What You Think

3×6 is 3 rows of 6.
That is 2 sixes plus 6 more.

2 sixes are 12.
1 six is 6.

$12 + 6 = 18$

$3 \times 6 = 18$.

There are 18 canoes in all.

TAKS Problem Solving

For **29** and **30**, use the table at the right.

29. What is the total number of stamps in a package of car stamps and a package of outer space stamps?

30. Cara bought 1 package of reptile stamps. What is the total number of reptile stamps she bought? Draw an array.

Data

Number of Stamps in Different Packages

Kind of Stamp	Number of Rows	Number in Each Row
Dinosaurs	3	7
Cars	3	9
Outer Space	3	8
Reptiles	5	6

31. Number Sense Suppose you need to find 3×9.

a What two multiplication facts can help you find 3×9?

b How could you use 3×9 to help you find 9×3?

32. It takes about 3 years for Comet Encke to orbit the Sun. About how many years will it take Comet Encke to orbit the Sun 5 times?

A About 5 years

B About 10 years

C About 15 years

D About 20 years

33. Mr. Torres had packages of tomatoes on the counter. Each package had 3 tomatoes in it.

If Mr. Torres counted the tomatoes in groups of 3, which list shows numbers he could have named?

F 6, 12, 16, 19

G 6, 9, 12, 15

H 3, 6, 10, 13

J 3, 7, 11, 15

Lesson

8-2

TEKS 3.4A: Learn and apply multiplication facts through 12 by 12 using concrete models and objects.
Also TEKS 3.4B.

4 as a Factor

counters

How can you use doubles to multiply with 4?

Anna painted piggy banks to sell at the student art show. She painted a bank on each of the 7 days of the week for 4 weeks. How many piggy banks did she paint in all?

Find 4×7.

Choose an Operation Multiply to find the total for an array.

Guided Practice*

Do you know HOW?

In **1–6**, multiply. You may use counters or draw pictures to help.

1. 4×6

2. 5×4

3. 4×12

4. 1×4

5. $\begin{array}{r} 11 \\ \times\ 4 \\ \hline \end{array}$

6. $\begin{array}{r} 10 \\ \times\ 4 \\ \hline \end{array}$

Do you UNDERSTAND?

7. Besides the way shown above, what is another way to break apart 4×7 using facts you know?

8. If you know $2 \times 8 = 16$, how can you find 4×8?

9. Nolan made lamps to sell at the school art show. He made 9 lamps each week for 4 weeks. How many lamps did Nolan make in all?

Independent Practice

In **10–29**, find the product. You may draw pictures to help.

10. 4×8 **11.** 3×8 **12.** 4×3 **13.** 6×4 **14.** 9×6

15. 4×4 **16.** 5×9 **17.** 11×4 **18.** 0×4 **19.** 2×11

20. 3×4 **21.** 2×8 **22.** 4×5 **23.** 7×4 **24.** 4×12

25. $\begin{array}{r} 2 \\ \times 4 \\ \hline \end{array}$ **26.** $\begin{array}{r} 7 \\ \times 4 \\ \hline \end{array}$ **27.** $\begin{array}{r} 9 \\ \times 4 \\ \hline \end{array}$ **28.** $\begin{array}{r} 10 \\ \times\ 7 \\ \hline \end{array}$ **29.** $\begin{array}{r} 4 \\ \times 8 \\ \hline \end{array}$

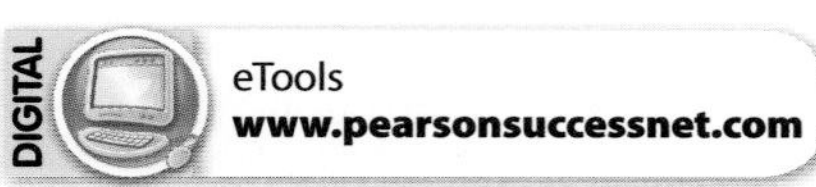

*For another example, see Set B on page 176.

What You Show

Find 4×7.

To multiply by 4, you can think of a 2s fact, then double it.

You can make arrays.

$2 \times 7 = 14$

$2 \times 7 = 14$

$14 + 14 = 28$

What You Think

4×7 is 4 rows of 7. That is 2 sevens plus 2 sevens.

2 sevens are 14.

$14 + 14 = 28$

So, $4 \times 7 = 28$.

Anna painted 28 piggy banks in all.

TAKS Problem Solving

For **30** and **31**, use the table at the right for the supplies James needs to buy for the Trail Walk trip.

Trail Walk Trip Supplies (Data)

Item	Number of Packages Needed	Number of Items in Each Package
Apples	2	8
Cereal Bars	4	6
Juice Drinks	4	3

30. What is the total number of cereal bars he needs to buy?

31. How many more apples than juice drinks does James need?

32. Martin studied slugs in science class. He learned that each slug has 4 feelers. That evening, he saw 8 slugs. How many feelers did the slugs have in all?

33. Writing to Explain Lila had 9 weeks of rock climbing lessons. She had 4 lessons each week. Explain why Lila can use 4×9 to find the product of 9×4.

34. Which of these best describes all the numbers on the shirts?

A They are all even numbers.

B They are all multiples of 3.

C They are all greater than 10.

D They are all 2-digit numbers.

35. Bess had boxes of candles on the table. Each box had 4 candles in it.

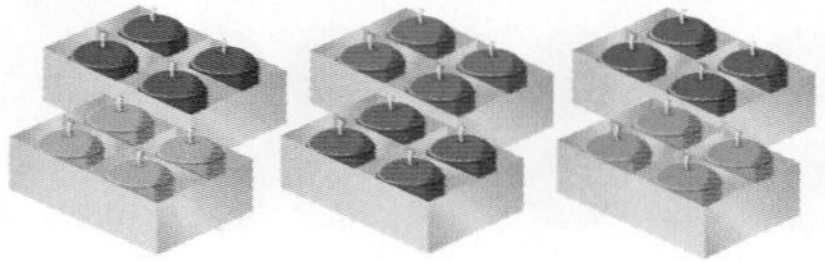

If Bess counted the candles in groups of 4, which list shows numbers she could have named?

F 8, 12, 16, 20

G 8, 12, 14, 18

H 4, 6, 12, 14

J 4, 8, 10, 14

Lesson

8-3

TEKS 3.4A: Learn and apply multiplication facts through 12 by 12 using concrete models and objects.
Also TEKS 3.4B.

6 and 7 as Factors

Hands-On
counters

How can you break apart arrays to multiply?

The musicians in the band march in 6 equal rows. There are 8 musicians in each row. How many musicians are in the band?

Find 6×8.

Choose an Operation Multiply to find the total for an array.

Another Example How can you break apart arrays to multiply by 7?

The singers in the chorus are standing in equal rows. There are 8 singers in each row. There are 7 rows. How many singers are in the chorus?

What You Show	What You Think
Find 7×8.	7×8 is 7 rows of 8.
Use 5s facts and 2s facts to help multiply with 7. Make an array for each multiplication sentence.	That is 5 eights plus 2 eights.

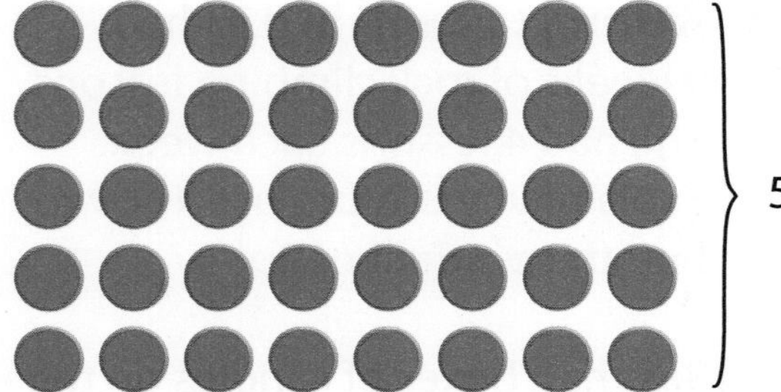

$5 \times 8 = 40$

$2 \times 8 = 16$

5 eights are 40.
2 eights are 16.

$40 + 16 = 56$

So, $7 \times 8 = 56$.

The chorus has 56 singers.

Explain It

1. What other multiplication facts might help to find 7×8?
2. How could you use 5×7 and 2×7 to find 7×7?

What You Show

Find 6×8.

Use 5s facts and 1s facts.

Make an array for each multiplication sentence.

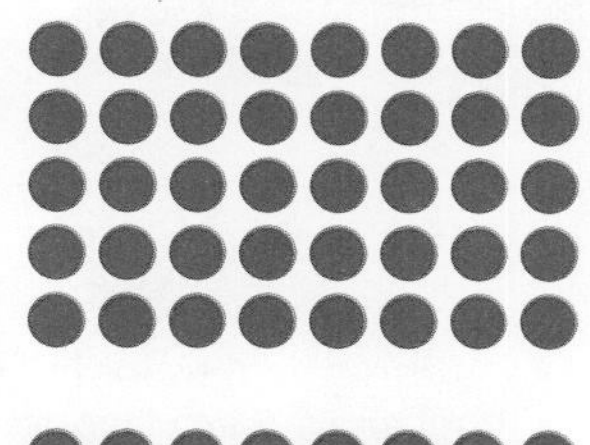

$5 \times 8 = 40$

$1 \times 8 = 8$

What You Think

6×8 is 6 rows of 8. That is 5 eights plus 1 more eight.

5 eights are 40.
8 more is 48.
$40 + 8 = 48$

So, $6 \times 8 = 48$.

The band has 48 musicians.

Guided Practice*

Do you know HOW?

In **1–6**, multiply. You may draw pictures or use counters to help.

1. 6×10

2. 7×6

3. $\begin{array}{r} 12 \\ \times\ 6 \\ \hline \end{array}$

4. $\begin{array}{r} 11 \\ \times\ 7 \\ \hline \end{array}$

5. Find 4 times 7.

6. Multiply 6 and 5.

Do you UNDERSTAND?

7. Draw a picture of two arrays that show that 6×9 is equal to 5×9 plus 1×9. Explain your drawing.

8. The students who are graduating are standing in 7 equal rows. There are 9 students in each row. How many students are graduating?

Independent Practice

In **9–23**, find the product. You may draw pictures to help.

9. 6×7 **10.** 7×9 **11.** 9×6 **12.** 12×7 **13.** 6×4

14. 6×6 **15.** 10×7 **16.** 8×6 **17.** 7×7 **18.** 7×3

19. $\begin{array}{r} 5 \\ \times 7 \\ \hline \end{array}$ **20.** $\begin{array}{r} 3 \\ \times 6 \\ \hline \end{array}$ **21.** $\begin{array}{r} 4 \\ \times 7 \\ \hline \end{array}$ **22.** $\begin{array}{r} 7 \\ \times 8 \\ \hline \end{array}$ **23.** $\begin{array}{r} 11 \\ \times\ 6 \\ \hline \end{array}$

DIGITAL eTools **www.pearsonsuccessnet.com**

For another example, see Set C on page 176.

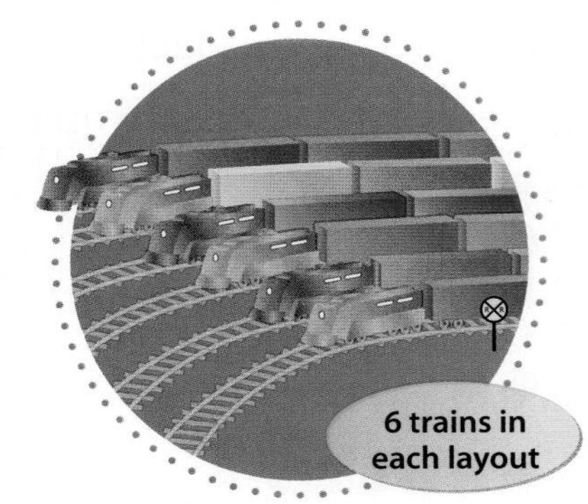

24. The National Toy Train Museum has 5 large layouts for trains. How many trains are at the museum?

25. **Number Sense** Marge says that the product 1×0 is the same as the sum $1 + 0$. Is she correct? Why or why not?

26. Miguel had baskets of oranges in his store. Each basket held 6 oranges.

If Miguel counted the oranges in groups of 6, which list shows numbers he could have named?

A 6, 12, 21, 26 **C** 12, 16, 20, 24

B 6, 11, 16, 21 **D** 12, 18, 24, 30

27. **Writing to Explain** Nan made the arrays shown to find 6×3. Explain how to change the arrays to find 7×3. Use objects and draw a picture.

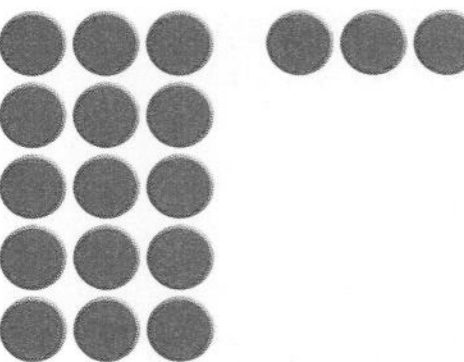

For **28** and **29**, use the drawings of the trains below.

28. A group of tourists needs 7 rows of seats in Car 5 of the Réseau train. How many seats are left for other passengers?

29. **Estimation** Use rounding to the nearest ten to find about how many seats in all are on the Atlantique and the Sud-Est trains.

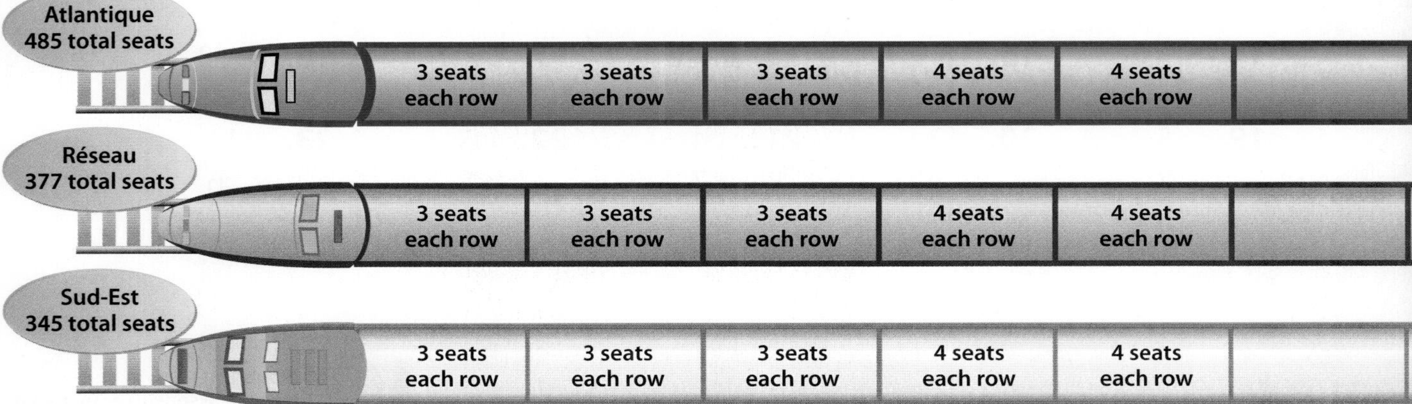

Algebra Connections

Number Sentences with More Than One Operation

Some number sentences have more than one operation. Rules called the *order of operations* tell the order in which you do the operations.

Rules for Order of Operations

- First, do operations inside the parentheses ( ).
- Next, do multiplications in order from left to right.
- Then do additions and subtractions in order from left to right.

Example: $(8 - 2) \times 7 = \square$

Think: Which operations are used? Are parentheses used?

Do operations inside the parentheses.

$(8 - 2) \times 7$

6×7

Next, do the multiplication.

$6 \times 7 = 42$

Example: $5 + 3 \times 6 = \square$

Do the multiplication. $5 + 3 \times 6$

$5 + 18$

Then do the addition. $5 + 18 = 23$

Copy and complete each number sentence using the order of operations.

1. $(5 + 3) \times 6 = \square$ **2.** $7 + 3 \times 2 = \square$ **3.** $(7 + 3) \times 2 = \square$

4. $(8 + 4) \times 2 = \square$ **5.** $3 + 2 \times 9 = \square$ **6.** $(7 - 1) \times 4 = \square$

7. $8 + 0 \times 6 = \square$ **8.** $(2 + 2) \times 7 = \square$ **9.** $(6 - 3) \times 4 = \square$

10. $16 - 4 \times 3 = \square$ **11.** $13 + 9 \times 0 = \square$ **12.** $45 - 3 \times 2 = \square$

For **13** and **14**, copy and complete the number sentence below each problem. Use it to help solve the problem.

13. Nat had 2 train sets that each had 7 cars. He took 3 cars away from each set. How many cars in all are in the train sets now?
$(7 - \square) \times 2 = \square$

14. Joan had 5 pencils. Then she bought 4 packs of pencils. Each pack had 6 pencils. What is the total number of pencils Joan has now?
$5 + 4 \times \square = \square$

15. Write a Problem Write a real-world problem that could be solved using the number sentence $3 + (6 \times 2) = \square$.

Lesson

8-4

TEKS 3.4A: Learn and apply multiplication facts through 12 by 12 using concrete models and objects.
Also **TEKS 3.4B**.

8 as a Factor

How can you use doubles to multiply with 8?

At the school fun fair, students try to toss a table tennis ball into a bowl. There are 8 rows of bowls. There are 8 bowls in each row. How many bowls are there in all?

Choose an Operation Multiply to find the total for an array. Find 8×8.

Guided Practice*

Do you know HOW?

In **1–6**, multiply.

1. 8×7

2. 8×12

3. 6×8

4. 10×8

5. 11×8

6. 8×3

Do you UNDERSTAND?

7. How could the fact that $5 \times 8 = 40$ help you find 8×8?

8. How can you use 4×7 to find 8×7?

9. Mrs. Reyes needs to order bricks for her garden. She needs 8 rows of bricks. Each row will have 7 bricks. How many bricks in all should Mrs. Reyes order?

Independent Practice

In **10–27**, find the product.

10. 8×4 **11.** 11×8 **12.** 2×9 **13.** 5×7 **14.** 8×2

15. 8×6 **16.** 5×9 **17.** 8×5 **18.** 0×8 **19.** 4×9

20. 10×8 **21.** 3×7 **22.** 8×8 **23.** 12×4 **24.** 9×8

25. Find 6 times 9. **26.** Multiply 8 and 1. **27.** Find 9 times 8.

For another example, see Set D on page 177.

One Way

Use 2s facts to find 8×8.

8×8 is 4 groups of 2 eights.

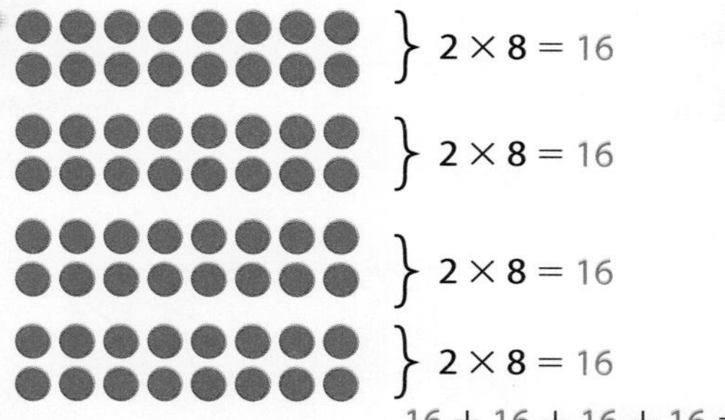

Another Way

Double a 4s fact to find 8×8.

8×8 is 4 eights plus 4 eights.

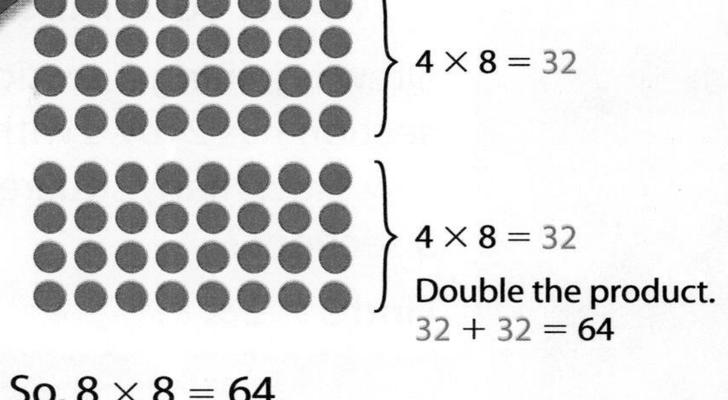

So, $8 \times 8 = 64$.

There are 64 bowls in all.

TAKS Problem Solving

For **28–30**, find the total number of tiles.

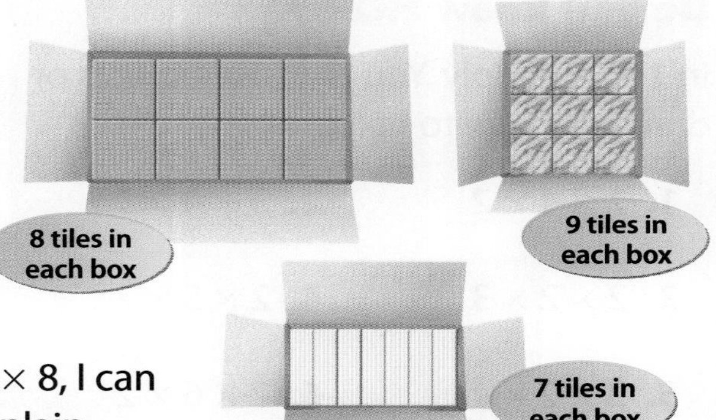

28. Mischa bought 8 boxes of checkered tiles.

29. Aaron bought 6 boxes of yellow tiles.

30. Liz bought 7 boxes of green tiles.

31. **Writing to Explain** Sophi says, "To find 8×8, I can find 2×8 and double it." Do you agree? Explain.

For **32** and **33**, use the table at the right.

32. **Algebra** The total amount of money Nate spent at the clothing sale is $(2 \times \$9) + \$42$. What did he buy?

33. Willa bought a shirt and a sweater. She had $14 left. How much money did she start with?

Data

Clothing Sale	
Shirt	$23
Belt	$9
Sweater	$38
Pair of Jeans	$42

34. Ms. Vero had boxes of crayons in a closet. Each box had 8 crayons in it.

 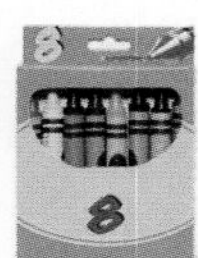 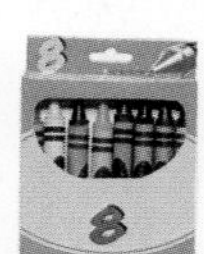   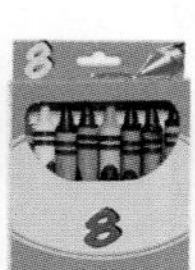

If Ms. Vero counted the crayons in groups of 8, which list shows numbers she could have named?

A 8, 16, 28, 32 **C** 16, 20, 24, 28

B 8, 14, 18, 24 **D** 16, 24, 32, 40

Lesson
8-5

TEKS 3.4A: Learn and apply multiplication facts through 12 by 12 using concrete models and objects.
Also TEKS 3.4B.

Multiplying with 3 Factors

How can you multiply 3 numbers?

Drew is joining 3 sections of a quilt. Each section has 2 rows with 4 squares in each row. How many squares in all are in these 3 sections?

Find $3 \times 2 \times 4$.

Guided Practice*

Do you know HOW?

In **1–6**, multiply. You may use objects or draw a picture to help.

1. $2 \times 4 \times 2$

2. $3 \times 4 \times 3$

3. $2 \times 2 \times 3$

4. $2 \times 5 \times 2$

5. $3 \times 2 \times 4$

6. $2 \times 6 \times 2$

Do you UNDERSTAND?

7. In the example above, if you find 3×4 first, do you get the same product? Explain.

8. Sara has 4 quilt pieces. Each piece has 3 rows with 3 squares in each row. How many squares are in Sara's quilt pieces?

Independent Practice

In **9–16**, find the product. You may draw a picture to help.

9. $2 \times 3 \times 2$

10. $5 \times 2 \times 2$

11. $3 \times 6 \times 1$

12. $3 \times 3 \times 2$

13. $2 \times 2 \times 2$

14. $2 \times 3 \times 4$

15. $3 \times 3 \times 3$

16. $6 \times 2 \times 2$

In **17–22**, write the missing number.

17. $3 \times (2 \times 5) = 30$, so $(3 \times 2) \times 5 = \square$

18. $5 \times (7 \times 2) = (7 \times 2) \times \square$

19. $4 \times (2 \times 2) = 16$, so $(4 \times 2) \times 2 = \square$

20. $8 \times (3 \times 6) = (8 \times 3) \times \square$

21. $(7 \times 3) \times 4 = \square \times (3 \times 4)$

22. $5 \times (2 \times 9) = (5 \times \square) \times 9$

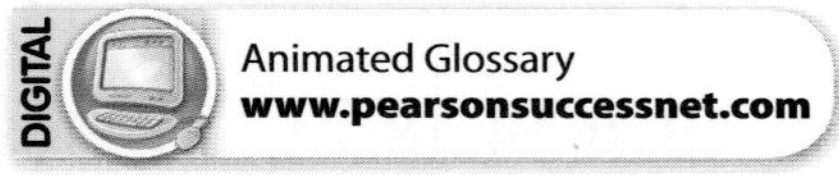

*For another example, see Set E on page 177.

One Way

Find 3×2 first.

$(3 \times 2) \times 4$

$6 \times 4 = 24$

6 rows, 4 squares in each row

There are 24 squares in all.

Another Way

Find 2×4 first.

$3 \times (2 \times 4)$

$3 \times 8 = 24$ 3 pieces, 8 squares in each piece

There are 24 squares in Drew's quilt pieces.

The Associative (Grouping) Property of Multiplication says that you can change the grouping of the factors and the product will be the same.

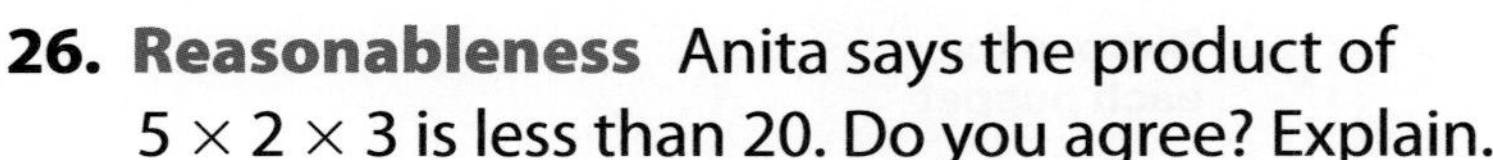

TAKS Problem Solving

For **23–25**, find the total number of eggs.

Mockingbirds lay 3 to 5 eggs.

23. There are 8 mockingbird nests at a park. Each nest has 5 eggs.

24. At another park, there are 3 mockingbird nests with 4 eggs in each nest, and 2 more nests with 3 eggs in each.

25. **Estimation** About how many eggs would you find in 10 nests?

26. **Reasonableness** Anita says the product of $5 \times 2 \times 3$ is less than 20. Do you agree? Explain.

For **27** and **28**, use the table at the right.

Sports Card Sale

Kind of Cards	Number of Cards in Each Pack
Baseball	8
Basketball	5
Football	7
Hockey	6

27. Ellis bought 3 packs of baseball cards and 2 packs of basketball cards. How many cards did he buy in all?

28. Mandy bought 1 pack of each of the four kinds of cards. What is the total number of cards she bought?

29. Which number makes this number sentence true?

$4 \times (3 \times 2) = (4 \times \square) \times 2$

A 12 **B** 7 **C** 3 **D** 2

Lesson

8-6

TEKS 3.14B: Solve problems that incorporate understanding the problem, making a plan, carrying out the plan, and evaluating the solution for reasonableness.

Problem Solving

Multiple-Step Problems

Some word problems have hidden questions that need to be answered before you can solve the problem.

Keisha bought 2 yards of felt to make some puppets. Tanya bought 6 yards of felt. The felt cost $3 a yard. How much did the two girls spend on felt?

Another Example

Keisha plans to make 3 puppets. Tanya will make 3 times as many puppets as Keisha. Each puppet needs 2 buttons for its eyes. How many buttons will Tanya need?

Find and solve the hidden question.

How many puppets will Tanya make?

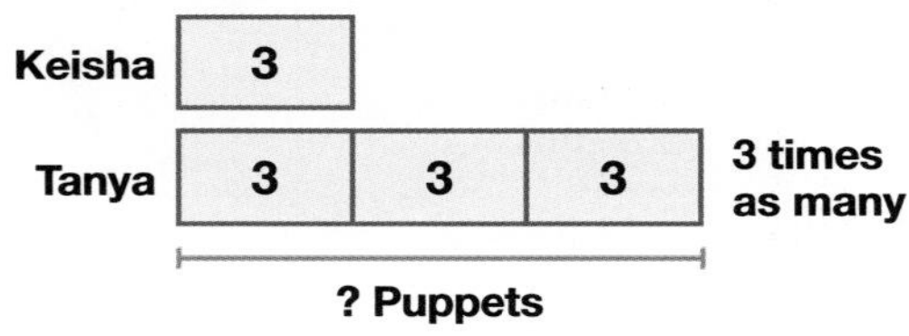

3×3 puppets $= 9$ puppets

Tanya will make 9 puppets.

Use the answer to the hidden question to solve the problem.

How many buttons will Tanya need?

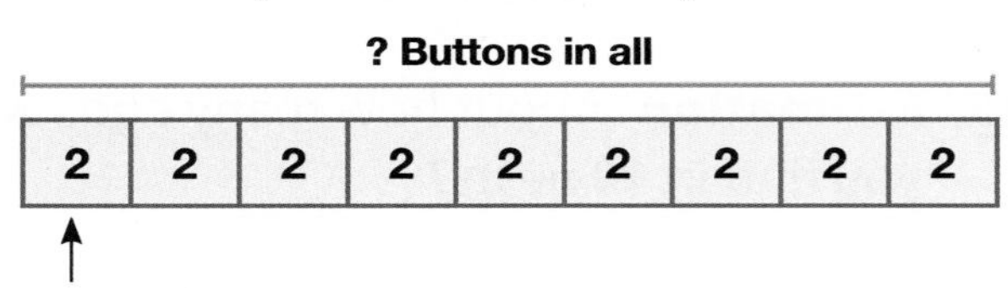

9×2 buttons $= 18$ buttons

Tanya will need 18 buttons.

Explain It

1. Philip wrote $3 + 3 + 3 = \square$ instead of $3 \times 3 = \square$ for the diagram for the hidden question. Is his number sentence correct? Why or why not?
2. **Number Sense** What multiplication sentences would you write to find how many buttons both girls need? Explain your thinking.

Find and solve the hidden question.

How much felt did the girls buy in all?

? Yards in all

2 yards	6 yards

2 yards + 6 yards = 8 yards

The girls bought 8 yards of felt.

Use the answer to the hidden question to solve the problem.

How much did the girls spend in all?

? Total cost

\$3	\$3	\$3	\$3	\$3	\$3	\$3	\$3

$8 \times \$3 = \$24$

The two girls spent \$24 on felt.

Guided Practice*

Do you know HOW?

1. Keisha bought glue for \$3, sequins for \$6, and lace for \$4 to decorate her puppets. She paid for these items with a \$20 bill. How much change should she get?

The hidden question is "What is the total cost of the three items?"

Do you UNDERSTAND?

2. Describe another way to solve the problem above about buying felt.

3. **Write a Problem** Write a problem that has a hidden question. Then solve your problem.

Independent Practice

4. The library has 4 videos and some books about dinosaurs. There are 5 times as many books as videos. How many dinosaur books does the library have?

Videos	4					
Books	4	4	4	4	4	5 times as many

? Books in all

Stuck? Try this....

- What do I know?
- What am I asked to find?
- What diagram can I use to help understand the problem?
- Can I use addition, subtraction, multiplication, or division?
- Is all of my work correct?
- Did I answer the right question?
- Is my answer reasonable?

*For another example, see Set F on page 177.

Independent Practice

Use the pictures for **5–8**.

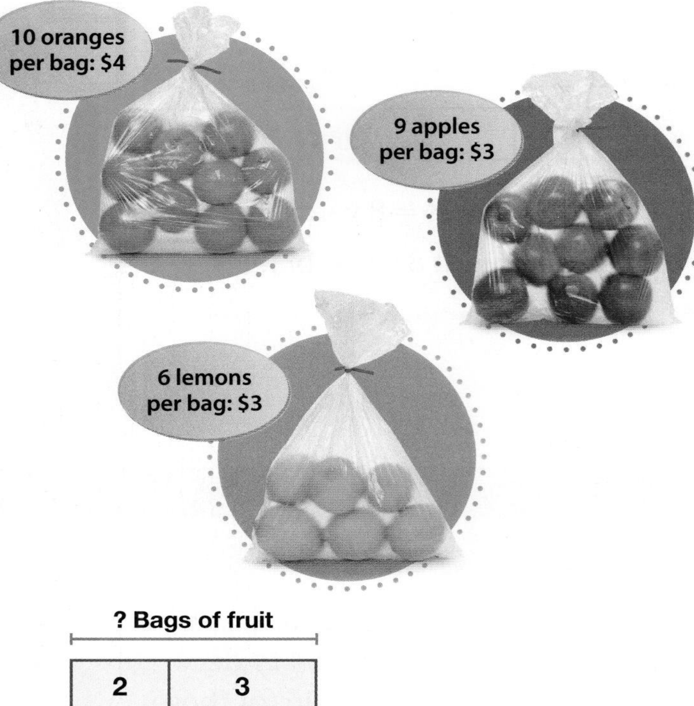

5. Craig bought 2 bags of oranges. After he ate 3 of the oranges, how many oranges were left?

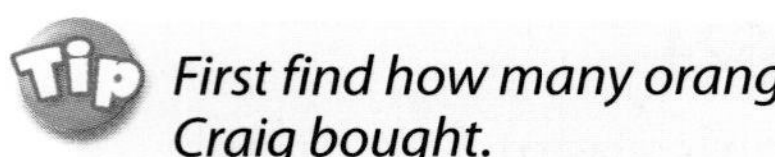

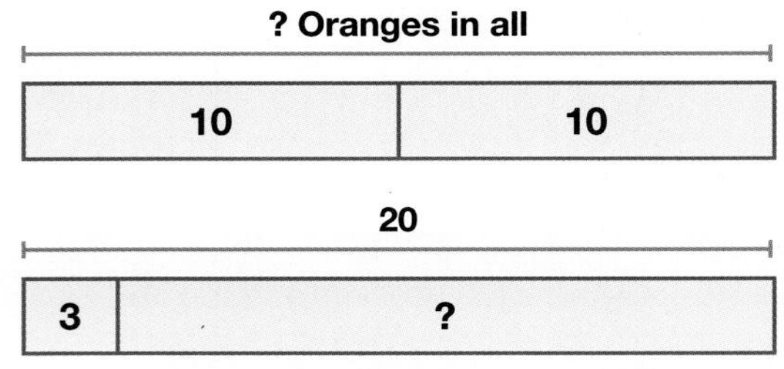

6. Delia bought 2 bags of lemons and 3 bags of apples. How much did she spend on fruit?

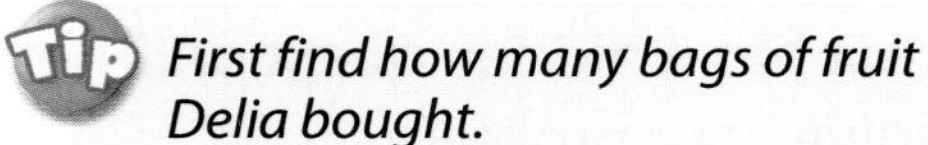

? Bags of fruit

2	3

? Total spent

3	3	3	3	3

7. Mr. Day bought a bag each of apples, oranges, and lemons. He paid with a $20 bill. What change should he get?

8. Mrs. Evans bought 2 bags of oranges and 2 bags of lemons. How many pieces of fruit did she buy?

Think About the Process

9. Al had $38. He spent $4 on an action figure and $10 on a board game. Which number sentence shows how much money Al has left?

A $38 + $4 + $10 = ☐

B $38 − ($4 + $10) = ☐

C $38 − $4 = ☐

D 38 + $10 = ☐

10. Jose has 4 action figures. His brother has 3 times as many action figures. Which number sentence shows how many figures the boys have in all?

F $4 + 3 =$ ☐

G $4 \times 3 =$ ☐

H $4 - 3 =$ ☐

J $4 + (3 \times 4) =$ ☐

Using Known Facts

Use eTools

Counters

Use known facts to find 4×6 and 6×7.

Step 1 Go to the Counters eTool. Select the two-part workspace. Use 2×6 to find 4×6. Select a counter. Show two rows of 6 counters in the left side. Look at the odometer. You see that $2 \times 6 = 12$. Show the same rows on the right side. There are 4 rows of 6 counters in all. $4 \times 6 = 24$, and $12 + 12 = 24$.

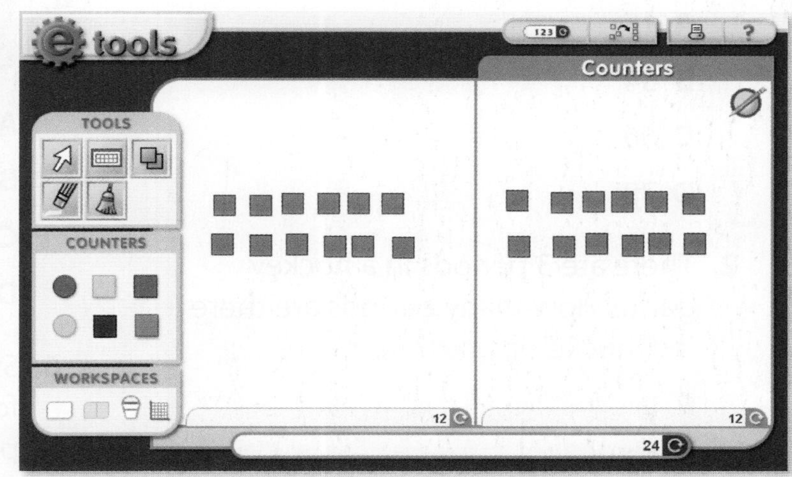

Step 2 Use the broom tool to clear one side of the workspace. Select the other side and use the broom tool again, to clear it. Use 5×7 and 1×7 to find 6×7. Show 5 rows of 7 counters on one side of the workspace. Look at the odometer to find that $5 \times 7 = 35$. Show 1 row of 7 counters on the other side. There are 6 rows of 7 counters in all. $6 \times 7 = 42$, and $35 + 7 = 42$.

Practice

Use the Counters eTool and known facts to find each product. Explain how you found the product.

1. 4×9

2. 8×8

3. 6×8

4. 7×7

TAKS Test Prep

1. Last summer, Martin walked the 8-mile Wolf Mountain Trail in Pedernales Falls State Park 7 times. How many total miles did he walk on the trail? (8-3)

   A 15

   B 54

   C 56

   D 78

2. There are 3 periods in a hockey game. How many periods are there in 5 hockey games? (8-1)

   F 8

   G 12

   H 15

   J 18

3. Which shows a way to find 4×6? (8-2)

   A $4 + 6$

   B $12 + 12$

   C $6 + 6 + 6$

   D $12 + 2$

4. Jon bought 3 packages of invitations. Each package had 8 invitations. He sent out 20 invitations. Which shows one way to find how many are left? (8-6)

   F Multiply 3 by 8 and then subtract 20.

   G Multiply 3 by 20 and then subtract 8.

   H Multiply 5 by 8 and then add 20.

   J Multiply 3 by 8 and then add 20.

5. Each box has 6 muffins. If you count the muffins in groups of 6, which list shows numbers you would name? (8-3)

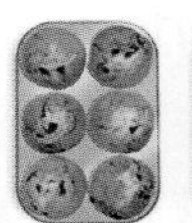 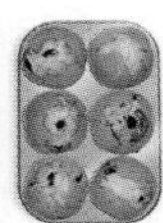    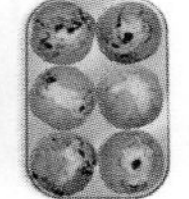

   A 6, 12, 16, 24

   B 6, 12, 16, 22

   C 12, 18, 24, 32

   D 12, 18, 24, 30

6. Sven feeds his fish 2 pellets of food 3 times a day. How many pellets of food does he feed his fish in 7 days? (8-5)

   F 13

   G 14

   H 21

   J 42

7. Mrs. Chavez put new light switch covers in her house. She put in 8 double light switch covers and 7 single light switch covers. The double covers use 4 screws and the single covers use 2 screws. How many screws did she use? (8-6)

   A 32

   B 39

   C 44

   D 46

8. Mr. Hernandez bought 8 bags of limes. Each bag had 4 limes. How many limes did he buy? (8-2)

F 32

G 28

H 24

J 12

9. What number makes the number sentence true? (8-5)

$6 \times (9 \times 2) = (6 \times 9) \times \square$

A 2

B 6

C 9

D 54

10. A marching band was in a parade. The band members marched in 8 rows. There were 6 band members in each row. Which shows a way to find 8×6? (8-4)

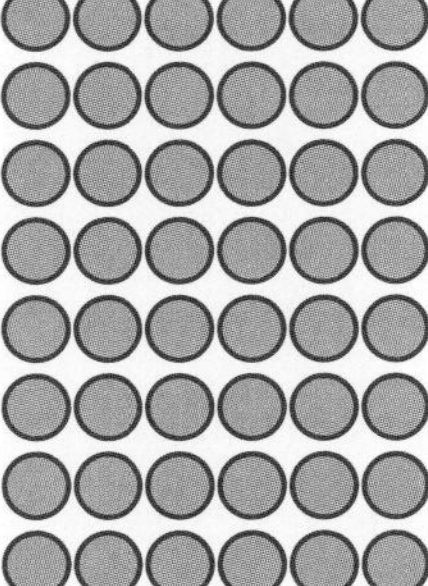

F $8 + 6$

G $24 + 24 + 24$

H $12 + 12 + 12 + 12$

J $16 + 16 + 16 + 16$

11. The Cougars basketball team has 8 players. The coach ordered 3 pairs of socks for each player. How many pairs did he order? (8-4)

A 16

B 24

C 32

D 48

12. Which of these best describes all the numbers on the mileage sign? (8-1)

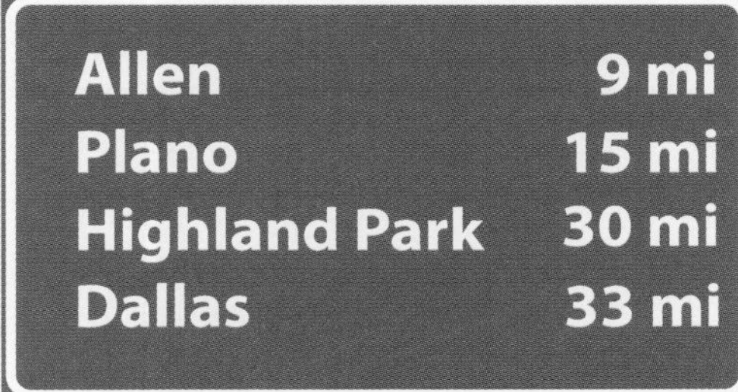

F They are all greater than 18.

G They are all multiples of 5.

H They are all multiples of 3.

J They are all less than 30.

13. Which is a way to find 7×6? (8-3)

A $35 + 14$

B $30 + 12$

C $35 + 6$

D $30 + 14$

14. **Griddable Response** Mrs. Kent drives a total of 4 miles 2 times a day to take her children to school. How many miles does she drive in 5 days? (8-5)

Reteaching

Set A, pages 158–159

Find 3×7.

You can break an array into facts you know.

$3 \times 7 = 3$ groups of 7
That is 2 sevens plus 1 more seven.

$2 \times 7 = 14$
$1 \times 7 = 7$
$14 + 7 = 21$

So, $3 \times 7 = 21$.

Remember that you can use facts you already know to help you multiply.

Find the product.

1. 3×8
2. 6×3
3. 4×3
4. 2×3
5. 9×3
6. 1×3
7. 3×3
8. 3×5
9. 10×3

Set B, pages 160–161

Find 4×7.

Think of a 2s fact, then double the product.

$4 \times 7 = 4$ groups of 7.

$2 \times 7 = 14$
$2 \times 7 = 14$
$14 + 14 = 28$

So, $4 \times 7 = 28$.

Remember that you can draw arrays to solve multiplication facts.

Find the product.

1. 4×10
2. 3×4
3. 6×4
4. 4×5
5. 4×4
6. 9×4
7. 8×4
8. 4×2
9. 11×4

Set C, pages 162–164

Find 7×6.

Use 5s facts and 2s facts to multiply with 7.

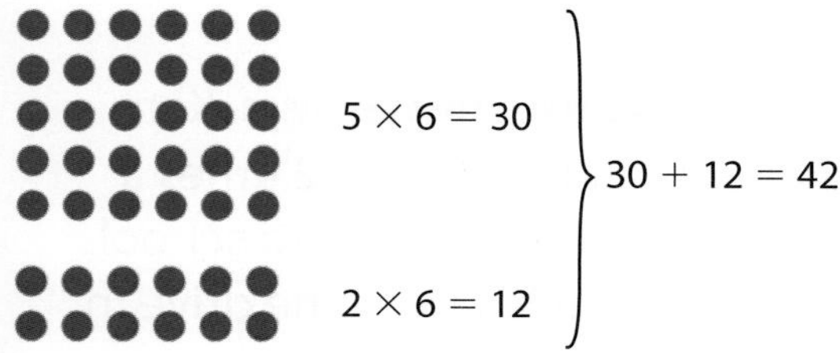

So, $7 \times 6 = 42$.

Remember that you can use known facts to multiply with 6 and 7.

Find the product.

1. 7×9
2. 8×7
3. 6×9
4. 3×6
5. 7×4
6. 6×8
7. 7×7
8. 6×2
9. 12×7

Set D, pages 166–167

Find 8×6. You can double a 4s fact.

Find 4×6. Then double the product.

$4 \times 6 = 24$

$4 \times 6 = 24$

$24 + 24 = 48$

So, $8 \times 6 = 48$.

Remember to check that your picture accurately shows the arrays for the numbers that are multiplied.

Find the product.

1. 7×8
2. 8×8
3. 1×8
4. 8×9
5. 10×8
6. 5×8
7. $\begin{array}{r} 2 \\ \times\ 8 \\ \hline \end{array}$
8. $\begin{array}{r} 3 \\ \times\ 8 \\ \hline \end{array}$
9. $\begin{array}{r} 11 \\ \times\ 8 \\ \hline \end{array}$

Set E, pages 168–169

Find $4 \times 5 \times 2$.

The Associative Property of Multiplication says that you can change the grouping of the factors, and the product will be the same.

One Way

$(4 \times 5) \times 2$

$20 \times 2 = 40$

Another Way

$4 \times (5 \times 2)$

$4 \times 10 = 40$

So, $4 \times 5 \times 2 = 40$.

Remember you may draw a picture to help you multiply 3 factors.

Find the product.

1. $3 \times 2 \times 5$
2. $5 \times 3 \times 4$
3. $1 \times 9 \times 8$
4. $7 \times 2 \times 5$
5. $6 \times 3 \times 4$
6. $4 \times 3 \times 2$

Set F, pages 170–172

Some problems have hidden questions.

Jeff charged \$10 to wash a car and \$7 to walk a dog. How much money did Jeff earn for washing 6 cars and walking 1 dog?

Find and solve the hidden question.
How much money did Jeff earn washing 6 cars?
$6 \times \$10 = \$60$
Then solve the problem.
How much money did Jeff earn in all?
$\$60 + \$7 = \$67$
Jeff earned \$67.

Remember to carefully read the order in which things happen.

1. At the fair, Bonnie wants to get 2 rings and 1 pen. Each ring costs 8 tickets, and each pen costs 6 tickets. How many tickets does she need in all?
2. Mrs. Green bought 2 bags of apples. Each bag had 10 apples. She used 4 apples. How many apples did she have left?

Topics 1–8

Spiral Review

Number and Operations

1. People are sitting in 73 seats in a movie theater. There are 39 empty seats in the theater. Which is the best estimate of the total number of seats in the movie theater?

A 110 **C** 100

B 30 **D** 20

2. Jeremy has a photo album with 12 pages. Each page has 6 pictures on it. How many pictures are in his photo album?

F 2 pictures

G 12 pictures

H 18 pictures

J 72 pictures

3. Write the expanded form of nine hundred twenty.

4. Find $160 + 27 + 391$.

5. Write a multiplication problem that means the same as $6 + 6 + 6$. Write the product.

6. Which number makes this number sentence true?

$\square \times 9 = 54$

7. **Writing to Explain** Explain how to find the product 7×4.

Geometry and Measurement

8. Which name best describes the figure?

A Sphere

B Cone

C Pyramid

D Cylinder

9. Draw a picture of a house, using at least 3 different shapes. Name each shape you used.

10. Which measurement best describes the length of a dollar bill?

F 6 centimeters

G 6 inches

H 6 feet

J 6 meters

11. Name two objects that weigh less than 1 pound.

12. What time is shown on the clock?

13. **Writing to Explain** At 1 P.M., the temperature was 78°F. At 9 P.M., it was 63°F. How many degrees did the temperature change? Did it increase or decrease? Explain.

Probability and Statistics

In **14** and **15**, use the table that shows the number of colored marbles in a bag.

Marble Colors

Color	Number in Bag
Yellow	9
Blue	3
Green	5
Purple	1

14. If Sarah takes 1 marble out of the bag without looking, which color will she most likely get?

A Yellow **C** Green
B Blue **D** Purple

15. Sarah takes the yellow and purple marbles out of the bag. How many blue marbles does she need to put in the bag to make it equally likely to choose a blue or green marble?

F 1 **G** 2 **H** 3 **J** 4

Use the picture graph for **16 and 17**.

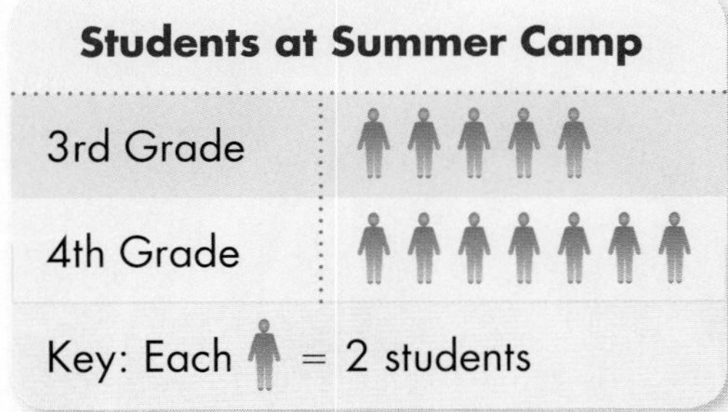

16. How many more 4th grade students than 3rd grade students are at camp?

17. Writing to Explain Explain how to use multiplication to find how many 4th graders are at camp.

Algebraic Thinking

18. Solve: 53 + ☐ = 70

A 7 **B** 10 **C** 17 **D** 123

19. Mr. Jenkins had paint boxes. Each paint box had 6 paints in it.

If Mr. Jenkins counted the paints in groups of 6, which list shows the numbers he could have named?

F 6, 7, 8, 9
G 6, 10, 14, 18
H 6, 10, 16, 20
J 6, 12, 18, 24

20. Jamie's brother is 17 years old and his sister is 15 years old. The sum of all three ages is 40. How old is Jamie?

21. Which number sentence is in the same fact family as $6 + 4 = 10$?

A $10 + 4 = 14$
B $6 \times 4 = 24$
C $6 - 4 = 2$
D $10 - 6 = 4$

22. Writing to Explain Andrew says that ☐ = 7 can make the number sentence ☐ + 5 = 11 true. Is he correct? Explain.

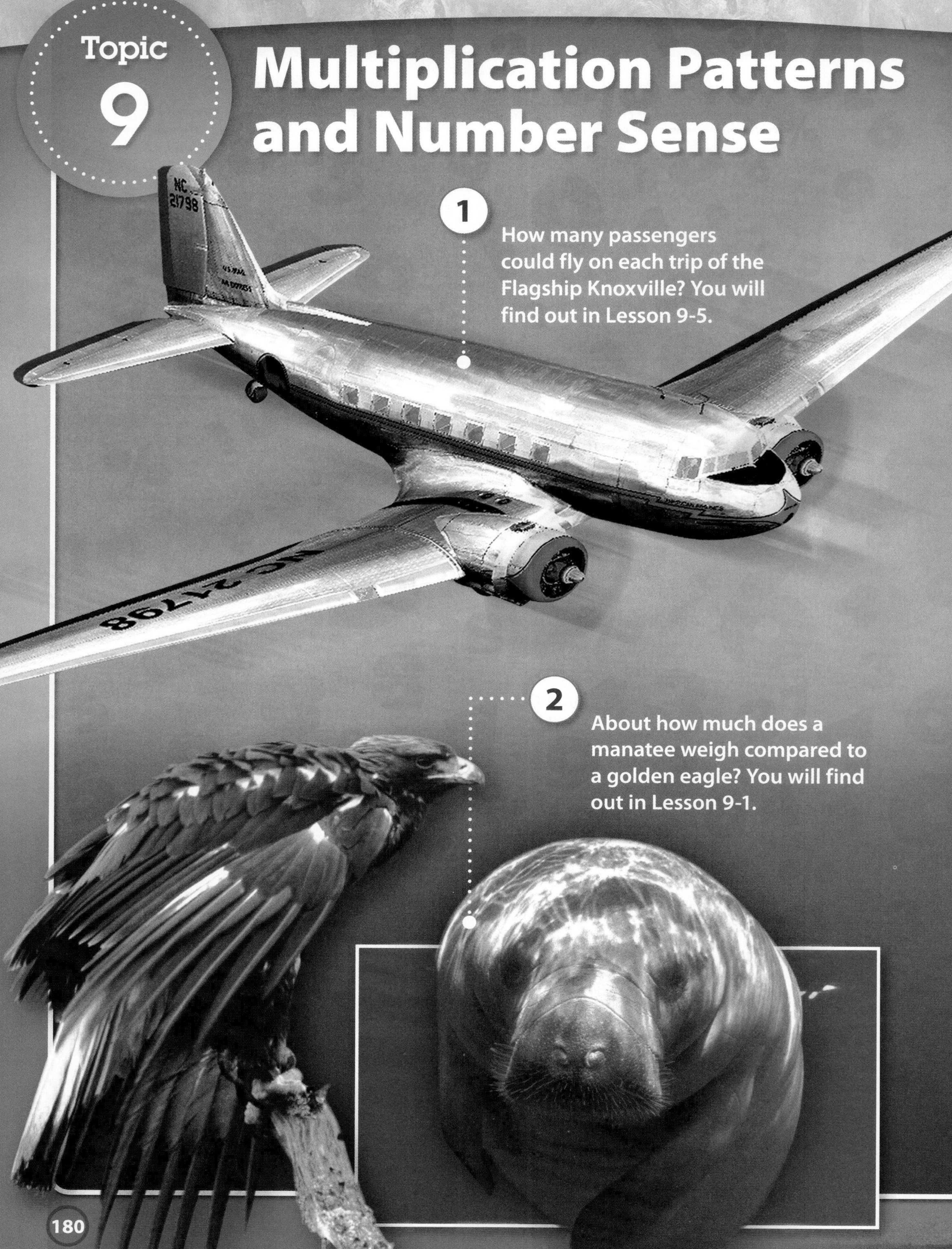

Topic 9 Multiplication Patterns and Number Sense

1. How many passengers could fly on each trip of the Flagship Knoxville? You will find out in Lesson 9-5.

2. About how much does a manatee weigh compared to a golden eagle? You will find out in Lesson 9-1.

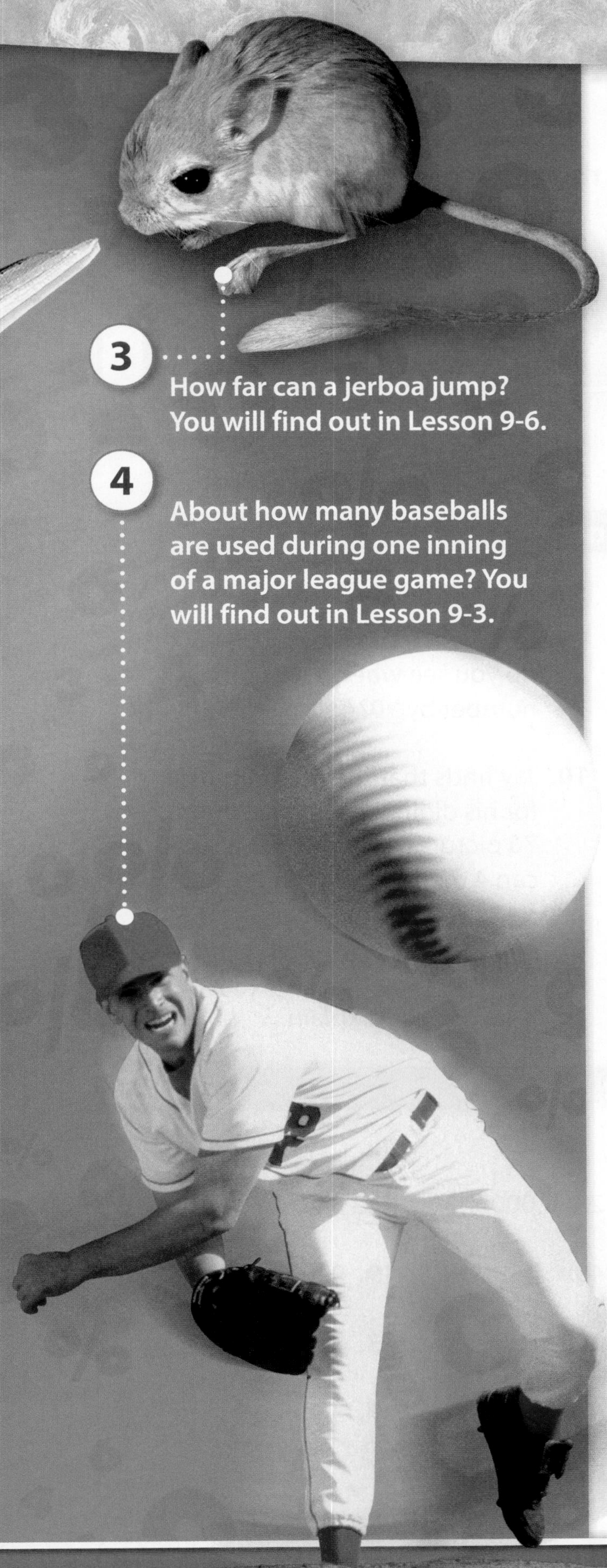

Review What You Know!

Vocabulary

Choose the best term from the box.

- addends
- factors
- product
- sum

1. When you add to combine numbers, another name for the total is the _?_.
2. The Commutative Property of Multiplication says that the _?_ can be multiplied in any order and the answer will be the same.
3. In the number sentence $9 \times 6 = 54$, the number 54 is called the _?_.

Multiplication

Multiply.

4. 3×9
5. 8×7
6. 6×6
7. 4×8
8. 7×5
9. 4×2
10. 7×6
11. 8×9
12. 6×8

Arrays

Draw an array of dots for each multiplication.

13. 3×9
14. 4×8
15. **Write a Problem** Write a problem for the number sentence 7×6.

Lesson

9-1

TEKS 3.4B: Solve and record multiplication problems (up to two digits times one digit). Also **TEKS 3.6B.**

Using Mental Math to Multiply

Hands-On
place-value blocks

How can you multiply by multiples of 10, 100, and 1,000?

Use place-value blocks to find each product.

6 × 100 is 6 groups of 1 hundred or 600. 5 × 1,000 is 5 groups of 1 thousand or 5,000.

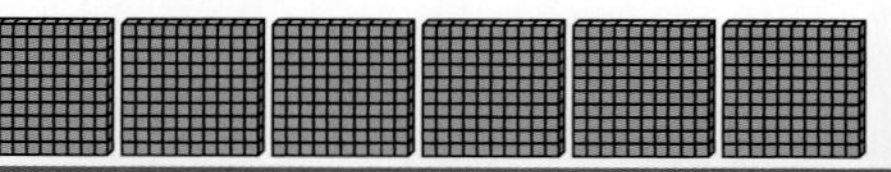

Guided Practice*

Do you know HOW?

In **1–8**, use place-value blocks or patterns to find each product.

1. 8 × 100 **2.** 7 × 1,000

3. 6 × 1,000 **4.** 9 × 100

5. 6 × 40 **6.** 3 × 700

7. 9 × 50 **8.** 5 × 3,000

Do you UNDERSTAND?

9. In the examples above, what pattern do you see when you multiply a number by 10? by 100? by 1,000?

10. Jay finds that the memory card for his digital camera can hold 70 pictures. How many pictures can 4 memory cards hold?

11. Your friend says, "The product 6 × 5 is 30, so 6 × 500 is 300." Is he correct? Explain.

Independent Practice

In **12–27,** use mental math to find the product.

12. 4 × 10 **13.** 9 × 100 **14.** 2 × 1,000 **15.** 3 × 60

16. 8 × 80 **17.** 6 × 50 **18.** 40 × 7 **19.** 900 × 4

20. 500 × 9 **21.** 70 × 5 **22.** 100 × 8 **23.** 2 × 6,000

24. 200 × 8 **25.** 300 × 6 **26.** 4 × 500 **27.** 3 × 400

*For another example, see Set A on page 202.

Find 3 × 70.

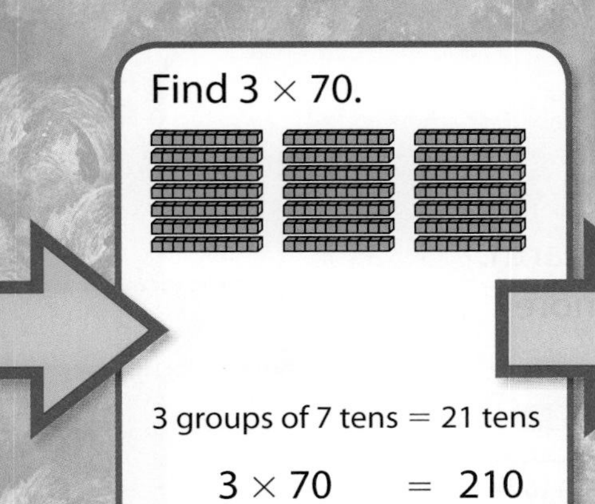

3 groups of 7 tens = 21 tens

3 × 70 = 210

Find 4 × 300.

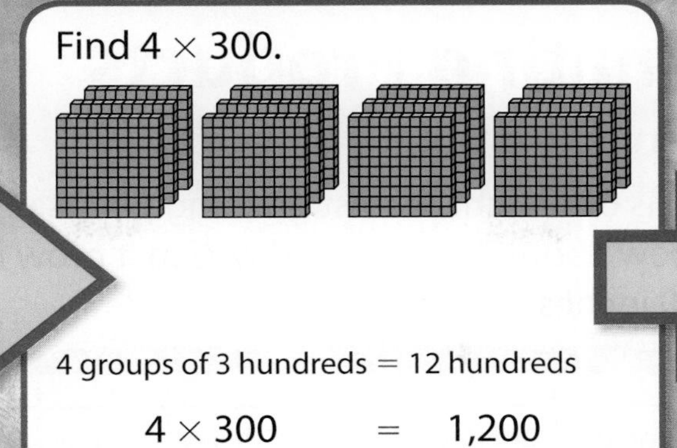

4 groups of 3 hundreds = 12 hundreds

4 × 300 = 1,200

Find 2 × 4,000.

Use a pattern.

2 × 4 = 8
2 × 40 = 80
2 × 400 = 800
2 × 4,000 = 8,000

TAKS Problem Solving

For **28** and **29**, use the table at the right.

Use of Water

Use	Estimated Number of Gallons
Bath	50
Dishwasher (1 load)	10
Shower (10 minutes)	20
Toilet (1 flush)	5
Washing Machine (1 load)	50

28. If you use a washing machine for 3 loads, how many gallons of water would you use? Draw pictures of place-value blocks to show the problem.

29. **Writing to Explain** How much water would you save if you took a 10-minute shower instead of a bath each day for 5 days? Explain how you solved the problem.

30. Each person in the United States uses about 200 gallons of water each day. About 125 gallons are used in the bathroom. How many gallons of water are used in other ways?

31. A golden eagle weighs about 11 pounds. A manatee can weigh 100 times as much as a golden eagle. How much can a manatee weigh?

32. An African elephant drinks about 50 gallons of water each day. How many gallons of water does the elephant drink in 7 days?

33. There are 6 floors in a building. Each floor has 20 windows. Some windows have 2 curtains. How many windows in all does the building have?

A 240 **C** 120

B 122 **D** 28

Lesson

9-2

TEKS 3.5A: Round whole numbers to the nearest ten or hundred to approximate reasonable results in problem situations.

Estimating Products

How can you estimate products?

Bamboo is one of the fastest growing plants on Earth. It can grow about 36 inches a day. Can it grow more than 200 inches in a week?

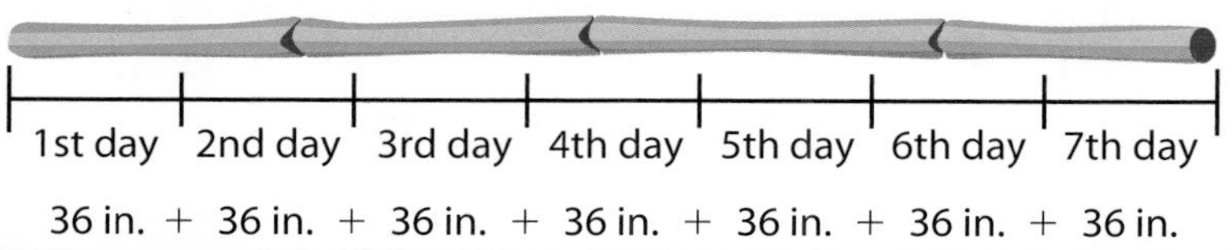

36 in. + 36 in. + 36 in. + 36 in. + 36 in. + 36 in. + 36 in.

Guided Practice*

Do you know HOW?

In **1–6**, estimate each product.

1. 6 × 18

2. 3 × 52

3. 5 × 79

4. 4 × 65

5. 7 × 23

6. 9 × 37

Do you UNDERSTAND?

7. In the example above, is the exact answer more than or less than the estimate of 280? How do you know?

8. The kudzu plant is a vine that can grow about 12 inches each day. Can it grow more than 100 inches in a week? Explain how to round to estimate.

Independent Practice

In **9–28**, estimate each product.

9. 2 × 46

10. 8 × 31

11. 5 × 84

12. 7 × 26

13. 4 × 58

14. 6 × 19

15. 3 × 67

16. 9 × 23

17. 8 × 44

18. 5 × 32

19. 9 × 47

20. 2 × 64

21. 4 × 71

22. 7 × 98

23. 6 × 85

24. 4 × 31

25. $\begin{array}{r} 56 \\ \times\ 2 \\ \hline \end{array}$

26. $\begin{array}{r} 73 \\ \times\ 5 \\ \hline \end{array}$

27. $\begin{array}{r} 29 \\ \times\ 3 \\ \hline \end{array}$

28. $\begin{array}{r} 47 \\ \times\ 6 \\ \hline \end{array}$

*For another example, see Set B on page 202.

Step 1

An estimate is enough to find out if the plant can grow more than 200 inches in a week.

Estimate 7×36.

Round 36 to the nearest ten.

7×36

36 rounds to 40.

$7 \times 40 = 280$

7×36 is about 280.

Step 2

Compare the estimate to 200 inches.

$280 > 200$

So, a bamboo plant can grow more than 200 inches in a week.

TAKS Problem Solving

For **29–31**, use the graph at the right.

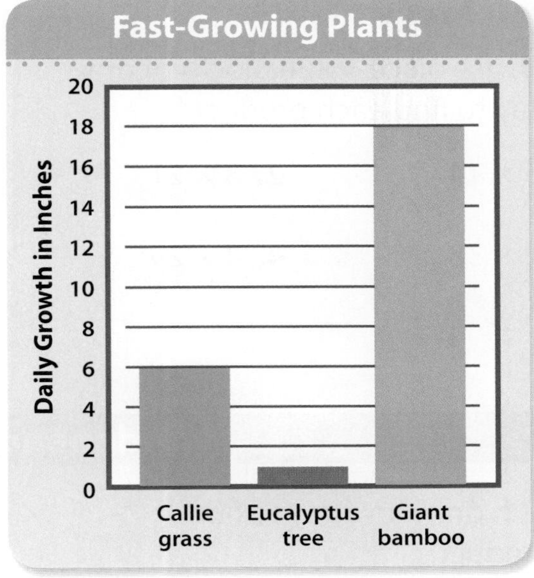

29. Writing to Explain Does a giant bamboo plant grow more than 100 inches in 6 days? Explain how to round to estimate the answer.

30. Reasonableness Jim says a eucalyptus tree grows more in 8 days than Callie grass grows in 2 days. Is his statement reasonable? Explain.

31. How much more does giant bamboo grow in one day than Callie grass?

32. Algebra Look for patterns in the table. Copy and complete.

2	3	4	5	7	9
40	60		100		

33. There are 18 rows of seats on an airplane. Each has 6 seats. Which is the best estimate of the number of seats on the plane?

A 20 **B** 60 **C** 120 **D** 200

34. Think About the Process Jamal is buying 5 books. Each book costs \$19. Which number sentence shows the best estimate of the total cost of the books?

F $5 \times \$10 = \$50$

G $\$5 + \$20 = \$25$

H $5 \times \$20 = \$100$

J $\$10 + \$20 = \$30$

Lesson

9-3

TEKS 3.4B: Solve and record multiplication problems (up to two digits times one digit).

Multiplication and Arrays

Hands-On
place-value blocks

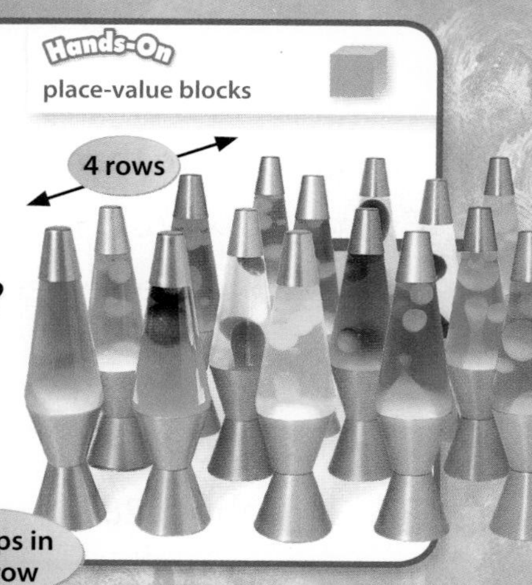

How can you use arrays to show how to multiply with greater numbers?

Lava lamps in a store are arranged in 4 equal rows. What is the total number of lava lamps?

Choose an Operation Multiply to find the total for an array.

Guided Practice*

Do you know HOW?

In **1–4**, use place-value blocks or draw an array to find each product.

1. 5×14

2. 3×21

3. 2×38

4. 4×29

Do you UNDERSTAND?

5. In the example above, what multiplication fact could you use to find the total number of ones?

6. Light bulbs are arranged in 3 equal rows on a shelf in the store. There are 17 bulbs in each row. What is the total number of bulbs on the shelf?

Independent Practice

In **7–11**, draw an array to find the product.

You can draw lines to show tens, and Xs to show ones. This picture shows 23.

———— ———— × ×

7. 3×26 **8.** 5×15 **9.** 2×18 **10.** 4×16 **11.** 7×21

In **12–21**, find each product. You may use place-value blocks or draw a picture to help.

12. 2×47 **13.** 6×28 **14.** 5×31 **15.** 3×45 **16.** 4×32

17. 8×15 **18.** 3×29 **19.** 5×22 **20.** 2×38 **21.** 4×19

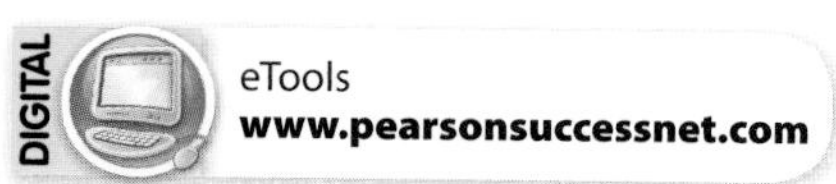

*For another example, see Set C on page 202.

Step 1

Use an array to show 4×13.

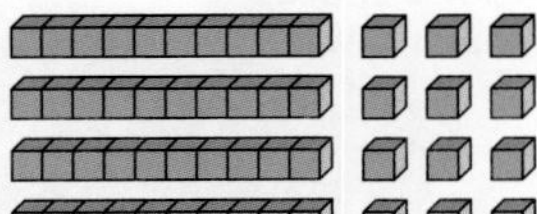

There are 4 rows with 1 ten and 3 ones in each row.

Step 2

Find how many in all.

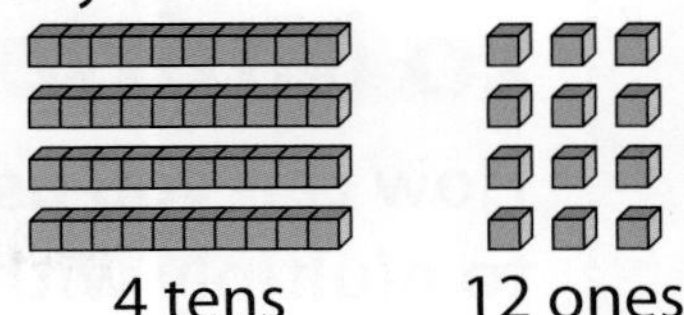

Count by tens and then count on with the ones to find the total.

10, 20, 30, 40

41, 42, 43, 44, 45, 46, 47, 48, 49, 50, 51, 52

There are 52 lava lamps.

TAKS Problem Solving

For **22** and **23**, use the table.

22. Jake walked for 1 minute. How many times did Jake's heart beat?

23. Strategy Focus Solve. Use the strategy Try, Check, and Revise.

While doing one of the activities, Jake counted his heartbeats. He found that his heart rate in one minute was greater than 120, but less than 130. Which activity was he doing? Explain how you solved the problem.

Jake's Heart Rate (Data)

Activity	Number of Heartbeats in 10 Seconds
Bicycling	21
Resting	13
Running	22
Walking	18

Tip *The number of heartbeats in 1 minute is 6 times as many as in 10 seconds.*

24. The soup cans in a store display were arranged in rows. There were 27 cans in each row. There were 3 rows. Which number sentence describes the array of soup cans?

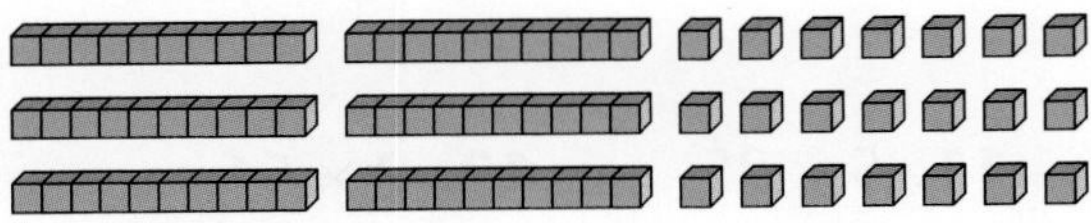

A $3 \times 27 = 81$

B $6 \times 21 = 126$

C $6 + 21 = 27$

D $2 \times 27 = 54$

25. What multiplication sentence could you write for this array?

_____ _____ _____

_____ _____ _____

26. In one inning, each baseball was used for 7 pitches. Write a number sentence that shows the total number of pitches thrown that inning.

4 baseballs are used each inning.

Lesson

9-4

TEKS 3.4B: Solve and record multiplication problems (up to two digits times one digit).

Breaking Apart to Multiply

place-value blocks

How can you use breaking apart to multiply with greater numbers?

A parking lot has the same number of spaces in each row. How many spaces are in the lot?

Choose an Operation Multiply to find the total for an array.

Guided Practice*

Do you know HOW?

In **1** and **2**, copy and complete.

1. 4×36
4×3 tens = ▢ tens or 120
4×6 ones = 24 ones or ▢
▢ + ▢ = ▢

2. 5×27
$5 \times 20 =$ ▢
$5 \times 7 =$ ▢
▢ + ▢ = ▢

In **3** and **4**, find each product. You may use place-value blocks or drawings to help.

3. 2×48 **4.** 6×34

Do you UNDERSTAND?

5. In the parking lot example above, into what two groups is the array broken?

6. The buses at a bus garage are parked in equal rows. There are 4 rows. There are 29 buses in each row. What is the total number of buses parked at the garage?

7. **Writing to Explain** Explain why you can break apart numbers to multiply without changing the product.

Independent Practice

In **8–17**, find each product. You may use place-value blocks or drawings to help.

8. 3×19 **9.** 4×31 **10.** 6×23 **11.** 5×25 **12.** 2×54

13. 3×49 **14.** 6×27 **15.** 5×43 **16.** 7×35 **17.** 4×62

Animated Glossary, eTools
www.pearsonsuccessnet.com

*For another example, see Set D on page 203.

Step 1

Use an array to show 4×24.

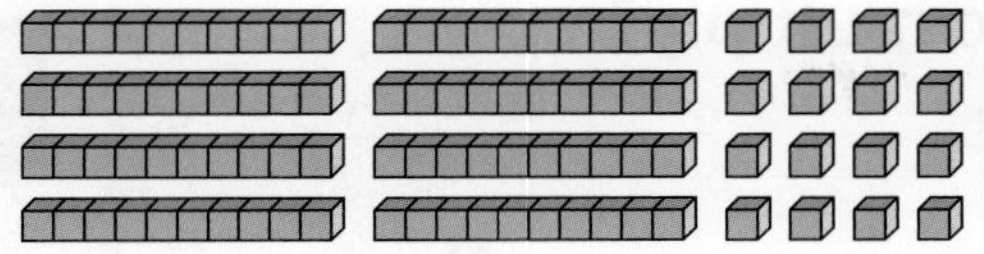

$4 \times 20 = 80$ $4 \times 4 = 16$

Step 2

Add each part to get the product.

$4 \times 20 = 80$ $4 \times 4 = 16$

$80 + 16 = 96$

80 and 16 are called partial products because they are parts of the product.

$4 \times 24 = 96$

There are 96 spaces in the parking lot.

TAKS Problem Solving

For **18–22**, find the total number of miles walked in the number of weeks given.

Kind of Job	Distance Walked in 1 Week
Doctor	16 miles
Mail carrier	21 miles
Nurse	18 miles
Police officer	32 miles
TV reporter	19 miles

18. Police officer: 4 weeks

19. Nurse: 6 weeks

20. Mail carrier: 7 weeks

21. Doctor: 3 weeks

22. TV reporter: 2 weeks

23. **Estimation** Walt has $80. Does he have enough money to buy a chair and a desk? Explain how to round to estimate.

24. Nilda bought a bookcase, a lamp, and a desk. What was the total cost of the items?

25. Raoul is counting the eggs in 8 rows. Each row has 36 eggs. Which number sentence shows the best way to estimate the total number of eggs in the rows?

A $8 + 30 = 38$ **C** $8 \times 30 = 240$

B $10 + 40 = 50$ **D** $8 \times 40 = 320$

Lesson

9-5

TEKS 3.4B: Solve and record multiplication problems (up to two digits times one digit).

Using an Expanded Algorithm

Hands-On place-value blocks

How can you use place value to multiply?

How many calories are in 3 peaches?

Find 3×46.

Estimate: $3 \times 50 = 150$

Calories	
Fruit	**Number of calories**
Peach	46
Orange	35
Pear	40

Guided Practice*

Do you know HOW?

In **1** and **2**, copy and complete. Use place-value blocks or draw pictures to help.

1. $\begin{array}{r} 16 \\ \times\ 3 \\ \hline 18 \\ \square\square \\ \hline \square\square \end{array}$

2. $\begin{array}{r} 34 \\ \times\ 5 \\ \hline 20 \\ \square\square\square \\ \hline \square\square\square \end{array}$

In **3** and **4**, find each product. You may use place-value blocks or drawings to help.

3. $\begin{array}{r} 67 \\ \times\ 2 \\ \hline \end{array}$

4. $\begin{array}{r} 54 \\ \times\ 7 \\ \hline \end{array}$

Do you UNDERSTAND?

For **5–7**, use the example above.

5. What factors give the partial product 18? What factors give the partial product 120?

6. What is the next step after you find the partial products?

7. How many calories are in 2 oranges?

Independent Practice

Leveled Practice In **8** and **9**, copy and complete. In **10–12**, find each product. You may use place-value blocks or drawings to help.

Tip *You can draw lines to show tens, and Xs to show ones. This picture shows 27.*

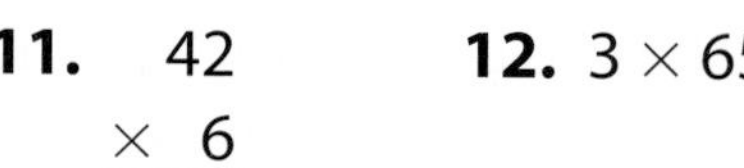

8. $\begin{array}{r} 36 \\ \times\ 2 \\ \hline 12 \\ \square\square \\ \hline \square\square \end{array}$

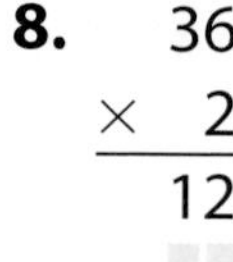

9. $\begin{array}{r} 53 \\ \times\ 4 \\ \hline 12 \\ \square\square\square \\ \hline \square\square\square \end{array}$

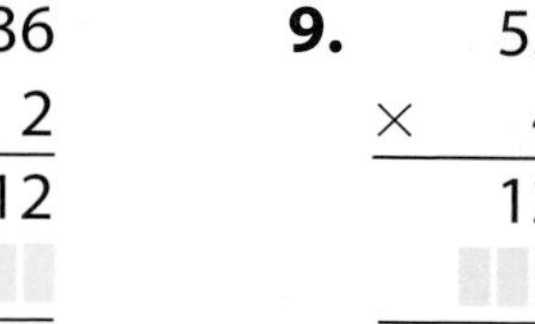

10. $\begin{array}{r} 18 \\ \times\ 7 \\ \hline \end{array}$

11. $\begin{array}{r} 42 \\ \times\ 6 \\ \hline \end{array}$

12. 3×65

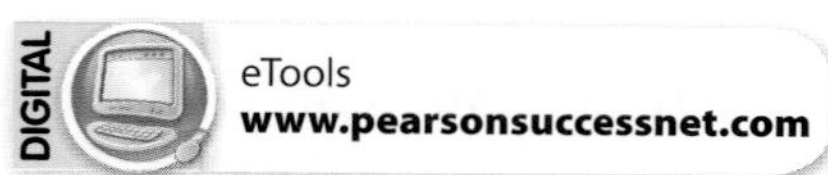

For another example, see Set E on page 203.

What You Show

Make an array for 3×46.

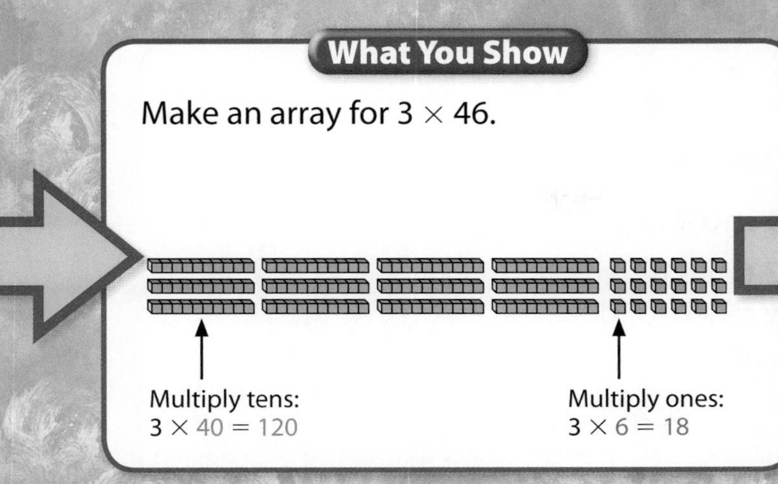

What You Write

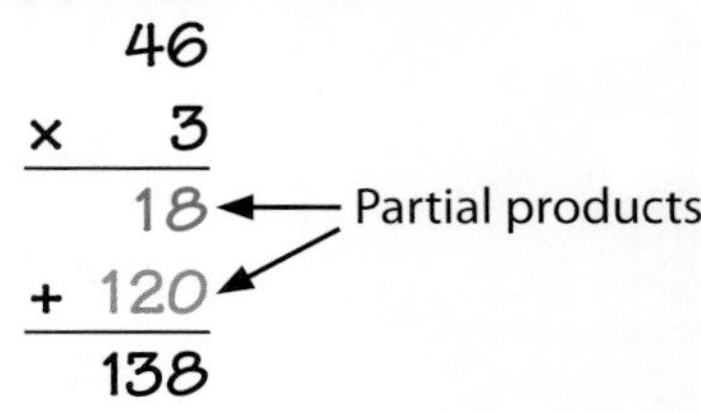

There are 138 calories in 3 peaches.

Is the answer reasonable?
Yes. 138 is close to the estimate of 150.

TAKS Problem Solving

13. Sam's family is planning a vacation. The table shows the cost of each one-way plane ticket from his town to three cities.

a How much more is a one-way ticket to Atlanta than a one-way ticket to Chicago?

b How much would Sam's family spend for 3 round-trip tickets to Kansas City?

A round-trip ticket costs twice as much as a one-way ticket.

Airfare

City	Cost of One-Way Ticket
Atlanta	$87
Chicago	$59
Kansas City	$49

14. Reasoning How can knowing that $5 \times 14 = 70$ help you find 5×16? Explain your strategy.

15. Algebra The product of this whole number and 25 is greater than 50 but less than 100. What's the number?

16. How many passengers could the *Flagship Knoxville* carry in all on 3 trips?

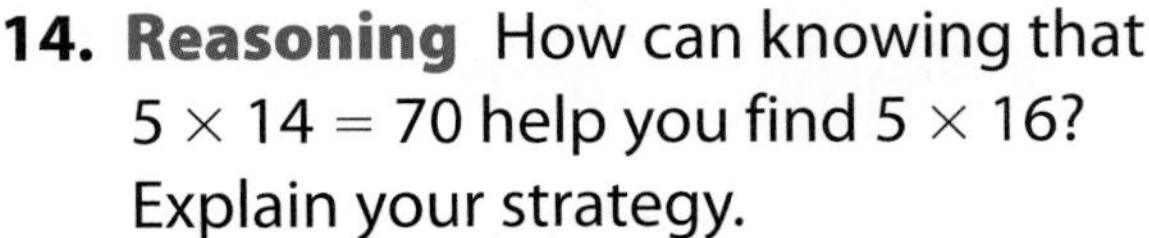

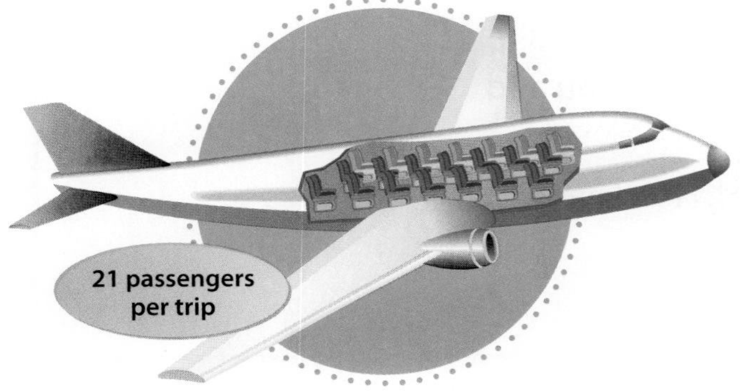

17. Writing to Explain To find 24×7, Joel adds the partial products 28 and 14. Is he correct? Explain.

18. Mr. Cruz weighed 8 cartons. Each carton weighed 17 pounds. How many pounds was this in all?

A 25 pounds
B 136 pounds
C 856 pounds
D 8,056 pounds

Lesson

9-6

TEKS 3.4B: Solve and record multiplication problems (up to two digits times one digit).

Multiplying 2-Digit by 1-Digit Numbers

Hands-On

place-value blocks

How do you regroup to multiply?

The grass carp fish can eat 3 times its weight in plant food each day. How much food can this grass carp eat each day?

Find 3×26.

Estimate: $3 \times 30 = 90$

This grass carp weighs 26 pounds.

Another Example How do you regroup to multiply without using place-value blocks?

A bluefin tuna can swim 67 feet in 1 second. How many feet can it swim in 4 seconds?

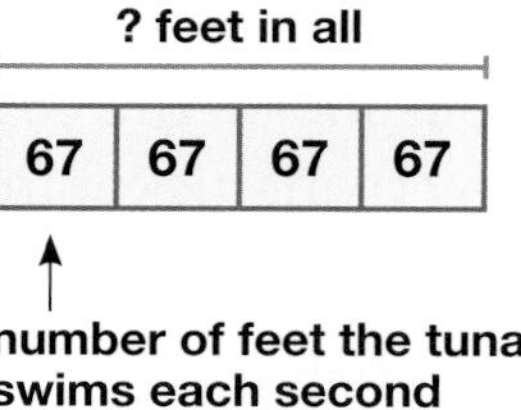

Find 4×67.

Estimate: $4 \times 70 = 280$

Step 1

Multiply the ones.
Regroup, if needed.

$4 \times 7 = 28$ ones
Regroup 28 ones as 2 tens 8 ones.

$$\begin{array}{r} {}^{2} \\ 67 \\ \times\ \ 4 \\ \hline 8 \end{array}$$

Step 2

Multiply the tens.
Add regrouped tens.

4×6 tens $= 24$ tens
24 tens + 2 tens = 26 tens

$$\begin{array}{r} {}^{2} \\ 67 \\ \times\ \ 4 \\ \hline 268 \end{array}$$

The tuna can swim 268 feet.

Is the answer reasonable?
Yes. 268 is close to the estimate of 280.

Explain It

1. Why is a small 2 written above the 6? Why do you add the 2 instead of multiply with it?
2. A dolphin can swim 44 feet in 1 second. How many feet can it swim in 5 seconds?

Step 1

Multiply the ones. Regroup, if needed.

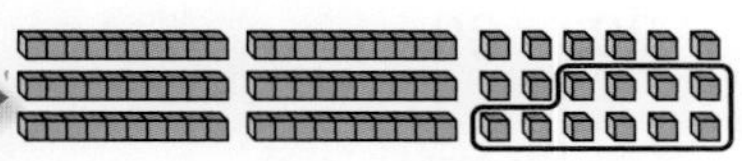

$$\begin{array}{r} {}^{1}\\ 26 \\ \times\ \ 3 \\ \hline 8 \end{array}$$

3 × 6 = 18 ones
Regroup 18 ones as 1 ten 8 ones.

Step 2

Multiply the tens. Add regrouped tens.

3 × 2 tens = 6 tens
6 tens + 1 ten = 7 tens

$$\begin{array}{r} {}^{1}\\ 26 \\ \times\ \ 3 \\ \hline 78 \end{array}$$

The fish would eat 78 pounds of food.

Guided Practice*

Do you know HOW?

In **1** and **2**, copy and complete. You may use drawings to help.

1.
$$\begin{array}{r} \square \\ 13 \\ \times\ \ 6 \\ \hline \square 8 \end{array}$$

2.
$$\begin{array}{r} \square \\ 24 \\ \times\ \ 7 \\ \hline \square\square 8 \end{array}$$

In **3** and **4**, find each product. You may use drawings to help.

3.
$$\begin{array}{r} 78 \\ \times\ \ 4 \\ \hline \end{array}$$

4.
$$\begin{array}{r} 35 \\ \times\ \ 8 \\ \hline \end{array}$$

Do you UNDERSTAND?

5. In the example above, why is the estimate greater than the exact answer?

6. In the example above, how much food could this grass carp eat in 4 days?

7. A blue shark can swim 36 feet in 1 second. How many feet can it swim in 3 seconds?

Independent Practice

In **8–15**, estimate and then find each product. You may use drawings to help.

8. $\begin{array}{r} 49 \\ \times\ 2 \\ \hline \end{array}$

9. $\begin{array}{r} 37 \\ \times\ 3 \\ \hline \end{array}$

10. $\begin{array}{r} 64 \\ \times\ 5 \\ \hline \end{array}$

11. $\begin{array}{r} 52 \\ \times\ 9 \\ \hline \end{array}$

12. 6 × 53

13. 7 × 38

14. 4 × 44

15. 5 × 42

DIGITAL eTools **www.pearsonsuccessnet.com**

For another example, see Set E on page 203.

Independent Practice

In **16–24**, find each product.

16. $\begin{array}{r} 46 \\ \times\ 7 \\ \hline \end{array}$ **17.** $\begin{array}{r} 23 \\ \times\ 9 \\ \hline \end{array}$ **18.** $\begin{array}{r} 85 \\ \times\ 4 \\ \hline \end{array}$ **19.** $\begin{array}{r} 19 \\ \times\ 6 \\ \hline \end{array}$ **20.** $\begin{array}{r} 89 \\ \times\ 2 \\ \hline \end{array}$

21. 2×48 **22.** 91×3 **23.** 86×5 **24.** 6×47

TAKS Problem Solving

25. The ostrich is the fastest bird on land. An ostrich can run 66 feet in 1 second. The cheetah is the fastest mammal on land. A cheetah can run 94 feet in 1 second. How many fewer feet can an ostrich run in 1 second than a cheetah?

26. The length of the body of this jerboa is shown in the picture. How far can this jerboa jump?

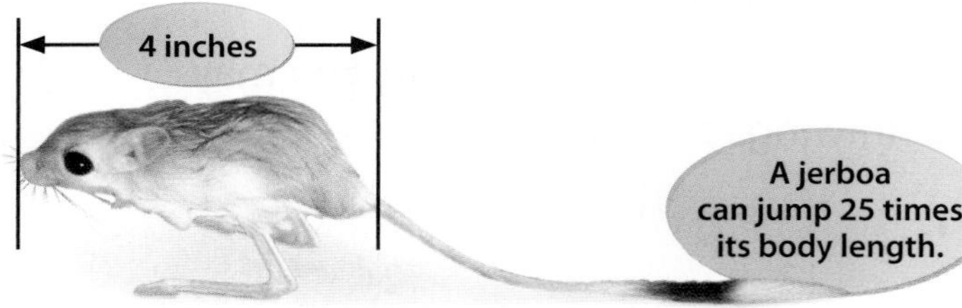

27. **Estimation** Dionne used rounding to estimate the product of 58 and another number. Her estimate of the product was 300. Which number is the best choice for the other factor?

A 3 **B** 5 **C** 8 **D** 10

28. At a museum, the visitors formed 8 tour groups to go on tours. Each group had 32 visitors. How many visitors were going on tours?

F 40 **G** 246

H 256 **J** 2,416

29. The Columbia Center building has 4 times as many floors as a 19-floor building. How many more floors does the Columbia Center building have than the 19-floor building?

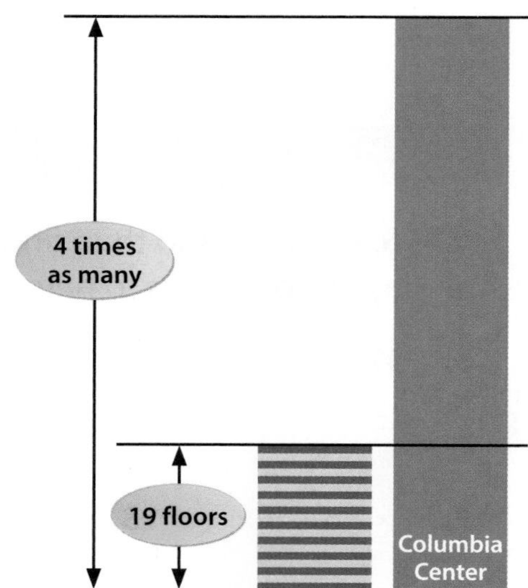

Algebra For **30–32**, copy and complete. Use $<$, $>$, or $=$.

30. 53×6 ◯ 308 **31.** 19×5 ◯ 145 **32.** 24×4 ◯ 12×8

Algebra Connections

Using Multiplication Properties

Remember to use the properties of multiplication to help you complete number sentences.

Commutative (Order) Property You can multiply factors in any order and the product is the same. $5 \times 9 = 9 \times 5$

Identity (One) Property When you multiply a number and 1, the product is that number. $1 \times 8 = 8$

Zero Property When you multiply a number and 0, the product is 0. $0 \times 7 = 0$

Associative (Grouping) Property You can change the grouping of the factors, and the product is the same. $(3 \times 2) \times 4 = 3 \times (2 \times 4)$

Example: $\square \times 8 = 0$

Think What number multiplied by 8 is equal to 0?

You can use the Zero Property.
$\underline{0} \times 8 = 0$

Example:
$6 \times (9 \times 7) = (6 \times \square) \times 7$

Think What number makes the two sides equal?

Use the Associative Property.
$6 \times (9 \times 7) = (6 \times \underline{9}) \times 7$

Copy and complete with the number that makes the two sides equal.

1. $10 \times \square = 10$

2. $12 \times 8 = 8 \times \square$

3. $6 \times (2 \times 5) = (6 \times \square) \times 5$

4. $\square \times 8 = 0$

5. $\square \times 7 = 7 \times 11$

6. $(4 \times 3) \times \square = 4 \times (3 \times 8)$

7. $6 \times \square = 9 \times 6$

8. $\square \times 9 = 9$

9. $(\square \times 7) \times 2 = 5 \times (7 \times 2)$

In **10** and **11**, copy and complete the number sentence. Solve the problem.

10. Gemma made 8 rows of stickers on a sheet with 9 stickers in each row. Then she placed the same number of stickers in 9 rows on another sheet. How many stickers were in each of these rows?

$8 \times 9 = 9 \times \square$

How many stickers did she have in all?

11. Hal and Den each have copies of the same photos. Hal arranges 5 photos on each of 6 pages in 2 albums. Den needs 5 pages in 2 albums for the same photos. How many photos are on each page in Den's albums?

$(6 \times 5) \times 2 = (5 \times \square) \times 2$

How many photos does each boy have?

12. **Write a Problem** Write a real-world problem to match the number sentence on the right.

$\square \times 12 = 12 \times 3$

Lesson
9-7

TEKS 3.14C Select or develop an appropriate problem solving plan or strategy including drawing a picture, looking for a pattern, systematic guessing and checking, acting it out, making a table, working a simpler problem, or working backwards to solve a problem.

Problem Solving

Draw a Picture and Write a Number Sentence

Oscar bought 5 cases of bottled water. How many bottles of water did Oscar buy?

Another Example

Melody wants to buy a case of juice boxes. There are 3 times as many boxes in a jumbo case as in a regular case. How many juice boxes are in a jumbo case?

Plan

Use a picture or a diagram to show what you know.

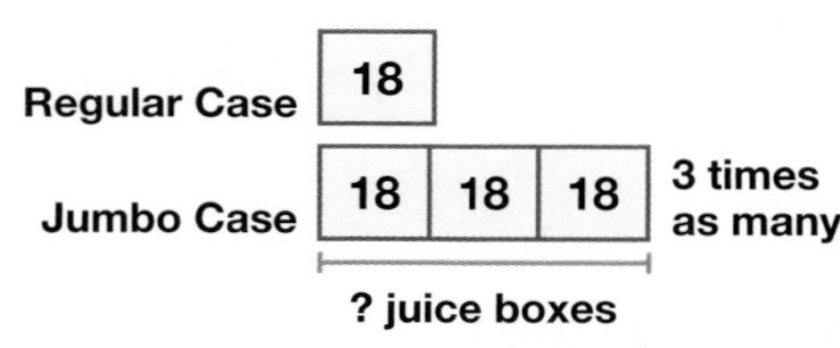

Write a Number Sentence
You want to find the number that is 3 times as many as 18.

$3 \times 18 = \square$

Solve

Find 3×18.

$$\begin{array}{r} \scriptstyle 2 \\ 18 \\ \times \; 3 \\ \hline 54 \end{array}$$

A jumbo case has 54 juice boxes.

Check

Make sure the answer is reasonable.

Estimate to check.

18 rounds to 20.

$20 \times 3 = 60$

54 is close to 60, so the answer is reasonable.

Explain It

1. **Number Sense** Why can't you use the same type of diagram for this problem as you used for the problem at the top of the page?
2. Describe another way that you could check that the answer to the problem above is correct.

Plan

Use a picture or a diagram to show what you know.

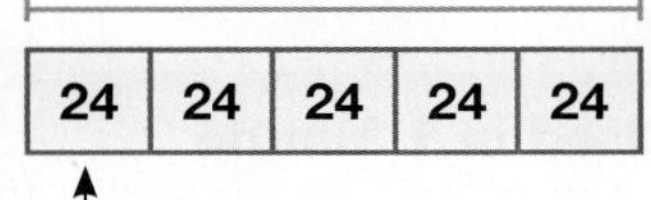

Number of bottles in each case

You know the number in each group and that the groups are equal. So you can multiply to find the total.

Solve

Find 5×24.

$$\begin{array}{r} {}^{2} \\ 24 \\ \times\ 5 \\ \hline 120 \end{array}$$

Oscar bought 120 bottles of water.

Check

Make sure the answer is reasonable.

Estimate to check.

24 rounds to 20.

$20 \times 5 = 100$

120 is close to 100, so the answer is reasonable.

Guided Practice*

Do you know HOW?

1. A doll collection is displayed in 8 rows with 16 dolls in each row. How many dolls are in the collection?

? dolls in all

16	16	16	16	16	16	16	16

Number of dolls in each row

Do you UNDERSTAND?

2. **Writing to Explain** Why do you multiply to solve Problem 1?

3. **Write a Problem** Write a problem that can be solved by drawing a picture. Draw the picture. Solve.

Independent Practice

4. Eduardo has 36 football cards. He has 3 times as many baseball cards. How many baseball cards does he have?

football cards: | 36 |

baseball cards: | 36 | 36 | 36 | 3 times as many

? baseball cards in all

5. **Writing to Explain** Noah has 95 books to put on 4 shelves. If he puts 24 books on each shelf, will all the books fit on the shelves?

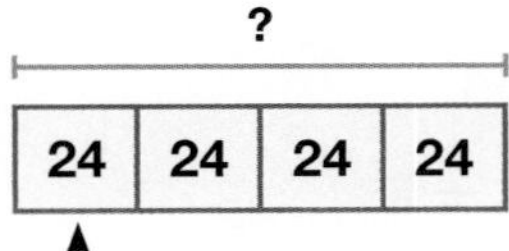

Number of books on each shelf

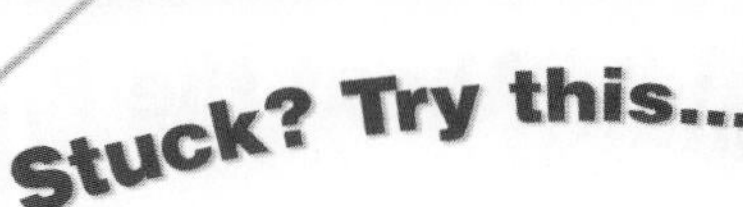

- What do I know?
- What am I asked to find?
- What diagram can I use to help understand the problem?
- Can I use addition, subtraction, multiplication, or division?
- Is all of my work correct?
- Did I answer the right question?
- Is my answer reasonable?

*For another example, see Set F on page 203.

Independent Practice

The table shows about how many calories a 100-pound person uses doing different activities. Use the table for **6–8**.

6. Martha went jogging for 15 minutes. How many calories did she use?

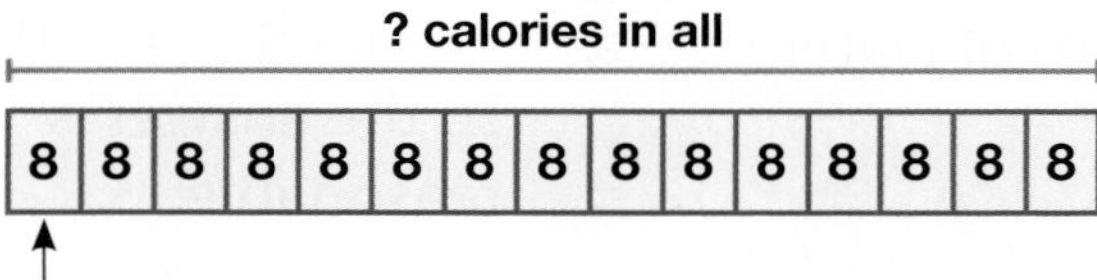

Data

Calories Used in 1 Minute	
Activity	**Number of Calories**
Biking	5
Jogging	8
Rollerblading	4
Walking	4

7. Julio walked for 25 minutes. Then he went rollerblading for 20 minutes. How many calories did he use?

8. Cathy plans to ride her bike for 15 minutes every day. How many calories will she use in a week?

9. Frank rode his bike for an hour. Then he went rollerblading for 25 minutes. How many more minutes did he spend riding his bike than rollerblading?

10. **Estimation** The U.S. Department of Health reports that many children spend about 32 hours each week in front of a computer screen. About how many hours is that in a month?

1 month is about 4 weeks.

11. Stacy has 3 bags of red beads. Cynthia has 2 more bags than Stacy. There are 24 beads in each bag.

a How many beads does each girl have?

b How many beads do the girls have all together?

Think About the Process

12. Mike earns \$4 an hour doing yard work. He worked 12 hours last week and 23 hours this week. Which number sentence shows how much he earned this week?

A $\$23 + \$12 = \square$

B $12 \times \$4 = \square$

C $23 \times \$4 = \square$

D $(23 \times \$4) \times 7 = \square$

13. Katy read 46 pages of a book on Monday. She read 25 pages on Tuesday. She still has 34 pages to read. Which number sentence shows how many pages are in the book?

F $46 + 25 = \square$

G $46 - 34 = \square$

H $(46 + 25) - 34 = \square$

J $46 + 25 + 34 = \square$

Arrays and Partial Products

Use eTools
Place-Value Blocks

Find 4×37. Use an array to tell the partial products.

Step 1 Go to the Place-Value Blocks eTool. Select a horizontal tens block. Click in the workspace 3 times to show the 3 tens in 37. Select a ones block. Click in the workspace 7 times to show the 7 ones in 37. Put all these blocks in one row.

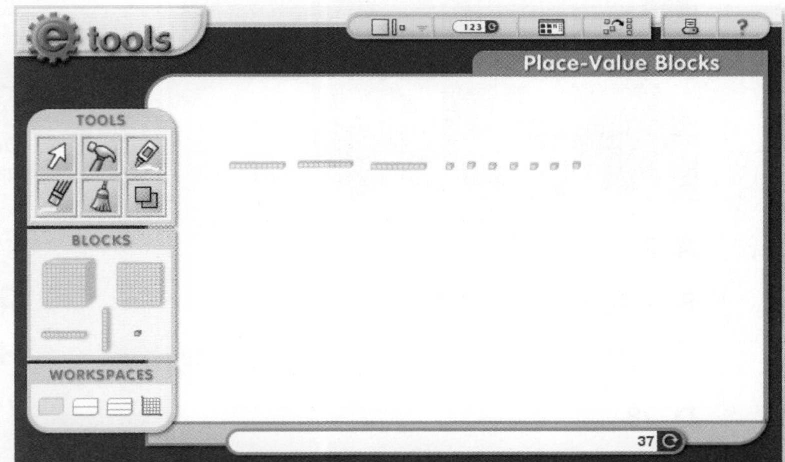

Step 2 Make 3 more rows with 37 in each, so you have 4 rows in all. Click on the odometer style button until you see the partial products 120 + 28 in the odometer. Click on the odometer style button again until the product is shown. The odometer should show 148. Now write a number sentence that shows the partial products and the product.
$4 \times 37 = 120 + 28 = 148$

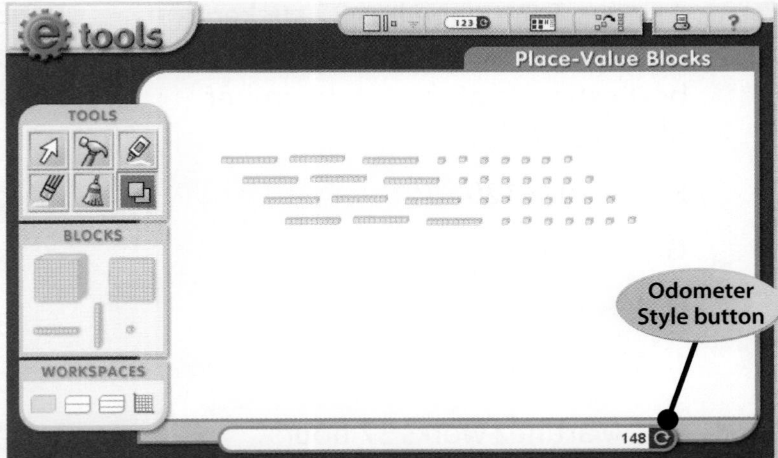

Practice

Use the Place-Value Blocks eTool to find the partial products and the product for each.

1. 3×56

2. 3×29

3. 2×68

4. 2×87

5. 3×98

6. 5×17

TAKS Test Prep

1. Jillian bought 7 packages of paper. Each package had 400 sheets. How many sheets of paper did Jillian buy? (9-1)

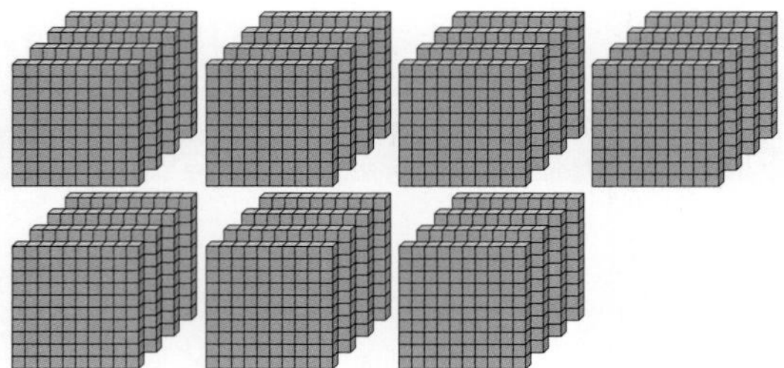

A 28,000

B 2,800

C 128

D 28

2. A package of stickers contains 4 pages. Each page has 32 stickers. Which number sentence shows the best estimate of the total number of stickers? (9-2)

F $4 \times 30 = 120$

G $4 \times 40 = 160$

H $4 + 30 = 34$

J $4 + 40 = 44$

3. Mrs. Martinez works 37 hours each week. How many hours does she work in 6 weeks? Find the product. (9-5)

$$\begin{array}{r} 37 \\ \times \quad 6 \\ \hline \end{array}$$

A 60

B 122

C 192

D 222

4. Vella's bookcase has 6 shelves. Each shelf displays 3 dolls. Which number sentence shows how many dolls are displayed in the bookcase? (9-7)

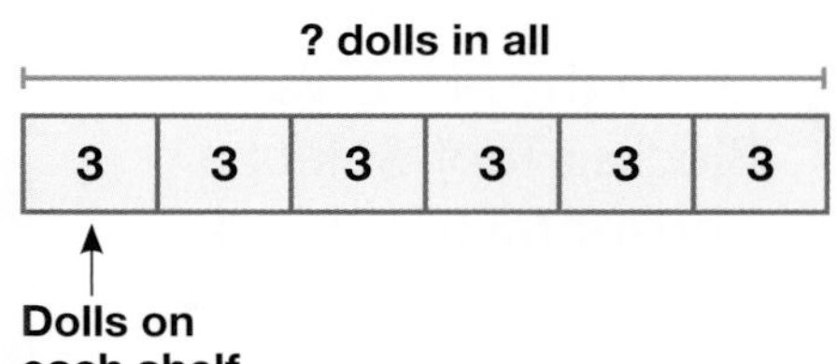

F $6 + 3 = 9$

G $6 - 3 = 3$

H $6 \times 3 = 18$

J $6 \div 3 = 2$

5. Henry bought 3 bags of oranges. Each bag had 16 oranges. How many oranges did he buy? Use the array to solve. (9-3)

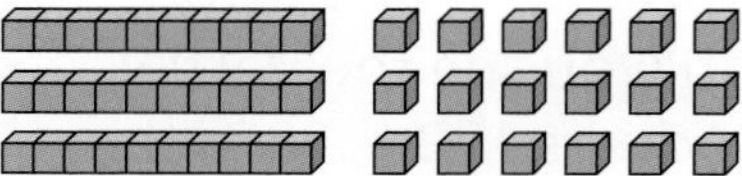

A 19

B 38

C 48

D 54

6. Mr. Gomez bought 26 packages of juice boxes for the school picnic. Each package had 8 juice boxes. How many juice boxes did he buy? (9-6)

F 214

G 208

H 202

J 168

7. Which addition sentence shows how to use partial products to find 5×17? (9-4)

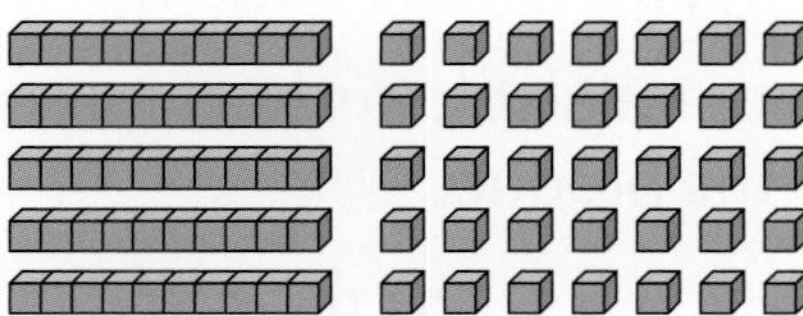

A $50 + 35 = 85$

B $5 + 35 = 38$

C $50 + 45 = 95$

D $50 + 5 = 55$

8. There are 46 students in Grade 3. Each student brought 6 balloons to use on the Grade 3 float in the parade. Which is the best estimate of the number of balloons that will be used on the float? (9-2)

F 50

G 100

H 150

J 300

9. Mrs. Kent bought 7 bags of sand for her daughter's sandbox. Each bag of sand weighed 25 pounds. How many pounds of sand did Mrs. Kent buy? (9-6)

A 32

B 145

C 175

D 180

10. Which number sentence comes next in the pattern? (9-1)

$8 \times 6 = 48$
$8 \times 60 = 480$
$8 \times 600 = 4{,}800$

F $8 \times 600 = 48{,}000$

G $8 \times 6{,}000 = 48{,}000$

H $80 \times 60 = 4{,}800$

J $80 \times 600 = 48{,}000$

11. Jo drinks 2 to 3 glasses of milk a day. Which is a reasonable number of glasses of milk Jo will drink in 7 days? (9-2)

A Fewer than 14

B Between 14 and 21

C Between 22 and 35

D More than 35

12. **Griddable Response** Ann needs 20 ceramic tiles to decorate one stepping stone. If she wants to decorate 4 stepping stones for her garden, how many ceramic tiles does she need? (9-1)

13. **Griddable Response** One package of fruit snacks contains 15 grams of sugar. If Stu ate one package of fruit snacks every day for 5 days, how many grams of sugar would he eat just from fruit snacks? (9-6)

Reteaching

Set A, pages 182–183

Find 7 × 5,000.

Use basic facts and patterns.

7 × 5 = 35 ← basic fact
7 × 50 = 350
7 × 500 = 3,500
7 × 5,000 = 35,000
} Pattern of zeros

Remember that when the product of a basic fact contains a zero, that zero is not part of the pattern.

Use place-value blocks or patterns to find the product.

1. 7 × 300 **2.** 9 × 6,000

3. 4 × 5,000 **4.** 5 × 200

5. 8 × 900 **6.** 3 × 3,000

Set B, pages 184–185

Estimate 6 × 57.

Round 57 to the nearest ten.
Then multiply.

6 × 57
↓ 57 rounds to 60.
6 × 60 = 360

6 × 57 is about 360.

Remember that you round to the greater ten if the digit in the ones place is 5 or greater. Round to the lesser ten if the ones digit is 4 or less.

Estimate each product.

1. 5 × 39 **2.** 8 × 67

3. 7 × 42 **4.** 2 × 76

5. 4 × 83 **6.** 9 × 25

Set C, pages 186–187

Draw an array to find 3 × 24.

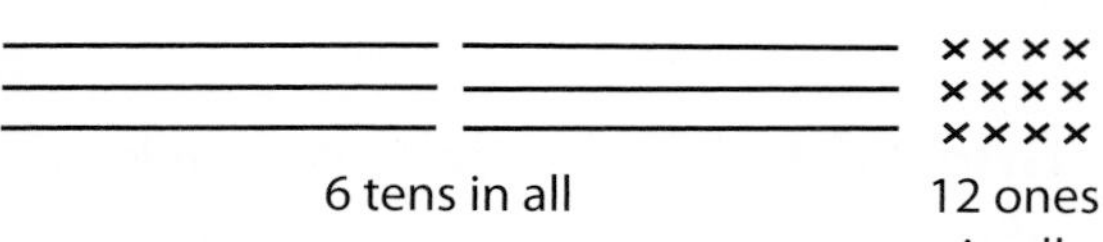

Count by tens.
10, 20, 30, 40, 50, 60

Then count by ones to find the total.
61, 62, 63, 64, 65, 66, 67, 68, 69, 70, 71, 72

So, 3 × 24 = 72.

Remember to keep your drawings simple.

Find each product. Use place-value blocks or draw a picture to help.

1. 3 × 27 **2.** 4 × 18

3. 5 × 14 **4.** 3 × 32

5. 7 × 31 **6.** 4 × 42

7. 8 × 22 **8.** 5 × 62

Set D, pages 188–189

Break apart numbers to find 2 × 17.

× × × × × × ×
× × × × × × ×

Two rows of 1 ten = 2 tens or 20
Two rows of 7 ones = 14 ones or 14
20 and 14 are partial products.

Add the partial products to find the product.
20 + 14 = 34

So, 2 × 17 = 34.

Remember to include a zero when you record the value of the tens.

Find each product. You may draw a picture to help.

1. 4 × 73
2. 2 × 59
3. 6 × 35
4. 3 × 81
5. 7 × 25
6. 5 × 34

Set E, pages 190–194

Find 27 × 6.

One Way

$$\begin{array}{r} 27 \\ \times\ \ 6 \\ \hline 42 \\ +\ 120 \\ \hline 162 \end{array}$$

42 and 120: partial products

Another Way

$$\begin{array}{r} {}^{4} \\ 27 \\ \times\ \ 6 \\ \hline 162 \end{array}$$

Multiply ones.
Regroup.
Multiply tens.

So, 27 × 6 = 162.

Remember you can estimate to check that your answer is reasonable.

Find each product. You may use drawings to help.

1. 29 × 6
2. 42 × 5
3. 79 × 4
4. 16 × 9
5. 55 × 8
6. 39 × 6

Set F, pages 196–198

Beth has 24 planet stickers. She has 4 times as many flower stickers as planet stickers. How many flower stickers does Beth have?

? Flower Stickers in all

Flower Stickers	24	24	24	24	4 times as many
Planet Stickers	24				

You know the number in each group and that the groups are equal. So you multiply.

24 × 4 = 96
Beth has 96 flower stickers.

Remember that drawing a picture can help you choose an operation.

Draw a picture to show what you know. Choose an operation and solve the problem.

1. Ty has his model car collection on shelves in his room. There are 9 shelves with 18 model cars on each shelf. How many model cars are on the shelves?

Topic 10

Division Meanings and Facts

1 How many strings are on the guitars used by Tejano musicians? You will find out in Lesson 10-2.

2 The same number of astronauts traveled on Apollo 11 and Apollo 12. How many astronauts traveled to the Moon on each space mission? You will find out in Lesson 10-3.

3

How much water might you use when you brush your teeth? You will find out in Lesson 10-5.

4

Each paddleboat can seat two people. Each person on shore has two friends. How many paddleboats will the entire group need? You will find out in Lesson 10-9.

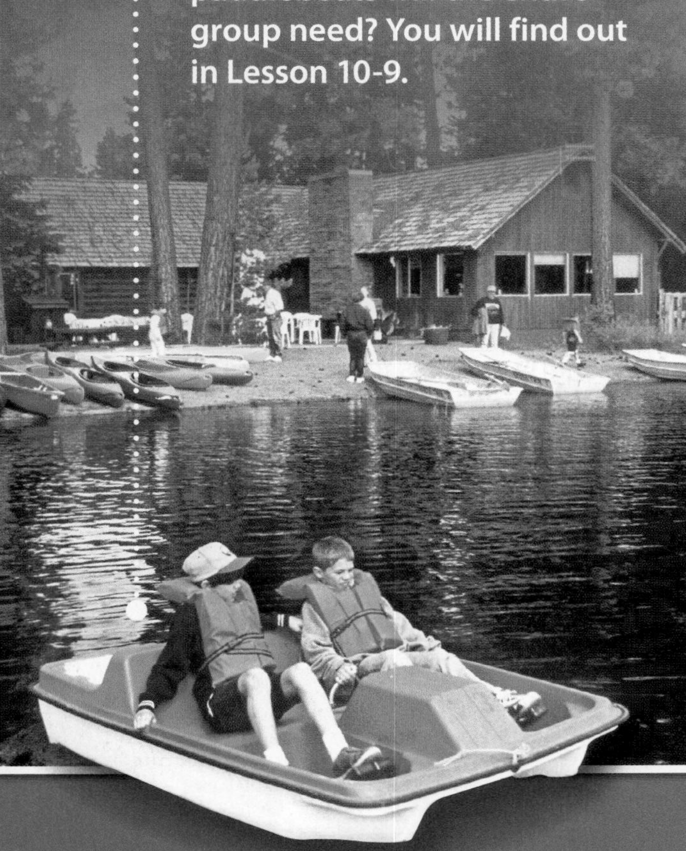

Review What You Know!

Vocabulary

Choose the best term from the box.

- array
- difference
- factor
- product

1. The answer in multiplication is the ___?___.

2. In $3 \times 5 = 15$, 5 is a ___?___.

3. When objects are placed in equal rows they form an ___?___.

Subtraction

Subtract.

4. $21 - 7$	**5.** $15 - 5$	**6.** $27 - 9$
$14 - 7$	$10 - 5$	$18 - 9$
$7 - 7$	$5 - 5$	$9 - 9$

Multiplication Facts

7. 5×4	**8.** 7×3	**9.** 3×8
10. 9×2	**11.** 6×5	**12.** 4×7
13. 6×7	**14.** 8×4	**15.** 5×9

Equal Groups

16. **Writing to Explain** The picture has 9 counters. Describe why this picture doesn't show equal groups. Then show how to change the drawing so it does show equal groups.

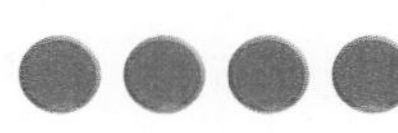

Lesson

10-1

TEKS 3.4C: Use models to solve division problems and use number sentences to record the solutions.

Division as Sharing

Hands-On
counters

How many are in each group?

Three friends have 12 toys to share equally. How many toys will each person get?

Think of putting 12 toys into 3 equal groups.

Division is an operation that is used to find how many equal groups or how many are in each group.

Guided Practice*

Do you know HOW?

Use counters or draw a picture to solve.

1. 15 bananas, 3 boxes
How many bananas in each box?

2. 16 plants, 4 pots
How many plants in each pot?

Do you UNDERSTAND?

3. Copy and complete.

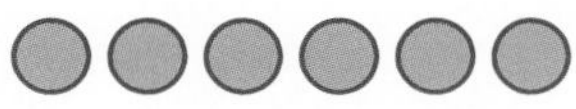

$18 \div 3 = \square$

4. Can 12 grapes be shared equally among 5 children? Explain.

Independent Practice

Use counters or draw a picture to solve.

5. 18 marbles, 6 sacks
How many marbles in each sack?

6. 36 stickers, 4 people
How many stickers for each person?

7. 16 crayons, 2 people
How many crayons for each person?

8. 12 pictures, 4 pages
How many pictures on each page?

9. 24 bottles, 4 cases
How many bottles in each case?

10. 27 CDs, 9 packages
How many CDs in each package?

Animated Glossary, eTools
www.pearsonsuccessnet.com

*For another example, see Set A on page 232.

What You Think

Put one at a time in each group.

When all the toys are grouped, there will be 4 in each group.

What You Write

You can write a division sentence to find the number in each group.

$12 \div 3 = 4$

12 — Total
3 — Number of equal groups
4 — Number in each group

Each person will get 4 toys.

Complete each division sentence.

11. 12

?	?

$12 \div 2 =$ ▢

12. 16

?	?	?	?	?	?	?	?

$16 \div 8 =$ ▢

TAKS Problem Solving

13. Writing to Explain James is putting 18 pens into equal groups. He says that there will be more pens in each of 2 equal groups than in each of 3 equal groups. Is he correct? Explain.

14. Joy has 12 shells. She gives 2 to her mom. Then she and her sister share the rest equally. How many shells does Joy get? How many shells does her sister get?

15. Max has the stickers shown. He wants to put an equal number of stickers on each of 2 posters. Which number sentence shows how many stickers Max should put on each poster?

A $7 + 2 = 9$

B $7 \times 2 = 14$

C $14 \div 7 = 2$

D $14 \div 2 = 7$

Lesson
10-2

TEKS 3.4C: Use models to solve division problems and use number sentences to record the solutions.

Division as Repeated Subtraction

Hands-On
counters

How many equal groups?

June has 10 strawberries to serve to her guests. If each guest eats 2 strawberries, how many guests can June serve?

Guided Practice*

Do you know HOW?

Use counters or draw a picture to solve.

1. 16 gloves
   2 gloves in each pair
   How many pairs?

2. 15 tennis balls
   3 balls in each can
   How many cans?

Do you UNDERSTAND?

3. Suppose June had 12 strawberries and each guest ate 2 strawberries. How many guests could she serve? Use counters or draw a picture to solve.

4. **Number Sense** Show how you can use repeated subtraction to find how many groups of 4 there are in 20. Then write the division sentence for the problem.

Independent Practice

Use counters or draw a picture to solve.

5. 12 wheels
   4 wheels on each wagon
   How many wagons?

6. 30 markers
   5 markers in each package
   How many packages?

7. 8 apples
   4 apples in each bag
   How many bags?

8. 18 pencils
   2 pencils on each desk
   How many desks?

*For another example, see Set A on page 232.

One Way

You can use repeated subtraction to find how many groups of 2 are in 10.

$10 - 2 = 8$
$8 - 2 = 6$
$6 - 2 = 4$
$4 - 2 = 2$
$2 - 2 = 0$

You can subtract 2, five times. There are five groups of 2 in 10.

There are no strawberries left.

June can serve 5 guests.

Another Way

You can write a division sentence to find the number of groups.

Write: $10 \div 2 = 5$

Read: Ten divided by 2 equals 5.

June can serve 5 guests.

TAKS Problem Solving

9. **Number Sense** Raymond has 16 model planes that he wants to display. Will he need more shelves if he puts 8 on a shelf or 4 on a shelf? Explain.

For **10–12**, match each problem to a picture or a repeated subtraction. Then write the division sentence to solve.

10. 24 books
6 in a box
How many boxes?

11. 24 books
3 in a box
How many boxes?

12. 24 books
8 in a box
How many boxes?

a

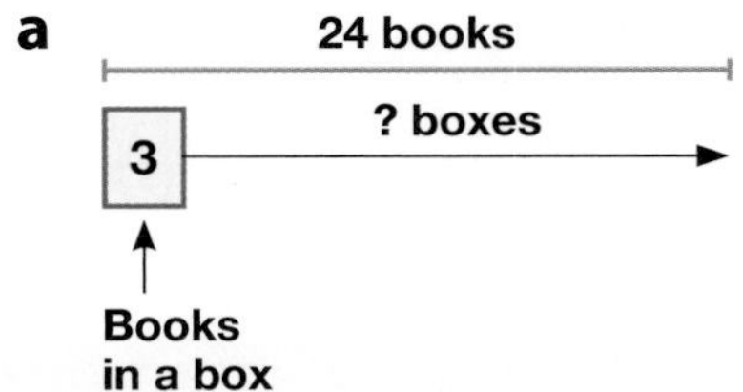

b $24 - 8 = 16$
$16 - 8 = 8$
$8 - 8 = 0$

c

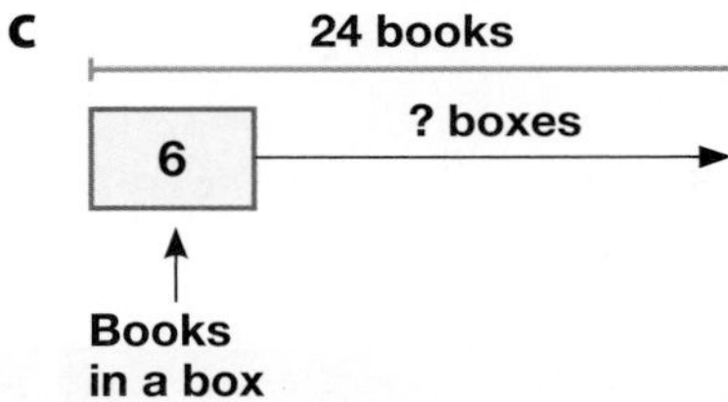

13. How many strings in all are used to make 4 twelve-string guitars?

14. Toni has 6 tulips and 6 daisies. She wants to put 4 flowers in each vase. Which number sentence shows how many vases she needs?

A $12 + 4 = 16$

B $12 - 4 = 8$

C $6 \times 4 = 24$

D $12 \div 4 = 3$

Lesson
10-3

TEKS 3.4C: Use models to solve division problems and use number sentences to record the solutions.

Writing Division Stories

What is the main idea of a division story?

Mrs. White asked her students to write a division story for the number sentence 15 ÷ 3 = ☐. Mike and Kia decided to write stories about putting roses in vases.

Guided Practice*

Do you know HOW?

Write a division story for each number sentence. Then use counters or draw a picture to solve.

1. 8 ÷ 4 = ☐
2. 10 ÷ 2 = ☐
3. 20 ÷ 5 = ☐
4. 14 ÷ 7 = ☐

Do you UNDERSTAND?

5. How are Mike's and Kia's stories alike? How are they different?
6. **Number Sense** When you write a division story, what information do you need to include?

Independent Practice

Write a division story for each number sentence. Then use counters or draw a picture to solve.

7. 18 ÷ 3 = ☐
8. 25 ÷ 5 = ☐
9. 16 ÷ 4 = ☐
10. 30 ÷ 6 = ☐

11. **Number Sense** Choose two of the stories you wrote for the exercises above. For each, tell whether you found the number in each group or the number of equal groups.

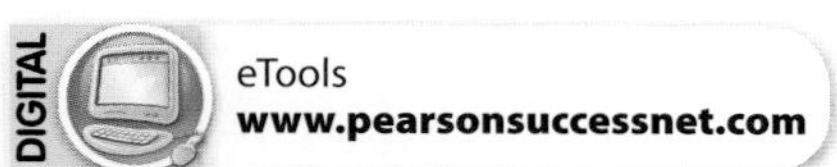

*For another example, see Set B on page 232.

Mike's Story

I have 15 roses. I want an equal number of roses in each of 3 vases. How many roses should I put in each vase?

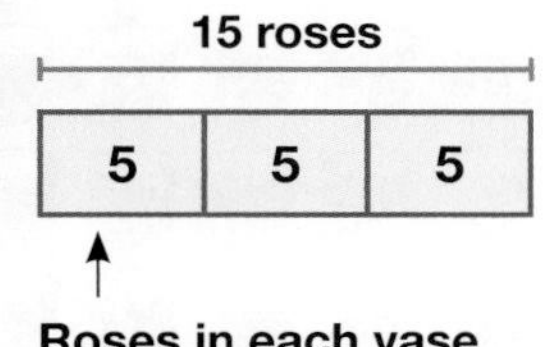

$15 \div 3 = 5$

I should put 5 roses in each vase.

Kia's Story

I have 15 roses to put into vases. I want to put 3 roses into each vase. How many vases will I need?

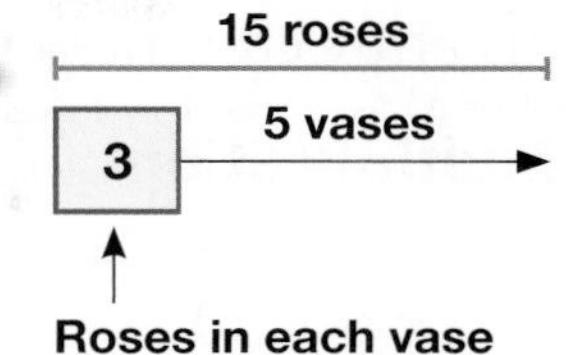

$15 \div 3 = 5$

I will need 5 vases.

TAKS Problem Solving

The table shows the number of players needed for each kind of sports team. Use the table for **12–14**.

There are 36 third graders at sports camp who want to play on different teams.

Data

Sports Team	Number
Baseball	9 players
Basketball	5 players
Tennis	2 players

12. If everyone wants to play baseball, how many teams will there be?

13. **Writing to Explain** Could everyone play basketball at the same time? Why or why not?

14. Twenty of the third graders went swimming. The rest of them played tennis. How many tennis teams were there?

15. In all, six astronauts traveled in space on Apollo 11 and Apollo 12. How many astronauts were on each mission?

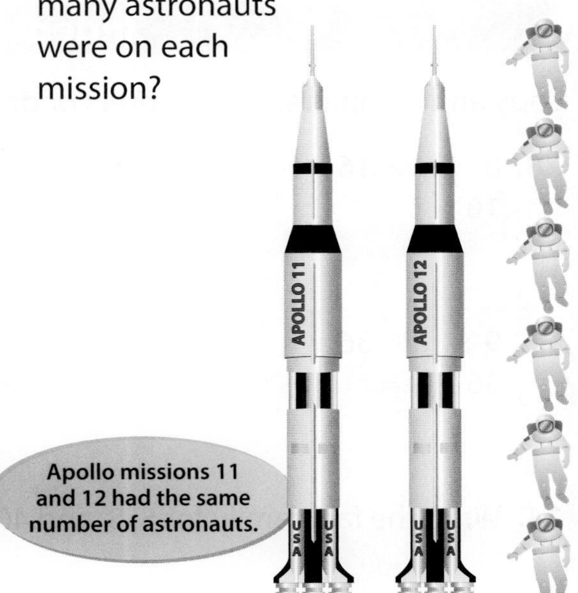

16. Carmen rides her bike to school from 3 to 5 times a week. Which is a reasonable number of times Carmen will ride her bike in 4 weeks?

A More than 28

B From 12 to 20

C From 14 to 28

D Fewer than 12

Lesson

10-4

TEKS 3.6C: Identify patterns in related multiplication and division sentences (fact families) such as 2 × 3 = 6, 3 × 2 = 6, 6 ÷ 2 = 3, 6 ÷ 3 = 2.

Relating Multiplication and Division

counters

How can multiplication facts help you divide?

This array can show multiplication and division.

Multiplication	Division
5 rows of 6 drums	30 drums in 5 equal rows
$5 \times 6 = 30$	$30 \div 5 = 6$
30 drums	6 drums in each row

Guided Practice*

Do you know HOW?

Copy and complete. Use counters or draw a picture to help.

1. $4 \times \square = 12$
$12 \div 4 = \square$

2. $6 \times \square = 36$
$36 \div 6 = \square$

3. $2 \times \square = 18$
$18 \div 2 = \square$

4. $8 \times \square = 32$
$32 \div 8 = \square$

Do you UNDERSTAND?

5. Number Sense What multiplication fact can help you find $54 \div 6$?

6. Look at the fact family for 5, 6, and 30. What do you notice about the products and the dividends?

7. Writing to Explain Is $4 \times 6 = 24$ part of the fact family for 3, 8, and 24? Explain.

Independent Practice

Copy and complete. Use counters or draw a picture to help.

8. $8 \times \square = 16$
$16 \div 8 = \square$

9. $5 \times \square = 35$
$35 \div 5 = \square$

10. $6 \times \square = 48$
$48 \div 6 = \square$

11. $9 \times \square = 36$
$36 \div 9 = \square$

12. $3 \times \square = 27$
$27 \div 3 = \square$

13. $8 \times \square = 56$
$56 \div 8 = \square$

14. Write the fact family for 5, 8, and 40.

*For another example, see Set C on page 232.

A fact family shows how multiplication and division are related.

Fact family for 5, 6, and 30:

$5 \times 6 = 30$	$30 \div 5 = 6$
$6 \times 5 = 30$	$30 \div 6 = 5$

dividend divisor quotient

The dividend is the number of objects to be divided.

The divisor is the number by which another number is divided.

The quotient is the answer to a division problem.

TAKS Problem Solving

15. Writing to Explain Why does the fact family for $2 \times 2 = 4$ have only two facts?

For **16** and **17**, write the rest of the fact family for each array.

16.

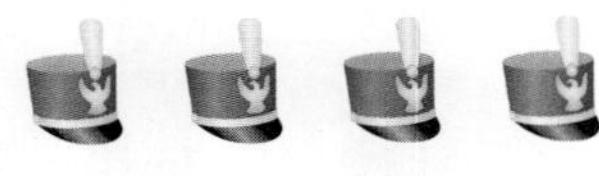

$3 \times 4 = 12$
$12 \div 3 = 4$

17.

$4 \times 5 = 20$
$20 \div 4 = 5$

18. There are 28 cheerleaders in a parade. They form lines with 4 cheerleaders in each line. How many lines are there?

19. There are 3 lines of clowns in a parade. Each line has 8 clowns in it. Near the end of the parade, 3 of the clowns leave. How many clowns are still in the parade?

20. Number Sense Draw an array. Then write a fact family to describe your array.

21. What number makes this number sentence true?

$\square \div 3 = 9$

A 3 **B** 12 **C** 18 **D** 27

Lesson 10-5

TEKS 3.6C: Identify patterns in related multiplication and division sentences (fact families) such as $2 \times 3 = 6$, $3 \times 2 = 6$, $6 \div 2 = 3$, $6 \div 3 = 2$.

Fact Families with 2, 3, 4, and 5

What multiplication fact can you use?

Dee has 14 noisemakers. She puts the same number on each of 2 tables. How many will be on each table?

What You Think	What You Write
2 times what number is 14? $2 \times 7 = 14$	$14 \div 2 = 7$ There will be 7 noisemakers on each table.

Another Example What is another way to write a division problem?

Dee is making balloon animals for her party. She has 24 balloons. It takes 4 balloons to make each animal. How many balloon animals can she make?

4 times what number is 24?
$4 \times 6 = 24$

There are two ways to write a division problem.

$24 \div 4 = 6$

24 ← dividend, 4 ← divisor, 6 ← quotient

$$4\overline{)24}$$

6 ← quotient; divisor → 4; 24 ← dividend

Dee can make 6 balloon animals.

Explain It

1. Copy and complete the fact family:

$4 \times 6 = 24$
$24 \div 4 = 6$

2. How do you know what multiplication fact to use to find $24 \div 4$?

3. **Number Sense** Dee says she could make more than 10 balloon animals if she was able to make an animal using only 3 balloons. Do you agree? Why or why not?

Dee has 40 stickers. She puts 5 stickers on each bag. How many bags can she decorate?

What You Think	What You Write
5 times what number is 40? $5 \times 8 = 40$	$40 \div 5 = 8$ Dee can decorate 8 bags.

Dee wants to put 15 cups in 3 rows on the table. How many cups will she put in each row?

What You Think	What You Write
3 times what number is 15? $3 \times 5 = 15$	$15 \div 3 = 5$ Dee will put 5 cups in each row.

Guided Practice*

Do you know HOW?

In **1–3**, copy and complete each fact family.

1. $2 \times 7 = 14$
$14 \div 2 = 7$

2. $5 \times 8 = 40$
$40 \div 5 = 8$

3. $3 \times 5 = 15$
$15 \div 3 = 5$

In **4–9**, find each quotient.

4. $27 \div 3$ **5.** $16 \div 4$ **6.** $40 \div 4$

7. $2\overline{)18}$ **8.** $4\overline{)28}$ **9.** $5\overline{)30}$

Do you UNDERSTAND?

10. Identify the dividend, divisor and quotient in Exercise 9.

11. **Number Sense** How can you tell without dividing that $15 \div 3$ will be greater than $15 \div 5$?

12. How can you use multiplication to help you find 36 divided by 4?

Independent Practice

Find each quotient.

13. $10 \div 2$ **14.** $25 \div 5$ **15.** $21 \div 3$ **16.** $18 \div 3$

17. $2\overline{)16}$ **18.** $5\overline{)50}$ **19.** $3\overline{)24}$ **20.** $4\overline{)36}$

*For another example, see Set C on page 232.

Independent Practice

Find each quotient.

21. $12 \div 4$

22. $45 \div 5$

23. $4\overline{)16}$

24. $5\overline{)40}$

25. Find 12 divided by 2.

26. Divide 20 by 5.

27. Find 32 divided by 4.

Algebra Find each missing number.

28. $2 \times \square = 8$

29. $15 \div 3 = \square$

30. $\square \div 3 = 2$

31. $7 \times 4 = \square$

32. $\square \times 5 = 40$

33. $32 \div \square = 8$

Number Sense Write < or > to compare.

34. $4 \times 2 \bigcirc 4 \div 2$

35. $2 \times 3 \bigcirc 6 \div 2$

36. $5 + 8 \bigcirc 5 \times 8$

TAKS Problem Solving

37. Writing to Explain Joey says, "I can't solve $8 \div 2$ by using the fact $2 \times 8 = 16$." Do you agree or disagree? Explain.

38. Anna wants to make one array with 2 rows of 8 tiles and another array with 3 rows of 5 tiles. How many tiles does she need all together?

39. You might use 2 gallons of water when you brush your teeth. There are 16 cups in a gallon. About how many cups of water might you use when brushing your teeth?

40. Bob has 15 pennies and 3 dimes. Miko has the same amount of money, but she has only nickels. How many nickels does Miko have?

41. Which number sentence is in the same fact family as $3 \times 6 = 18$?

A $3 \times 3 = 9$

B $2 \times 9 = 18$

C $6 \div 3 = 2$

D $18 \div 6 = 3$

42. Mike bought 3 bags of marbles with 5 marbles in each bag. He gave 4 marbles to Marsha. How many marbles did Mike have left?

F 11

G 15

H 19

J 21

43. Sammy wants to buy a remote control car for \$49 and 3 small cars for \$5 each. What will the total cost be?

Algebra Connections

Division and Number Sentences

Remember that the two sides of a number sentence can be equal or unequal. A symbol >, <, or = tells how the sides compare. Estimation or reasoning can help you tell if one side is greater without doing any computations.

> means *is greater than*
< means *is less than*
= means *is equal to*

Example: 10 ÷ 2 ◯ 8 ÷ 2

Each whole is being divided into 2 equal groups. The greater whole will have a greater number of items in each group.

Since 10 is greater than 8, the quotient on the left side is greater. Write the symbol >.

10 ÷ 2 (>) 8 ÷ 2

Copy and complete by writing >, <, or =.

1. 20 ÷ 5 ◯ 25 ÷ 5
2. 12 ÷ 3 ◯ 12 ÷ 4
3. 3 × 18 ◯ 3 × 21
4. 24 ÷ 2 ◯ 8
5. 19 + 19 ◯ 2 × 19
6. 100 ◯ 5 × 30
7. 1 × 53 ◯ 1 × 43
8. 9 ◯ 36 ÷ 4
9. 9 ÷ 3 ◯ 18 ÷ 3
10. 16 ÷ 2 ◯ 1 + 9
11. 35 ÷ 5 ◯ 2 + 3
12. 24 ÷ 4 ◯ 24 ÷ 2

In **13** and **14**, copy and complete the number sentence below each problem. Use it to help explain your answer.

13. Mara and Bobby each have 40 pages to read. Mara will read 4 pages each day. Bobby will read 5 pages each day. Who needs more days to read 40 pages?

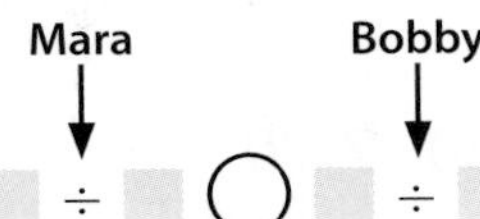

14. Tim had a board that was 12 feet long. He cut the board into 3 equal pieces. Ellen had a board that was 18 feet long. She cut the board into 3 equal pieces. Who had the longer pieces?

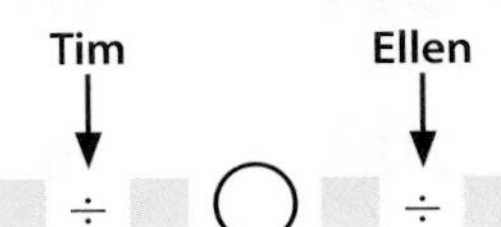

15. Write a Problem Write a real-world problem described by 16 ÷ 2 > 14 ÷ 2.

Lesson
10-6

TEKS 3.6C: Identify patterns in related multiplication and division sentences (fact families) such as
$2 \times 3 = 6$,
$3 \times 2 = 6$,
$6 \div 2 = 3$,
$6 \div 3 = 2$.

Fact Families with 6 and 7

How do you divide with 6 and 7?

There are 48 dogs entered in a dog show. The judge wants 6 dogs in each group. How many groups will there be?

Choose an Operation Divide to find how many groups.

Guided Practice*

Do you know HOW?

1. Copy and complete the fact family.

$8 \times 6 = 48$
$48 \div 6 = 8$

In **2–10**, find each quotient.

2. $12 \div 6$ **3.** $30 \div 6$ **4.** $42 \div 6$

5. $14 \div 7$ **6.** $42 \div 7$ **7.** $63 \div 7$

8. $6\overline{)24}$ **9.** $6\overline{)54}$ **10.** $6\overline{)60}$

Do you UNDERSTAND?

11. Number Sense How can you tell without dividing that $42 \div 6$ will be greater than $42 \div 7$?

12. Write the fact family for 7, 8, and 56.

13. There are 54 children in 6 ballet classes. Each class is the same size. How many children are in each class?

Independent Practice

Find each quotient.

14. $18 \div 6$ **15.** $36 \div 4$ **16.** $21 \div 7$ **17.** $36 \div 6$ **18.** $27 \div 3$

19. $6\overline{)48}$ **20.** $2\overline{)24}$ **21.** $7\overline{)56}$ **22.** $5\overline{)35}$ **23.** $6\overline{)36}$

24. $6\overline{)72}$ **25.** $7\overline{)84}$ **26.** $6\overline{)66}$ **27.** $7\overline{)77}$ **28.** $7\overline{)70}$

29. Find 49 divided by 7. **30.** Divide 72 by 6. **31.** Find 56 divided by 7.

32. Find 60 divided by 6. **33.** Divide 21 by 7. **34.** Find 48 divided by 6.

*For another example, see Set C on page 232.

Find 48 ÷ 6.

What You Think	What You Write
What number times 6 is 48? $8 \times 6 = 48$	$48 \div 6 = 8$ There will be 8 groups.

Another dog was entered. There will now be 7 dogs in each group. How many groups will there be now?

Find 49 ÷ 7.

What You Think	What You Write
What number times 7 is 49? $7 \times 7 = 49$	$49 \div 7 = 7$ There will be 7 groups.

TAKS Problem Solving

Use the pictures below for **35–38**.

35. Rita needs 15 gold beads for an art project.

a How many packages of beads does she need?

b How much do the beads cost?

36. Eve bought 2 packages of red beads and 2 packages of blue beads.

a How many beads did she buy?

b How much did she spend?

37. **Writing to Explain** Guy bought 28 red beads and 18 blue beads. How many packages did he buy? Explain how you solved the problem.

38. **Number Sense** Andy bought exactly 35 beads. Which color beads could he have bought? Explain your thinking.

39. There are 6 rafts on the river. Each raft holds 8 people. Which number sentence is in the fact family for these numbers?

A 48 – 6 = 42 **C** 48 + 6 = 54

B 48 ÷ 6 = 8 **D** 48 – 8 = 40

40. The school auditorium has 182 seats. People are sitting in 56 of the seats. Which is the best estimate of the number of seats that do **NOT** have people sitting in them?

F 20 **G** 120 **H** 240 **J** 250

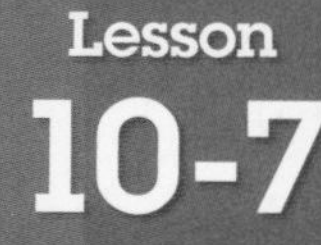

TEKS 3.6C: Identify patterns in related multiplication and division sentences (fact families) such as
$2 \times 3 = 6$,
$3 \times 2 = 6$,
$6 \div 2 = 3$,
$6 \div 3 = 2$.

Fact Families with 8 and 9

What multiplication fact can you use?

John has 56 straws. How many spiders can he make?

Find $56 \div 8$.

What number times 8 is 56?

$7 \times 8 = 56$

John can make 7 spiders.

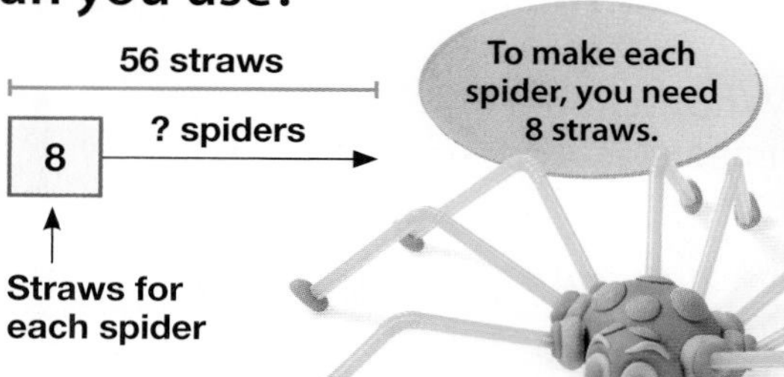

Guided Practice*

Do you know HOW?

Find each quotient.

1. $16 \div 8$ **2.** $64 \div 8$ **3.** $36 \div 9$

4. $27 \div 9$ **5.** $45 \div 9$ **6.** $63 \div 9$

7. $8\overline{)24}$ **8.** $8\overline{)72}$ **9.** $8\overline{)80}$

Do you UNDERSTAND?

10. What multiplication fact could you use to find $18 \div 9$?

11. **Number Sense** Carla and Jeff each use 72 straws. Carla makes animals with 9 legs. Jeff makes animals with 8 legs. Who makes more animals? Explain.

Independent Practice

Find each quotient.

12. $32 \div 8$ **13.** $28 \div 7$ **14.** $18 \div 9$ **15.** $48 \div 8$ **16.** $81 \div 9$

17. $5\overline{)45}$ **18.** $9\overline{)54}$ **19.** $7\overline{)56}$ **20.** $4\overline{)28}$ **21.** $8\overline{)56}$

22. $9\overline{)27}$ **23.** $9\overline{)90}$ **24.** $8\overline{)16}$ **25.** $8\overline{)64}$ **26.** $8\overline{)48}$

27. Find 72 divided by 9. **28.** Divide 40 by 8. **29.** Find 56 divided by 8.

30. Find 81 divided by 9. **31.** Divide 45 by 9. **32.** Find 64 divided by 8.

33. Write fact families for the numbers in **30** and **31**. How are the fact families different?

*For another example, see Set C on page 232.

Luz made 9 animals. She used 54 straws. She used the same number of straws for each animal. How many straws did Luz use for each animal?

Find $54 \div 9$.

54 straws

?	?	?	?	?	?	?	?	?

Number of straws for one animal

What You Think	What You Write
9 times what number is 54?	$54 \div 9 = 6$
$9 \times 6 = 54$	Luz used 6 straws for each animal.

TAKS Problem Solving

Algebra Write $<$ or $>$ to compare.

34. $36 \div 9 \bigcirc 9$

35. $65 \bigcirc 8 \times 8$

36. $63 \div 9 \bigcirc 8$

Use the ticket prices at the right for **37–40**.

37. The clerk at the playhouse sold \$64 worth of youth tickets. How many youth tickets did the clerk sell?

38. Melinda bought 2 children's tickets and 2 adult tickets. How much did she spend?

Data

Playhouse Ticket Prices

Type of Ticket	Price of Ticket
Child	\$4
Youth	\$8
Adult	\$9

39. Reasoning The clerk at the playhouse sold \$72 worth of adult tickets. Ten people bought adult tickets online. Did more people buy tickets at the playhouse or online? Tell how you know.

40. Writing to Explain Mr. Stern bought 4 children's tickets and 2 adult tickets. How much more did he spend for the adult tickets than the children's tickets? Explain.

41. Which number sentence is **NOT** in the same fact family as the others?

A $8 \times 4 = 32$

B $32 \div 8 = 4$

C $2 \times 4 = 8$

D $4 \times 8 = 32$

42. Baby pigs are born with 8 small teeth called "needle teeth." How many needle teeth do 5 baby pigs have all together?

Lesson

10-8

TEKS 3.6C: Identify patterns in related multiplication and division sentences (fact families) such as $2 \times 3 = 6$, $3 \times 2 = 6$, $6 \div 2 = 3$, $6 \div 3 = 2$.

Dividing with 0 and 1

How do you divide with 1 or 0?

Dividing by 1

Find $3 \div 1$

What number times 1 is 3?

$3 \times 1 = 3$

So, $3 \div 1 = 3$.

Rule: Any number divided by 1 is itself.

Guided Practice*

Do you know HOW?

Find each quotient.

1. $8 \div 8$ **2.** $2 \div 1$ **3.** $0 \div 5$

4. $1\overline{)8}$ **5.** $6\overline{)6}$ **6.** $10\overline{)0}$

Do you UNDERSTAND?

7. How can you tell without dividing that $375 \div 375 = 1$?

8. Writing to Explain Describe how you can find $0 \div 267$, without dividing.

Independent Practice

Find each quotient.

9. $7 \div 7$ **10.** $0 \div 4$ **11.** $10 \div 1$ **12.** $0 \div 6$ **13.** $10 \div 10$

14. $1\overline{)4}$ **15.** $1\overline{)7}$ **16.** $8\overline{)0}$ **17.** $5\overline{)5}$ **18.** $1\overline{)5}$

19. $2\overline{)14}$ **20.** $5\overline{)25}$ **21.** $7\overline{)56}$ **22.** $4\overline{)24}$ **23.** $9\overline{)81}$

24. $6\overline{)36}$ **25.** $7\overline{)49}$ **26.** $8\overline{)64}$ **27.** $9\overline{)90}$ **28.** $5\overline{)20}$

29. $7\overline{)56}$ **30.** $8\overline{)48}$ **31.** $7\overline{)42}$ **32.** $7\overline{)70}$ **33.** $4\overline{)32}$

34. Divide 0 by 9. **35.** Find 9 divided by 9. **36.** Find 6 divided by 1.

37. Divide 3 by 3. **38.** Find 0 divided by 8. **39.** Find 7 divided by 1.

*For another example, see Set D on page 233.

1 as a Quotient

Find $3 \div 3$.

Think: 3 times what number equals 3?

$3 \times 1 = 3$

So, $3 \div 3 = 1$.

Rule: Any number (except 0) divided by itself is 1.

Dividing 0 by a Number

Find $0 \div 3$.

Think: 3 times what number equals 0?

$3 \times 0 = 0$

So, $0 \div 3 = 0$.

Rule: 0 divided by any number (except 0) is 0.

Dividing by 0

Find $3 \div 0$.

Think: 0 times what number equals 3?

There is no such number.

So, $3 \div 0$ can't be done.

Rule: You cannot divide by 0.

TAKS Problem Solving

Algebra In **40–43**, copy and complete.

40. $3 \div 3 \bigcirc 3 \times 0$

41. $17 \div 17 \bigcirc 1 \div 1$

42. $0 \div 6 \bigcirc 0 \div 1$

43. $6 \times 1 \bigcirc 6 \div 1$

Use the sign at the right for **44–47**.

44. Paul hiked one trail 3 times for a total distance of 12 miles. Which trail did he hike?

45. Reasoning Addie hiked 3 different trails for a total distance of 11 miles. Which trails did she hike?

46. Yoko hiked the blue trail once and the green trail twice. How many miles did she hike on the green trail?

47. Writing to Explain Marty hiked one trail 4 times. He hiked more than 10 miles but less than 16 miles. Which trail did he hike? Explain.

48. Which number will make the number sentence below true?

$54 \div \square = 9$

A 5

B 6

C 7

D 8

49. Which number makes the number sentence below true?

$\square \times 6 = 42$

F 48

G 36

H 6

J 7

TEKS 3.6C: Identify patterns in related multiplication and division sentences (fact families) such as $2 \times 3 = 6$, $3 \times 2 = 6$, $6 \div 2 = 3$, $6 \div 3 = 2$.

Division Patterns

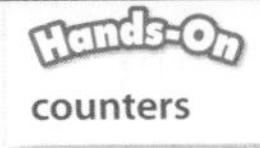

counters

What are some division patterns for 10 and 11?

Dan is filling baskets with apples and oranges. How many baskets will he use for 90 apples and 99 oranges?

Number of Baskets	1	2	3	4	5	6	7	8	9	10	11
Number of Apples	10	20	30	40	50	60	70	80	90	100	110
Number of Oranges	11	22	33	44	55	66	77	88	99	110	121

Guided Practice*

Do you know HOW?

Find each quotient. You may use a multiplication table, counters, or a picture to help.

1. $70 \div 10$
2. $44 \div 11$
3. $121 \div 11$
4. $110 \div 10$

Do you UNDERSTAND?

5. **Number Sense** Write the fact family for 8, 11, and 88.
6. Make a drawing to show how you can find $44 \div 11$.

Independent Practice

For **7–19**, find each quotient. You may use a multiplication table, counters, or a picture to help.

7. $40 \div 10$
8. $77 \div 11$
9. $120 \div 10$
10. $22 \div 11$
11. $100 \div 10$
12. $8\overline{)24}$
13. $6\overline{)36}$
14. $7\overline{)28}$
15. $9\overline{)63}$
16. $6\overline{)42}$
17. Divide 99 by 9.
18. Find 11 divided by 11.
19. Find 30 divided by 10.

Number Sense For **20–22**, use patterns to find each quotient.

20. $10 \div 5 = \square$
    $20 \div 10 = \square$
21. $40 \div 5 = \square$
    $80 \div 10 = \square$
22. $30 \div 5 = \square$
    $60 \div 10 = \square$

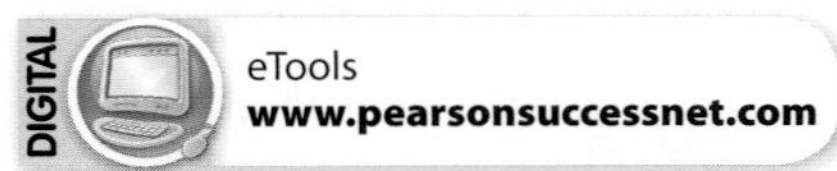

*For another example, see Set E on page 233.

Dividing by 10

$50 \div 10 = 5$

$70 \div 10 = 7$

$90 \div 10 = 9$

$110 \div 10 = 11$

The quotient is the same as the dividend without its ending zero.

Dividing by 11

$33 \div 11 = 3$

$55 \div 11 = 5$

$77 \div 11 = 7$

$99 \div 11 = 9$

The quotient is the same as each of the digits in the dividend.

$90 \div 10 = 9$

$99 \div 11 = 9$

Dan will need 9 baskets for 90 apples and 99 oranges.

TAKS Problem Solving

23. Look back at **20–22**. What do you notice about the dividends, divisors, and quotients in each pair of number sentences?

24. How many paddleboats are needed for 18 people if each paddleboat is full?

25. For a field trip, 88 students were divided into 8 equal groups. How many students were in each group?

26. A photo album has 10 pages with 4 photos on each page. Two other pages have 3 photos each. How many photos are there in all?

27. **Writing to Explain** Kyle exercised for 40 minutes each day for 5 days. Was his total exercise time more than or less than 4 hours? Explain.

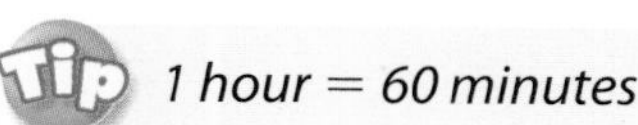

28. At the end of the day, the baker counted 12 rolls, 24 bagels, and 10 muffins that were not sold. How many rolls and bagels were not sold?

A 12 **C** 36

B 24 **D** 40

29. What fact family could you use to help you find $110 \div 11 = 10$?

Lesson

10-10

TEKS 3.14C: Select or develop an appropriate problem solving strategy, including drawing a picture, looking for a pattern, systematic guessing and checking, acting it out, making a table, working a simpler problem, or working backwards to solve a problem.

Problem Solving

Draw a Picture and Write a Number Sentence

Jeff is setting up the sand-painting booth at the school carnival. He put the sand from one bag of sand into 5 buckets. If each bucket has the same amount of sand, how much sand is in each bucket?

45 pounds of sand

Another Example Are there other types of division situations?

Alison is setting up the prize booth. She has 48 prizes. She will put 8 prizes in each row. How many rows can she make?

Plan and Solve

Use a diagram to show what you know.

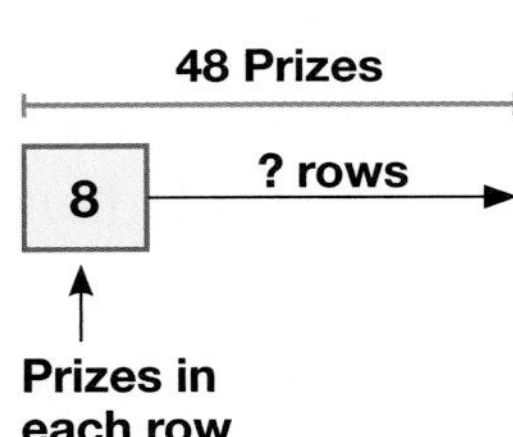

Answer

Write a number sentence

$48 \div 8 = 6$

Alison can make 6 rows.

Check

Make sure the answer is reasonable.

Use multiplication or repeated addition to check.

$6 \times 8 = 48$

or

$8 + 8 + 8 + 8 + 8 + 8 = 48$

Explain It

1. Explain how you can check the quotient in division by using either multiplication or addition.
2. **Number Sense** If Alison wants fewer than 6 rows of prizes, should she put more or fewer prizes in each row? Explain your thinking.

Plan and Solve

Use a diagram to show what you know.

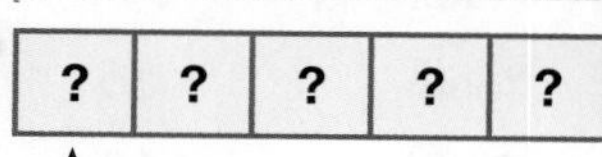

You know the total amount of sand and that there are 5 buckets. Divide to find how much sand is in each bucket.

Answer

Write a number sentence.

$45 \div 5 = 9$

There are 9 pounds of sand in each bucket.

Check

Make sure the answer is reasonable.

Use multiplication or repeated addition to check.

$5 \times 9 = 45$

or

$9 + 9 + 9 + 9 + 9 = 45$

Guided Practice*

Do you know HOW?

1. Larry and Pat made 18 posters. Each made the same number. How many did each make? Write a number sentence and solve.

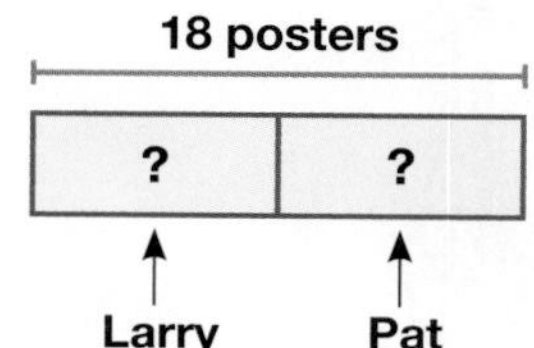

Do you UNDERSTAND?

2. What operation did you use for Problem 1? Tell why.

3. **Write a Problem** Write a real-world problem that you can solve by subtracting. Draw a diagram. Write a number sentence and solve.

Independent Practice

For **4** and **5**, draw a diagram to show what you know. Then write a number sentence and solve.

4. There are 8 cars on a Ferris wheel. Each car holds 3 people. How many people can ride the Ferris wheel at the same time?

5. There were 24 children in a relay race. There were 6 teams in all. How many children are on each team?

- What do I know?
- What am I asked to find?
- What diagram can I use to help understand the problem?
- Can I use addition, subtraction, multiplication, or division?
- Is all of my work correct?
- Did I answer the right question?
- Is my answer reasonable?

*For another example, see Set F on page 233.

Independent Practice

Use the table at the right for **6** and **7**. Solve each problem.

Cost of Tickets	
Adult	$10
Youth	$5
Child	$3

6. Mr. Niglio bought 2 youth tickets and 2 adult tickets. He gave the clerk a $50 bill. How much change did he get back?

7. **Number Sense** Dan, Sue, and Joe each bought a different kind of ticket. Dan spent the least. Sue spent twice as much as Joe. How much did Joe spend?

For **8** and **9**, use the animal pictures at the right. Write a number sentence and solve.

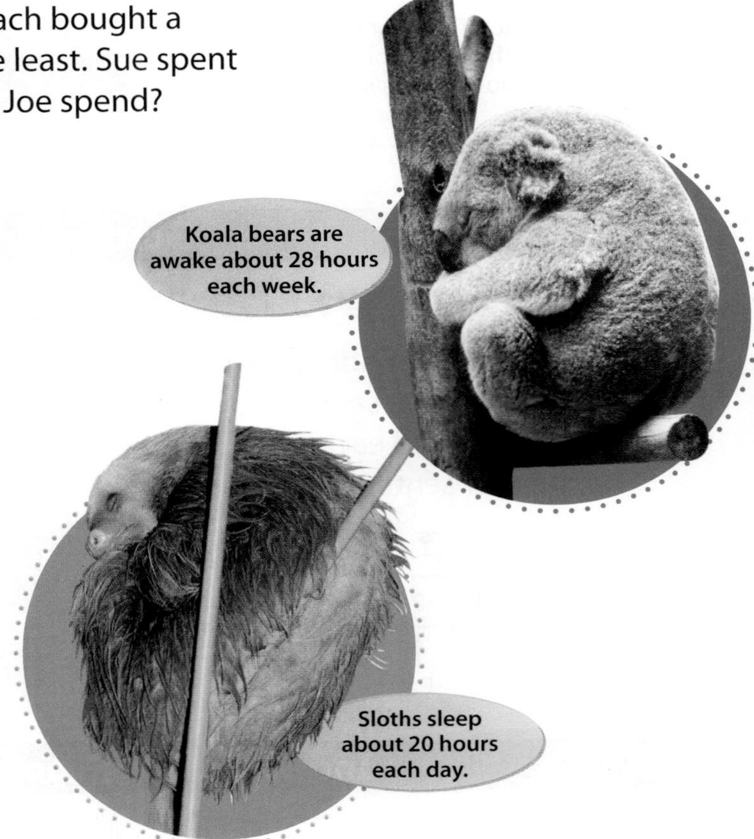

8. About how many hours is a sloth awake each day?

Tip *There are 24 hours in a day.*

9. About how many hours is a koala bear awake each day?

Tip *There are 7 days in a week.*

Think About the Process

10. Alma bought 2 bracelets for $6 at the craft fair. Each bracelet cost the same amount. Which number sentence shows how much each bracelet cost?

A $2 \times \$6 = \square$

B $2 + \$6 = \square$

C $\$6 - 2 = \square$

D $\$6 \div 2 = \square$

11. Tomas bought a book for $4, crayons for $2, and a pen for $1. He gave the clerk $10. Which number sentence shows how to find his change?

F $\$4 + \$2 + \$1 = \square$

G $\$4 \times \$2 \times \$1 = \square$

H $\$10 - \$6 = \square$

J $\$10 - (\$4 + \$2 + \$1) = \square$

Choosing an Operation and a Computation Method

The tallest building in Dallas is the Bank of America Plaza. It is 921 feet tall. The second tallest building is the Renaissance Tower. It is 886 feet tall. How much taller is the Bank of America Plaza than the Renaissance Tower?

Step 1 Draw a picture and choose an operation.

921 feet	
886	?

Subtract. Find 921 − 886.

Step 2 Choose the best computation method. Decide whether to use mental math, paper and pencil, or a calculator.

Since there is more than 1 regrouping, use a calculator.

Step 3 Solve.

Press: 921 [−] 886 [ENTER =]

Display: 35

The Bank of America Plaza is 35 feet taller than the Renaissance Tower.

Practice

For each problem, draw a picture and choose an operation. Then use the best computation method to solve.

1. The Bank of America Plaza has 72 floors. An elevator stopped at every 9th floor as it came down from the top floor to the bottom. How many times did it stop?

2. The JP Morgan Chase Tower in Houston could be divided into 3 sections with 25 floors in each section. How many floors does the tower have?

3. The Lincoln Plaza in Dallas is 579 feet tall. Fountain Place is 142 feet taller. How tall is Fountain Place?

4. In Houston, the JP Morgan Chase Tower is 1,002 feet tall. The Wells Fargo Plaza is 972 feet tall. How much taller is the JP Morgan Tower than the Wells Fargo Plaza?

TAKS Test Prep

1. Five friends have 15 pencils to share equally. Which number sentence shows how many pencils each friend will get? (10-1)

A $15 \div 5 = 3$

B $15 + 5 = 20$

C $15 \times 5 = 75$

D $15 - 5 = 10$

2. Which makes both number sentences true? (10-4)

$9 \times \square = 54$ and $54 \div 9 = \square$

F 8

G 7

H 6

J 5

3. Which number sentence is true? (10-8)

A $6 \div 6 = 0$

B $5 \div 1 = 1$

C $4 \div 0 = 4$

D $7 \div 1 = 7$

4. Nancy has 4 CDs. Each CD has 8 songs. Which number sentence is in this fact family? (10-5)

F $32 \div 4 = 8$

G $32 - 8 = 24$

H $8 - 4 = 4$

J $2 \times 4 = 8$

5. Mrs. Vincent bought 16 kiwis for her 4 children to share equally. How many kiwis will each child get? (10-1)

A 3

B 4

C 5

D 12

6. Mason has 12 pinecones. His birdfeeder design uses 3 pinecones. Which number sentence shows how many birdfeeders he can make? (10-2)

F $12 + 3 = 15$

G $12 \div 3 = 4$

H $12 - 3 = 9$

J $12 \times 3 = 36$

7. Nick has 60 chairs to put in rows. Each row needs 10 chairs. How many rows will he make? (10-9)

A 6

B 50

C 70

D 600

8. Mrs. Hendrix bought 45 pounds of modeling clay. She wants to divide it evenly between her 5 art classes. How many pounds of modeling clay will each class get? (10-5)

   F 40

   G 9

   H 8

   J 7

9. Beth bought a box of dog treats. The box had 48 treats. If Beth gives her dog 6 treats a day, how many days will the box of treats last? (10-6)

   A 6

   B 7

   C 8

   D 9

10. Which story could be solved with $20 \div 4$? (10-3)

   F Harold caught 20 fish. All but 4 of them were catfish. How many of the fish were something other than catfish?

   G Becky bought 20 bags of crystal beads. Each bag had 4 crystal beads. How many crystal beads did she buy?

   H Batina has made 20 doll dresses. If she makes 4 more, how many doll dresses will she have made?

   J Coach Sid has 20 baseballs. Each group needs 4 balls for the practice drill. How many groups can he form?

11. Gavin has 7 pages of his picture album filled. Each page has 6 pictures, for a total of 42 pictures. Which number sentence is **NOT** in the same fact family as the others? (10-6)

   A $7 \times 6 = 42$

   B $6 \times 7 = 42$

   C $42 \div 7 = 6$

   D $5 \times 7 = 35$

12. Neil has 30 nails and 6 boards. Which number sentence shows how many nails he can put in each board if he puts the same number in each? (10-10)

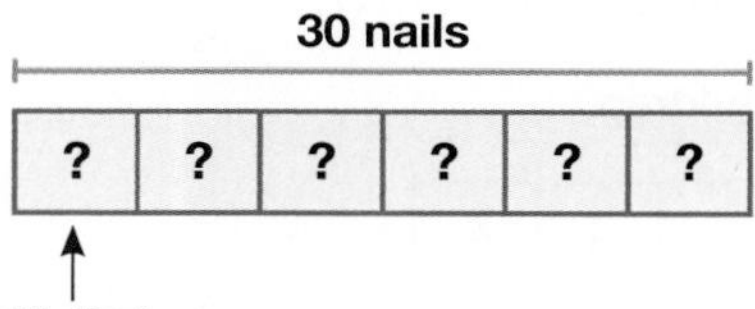

   F $30 + 6 = 36$

   G $30 - 6 = 24$

   H $30 \div 6 = 5$

   J $6 \times 30 = 180$

13. **Griddable Response** What number makes this number sentence true? (10-7)

   $\square \div 9 = 8$

14. **Griddable Response** Peg put 18 rocks into 2 equal piles. How many rocks were in each pile? (10-5)

Reteaching

Set A, pages 206–209

Don has 12 model cars. If 4 model cars fit in each case, how many cases does he need?

$12 - 4 = 8$ Use repeated subtraction to find how many groups.
$8 - 4 = 4$
$4 - 4 = 0$ You can subtract 4 three times.

$12 \div 4 = 3$ You can also divide to find the number of groups.

Don needs 3 cases.

Remember that you can also think of division as sharing equally.

Use counters or draw a picture to solve each problem.

1. 6 books
   3 books on each shelf
   How many shelves?
2. 18 students
   2 equal groups
   How many in each group?

Set B, pages 210–211

Write a division story for $20 \div 5$.

If 20 children form 5 equal teams, how many children are on each team?

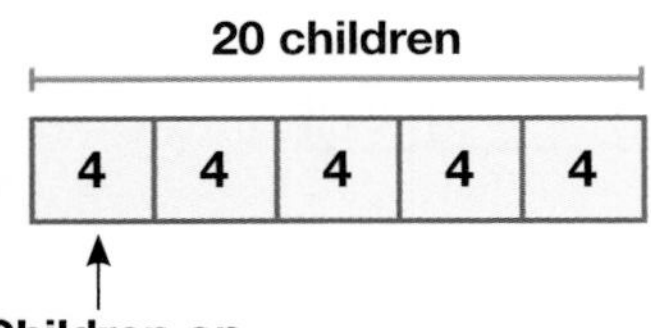

$20 \div 5 = 4$

There are 4 children on each team.

Remember that division stories can ask for the number in each group or the number of equal groups.

Write a division story for each number sentence. Draw a picture to help.

1. $15 \div 3 = \square$
2. $21 \div 7 = \square$
3. $24 \div 6 = \square$
4. $30 \div 5 = \square$

Set C, pages 212–216, 218–221

Hanna read 21 pages of a book in 3 days. If Hanna read the same number of pages each day, how many pages did she read each day?

Find $21 \div 3$.

What number times 3 equals 21?

$7 \times 3 = 21$

Write: $21 \div 3 = 7$

Hanna read 7 pages each day.

Remember to think of a related multiplication fact to solve a division problem.

Find each quotient.

1. $27 \div 3$
2. $63 \div 9$
3. $42 \div 7$
4. $35 \div 5$
5. $60 \div 6$
6. $8 \div 2$
7. $20 \div 4$
8. $48 \div 8$

Reteaching

Set D, pages 222–223

Find 8 ÷ 1, 8 ÷ 8, and 0 ÷ 8.

When any number is divided by 1, the quotient is that number. **8 ÷ 1 = 8**

When any number (except 0) is divided by itself, the quotient is 1. **8 ÷ 8 = 1**

When zero is divided by any number (except 0), the quotient is 0. **0 ÷ 8 = 0**

Remember that you cannot divide any number by 0.

Find each quotient.

1. 4 ÷ 1 **2.** 7 ÷ 7 **3.** 0 ÷ 5

4. $1\overline{)5}$ **5.** $3\overline{)0}$ **6.** $9\overline{)9}$

7. $6\overline{)6}$ **8.** $1\overline{)7}$ **9.** $4\overline{)0}$

Set E, pages 224–225

Find 55 ÷ 11.

When the dividend is a two-digit number, you can use a pattern to divide by 11s.

11 ÷ 11 = 1	44 ÷ 11 = 4	77 ÷ 11 = 7
22 ÷ 11 = 2	55 ÷ 11 = 5	88 ÷ 11 = 8
33 ÷ 11 = 3	66 ÷ 11 = 6	99 ÷ 11 = 9

The quotient is the same as each of the digits in the dividend.

55 ÷ 11= 5

Remember that all numbers divisible by 10 will end in a 0.

Divide. You may use a multiplication table, counters, or a picture.

1. 40 ÷ 10 **2.** 66 ÷ 11

3. $11\overline{)77}$ **4.** $10\overline{)30}$ **5.** $10\overline{)50}$

6. $11\overline{)22}$ **7.** $10\overline{)70}$ **8.** $11\overline{)44}$

Set F, pages 226–228

Carl has 48 balloons to tie in 6 equal groups. How many balloons will be in each group?

48 balloons

?	?	?	?	?	?

Balloons in each group

Draw a diagram to show what you know.

Write a number sentence.
48 ÷ 6 = 8
There will be 8 balloons in each group.

Remember to read carefully.

Draw a diagram and write a number sentence to solve.

1. A roller coaster has 10 cars that each hold 6 people. How many people can ride the roller coaster at one time?
2. There were 36 children on a field trip. The children formed 6 equal groups. How many children were in each group?

Topics 1–10

Spiral Review

Number and Operations

1. Which of the following is another way to write 2,508?

A 2,000 + 500 + 80

B Two thousand, five hundred eight

C 2,000 + 50 + 8

D Two thousand, five hundred eighty

2. Which number completes the division sentence shown below?

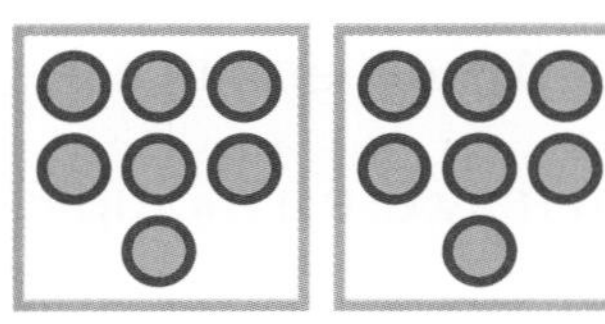

$14 \div 2 = \square$

F 7 **H** 16

G 12 **J** 28

3. Which number sentence is **NOT** part of the same fact family as the others?

A $48 \div 6 = 8$ **C** $8 + 6 = 14$

B $8 \times 6 = 48$ **D** $48 \div 8 = 6$

4. Show two different ways to find 28×7. Write the product.

5. Thomas put 24 tennis balls into 8 cans. He put the same number of tennis balls in each can. How many tennis balls are in each can?

6. **Writing to Explain** Explain how you can use mental math to find $8 \times 1{,}200$. Write the product.

Geometry and Measurement

7. What number does Point *A* best represent on the number line?

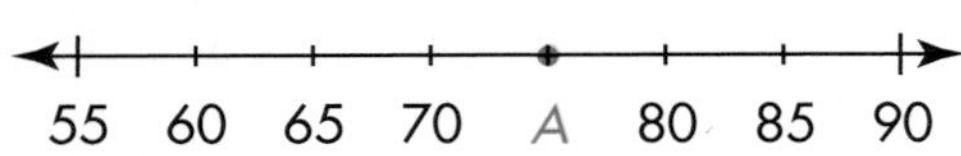

8. How many vertices does a cube have?

F 6 **H** 10

G 8 **J** 12

9. Which tool would be best to use to measure the capacity of a bowl?

A 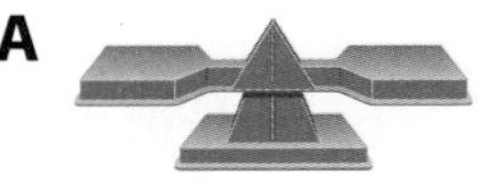 **C** 

B INCHES 0 1 2 3 **D** 

10. Which might take about 1 minute to do?

F Sleep all night **H** Eat dinner

G Tie shoes **J** Write a story

11. What time is shown on the clock?

12. Would you use inches, cups, or pounds to measure length?

13. **Writing to Explain** The thermometer shows that it is 33°F outside. What type of clothing should you wear outside? Explain.

Probability and Statistics

14. On which of the following is the spinner more likely to land?

A A number less than 5

B An even number

C An odd number

D A number greater than 4

Use the bar graph for questions **15–17**.

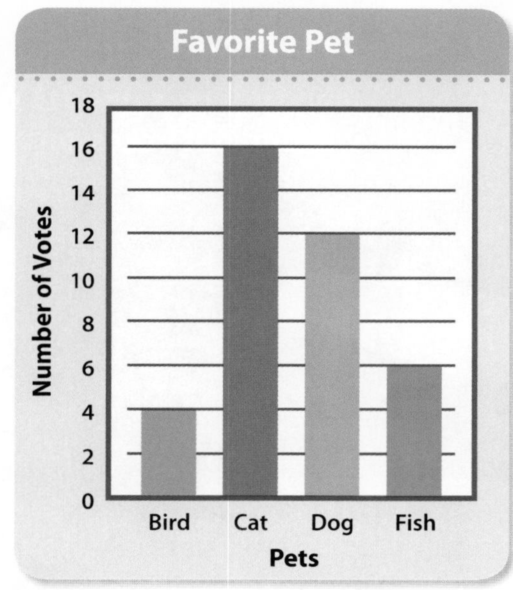

15. How many more students chose dog than fish?

16. How many students voted in all?

17. **Writing to Explain** Suppose 10 students voted for gerbil. Explain how you would show this on the graph.

Algebraic Thinking

18. Which number completes the pattern?

27, 24, 21, ☐, 15

F 16   **H** 18

G 17   **J** 20

19. What is the missing number?

$24 \div \square = 8$

A 2   **C** 4

B 3   **D** 6

20. What number makes this number sentence true?

$6 + \square = 20$

21. Linda is playing a counting game. She counts 50, 45, 40, 35, 30. If her pattern continues, what are the next three numbers she will count?

22. Two pens cost \$4. Three pens cost \$6. Four pens cost \$8. How much will nine pens cost?

23. **Writing to Explain** How many dots will be in the sixth figure in this pattern? Explain how you found your answer.

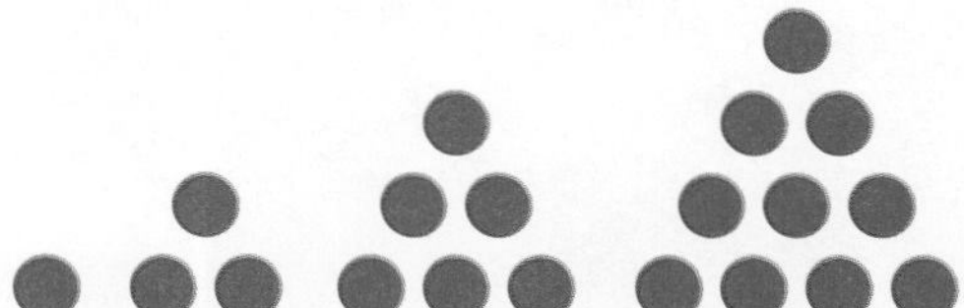

Topic 11

Fraction Concepts

1 What fraction of the statues in the Children's Monument in Texas are girls? You will find out in Lesson 11-3.

2 What fraction of Earth's land surface is desert? You will find out in Lesson 11-7.

3 What fraction of the bones in your body are in your feet? You will find out in Lesson 11-4.

4 Is the flag of Nigeria made up of equal parts? You will find out in Lesson 11-1.

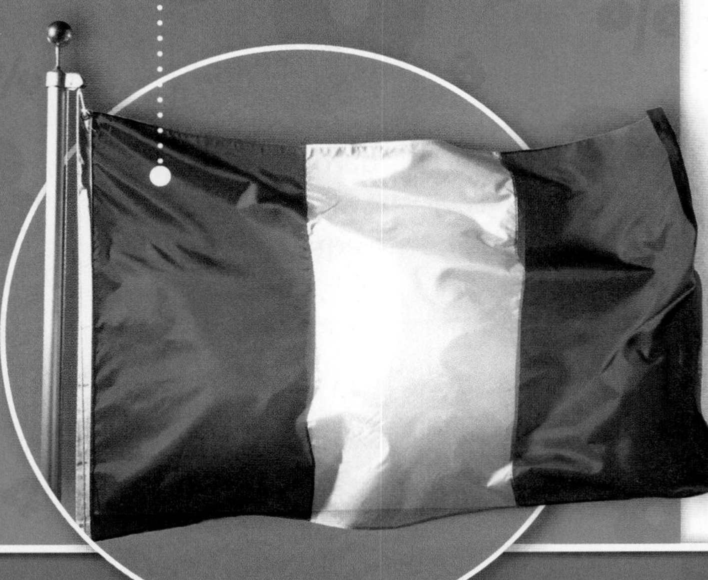

Review What You Know!

Vocabulary

Choose the best term from the box.

- compare
- greater
- less
- multiply

1. The number 219 is __?__ than the number 392.

2. The number 38 is __?__ than the number 19.

3. When you decide if 15 has more tens or fewer tens than 24, you __?__ the numbers.

Arrays

Find the product for each array.

4.

5.

Compare Numbers

Compare. Write $>$, $<$, or $=$.

6. 427 ◯ 583
7. 910 ◯ 906
8. 139 ◯ 136
9. 4,500 ◯ 4,500
10. 693 ◯ 734
11. 1,050 ◯ 1,005

12. **Writing to Explain** Which number is greater, 595 or 565? Explain which digits you used to decide.

TEKS 3.2A: Construct concrete models of fractions.

Dividing Regions into Equal Parts

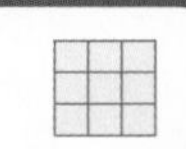
grid paper

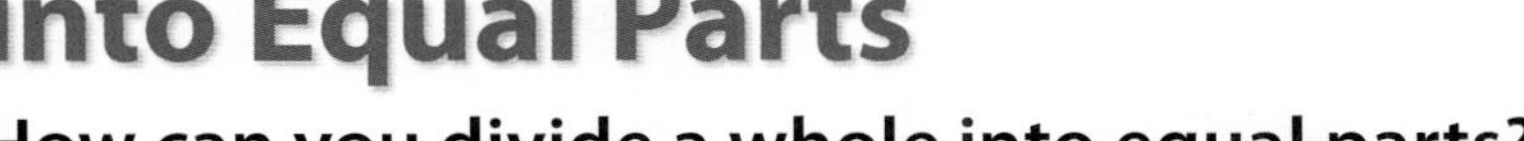

How can you divide a whole into equal parts?

Show two ways to divide the grid paper into equal parts.

When a region is divided into two equal parts, the parts are called halves.

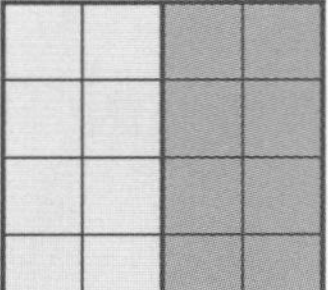
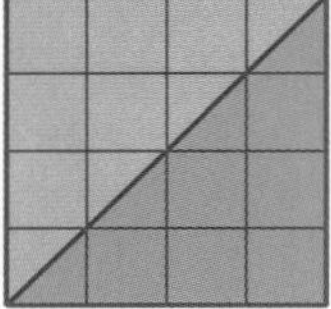

The parts do not need to be the same shape, but they must be equal in area.

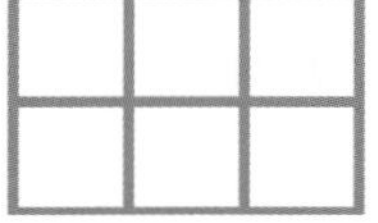
6 equal parts
sixths

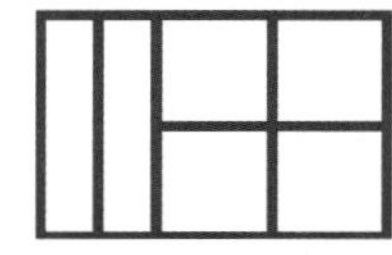
6 equal parts
sixths

10 equal parts
tenths

10 equal parts
tenths

Guided Practice*

Do you know HOW?

In **1–4**, tell if each shows equal or unequal parts. If the parts are equal, name them.

1. 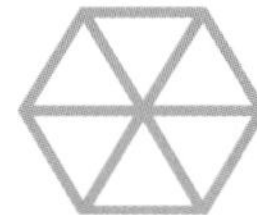

2. 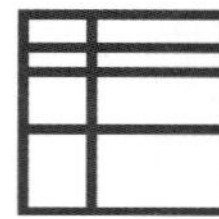
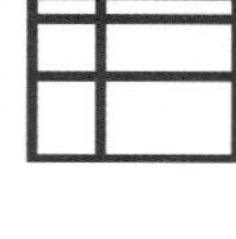

3. 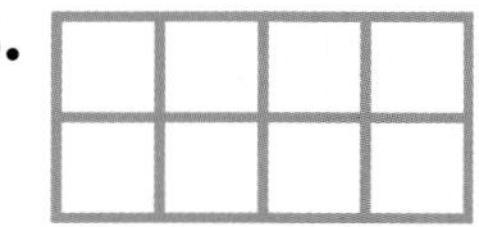

4. 

Do you UNDERSTAND?

5. In the examples on grid paper above, explain how you know the two parts are equal.

6. Use grid paper. Draw a picture to show sixths.

7. Amar divided his garden into equal areas, as shown below. What is the name of the equal parts of the whole?

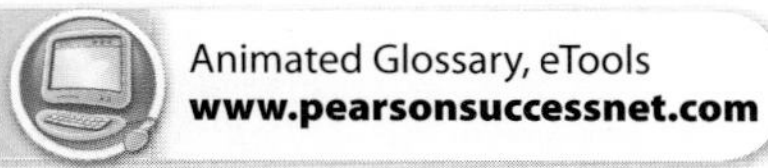

*For another example, see Set A on page 258.

Here are some names of equal parts of a whole.

2 equal parts	3 equal parts	4 equal parts	5 equal parts
halves	thirds	fourths	fifths

6 equal parts	8 equal parts	10 equal parts	12 equal parts
sixths	eighths	tenths	twelfths

Independent Practice

In **8–11**, tell if each shows equal or unequal parts. If the parts are equal, name them.

8. 

9. 

10. 

11. 

In **12–15**, use grid paper. Draw a region showing the equal parts named.

12. fourths **13.** halves **14.** tenths **15.** eighths

TAKS Problem Solving

In **16–18**, use the table of flags.

16. **Reasoning** The flag of this nation has more than three parts. The parts are equal. Which nation is this?

17. The flag of Nigeria is made up of equal parts. What is the name of the parts of this flag?

18. Which flag does **NOT** have equal parts?

Flags of Different Nations

Nation	Flag
Mauritius	
Nigeria	
Poland	
Seychelles	

19. Which shape is **NOT** divided into equal parts?

A 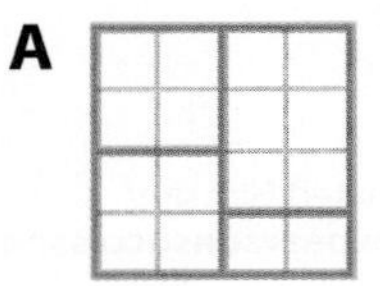

B 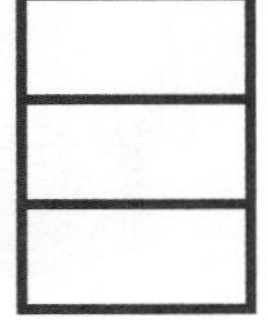

C 

D

Lesson
11-2

TEKS 3.2C: Use fraction names and symbols to describe fractional parts of whole objects or sets of objects.

Fractions and Regions

How can you show and name part of a region?

Mr. Kim made a pan of fruit bars. He served part of the pan of bars to friends. What part of the whole pan was served? What part was left?

A fraction is a symbol, such as $\frac{1}{2}$ or $\frac{2}{3}$, that names equal parts of a whole.

Guided Practice*

Do you know HOW?

In **1** and **2**, write the fraction of each figure that is orange.

1.

2. 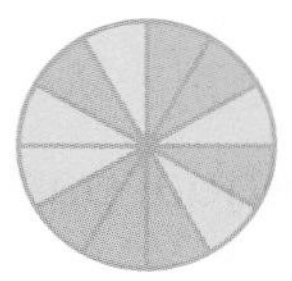

In **3** and **4**, draw a picture to show each fraction.

3. $\frac{3}{4}$ **4.** $\frac{4}{7}$

Do you UNDERSTAND?

5. In the example above, what fraction names all of the parts in the pan of bars?

6. Mrs. Gupta bought a pizza. She ate part of it. What fraction of the pizza did she eat? What fraction of the pizza was left?

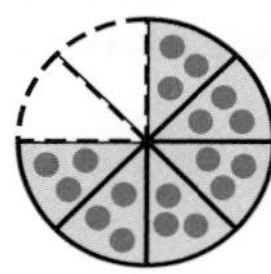

Independent Practice

In **7–10**, write the fraction of each figure that is green.

7. 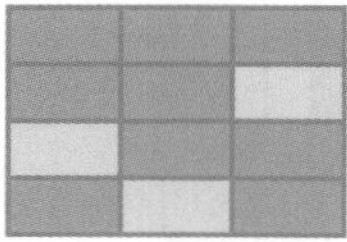

8. 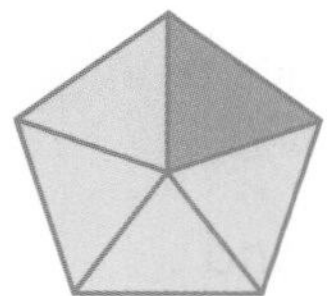

9. 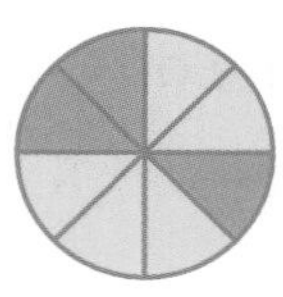

10. 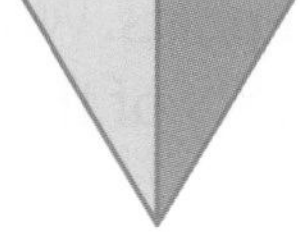

In **11–15**, draw a picture to show each fraction.

11. $\frac{1}{3}$ **12.** $\frac{2}{4}$ **13.** $\frac{1}{6}$ **14.** $\frac{7}{10}$ **15.** $\frac{2}{2}$

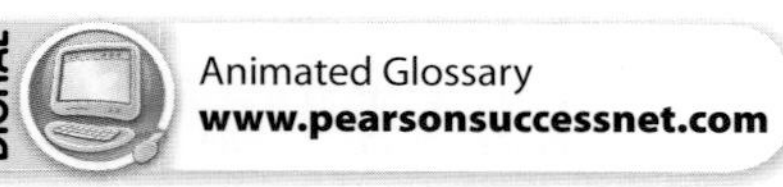

*For another example, see Set B on page 258.

What You Write

Numerator → $\frac{4}{9}$ ← 4 equal parts served
Denominator → ← 9 equal parts **in all**

Numerator → $\frac{5}{9}$ ← 5 equal parts left
Denominator → ← 9 equal parts **in all**

The numerator tells how many equal parts are described. It is the number above the fraction bar.

The denominator tells the total number of equal parts. It is the number below the bar.

What You Say

Four ninths of the pan of fruit bars was served.

Five ninths of the pan of fruit bars was left.

TAKS Problem Solving

For **16–19**, use the sign at the right.

Size of Pizza	Price
Small	$7
Medium	$9
Large	$11

16. Ben and his friends ordered a medium pizza. Ben ate 1 slice of the pizza. What fraction of the pizza did Ben eat?

17. Aida's family bought a large pizza. The family ate 4 slices of the pizza. What fraction of the pizza was left?

18. Tami's family bought 3 small pizzas. Leo's family bought 2 medium pizzas. How much more did Tami's family spend than Leo's family?

19. Which costs more, 6 small pizzas or 4 large pizzas? How much more?

20. **Reasonableness** A pan of macaroni and cheese is divided into 12 unequal parts. Alana serves 3 of the parts. Is it reasonable to say she has served $\frac{3}{12}$ of the macaroni and cheese? Explain.

21. Look at the picture of the quilt. What fraction of the quilt is white?

A 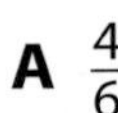 $\frac{4}{6}$ **C** $\frac{6}{10}$

B $\frac{6}{6}$ **D** $\frac{2}{5}$

Lesson
11-3

TEKS 3.2C: Use fraction names and symbols to describe fractional parts of whole objects or sets of objects.
Also TEKS 3.2A

Fractions and Sets

Hands-On
counters

How can a fraction name part of a group?

A group of 12 people is in line for movie tickets. What fraction of the group of people are wearing red? What fraction of the people are not wearing red?

A fraction can name equal parts of a set, or group, of objects.

8 of the people are wearing red.

Guided Practice*

Do you know HOW?

In **1** and **2**, write the fraction of the counters that are red.

1.

2.

In **3** and **4**, draw counters to show the fraction given.

3. $\frac{4}{5}$

4. $\frac{3}{8}$

Do you UNDERSTAND?

5. In the example above, why is the denominator the same for the part of the group wearing red and for the part of the group not wearing red?

6. A group of 9 students is waiting for a bus. Six of them are wearing jackets. What fraction of the students in the group are wearing jackets? What fraction of the students are not wearing jackets?

Independent Practice

In **7–9**, write the fraction of the counters that are yellow.

7.

8.

9.

In **10–12**, draw a picture of the set described.

10. 5 shapes, $\frac{3}{5}$ of the shapes are circles

11. 8 shapes, $\frac{5}{8}$ of the shapes are triangles

12. 2 shapes, $\frac{1}{2}$ of the shapes are squares

*For another example, see Set B on page 258.

What You Write

$\frac{8}{12}$ ← Number of people wearing red
← Total number of people

$\frac{4}{12}$ ← Number of people **not** wearing red
← Total number of people

What You Say

Eight twelfths of the people are wearing red.

Four twelfths of the people are not wearing red.

TAKS Problem Solving

For **13–15**, write the fraction of the group of buttons described.

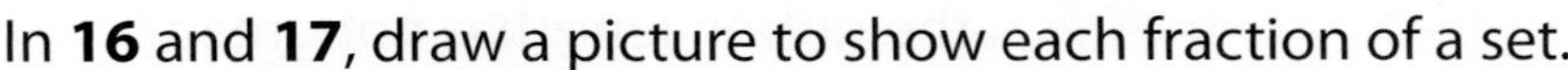

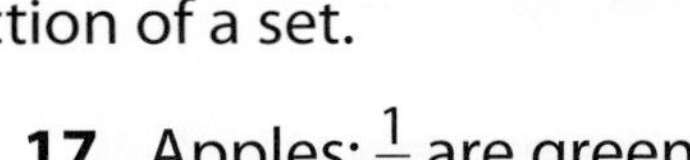

13. Pink buttons

14. Blue buttons

15. Buttons with only two holes

In **16** and **17**, draw a picture to show each fraction of a set.

16. Flowers: $\frac{3}{4}$ are yellow

17. Apples: $\frac{1}{2}$ are green

18. The Children's Monument at the State Capitol in Austin, Texas, has six statues of children. How many are statues of girls?

$\frac{3}{6}$ of the statues are statues of girls.

19. Number Sense A family of 5 is buying concert tickets. If $\frac{2}{5}$ of the tickets they buy are for adults, how many adult tickets does the family need?

20. What fraction of the flower petals have fallen off the flower?

A $\frac{3}{5}$

B $\frac{2}{8}$

C $\frac{8}{10}$

D $\frac{2}{10}$

Lesson
11-4

TEKS 3.2C: Use fraction names and symbols to describe fractional parts of whole objects or sets of objects.
Also **TEKS 3.2A**

Fractions and Length

Hands-On
fraction strips

How can a fraction name part of a length?

What fraction of this necklace length is blue? What fraction is not blue?

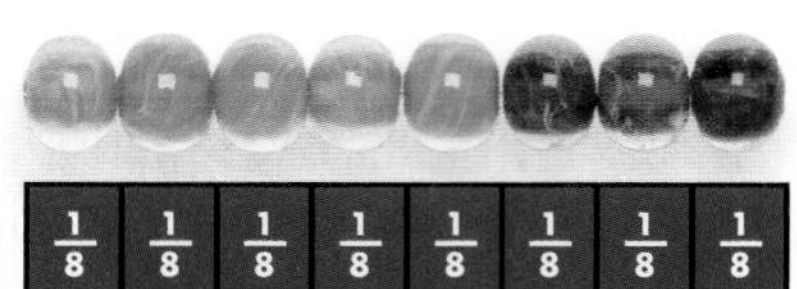

A fraction can name part of a length.

Guided Practice*

Do you know HOW?

In **1** and **2**, what fraction of the length of the 1 strip do the other strips show? Use fraction strips to help.

1.

2.

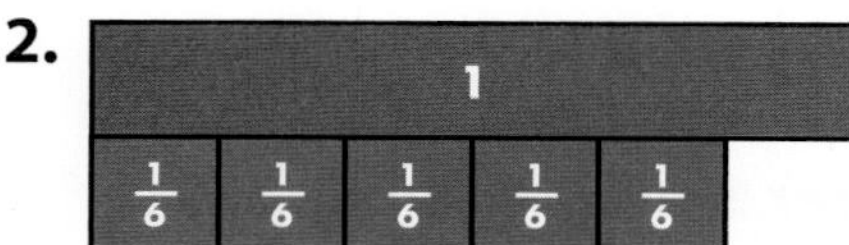

Do you UNDERSTAND?

3. In the example above, how do the fraction strips help you solve the problem?

4. What fraction of the ribbon length below is green? What fraction of the ribbon length is not green?

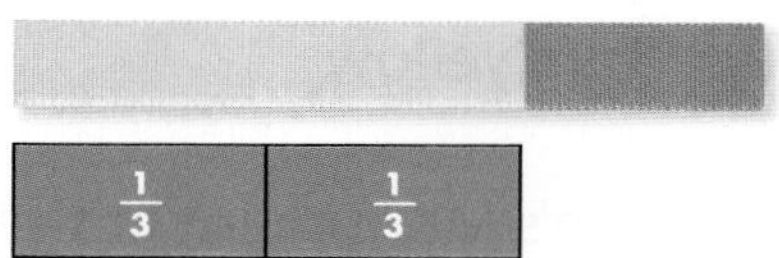

Independent Practice

In **5–8**, what fraction of the length of the 1 strip do the other strips show? Use fraction strips to help.

5.

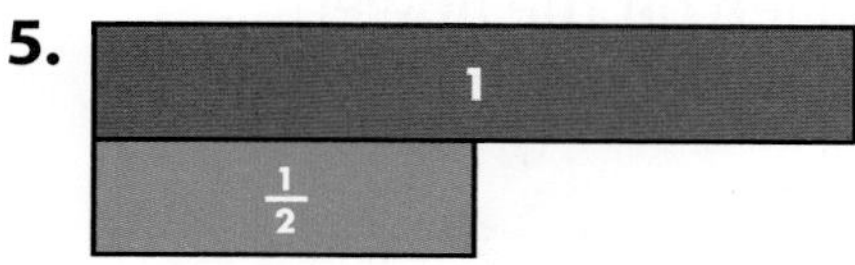

6.

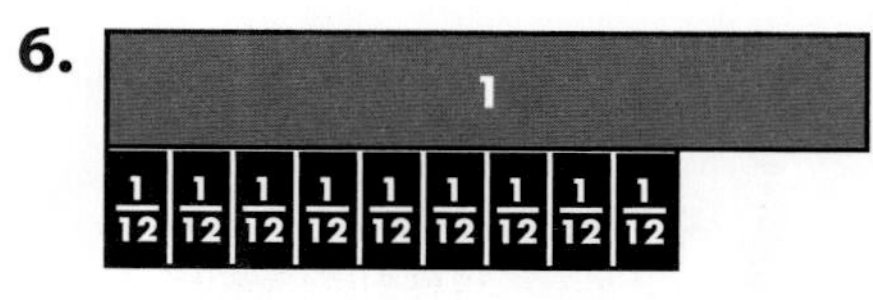

7.

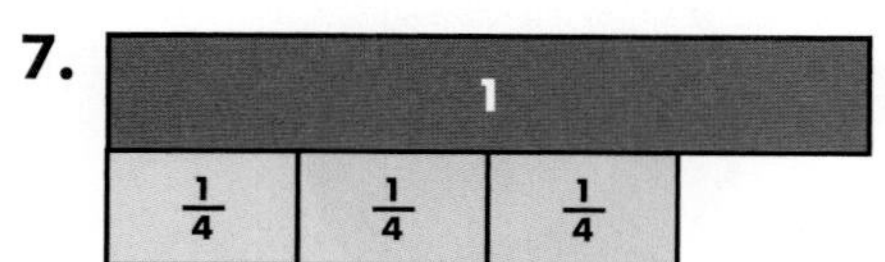

8.

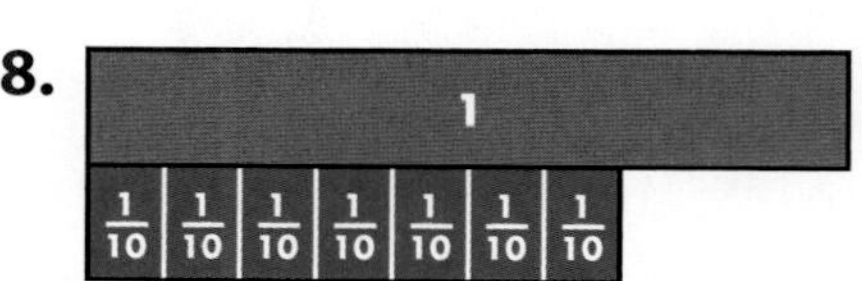

*For another example, see Set C on page 258.

What You Write

$\frac{5}{8}$ ← Number of parts of the length that are blue
← Total number of parts in the necklace length

$\frac{3}{8}$ ← Number of parts of the length that are **not** blue
← Total number of parts in the necklace length

What You Say

Five eighths of the necklace length is blue.

Three eighths of the necklace length is not blue.

TAKS Problem Solving

For **9** and **10**, what fraction of each length of yarn is green?

9.

$\frac{1}{12}$	$\frac{1}{12}$	$\frac{1}{12}$	$\frac{1}{12}$	$\frac{1}{12}$	$\frac{1}{12}$	$\frac{1}{12}$	$\frac{1}{12}$

10.

$\frac{1}{4}$	$\frac{1}{4}$

11. Estimation Nick wants to buy two items. He estimated that the total cost of the items is \$100. One item costs \$58. What is one reasonable price of the other item?

12. For her part in the school play, Carmen must memorize 10 lines. Each line has about 10 words. About how many words does Carmen need to memorize?

13. Which group shows fewer than $\frac{3}{5}$ of the shapes shaded?

A ◆ ◇ ◆ ◇ ◆

B ◆ ◇ ◆ ◆ ◆

C ◆ ◆ ◆ ◆ ◆

D ◆ ◇ ◇ ◇ ◆

14. What fraction of your body's bones are **NOT** in your feet?

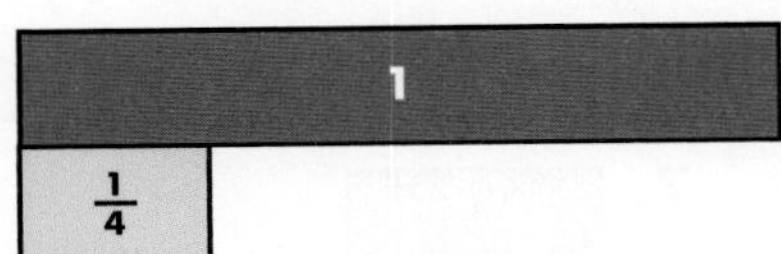

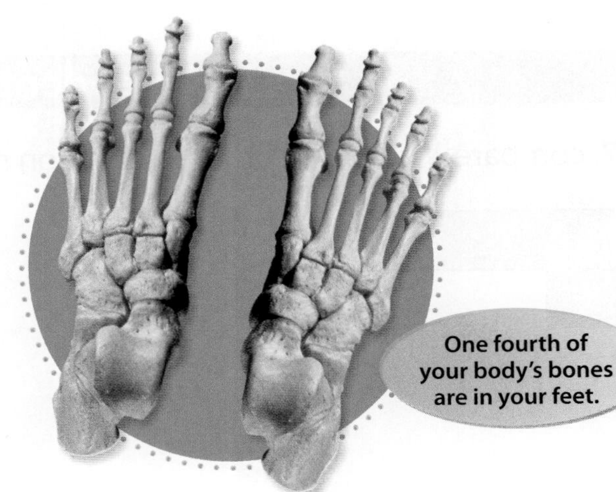

Lesson

11-5

TEKS 3.2B: Compare fractional parts of whole objects or sets of objects in a problem situation using concrete models.

Using Models to Compare Fractions

Hands-On
fraction strips

How can you compare fractions?

Nola and Edwin are painting two boards that are the same size and the same shape. Who painted a greater amount—Nola or Edwin?

Compare $\frac{1}{2}$ and $\frac{2}{5}$.

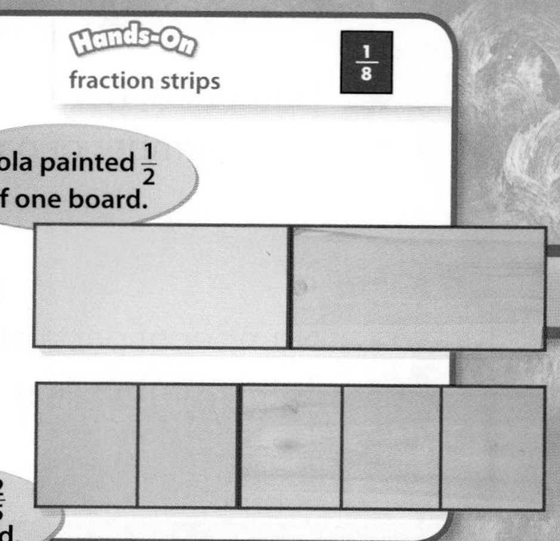

Guided Practice*

Do you know HOW?

In **1** and **2**, compare. Write >, <, or =. Use fraction strips to help.

1. 

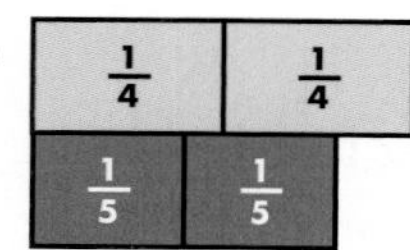

$\frac{2}{4} \bigcirc \frac{2}{5}$

2.

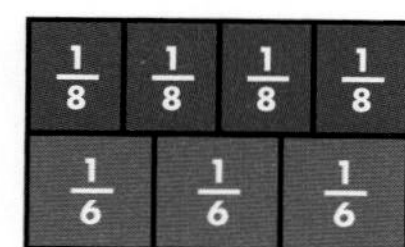

$\frac{4}{8} \bigcirc \frac{3}{6}$

Do you UNDERSTAND?

3. In the problem above about Zoe and Nat, can you tell who painted a greater area of board? Explain.

4. Bob and Irene are painting two walls that are the same size and shape. Irene painted $\frac{2}{3}$ of one wall. Bob painted $\frac{3}{4}$ of the other wall. Who painted a greater amount?

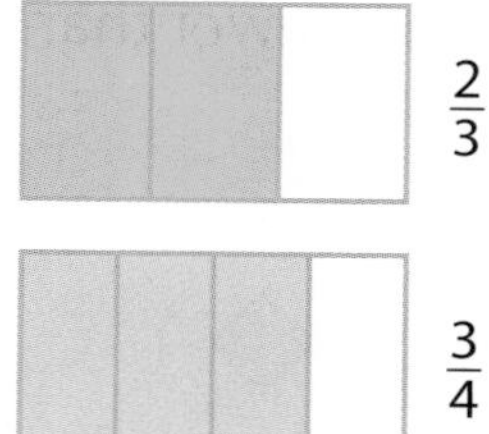

Independent Practice

In **5–7**, compare. Write >, <, or =. Use fraction strips to help.

5.

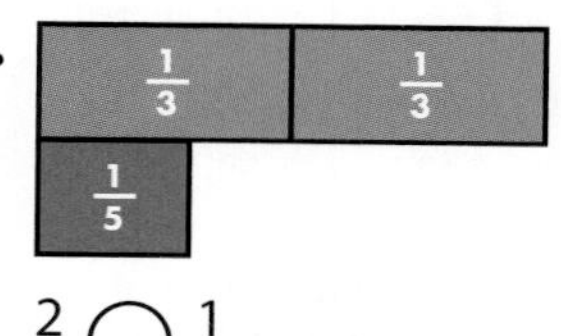

$\frac{2}{3} \bigcirc \frac{1}{5}$

6.

$\frac{3}{12} \bigcirc \frac{1}{4}$

7.

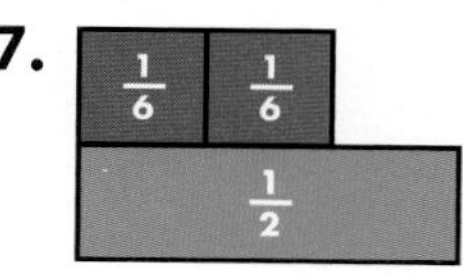

$\frac{2}{6} \bigcirc \frac{1}{2}$

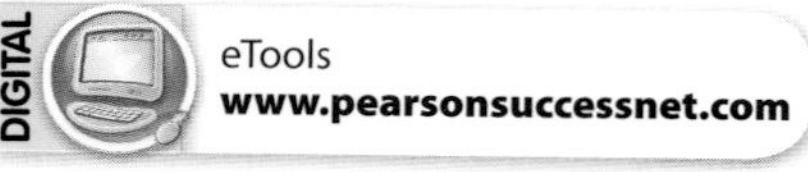

*For another example, see Set D on page 259.

You can use fraction strips.

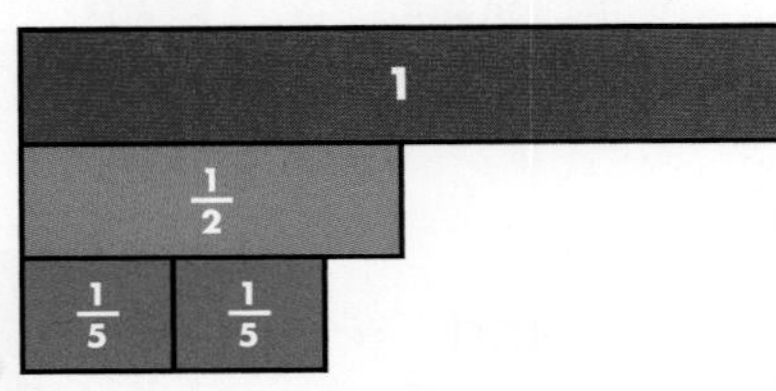

Compare the fraction strips.

$\frac{1}{2}$ is greater than $\frac{2}{5}$.

$\frac{1}{2} > \frac{2}{5}$

Nola painted a greater amount.

Zoe painted $\frac{1}{2}$ of one board. Nat painted $\frac{1}{2}$ of a board with a different area. Is the half Zoe painted equal to the half Nat painted?

Draw a picture.

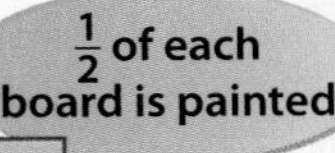

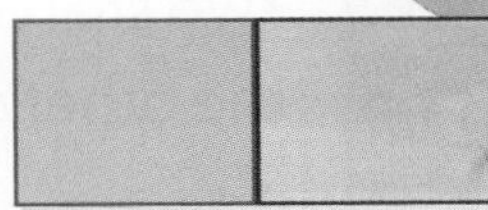

The boards have different areas. Zoe's half is not equal to Nat's half.

TAKS Problem Solving

The fraction strips at the right represent three loaves of bread that Mrs. Rai sliced for a meal. The strips show how much of each loaf was left after the meal.

For **8** and **9**, copy and complete each number sentence to find the loaf with the greater amount left after the meal.

8. The loaf cut in sixths or the loaf cut in thirds

$\frac{5}{6} \bigcirc \frac{2}{3}$

9. The loaf cut in eighths or the loaf cut in thirds

$\frac{3}{8} \bigcirc \frac{2}{3}$

10. **Writing to Explain** Lupe ate $\frac{1}{3}$ of a sandwich. Jed ate $\frac{1}{3}$ of a different sandwich. Jed ate more than Lupe. How is that possible?

11. Kobe fed his hamster and his rabbit. He gave the rabbit 3 carrot pieces for each 2 carrot pieces he gave the hamster. If the hamster got 8 carrot pieces, how many carrot pieces did the rabbit get?

12. Which group shows more than $\frac{5}{7}$ of the shapes shaded?

A 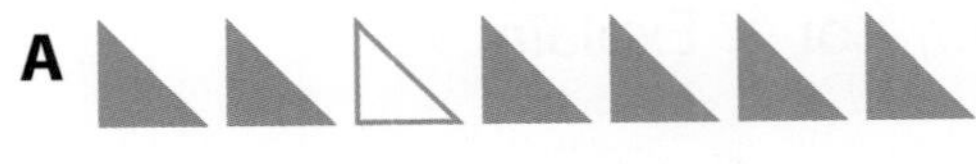

C 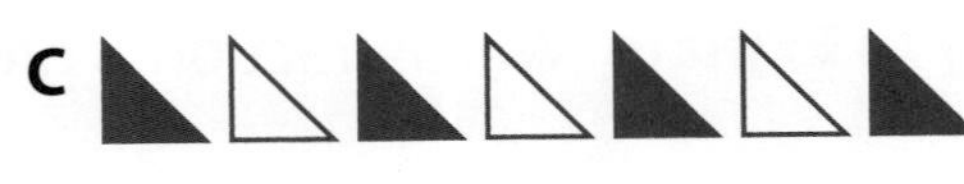

B 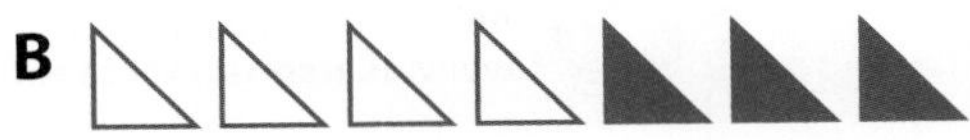

D 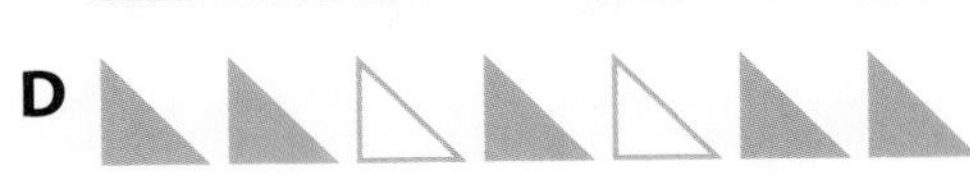

Lesson

11-6

TEKS 3.2B: Compare fractional parts of whole objects or sets of objects in a problem situation using concrete models.

Comparing Fractions

Hands-On
fraction strips

$\frac{1}{5}$

How can you compare fractions with the same numerator or the same denominator?

Two scarves are the same size. One scarf is $\frac{4}{5}$ green, and the other scarf is $\frac{2}{5}$ green.

Which is greater, $\frac{4}{5}$ or $\frac{2}{5}$?

Compare $\frac{4}{5}$ and $\frac{2}{5}$.

$\frac{4}{5}$ of this scarf is green.

$\frac{2}{5}$ of this scarf is green.

Another Example

How can you compare fractions with the same numerator?

Two scarves are the same size. Each scarf has a blue part and a white part. One scarf is $\frac{1}{6}$ blue, and the other scarf is $\frac{1}{4}$ blue. Which fraction is less, $\frac{1}{6}$ or $\frac{1}{4}$?

$\frac{1}{6}$ and $\frac{1}{4}$ are unit fractions. A unit fraction is a fraction with a numerator of 1.

What You Show

You can use fraction strips.

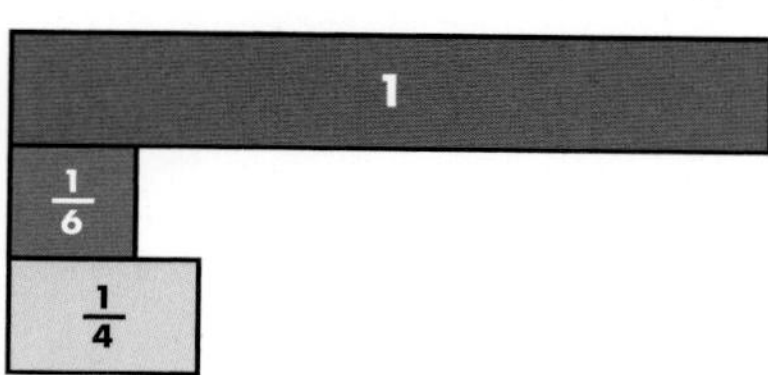

Compare the fraction strips.

What You Write

$\frac{1}{6} < \frac{1}{4}$

One sixth is less than *one fourth*.

If two fractions have the same numerator, the fraction with the greater denominator is less than the other fraction.

Explain It

1. **Reasonableness** Can $\frac{1}{6}$ and $\frac{1}{3}$ of the same scarf be equal? Why or why not?

2. **Writing to Explain** Which fraction is greater, $\frac{2}{6}$ or $\frac{2}{5}$? Explain.

What You Show

You can use fraction strips.

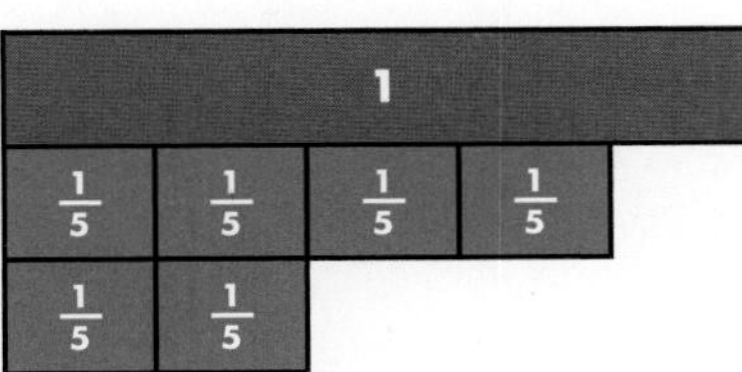

Compare the fraction strips.

What You Write

$\frac{4}{5} > \frac{2}{5}$

Four fifths is greater than *two fifths*.

If two fractions have the same denominator, the fraction with the greater numerator is the greater fraction.

Guided Practice*

Do you know HOW?

In **1** and **2**, compare. Write $>$, $<$, or $=$. Use fraction strips to help.

1.

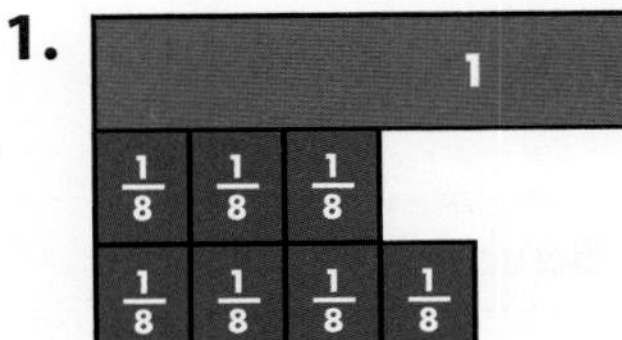

$\frac{3}{8} \bigcirc \frac{4}{8}$

2.

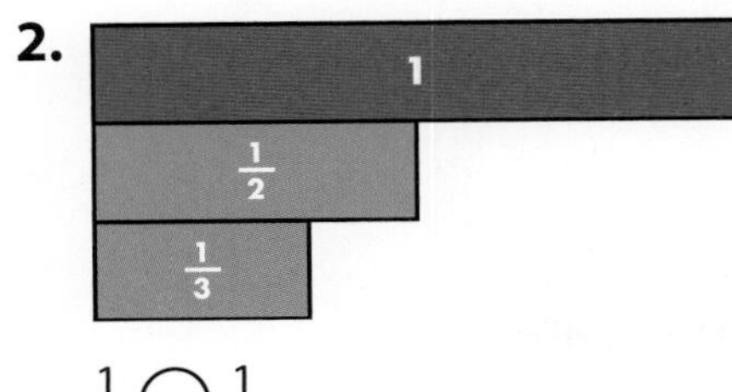

$\frac{1}{2} \bigcirc \frac{1}{3}$

Do you UNDERSTAND?

3. In the example above, how can models show that if two fractions have the same denominator, the fraction with the greater numerator is greater?

4. Two ribbons are the same length. Each has a pink part and a yellow part. One ribbon is $\frac{2}{4}$ pink, and the other is $\frac{3}{4}$ pink. Which fraction is greater, $\frac{2}{4}$ or $\frac{3}{4}$?

Independent Practice

In **5** and **6**, compare. Write $>$, $<$, or $=$. Use fraction strips to help.

5.

1

1/5

1/8

$\frac{1}{5} \bigcirc \frac{1}{8}$

6.

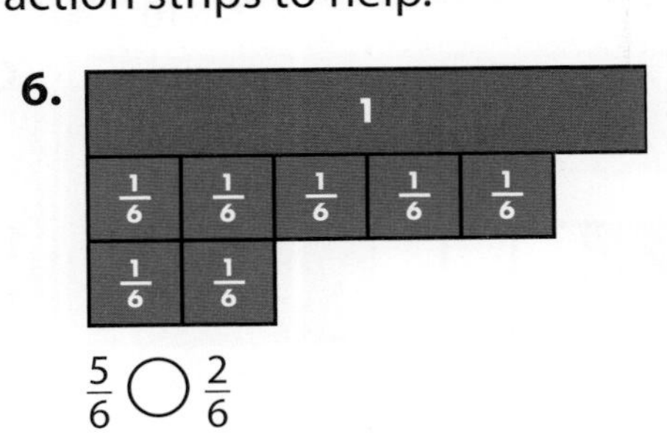

$\frac{5}{6} \bigcirc \frac{2}{6}$

*For another example, see Set D on page 259.

Independent Practice

In **7–10**, copy and complete. Use <, >, or = to compare.

7. $\frac{4}{5} \bigcirc \frac{4}{10}$ **8.** $\frac{5}{8} \bigcirc \frac{7}{8}$ **9.** $\frac{1}{2} \bigcirc \frac{1}{10}$ **10.** $\frac{3}{8} \bigcirc \frac{3}{6}$

For **11–14**, the drawing shows four fence posts that are partly painted. Copy and complete each number sentence to compare painted parts of the fence posts.

$\frac{1}{6}$ $\frac{1}{3}$ $\frac{3}{4}$ $\frac{2}{4}$

11. Fence posts painted green:

$\frac{1}{3} \bigcirc \frac{1}{6}$

12. Fence posts painted yellow:

$\frac{3}{4} \bigcirc \frac{2}{4}$

13. First post and last post:

$\frac{1}{6} \bigcirc \frac{2}{4}$

14. Estimation Roy has saved some money to buy a kit that costs $54.

a Use an estimate to decide if he has saved enough to buy the kit. Explain.

b How much money has Roy saved so far?

c How much more money does he need to buy the kit?

Money Saved (Data)

Month	Amount
June	$12
July	$13
August	$21

15. Writing to Explain A vegetable pizza and a cheese pizza are the same size. The vegetable pizza is cut into 8 equal pieces. The cheese pizza is cut into 12 equal pieces. Which pizza has larger pieces? Explain.

16. Which region shows more than $\frac{6}{10}$ of the region shaded?

A

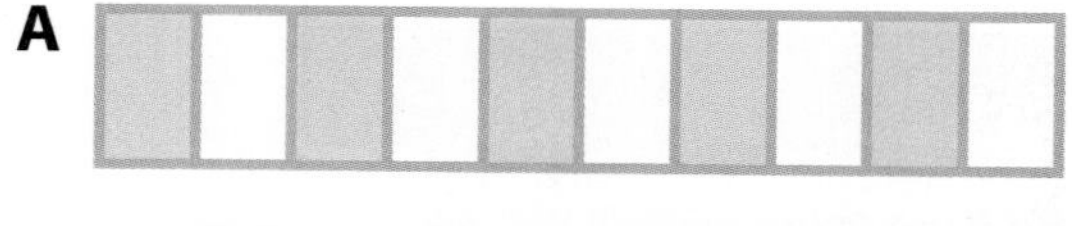

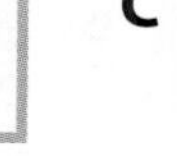

C

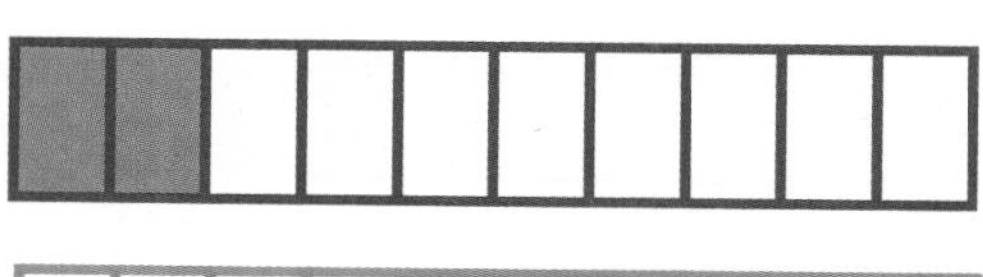

B

D

Comparing Fractions

Use eTools

Fractions

Model each fraction using the Fractions eTool and write $>$ or $<$ for each ◯.

$\frac{1}{3}$ ◯ $\frac{1}{4}$ $\frac{3}{8}$ ◯ $\frac{1}{8}$

Step 1 Go to the Fractions eTool. Select the equivalents workspace mode by using the pull-down menu at the top of the page. Select $\frac{1}{3}$, to show $\frac{1}{3}$ in the first circle.

Step 2 Select the second circle by clicking on it. Select $\frac{1}{4}$, to show $\frac{1}{4}$ in the second circle. Notice that more of the first circle is shaded than the second circle. Also, see the symbol in the middle of the workspace. Both show that $\frac{1}{3} > \frac{1}{4}$.

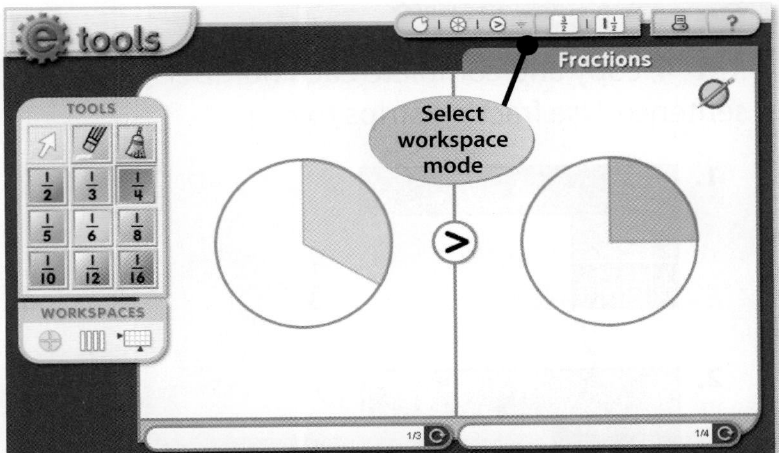

Step 3 Use the broom tool to clear the workspace before starting another problem. Click on the first circle. Then click on $\frac{1}{8}$ three times to show $\frac{3}{8}$. Click on the second circle and then on $\frac{1}{8}$. This shows $\frac{3}{8} > \frac{1}{8}$.

Practice

Model each fraction using the Fractions eTool and write $>$ or $<$ for each ◯.

1. $\frac{2}{3}$ ◯ $\frac{1}{3}$

2. $\frac{1}{5}$ ◯ $\frac{3}{5}$

3. $\frac{1}{8}$ ◯ $\frac{1}{6}$

4. $\frac{5}{6}$ ◯ $\frac{1}{6}$

5. $\frac{1}{4}$ ◯ $\frac{1}{5}$

6. $\frac{4}{5}$ ◯ $\frac{3}{5}$

7. $\frac{1}{3}$ ◯ $\frac{1}{2}$

8. $\frac{3}{10}$ ◯ $\frac{7}{10}$

9. $\frac{5}{12}$ ◯ $\frac{7}{12}$

Lesson

11-7

TEKS 3.2D: Construct concrete models of equivalent fractions for fractional parts of whole objects.

Finding Equivalent Fractions

Hands-On fraction strips

How can different fractions name the same part of a whole?

Sonya has colored $\frac{1}{2}$ of the border. What are two other ways to name $\frac{1}{2}$? Different fractions can name the same part of a whole.

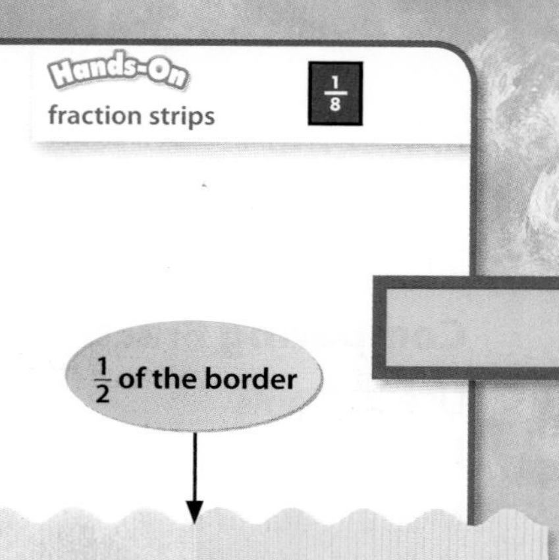

Guided Practice*

Do you know HOW?

In **1–4**, copy and complete each number sentence. Use fraction strips to help.

1.

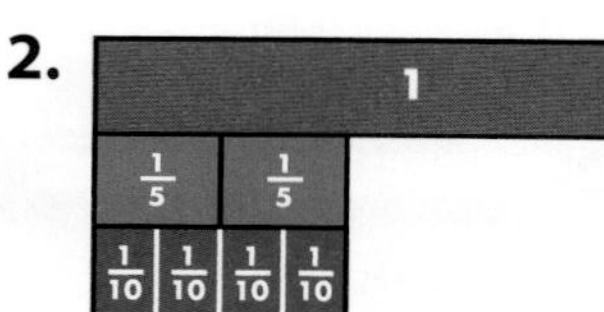

$\frac{1}{3} = \frac{\square}{12}$

2. (1; $\frac{1}{5}$ $\frac{1}{5}$; $\frac{1}{10}$ $\frac{1}{10}$ $\frac{1}{10}$ $\frac{1}{10}$)

$\frac{2}{5} = \frac{\square}{10}$

3. $\frac{1}{2} = \frac{5}{\square}$

4. $\frac{2}{4} = \frac{\square}{6}$

Do you UNDERSTAND?

5. In the example above, what pattern do you see in the numerator and denominator of fractions that name $\frac{1}{2}$?

6. Vijay folded a rope into fourths. Then he showed $\frac{1}{4}$ of the length. Write $\frac{1}{4}$ one other way.

Independent Practice

In **7–9**, copy and complete each number sentence. Use fraction strips to help.

7.

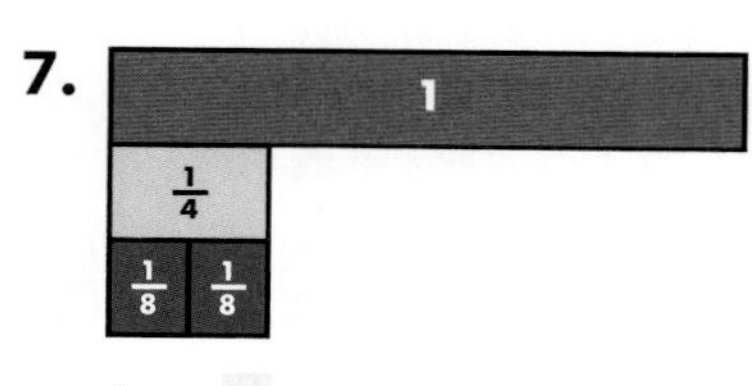

$\frac{1}{4} = \frac{\square}{8}$

8.

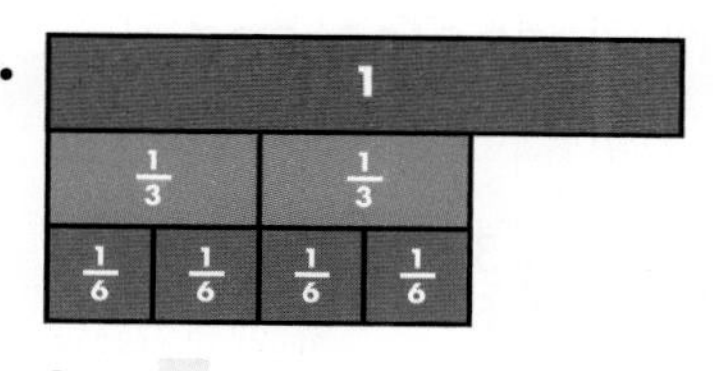

$\frac{2}{3} = \frac{\square}{6}$

9.

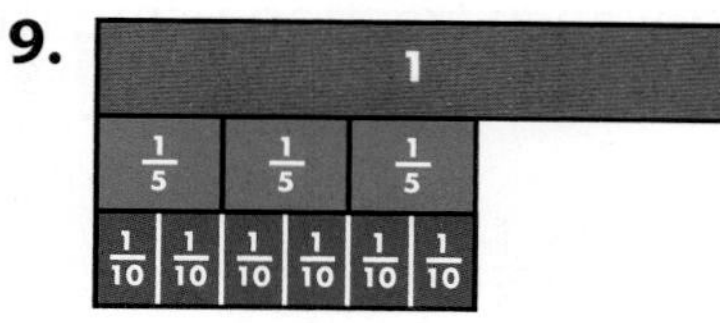

$\frac{3}{5} = \frac{\square}{10}$

*For another example, see Set E on page 259.

$\frac{1}{2} = \frac{\square}{8}$ You can use fraction strips. The denominators of the fractions tell which fraction strips to use.

Find how many $\frac{1}{8}$s are equal to $\frac{1}{2}$.

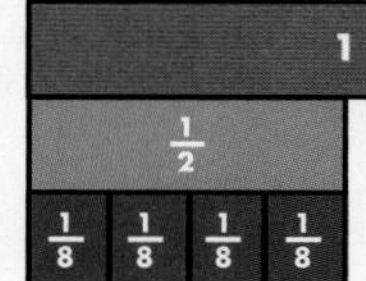

Four $\frac{1}{8}$ strips are equal to $\frac{1}{2}$, so $\frac{1}{2} = \frac{4}{8}$.
Another name for $\frac{1}{2}$ is $\frac{4}{8}$.

$\frac{1}{2} = \frac{\square}{6}$ You can use fraction strips. The denominator is 6, so use $\frac{1}{6}$ strips.

Find how many $\frac{1}{6}$s are equal to $\frac{1}{2}$.

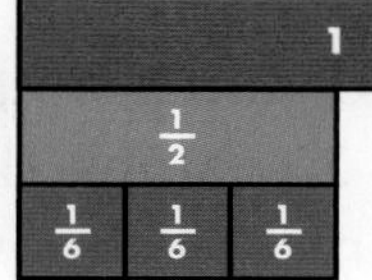

Three $\frac{1}{6}$ strips are equal to $\frac{1}{2}$, so $\frac{1}{2} = \frac{3}{6}$.
Another name for $\frac{1}{2}$ is $\frac{3}{6}$.

TAKS Problem Solving

In **10–12**, copy and complete. Use >, <, or = to compare.

10. $\frac{6}{12} \bigcirc \frac{6}{10}$ **11.** $\frac{1}{5} \bigcirc \frac{2}{10}$ **12.** $\frac{1}{3} \bigcirc \frac{2}{6}$

For **13** and **14**, name a fraction to solve each problem.

13. Evie painted $\frac{1}{6}$ of the length of a board. What is one other way to name $\frac{1}{6}$?

14. Two eighths of a necklace is red. What part of the necklace length is not red?

Algebra For **15–17**, copy and complete to continue each pattern.

15. $\frac{1}{2}, \frac{2}{4}, \frac{3}{6}, \frac{4}{\square}, \frac{5}{\square}, \frac{6}{\square}$ **16.** $\frac{2}{3}, \frac{4}{6}, \frac{6}{9}, \frac{\square}{12}$ **17.** $\frac{1}{4}, \frac{2}{8}, \frac{3}{12}, \frac{\square}{16}, \frac{\square}{20}, \frac{\square}{24}$

18. Reasonableness Jan reads 4 to 6 books every month. About how many books would Jan read in 7 months? Explain your answer.

19. Which fraction names the part of Earth's land surface that is desert?

A $\frac{1}{2}$
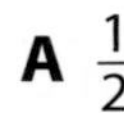

B $\frac{1}{3}$
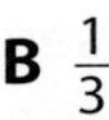

C $\frac{1}{5}$

D $\frac{4}{6}$
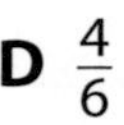

About $\frac{2}{6}$ of the Earth's land surface is desert.

20. The shaded part of which rectangle is a fraction equal to $\frac{1}{4}$?

F

H

G

J
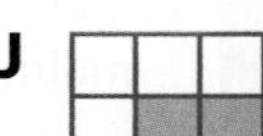

Lesson
11-8

TEKS 3.14C: Select or develop an appropriate problem solving plan or strategy, including drawing a picture, looking for a pattern, systematic guessing and checking, acting it out, making a table, working a simpler problem, or working backwards to solve a problem.

Problem Solving

Make a Table and Look for a Pattern

A video game company tested 20 games. Three of the games did not work. If 120 games are tested, how many of them might not work?

Guided Practice*

Do you know HOW?

Copy and complete the table to solve.

1. Ms Simms is buying bags of blocks. Out of the 50 blocks in each bag, 3 are cubes. If Ms Simms buys 250 blocks, how many will be cubes?

Cubes	3				
Total Blocks	50				

Do you UNDERSTAND?

2. Look at the example above. If the video game store bought 50 games, about how many games might not work? Explain.

3. **Write a Problem** Write a problem that can be solved by making a table and using a pattern. Then solve the problem.

Independent Practice

Copy and complete the table to solve.

4. Erasers are sold in packages of 6. In each package, 2 of the erasers are pink. How many pink erasers will you get if you buy 30 erasers?

Pink Erasers	2				
Total Erasers	6				

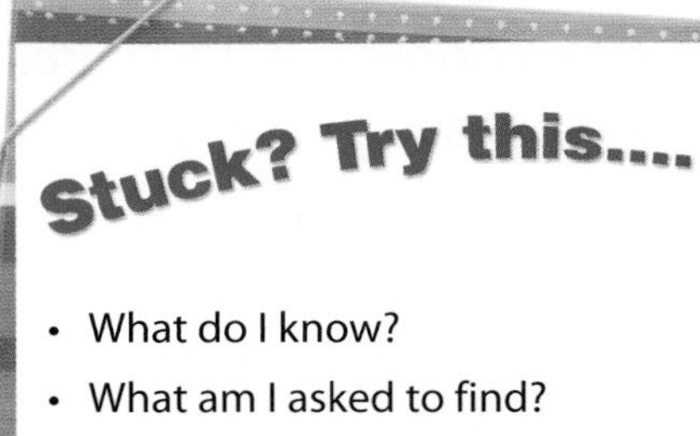

Stuck? Try this....

- What do I know?
- What am I asked to find?
- What diagram can I use to help understand the problem?
- Can I use addition, subtraction, multiplication, or division?
- Is all of my work correct?
- Did I answer the right question?
- Is my answer reasonable?

*For another example, see Set F on page 259.

Plan

Make a table.

Then, write in the information you know.

Might Not Work	3					
Total Games	20					

Solve

Extend the table. Look for a pattern to help. Then find the answer in the table.

Might Not Work	3	6	9	12	15	18
Total Games	20	40	60	80	100	120

If 120 games are tested, 18 might not work.

In **5** and **6**, copy and complete each table to solve.

5. Sue planted 8 daffodil bulbs. Two of the bulbs didn't grow. Suppose that pattern continues and Sue plants 32 bulbs. How many bulbs most likely won't grow?

Didn't Grow	2	■	■	■
Total Bulbs	8	■	■	■

6. Sue planted 12 tulip bulbs of mixed colors. When the bulbs grew, there were 4 red tulips. Suppose that pattern continues and Sue plants 48 bulbs. How many of the tulips will likely be red?

Red Tulips	4	■	■	■
Total Tulips	12	■	■	■

7. Reasoning Tad planted 15 tulips in a row. He followed the pattern shown below. What is the color of the last tulip in the row?

8. Reasoning Look back at Problem 5. Suppose Sue decided to plant 20 daffodil bulbs.

a How many bulbs would most likely not grow?

b How many bulbs would most likely grow?

9. Which equivalent fraction completes the pattern below?

$\frac{1}{4}$ $\frac{2}{8}$ $\frac{3}{12}$ $\frac{■}{■}$

A $\frac{3}{14}$

B $\frac{4}{14}$

C $\frac{3}{16}$

D $\frac{4}{16}$

10. Number Sense Suppose Sue wants 10 red tulips. How many tulip bulbs should she plant? See Problem 6.

11. Look back at Problem 6. If Sue planted 48 tulip bulbs, how many of the tulips will **NOT** be red?

TAKS Test Prep

1. What is the name of the equal parts of the whole pizza? (11-1)

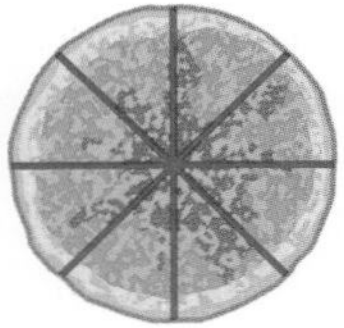

A Sixths

B Sevenths

C Eighths

D Ninths

2. The stage was divided into equal parts. What fractional part of the stage was used for flute players? (11-2)

Trombones	Drums	Trombones
Clarinets	Trombones	Clarinets
Flutes	Triangles	Flutes

F $\frac{1}{9}$

G $\frac{2}{9}$

H $\frac{2}{7}$

J $\frac{3}{9}$

3. Blair bought the fruit shown below. What fraction of the pieces of fruit are oranges? (11-3)

A $\frac{5}{7}$

B $\frac{6}{12}$

C $\frac{5}{12}$

D $\frac{1}{5}$

4. What color is $\frac{7}{15}$ of the rug Ted bought for the reading corner in his classroom? (11-2)

F Purple

G Orange

H Light blue

J White

5. Which comparison is true? (11-6)

A $\frac{3}{5} < \frac{3}{8}$

B $\frac{3}{8} > \frac{3}{4}$

C $\frac{3}{4} < \frac{3}{5}$

D $\frac{3}{5} > \frac{3}{8}$

6. What fraction of the board length has wire attached? (11-4)

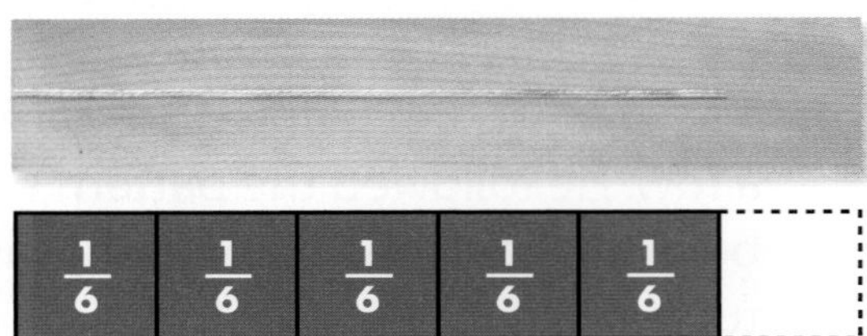

F $\frac{6}{6}$

G $\frac{4}{5}$

H $\frac{5}{6}$

J $\frac{1}{6}$

7. During the time allowed, Deja swam $\frac{3}{4}$ of the length of the pool. Loren finished $\frac{4}{5}$ of it. Use the models to find which symbol makes the comparison true. (11-5)

$\frac{3}{4} \bigcirc \frac{4}{5}$

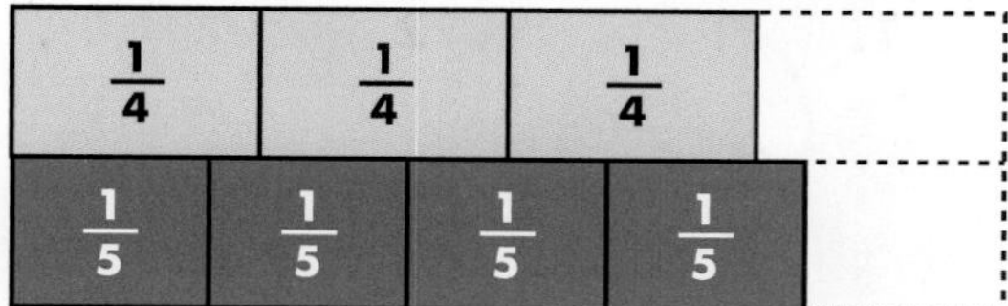

A =

B ×

C >

D <

8. What number makes the statement true? (11-7)

$\frac{1}{4} = \frac{\square}{12}$

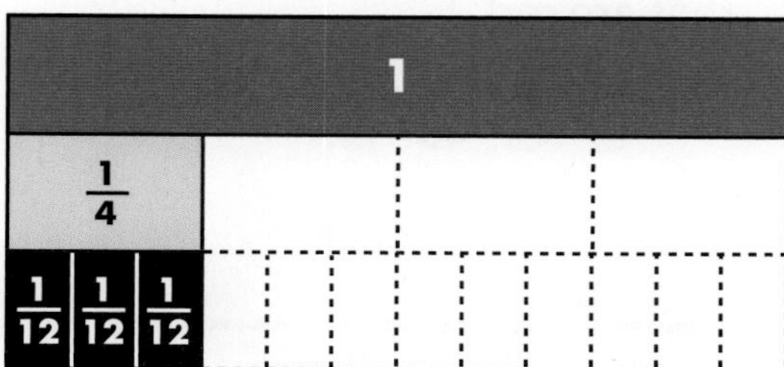

F 12

G 9

H 4

J 3

9. Alfred has 7 coins. Which shows $\frac{3}{7}$ of the coins are dimes? (11-3)

A

B

C

D

10. Griddable Response Allison is buying packages of sliced meat for the picnic. Each package has 20 slices of meat. Out of the 20 slices, 5 are turkey. If Allison buys 80 slices, how many are turkey? (11-8)

Turkey Slices	5	10		
Total Slices	20	40	60	80

Reteaching

Set A, pages 238–239

Tell if the shape is divided into equal parts of a whole and name them.

There are 8 equal parts.

The equal parts are called eighths.

Remember that equal parts do not need to be the same shape, but they must be equal in area.

Tell if each shows equal or unequal parts. If the parts are equal, name them.

1. 

2. 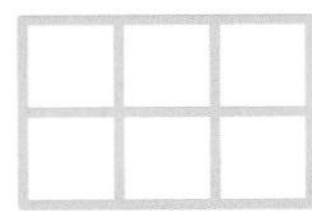

Set B, pages 240–243

What fraction of the triangles are pink?

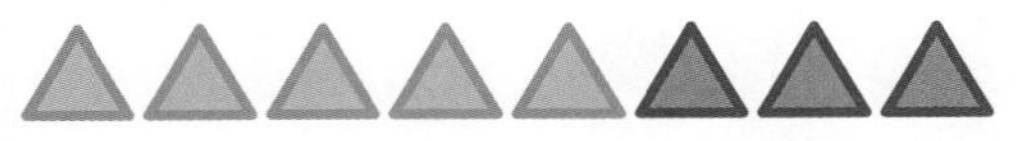

$\frac{\text{numerator}}{\text{denominator}} = \frac{\text{number of pink triangles}}{\text{total number of triangles}} = \frac{5}{8}$

$\frac{5}{8}$ of the triangles are pink.

Remember that fractions can name regions or sets.

Write the fraction of the figure that is red.

1.

Write the fraction of the counters that are red.

2.

Set C, pages 244–245

What fraction of the length of the 1 strip do the other strips show?

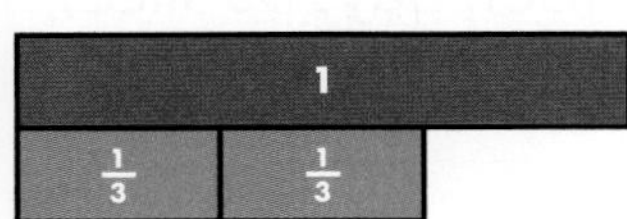

Two $\frac{1}{3}$ strips show $\frac{2}{3}$ of the 1 strip.

Remember that fraction strips divide the whole strip into equal parts.

What fraction of the length of the 1 strip do the other strips show?

1. 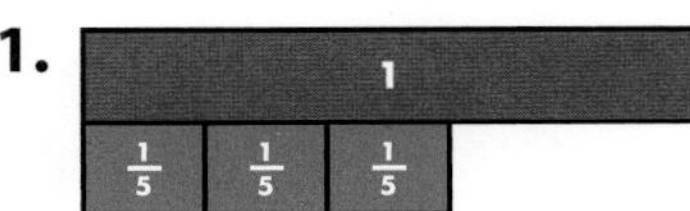

2. 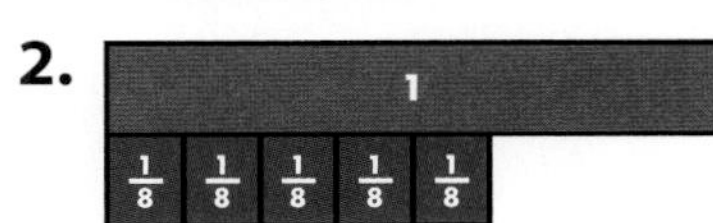

Set D, pages 246–250

Compare $\frac{3}{8}$ and $\frac{1}{2}$.

$\frac{3}{8} \bigcirc \frac{1}{2}$

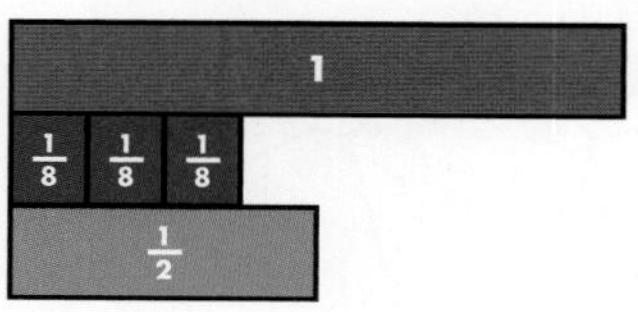

$\frac{3}{8} < \frac{1}{2}$

Remember that if two fractions have the same denominator, the fraction with the greater numerator is the greater fraction.

Compare. Write <, >, or =.

1. 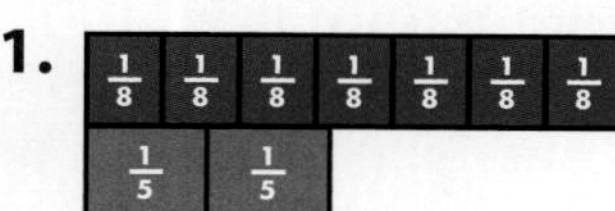

$\frac{7}{8} \bigcirc \frac{2}{5}$

Set E, pages 252–253

Complete the number sentence.

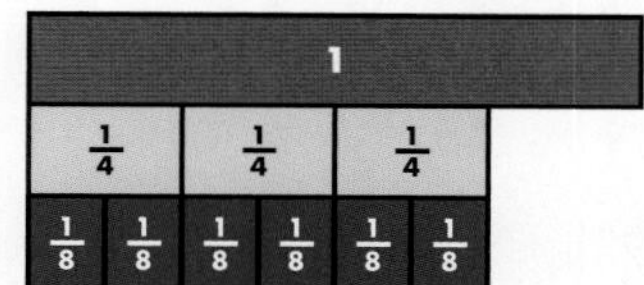

$\frac{3}{4} = \frac{\square}{8}$

$\frac{3}{4} = \frac{6}{8}$

Remember that different fractions can name the same part of a whole.

1. 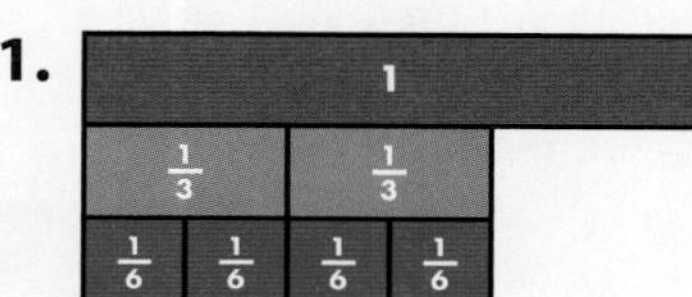

$\frac{2}{3} = \frac{\square}{6}$

Set F, pages 254–255

Make a table to solve the problem.

Bags of marbles have 20 marbles in each bag. Out of the 20 marbles, 4 are green. If you buy 80 marbles, how many are green?

Make a table showing what you know. Look for a pattern and continue it.

Green Marbles	4	8	12	16
Total Marbles	20	40	60	80

Out of 80 marbles, 16 are green.

Remember it can help to make a table when the amounts change according to a pattern.

1. Pens are sold in packages of 8. In each package there are 2 red pens. How many red pens will you get if you buy 40 pens?

Red Pens	2				
Total Pens	8				

Topic 12 Patterns and Relationships

1 How many years will it take an animal symbol to repeat in the Chinese calendar? You will find out in Lesson 12-2.

2 How fast can a penguin swim? You will find out in Lesson 12-3.

3 Are the rocks of Stonehenge arranged in a pattern? You will find out in Lesson 12-5.

4

How many eggs can an ostrich hen lay in a year? You will find out in Lesson 12-4.

Review What You Know!

Vocabulary

Choose the best term from the box.

- compare
- divide
- multiply
- regroup

1. To put together equal groups to find the total number, you ? .

2. To decide if 4 has more ones or fewer ones than 8, ? the numbers.

3. To separate into equal groups, you ? .

Number Patterns

Write the missing number in each pattern.

4. 3, 6, 9, 12, ▢, 18

5. 4, 8, 12, ▢, 20, 24

6. 8, 7, 6, ▢, 4, 3

7. 30, 25, 20, 15, ▢, 5

Multiplication Facts

Find each product.

8. 4×3

9. 3×5

10. 7×2

11. 5×6

12. 2×4

13. 3×7

Division Facts

Find each quotient.

14. $20 \div 4$

15. $10 \div 5$

16. $18 \div 6$

17. $28 \div 4$

18. $24 \div 6$

19. $56 \div 8$

20. **Writing to Explain** Janelle bought 4 cans of tennis balls. There are 3 balls in each can. How many tennis balls did she buy? Explain how you solved the problem.

Lesson
12-1

TEKS 3.6A: Identify and extend whole-number and geometric patterns to make predictions and solve problems.

Repeating Patterns

How can you continue a repeating pattern?

Rashad is making patterns with shapes. What three shapes should come next in this pattern?

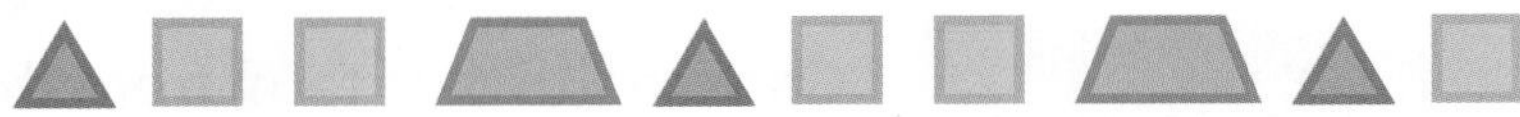

A repeating pattern is made up of shapes or numbers that form a part that repeats.

Guided Practice*

Do you know HOW?

1. Draw the next three shapes to continue the pattern.

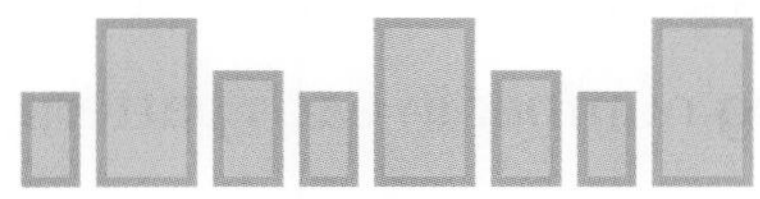

2. Write the next three numbers to continue the pattern.
9, 2, 7, 6, 9, 2, 7, 6, 9

Do you UNDERSTAND?

3. In the example above, describe the pattern using words.

4. What is the 10th shape in the pattern below? How do you know?

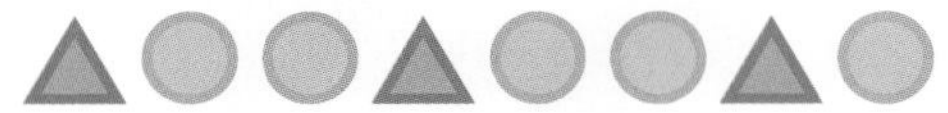

Independent Practice

In **5–8**, draw the next three shapes to continue the pattern.

5.

6.

7.

8.

In **9–12**, write the next three numbers to continue the pattern.

9. 1, 1, 2, 1, 1, 2, 1, 1, 2

10. 5, 7, 4, 8, 5, 7, 4, 8, 5, 7, 4

11. 2, 8, 2, 9, 2, 8, 2, 9, 2, 8, 2, 9

12. 4, 0, 3, 3, 4, 0, 3, 3, 4, 0, 3

Animated Glossary
www.pearsonsuccessnet.com

*For another example, see Set A on page 282.

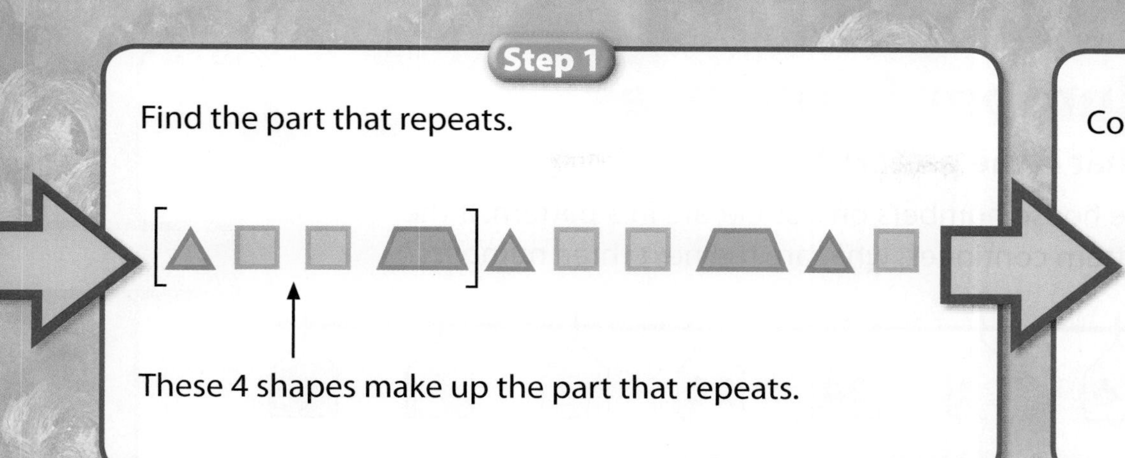

TAKS Problem Solving

13. Hilda is making a pattern with the shapes below. If she continues the pattern, what will the 11th shape in the pattern be? Draw a picture to show the shape.

14. Marcus is using shapes to make the pattern below. He wants the completed pattern to show the part that repeats 5 times. How many circles will be in Marcus' finished pattern?

15. Louisa put beads on a string to make a bracelet. She used a blue bead, then three green beads, then a blue bead, then three green beads, and so on, until she used 18 green beads. How many beads did she use in all?

16. **Estimation** A box of toy blocks has 108 blocks. Jiang used 72 of the blocks to make a building. About how many blocks are left in the box? Explain how you estimated.

17. The table shows the number of students in each grade at a school.

Which grade has more than 145 but fewer than 149 students?

A First　　**C** Second

B Third　　**D** Fourth

Data

Grade	Number of Students
First	142
Second	158
Third	146
Fourth	139

18. **Writing to Explain** Balloons are sold in bags of 30. There are 4 giant balloons in each bag. How many giant balloons will you get if you buy 120 balloons? Explain.

Lesson
12-2

TEKS 3.6A: Identify and extend whole-number and geometric patterns to make predictions and solve problems.

Number Sequences

What is the pattern?

The house numbers on a street are in a pattern. If the pattern continues, what are the next three numbers?

Guided Practice*

Do you know HOW?

In **1** and **2**, find a rule for the pattern. Use your rule to continue each pattern.

1. 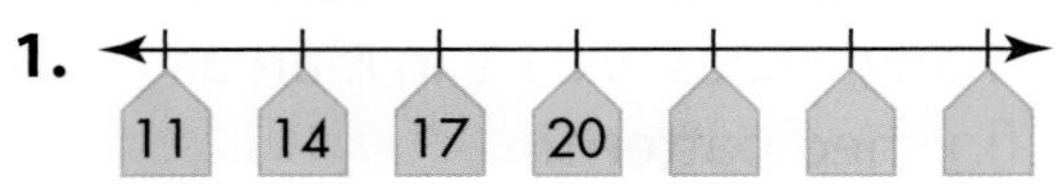

2. 48, 42, 36, 30, 24, ▢, ▢, ▢

Do you UNDERSTAND?

3. In the example above, if 16 is the 1st number in the pattern, what is the 10th number?

4. Rudy is using "add 2" as his rule to make a pattern. He started with 4 and wrote the numbers below for his pattern. Which number does not belong in the pattern? Explain.

4, 6, 8, 9, 10, 12

Independent Practice

In **5–16**, find a rule for the pattern. Use your rule to continue each pattern.

5. 21, 18, 15, ▢, ▢

6. 4, 11, 18, ▢, ▢

7. 5, 10, 15, ▢, ▢

8. 5, 7, 9, ▢, ▢, 15

9. 250, 300, 350, ▢, ▢

10. 92, 80, 68, ▢, ▢

11. 790, 780, 770, ▢, ▢

12. 16, 27, 38, ▢, ▢

13. 96, 101, 106, ▢, 116, ▢

14. 43, 47, 51, ▢, ▢, 63

15. 120, 105, 90, ▢, ▢, 45

16. 99, 90, 81, 72, ▢, ▢

*For another example, see Set B on page 282.

Step 1

Find a rule for the pattern.

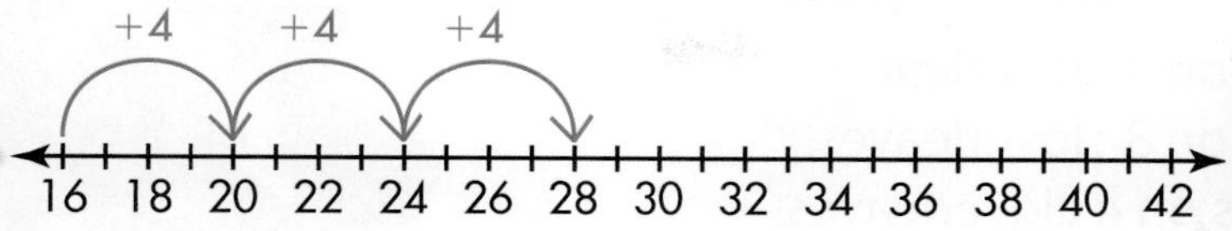

Each number is 4 more than the number before it.

Step 2

Use your rule to continue the pattern.

Rule: Add 4

$28 + 4 = 32$

$32 + 4 = 36$

$36 + 4 = 40$

The next numbers in the pattern are 32, 36, and 40.

TAKS Problem Solving

17. Orlando delivers mail. He sees that one mailbox does not have a number. If the numbers are in a pattern, what is the missing number?

18. In the Chinese calendar, each year has an animal as a symbol. There are 12 animals. It was the year of the snake in 2001 and will be again in 2013. The year 2005 was the year of the rooster. When is the next year of the rooster?

19. Suppose you were born in the year of the snake. How old will you be the next time the year of the snake is celebrated?

The pattern of animals repeats every 12 years.

20. **Reasoning** The numbers below are in a pattern.

24, 27, 30, 33

Which number would be part of the pattern?

A 34 **C** 39

B 38 **D** 44

21. Mia counted the pencils in a box.

If she counted the pencils in groups of 6, which list shows numbers Mia could have named?

F 24, 36, 48, 52 **H** 6, 12, 24, 32

G 6, 24, 48, 56 **J** 12, 18, 24, 30

Lesson

12-3

TEKS 3.7A: Generate a table of paired numbers based on a real-life situation such as insects and legs.

Extending Tables

What pairs of numbers fit a pattern?

There are 3 leaflets on 1 cloverleaf.
There are 9 leaflets on 3 cloverleaves.
There are 12 leaflets on 4 cloverleaves.
How many leaflets are there on 2 cloverleaves? on 5 cloverleaves?

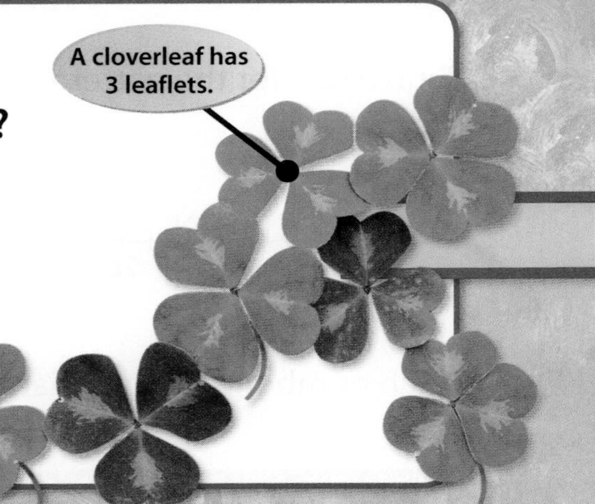

Guided Practice*

Do you know HOW?

In **1** and **2**, copy and complete each table.

1.

Number of Boxes	*Total Number of Hats*
2	6
5	15
7	21
	27

2.

Number of Cars	2	3	5	9
Total Number of Wheels	8	12	20	

Do you UNDERSTAND?

3. In the example above, 4 and 12 are a pair of numbers that fit the pattern. Does the pair 6 and 16 fit the pattern? Explain.

4. **Reasonableness** A rule for this table is "add 5 to my age."

My Age	*Joe's Age*
5	10
8	13
9	15

Which number does not belong?

Independent Practice

In **5–7**, copy and complete each table.

5.

Number of Spiders	*Number of Legs*
1	8
2	
3	24
4	32
	56

6.

Regular Price	*Sale Price*
$29	$22
$25	$18
	$16
$22	
$19	$12

7.

Weight of Book in Ounces	9	11	12	16
Total Weight of Carton in Ounces	18	20	21	

8. For each table in 5–7, write another pair of numbers that belongs in the table.

*For another example, see Set C on page 282.

One Way

Draw pictures and count the leaves.

2 cloverleaves have 6 leaflets.

5 cloverleaves have 15 leaflets.

Another Way

Fill in a table by using a rule.

Rule: Multiply by 3

Number of Cloverleaves	Number of Leaflets
1	3
2	6
3	9
4	12
5	15

TAKS Problem Solving

For **9** and **10**, the table at the right shows the number of batteries needed for different numbers of one kind of flashlight.

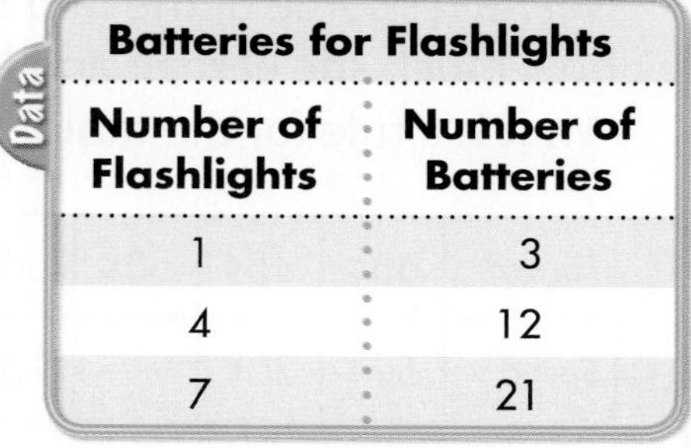

Batteries for Flashlights

Number of Flashlights	Number of Batteries
1	3
4	12
7	21

9. How many batteries do 8 flashlights need? 10 flashlights?

10. **Writing to Explain** How many more batteries do 6 flashlights need than 4 flashlights? Explain how you found your answer.

11. **Number Sense** What is the greatest number you can make using each of the digits 1, 7, 0, and 6 once?

12. A penguin can swim 11 miles per hour. At this speed, how far can it swim in 3 hours? Use a table to help.

13. Alan has 35 fewer coins than Suzy has. Which of these shows the number of coins that Alan and Suzy could have?

A Alan 65, Suzy 105

B Alan 105, Suzy 70

C Alan 105, Suzy 65

D Alan 70, Suzy 105

14. If the pattern at the right continues, how long will each side of the next square be?

F 8 feet

G 9 feet

H 10 feet

J 11 feet

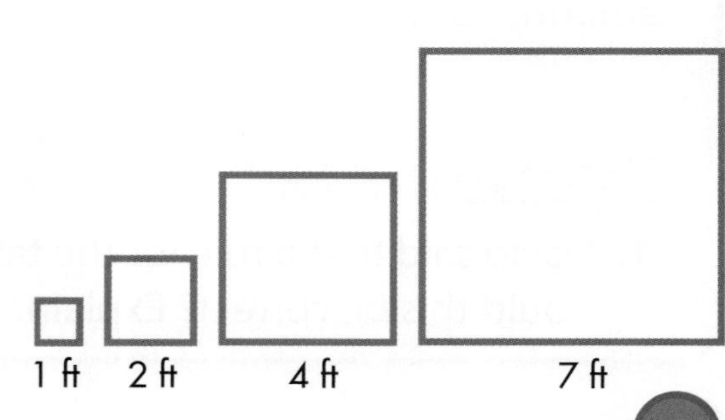

Lesson
12-4

TEKS 3.7B: Identify and describe patterns in a table of related number pairs based on a meaningful problem and extend the table.

Writing Rules for Situations

What is a math rule for the situation?

Alex and his older brother Andy have the same birthday. If you know Alex's age, how can you find Andy's age? Look for a pattern in the table and find a rule.

Alex's age	2	4	6	7	9
Andy's age	8	10	12	13	15

Another Example What other rules are there for pairs of numbers?

Nell saves some of the money she earns. The table shows how much she earned and how much she saved for five days. What is a rule for the table? What are the missing numbers?

Earned	65¢	45¢	50¢	30¢	
Saved	50¢	30¢		15¢	25¢

Step 1

Find a rule for the table.

Look for a pattern.

Earned	65¢	45¢	50¢	30¢	
Saved	50¢	30¢		15¢	25¢

Each time, the amount saved is 15¢ less than the amount earned.

A rule is "subtract 15¢ from the amount earned."

Step 2

Check that your rule works for all pairs.

Rule: Subtract 15¢ from the amount earned.

65¢ − 15¢ = 50¢
45¢ − 15¢ = 30¢
30¢ − 15¢ = 15¢

The rule works for each pair.

What amount is 15¢ less than 50¢?
50¢ − 15¢ = 35¢

25¢ is 15¢ less than what amount?
25¢ = ☐ − 15¢   15¢ + 25¢ = 40¢

The missing amounts are 35¢ and 40¢.

Explain It

1. David said that a rule for the table above is "Add 15¢." Could this be correct? Explain.

Step 1

Find a rule for the table.

Compare each pair of numbers. Look for a pattern.

Alex's age	2	4	6	7	9
Andy's age	8	10	12	13	15

In each pair, Andy's age is 6 more than Alex's age. The rule is "add 6."

Step 2

Check that your rule works for all pairs.

Rule: Add 6

$2 + 6 = 8$
$4 + 6 = 10$
$6 + 6 = 12$
$7 + 6 = 13$
$9 + 6 = 15$

Your rule works for each pair.

Guided Practice*

Do you know HOW?

In **1** and **2**, use the table below.

Hours Worked	4	8	7	2	6
Amount Earned	$24	$48	▢	$12	▢

1. Write a rule for the table.

2. Write the missing numbers.

Do you UNDERSTAND?

3. In the example above, what does the rule "add 6" mean in the problem?

4. Marty uses the rule "subtract 9" for his table. If the first number is 11, what is the second number in the number pair?

Independent Practice

In **5–9**, find a rule for the table. Use your rule to complete the table.

5.

Earned	$15	$12	$17	$9	$11
Spent	$7	▢	$9	▢	$3

6.

Earned	$14	$18	$12	$16	$8
Saved	$7	$9	▢	▢	$4

7.

Price	$36	$28	$33	$40	$25
Discount	$24	$16	▢	$28	▢

8.

Number of Chairs	*Number of Legs*
3	12
2	8
5	20
7	▢
▢	36

9.

Number of Teams	*Number of Players*
4	20
3	15
5	▢
6	30
8	▢

****For another example, see Set C on page 282.**

TAKS Problem Solving

For **10** and **11**, use the table at the right.

Plant's Age in Years	
Velvet Mesquite Tree	**Saguaro Cactus**
1 year	36
15	50
67	102
48	

10. The table shows the ages of a Velvet mesquite tree and a Saguaro cactus plant at a garden. When the Velvet mesquite tree was 48 years old, how old was the Saguaro cactus?

11. Reasonableness Phil says the Saguaro cactus is about 100 years older than the Velvet mesquite tree. Is his estimate reasonable? Explain.

12. Use the table below. How many eggs can 4 ostrich hens lay in a year? 5 ostrich hens?

Number of Ostrich Hens	1	2	3	4	5
Number of Eggs	50	100	150		

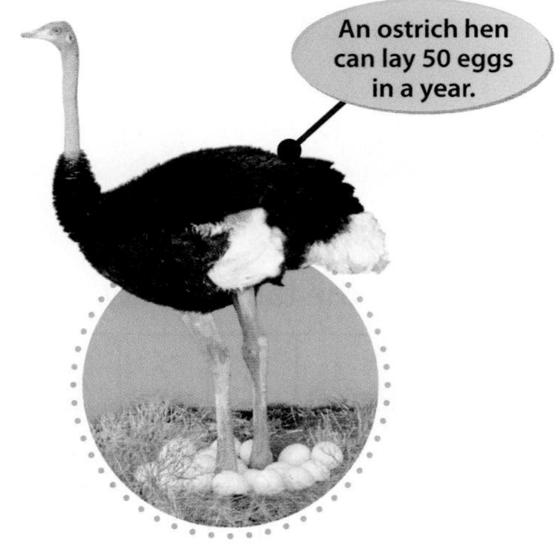

For **13** and **14**, the table shows the number of baskets that Betty needs for different numbers of apples. She needs to put an equal number of apples into each basket.

Betty's Apple Baskets					
Number of Apples	28	56	7	21	14
Number of Baskets	4		1	3	2

13. How many baskets does Betty need for 56 apples?

A 8 **B** 7 **C** 6 **D** 5

14. What is the rule for the table?

F Subtract 24
G Subtract 6
H Divide by 7
J Add 12

15. An art museum has 47 paintings in one room and 24 paintings in another room. Which is the best estimate of the total number of paintings?

A 50
B 70
C 80
D 100

16. Esther is 8 years older than Manuel. Which of these shows the ages that Esther and Manuel each could be?

F Esther 15, Manuel 23
G Esther 16, Manuel 15
H Esther 15, Manuel 7
J Esther 7, Manuel 15

Mixed Problem Solving

In the 1800s and 1900s, several inventions helped to change life around the world. The time line shows the dates of some of these inventions and discoveries.

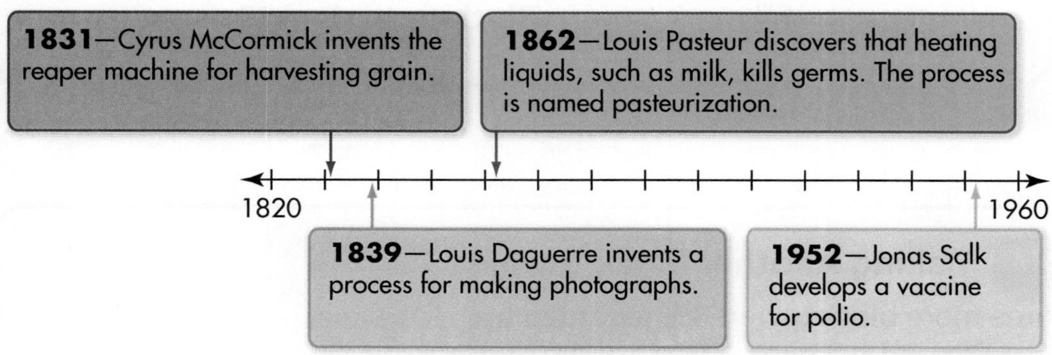

1. Which invention was made about 10 years before a process for making photographs was invented?

2. About how many years after the development of pasteurization was the development of a polio vaccine?

3. Which invention or discovery was made before 1900 but after 1850?

4. How many years have passed since the year that a polio vaccine was developed?

5. Look at the table below.

Data

Year	Number of Polio Cases in the World
1988	350,000
1996	4,074
2000	2,971
2004	1,258

How many fewer cases of polio were there in 2004 than in 1996?

6. **Strategy Focus** Solve the problem. Use the strategy Make a Table.

The reaper machine could cut wheat and move it to the side for harvesting. One reaper machine could do the work of 5 people. How many reapers could do the work of 20 people?

Lesson
12-5

TEKS 3.6A: Identify and extend whole-number and geometric patterns to make predictions and solve problems.

Geometric Patterns

Hands-On
grid paper

How can you describe block towers?

Talisa made three block towers. She recorded her pattern. If she continued the pattern, how many blocks would be in a 10-story tower? a 100-story tower?

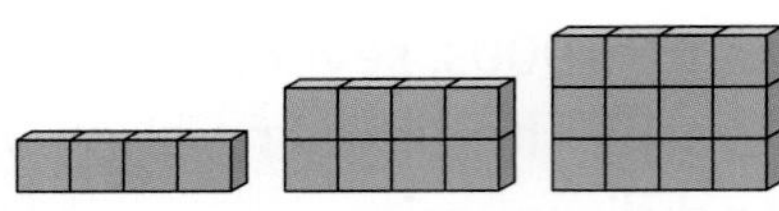

Stories:	1	2	3
Blocks:	4	8	12

Another Example Making Another Block Tower

Luis made three more block towers. He recorded his pattern. If he continued the pattern, how many blocks would a 5-story tower have?

Number of Stories	1	2	3
Number of Blocks	1	3	6

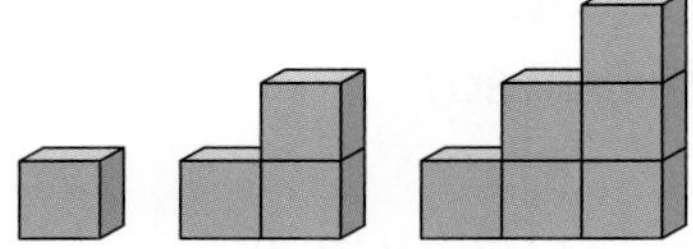

Build the next two towers.

Number of Stories	1	2	3	4	5
Number of Blocks	1	3	6	?	?

A 4-story tower has 10 blocks, and a 5-story tower has 15 blocks.

Explain It

1. How many blocks would Luis need for a 6-story tower? Explain.
2. How many stories is a tower made of 36 blocks?

Build the next two towers.

Number of Stories	1	2	3	4	5
Number of Blocks	4	8	12		

1 story
4 blocks

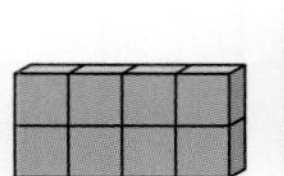
2 stories
8 blocks

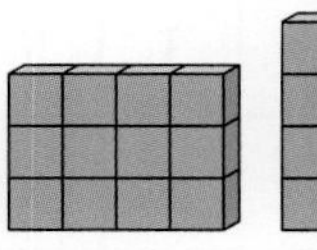
3 stories
12 blocks

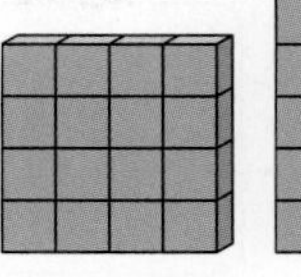
4 stories
16 blocks

5 stories
20 blocks

The pattern in the table is "multiply by 4."

$$5 \times 4 = 20$$
$$10 \times 4 = 40$$
$$100 \times 4 = 400$$

A 10-story tower would have 40 blocks.

A 100-story tower would have 400 blocks.

Guided Practice*

Do you know HOW?

In **1** and **2**, draw the next two towers in the pattern. Use grid paper. Find the missing numbers in each table.

1.

Number of Stories	1	2	3	4	5
Number of Blocks	2	4	6		

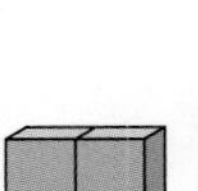

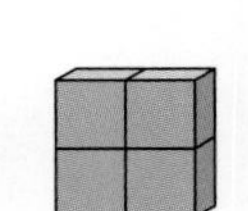

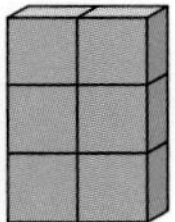

2.

Number of Stories	1	2	3	4	5	
Number of Blocks	2	3	4	5		7

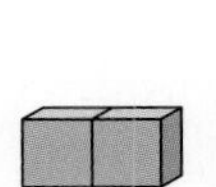

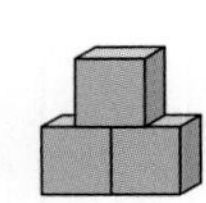

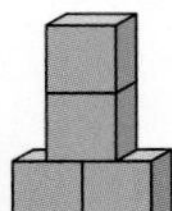

Do you UNDERSTAND?

3. In the example above, why does multiplication work to get from the first number to the second number in a number pair?

4. In Exercise 1, how many blocks would a 10-story tower have?

5. Lionel made the three block towers below. If he continued the pattern, how many blocks would a 100-story tower have?

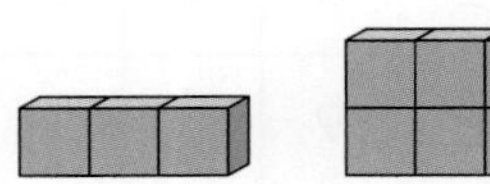

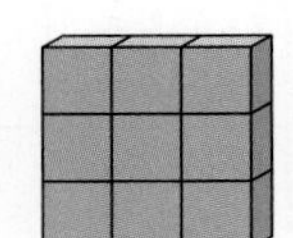

6. Writing to Explain How many blocks would you need to make a 15-story tower in Exercise 2? Explain how you know.

DIGITAL
eTools
www.pearsonsuccessnet.com

For another example, see Set D on page 283.

Independent Practice

In **7–10**, draw the next two figures in the pattern.
Use grid paper to help. Find the missing numbers in each table.

7.

Number of Stories	7	6	5	4	3
Number of Blocks	21	18	15		

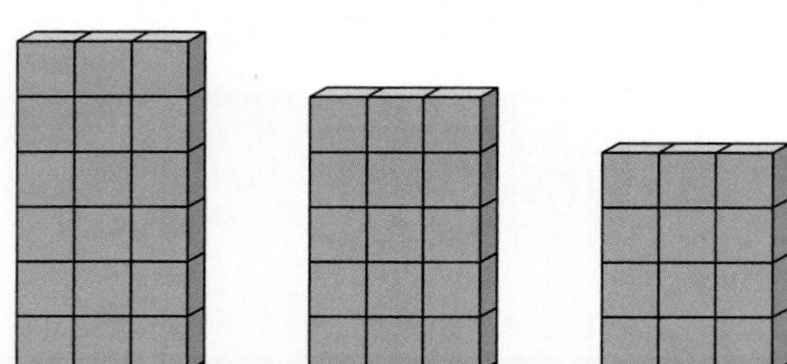

8.

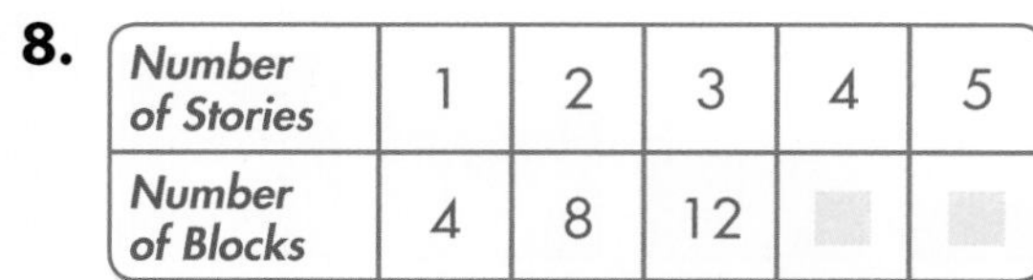

Number of Stories	1	2	3	4	5
Number of Blocks	4	8	12		

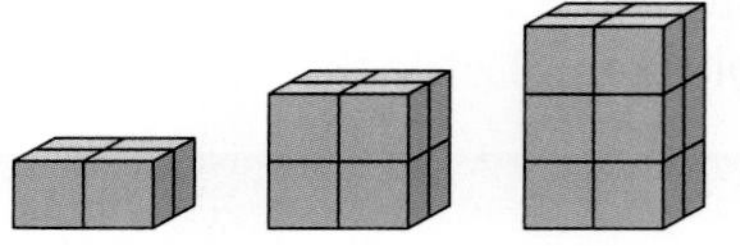

9.

Number of Rows	2	3	4	5	6
Number of Squares	3	5	7		

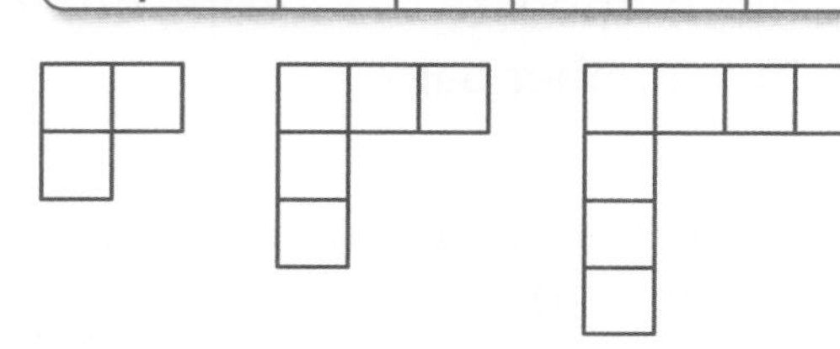

10.

Number of Rows	1	2	3	4	5
Number of Small Triangles	1	4	9		

In **11–13**, use the patterns in the figures to copy and complete each table.

11.

Number of Stories	1	2	3	4	5	
Number of Blocks	3	6	9			30

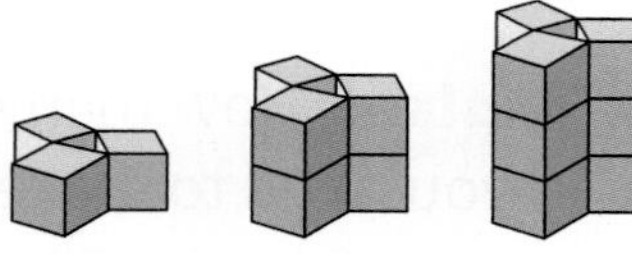

12.

Length of Side	1	2	4	6	9
Sum of All Sides	4	8	16		

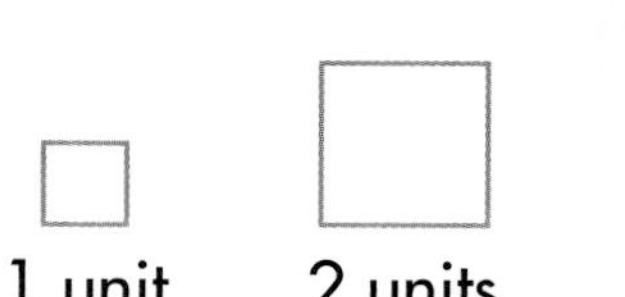

1 unit 2 units 4 units

13.

Number of Stories	1	2	3	4	5
Number of Blocks	2	6	12		

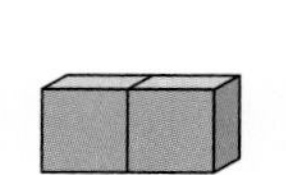

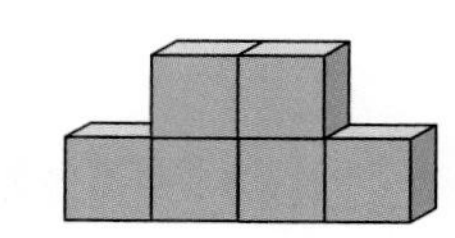

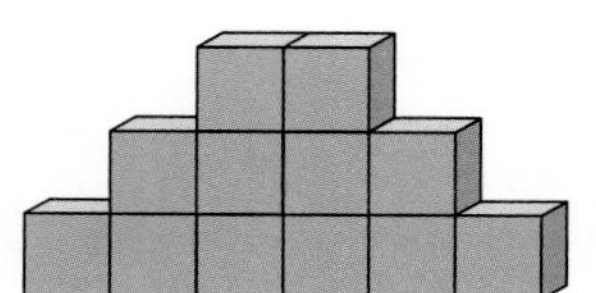

14. Jon used 15 blocks to make a tower. Then he used 12 blocks to make a tower, and then 9 blocks to make a tower. If he continued the pattern, what rule could he use for this table?

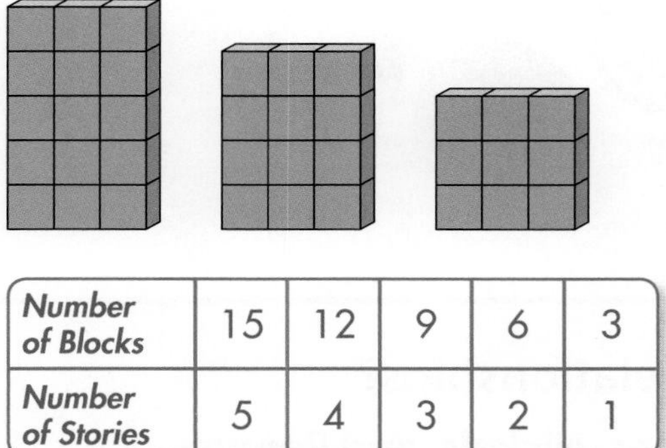

Number of Blocks	15	12	9	6	3
Number of Stories	5	4	3	2	1

15. Dean is making picture frames. He uses the same number of wood pieces in each frame. The table shows the number of wood pieces that he needs for different numbers of frames.

Number of Frames	6	7	8	9	10
Number of Wood Pieces	24	28	■	36	40

How many wood pieces does Dean need for 8 picture frames?

A 30 **C** 34

B 32 **D** 36

16. Stonehenge is an ancient monument in England made up of a pattern of rocks that looks like this:

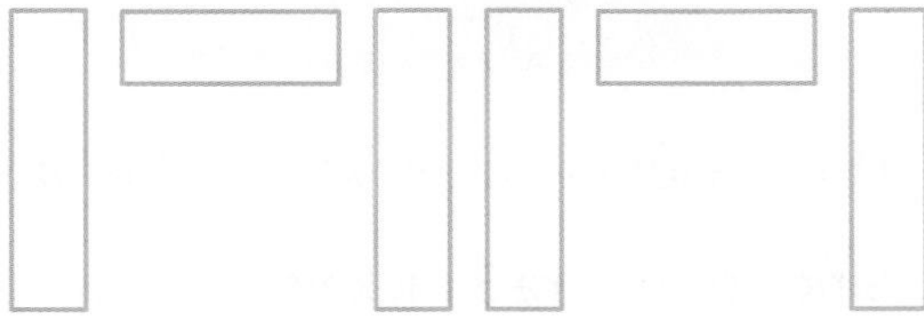

Draw the shape that comes next in this pattern.

17. Maura made these three block towers. If she continued the pattern, how many blocks would a 10-story tower have? How many blocks would a 100-story tower have?

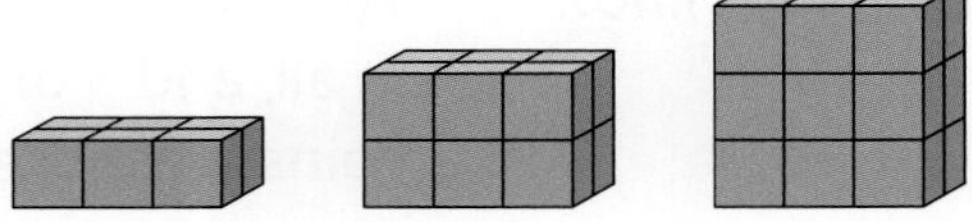

18. **Algebra** What two 1-digit factors could you multiply to get a product of 48?

19. **Writing to Explain** Which product is greater, 9×15 or 9×17? Explain how you can tell without finding the products.

20. **Estimation** Lily has 75¢. A stamp costs 39¢. Does she have enough money to buy 2 stamps? Explain.

21. Leon ran twice as many laps around the track as Sam. Sam ran 6 laps. How many laps did they run in all?

Lesson

12-6

TEKS 3.14C: Select or develop an appropriate problem-solving plan or strategy, including drawing a picture, looking for a pattern, systematic guessing and checking, acting it out, making a table, working a simpler problem, or working backwards to solve a problem.

Problem Solving

Act It Out and Use Reasoning

Hands-On
counter

Juana collected old pennies, nickels, and dimes. Her collection has at least one of each kind of coin.

How many of each kind of coin does Juana have?

Juana's Collection
2 pennies
2 fewer nickels than dimes
10 coins in all

nickel

penny

dime

Another Example What are other kinds of relationships?

Ken's Collection of Dimes, Nickels, and Pennies
3 nickels
4 more dimes than nickels
15 coins in all

How many of each coin are in his collection?

Read and Understand

What do I know? There are 15 coins in all, and 3 of the coins are nickels.

There are 4 more dimes than nickels.

Use objects to show what you know.

Plan and Solve

Use reasoning to make conclusions.

Since there are 3 nickels, there are 12 pennies and dimes together.

Try 3 nickels, 7 dimes, and 5 pennies. Since $3 + 7 + 5 = 15$, this is correct.

There are 5 pennies, 3 nickels, and 7 dimes in the collection.

Explain It

1. Which number of coins in Ken's collection is given to you? Which information do you need to find?
2. Explain how you know 7 is the number of dimes in the solution above.

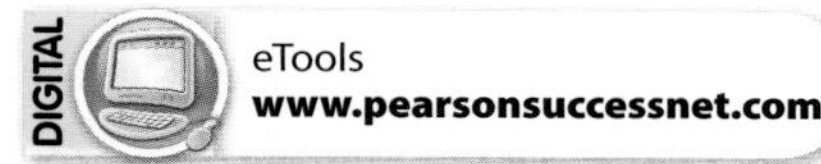

Read and Understand

What do I know? Juana has 10 coins in all, and 2 of the coins are pennies.

There are 2 fewer nickels than dimes.

Use objects to show what you know.

Plan and Solve

Use reasoning to make conclusions.

She has 2 pennies, so there are 8 nickels and dimes together.

Try 2 nickels and 4 dimes. But $2 + 2 + 4$ is not equal to 10.

Try 3 nickels and 5 dimes. Since $2 + 3 + 5 = 10$, this is correct.

There are 2 pennies, 3 nickels, and 5 dimes in Juana's collection.

Guided Practice*

Do you know HOW?

Find the number of each kind of stamp in the collection. Use counters.

1. Ricardo has 9 stamps in all. He has 2 nation stamps and 3 more inventor stamps than flower stamps.

Nation Stamps = ☐
Inventor Stamps = ☐
Flower Stamps = ☐

Do you UNDERSTAND?

2. What did you do to find the number of inventor stamps in Ricardo's collection?

3. **Write a Problem** Write a problem about coin collections that you can solve by using logical reasoning.

Independent Practice

Find the number of each kind of object in Anya's collection. Use counters or draw pictures to help.

4. **Anya's Collection of Minerals, Gemstones and Rocks**
6 minerals
3 fewer gemstones than rocks.
15 objects in all.

Minerals = ☐
Gemstones = ☐
Rocks = ☐

Stuck? Try this....

- What do I know?
- What am I asked to find?
- What diagram can I use to help understand the problem?
- Can I use addition, subtraction, multiplication, or division?
- Is all of my work correct?
- Did I answer the right question?
- Is my answer reasonable?

*For another example, see Set E on page 283.

5. There are 10 fish in all in Percy's fish tank. Four of the fish are angel fish. There are 4 more mollie fish than tetra fish. How many of each kind of fish are in the tank?

6. Norah's dog weighs 9 pounds more than her cat. Her dog weighs 6 pounds less than Jeff's dog. Norah's cat weighs 7 pounds. How much does Jeff's dog weigh?

7. The students in Mr. Cole's class voted on which kind of collection they should start as a class. The graph shows the results. How many more votes did the collection with the greatest number of votes get than the collection with the least number of votes?

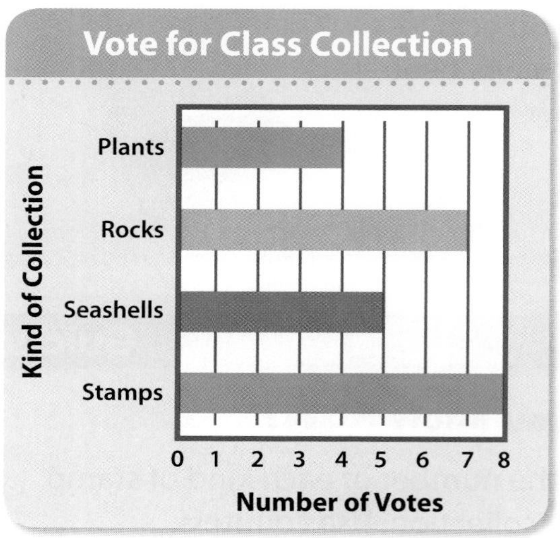

8. Isadora has 15 seashells in her collection. The seashells are oyster shells, clam shells, and conch shells. There are 6 clam shells. There are 2 fewer clam shells than oyster shells. How many conch shells are in the collection?

9. Lyn, Kurt, and Steve wrote a riddle about their ages. Lyn is 7 years older than Steve. Steve is 5 years old. The sum of their ages is 25 years. How old is Kurt?

10. Sondra wants to buy 2 plates and 3 towels. What is the total cost of her items?

Data

Item	Price
Flashlight	\$9
Plate	\$7
Towel	\$4
Fishing net	\$8
Umbrella	\$3

11. **Think About the Process** At the town pet show, Dina saw 48 pets. There were 6 birds and 7 cats. The remaining pets were dogs. Which number sentence shows one way to find the number of pets that were dogs?

A $48 - 6 - 7 = \square$

B $48 + 6 \div 7 = \square$

C $48 - 6 \times 7 = \square$

D $6 \times 7 \times 48 = \square$

Extending Tables

Use e tools

Spreadsheet/Data/Grapher eTool

Use a rule to complete the table.

Number of Lions	1	2	3	4	5
Number of Legs	4	8		16	20

Step 1 Go to the Spreadsheet/Data/Grapher eTool. Use the arrow tool to select at least 2 rows and 6 columns. Set the number of decimal places at zero using the .00 pull-down menu. Enter *Lions*, *1*, *2*, *3*, *4*, *5* in row A. Enter *Legs* in the first column of row B.

Step 2 Try the rule "multiply by 4." Cell B2 is in column B, row 2. In cell B2, type = *4*B1*. This will multiply 4 times 1 and show the product in cell B1. In cell C2, type = *4*C1*. Do the same for cells D2, E2, and F2.

Step 3 Check that the numbers match those in the above table. This means the rule "multiply by 4" is correct. The missing number is 12.

Set number of decimal places

F2	20					
	A	B	C	D	E	F
1	Lions	1.00	2.00	3.00	4.00	5.00
2	Legs	4.00	8.00	12.00	16.00	20.00

Practice

Copy each table, find the rule, and fill in the missing cell.

1.

Bud's Age	2	4	6	9
Spot's Age	7	9		14

2.

Days	1	2	3	4
Toys Made	7		21	28

TAKS Test Prep

1. Mrs. Inez made loaves of banana bread for the bake sale. The list below shows the number of eggs she had used after making each loaf starting with 5 loaves.

   15, 18, 21, 24

   How many eggs will she have used after she makes one more loaf? (12-2)

   A 25

   B 27

   C 28

   D 30

2. What are the next 3 numbers in this pattern? (12-1)

   6, 5, 3, 1, 6, 5, 3, 1, 6, 5, 3

   F 6, 3, 1

   G 6, 5, 3

   H 1, 5, 3

   J 1, 6, 5

3. What rule can be used to find the number of legs on 7 grasshoppers? (12-4)

Number of Grasshoppers	3	5	7	9
Number of Legs	18	30		54

   A Add 15

   B Divide by 6

   C Multiply by 5

   D Multiply by 6

4. Coach Kim needs to form equal sized teams. The table shows the number of teams formed for different numbers of players.

Number of Players	24	32	40	72
Number of Teams	3	4		9

   What rule can be used to find how many teams are formed if there are 40 players? (12-4)

   F Divide by 8

   G Divide by 6

   H Multiply by 8

   J Multiply by 6

5. Kayla is cutting ribbon to go around picture holders, which are in the shape of a triangle, with all sides the same length. How many inches of ribbon does she need for a picture holder with sides that are 7 inches long? (12-5)

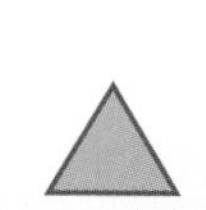
2 inches

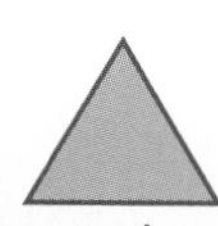
3 inches

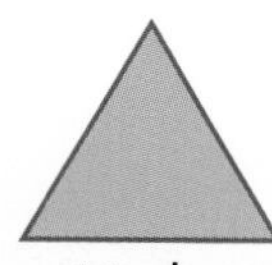
4 inches

Inches in One Side	2	3	4	7
Inches of Ribbon	6	9	12	

   A 15

   B 18

   C 21

   D 24

6. Hank had a party at the zoo. Below is a guide to find the total price of admission for different size parties.

Total Number of Children	*Total Admission Price*
3	$21
5	$35
7	
9	$63

What is the cost for 7 children? (12-3)

F $37

G $48

H $49

J $56

7. Jasmine has a wallpaper border in her room. Which shows the next 3 objects in the pattern? (12-1)

A 

B 

C 

D 

8. Joe has 18 pets. Ten are fish. The rest are birds or hamsters. He has 2 fewer birds than hamsters. How many birds does he have? (12-6)

F 2

G 3

H 4

J 5

9. What is the rule for the pattern? (12-2)

29, 24, 19, 14, 9

A Subtract 4

B Subtract 5

C Add 4

D Add 5

10. Griddable Response The table shows how many ounces of juice are in different numbers of cans. The cans are exactly alike.

Number of Cans	3	6	9	12
Number of Ounces	18	36		72

How many ounces are in 9 cans of juice? (12-3)

11. Griddable Response Football players came out of the locker room in the pattern below.

What number belongs on the blank shirt? (12-2)

Reteaching

Set A, pages 262–263

Draw the next three shapes to continue the pattern.

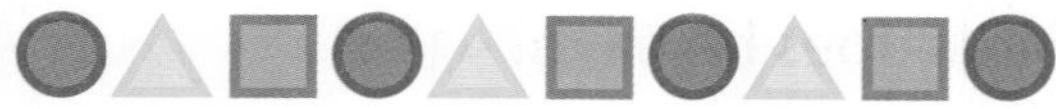

Find the part of the pattern that repeats.

Then continue the pattern.

Remember to first find the part of the pattern that repeats.

Draw the next three shapes or numbers to continue the pattern.

1. 

2. 3, 5, 7, 9, 3, 5, 7, 9, 3, 5, 7

Set B, pages 264–265

Find a rule for the pattern. Use the rule to continue the pattern.

24, 21, 18, 15, 12, ▢, ▢, ▢,

−3 −3 −3 −3 −3 −3 −3

Rule: Subtract 3

$12 - 3 = 9$ $9 - 3 = 6$ $6 - 3 = 3$

The next numbers in the pattern are 9, 6, and 3.

Remember to check that your rule works with all of the given numbers for the pattern.

Find a rule for each pattern. Use the rule to continue the pattern.

1. 5, 7, 9, ▢, ▢, ▢

2. 22, 18, 14, ▢, ▢, ▢

Set C, pages 266–270

Find a rule and fill in the table.

Number of Ants	1	2	3	4	5
Number of Legs	6	▢	18	24	▢

A rule is multiply the number of ants by 6.

Number of Ants	1	2	3	4	5
Number of Legs	6	12	18	24	30

The missing numbers are 12 and 30.

Remember to use the number pairs in a table to find a rule.

Find the missing numbers. Write a rule.

1.

Number of Cars	1	2	3	4
Number of Wheels	4	8	▢	▢

2.

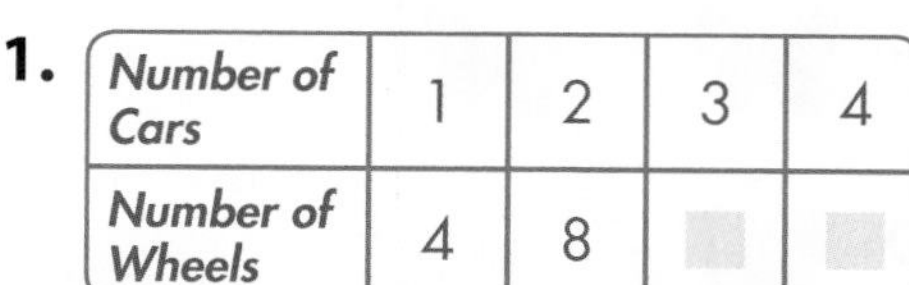

Saved	\$8	\$12	\$15	\$6	\$10
Earned	\$16	\$24	▢	▢	\$20

Set D, pages 272–275

Sam made three block towers. He recorded his pattern. If he continued the pattern, how many blocks would a 5-story tower have?

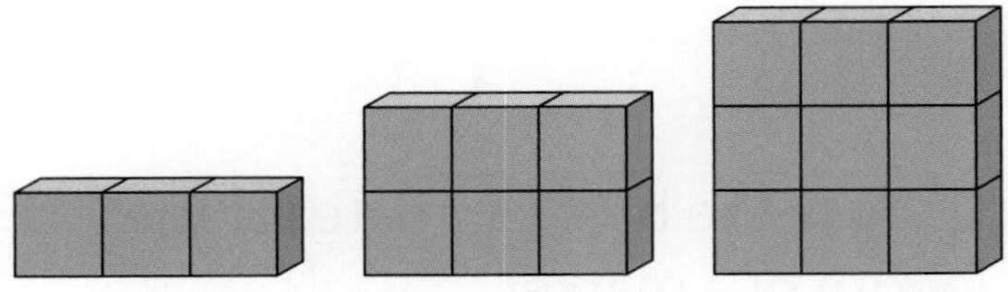

Number of Stories	1	2	3
Number of Blocks	3	6	9

The pattern in the table is multiply by 3.

So, use 5×3 to find the number of blocks in a 5 story tower.

$5 \times 3 = 15$.

There are 15 blocks in a 5-story tower.

Remember to be sure you are using the correct operation to find the number of blocks.

1. Draw the next two figures in the pattern. Use grid paper. Find the missing numbers in the table, and write the rule.

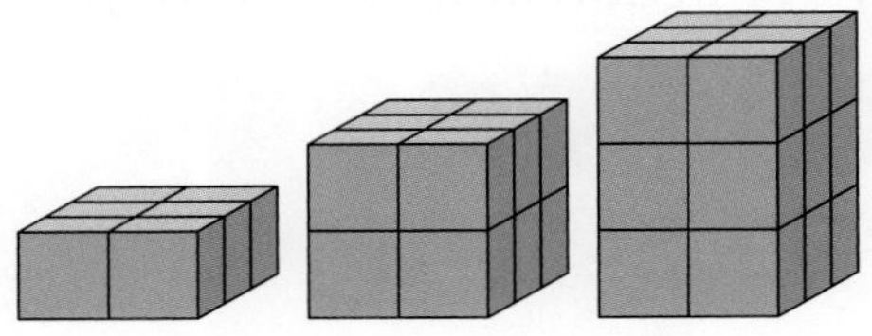

Number of Stories	1	2	3	4	5
Number of Blocks	6	12	18		

Set E, pages 276–278

When you solve a problem by acting it out, follow these steps.

Step 1

Choose objects to act out the problem.

Step 2

Show what you know using the objects.

Step 3

Act out the problem.

Step 4

Find the answer.

Remember to decide what the objects represent before you act out the problem.

Solve. Find the number of each kind of object in the collection.

1. **Ben's Sticker Collection**
   - 17 stickers in all
   - 6 star stickers
   - 3 fewer smiley face stickers than planet stickers

   Star Stickers = ▢
   Smiley Face Stickers = ▢
   Planet Stickers = ▢

Spiral Review

Number and Operations

1. Which number makes this number sentence true?

$3{,}535 < \square$

A 3,525 **C** 3,355

B 3,553 **D** 3,532

2. What fraction of the balls are yellow?

F $\frac{3}{5}$ **H** $\frac{5}{8}$

G $\frac{5}{3}$ **J** $\frac{3}{8}$

3. Estimate the difference.

$892 - 129$

A 900 **C** 800

B 825 **D** 700

4. Copy and complete the number sentence below.

$\frac{1}{2} = \frac{3}{\square}$

5. Hector made a tower using blocks. Each story of the tower was made of 3 rows. Each row had 2 blocks. The tower was 6 stories tall. How many blocks did Hector use?

6. Writing to Explain Explain how thinking about multiplication can help you find $28 \div 4$. Then find the quotient.

Geometry and Measurement

7. How many sides does a triangle have?

F 2 **H** 4

G 3 **J** 8

8. Choose the best estimate for the length of a marker.

A 1 inch **C** 8 inches

B 2 feet **D** 24 inches

9. This paper clip is about 1 inch long. How long is the ribbon?

F about 3 inches

G about 2 inches

H about 5 inches

J about 6 inches

10. Kevin woke up at 7:30 A.M. It took him 30 minutes to get ready for school. At what time did he finish getting ready?

11. What is the area of the shaded part of the figure?

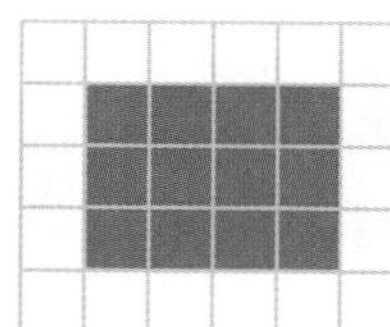

12. Writing to Explain How many ways can you make $0.11 using pennies, nickels, and dimes? Make an organized list to solve.

Probability and Statistics

13. Martin made a pictograph. Each symbol on his graph stands for 2 votes. How many symbols did he use for 12 votes?

A 2 **C** 6
B 4 **D** 8

14. When it is snowing, which temperature is more likely than the others?

F 30°F **H** 65°F
G 50°F **J** 80°F

Use the bar graph for **15** and **16**.

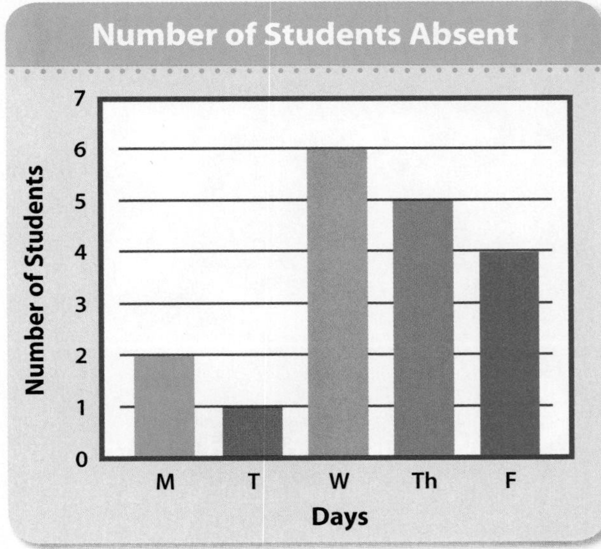

15. How many were absent on Friday?

16. When were 6 students absent?

17. **Writing to Explain** There are 10 blue, 3 yellow, and 5 red marbles in a bag. If you take a marble without looking, which color are you less likely to pick than the others? Explain.

Algebraic Thinking

18. What number is missing in the pattern below?

7, 9, 12, 7, 9, 12, 7, ▢

A 8 **C** 10
B 9 **D** 12

19. What number is missing from the table?

Number of Bikes	1	4	7	10
Number of Wheels	2	8	▢	20

F 9 **H** 12
G 10 **J** 14

20. What multiplication property says that $5 \times 1 = 5$?

A Commutative (order) Property
B Associative (grouping) Property
C Identity Property
D Zero Property

21. Draw the next three shapes in this pattern.

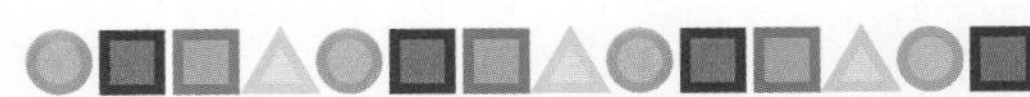

22. **Writing to Explain** A hospital has 2 nurses on duty for every 10 patients. If there are 70 patients in the hospital, how many nurses are on duty? Explain how you found your answer.

Topic 13

Whole Numbers and Fractions on the Number Line

1 On August 7, 2004, a record for the world's longest sandwich was set. How long was the sandwich? You will find out in Lesson 13-2.

2 What is the record length of the "World's Longest Apple Peel?" You will find out in Lesson 13-1.

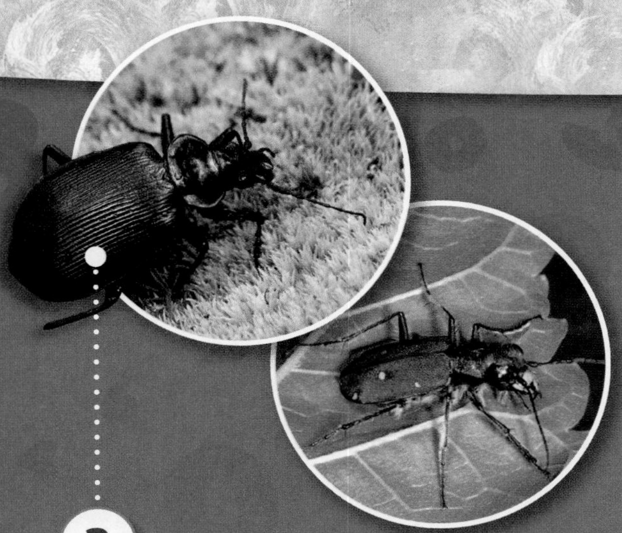

3

The tiger beetle and the caterpillar hunter beetle are helpful insects that live in Texas. Which type of beetle is longer? You will find out in Lesson 13-4.

4

How many centimeters does the shore of Iceland grow each year? You will find out in Lesson 13-3.

Review What You Know!

Vocabulary

Choose the best term from the box.

- compare
- half
- fraction
- order

1. When you decide one number is greater than another number, you __?__ the numbers.

2. A number that names part of a whole is a __?__.

3. When numbers are written from greatest to least, the numbers are in __?__.

Skip Counting

Write the missing numbers.

4. 2, 4, 6, ▢, ▢, 12, ▢

5. 4, 8, 12, ▢, ▢, ▢

Compare Numbers

Compare. Write < or >.

6. 5 ◯ 7

7. 18 ◯ 13

8. 86 ◯ 87

9. 128 ◯ 124

Equivalent Fractions

10. **Writing to Explain** Describe what the drawing below shows.

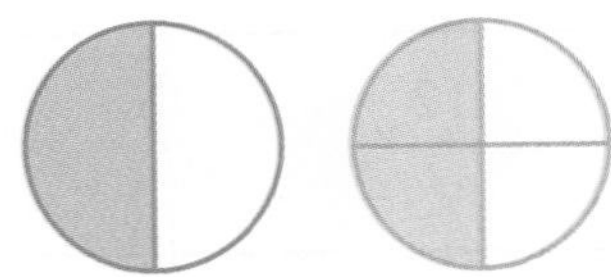

Lesson
13-1

TEKS 3.10: Locate and name points on a number line using whole numbers and fractions, including halves and fourths.

Understanding Number Lines

How can you locate and write numbers on a number line?

Look at this number line.

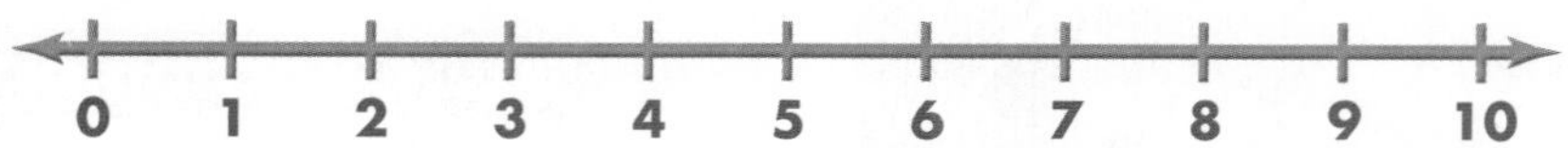

- Each whole number has its own point on the number line.
- Zero is the least whole number on the number line.
- A number line goes on forever, so there is no greatest number.

Guided Practice*

Do you know HOW?

In **1** and **2**, write the number for each lettered point on the number line.

1. 

2.
10 A B 13

Do you UNDERSTAND?

3. How are the number lines for Exercises 1 and 2 the same? How are they different?

4. Writing to Explain Why are there 5 numbers on the number line in Exercise 1 and only 4 numbers on the number line in Exercise 2?

Independent Practice

In **5–9**, write the number for each lettered point on the number line.

5. 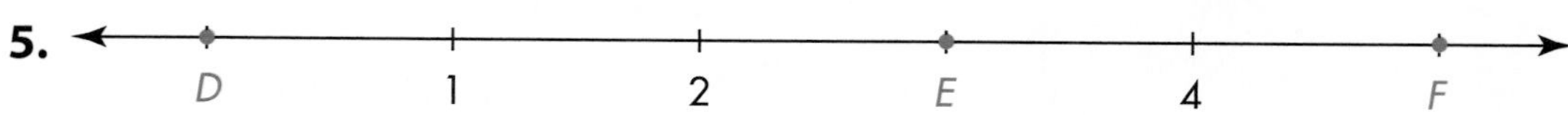

6. 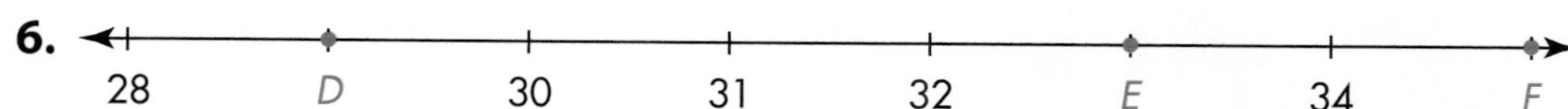

7. 

8. 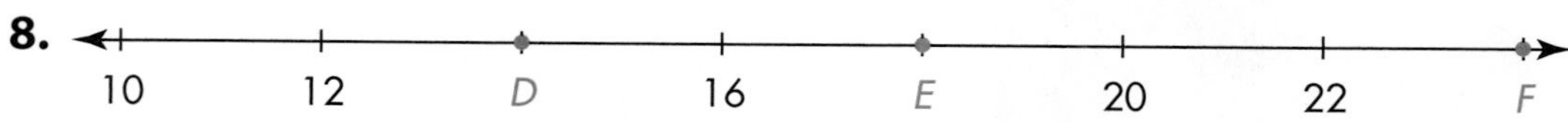

9. 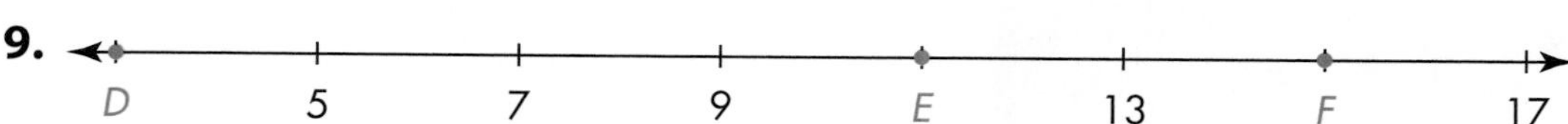

*For another example, see Set A on page 302.

On a number line, the distance between any whole number and the next whole number is the same.

Both of these number lines show the numbers 5 through 9.

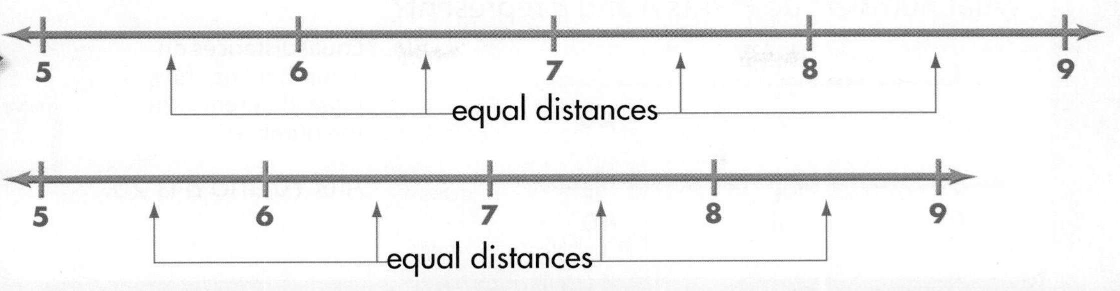

TAKS Problem Solving

10. In 1976, the world record was set for the "World's Longest Apple Peel," measuring at about 170 feet. Which lettered point best represents the length of the "World's Longest Apple Peel"?

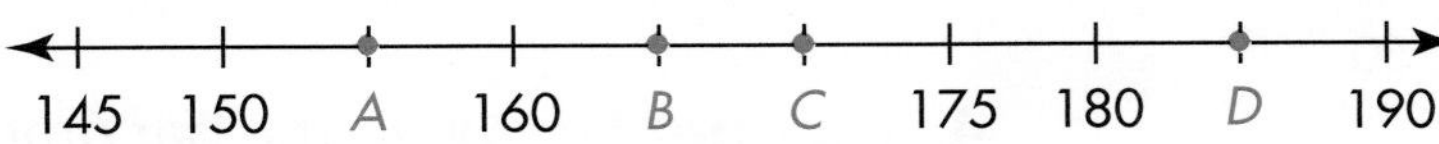

11. Number Sense Maryanne marked and labeled the points on the number line below. Explain what is wrong with her work.

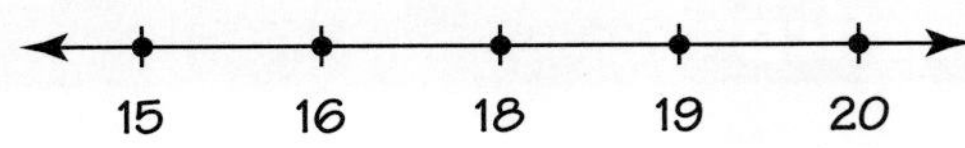

12. Number Sense Tito marked and labeled the points on the number line below. Explain what is wrong with his work.

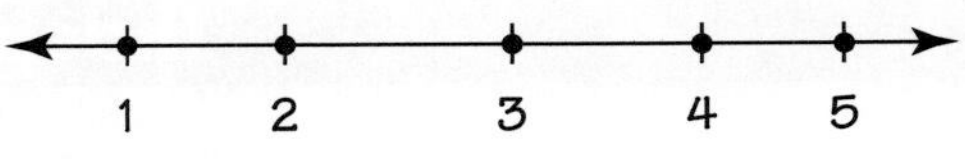

13. Which lettered point on the number line represents 30?

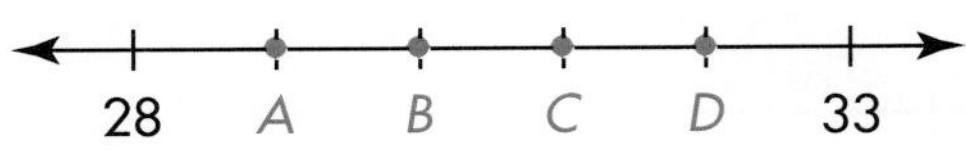

A Point *A*

B Point *B*

C Point *C*

D Point *D*

14. What number does Point *C* on the number line represent?

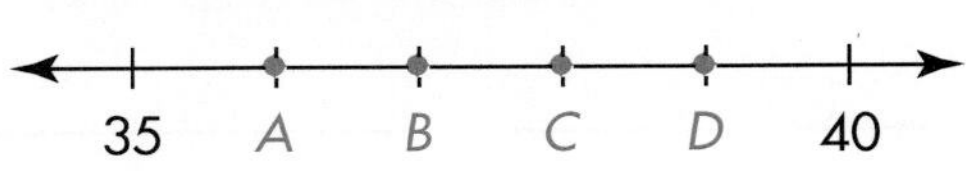

F 36

G 37

H 38

J 39

15. Writing to Explain Explain why Points *A* and *B* both represent the number 6.

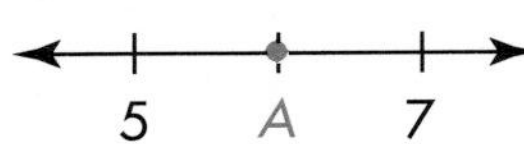

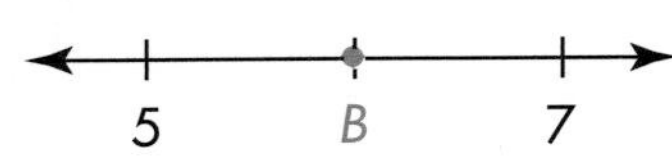

Lesson

13-2

TEKS 3.10: Locate and name points on a number line using whole numbers and fractions, including halves and fourths.

Patterns on the Number Line

How can you complete the pattern on a number line?

What numbers do Points *A* and *B* represent?

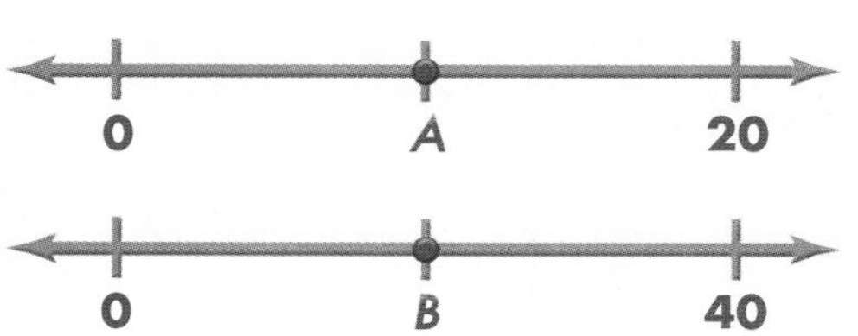

Equal distances on a number line show equal differences in the numbers.

A is 10 and *B* is 20.

Guided Practice*

Do you know HOW?

1. What whole numbers are missing on this part of a number line?

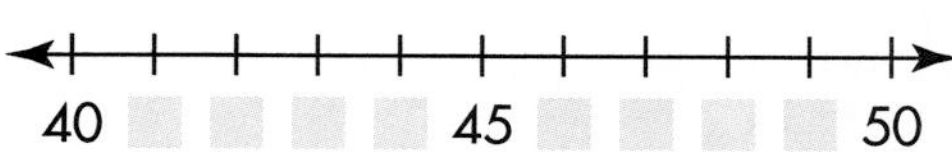

2. What whole numbers are missing from this number line?

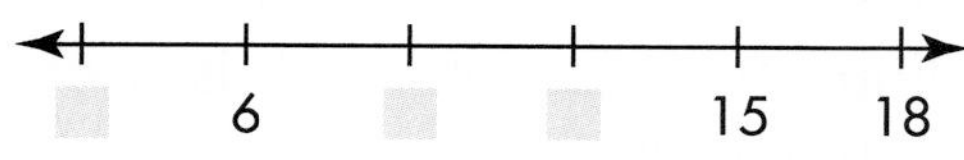

Do you UNDERSTAND?

3. **Writing to Explain** Describe how you found the pattern in the number line in Exercise 2.

4. **Number Sense** In the bar graph above, how much taller was Plant 2 than Plant 1?

Independent Practice

Write the missing whole numbers for each number line.

5. 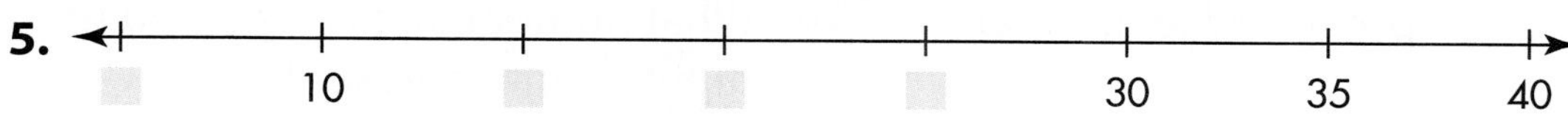

6. 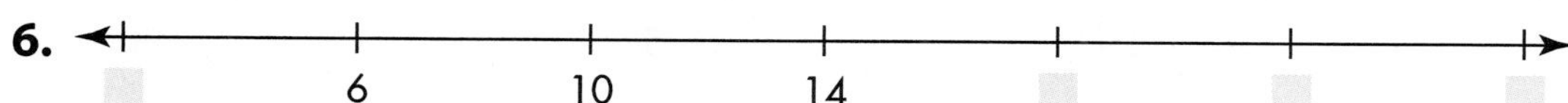

7. 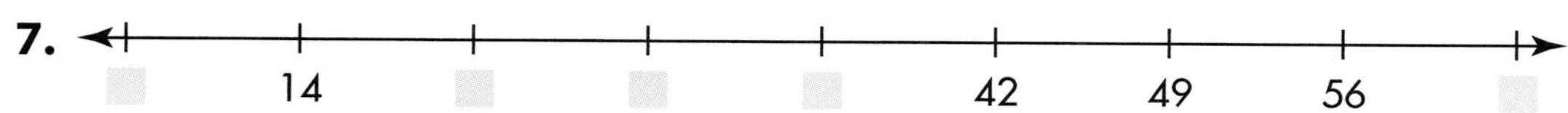

8. 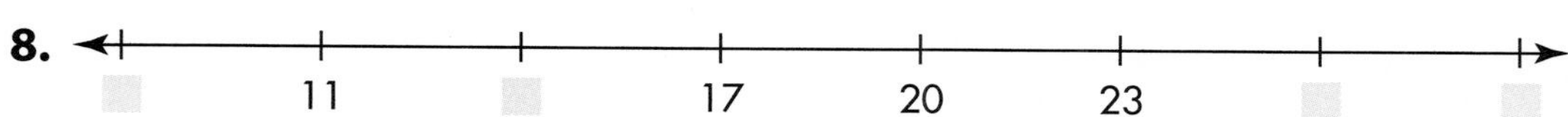

*For another example, see Set B on page 302.

The scale on some bar graphs is a number line. This graph shows the height of two plants. Which plant is taller?

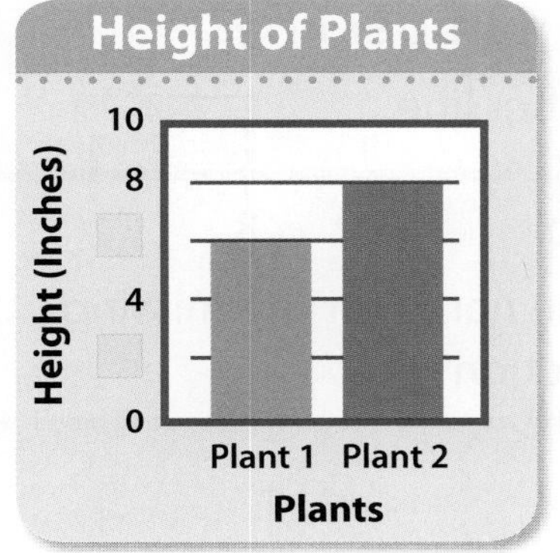

Step 1

Find the missing numbers on the scale.

Skip count by different numbers until you find numbers that fit the pattern.

Each line on the scale represents 2 inches. So, the missing numbers are 2 and 6.

Step 2

Compare the bars for the two plants.

Plant 1: Bar ends at the mark for 6 inches
Plant 2: Bar ends at the mark for 8 inches

Plant 2 is taller.

TAKS Problem Solving

9. On August 7, 2004, a sandwich that was 2,081 feet long was made in Italy. Make a number line like the one below. Then draw a point to show where 2,081 is on the number line.

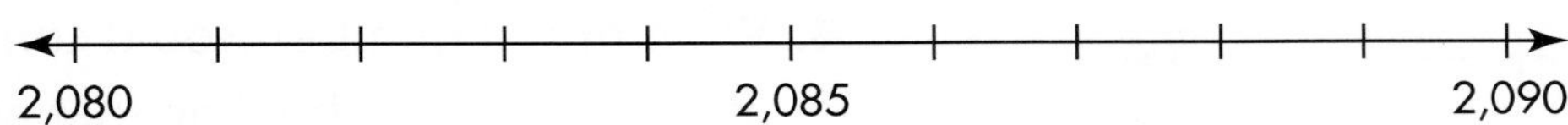

The graph shows how many books four students have read this year. Use the graph for **10–13**.

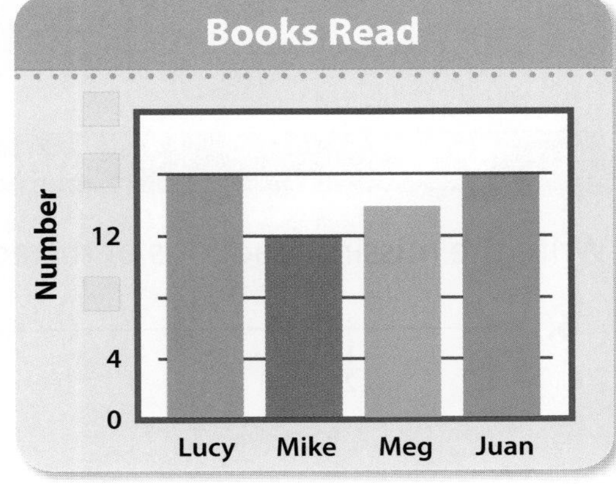

10. What numbers are missing from the scale?

11. Who read sixteen books?

12. **Writing to Explain** How many books did Meg read? How do you know?

13. Ed read twice as many books as Mike. How many books did Ed read?

14. What point on the number line represents 24?

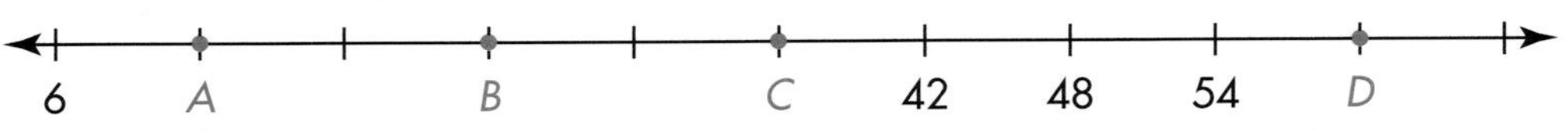

A Point *A** **B** Point *B* **C** Point *C* **D** Point *D*

Lesson

13-3

TEKS 3.10: Locate and name points on a number line using whole numbers and fractions, including halves and fourths.

Locating Fractions on the Number Line

How can you find fractions on a number line?

Each fraction names a point on a number line.

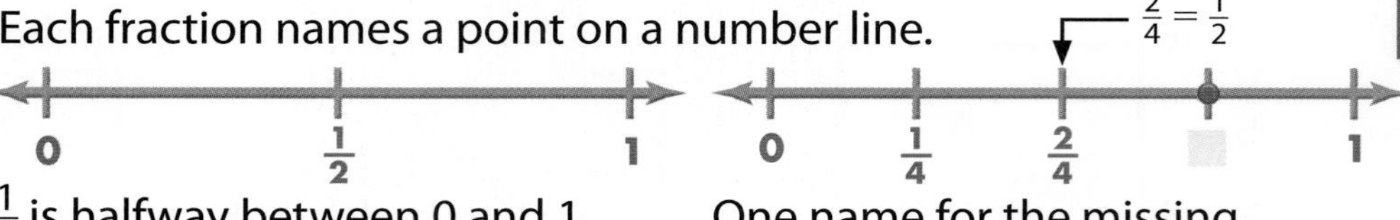

$\frac{1}{2}$ is halfway between 0 and 1.

One name for the missing fraction is $\frac{3}{4}$.

Guided Practice*

Do you know HOW?

Write the missing fractions or mixed numbers for each number line.

1. 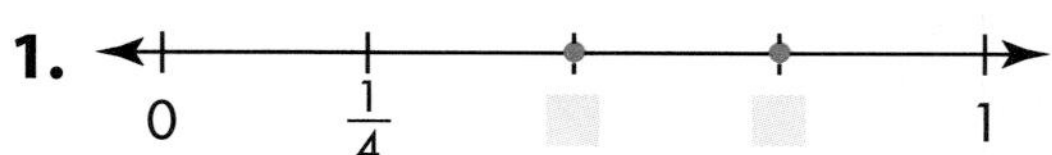

2. 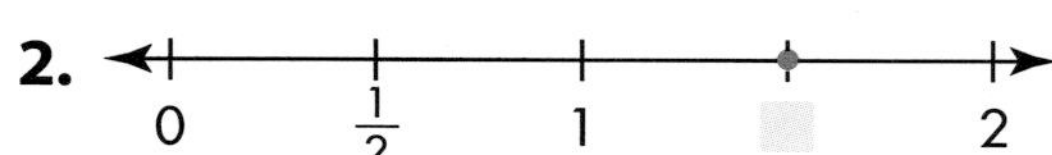

Do you UNDERSTAND?

3. What whole number equals $\frac{4}{4}$?

4. What mixed number would come after $1\frac{2}{4}$ on a number line that was divided into fourths?

5. **Number Sense** Chris says that $\frac{8}{4}$ is the same as 2. Do you agree? Why or why not?

Independent Practice

Write the missing fractions or mixed numbers for each number line.

6. 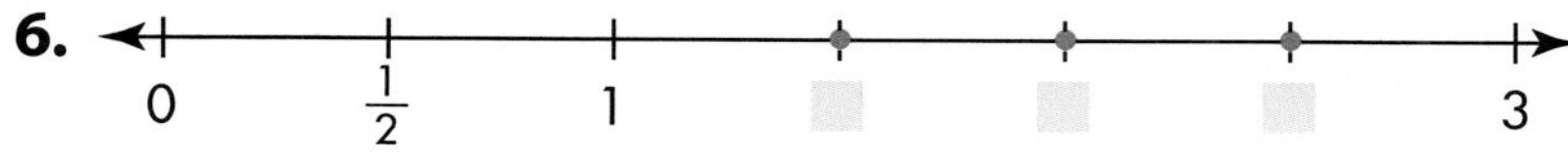

7. 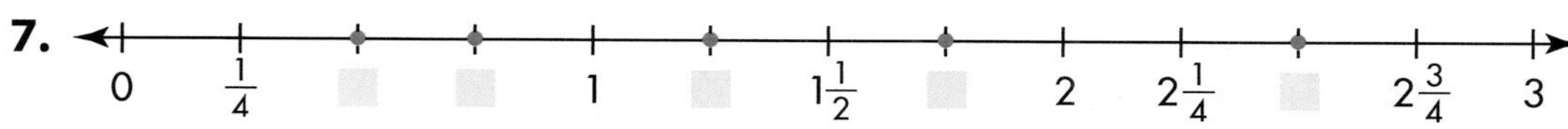

8. 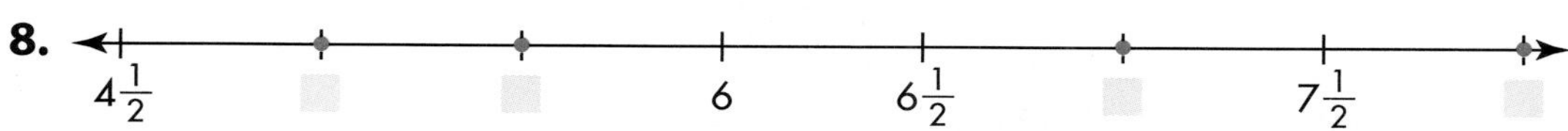

*For another example, see Set C on page 302.

Mixed numbers are numbers that have a whole number part and a fraction part.

You can use mixed numbers to name points on a number line.

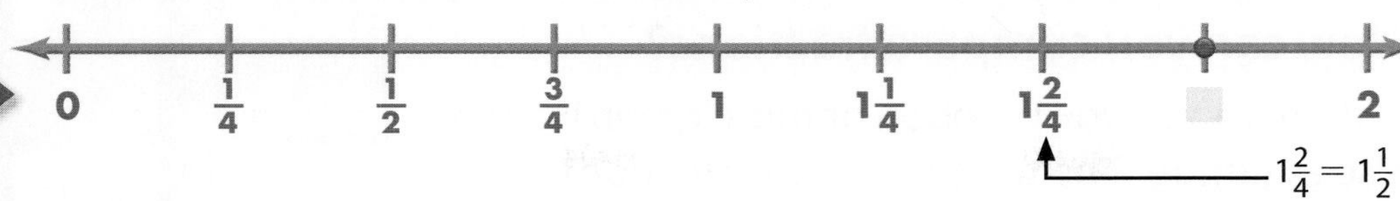

Each mixed number names a point on the number line. One name for the missing mixed number on the number line is $1\frac{3}{4}$.

TAKS Problem Solving

The number line below shows how many miles several places are from Oliver's house. Use the number line for **9** and **10**.

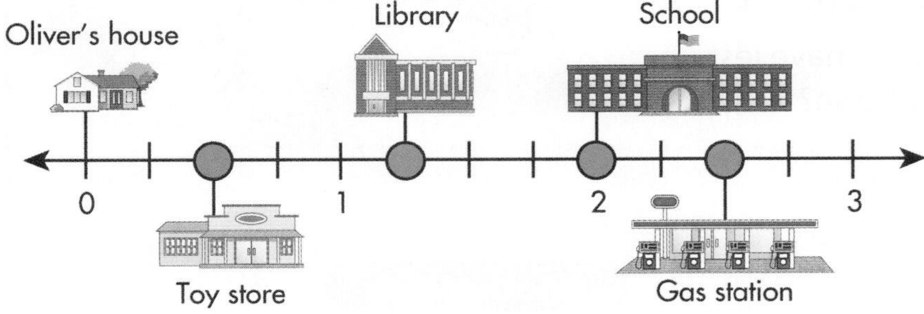

9. How many miles from Oliver's house are these places?

a library **b** store **c** gas station

10. A bank is twice as far from Oliver's house as the toy store. How many miles from Oliver's house is the bank?

11. Which letter on the ruler below represents the number of centimeters that Iceland could grow in a year?

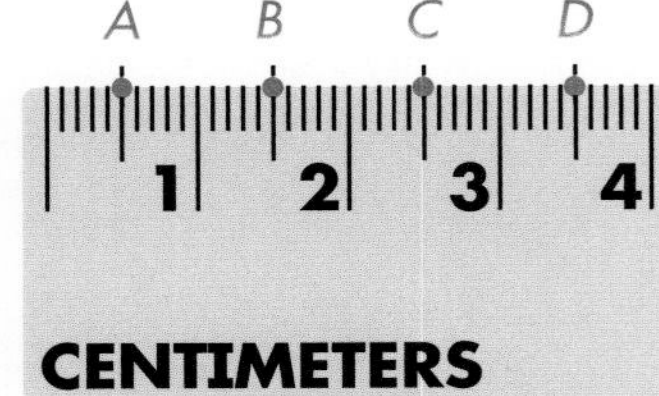

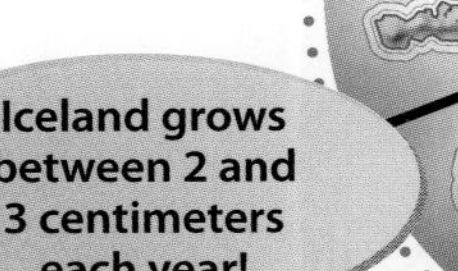

12. Which number makes this number sentence true?

$\square \div 9 = 6$

A 18 **B** 28 **C** 36 **D** 54

Lesson

13-4

TEKS 3.2B: Compare fractional parts of whole objects or sets of objects in a problem situation using concrete models. Also **TEKS 3.10.**

Comparing Fractions on the Number Line

How can you compare fractions?

Is there more brown ribbon or more green ribbon? Use a number line to compare the fractions.

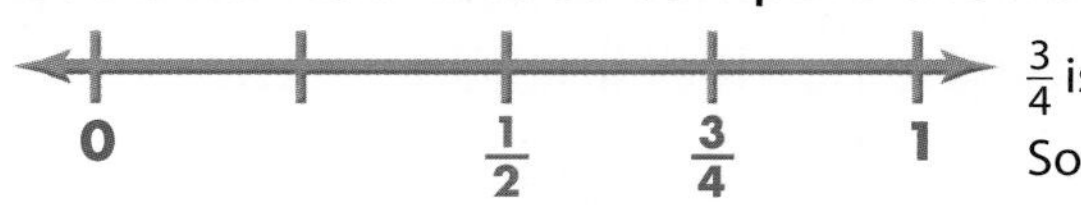

$\frac{3}{4}$ is farther to the right than $\frac{1}{2}$.
So $\frac{3}{4} > \frac{1}{2}$.

There is more green ribbon.

Another Example

How can you compare mixed numbers that have the same fractional parts?

Nancy has two pieces of ribbon that she will use for an art project. Does she have less pink ribbon or less orange ribbon?

$1\frac{1}{4}$ yard

$2\frac{1}{4}$ yard

Compare $1\frac{1}{4}$ and $2\frac{1}{4}$.

One Way

You can use a number line to compare the mixed numbers.

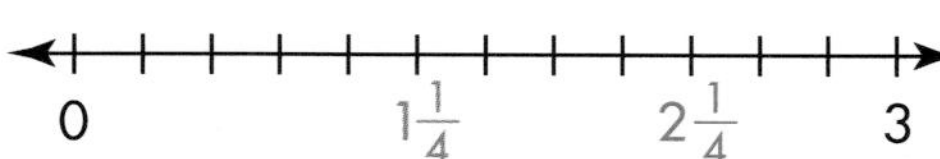

$1\frac{1}{4}$ is farther to the left than $2\frac{1}{4}$.

So, $1\frac{1}{4} < 2\frac{1}{4}$.

Another Way

The fractional parts of the mixed numbers are the same.

You can compare just the whole number parts of the mixed numbers.

$1 < 2$

So, $1\frac{1}{4} < 2\frac{1}{4}$.

Explain It

1. Describe how you would compare $4\frac{1}{2}$ and $2\frac{1}{2}$.
2. Why is $3\frac{1}{4}$ greater than $1\frac{3}{4}$, even though $\frac{1}{4}$ is less than $\frac{3}{4}$?
3. Describe how to compare $9\frac{2}{4}$ and $9\frac{3}{4}$.

One Way

You can use a number line to compare mixed numbers. Compare $1\frac{3}{4}$ and $1\frac{1}{4}$.

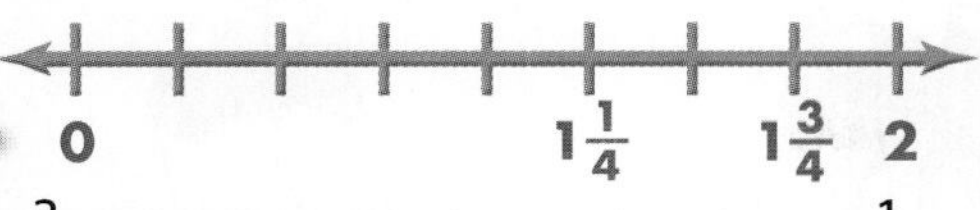

$1\frac{3}{4}$ is farther to the right than $1\frac{1}{4}$.

So, $1\frac{3}{4} > 1\frac{1}{4}$.

Another Way

The whole number parts of $1\frac{3}{4}$ and $1\frac{1}{4}$ are the same.

You can compare just the fractional parts.

$\frac{3}{4} > \frac{1}{4}$

So, $1\frac{3}{4} > 1\frac{1}{4}$.

Guided Practice*

Do you know HOW?

Compare. Write <, >, or =.

1. $\frac{1}{2} \bigcirc \frac{3}{4}$
2. $\frac{2}{4} \bigcirc \frac{1}{4}$
3. $4\frac{1}{2} \bigcirc 4\frac{2}{4}$
4. $8\frac{1}{4} \bigcirc 8\frac{3}{4}$
5. $6\frac{1}{2} \bigcirc 8\frac{1}{2}$
6. $5\frac{3}{4} \bigcirc 4\frac{3}{4}$

Do you UNDERSTAND?

7. **Number Sense** Look at Exercise 1. How do you know which fraction is less?

8. **Writing to Explain** Look at Exercise 6. How can you tell which mixed number is greater without looking at the fractional part of the mixed numbers?

Independent Practice

Use the number line to compare. Write <, >, or =.

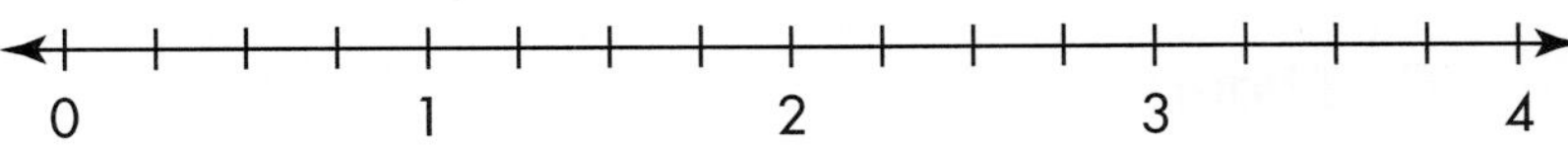

9. $\frac{1}{2} \bigcirc \frac{1}{4}$
10. $\frac{2}{4} \bigcirc \frac{4}{4}$
11. $\frac{1}{4} \bigcirc \frac{3}{4}$
12. $1\frac{2}{4} \bigcirc 1\frac{1}{2}$
13. $4\frac{3}{4} \bigcirc 4\frac{1}{4}$
14. $9\frac{1}{2} \bigcirc 9\frac{3}{4}$
15. $3\frac{1}{4} \bigcirc 7\frac{1}{4}$
16. $9\frac{3}{4} \bigcirc 7\frac{3}{4}$
17. $\frac{1}{2} \bigcirc \frac{2}{2}$
18. $\frac{2}{4} \bigcirc \frac{1}{2}$
19. $8\frac{1}{4} \bigcirc 9\frac{1}{4}$
20. $8\frac{1}{2} \bigcirc 6\frac{1}{2}$
21. $6\frac{1}{4} \bigcirc 6\frac{3}{4}$
22. $3\frac{1}{4} \bigcirc 2\frac{3}{4}$
23. $\frac{1}{1} \bigcirc \frac{2}{2}$
24. $5\frac{1}{2} \bigcirc 5\frac{1}{4}$

*For another example, see Set D on page 303.

TAKS Problem Solving

Use the pictures and number line below for **25** through **28**.

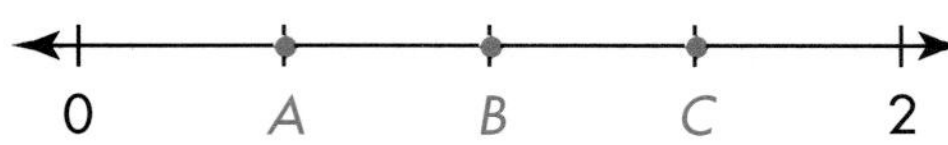

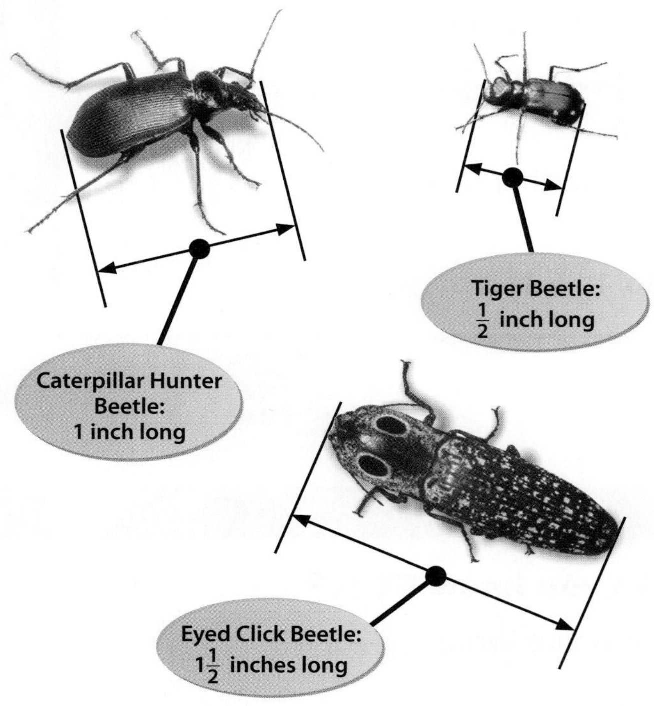

25. Write the name of the beetle whose length matches each lettered point on the number line.

- **a** Point *A*
- **b** Point *B*
- **c** Point *C*

26. **Writing to Explain** How does the number line show which beetle is the longest?

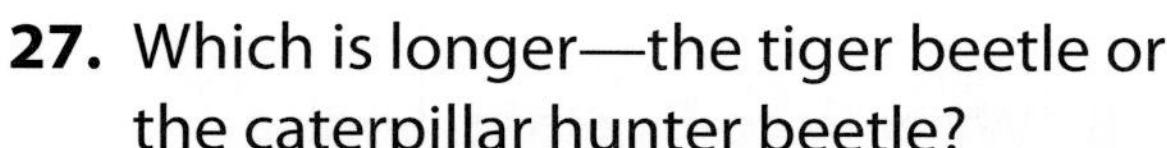

27. Which is longer—the tiger beetle or the caterpillar hunter beetle?

28. Which beetle is the shortest?

29. Show 3 different ways to divide a square into fourths.

30. What fraction of the letters in the word *TENNESSEE* are *E*s?

31. Write a fact family for the numbers 4, 5, and 9.

32. Write a fact family for the numbers 5, 9, and 45.

33. Felipe's party started at 1:00 P.M. and ended at 4:00 P.M. What was the total amount of time his party lasted?

A 2 hours
B 2 hours 30 minutes
C 3 hours
D 3 hours 30 minutes

34. What number is missing from the pattern below?

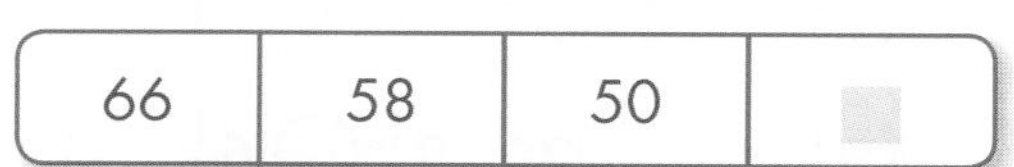

F 48 **G** 46 **H** 44 **J** 42

Algebra Connections

Using Number Sentences to Compare

You know that the two sides of a number sentence can be equal or unequal. Estimation, a number line, or reasoning can help you decide which symbol (>, <, or =) shows how the sides compare.

> means is greater than
< means is less than
= means is equal to

Example: $3 \times 16 \bigcirc 3 \times 20$

Is 3 groups of 16 more than 3 groups of 20?

Since 16 is less than 20, the left side is less. Write "<".

$3 \times 16 \bigcirc 3 \times 20$

Copy and complete by writing <, >, or =.

1. $3 \times 25 \bigcirc 3 \times 19$

2. $5\frac{1}{2} \times 1 \bigcirc 5\frac{1}{2}$

3. $38 + 38 \bigcirc 2 \times 38$

4. $10 \div 2 \bigcirc 8\frac{1}{2}$

5. $6 \times 47 \bigcirc 7 \times 47$

6. $300 \bigcirc 9 \times 30$

7. $16 \times 0 \bigcirc 15 \times 0$

8. $80 \bigcirc 5 \times 13$

9. $17 + \frac{1}{2} \bigcirc 4 + \frac{1}{2}$

10. $1 \times 52 \bigcirc 1\frac{3}{4} + 52$

11. $2 \times 15 \bigcirc 2 + 15$

12. $6 \times 40 \bigcirc 4 \times 60$

For **13** and **14**, copy and complete the number sentence below each problem. Use it to help explain your answer.

13. Jamie scored 2 points on each of 3 basketball tosses. Al scored 3 points on each of 4 basketball tosses. Who scored more points?

Jamie's score Al's score

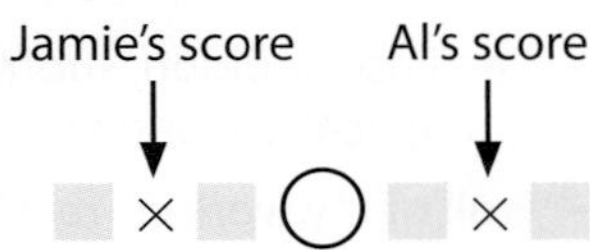

14. Look at the items for sale below. Mrs. Tom bought 2 sweaters. Mrs. Lum bought 2 shirts. Who spent more?

Mrs. Tom Mrs. Lum

$\square \times \square \bigcirc \square \times \square$

15. Write a Problem Write a problem using this number sentence: $5 \times 24 > 5 \times 21$.

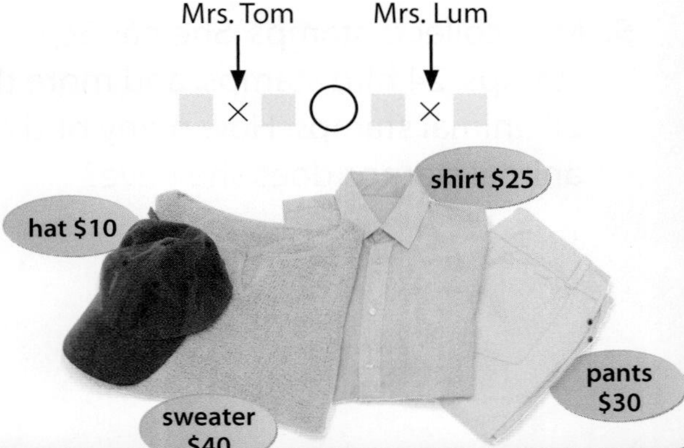

Lesson

13-5

TEKS 3.14B: Solve problems that incorporate understanding the problem, making a plan, carrying out the plan, and evaluating the solution for reasonableness.

Problem Solving

Missing or Extra Information

Ruth bought one CD, one DVD, and one package of blank tapes. She spent a total of $25 on the CD and DVD. If Ruth started with $45, how much money did she have left?

Guided Practice*

Do you know HOW?

Tell what information is missing.

1. Brad bought 3 tapes for a total of $9. He also bought some CDs that cost $10 each. How much did Brad spend in all?

Do you UNDERSTAND?

2. For Problem 1, make up the missing information and solve.

3. **Write a Problem** Write a problem that has extra information about the cost of school supplies.

Independent Practice

Decide if the problem has extra or missing information. Solve if you have enough information.

4. Pablo collects coins. He has 24 coins from Mexico, 14 coins from Canada, and 6 coins from Italy. How many more coins does he have from Mexico than from Canada?

5. Meg collects stamps. She has 36 flower stamps, 24 bird stamps, and more than 20 animal stamps. How many bird and animal stamps does she have?

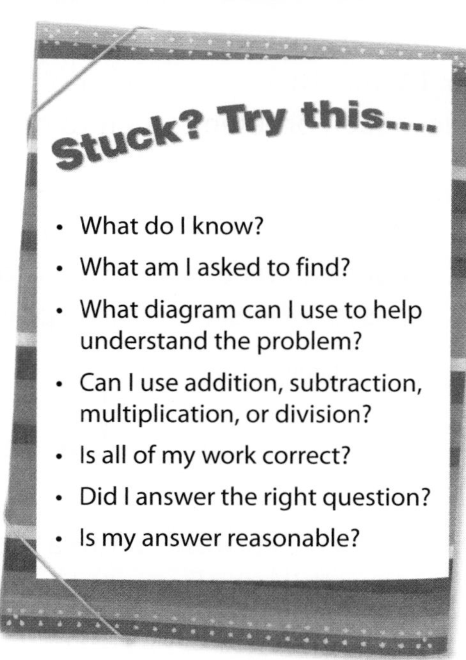

Stuck? Try this....

- What do I know?
- What am I asked to find?
- What diagram can I use to help understand the problem?
- Can I use addition, subtraction, multiplication, or division?
- Is all of my work correct?
- Did I answer the right question?
- Is my answer reasonable?

*For another example, see Set E on page 303.

Plan and Solve

Draw a diagram to show what you know and what you want to find.

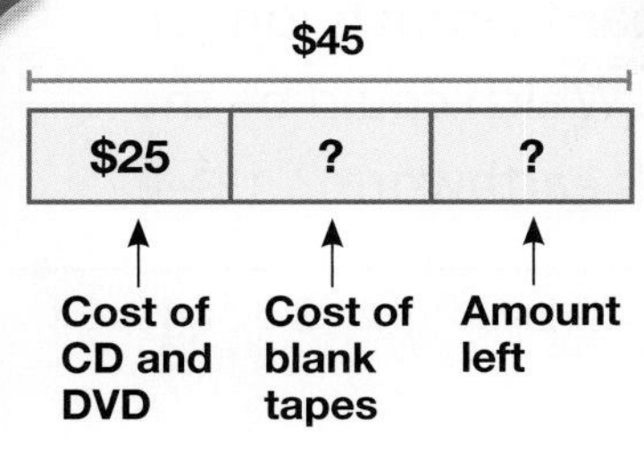

Is any information missing that you need to solve the problem?

Yes, I need to know the cost of the blank tapes so I can find the total Ruth spent. Then I can find how much she had left.

Is there extra information not needed to solve the problem?

No, there is no extra information.

For **6–9**, decide if each problem has extra or missing information. If information is missing, make up the information. Then solve.

Use the pictograph for **6** and **7**.

Trees Planted by Scouts

Oak	
Maple	
Walnut	

stands for 3 trees

6. The scouts spent 2 hours planting oak trees and 4 hours planting maple trees. How many oak and maple trees did they plant?

7. The scouts also planted twice as many pine trees as walnut trees. How many pine trees did they plant?

8. Stacy spent $24 on 20 yards of material to make curtains. She used all of the material to make 4 identical curtains. How much material did she use for each curtain?

9. Nick is planting 36 flowers in rows in his garden. His garden is 10 feet long and 2 feet wide. How many rows of flowers can Nick plant?

10. Francis has 24 colored pencils and 14 markers. What information is needed to find the number of her pencils that are **NOT** red?

A The total number of pencils and markers

B The number of pencils that are red

C The number of markers that are blue

D The number of markers that are red

1. The students at music camp marked their ages on the number line. Miguel marked his age with the letter M. How old is Miguel? (13-1)

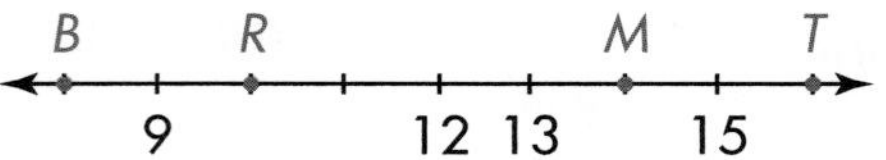

A 8

B 10

C 14

D 16

2. Four friends guessed the average length, in inches, of the most common scorpion found in Texas, the striped bark scorpion. Ty's guess was correct. Which number is represented by his guess? (13-3)

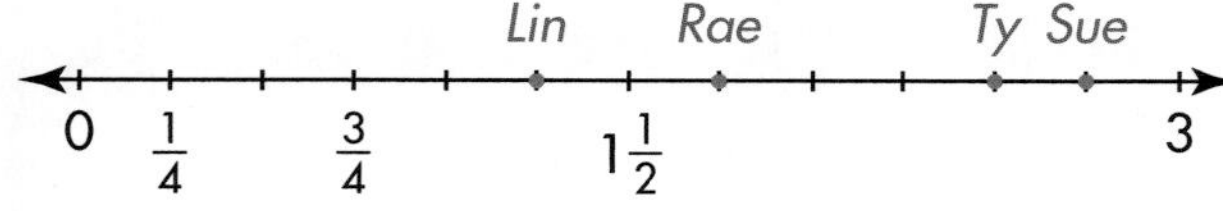

F $1\frac{1}{4}$

G $1\frac{3}{4}$

H $2\frac{1}{2}$

J $2\frac{3}{4}$

3. Elena has 6 tennis balls, 12 golf balls, 2 basketballs, and some softballs in the gym closet. What other information is needed to find how many softballs Elena has? (13-5)

A How many balls she has in all

B How many soccer balls she has

C How big the ball bin is

D How often she plays softball

4. Rachel's earthworm is $3\frac{1}{2}$ inches long. Elle says her earthworm is longer than Rachel's. Which could be the length of Elle's earthworm? (13-4)

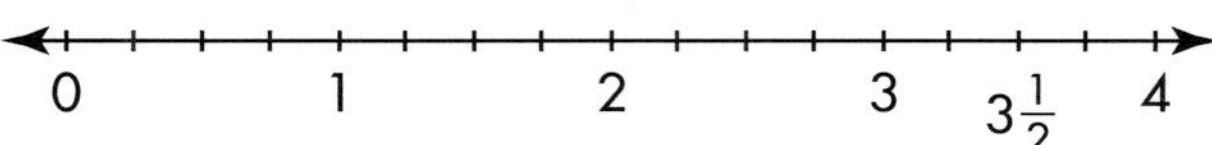

F $3\frac{3}{4}$

G $2\frac{3}{4}$

H 3

J $3\frac{1}{4}$

5. Which statement is true about the number line? (13-1)

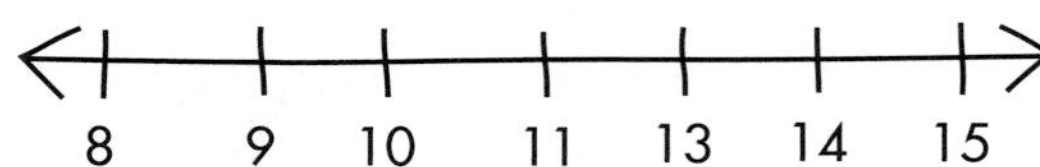

A The only thing wrong is that the number 12 was skipped.

B It is correct because the points were evenly spaced.

C It is wrong because the number 12 was skipped, and the points were not spaced evenly.

D There is nothing wrong with the number line.

6. Which point on the number line represents 28? (13-2)

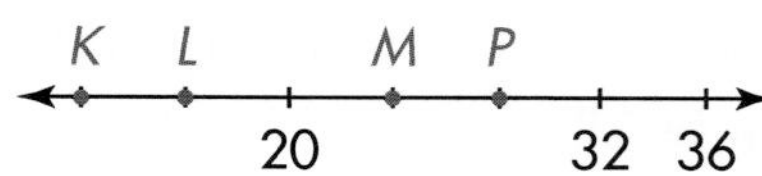

F *K*

G *L*

H *M*

J *P*

7. What point on the number line best represents 46? (13-1)

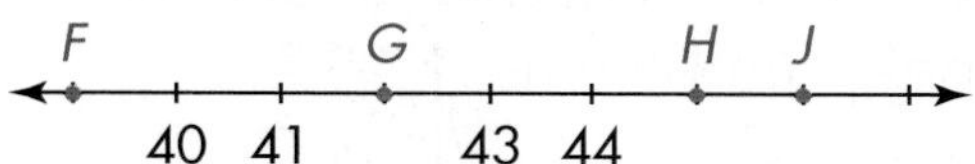

A *F*

B *G*

C *H*

D *J*

8. On sunny days, Jan likes to ride her bike to school. She rides about $1\frac{1}{2}$ miles each way. Which point best represents $1\frac{1}{2}$ on the number line? (13-3)

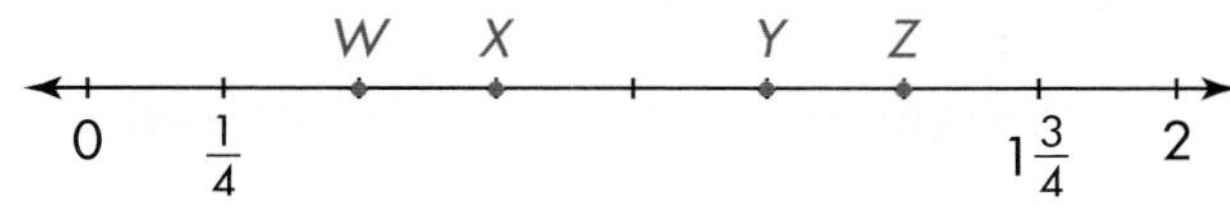

F *W*

G *X*

H *Y*

J *Z*

9. Rashawn adds the same number of flowers to his collection every week. The number line shows how his collection is growing. What number does the point *N* represent? (13-2)

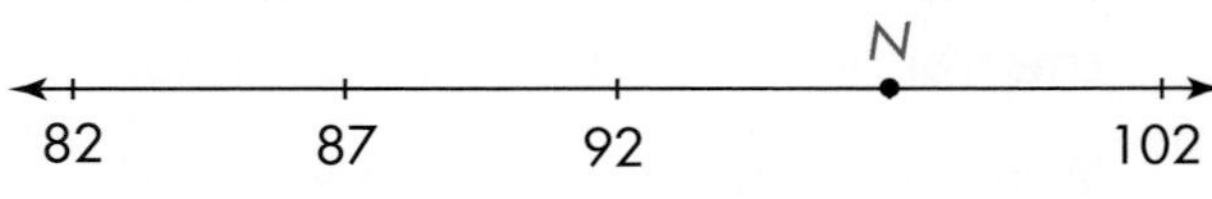

A 95

B 97

C 98

D 100

10. Poison dart frogs are some of the most dangerous animals in a tropical rain forest. They range in length from $\frac{1}{2}$ inch to 2 inches. The zoo has a blue poison dart frog that measures $1\frac{1}{4}$ inches long and a golden one that is $1\frac{3}{4}$ inches long. Which symbol makes the number sentence true? (13-4)

$1\frac{1}{4} \bigcirc 1\frac{3}{4}$

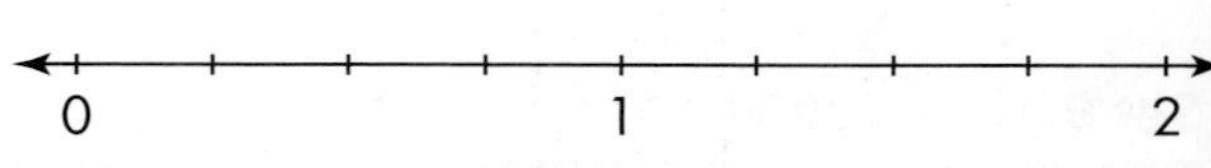

F $>$

G $<$

H $\times$

J $=$

11. Maria spent \$11 on a shirt, \$25 on pants, \$12 on a CD, and \$19 on sandals. How much did Maria spend in all on things to wear? (13-5)

A \$48

B \$55

C \$56

D \$67

12. Griddable Response What number does point *G* represent on the number line? (13-2)

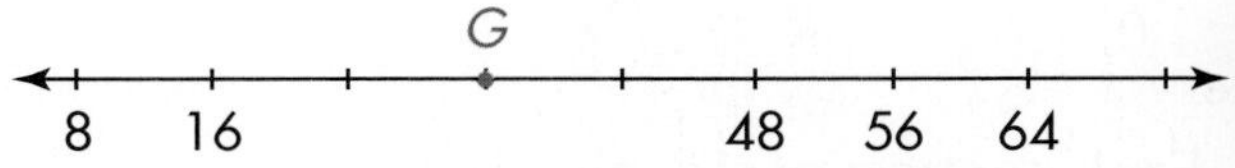

Reteaching

Set A, pages 288–289

What numbers are shown by Points *A* and *B* on the number line?

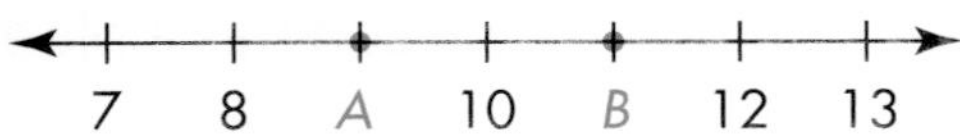

The distance between any whole number and the next whole number on a number line is the same.

Point *A* stands for 9.
Point *B* stands for 11.

Remember that numbers may be very close together or far apart on a number line.

Write the number for each lettered point on the number line.

1. 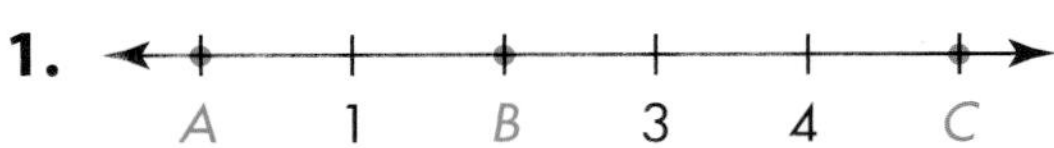

2. 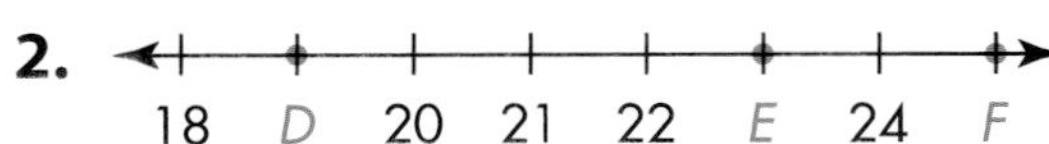

Set B, pages 290–291

Look at these number lines. What numbers are shown by Points *A* and *B*?

Point *A* stands for 20.

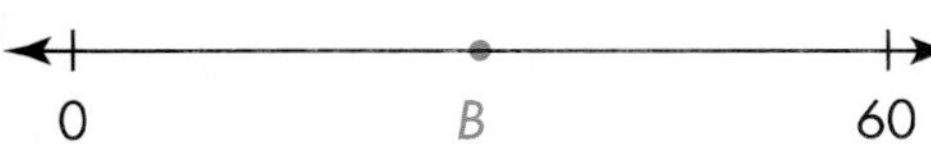

Point *B* stands for 30.

Equal distances on a number line show equal differences in the numbers.

Remember to find a pattern that fits all of the points on the number line.

Write the number for each lettered point on the number line.

1. A 20 B C D 100 120 140

2. E 12 20 28 F G H

3. J 12 K L M 36 42 48 N

Set C, pages 292–293

What fractions are shown by Points *A* and *B* on the number line?

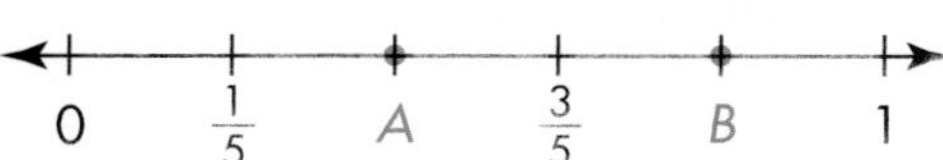

Each section of the number line is $\frac{1}{5}$.

Point *A* stands for $\frac{2}{5}$. Point *B* stands for $\frac{4}{5}$.

Remember to look for a pattern in the fractions on your number line.

Write the fraction for each lettered point on the number line.

1. 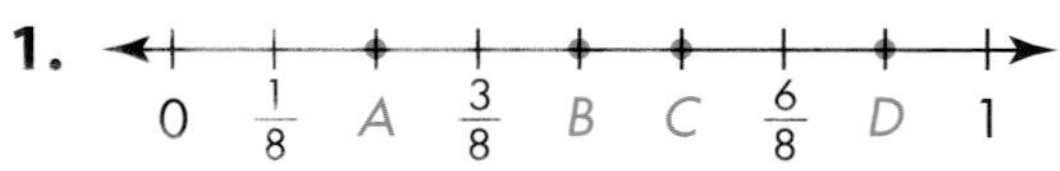

2. 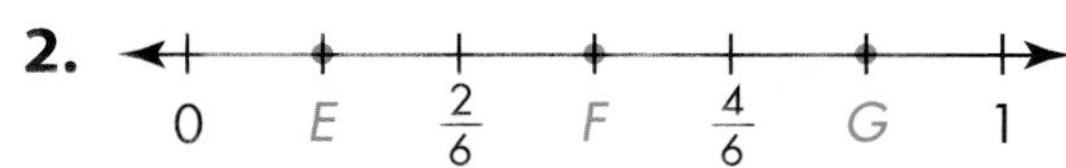

Set D, pages 294–296

Use a number line to compare $1\frac{1}{2}$ and $1\frac{3}{4}$.

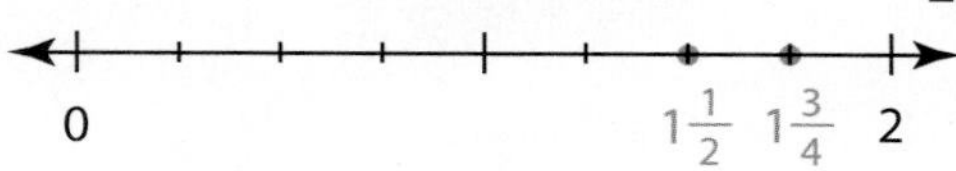

$1\frac{3}{4}$ is farther to the right than $1\frac{1}{2}$.

So $1\frac{3}{4} > 1\frac{1}{2}$.

Remember to correctly place the fractions or mixed numbers on the number line before comparing them.

Compare. Write <, >, or =.

1. $\frac{1}{4} \bigcirc \frac{1}{2}$ **2.** $\frac{3}{4} \bigcirc \frac{1}{4}$

3. $3\frac{3}{4} \bigcirc 3\frac{2}{4}$ **4.** $5\frac{1}{4} \bigcirc 5\frac{2}{4}$

5. $2\frac{1}{4} \bigcirc 2\frac{1}{2}$ **6.** $7\frac{2}{4} \bigcirc 7\frac{3}{4}$

7. $5\frac{1}{2} \bigcirc 3\frac{1}{4}$ **8.** $4\frac{3}{4} \bigcirc 5\frac{1}{4}$

Set E, pages 298–299

To solve a problem with a lot of information, follow these steps.

Step 1

Find the main idea and the key facts and details in the problem.

Step 2

Cross out any extra information.

Step 3

Solve the problem if you have enough information.

Does this problem have extra information? Is there missing information that is needed?

Meg collects stamps. She has 36 flower stamps, 24 bird stamps, and more than 20 fish stamps. How many bird and fish stamps does she have?

The number of flower stamps is extra information. The exact number of fish stamps is missing information that is needed to solve the problem.

Remember to make sure you understand what information you need to find to solve the problem.

Decide if each problem has extra information or missing information. If there is enough information, solve the problem. If not, tell what is missing.

1. Three friends spent \$24 to buy lunch. They also bought a magazine for \$4. They shared the cost of buying lunch equally. How much did each person spend on lunch?

2. Anna bought 4 yards of cloth to make pillows. She paid \$4 per yard for the cloth. How many pillows can Anna make?

Topic 14

Solids and Shapes

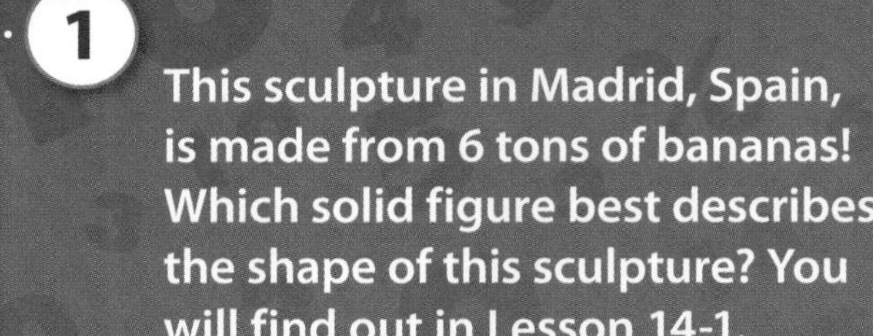

1 This sculpture in Madrid, Spain, is made from 6 tons of bananas! Which solid figure best describes the shape of this sculpture? You will find out in Lesson 14-1.

2 Which geometric term describes the wings of a biplane? You will find out in Lesson 14-3.

3 Which polygons did famous architect Frank Lloyd Wright use in designing this building ? You will find out in Lesson 14-5.

4 What is the first thing you notice about this bicycle? You will find out what is unusual in Lesson 14-7.

Review What You Know!

Vocabulary

Choose the best term from the box.

• circle	• square
• cube	• triangle

1. A shape that has 4 sides all the same length is called a ? .
2. A solid that has six square faces is called a ? .
3. A shape with 3 sides is called a ? .

Name Solids and Shapes

Write the name of each figure.

4. 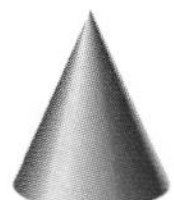
5. 
6. 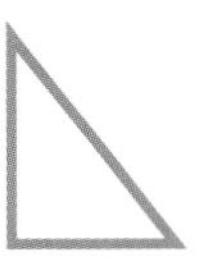
7. 

Shapes

Write the number of sides each figure has.

8. 
9. 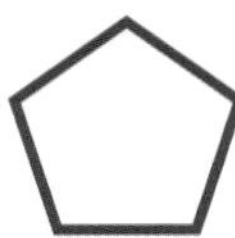
10. 
11. 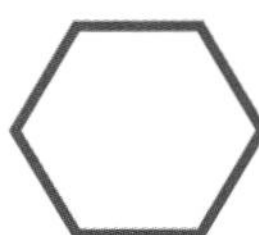

12. **Writing to Explain** Which solid rolls, a cone or a cube? Explain why it rolls.

Lesson

14-1

TEKS 3.8: Identify, classify, and describe two- and three-dimensional geometric figures by their attributes. Compare two-dimensional figures, three-dimensional figures, or both by their attributes using formal geometry vocabulary.

Solid Figures

What is a solid figure?

A solid figure is a geometric figure that has length, width, and height.

Some common solid figures and their names are shown at the right.

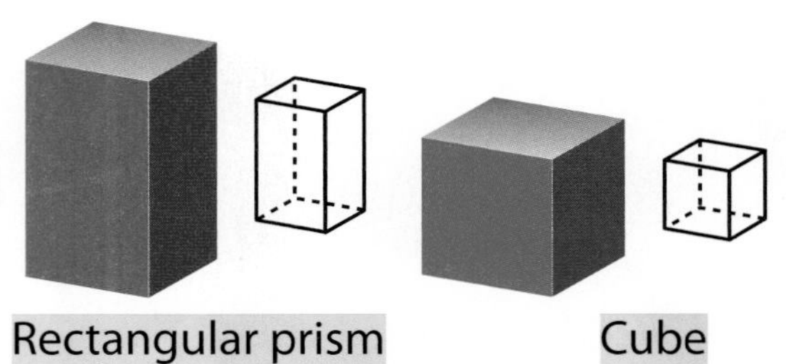

Rectangular prism

Cube

Another Example **How do solid figures help you describe objects in the world around you?**

Many things in the real world are shaped like the solid figures shown above. Name the solid figure each object looks like.

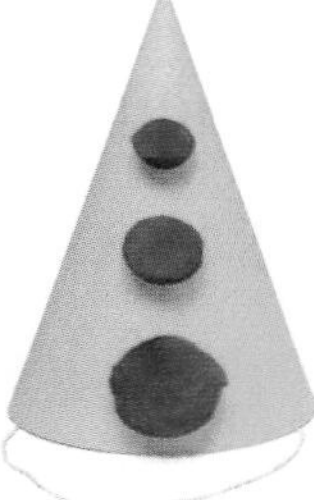

The clown's hat looks like a cone.

The cereal box looks like a rectangular prism.

The tennis ball looks like a sphere.

The glue stick looks like a cylinder.

Explain It

1. Explain why the clown's hat looks like a cone.
2. Why is it wrong to say that the cereal box looks like a cube?
3. Which of the 4 objects pictured can roll? Explain.

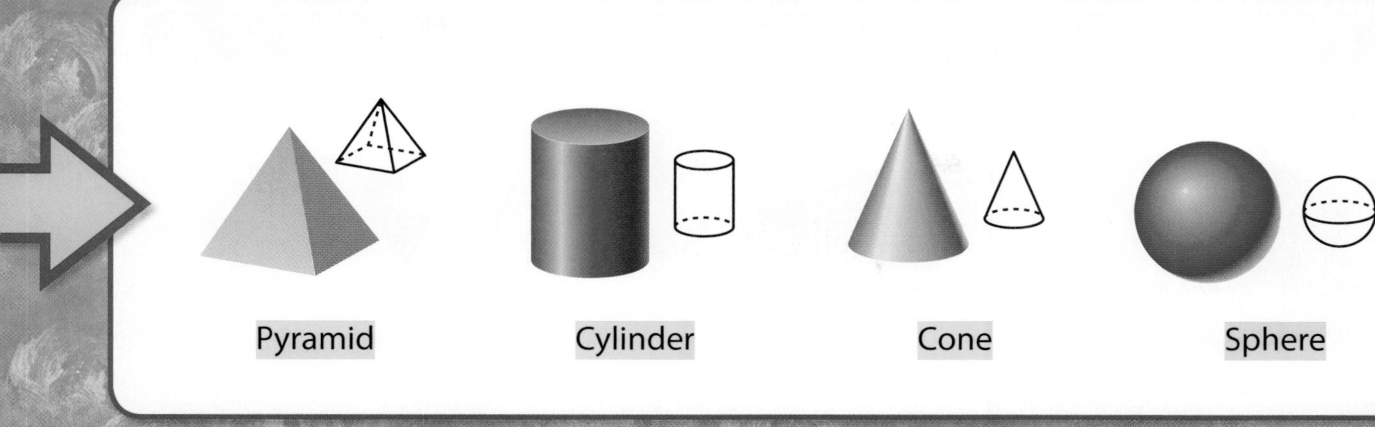

Guided Practice*

Do you know HOW?

Name the solid figure.

1. 

2. 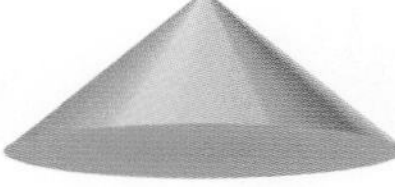

Name the solid figure that each object looks like.

3. 

4. 

5. 

6. 

Do you UNDERSTAND?

For **7–10**, look at the solid figures above.

7. Which solid figure has no flat surfaces?

8. Which solid figures can roll? Which cannot roll?

9. How are the cone and the cylinder alike? How are they different?

10. How are the cone and the pyramid alike? How are they different?

11. **Writing to Explain** Look at the pictures below. Does the name of a solid figure change if the figure is turned on its side? Explain.

DIGITAL Animated Glossary **www.pearsonsuccessnet.com**

**For another example, see Set A on page 328.*

Independent Practice

In **12–17**, name the solid figure.

12. 

13. 

14. 

15. 

16. 

17. 

In **18–26**, name the solid figure that each object looks like.

18. 

19. 

20. 

21. 

22. 

23. 

24. 

25. 

26. 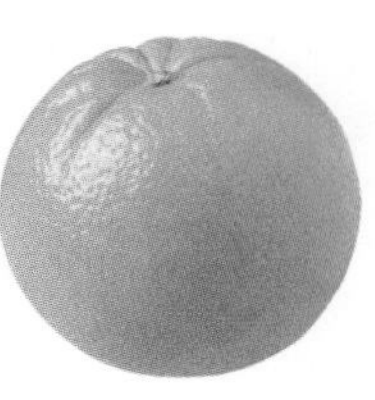

In **27–32**, name an object in your classroom or at home that is shaped like each solid figure.

27. Sphere

28. Cube

29. Cylinder

30. Rectangular prism

31. Pyramid

32. Cone

TAKS Problem Solving

33. Kayla used blocks to make this train. Give the solid figure name for each type of block. Tell how many blocks of each type Kayla used.

34. What solid figures do you get if you cut a cube as shown?

35. Three pizzas were cut into 8 slices each. Six friends ate all of the pizza, and each person ate the same number of slices. How many slices did each person eat?

36. **Writing to Explain** Spheres and cylinders are both solid figures that can roll. Why are so many sports played with objects shaped like spheres rather than objects shaped like cylinders?

37. What solid figure would you make if you stacked two rectangular prisms of the same size?

38. What solid figures can be stacked to make a round tower with a flat top?

39. Which solid figure name best describes the shape of the banana sculpture shown at the right?

A Cylinder

B Pyramid

C Rectangular prism

D Sphere

40. **Number Sense** Catherine has 2 hamsters, 1 cat, 2 dogs, and 4 fish. What fraction of her pets are dogs?

Lesson
14-2

TEKS 3.8: Identify, classify, and describe two- and three-dimensional geometric figures by their attributes. Compare two-dimensional figures, three-dimensional figures, or both by their attributes using formal geometry vocabulary.

Relating Solids and Shapes

How can you describe parts of solid figures?

Some solid figures have faces, vertices, and edges.

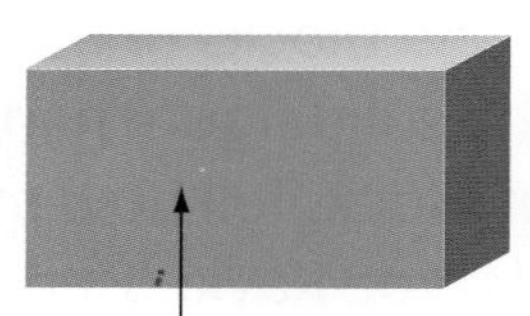

Each flat surface is a face.

A rectangular prism has 6 faces.
The shape of each face is a rectangle.

Another Example Do all solid figures have faces, edges, and vertices?

Flat surfaces of solid figures that can roll are not called faces.

A cylinder has two flat surfaces.

But a cylinder can roll.

So, the flat surfaces of a cylinder are not faces.

Remember, an edge is where 2 faces meet. So, a cylinder does not have edges or vertices.

A cone does not have faces or edges. A cone has one vertex.

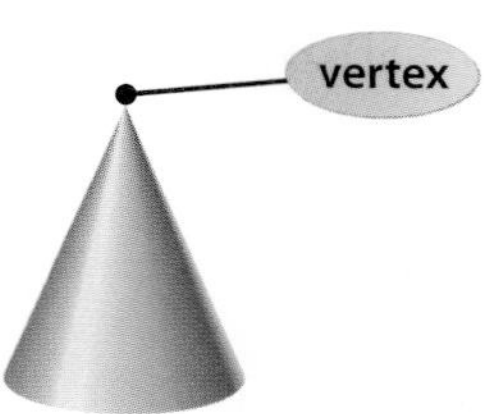

Explain It

1. Explain why the flat surface of a cone is not called a face.
2. Do you think that the flat surfaces of a pyramid are called faces? Explain.

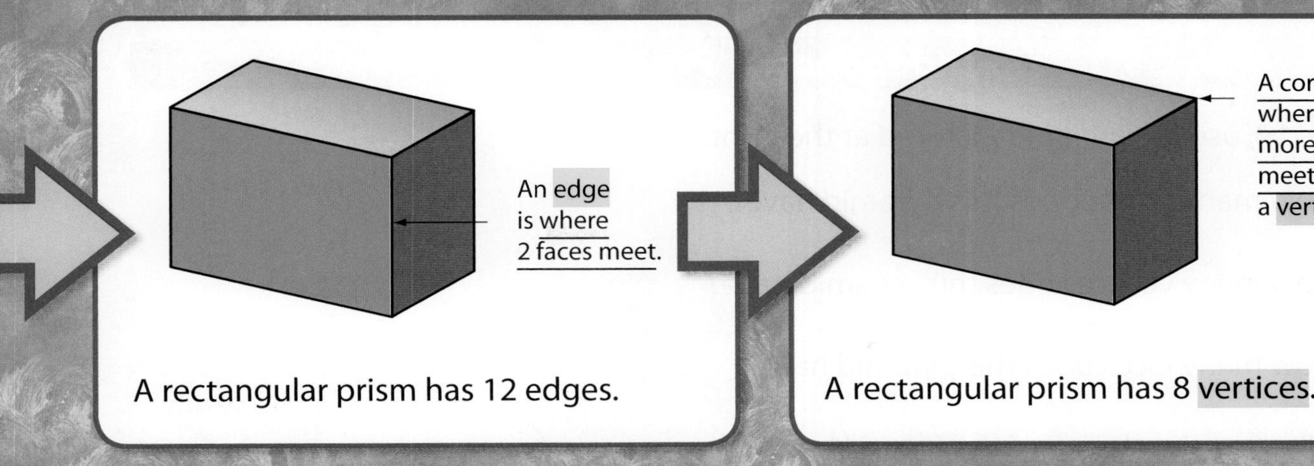

Guided Practice*

Do you know HOW?

For **1–6**, use the cube and cone pictured below.

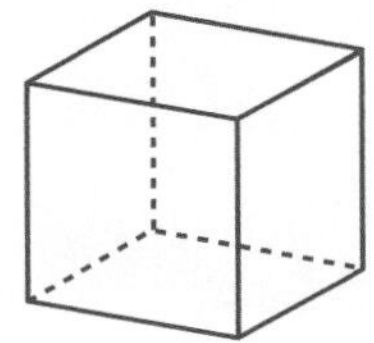
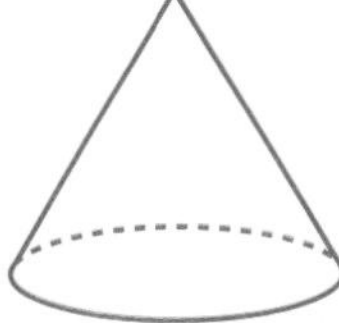

1. How many faces does the cube have in all?

2. What is the shape of each face of the cube?

3. How many edges does the cube have?

4. How many vertices does the cube have?

5. How many edges does the cone have?

6. How many vertices does the cone have?

Do you UNDERSTAND?

For **7–10**, use the solids pictured below.

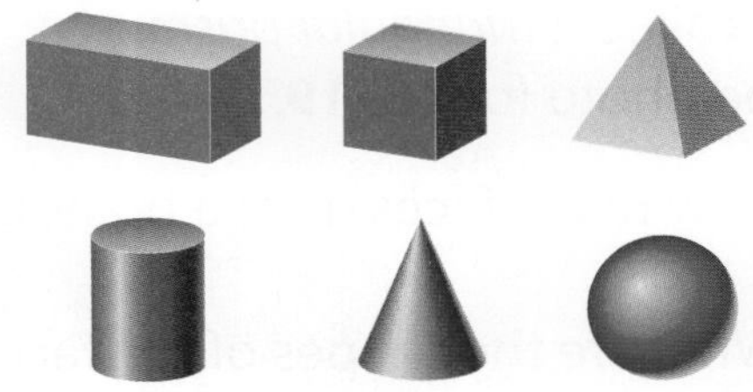

7. Which solid has faces that are all the same size and shape? What is the name of this shape?

8. Which two solids have the same number of edges?

9. Which of these solid figures do not have faces?

10. Besides the rectangular prism, which solid has 6 faces, 12 edges, and 8 vertices?

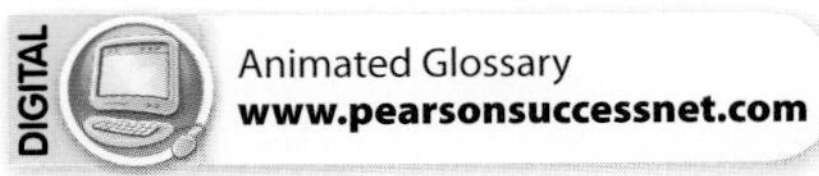

For another example, see Set B on page 328.

Independent Practice

For **11–14**, use the pyramid pictured at the right.

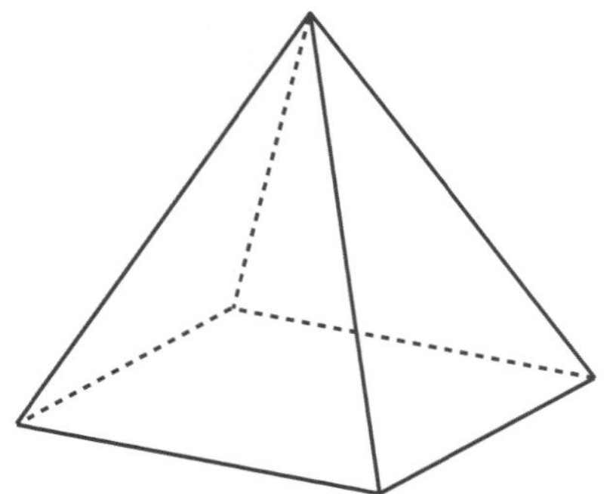

11. How many edges does this pyramid have?

12. How many vertices does this pyramid have?

13. How many faces does this pyramid have?

14. What are the shapes of the faces? How many faces of each shape are there?

TAKS Problem Solving

15. Writing to Explain Why does a cube have the same number of faces, edges, and vertices as a rectangular prism?

This wedge of cheese looks like a solid figure called a *triangular prism*. Use the photo for **16–19**.

16. How many faces does a triangular prism have?

17. What are the shapes of the faces?

18. How many vertices does a triangular prism have?

19. How many edges does a triangular prism have?

20. Tran bought a bag of 24 stickers. He plans to put one sticker on each face of this cube. How many stickers will be left over?

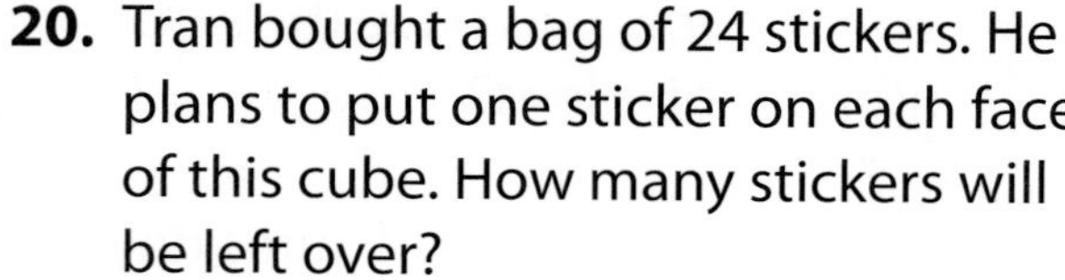

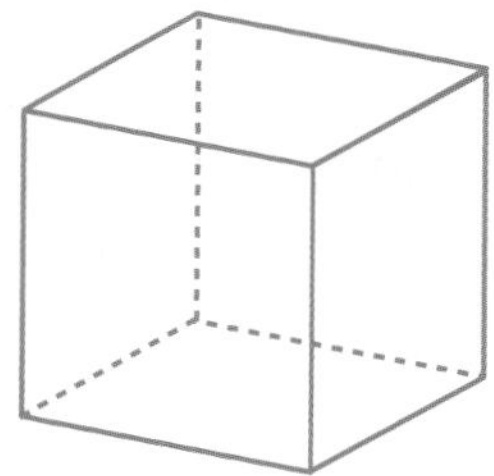

A 12 **C** 18

B 16 **D** 21

21. What is the total value of the 8 coins shown below?

F 36¢ **H** 56¢

G 46¢ **J** 71¢

Mixed Problem Solving

Different musical instruments make different sounds. The shape of an instrument can affect how it sounds. Use the table at the right to answer **1–5**.

1. Which instrument is made up of a long, narrow rectangular prism and a short cylinder?

2. Which of the percussion instruments has a cylinder shape?

3. Which instrument has the shape of a 3-sided figure?

4. What solid figure does the recorder look like?

5. The instrument that makes the sound with the greatest number of decibels is the loudest. Which instrument in the table below can make the loudest sound?

Data

Instrument	Maximum Loudness (in decibels)
Trumpet	95
Cymbal	110
Bass drum	115
Piano	100

Musical Instruments

Name of Instrument	Group of Instruments
Banjo	String
Drum	Percussion
Recorder	Woodwind
Triangle	Percussion

6. Strategy Focus Solve. Use the strategy Try, Check, and Revise.

Elian plays three instruments. The drum weighs 5 pounds more than the guitar. The trumpet weighs 5 pounds less than the guitar. The trumpet weighs 3 pounds. How many pounds does the drum weigh?

Lesson
14-3

TEKS 3.8: Identify, classify, and describe . . . figures by their attributes using formal geometry vocabulary.

Lines and Line Segments

What is important to know about lines?

Lines and parts of lines are used to describe shapes and solid figures.

A point is an exact position.

A line is a set of points that is endless in two directions.

A line segment is a part of a line with two endpoints.

Guided Practice*

Do you know HOW?

Write the name for each.

1.

2.

3.

Do you UNDERSTAND?

4. What do the arrows in the drawing of a line tell you?

5. What type of lines do the railroad tracks look like?

Independent Practice

Write the name for each.

6.

7.

8.

9.

10.

11.

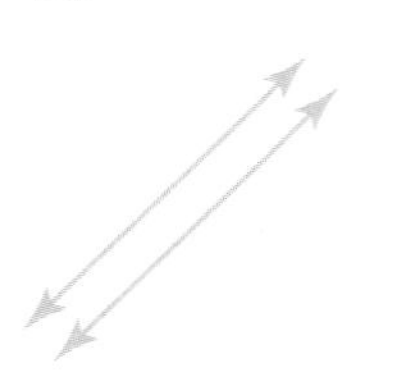

*For another example, see Set C on page 328.

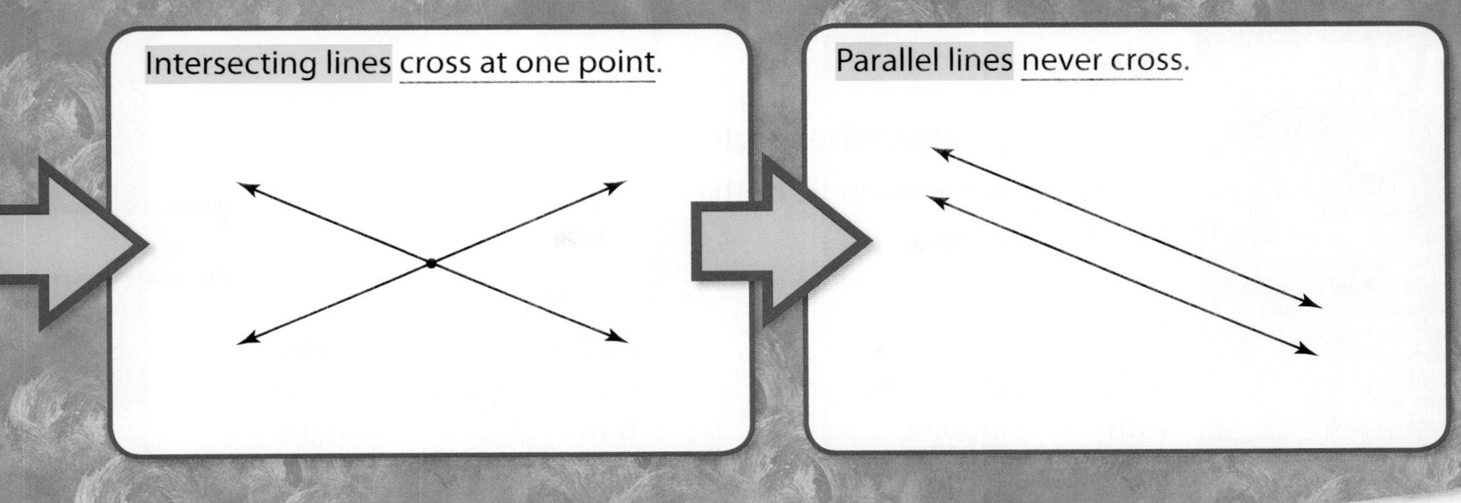

Draw and label a picture of each.

12. Line segment **13.** Line **14.** Parallel lines **15.** Intersecting lines

For **16** and **17**, use the map at the right. Tell if the two streets named look like intersecting lines or parallel lines.

Park
Birch Street
Elm Street
Oak Street
School

16. Oak Street and Birch Street

17. Birch Street and Elm Street

18. **Writing to Explain** Rosa bought 3 packs of 6 baseball cards. Luis bought 4 packs of 3 baseball cards. Who bought more baseball cards? Explain.

19. Look at the wings on the plane. What geometric term can you use to describe them?

20. Which best describes the place where these two lines intersect?

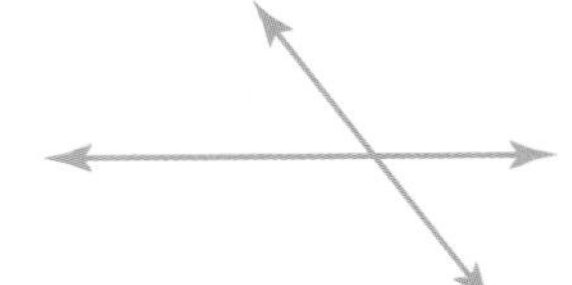

A Line

B Point

C Line segment

D Parallel line

Lesson

14-4

TEKS 3.8: Identify, classify, and describe two- and three-dimensional geometric figures by their attributes. Compare two-dimensional figures, three-dimensional figures, or both by their attributes using formal geometry vocabulary.

Angles

How do you describe angles?

You can describe an angle by the size of its opening.

A ray is a part of a line with one endpoint.

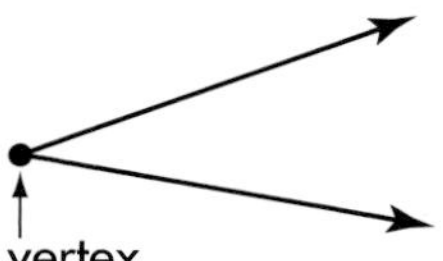

An angle is two rays with the same endpoint. That endpoint is the vertex of the angle.

Guided Practice*

Do you know HOW?

Write the name for each.

1. 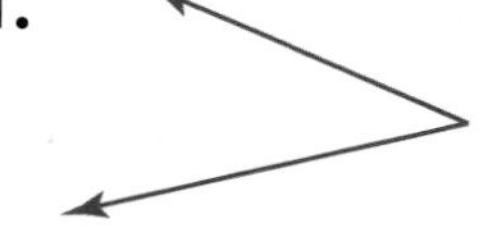

2. 

Tell if each angle is right, acute, or obtuse.

3. 

4. 

Do you UNDERSTAND?

5. How can you use the corner of a note card to decide if an angle is acute, right, or obtuse?

6. Explain why these two rays do not form an angle.

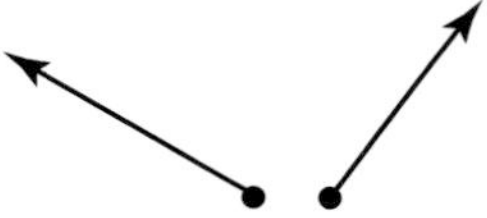

7. Describe something in your classroom that reminds you of perpendicular line segments.

Independent Practice

Tell if each angle is right, acute, or obtuse.

8. 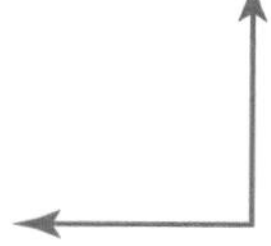

9. 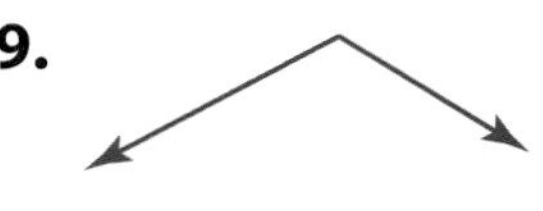

10. 

11. 

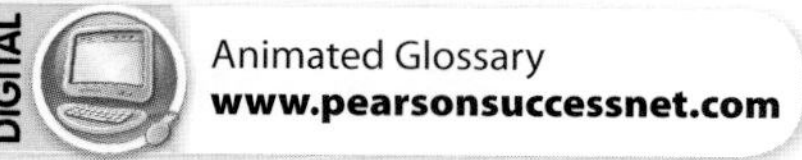

*For another example, see Set D on page 328.

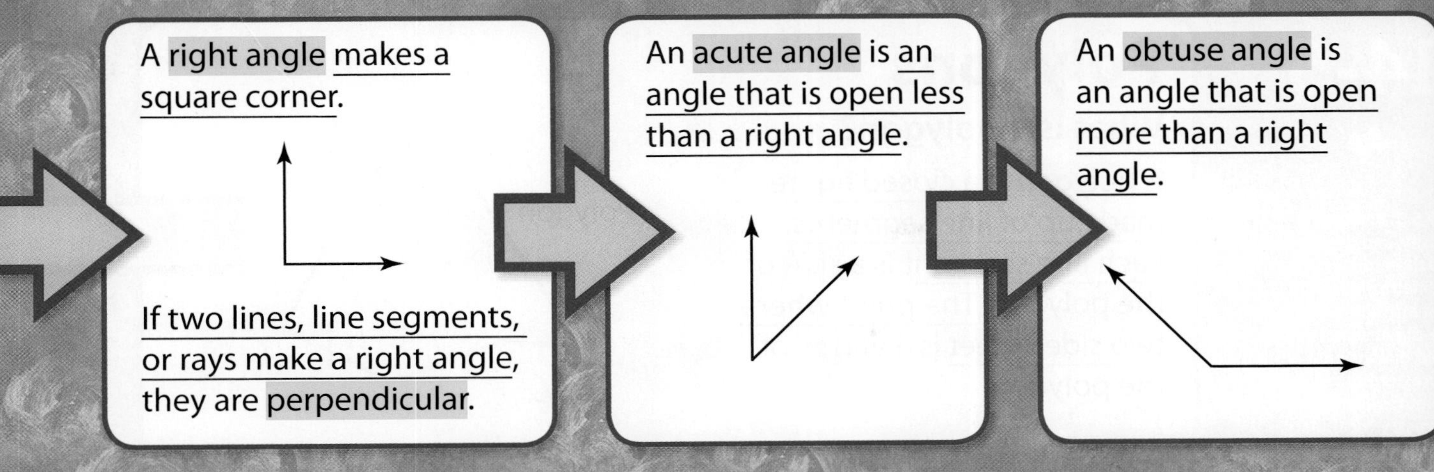

In **12–15**, draw and label a picture of each.

12. Obtuse angle **13.** Right angle **14.** Ray **15.** Acute angle

TAKS Problem Solving

In **16–18**, tell the time on each clock. Then tell what type of angle is formed by the hands of the clock.

16.

17.

18.

19. Writing to Explain Are all obtuse angles the same size? Draw a picture to explain your answer.

20. Which picture shows a pair of perpendicular line segments?

A

B

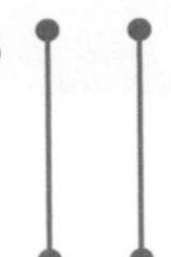

C

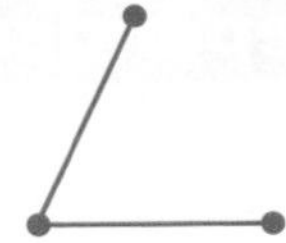

D

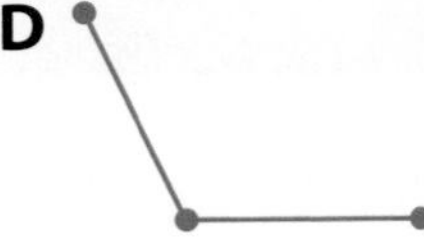

21. Reasoning Are these lines parallel or intersecting? Explain.

Remember that a line does not end.

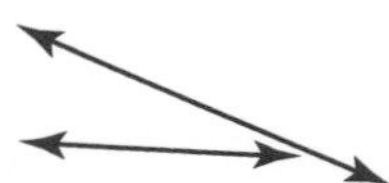

Lesson

14-5

TEKS 3.8: Identify, classify, and describe two- and three-dimensional geometric figures by their attributes. Compare two-dimensional figures, three-dimensional figures, or both by their attributes using formal geometry vocabulary.

Polygons

What is a polygon?

A polygon is a closed figure made up of line segments. Each line segment is a side of the polygon. The point where two sides meet is a vertex of the polygon.

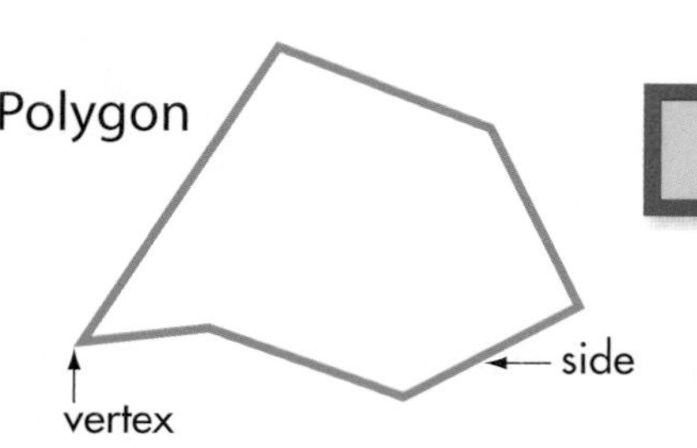

Guided Practice*

Do you know HOW?

Name the polygon.

1. 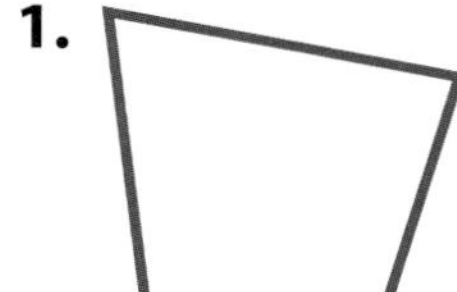

2. 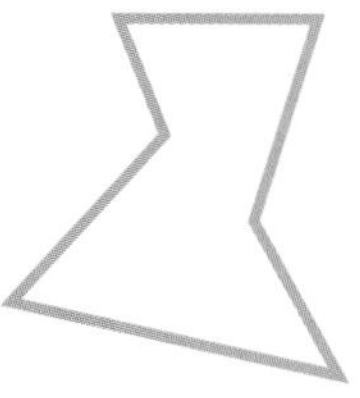

Is each figure a polygon? If it is not, explain why.

3. 

4. 

Do you UNDERSTAND?

Draw a polygon with 3 sides. Use the polygon for Exercises **5–7**.

5. How many vertices are there?

6. How many angles are there?

7. What is the name of the polygon?

8. Suppose that a polygon has 10 sides. How many angles does it have?

9. Describe an everyday object that is a model of a polygon. What is the name of the polygon?

Independent Practice

Name the polygon.

10. 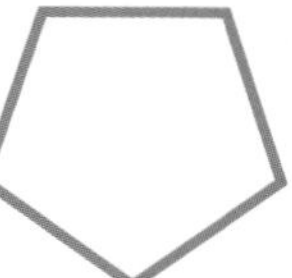

11. 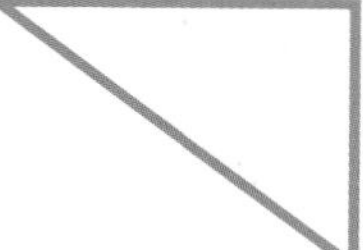

12. 

13. 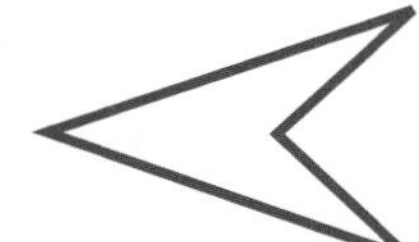

*For another example, see Set E on page 329.

Polygons are named by the number of sides they have. The sides form an angle at each vertex.

Data

Polygon	Number of Sides	Number of Vertices
Triangle	3	3
Quadrilateral	4	4
Pentagon	5	5
Hexagon	6	6
Octagon	8	8

Is each figure a polygon? If not, explain why.

14. 

15. 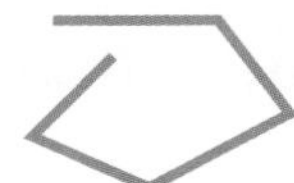

16. 

17. 

TAKS Problem Solving

In **18–21**, name the polygon that each traffic sign looks most like.

18. 

19. 

20. 

21. 

22. Reasoning Which polygon comes next in the pattern? Explain your answer.

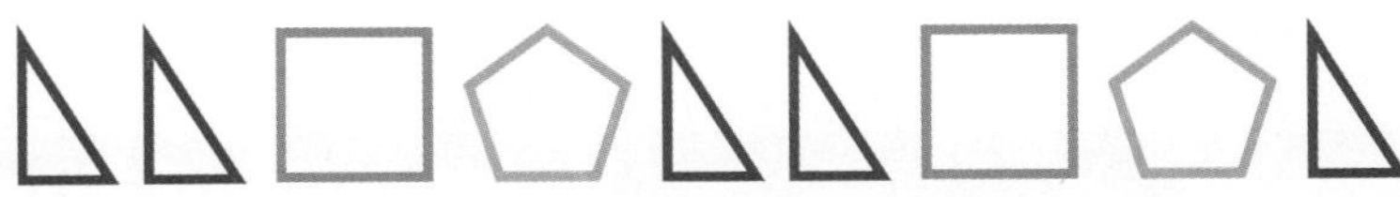

23. What polygons were used to design this house?

24. Which polygon best represents the top of the box?

A Quadrilateral **C** Pentagon

B Octagon **D** Hexagon

Lesson

14-6

TEKS 3.8: Identify, classify, and describe two- and three-dimensional geometric figures by their attributes. Compare two-dimensional figures, three-dimensional figures, or both by their attributes using formal geometry vocabulary.

Triangles

How can you describe triangles?

Triangles can be described by their sides.

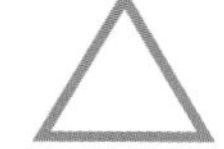

Equilateral triangle

All three sides are the same length.

Isosceles triangle

At least two sides are the same length.

Scalene triangle

No sides are the the same length.

Guided Practice*

Do you know HOW?

Tell if each triangle is equilateral, isosceles, or scalene.

1. 

2. 

Tell if each triangle is right, acute, or obtuse.

3. 

4. 

Do you UNDERSTAND?

5. How many acute angles are in an acute triangle?

6. How many obtuse angles are in an obtuse triangle?

7. Can a right triangle also be
   - a an isosceles triangle? Explain.
   - b an equilateral triangle? Explain.

8. Can an isosceles triangle also be equilateral? Explain.

Independent Practice

In **9–12**, tell if each triangle is equilateral, isosceles, or scalene. If a triangle has two names, give the name that best describes it.

9. 

10. 

11. 

12. 

*For another example, see Set F on page 329.

Triangles can be described by their angles.

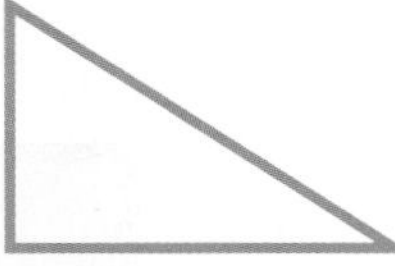

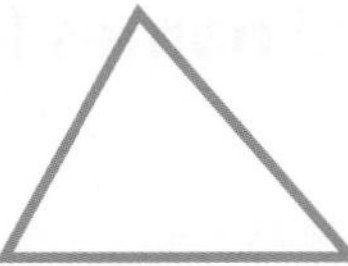

Right triangle
One angle is a right angle.

Acute triangle
All three angles are acute angles.

Obtuse triangle
One angle is an obtuse angle.

In **13–16**, tell if each triangle is right, acute, or obtuse.

13. 

14. 

15. 

16. 

TAKS Problem Solving

For **17** and **18**, use the picture of the musical triangle.

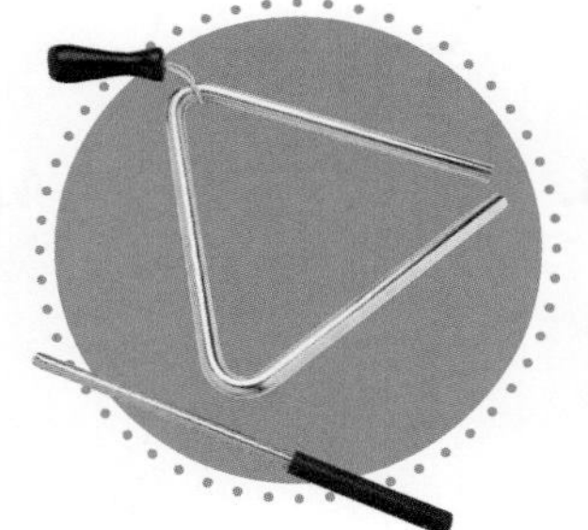

17. Does the musical triangle look most like an equilateral triangle, an isosceles triangle, or a scalene triangle?

18. Reasoning The shape of the musical triangle is not a geometric triangle. Explain why not.

19. Look at the sentence below. Write the word that will make it true.

An obtuse triangle has one obtuse angle and two __?__ angles.

20. Draw a picture to show how you could make one straight cut in a rectangle to form two right triangles.

21. Which pair of triangle names best describes this pennant?

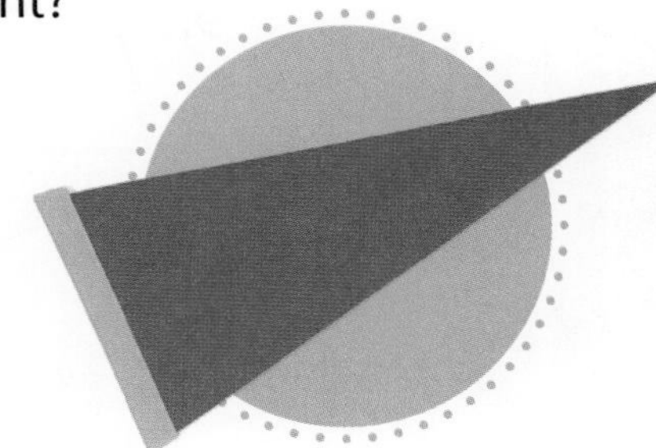

A Equilateral triangle, acute triangle

B Equilateral triangle, right triangle

C Isosceles triangle, acute triangle

D Isosceles triangle, obtuse triangle

22. Writing to Explain Why is it impossible for a triangle to have two right angles?

Lesson
14-7

TEKS 3.8: Identify, classify, and describe two- and three-dimensional geometric figures by their attributes. Compare two-dimensional figures, three-dimensional figures, or both by their attributes using formal geometry vocabulary.

Quadrilaterals

What are some special names for quadrilaterals?

Trapezoid

Exactly one pair of parallel sides

Parallelogram

Two pairs of parallel sides

Opposite sides are the same length.
Opposite angles are the same size.

Guided Practice*

Do you know HOW?

In **1–4**, write as many special names as possible for each quadrilateral.

1. 

2. 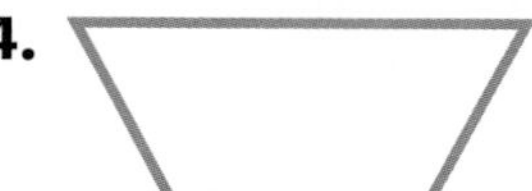

3.

4.

Do you UNDERSTAND?

5. This figure is a rectangle, but it is not a square. Why?

6. Draw a parallelogram with all four sides the same length. What is its special name?

7. Why is a square a parallelogram?

Independent Practice

In **8–12**, write as many special names as possible for each quadrilateral.

8. 

9. 

10. 

11. 

12. 

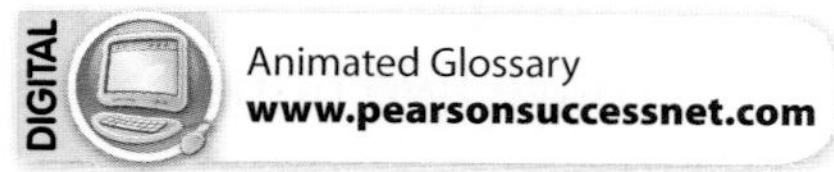

*For another example, see Set G on page 329.

Some quadrilaterals have more than one special name.

Rectangle

Four right angles

A *rectangle* is a special *parallelogram*.

Rhombus

All sides the same length

A *rhombus* is a special *parallelogram*.

Square

Four right angles and all sides the same length

A *square* is a special *parallelogram*. It is a combination of a *rectangle* and a *rhombus*.

In **13–16**, write the name that best describes the quadrilateral. Draw a picture to help.

13. A rectangle with all sides the same length

14. A quadrilateral with only one pair of parallel sides

15. A parallelogram with four right angles

16. A rhombus with four right angles

TAKS Problem Solving

17. The bike in the photo was designed with square wheels instead of round ones. How is a square different from a circle?

18. Reasoning I am a special quadrilateral with opposite sides the same length. What special quadrilateral could I be? (*Hint:* There is more than one correct answer.)

19. Writing to Explain How are a rectangle and a rhombus alike? How are they different?

20. Which picture shows more than $\frac{5}{8}$ of the square shaded?

A 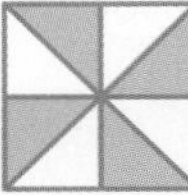

B 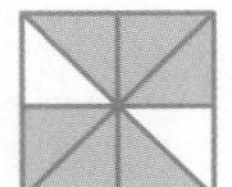

C 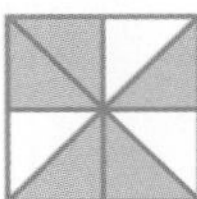

D 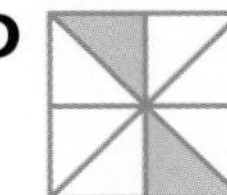

Lesson
14-8

TEKS 3.16A: Make generalizations from patterns or sets of examples and nonexamples.

Problem Solving

Make and Test Generalizations

What is the same in all these polygons?

Guided Practice*

Do you know HOW?

Make and test a generalization for each set of polygons.

1.

2.

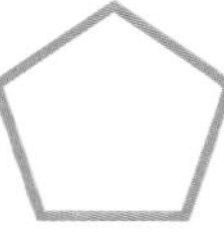
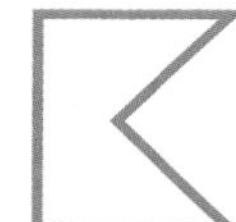
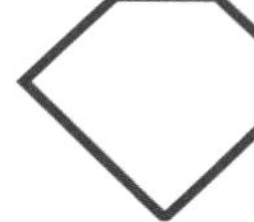

Do you UNDERSTAND?

3. Look at the polygons above. All sides of the second and third polygons **are** the same length. So why is the friend's generalization incorrect?

4. Draw a set of polygons that you can make a generalization about. Include a picture.

Independent Practice

In **5–7**, make a generalization for each set of polygons.

5.

6.

7.

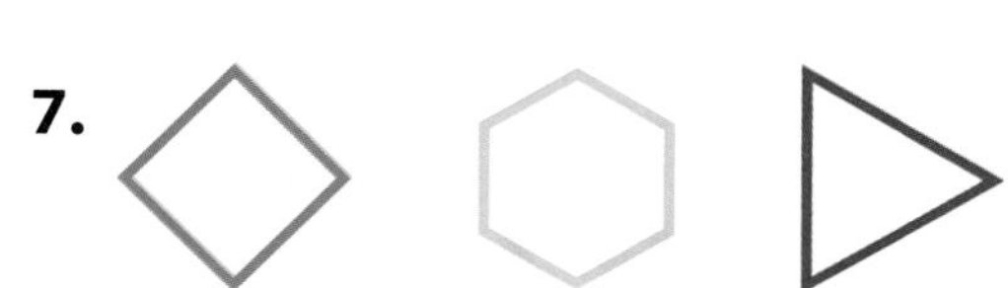

Stuck? Try this....

- What do I know?
- What am I asked to find?
- What diagram can I use to help understand the problem?
- Can I use addition, subtraction, multiplication, or division?
- Is all of my work correct?
- Did I answer the right question?
- Is my answer reasonable?

*For another example, see Set H on page 329.

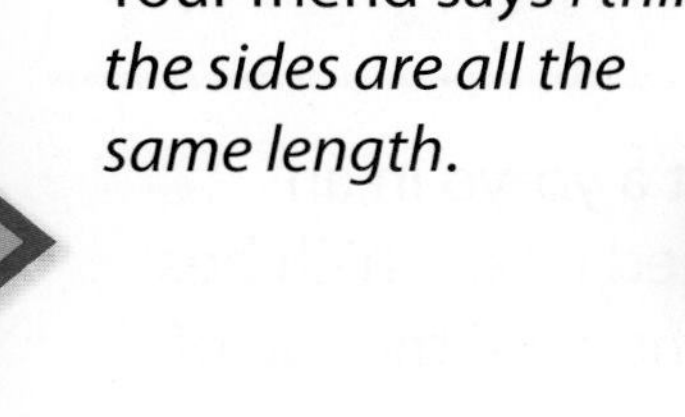

Make a Generalization

Your friend says *I think the sides are all the same length.*

You say *I think they all have 4 sides.*

Test the Generalization

Your friend says *Wait! The top and bottom of this polygon are not the same length. My generalization is not correct!*

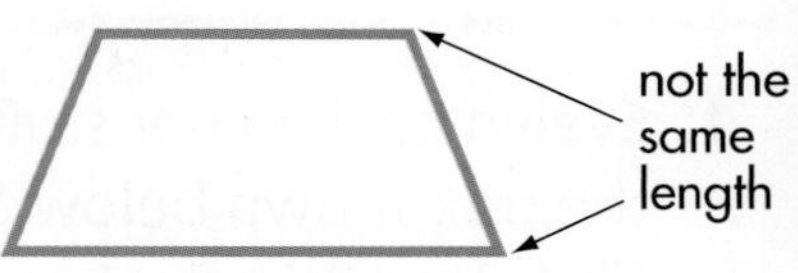

You say *The first polygon has 4 sides. The second has 4 sides. So does the third. My generalization is correct!*

8. Mr. Redbird makes tables that have 3 legs and tables that have 4 legs. The tables that he made this month have 18 legs in all. How many tables of each kind did he make?

9. Anna earns $4 for each hour that she babysits. She babysat for 2 hours last week and 5 hours this week. How much did she earn in all?

10. How are these four numbers alike?

18 24 16 40

11. Compare each sum to its addends in these number sentences:

$34 + 65 = 99$

$8 + 87 = 95$

$435 + 0 = 435$

Make a generalization about addends and sums for whole numbers.

12. **Writing to Explain** Is this generalization true? If not, draw a picture to show why not.

If a shape is made up of line segments, then it is a polygon.

13. Ari gave his friends these clues about a secret number.

- The number has three digits.
- The hundreds digit is less than 3.
- The tens digit is twice the ones digit.
- The number is odd.

What are all the possible secret numbers?

14. What is the same in all these polygons?

  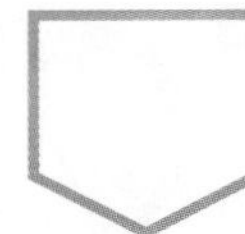

A All have a pair of parallel sides.

B All have two right angles.

C All have one acute angle.

D All have four sides.

1. Evelyn packed her stuffed animals in the box shown below. Which solid best describes the box? (14-1)

A Cylinder
B Cube
C Pyramid
D Cone

2. The angles below are examples of acute angles. (14-4)

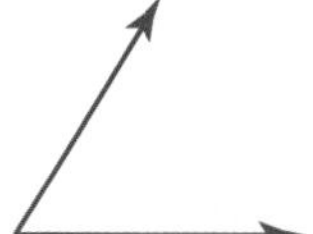

Which clock face below shows the hands in an acute angle?

F

G

H

J

3. Keenan bought a yo-yo in an unusually shaped box. Which best describes the shape of the top of the box? (14-5)

A Hexagon
B Pentagon
C Octagon
D Quadrilateral

4. Which best describes the triangles? (14-8)

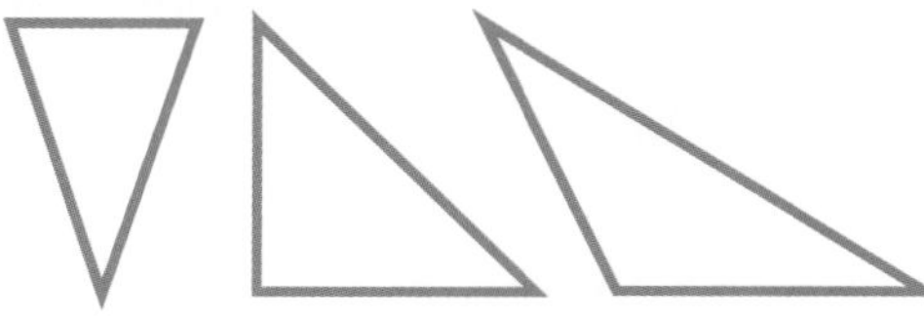

F They are all acute triangles.
G They are all isosceles triangles.
H They are all obtuse triangles.
J They are all scalene triangles.

5. Which figure is a polygon? (14-5)

A

B

C
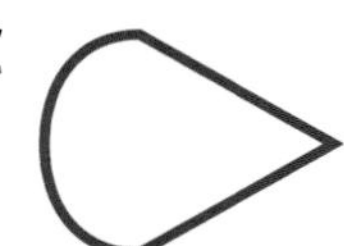

D

6. Four friends made quadrilateral shapes out of modeling clay. Whose shape has only one set of parallel sides? (14-7)

F Melissa's

G Nigel's

H Pat's

J Rahmi's

7. Below is part of a nature trail map. Which two trails represent parallel lines? (14-3)

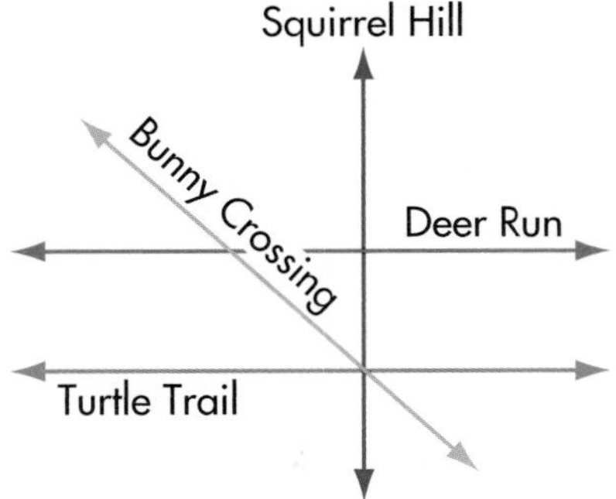

A Deer Run and Turtle Trail

B Deer Run and Squirrel Hill

C Bunny Crossing and Squirrel Hill

D Bunny Crossing and Deer Run

8. The students ran a course from the flag to the tree, to the trash can, and then back to the flag. What type of triangle did the course form? (14-6)

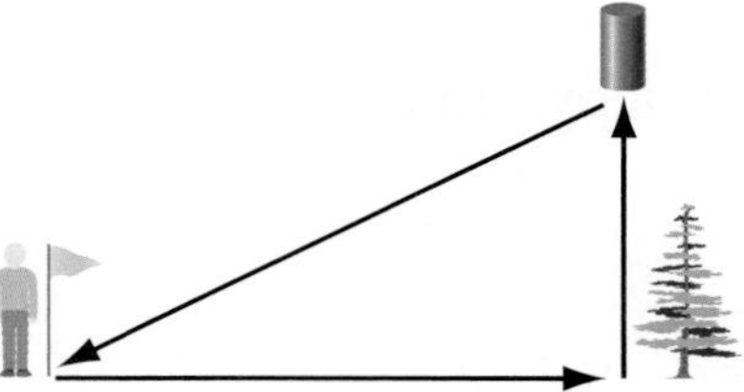

F Scalene

G Isosceles

H Equilateral

J Acute

9. Xavier bought this rug to put by his bed. What two quadrilaterals make up the rug design? (14-7)

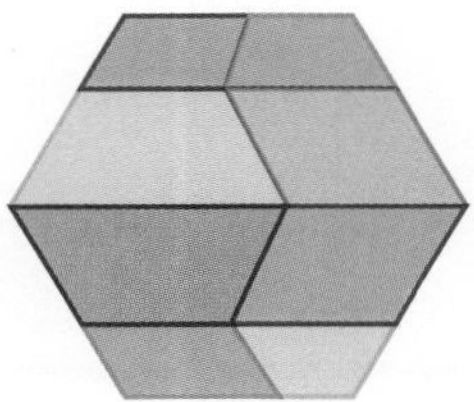

A Rhombus and parallelogram

B Rhombus and trapezoid

C Parallelogram and trapezoid

D Parallelogram and hexagon

10. **Griddable Response** Claire made a decorative pillow in the shape of a rectangular prism. If she sews a tassel at each vertex, how many tassels will she need? (14-2)

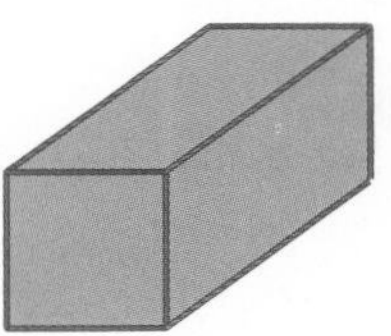

Reteaching

Set A, pages 306–309

Name this solid figure.

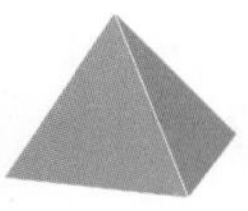
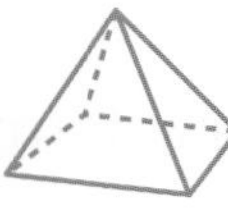

The figure has flat surfaces and a point at the top.

The figure is a pyramid.

Remember that some solid figures roll and some do not.

Name the solid figure.

1. 

2. 

Set B, pages 310–312

How many faces, edges, and vertices does the following solid figure have?

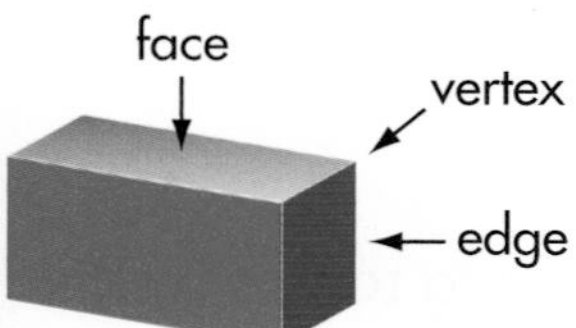

A rectangular prism has 6 faces, 12 edges, and 8 vertices.

Remember that a vertex is where three or more edges meet.

For **1** and **2**, use the cube below.

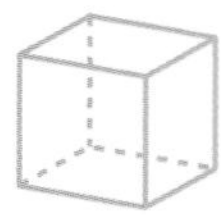

1. How many faces, edges, and vertices does this cube have?
2. Describe the shape of each face.

Set C, pages 314–315

Write the name for the following.

The lines cross at one point. They are intersecting lines.

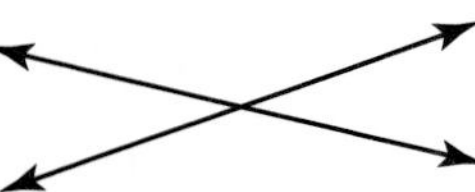

Remember that a line never ends.

Write the name for each.

1. •——→ **2.** •——•

Set D, pages 316–317

Describe the angle as right, acute, or obtuse.

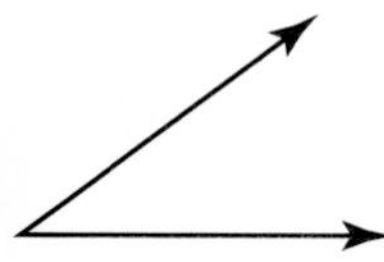

The angle is open less than a right angle.

It is an acute angle.

Remember that the opening of a right angle makes a square corner.

Describe each angle.

1. **2.**

Reteaching

Set E, pages 318–319

Is the figure a polygon? If it is a polygon, give its name. If not, explain why.

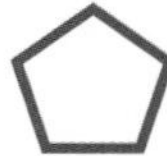

The figure is closed and is made up of line segments. It is a polygon.

The figure has 5 sides. It is a pentagon.

Remember that a polygon is made up of line segments.

Is each figure a polygon? If so, give its name. If not, explain why.

1. 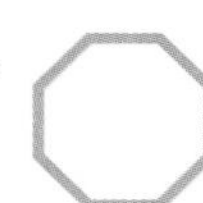

2.

Set F, pages 320–321

Tell if the triangle below is equilateral, isosceles, or scalene. Then tell if the triangle is right, acute, or obtuse.

None of the sides are the same length. The triangle is a scalene triangle. One angle is an obtuse angle.

The triangle is an obtuse triangle.

Remember that no sides of a scalene triangle are congruent.

Describe each triangle by its sides and by its angles.

1. 

2. 

Set G, pages 322–323

Name the following quadrilateral.

Opposite sides are parallel and opposite sides have the same length.

The figure is a parallelogram.

Remember that all quadrilaterals have four sides.

Write as many special names as possible for each quadrilateral.

1.

2. 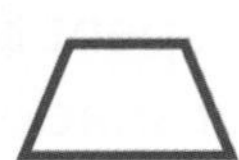

Set H, pages 324–325

Make and test a generalization for the set of polygons.

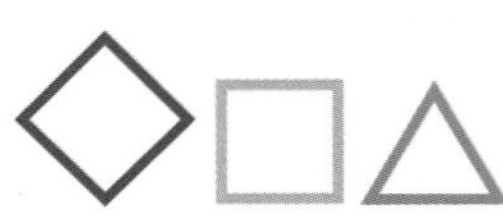

Make a generalization. *Each polygon has sides that are the same length.*

Test the generalization. *The polygons have sides that are the same length.*

Remember that a generalization has to apply to the entire set.

Make and test a generalization for this set of polygons.

1.

Number and Operations

1. Which of the following numbers are written in order from least to greatest?

A 1,797 1,979 1,977

B 1,977 1,797 1,979

C 1,797 1,977 1,979

D 1,979 1,977 1,797

2. Karen bought 12 of the same kind of muffins at the bakery. She spent $24. How much did each muffin cost?

F $36 **H** $4

G $6 **J** $2

3. Which number sentence is true?

A $\frac{1}{4} < \frac{1}{2}$ **C** $\frac{3}{4} = \frac{1}{2}$

B $\frac{1}{2} < \frac{1}{4}$ **D** $\frac{3}{4} < \frac{1}{2}$

4. What fraction of this figure is shaded blue?

5. Mike spent $5 to see a movie and $2 for snacks. He had $8 in his pocket when he got home. Work backward to find out how much money he had before the movie.

6. **Writing to Explain** Mrs. Coleman bought 3 boxes of pencils. What do you need to know to find out how many pencils she bought in all? Explain your answer.

Geometry and Measurement

7. Identify the figure shown below.

F Line **H** Ray

G Line segment **J** Angle

8. Which triangle is an equilateral triangle?

A **C** 

B **D** 

9. Look at the figures below.

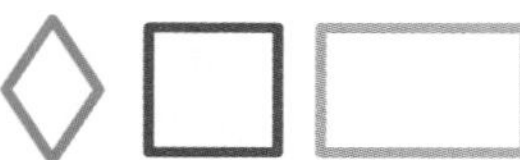

Which statement about these figures is true?

F They are all squares.

G They are all quadrilaterals.

H They are all pentagons.

J They all have one right angle.

10. **Writing to Explain** How are figures *A* and *B* the same? How are they different?

A.  **B.** 

11. **Writing to Explain** Describe the positions of the hands on a clock when it is 10:30.

Probability and Statistics

12. Which event is less likely to happen than the others?

A It will rain next Monday.

B Next week will have 7 days.

C Tuesday will follow Monday.

D The Sun will set tonight.

13. On which of the following is this spinner more likely to land?

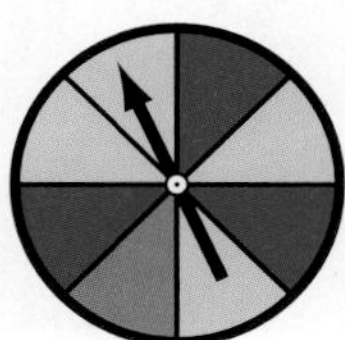

F Red　　**H** Yellow

G Green　　**J** Blue

Use the pictograph for **14–16.**

School Car Wash	
Friday	🚗 🚗
Saturday	🚗 🚗 🚗 🚗 🚗
Key: Each 🚗 = 5 cars washed	

14. On which day were more cars washed?

15. How many cars were washed on Friday?

16. **Writing to Explain** Thomas says the total number of cars washed was 7. Do you agree? Explain why or why not.

Algebraic Thinking

17. What number is missing in the pattern below?

52, 56, 60, $\square$, 68, 72

A 62　　**C** 73

B 64　　**D** 80

18. What number makes this number sentence true?

$\square \times 5 = 0$

F 0　　**H** 5

G 1　　**J** 10

19. In Art class, students made pictures using their hand prints.

If the students counted the total number of fingers by 5s, which list shows numbers the students could have named?

A 5, 10, 12, 15, 20, 22

B 3, 6, 9, 12, 15, 18

C 5, 10, 15, 20, 25, 30

D 2, 4, 6, 8, 10, 12

20. **Writing to Explain** Which fraction is closer to zero, $\frac{1}{4}$ or $\frac{3}{4}$? Explain.

Topic 15

Congruence and Symmetry

1 Are snowflakes symmetric? You will find out in Lesson 15-3.

2 Are the windows of the Taj Mahal congruent? You will find out in Lesson 15-1.

3 Where is the line of symmetry in the picture of a mountain and its reflection? You will find out in Lesson 15-2.

4 Does fruit such as a grapefruit or an orange have lines of symmetry? You will find out in Lesson 15-3.

Review What You Know!

Vocabulary

Choose the best term from the box.

- difference
- estimate
- line
- rounding

1. When you subtract two numbers, the answer is called the __?__.
2. When you replace a number with a number that tells about how many to the nearest ten, you are __?__ the number.
3. A __?__ is a straight path of points that is endless in both directions.

Repeating Patterns

Draw the next three shapes to continue each pattern.

4. ○ ◯ △ △ ○ ◯ △

5. □ ▯ □ ○ □ ▯ □

Division Facts

Find each quotient.

6. 24 ÷ 3
7. 36 ÷ 9
8. 16 ÷ 4
9. 54 ÷ 6
10. 81 ÷ 9
11. 48 ÷ 8
12. **Writing to Explain** Is the figure below a polygon? Explain how you can draw the figure to make it a polygon.

Lesson
15-1

TEKS 3.9A
Identify congruent two-dimensional figures.

Congruent Figures and Motion

What are congruent figures?

Figures that have the same size and shape are congruent figures. You can move a figure to make a new figure that is congruent to it.
When a figure is moved up, down, left, or right, the motion is a translation.

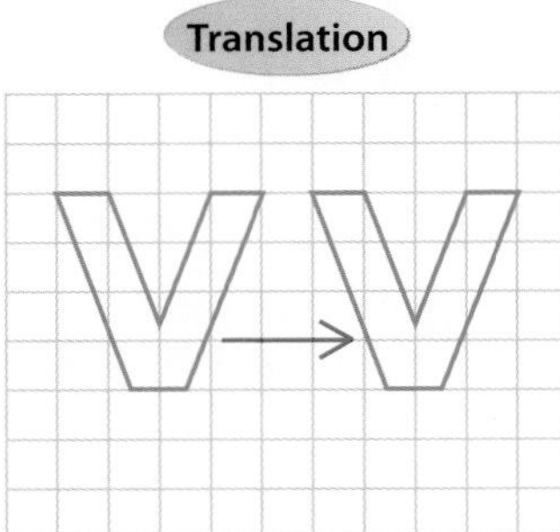

Another Example How can you decide if two figures are congruent?

To decide if two figures are congruent, trace one of the figures and place the tracing on top of the other figure.

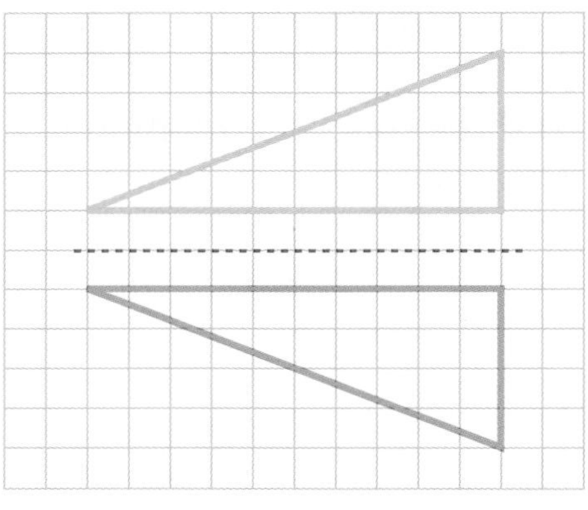

Yes, the figures are congruent.

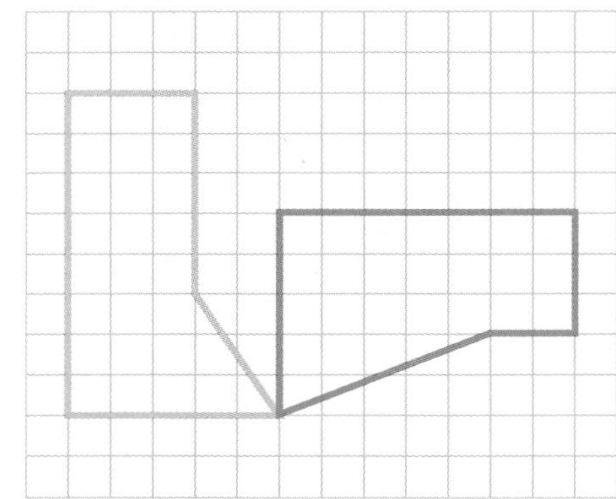

No, the figures are not congruent.

Explain It

1. Look at the two triangles. How could you move one triangle to match it to the other?
2. Look at the two pentagons. How could you move one to show that it does not match the other?

When a figure is picked up and turned over, the motion is a reflection.

Reflection

When a figure is moved around a point, the motion is a rotation.

Rotation

Guided Practice*

Do you know HOW?

Write *translation, reflection,* or *rotation* for each.

1.

2. 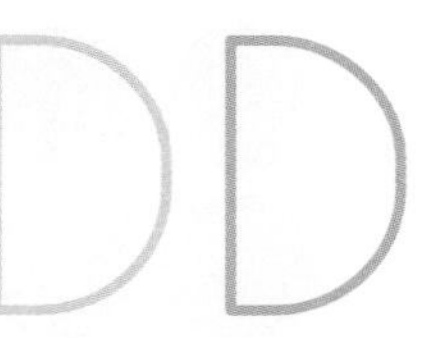

Are the figures congruent? Write *yes* or *no*. You may trace to decide.

3.

4. 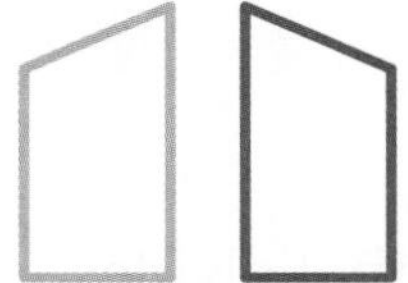

Do you UNDERSTAND?

5. Could a triangle and a square be congruent? Explain your answer.

6. Are all triangles congruent? Explain your answer.

7. Are all squares congruent? Explain your answer.

8. Trace this pentagon. Then show what it would look like after reflecting it to the right.

Independent Practice

For **9–11**, write *translation, reflection,* or *rotation* for each pair of congruent figures.

9. 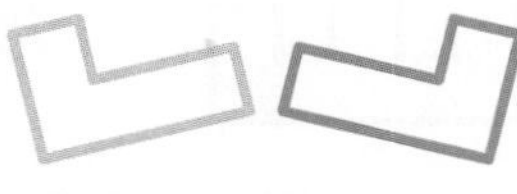

10. 

11. 

DIGITAL Animated Glossary **www.pearsonsuccessnet.com**

For another example, see Set A on page 346.

Independent Practice

For **12–14**, are the figures congruent? Write *yes* or *no*. You may trace to decide.

12. 

13. 

14. 

TAKS Problem Solving

15. Manny says the windows of the Taj Mahal are congruent because they are all shaped like the window in the picture below. Do you agree? Why or why not?

16. Think About the Process Samantha arranged some pennies in the pattern shown below. What operation best shows how she arranged them?

A $3 + 6$ **C** 3×6

B $3 + 9$ **D** 3×9

17. Draw a rectangle. Then draw a line segment that divides the rectangle into two congruent figures. Describe the two figures.

18. **Writing to Explain** Are all rectangles congruent? Explain your answer.

19. Which figure below is congruent to the figure at the right?

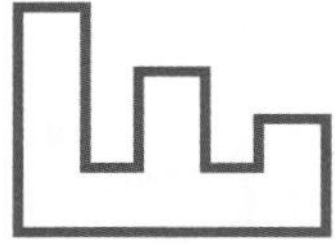

F 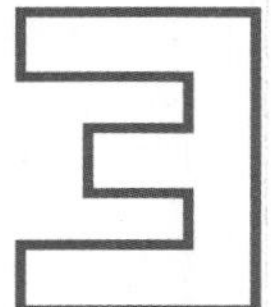

G 

H 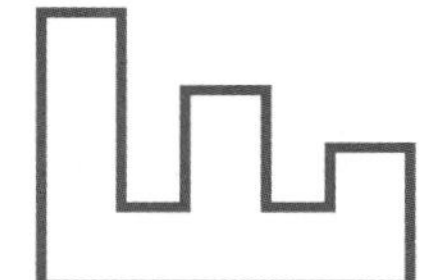

J 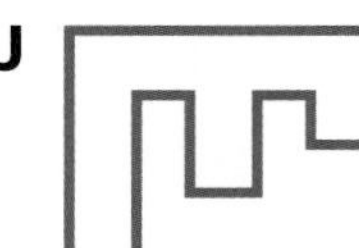

Motions

Use eTools

Geometry Shapes

Write *translation*, *reflection*, or *rotation* for each pair of figures.

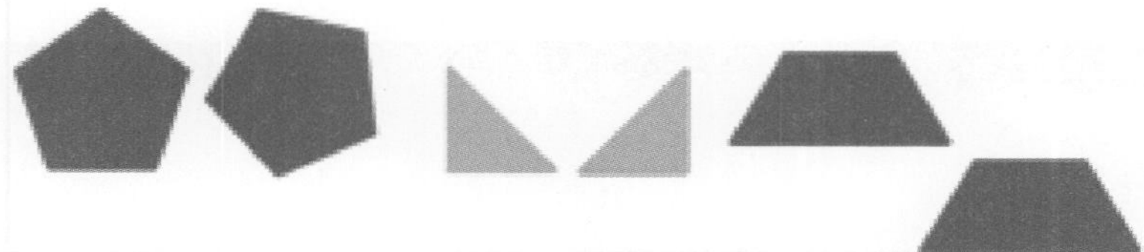

Step 1 Go to the Geometry Shapes eTool. Click on the pentagon, and then click in the workspace twice to create two pentagons side-by-side.

Step 2 Click on the rotate tool and then click on the second pentagon until it looks like the second pentagon pictured above. This shows that the second pentagon is the result of rotating the first. Write *rotation*.

Step 3 Make two copies of the right triangle in the workspace. Click on the reflection (flip vertical) tool and then on the second triangle. This shows that the second triangle is a reflection of the first. Write *reflection*.

Step 4 Make two copies of the trapezoid in the workspace. Use the arrow tool to move the second trapezoid like the one pictured above. This shows that the second trapezoid is a translation of the first. Write *translation*. Use the broom tool to clear the workspace.

Practice

Write *translation, reflection,* or *rotation* for each pair of figures.

1. 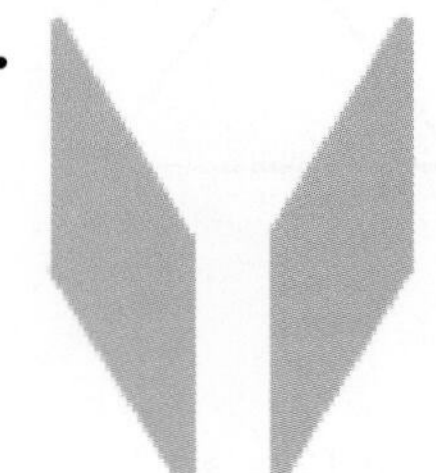

2. 

3. 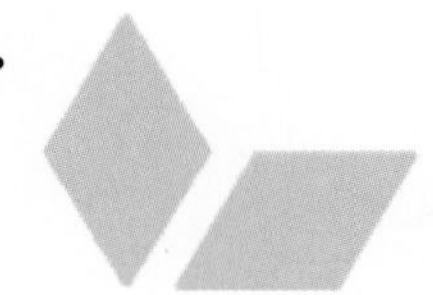

Lesson
15-2

TEKS 3.9C Identify lines of symmetry in two-dimensional geometric figures.

Line Symmetry

What are symmetric figures?

A line of symmetry is a line on which a figure can be folded so the two parts match exactly. A symmetric figure has at least one line of symmetry.

A figure can have just one line of symmetry.

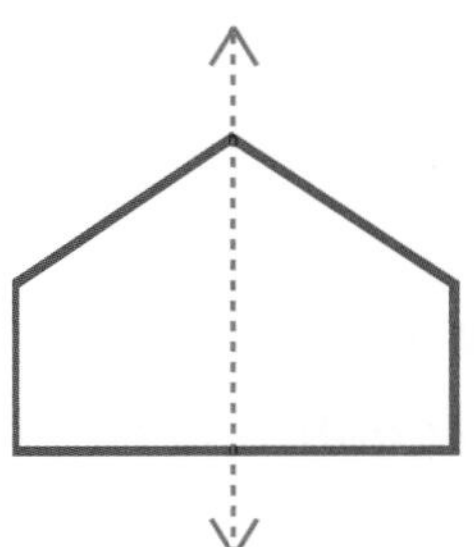

Guided Practice*

Do you know HOW?

Is the figure symmetric? Write *yes* or *no*. You may trace to decide.

1. 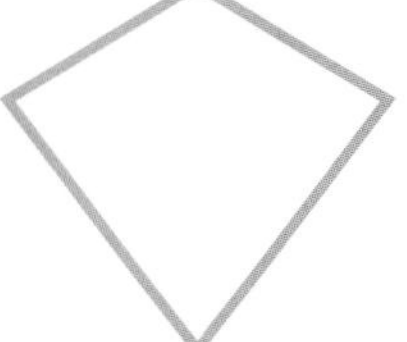

2. 

3. 

4. 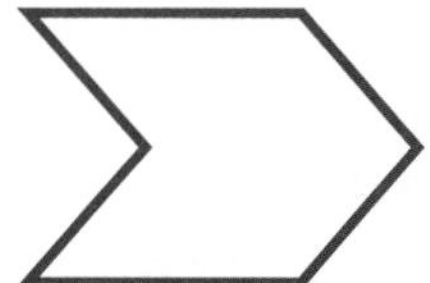

Do you UNDERSTAND?

5. Explain how you can test a figure to decide if it has a line of symmetry.

6. Is the dashed line a line of symmetry for the rectangle? Explain.

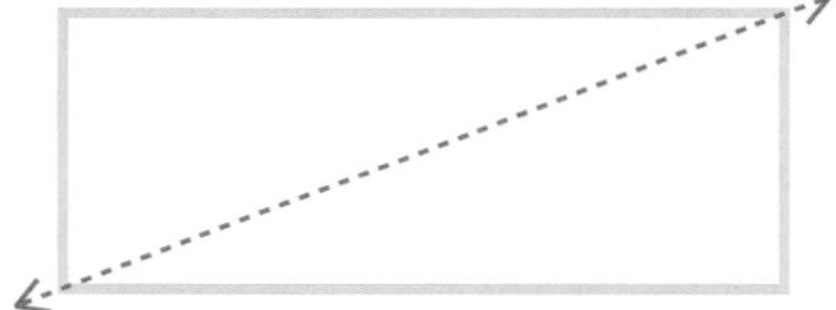

Independent Practice

Is the figure symmetric? Write *yes* or *no*. You may trace to decide.

7. 

8. 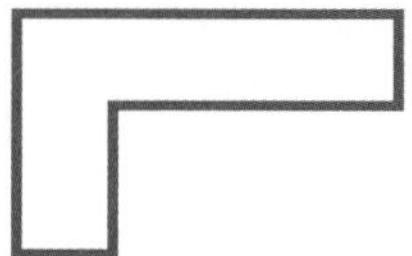

9. 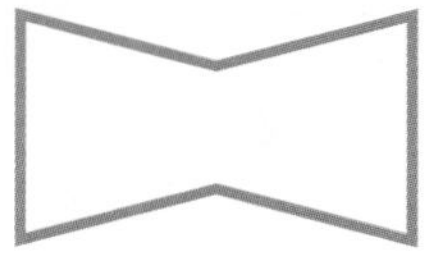

10. 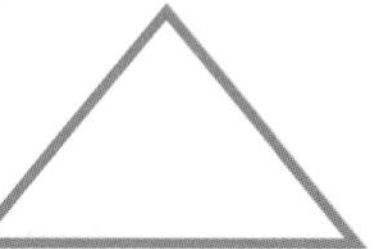

*For another example, see Set B on page 346.

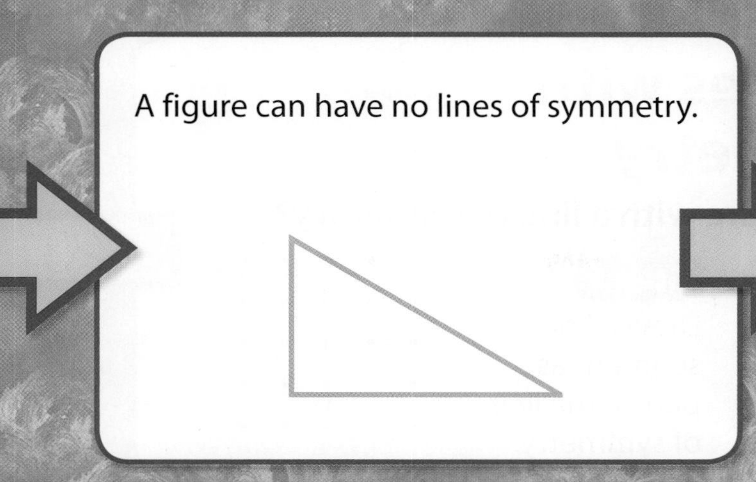

A figure can have more than one line of symmetry.

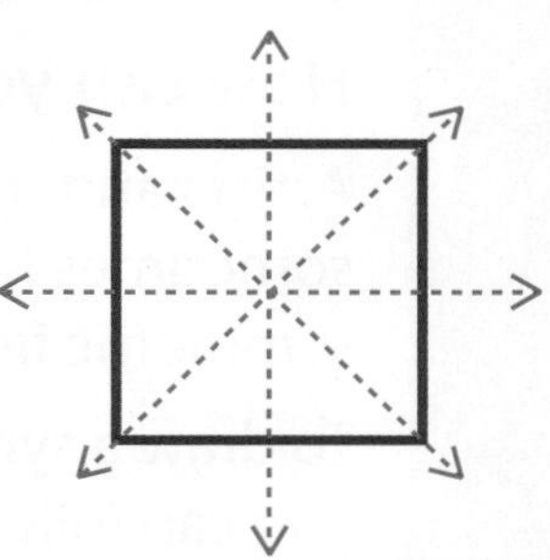

Tell whether each object is symmetric. Write *yes* or *no*.

11. 

12. 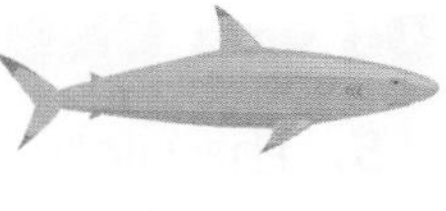

13. 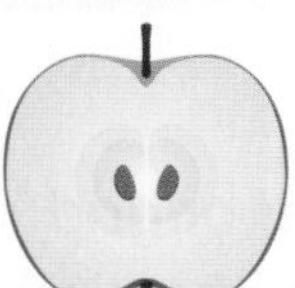

14. 

TAKS Problem Solving

15. Trace this picture of a mountain and its reflection. Then fold your tracing and draw the line of symmetry.

16. Which figure below does **NOT** have at least one line of symmetry?

A 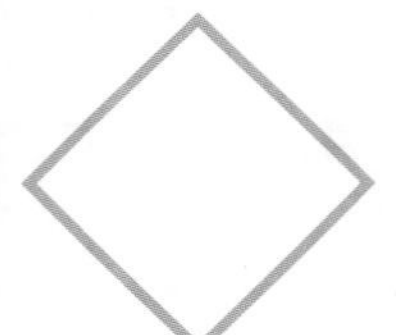

C 

B 

D 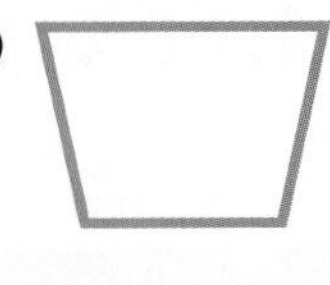

17. Writing to Explain You have learned that a square is a type of rectangle. Do all rectangles and squares have the same number of lines of symmetry? Explain your answer.

18. Sue has some nickels, dimes, and quarters in her pocket.

- There are 3 quarters.
- There are 2 more dimes than nickels.
- There are 15 coins in all.

What is the total value of the coins?

Lesson

15-3

TEKS 3.9B Create two-dimensional figures with lines of symmetry using concrete models and technology.

Drawing Shapes with Lines of Symmetry

Hands-On
grid paper

How can you draw a figure with a line of symmetry?

Artists and other workers sometimes have to draw symmetric figures.

To draw a symmetric figure, you can follow these steps.

Step 1

Draw a line segment as part of the line of symmetry.

Guided Practice*

Do you know HOW?

Trace the figure onto dot paper or grid paper. Then complete it so the blue line segment is part of a line of symmetry.

1. 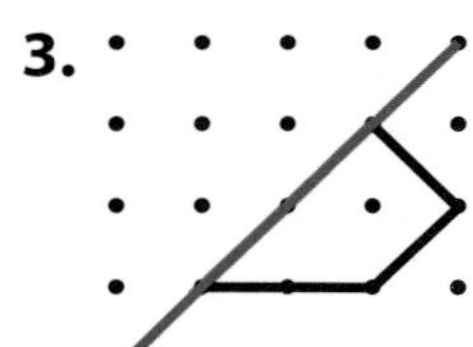

2. 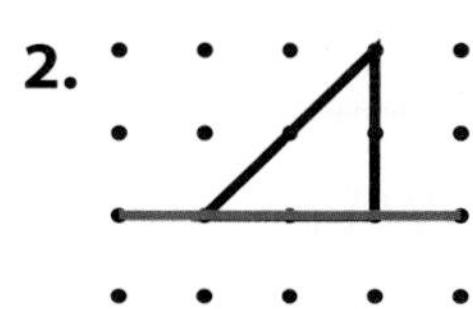

3.

4. 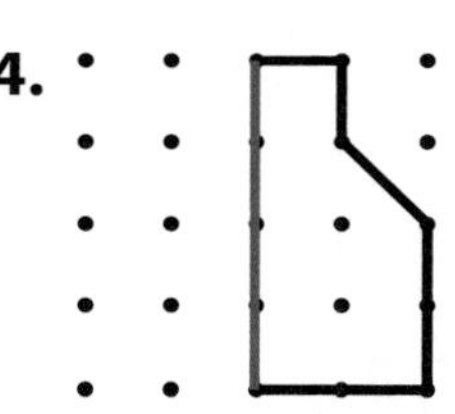

Do you UNDERSTAND?

5. The picture below shows two parts of a figure on dot paper.

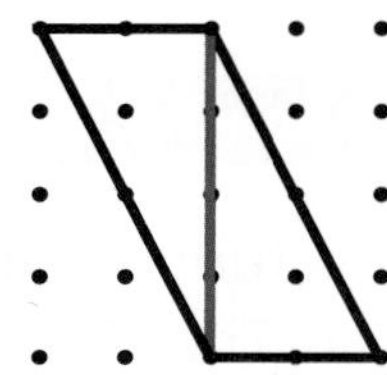

Explain why the blue line segment is not part of a line of symmetry.

6. How would you draw a figure that has two lines of symmetry?

Independent Practice

Trace the figure. Then complete it so the blue line segment is part of a line of symmetry. You may use dot paper or fold and trace.

7.

8. 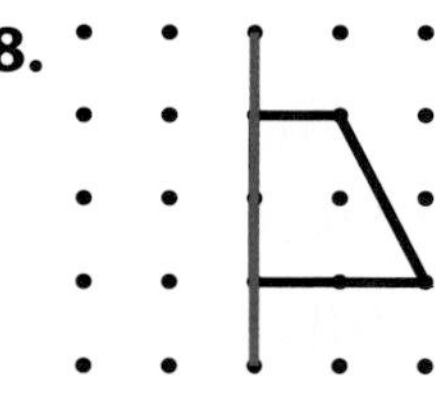

9.  

10. 

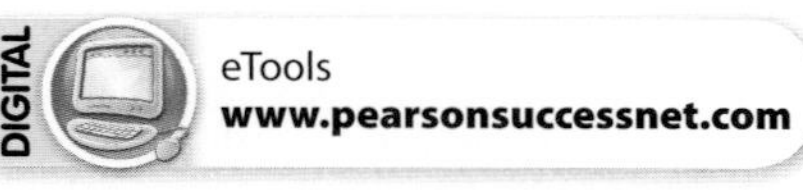

*For another example, see Set C on page 347.

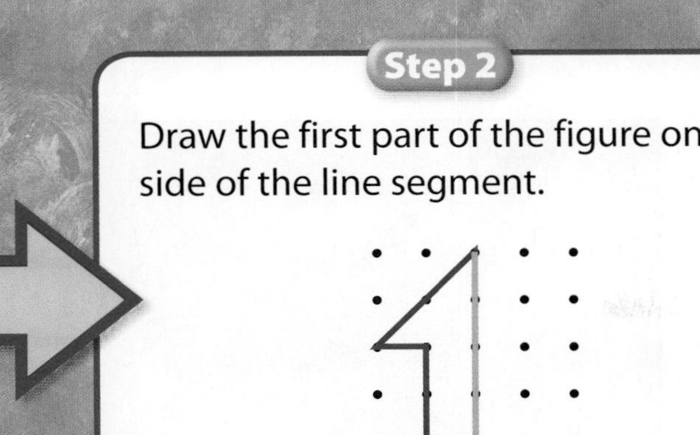

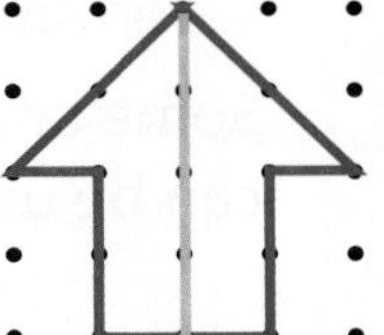

Step 3

Copy the first part exactly on the other side of the line segment.

TAKS Problem Solving

11. **Estimation** Jeremy is reading a book that has 121 pages. He read 19 pages yesterday and 33 pages today. About how many more pages are left to read?

13. **Writing to Explain** Explain how you can use this shape to make a symmetric quadrilateral. What type of quadrilateral will it be?

14. The picture shows a sliced ruby red grapefruit and an outline of part of the grapefruit sections.

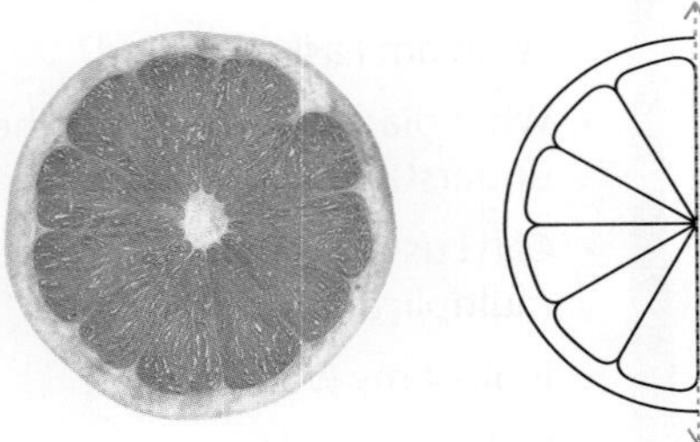

Trace the outline onto a sheet of paper. Complete the outline so the dashed line is a line of symmetry.

12. A perfectly formed snowflake has 6 sides and is symmetric.

Draw your own snowflake. Color the lines of symmetry on your drawing. How many lines of symmetry does it have?

15. The green line segment is part of a line of symmetry. Which picture below shows the complete figure?

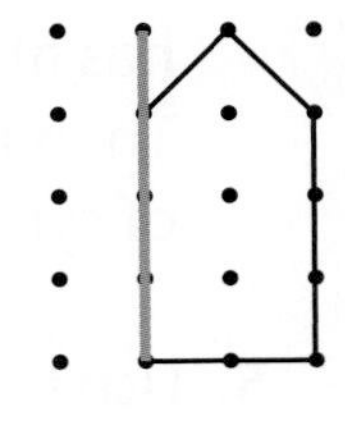

A

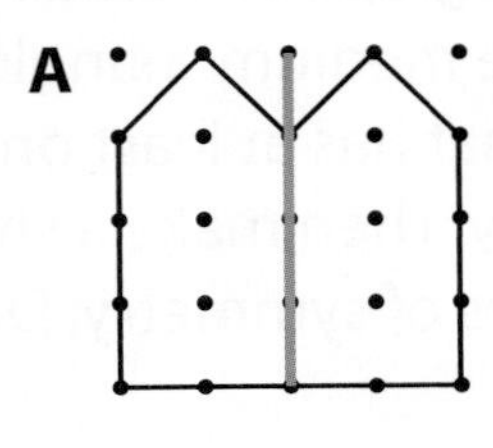

C

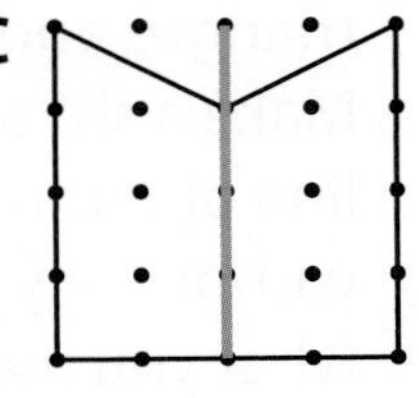

B

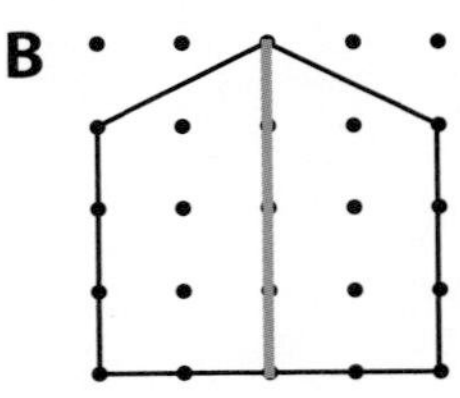

D

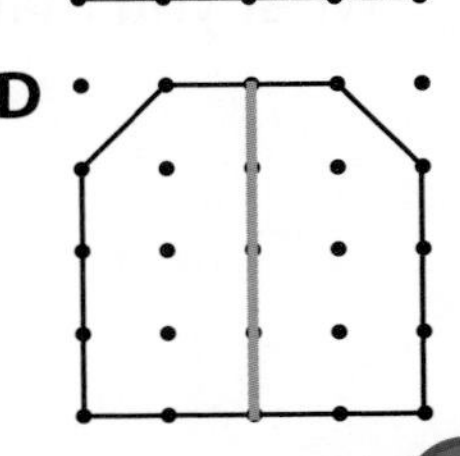

Lesson

15-4

TEKS 3.14D Use tools such as real objects, manipulatives, and technology to solve problems.
TEKS 3.9B Create two-dimensional geometric figures with lines of symmetry using concrete models and technology.

Problem Solving

Use Objects

A tangram is a square made up of seven smaller shapes.

Some or all of the smaller shapes can be used to make other shapes.

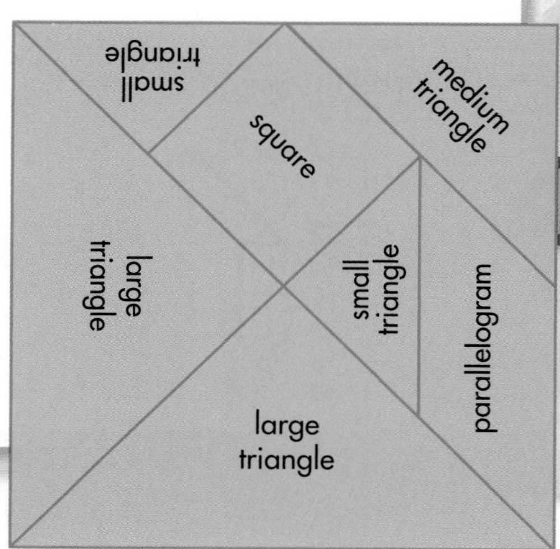

Guided Practice*

Do you know HOW?

Use the tangram to make the shape. Draw what you made.

1. Use the parallelogram and one small triangle. Make a shape that has at least one line of symmetry. Then make a shape without any lines of symmetry.

Do you UNDERSTAND?

For **2** and **3**, look at the problem above.

2. Where are the two lines of symmetry in the rectangle?

3. **Write a Problem** Write a problem that you can solve by making a shape from tangram pieces.

Independent Practice

4. Use the parallelogram and the medium triangle. Make a shape that has at least one line of symmetry. Then make a shape without any lines of symmetry. Draw what you made.

5. Use the parallelogram, one small triangle, and the medium triangle. Make a shape that has at least one line of symmetry. Then make a shape without any lines of symmetry. Draw what you made.

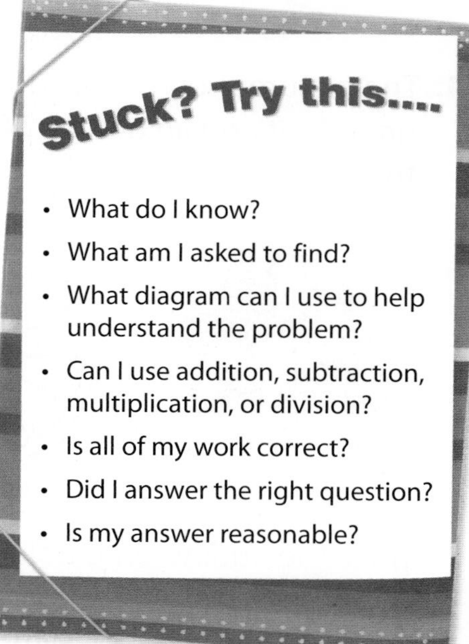

*For another example, see Set D on page 347.

Read and Understand

Make two different shapes using the two small triangles and the medium triangle.

- Make one shape that has at least one line of symmetry.
- Make the other shape without any lines of symmetry.

Plan and Solve

This shape is a rectangle. It has two lines of symmetry.

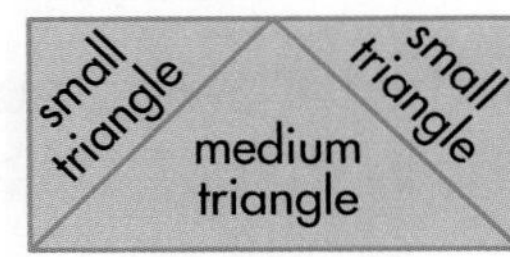

This shape is a parallelogram. It does not have a line of symmetry.

For **6–8**, use the two small triangles and the parallelogram to make each shape. For each shape, use all three pieces. Then draw what you made.

6. A rectangle

7. A triangle

8. A parallelogram

For **9–11**, use the two small triangles, the parallelogram, and the square. Make each shape using all four pieces. Then draw what you made.

9. A rectangle

10. A parallelogram

11. A hexagon

12. **Writing to Explain** Show and explain how you can make a triangle and two types of quadrilaterals using just the two small triangles.

13. Use all five triangles from a set of tangram shapes. Make at least three different shapes. Draw what you made.

14. Timothy sold some tickets to the school play. The tickets were numbered in order. The numbers started at 16 and ended at 45. How many tickets did Timothy sell?

15. Jessica is standing in a line of 10 people. There are twice as many people ahead of her as there are behind her. How many people are ahead of Jessica in the line?

16. David's mother brought 24 cartons of orange and grape juice to the class picnic. There were twice as many cartons of orange juice as cartons of grape juice. How many of each kind were there?

A 12 orange, 6 grape

B 12 grape, 6 orange

C 16 orange, 8 grape

D 16 grape, 8 orange

TAKS Test Prep

1. Which of the following numbers is symmetric in shape? (15-2)

   A 2

   B 5

   C 0

   D 7

2. Which moves one outline of the state of Texas to match the other one? (15-1)

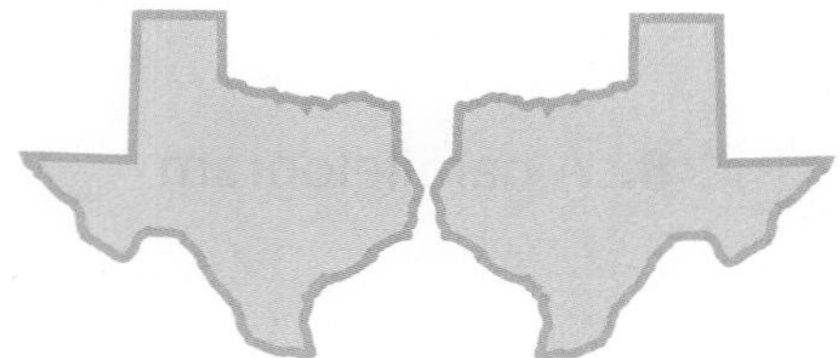

   F Reflection

   G Symmetry

   H Translation

   J Rotation

3. Below are examples of the small triangle tangram shape turned to several different positions.

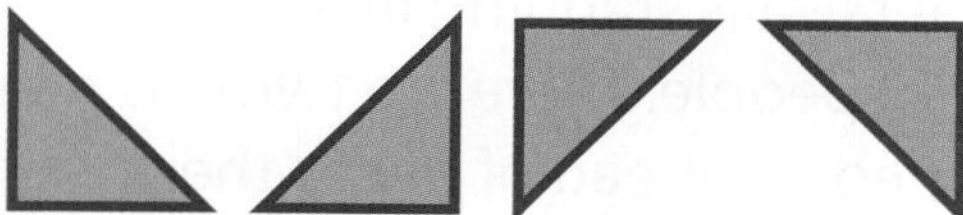

   Which of the following shapes can **NOT** be made by joining two of the triangles? (15-4)

   A A square

   B A parallelogram

   C A triangle

   D A trapezoid

4. Katherine designed the body of a kite.

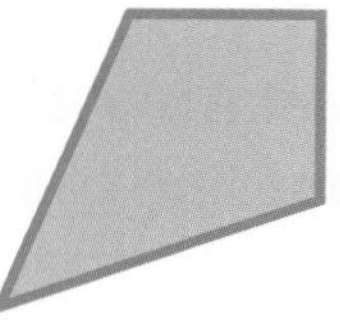

   Which shape is congruent to her kite design? (15-1)

   F

   G

   H

   J

5. Which of the following shows a rotation? (15-1)

   A

   B

   C

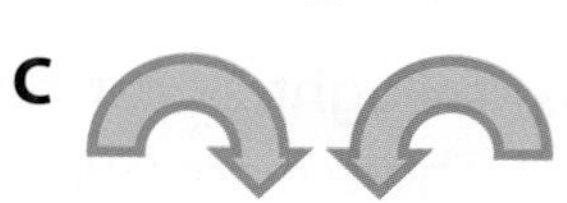

   D

6. While on a nature hike, Nolan saw the items below. Which item does **NOT** show a line of symmetry? (15-2)

F

G

H

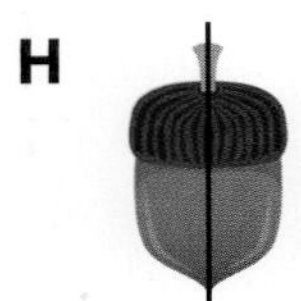

J

7. Which moves one flag of Texas to match the other one? (15-1)

A Translation

B Rotation

C Congruent

D Reflection

8. Danny drew the left half of his playground design on dot paper.

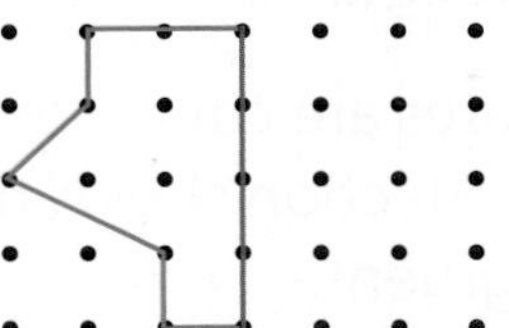

Which completes the right half of his playground design if the blue line is the line of symmetry? (15-3)

F

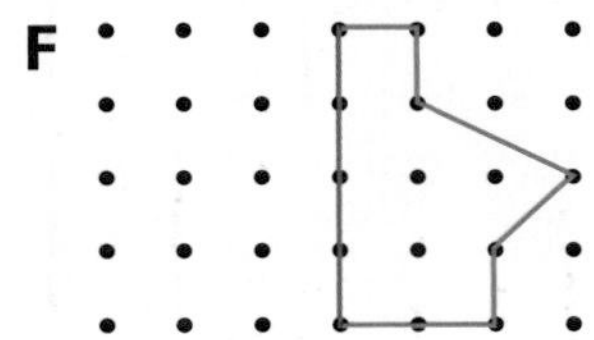

G

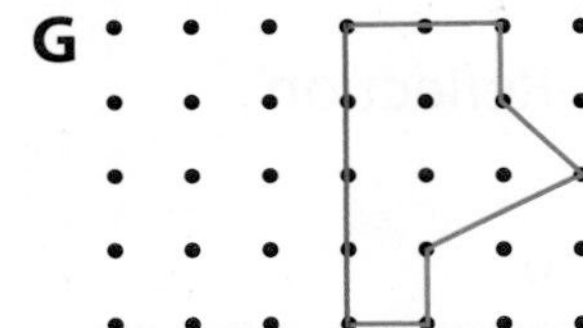

H

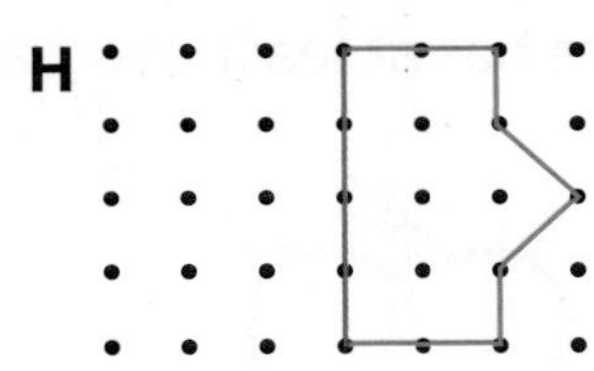

J

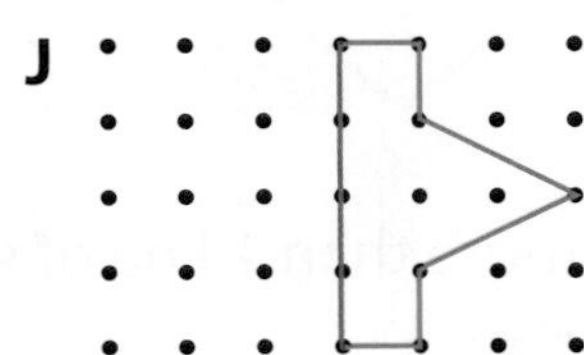

9. **Griddable Response** How many letters in the word below have at least one line of symmetry? (15-2)

TEXAS

Reteaching

Set A, pages 334–336

Figures that have the same size and same shape are congruent figures.

You can check if figures are congruent by moving them. This reflection shows that these two figures are congruent.

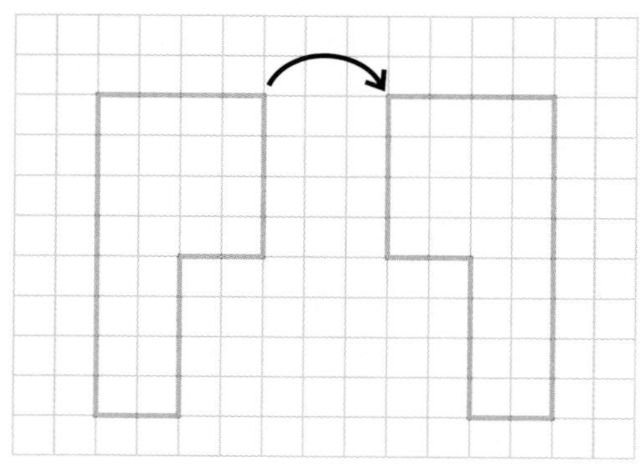

Reflection

Remember that figures need to be the same shape and same size to be congruent.

Are the figures congruent? Write *yes* or *no*. If yes, write *translation*, *rotation*, or *reflection* for each.

1. 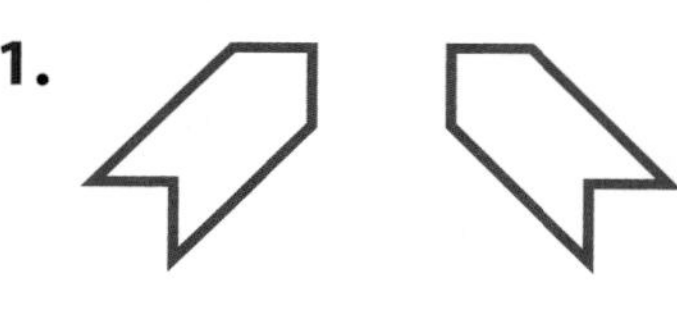

2. 

Set B, pages 338–339

A symmetric figure has at least two parts that match exactly.

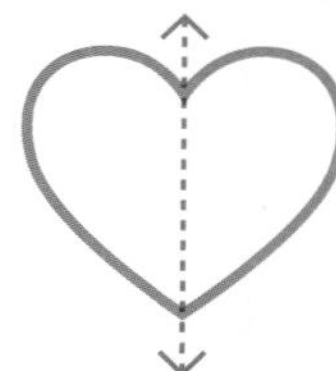

A figure can have more than 1 line of symmetry.

This figure has 5 lines of symmetry.

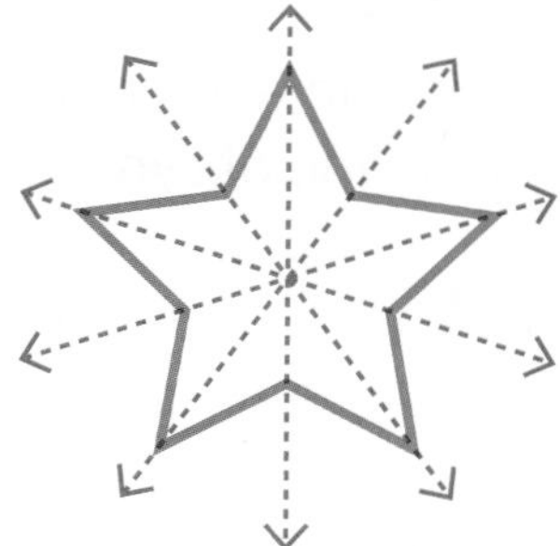

Remember that a symmetric figure has at least 1 line of symmetry, showing two parts that match exactly.

Tell whether each figure is symmetric. Write *yes* or *no*.

1. 

2. 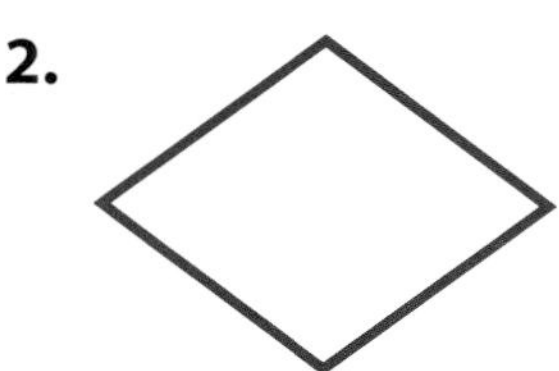

Set C, pages 340–341

To draw a symmetric figure, draw the first part of the figure on one side of a line segment.

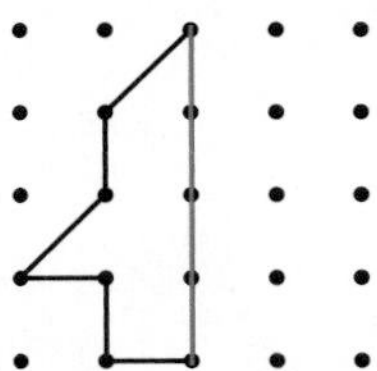

Copy the first part exactly on the other side of the line segment.

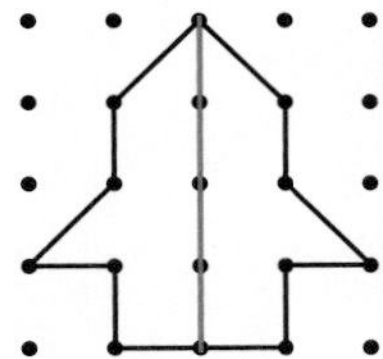

Remember to match each part of the figure exactly.

Copy the figure onto dot paper. Then complete it so the red line segment is part of a line of symmetry.

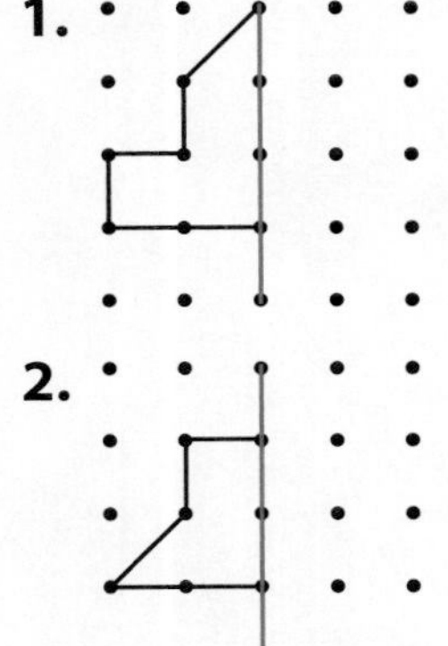

Set D, pages 342–343

Use the two large triangle tangram shapes. Make one shape that has at least one line of symmetry. Make another shape that does not have a line of symmetry.

This shape is a triangle. It has one line of symmetry.

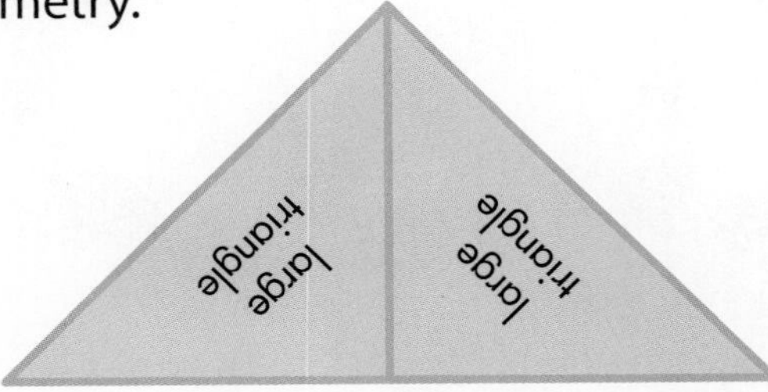

This shape is a polygon. It does not have a line of symmetry.

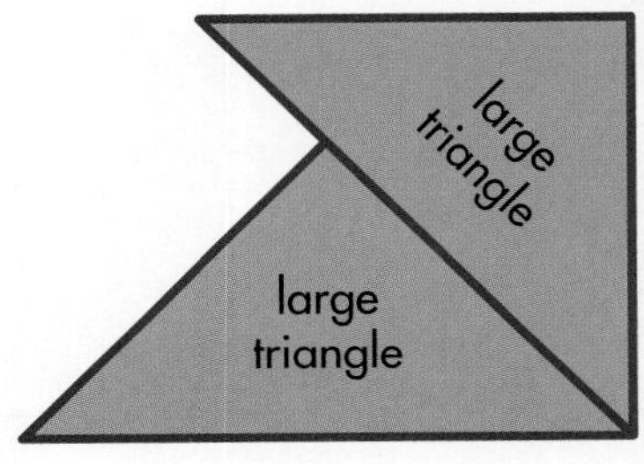

Remember to check that your new shape matches the directions given.

Use the two small triangles and the square. Make the shape. Draw what you made.

1. A shape with a line of symmetry
2. A parallelogram
3. A trapezoid

Topic 16

Estimating and Measuring Length

1 What is the length in meters and centimeters of the footbridge on Tower Bridge in London, England? You will find out in Lesson 16-5.

2 How long are the horns of Texas Longhorn cattle? You will find out in Lesson 16-3.

3 Mark Twain is a famous author. What does his name have to do with a unit of measure? You will find out in Lesson 16-1.

4 What is the length of the world's smallest seahorse? You will find out in Lesson 16-4.

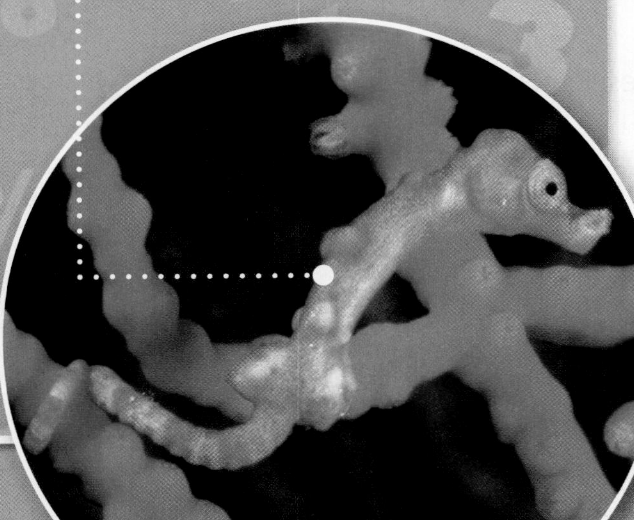

Review What You Know!

Vocabulary

Choose the best term from the box.

- estimate
- fraction
- factor
- multiply

1. When you find 3×4, you _?_.
2. When you find a number that is about how many, you _?_.
3. If a whole is divided into equal parts, each part is a _?_ of the whole.

Fractions and Length

Find what part of the length of the 1 strip the other strips show. Write the fraction.

4. 1; $\frac{1}{12}$ $\frac{1}{12}$ $\frac{1}{12}$ $\frac{1}{12}$ $\frac{1}{12}$ $\frac{1}{12}$ $\frac{1}{12}$

5. 1; $\frac{1}{4}$ $\frac{1}{4}$ $\frac{1}{4}$

Multiplication

Find each product.

6. 3×12
7. 6×10
8. 5×3
9. 2×100
10. 4×36
11. 6×12
12. **Writing to Explain** Kim has had 3 skating lessons each month for 12 months. How many lessons has she had? Explain how an array could help you solve this problem. Then solve the problem.

Lesson

16-1

TEKS 3.11A: Use linear measurement tools to estimate and measure lengths using standard units.

Understanding Measurement

Hands-On
inch ruler

How can you describe the length of an object in different ways?

Measure the length of your desktop in pencil-lengths and in crayon-lengths.

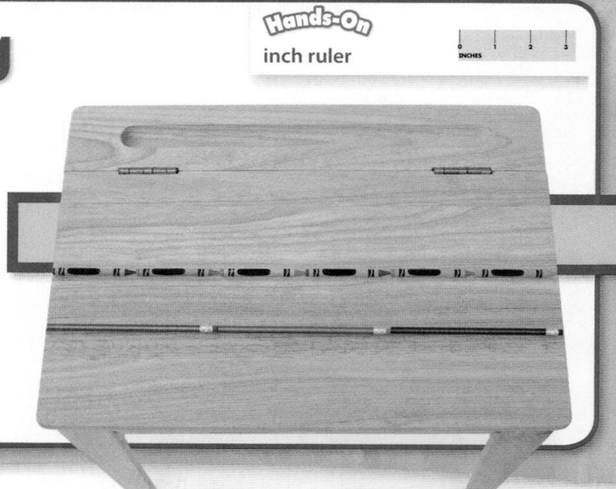

Another Example How can you use inches to measure?

Find the length of the desktop in inches.

To use a ruler, line up the object with the 0 mark.

You may need to move the ruler to continue measuring. If so, make sure that you mark where the ruler ends before you move it.

When the ruler on the desk is moved, it will show about 6 more inches.

$12 + 6 = 18$

To the nearest inch, this desktop is 18 inches long.

Explain It

1. Estimate the length of your shoe in inches. Explain how you got your estimate.
2. Find the length of a pen to the nearest inch.
3. Explain why using a ruler is a better way to measure length than using a crayon.

Find the length.

More crayon-lengths than pencil-lengths equal the length of the desktop.

The desktop is 3 pencil-lengths or 6 crayon-lengths long.

Compare the units.

The crayon-length is a smaller unit than the pencil-length.

The smaller the unit used, the more units are needed to equal a given length.

Use a standard unit.

People use standard units to describe measurements.

A standard unit for measuring length is the inch (in.).

1 inch

Guided Practice*

Do you know HOW?

Estimate each length. Then measure to the nearest inch.

1.

2.

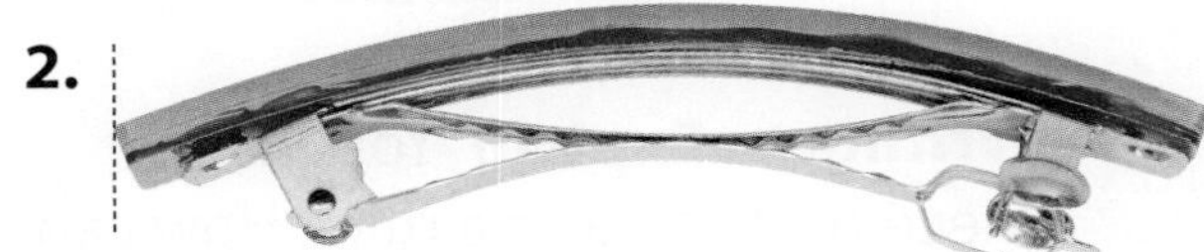

3.

Do you UNDERSTAND?

4. In the example above, are more pencil-lengths or crayon-lengths equal to the length of the desktop?

5. Find the length of your desktop in paper clip-lengths. First estimate the length in paper clips.

6. What is the length of the candle to the nearest inch?

Independent Practice

In **7–10**, estimate each length. Then measure to the nearest inch.

7. 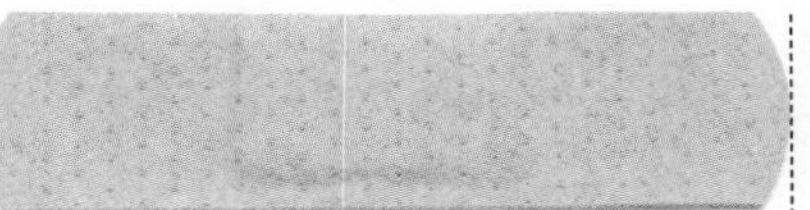

8. 

9.

10. 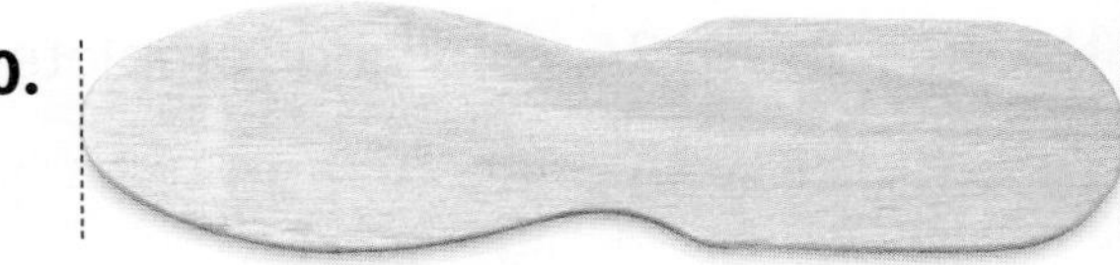

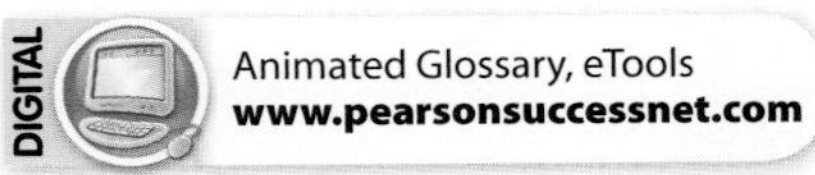

For another example, see Set A on page 370.

Independent Practice

In **11–13**, estimate each length. Then measure to the nearest inch.

11. 

12. 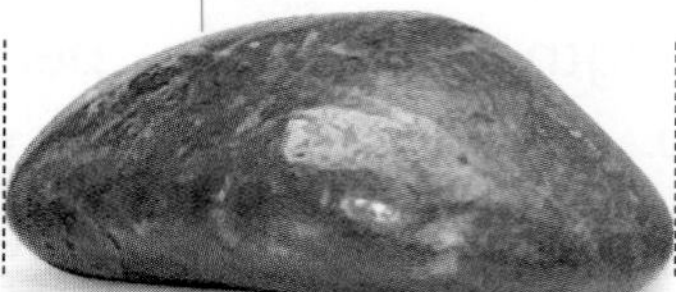

13. 

TAKS Problem Solving

14. A marker is 4 times as long as a piece of chalk. The piece of chalk is 2 inches long. How long is the marker?

marker |—|—|—|—|
chalk |—|

15. Kevin's father is 72 inches tall. He is 26 inches taller than Kevin. How tall is Kevin?

Kevin's father	72	
Kevin	?	26

16. **Number Sense** Jeff's hand is 3 large paper clips long. Alan's hand is 8 small paper clips long. Could their hands be the same size? Explain. How would standard units help?

17. **Writing to Explain** You have a piece of string and a ruler. How can you decide how long this curve is?

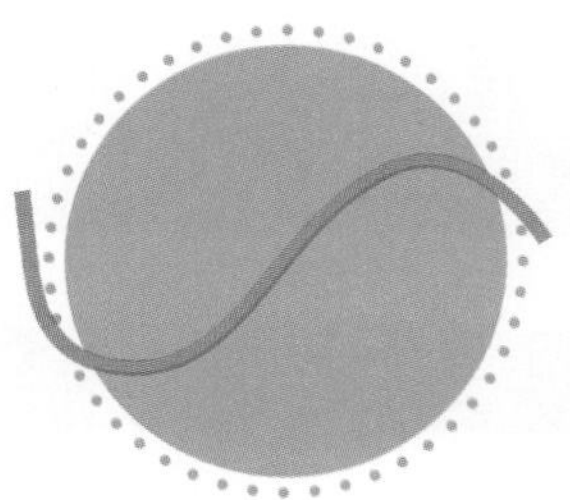

18. **Reasoning** The author Mark Twain's name is taken from riverboat slang. "Mark twain" meant "Mark two" for 2 fathoms. Two fathoms are equal to 12 feet. Which measurement unit is longer, a fathom or a foot?

Algebra In **19–24**, copy and complete each number sentence.

19. 35 + ☐ = 50 + 5

20. ☐ − 10 = 38 + 1

21. 40 − ☐ = 30 + 1

22. ☐ + 22 = 30 − 2

23. 50 − ☐ = 46 + 3

24. 32 − ☐ = 20 + 4

25. Without using a ruler, draw a line about 4 inches long. Then measure it to the nearest inch.

26. Al fed his friend's dog for 4 days. He used 2 cups of food 2 times each day. How many cups of food did he use?

27. Juan has 15 pennies and 3 dimes. Olivia has the same amount of money, but she has only nickels. How many nickels does Olivia have?

28. Alberto had 104 peacock stickers. He put 68 of them in his old sticker book and gave 18 away. How many peacock stickers does Alberto have left to put in his new sticker book?

29. **Number Sense** Suppose two pizzas are the same size. One pizza is cut into eighths and the other pizza is cut into tenths. Which pizza has larger pieces?

30. **Reasoning** Ken has 8 quarters, 5 dimes, 5 nickels, and 5 pennies. This is all the money he has. Explain why the total value of all of Ken's coins could not be $2.81. Then find the correct amount he had.

31. Which of the pencil stickers below is 2 inches high? Use a ruler to measure.

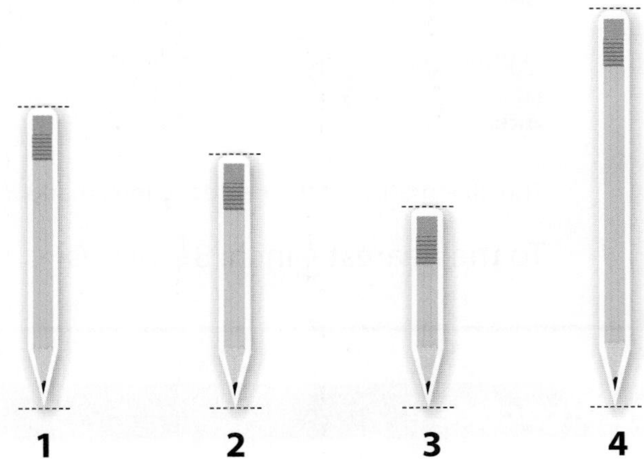

A Sticker 1 **C** Sticker 3
B Sticker 2 **D** Sticker 4

32. Ruth did 63 extra math problems in 7 days. She did the same number of problems each day. Which number sentence would you use to find the number of problems she did each day?

F $63 + 7 = \square$ **H** $63 \times 7 = \square$
G $63 - 7 = \square$ **J** $63 \div 7 = \square$

Lesson

16-2

TEKS 3.11A: Use linear measurement tools to estimate and measure lengths using standard units.

Fractions of an Inch

Hands-On
inch ruler

How do you measure to a fraction of an inch?

In the picture, what is the length of the red pepper to the nearest $\frac{1}{2}$ inch and to the nearest $\frac{1}{4}$ inch?

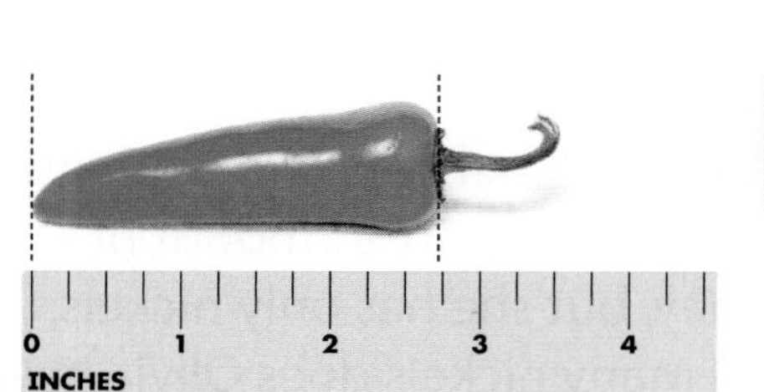

Other Examples

The nearest $\frac{1}{2}$ inch and $\frac{1}{4}$ inch can be the same.

In the picture, the length of the green bean is measured to the nearest $\frac{1}{2}$ inch and $\frac{1}{4}$ inch.

To the nearest $\frac{1}{2}$ inch:

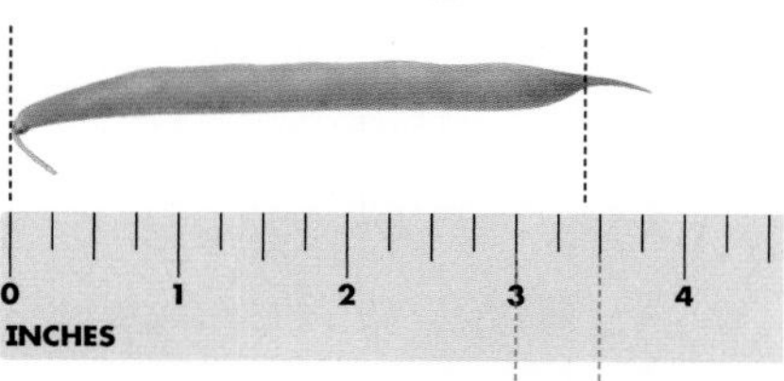

The red marks are the nearest $\frac{1}{2}$-inch marks.

To the nearest $\frac{1}{2}$ inch: $3\frac{1}{2}$ inches

To the nearest $\frac{1}{4}$ inch:

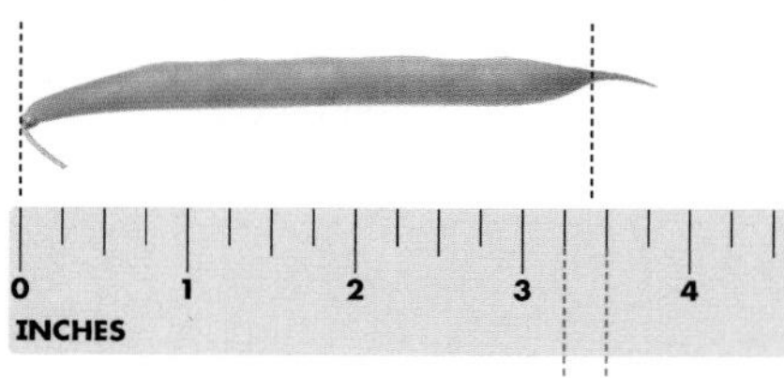

The blue marks are the nearest $\frac{1}{4}$-inch marks.

To the nearest $\frac{1}{4}$ inch: $3\frac{1}{2}$ inches

Guided Practice*

Do you know HOW?

Measure the length of each object to the nearest $\frac{1}{2}$ inch and $\frac{1}{4}$ inch.

1.

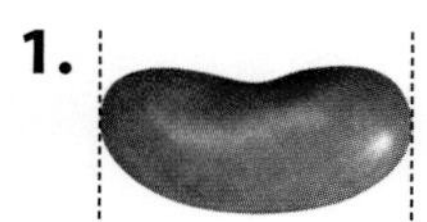

2.

Do you UNDERSTAND?

3. In measuring the red pepper above, between which two $\frac{1}{2}$-inch marks does the pepper end?

4. Is $2\frac{1}{2}$ inches or $2\frac{3}{4}$ inches nearer to the actual length of the pepper? Explain.

*For another example, see Set B on page 370.

Measure to the nearest $\frac{1}{2}$ inch.

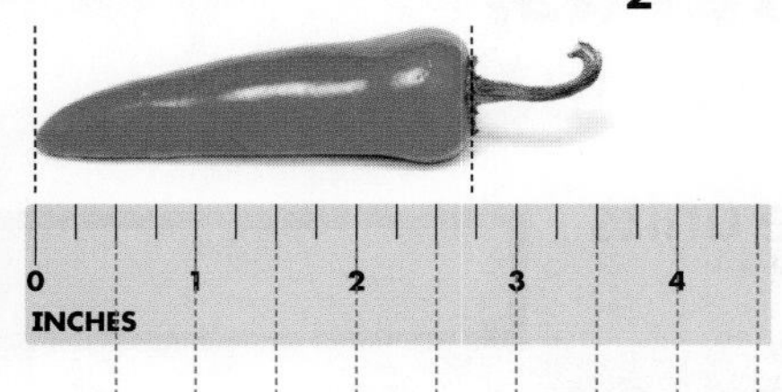

The red marks are all $\frac{1}{2}$-inch marks. The nearest $\frac{1}{2}$-inch marks are $2\frac{1}{2}$ inches and 3 inches.

To the nearest $\frac{1}{2}$ inch: $2\frac{1}{2}$ inches

Measure to the nearest $\frac{1}{4}$ inch.

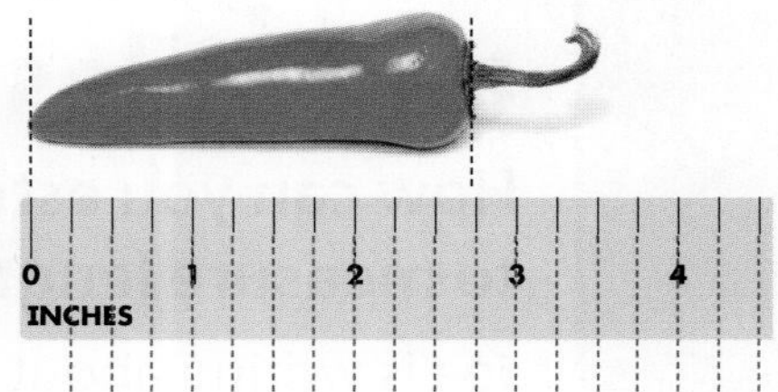

The blue marks are all $\frac{1}{4}$-inch marks. The nearest $\frac{1}{4}$-inch marks are $2\frac{1}{2}$ inches and $2\frac{3}{4}$ inches.

To the nearest $\frac{1}{4}$ inch: $2\frac{3}{4}$ inches

Independent Practice

Measure the length of each object to the nearest $\frac{1}{2}$ inch and $\frac{1}{4}$ inch.

5. 

6. 

7. 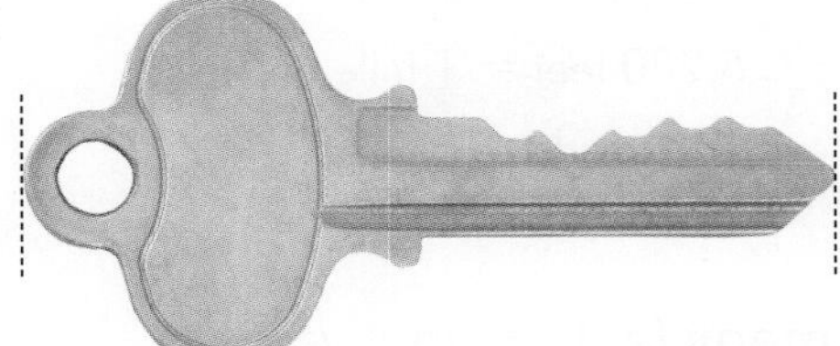

8. 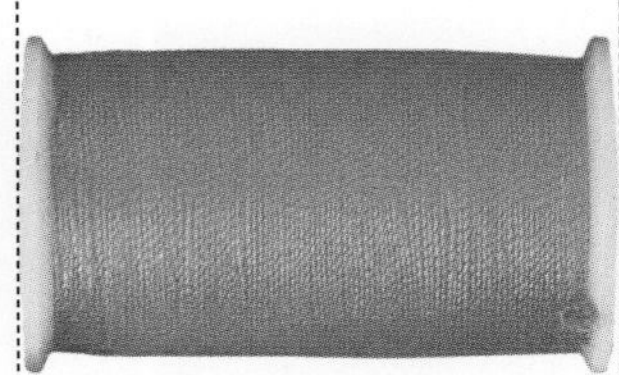

TAKS Problem Solving

9. Reasoning Can a piece of carrot be 3 inches long to the nearest inch, nearest $\frac{1}{2}$ inch, and nearest $\frac{1}{4}$ inch? Explain.

10. Karina has 3 rows of tomato plants in her garden. There are 9 plants in each row. How many tomato plants are in her garden?

11. What is the length of the asparagus to the nearest $\frac{1}{2}$ inch? Use a ruler to measure.

A 5 inches **B** $5\frac{1}{2}$ inches **C** 6 inches **D** $6\frac{1}{2}$ inches

Lesson
16-3

TEKS 3.11A: Use linear measurement tools to estimate and measure lengths using standard units.

Using Inches, Feet, Yards, and Miles

How can you estimate and choose units to measure length?

Joe is writing about fire trucks. What units of length or distance might he use?

Another Example How can you change from one unit of length to a different unit of length?

The table at the right shows how some units of length are related.

Customary Units of Length
12 inches = 1 foot (ft)
3 feet = 1 yard (yd)
36 inches = 1 yard
5,280 feet = 1 mile (mi)
1,760 yards = 1 mile

3 feet, 2 inches = ▢ inches

1 foot = 12 inches

Multiply, then add:
3 × 12 inches = 36 inches
36 inches + 2 inches = 38 inches

3 feet, 2 inches = 38 inches

How many feet are in 4 yards?

1 yard = 3 feet

Multiply:
4 × 3 feet = 12 feet

There are 12 feet in 4 yards.

Explain It

1. How could you make a table to help find the number of inches in 3 feet, 2 inches?
2. How many inches are in 2 feet, 7 inches?

Besides the inch, some customary units of length are the foot (ft), yard (yd), and mile (mi).

A loaf of bread is about a foot long.

A baseball bat is about a yard long.

Most people can walk a mile in 15 minutes.

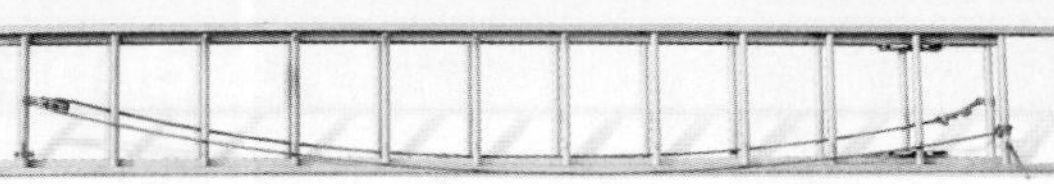

The length of the ladder on the fire truck is best measured in feet.

The length of the fire hose is best measured in yards. The width of the fire hose is best measured in inches.

The distance a fire truck travels is best measured in miles.

Guided Practice*

Do you know HOW?

Which is the best unit to use? Choose inches, feet, yards, or miles.

1. The distance between two cities
2. The length of your classroom

Do you UNDERSTAND?

3. In the example above, why would the width of the hose be measured in inches instead of feet?
4. What unit is best used for the height of a bookcase? Why?

Independent Practice

In **5–7**, tell which is the best unit to use. Choose inches, feet, yards, or miles.

5. The length of a toothbrush
6. The distance driven on a road trip
7. The length of a playground

Leveled Practice In **8–11**, change the units.

8. Change 2 feet, 9 inches to inches.
   1 foot = 12 inches
   2 × 12 inches = 24 inches
   24 inches + ▢ inches = ▢ inches

9. Change 2 yards, 2 feet to feet.
   1 yard = 3 feet
   2 × 3 feet = ▢ feet
   ▢ + 2 feet = ▢ feet

10. How many feet are in 6 yards?

11. 4 feet, 5 inches = ▢ inches

DIGITAL Animated Glossary **www.pearsonsuccessnet.com**

For another example, see Set C on page 370.

Independent Practice

In **12–15**, choose the better estimate.

12. A child's height
4 feet or 9 feet

13. The distance you travel on a train
70 yards or 70 miles

14. The length of a car's license plate
9 inches or 9 yards

15. The distance across your hand
3 inches or 8 inches

TAKS Problem Solving

16. Mr. Berry put up the fence shown below. How many inches long is the fence?

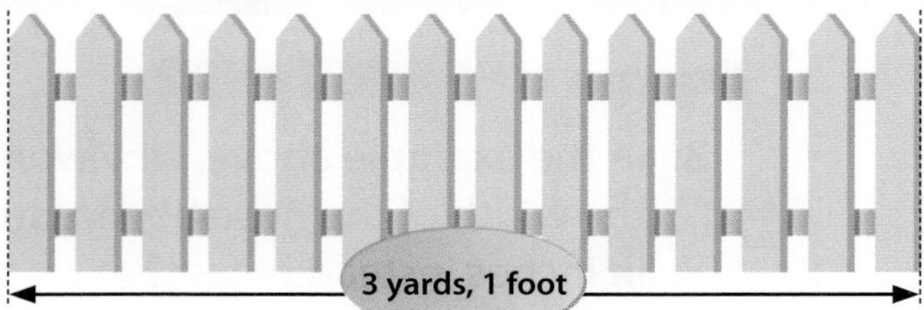

17. Angie needs 8 inches of ribbon for each of the 9 bows she is making. The ribbon is sold by the yard. How many yards of ribbon should Angie buy?

18. **Writing to Explain** West Side Park is 2,000 feet long. East Side Park is 1 mile long. Which park is longer? Explain your answer.

19. **Reasonableness** Choose the better estimate. Do the horns of a Texas Longhorn cow measure 5 feet long or 5 yards from tip to tip? Explain your answer.

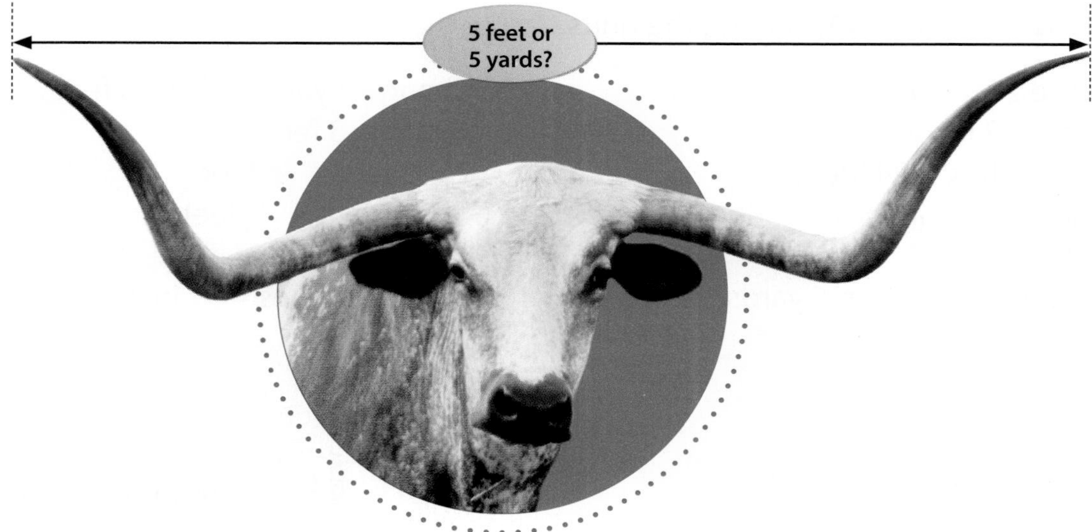

20. **Writing to Explain** Judy broke one of her shoelaces. She measured the unbroken lace and found it was 2 feet long. She bought a pair of 27-inch shoelaces. How does the length of her new laces compare to the length of her old laces? Explain.

21. **Number Sense** Would you measure the length of a soccer field in yards or inches? Explain.

22. **Geometry** Which shape is a scalene triangle?

A  **B** 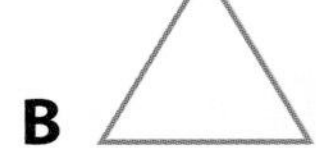 **C**  **D** 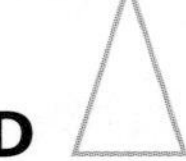

23. Look at the poster below. What fraction of the squares on this poster show food?

F $\frac{1}{15}$

G $\frac{7}{15}$

H $\frac{8}{15}$

J $\frac{3}{5}$

24. The table shows the long-jump distances for Juanita, Tom, and Margo. Write these distances in order from shortest to longest.

Long Jump

Student	Distance
Juanita	2 ft, 4 in.
Tom	23 in.
Margo	2 ft

25. Which measurement best describes the length of a couch?

A 6 miles

B 6 yards

C 6 feet

D 6 inches

26. Which measurement best describes the height of a kitchen table?

F 1 foot

G 3 feet

H 6 feet

J 12 feet

Lesson

16-4

TEKS 3.11A: Use linear measurement tools to estimate and measure lengths using standard units.

Using Centimeters and Decimeters

Hands-On
metric ruler

How can you estimate and measure in metric units?

What is the length of the grasshopper, to the nearest centimeter?

Other Examples

Some other metric units of length are the decimeter (dm) and the millimeter (mm).

10 centimeters = 1 decimeter
10 cm = 1 dm

10 millimeters = 1 centimeter
10 mm = 1 cm

This wrench is 1 dm long.

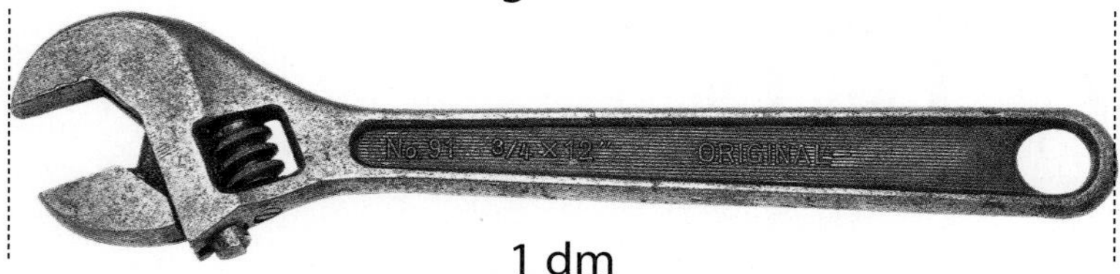

1 dm

A dime is about 1 mm thick.

1 mm

Guided Practice*

Do you know HOW?

In **1** and **2**, estimate each length. Then measure to the nearest centimeter.

1.

2.

Do you UNDERSTAND?

3. A cricket is 1 cm shorter than the grasshopper above. Draw a line segment that is the same length as the cricket.

4. What is the length of the clamshell to the nearest centimeter?

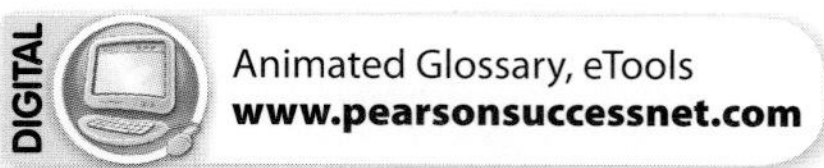

*For another example, see Set D on page 371.

A metric unit for measuring length is the centimeter (cm).

Your finger is about 1 cm wide. Use your finger width to help estimate the lengths.

1 cm

Use the centimeter ruler to measure.

The grasshopper is 4 cm long, to the nearest centimeter.

Independent Practice

In **5–7**, estimate each length. Then measure to the nearest centimeter.

5. 

6. 

7. 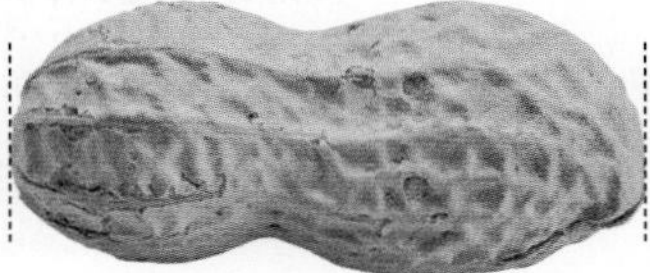

TAKS Problem Solving

8. What is the length of the flower to the nearest centimeter?

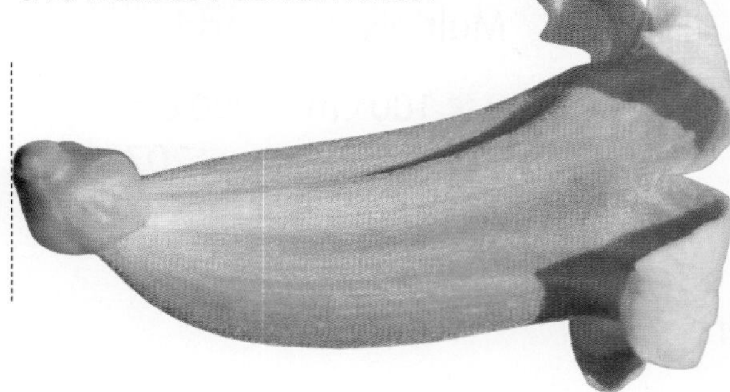

9. What is the length of the world's smallest seahorse to the nearest centimeter?

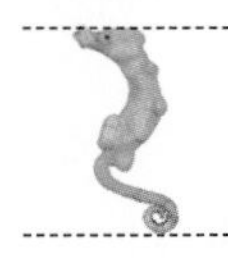

Algebra In **10–12**, copy and complete each number sentence.

10. $36 = 9 \times \square$

11. $7 \times \square = 56$

12. $60 = \square \times 10$

13. Which is the length of the crayon below? Use a centimeter ruler to measure.

A 1 cm **B** 4 cm **C** 8 cm **D** 1 dm

Lesson
16-5

TEKS 3.11A: Use linear measurement tools to estimate and measure lengths using standard units.

Using Meters and Kilometers

How can you estimate and choose units to measure length?

Lou needs to tell a friend in another country about the length of a truck and the road it travels on. What units can Lou use?

Another Example How can you change units?

Metric Units of Length
1 meter (m) = 100 centimeters (cm)
1 kilometer (km) = 1,000 meters (m)

Data

2 meters, 7 centimeters = ▢ centimeters

One Way

Make a table.

Meters	1	2	3	4
Centimeters	100	200	300	400

2 meters, 7 centimeters = 207 centimeters

Another Way

Multiply. Then add.

2×100 cm = 200 cm
200 cm + 7 cm = 207 cm

Explain It

1. How could you make a table to help find the number of centimeters in 6 meters, 5 centimeters?
2. How many centimeters are in 4 meters, 17 centimeters?

Metric units used for measuring longer lengths are the meter (m) and the kilometer (km).

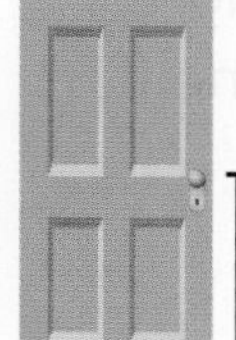

A doorknob is about 1 meter above the floor.

Most people can walk a kilometer in about 10 minutes.

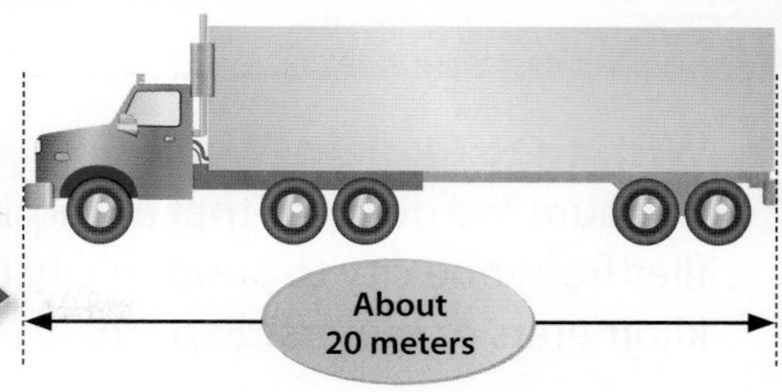

The length of a truck is best measured in meters.

The distance a truck travels on a road is best measured in kilometers.

Guided Practice*

Do you know HOW?

Which is the best unit to use? Choose meter or kilometer.

1. The length of a classroom
2. The length of a table in the lunchroom
3. The distance across your state

Do you UNDERSTAND?

4. In the example above, why is a kilometer the better unit to use to measure the length of the road?
5. **Writing to Explain** Which distance is greater, 850 meters or 1 kilometer? How do you know?

Independent Practice

In **6** and **7** tell if meter or kilometer is the better unit to use.

6. The height of a flagpole
7. The length of a bike trail

In **8** and **9**, change the units. Copy and complete.

8. How many centimeters are in 3 meters, 8 centimeters?
9. 4 meters = ☐ centimeters

In **10** and **11**, choose the better estimate.

10. The height of an adult
    2 kilometers or 2 meters
11. The length of your foot
    20 centimeters or 20 meters

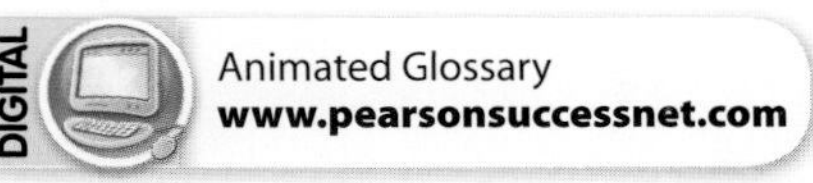

*For another example, see Set D on page 371.

12. Writing to Explain Would you measure the distance that an airplane flies from one city to another city in kilometers or meters? Explain.

13. Number Sense A tree is 4 meters, 10 centimeters tall. Is this more than or less than 500 centimeters? Explain.

14. Change the units. Copy and complete the table to help.

Meters	1	2	3	4
Centimeters	100	200		

3 meters, 15 centimeters = ▢ centimeters
4 meters, 63 centimeters = ▢ centimeters

In **15** and **16**, use the table at the right.

Sale on Fence Posts

Length	Price
36 inches	$8
40 inches	$11
48 inches	$19

15. Estimation About how much would the total cost be for two 48-inch posts and two 36-inch posts?

16. How much more is the price of one 40-inch post than the price of one 36-inch post?

17. Which measurement best describes the length of a car?

A 5 centimeters
B 5 kilometers
C 5 meters
D 5 millimeters

18. The footbridge on Tower Bridge was built so workers could cross the River Thames in London, even when the main part of the bridge was open to let a boat pass. How many centimeters long is the footbridge?

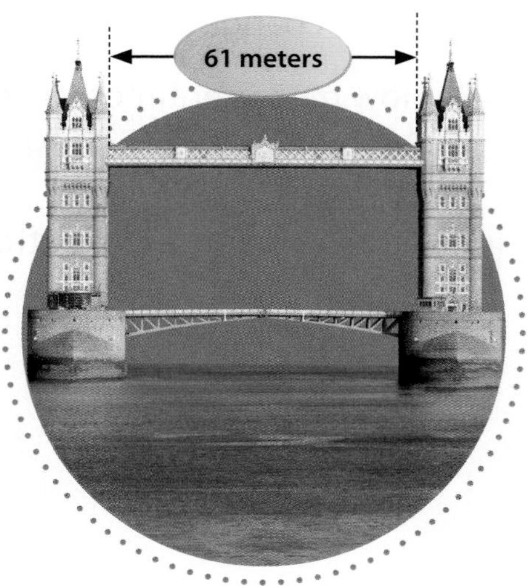

Changing Units

How many inches are in 4 feet 8 inches?

There are 12 inches in a foot. To find how many inches are in 4 feet 8 inches, multiply 4×12 and then add 8.

One Way Multiply first and then add.

Press: 4 × 12 ENTER = 48 + 8 ENTER =

Display: 48 Display: 56

Another Way Multiply and add in the same step.

Press: 4 × 12 + 8 ENTER =

Display: 56

4 feet 8 inches = 56 inches

How many centimeters are in 2 meters 45 centimeters?

There are 100 centimeters in a meter. To find how many centimeters are in 2 meters 45 centimeters, multiply 2×100 and then add 45.

Press: 2 × 100 + 45 ENTER =

Display: 245

2 meters 45 centimeters = 245 centimeters

Practice

1. How many inches are in 3 feet 9 inches?
2. How many centimeters are in 2 meters 74 centimeters?
3. How many inches are in 7 yards 16 inches?
4. How many feet are in 4 yards 2 feet?
5. How many meters are in 5 kilometers 25 meters?

Lesson
16-6

TEKS 3.14C: Select or develop an appropriate problem-solving strategy, including drawing a picture, looking for a pattern, systematic guessing and checking, acting it out, making a table, working a simpler problem, or working backwards to solve a problem.
Also **TEKS 3.16**

Problem Solving

Make a Table and Look for a Pattern

Livia is training for a 25 km walk. She recorded how far she walked each day. If she continues the pattern, how far will Livia walk on Day 4? How far will she walk on Day 5?

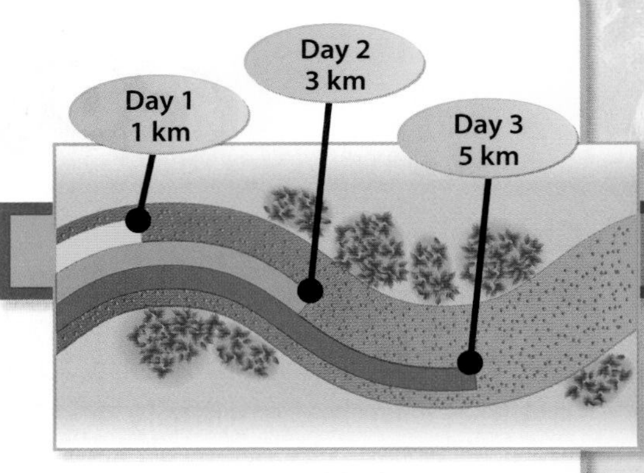

Guided Practice*

Do you know HOW?

Copy and complete the table. Write to explain the pattern. Solve.

1. Nat has a pole that is 1 meter long. He is cutting it into 20-centimeter long pieces. What length of pole is left after 3 cuts? after 4 cuts?

Cuts	0	1	2	3	4
Length (cm)	100	80	60		

Do you UNDERSTAND?

2. In the example above, how did the table help you to explain the pattern?

3. **Write a Problem** Write a problem that you can solve by writing an explanation of a pattern.

Independent Practice

In **4–7**, Copy and complete the table. Write to explain the pattern. Solve.

4. Nola is putting tiles in a row. Each tile is a square and the length of its side is 4 centimeters. What is the length of 4 tiles together? 5 tiles?

Number of Tiles	1	2	3	4	5
Total Length (cm)	4	8	12		

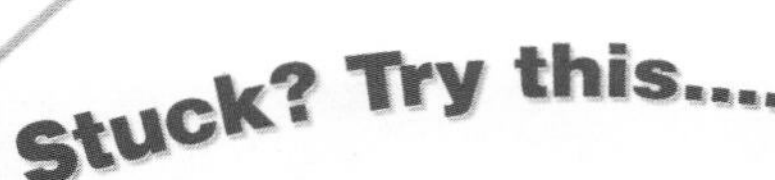

- What do I know?
- What am I asked to find?
- What diagram can I use to help understand the problem?
- Can I use addition, subtraction, multiplication, or division?
- Is all of my work correct?
- Did I answer the right question?
- Is my answer reasonable?

*For another example, see Set E on page 371.

Plan

You can make a table to show what you know. Then look for a pattern.

Day	1	2	3	4	5
Distance walked (km)	1	3	5	■	■

Explain the pattern.

Each day Livia increased the distance she walked by 2 km.

Solve

Use the pattern to complete the table and solve the problem.

Day 3: 5 km
Day 4: 5 km + 2 km = 7 km
Day 5: 7 km + 2 km = 9 km

Day	1	2	3	4	5
Distance walked (km)	1	3	5	7	9

Livia will walk 7 km on Day 4 and 9 km on Day 5.

5. Talia is cutting up a sheet of paper that is 24 centimeters long. She is cutting the sheet into pieces that are each 3 centimeters long. What is the length of the sheet that is left after Talia has made 3 cuts? 4 cuts?

Number of Cuts	0	1	2	3	4
Length Left (cm)	24	21	18	■	■

6. Mr. Lum is putting fence rails together in a row. Each rail is 2 meters long. What is the length of 5 rails together? 6 rails?

Number of Rails	1	2	3	4	5	6
Total Length (m)	2	4	6	8	■	■

7. Evan makes picture frames using wood. For each frame, he needs 60 cm of wood. What is the total length of wood he needs to make 4 frames? 5 frames?

Number of Frames	1	2	3	4	5
Total Length (cm)	60	120	180	■	■

8. Nick earns money doing chores. How much would he earn if he washes windows, washes dishes, and does laundry?

Data

Item	Price
Clean yard	\$8
Do laundry	\$5
Vacuum floors	\$3
Wash dishes	\$2
Wash windows	\$7

9. In the morning, Ray painted 12 windows. By the end of the day he had painted all 26 windows in the house. Which of these shows one way to find how many windows he painted in the afternoon?

A 26 + 12 **B** 26 − 12 **C** 26 × 12 **D** 26 ÷ 12

TAKS Test Prep

1. What is the length of the leaf to the nearest $\frac{1}{2}$ inch? (16-2)

A $3\frac{1}{2}$ inches

B 3 inches

C $2\frac{1}{2}$ inches

D 2 inches

2. Which of the following is about 2 meters? (16-5)

F The length of a bumble bee

G The distance from your home to the school

H The height of a one-story house

J The height of a classroom door

3. What is the length of the apple core to the nearest centimeter? (16-4)

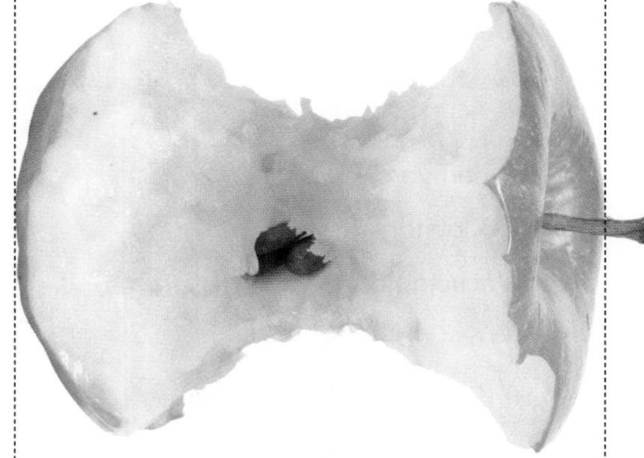

A 3 centimeters

B 6 centimeters

C 7 centimeters

D 8 centimeters

4. Which is the best unit to measure the length of the Mississippi River? (16-3)

F Miles

G Yards

H Feet

J Inches

5. Juana's goldfish is 2 inches long. Which could be Juana's goldfish? (16-1)

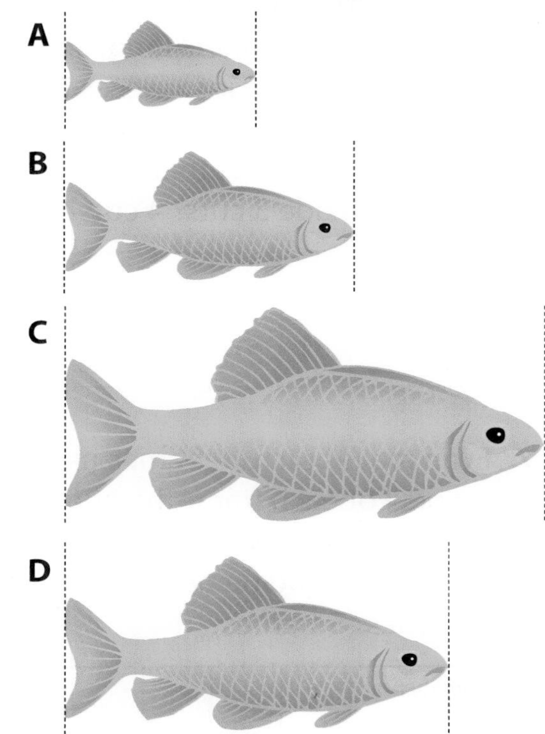

6. Which best describes the length of a large school bus? (16-3)

F 12 inches

G 12 feet

H 12 yards

J 12 miles

7. Which best describes the length of a new crayon? (16-4)

A 7 millimeters

B 7 centimeters

C 7 decimeters

D 7 feet

8. What is the length of the screwdriver to the nearest $\frac{1}{2}$ inch? (16-2)

F $1\frac{1}{4}$ inches

G $1\frac{1}{2}$ inches

H $1\frac{3}{4}$ inches

J 2 inches

9. Pat bought a party-size sub sandwich that was 36 inches long. She cut it into pieces that were 4 inches long. What was the length of the sandwich that was left after Pat cut off 5 pieces? (16-6)

Pieces Cut Off	0	1	2	3	4	5
Inches Left	36	32	28	24		

A 20 inches

B 18 inches

C 16 inches

D 12 inches

10. Which unit would be best to use for the distance from New York to Chicago? (16-5)

F centimeters

G kilometers

H meters

J millimeters

11. Which is the best estimate of the length of the almond? (16-1)

A 1 inch

B 2 inches

C 3 inches

D 4 inches

12. Which bug could be about 5 centimeters long? (16-4)

F Ladybug

G Flea

H Ant

J Dragonfly

13. **Griddable Response** Is a school hallway about 3 feet long or about 30 feet long? (16-3)

14. **Griddable Response** What number is missing in the table below? (16-6)

Number of Weeks	1	2	3	4	5	6
Number of Days	7	14	21	28	35	

Reteaching

Set A, pages 350–353

You can use different units to measure length.

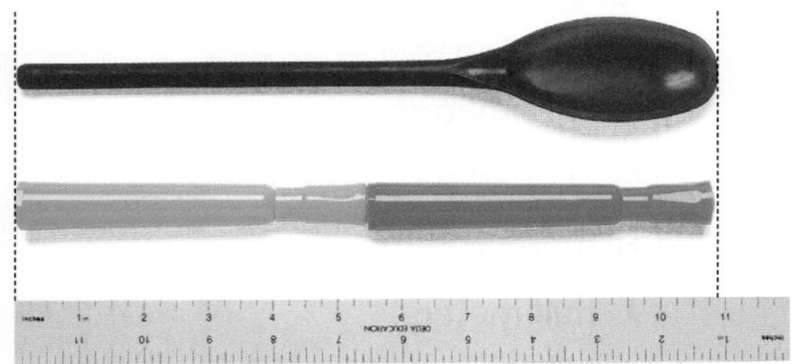

The spoon is about 2 marker-lengths long and about 11 inches long, to the nearest inch.

Remember to line up the object with the 0 mark on the ruler.

Use an inch ruler to measure each length to the nearest inch.

1. 

2. 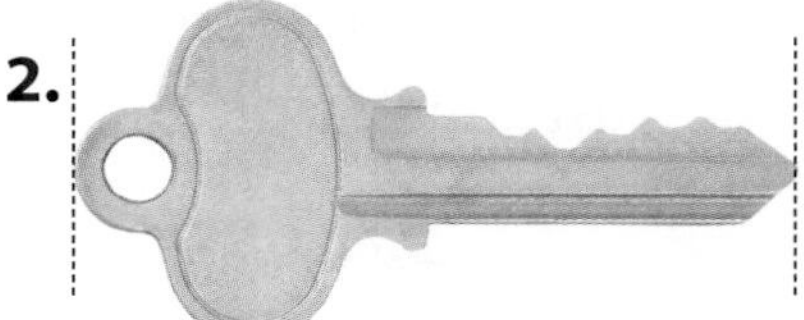

Set B, pages 354–355

Use the picture to measure the ribbon to the nearest $\frac{1}{2}$ inch.

Look for the two nearest $\frac{1}{2}$ inch marks.
To the nearest $\frac{1}{2}$ inch ⟶ $3\frac{1}{2}$ inches

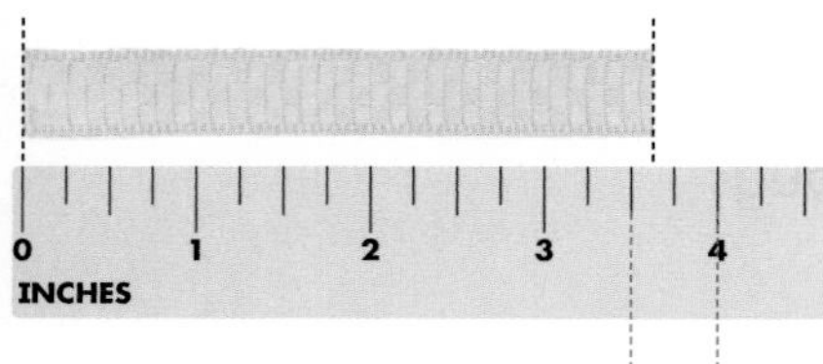

Use the picture to measure to the nearest $\frac{1}{4}$ inch, look for the two nearest $\frac{1}{4}$ inch marks.
To the nearest $\frac{1}{4}$ inch ⟶ $3\frac{3}{4}$ inches

Remember that the nearest $\frac{1}{2}$ inch and nearest $\frac{1}{4}$ inch for an object can be the same.

Measure the length of each object to the nearest $\frac{1}{2}$ inch and $\frac{1}{4}$ inch.

1. 

2. 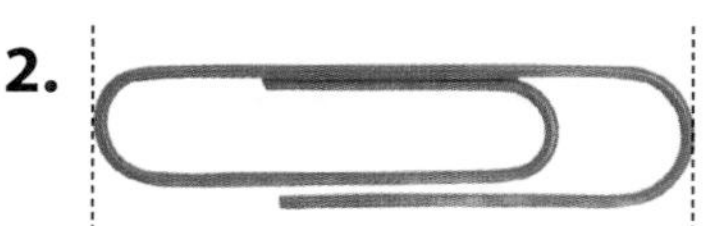

Set C, pages 356–359

Change the unit.

2 feet, 6 inches = ☐ inches

Tip *1 foot = 12 inches*

Multiply: 2×12 inches = 24 inches
Then add: 24 inches + 6 inches = 30 inches

2 feet, 6 inches = 30 inches

Remember that 1 yard equals 3 feet.

Change the units.

1. 4 feet, 3 inches = ☐ inches

2. 6 feet, 4 inches = ☐ inches

3. 5 yards, 2 feet = ☐ feet

Topic 16

Reteaching

Set D, pages 360–364

Estimate the length of the bead in centimeters. Then measure to the nearest centimeter.

You can use your finger width as 1 centimeter to help estimate.

Estimate: about 3 centimeters long

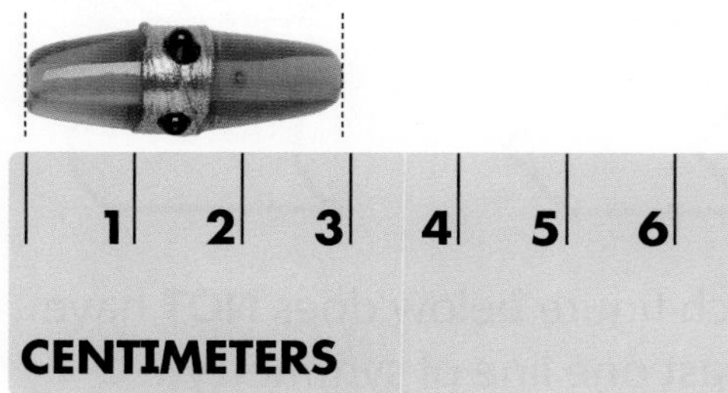

The bead is 3 centimeters long, to the nearest centimeter.

Remember to line up the object with the 0 mark on the ruler.

Estimate the length. Then measure to the nearest centimeter.

1. 

Choose the better estimate.

2. The length of a truck
10 meters or 10 kilometers

3. The height of a house
4 centimeters or 4 meters

Change the units.

4. 5 meters = ▢ centimeters

5. How many centimeters are in 4 meters, 3 centimeters?

Set E, pages 366–367

Vita makes bows using ribbon. What is the total length of ribbon she needs to make 4 bows? 5 bows?

Make a table and look for a pattern.

Explain the pattern.
Solve the problem.

Number of Bows	1	2	3	4	5
Total Length of Ribbon	30 cm	60 cm	90 cm	120 cm	150 cm

Vita needs 30 cm of ribbon for each bow she makes.

Vita needs 120 cm for 4 bows and 150 cm for 5 bows.

Remember to check your answers. Make sure all of your numbers fit the pattern.

Copy and complete the table.
Write to explain the pattern.
Solve the problem.

Ned is training for a 40 km bike race. If he continues his pattern, how far will he ride on Day 4? On Day 5?

Day	1	2	3	4	5
Distance Ned Rode	1 km	4 km	7 km	▢	▢

Spiral Review

Numbers and Operations

1. Which means the same as 70,000 + 3,000 + 10 + 7?

A 7,317

B 17,317

C 70,317

D 73,017

2. What fraction of the plates do **NOT** have muffins?

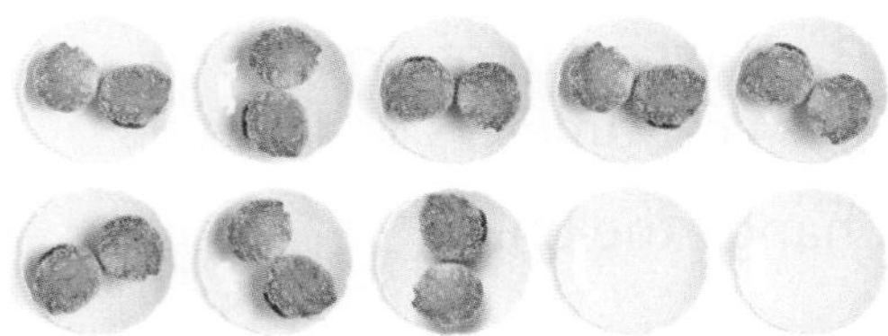

F $\frac{2}{10}$

G $\frac{2}{8}$

H $\frac{8}{10}$

J $\frac{8}{2}$

3. Elly bought 2 books of tickets with 8 tickets in each book. She and 3 friends used 4 tickets. How many tickets does Elly have left?

A 19

B 12

C 10

D 4

4. Keith has 42 stamps. He wants to put 6 stamps in each row on a page. How many rows can he make?

5. **Writing to Explain** How can you use multiplication facts you know to help you find a fact you don't know? To explain, use 6 × 9 as the fact you don't know.

Geometry and Measurement

6. Look at the figure below. Which figure is congruent to it?

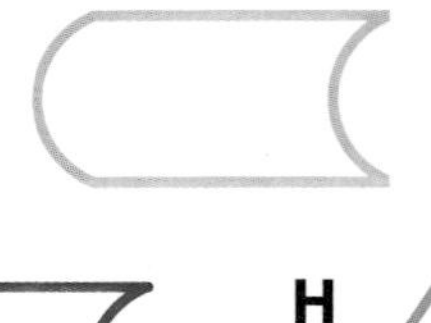

F **H**

G **J**

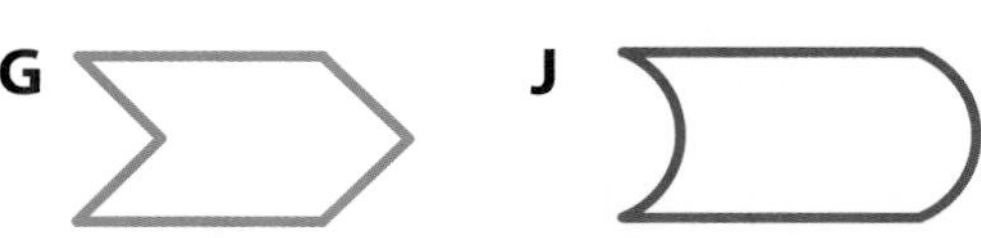

7. Which figure below does **NOT** have at least one line of symmetry?

A **C**

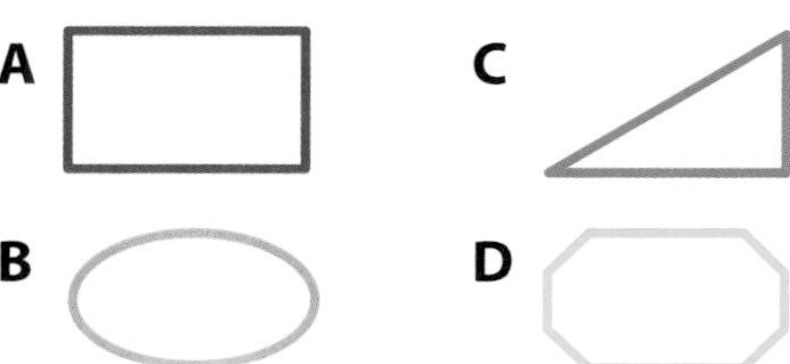

B **D**

8. Which line segment below is 1 inch long? Use a ruler to measure.

F ______________________

G ___________

H _____

J ________

9. Estimate the length of the pin to the nearest inch. Use a ruler to measure.

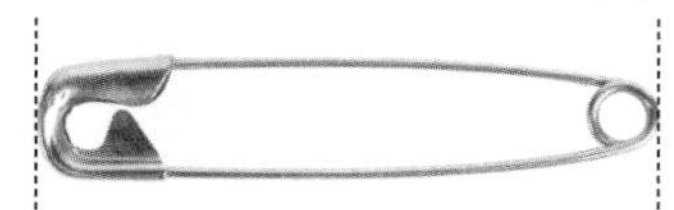

10. **Writing to Explain** Explain how you could use a ruler to measure the length of a string.

Probability and Statistics

11. A box has 16 straws. It has 5 blue, 4 green, 3 pink, and 4 red straws. If Ira takes 1 straw from the box without looking, which color is he less likely to get than the others?

A Blue **C** Pink

B Green **D** Red

For **12** and **13**, use the bar graph below.

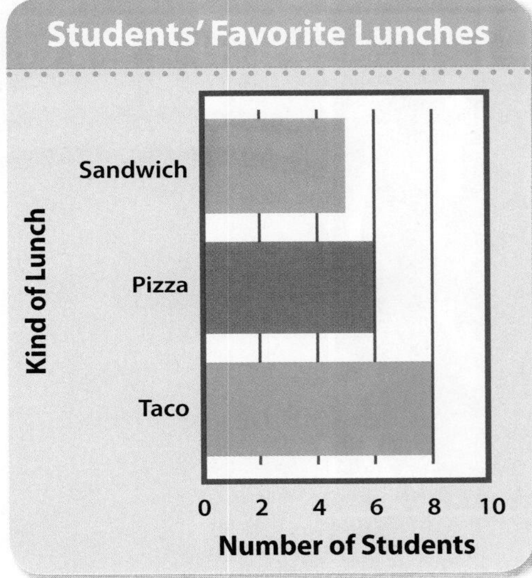

12. How many students voted in all?

F 11 **G** 13 **H** 14 **J** 19

13. How many more students voted for a taco lunch than a sandwich lunch?

A 3 **C** 6

B 5 **D** 8

14. **Writing to Explain** The temperature is 56° F today. Which is more likely to happen today—it will rain or it will snow? Explain.

Algebra

15. If the staircase pattern continues, how many blocks will the next staircase have?

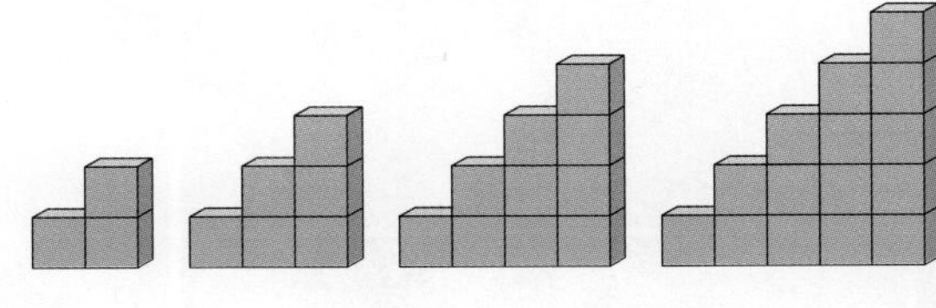

F 16 **H** 20

G 19 **J** 21

16. What number is missing in the pattern?

18, 27, 36, 45, ▒

A 46 **C** 54

B 50 **D** 56

17. Ava makes hats with an equal number of bows on each hat.

Number of Hats	3	4	5	6	7
Number of Bows	18	24	30	▒	42

How many bows does Ava need for 6 hats?

F 36 **H** 18

G 32 **J** 6

18. Each spider has 8 legs. Make a table to show the number of legs on 1, 2, 3, 4, 5, and 6 spiders.

19. **Writing to Explain** Which number sentence completes this fact family? Explain how you found your answer.
$4 \times 6 = 24, 6 \times 4 = 24, 24 \div 4 = 6$

Topic 17

Perimeter and Area

1

How far would you need to walk to go around the outside of this maze in Williamsburg, Virginia? You will find out in Lesson 17-1.

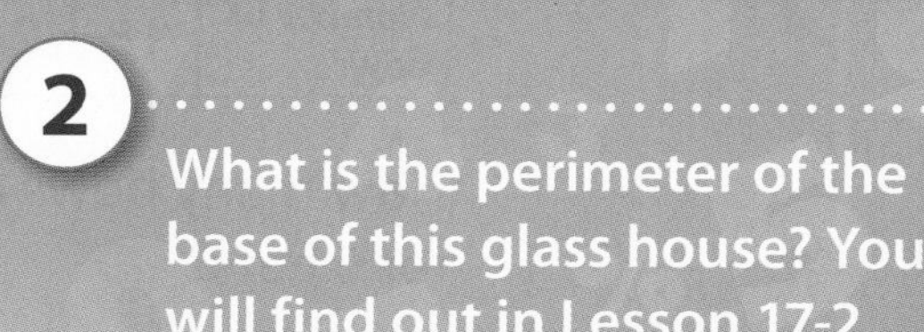

2

What is the perimeter of the base of this glass house? You will find out in Lesson 17-2.

3

How long is one side of this small chess board? You will find out in Lesson 17-4.

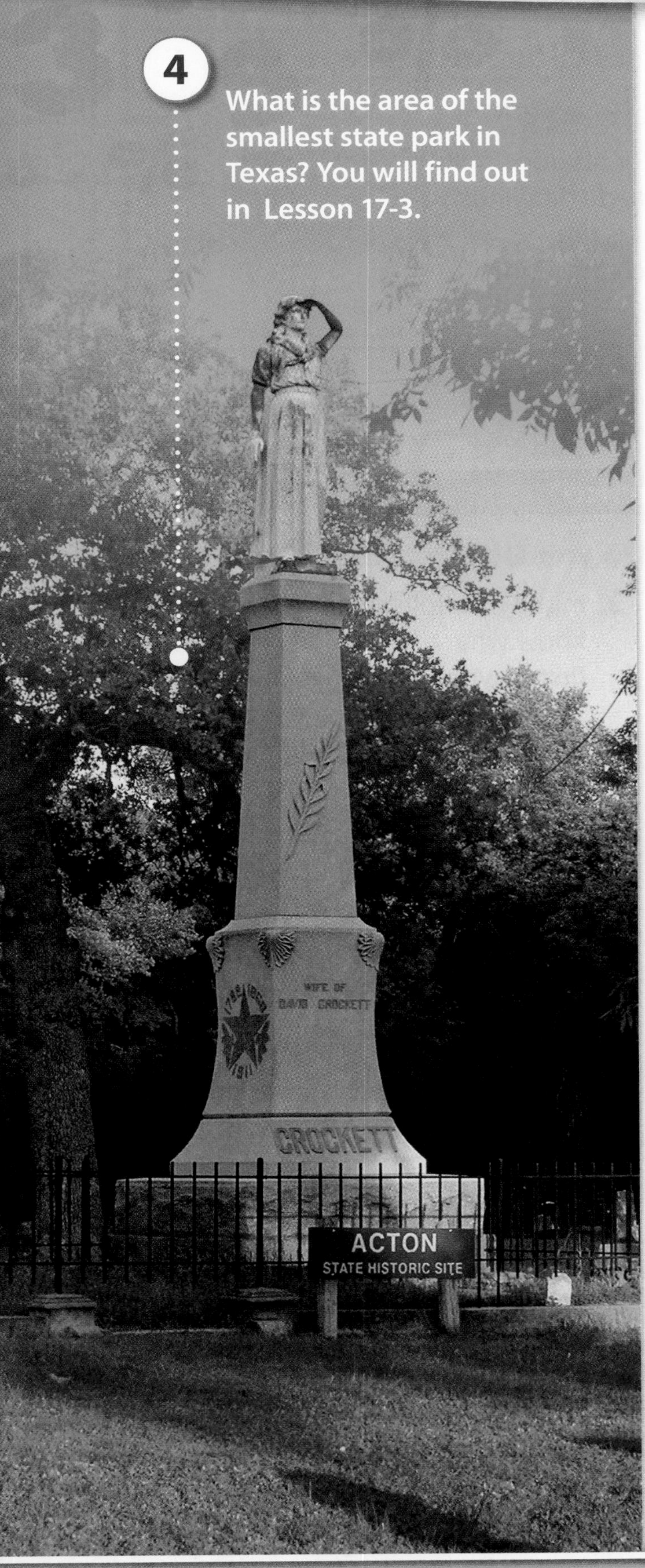

Review What You Know!

Vocabulary

Choose the best term from the box.

- equilateral
- quadrilateral
- polygon
- trapezoid

1. A _?_ could have 5 sides.
2. A triangle with all three sides the same length is called a(n) _?_ triangle.
3. A rectangle is a special _?_ with 4 right angles.

Multiplication Facts

Find each product.

4. 3×8	5. 6×4	6. 5×7
7. 2×9	8. 7×3	9. 4×8
10. 7×5	11. 4×4	12. 9×8

Geometry

Write the name that best describes each figure.

13. A quadrilateral with only one pair of parallel sides
14. A quadrilateral with four right angles and all sides the same length
15. A triangle with no sides the same length

Arrays

16. **Writing to Explain** Explain how to draw an array to show 3×6. Draw the array.

Lesson
17-1

TEKS 3.11B: Use standard units to find the perimeter of a shape.

Understanding Perimeter

How do you find perimeter?

Gus wants to make a playpen for his dog and put a fence around it. He made drawings of two different playpens. What is the perimeter of the playpen in each drawing?

The distance around a figure is its **perimeter**.

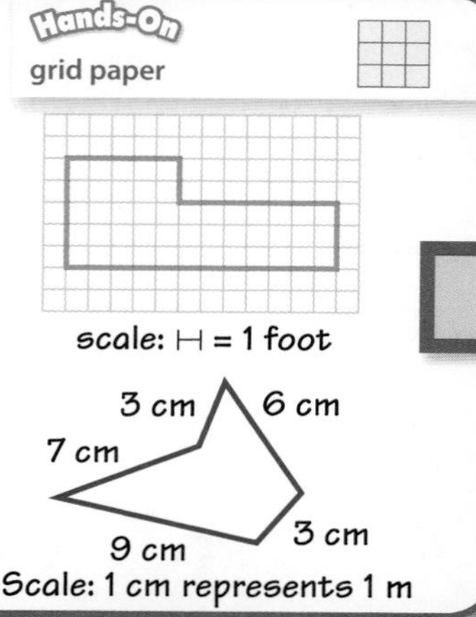

Guided Practice*

Do you know HOW?

In **1** and **2**, find the perimeter.

1.

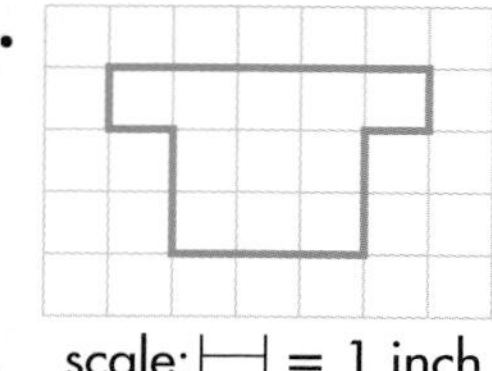

2.

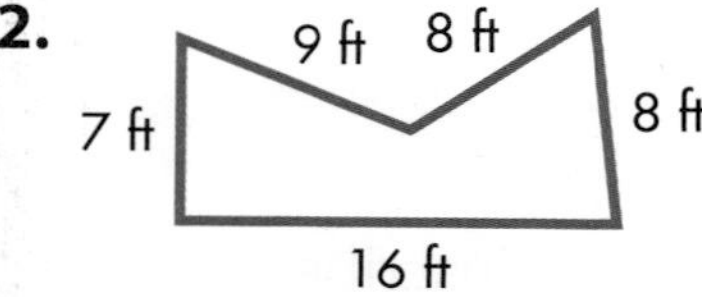

Do you UNDERSTAND?

3. In the example above, how do you know what unit Gus used for the first playpen?

4. What is the perimeter of the garden shown in the diagram below?

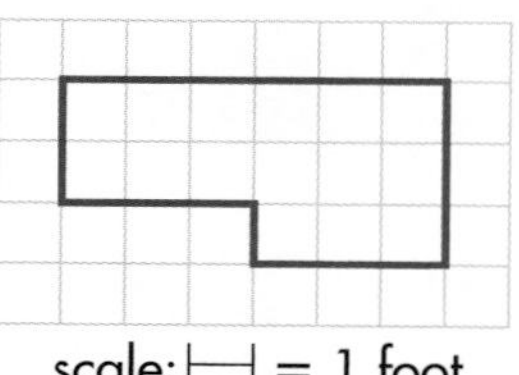

Independent Practice

In **5–7**, find the perimeter of each polygon.

5.

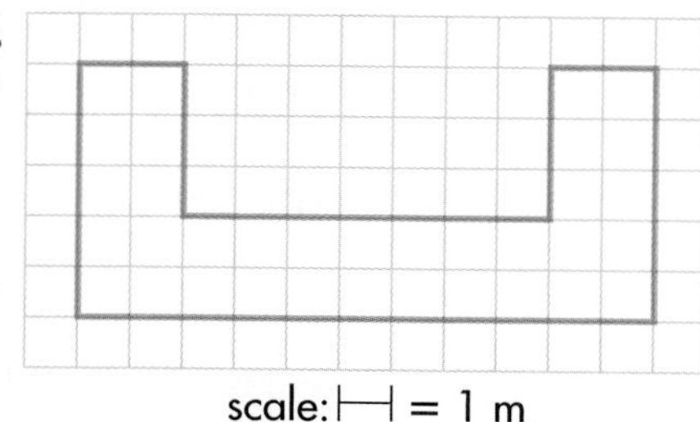

6.

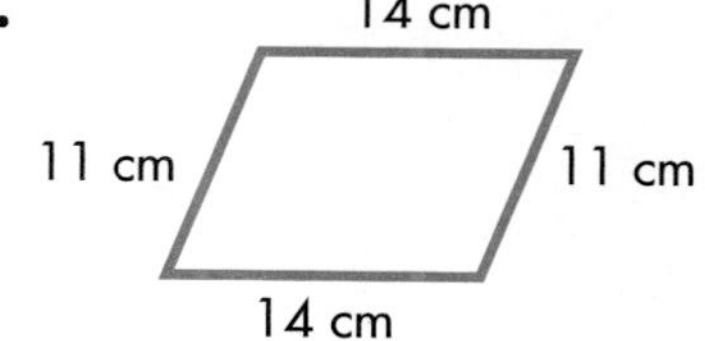

7.

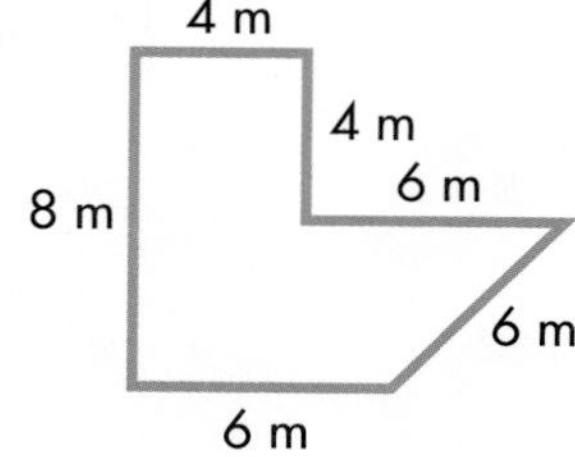

In **8–10**, draw a figure with the given perimeter. Use grid paper.

8. 14 units

9. 8 units

10. 20 units

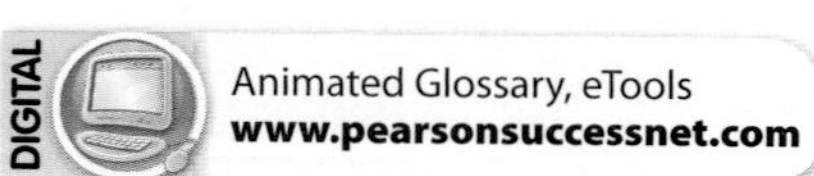

*For another example, see Set A on page 388.

One Way

You can find the perimeter by counting unit segments.

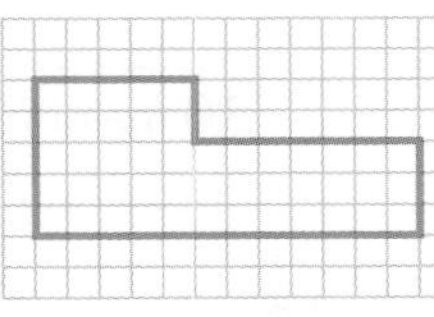

scale: ├┤ = 1 foot

The perimeter of this playpen is 34 feet.

Another Way

Add the lengths of the sides to find the perimeter.

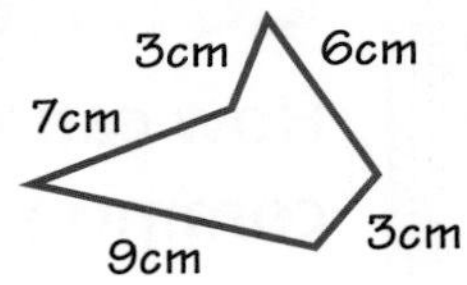

$3 + 9 + 7 + 3 + 6 = 28$

The perimeter of this playpen is 28 meters.

TAKS Problem Solving

11. Mr. Karas needs to find the perimeter of the playground to build a fence around it. What is the perimeter of the playground?

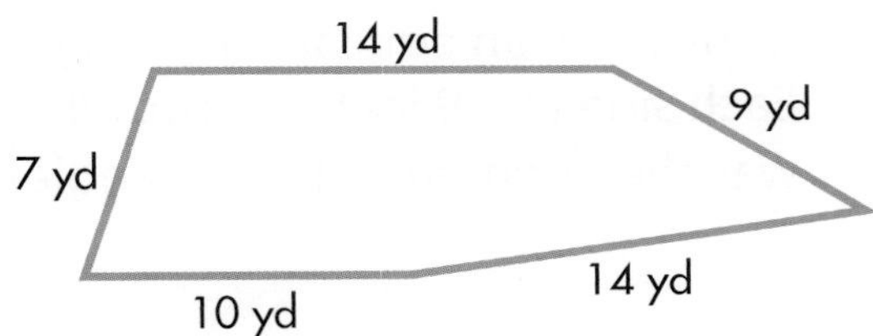

12. Mike needs to find the perimeter of the pool so he knows how many tiles to put around the edge. What is the perimeter of the pool?

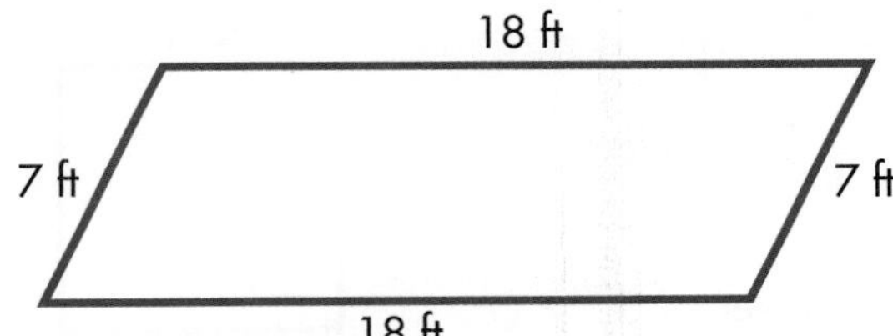

13. The distance around the outside of this maze in Williamsburg, Virginia, is the same as the perimeter of a rectangle. The picture shows the lengths of the sides of the rectangle. What is the perimeter of the maze?

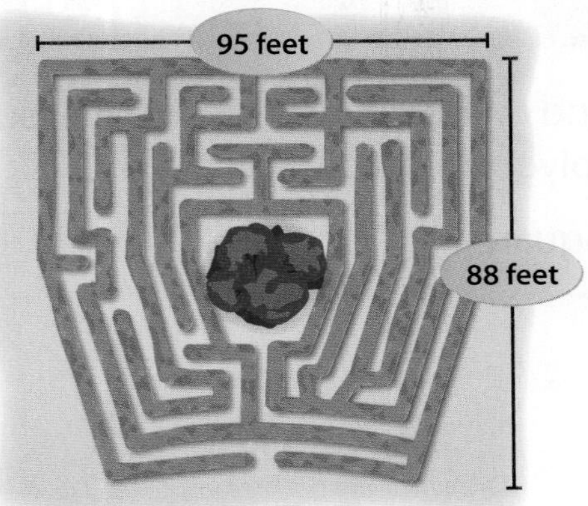

14. Jani has a magnet shown below.

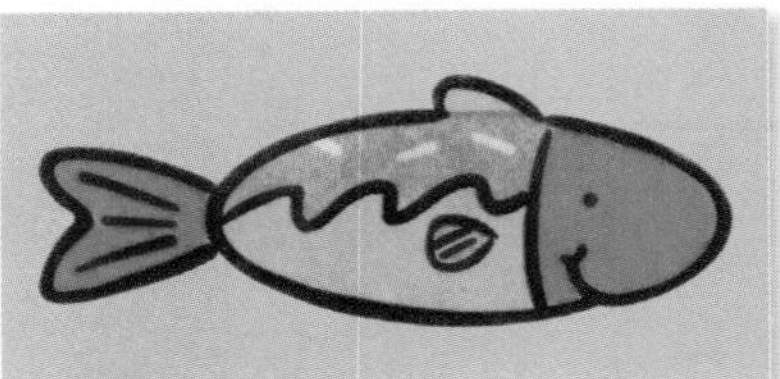

What is the perimeter of Jani's magnet to the nearest inch? Use a ruler to measure.

A 2 in. **B** 4 in. **C** 5 in. **D** 6 in.

15. **Writing to Explain** Roberto has a magnet that is twice as long and twice as wide as Jani's magnet in Problem 14. Find the perimeter of Roberto's magnet. Explain your work.

Lesson
17-2

TEKS 3.11B: Use standard units to find the perimeter of a shape.

Perimeter of Common Shapes

How can you find the perimeter of common shapes?

Mr. Coe needs to find the perimeter of two swimming pool designs. One pool shape is a rectangle. The other pool shape is a square. What is the perimeter of each pool?

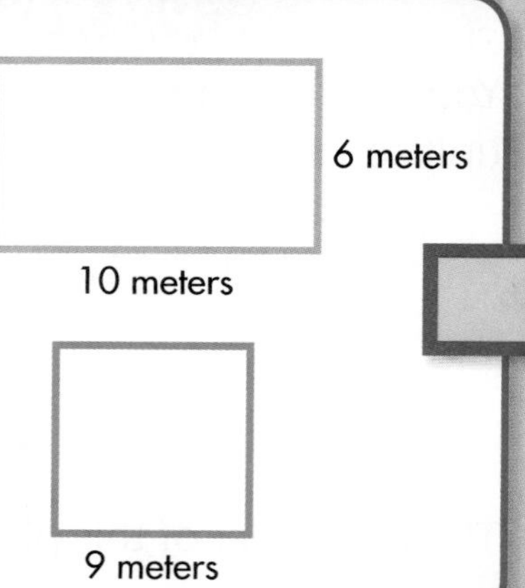

Guided Practice*

Do you know HOW?

For **1** and **2**, find the perimeter.

1. Rectangle

2. Square

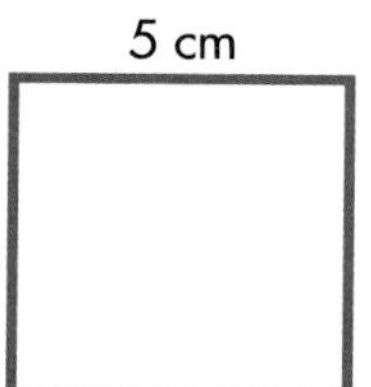

Do you UNDERSTAND?

3. In the examples above, explain how to find the missing lengths.

4. Darla drew an equilateral triangle. Each side was 9 inches long. What was the perimeter of the triangle?

Independent Practice

In **5** and **6**, use an inch ruler to measure the length of the sides of the polygon. Find the perimeter.

5. Square

6. Rectangle

In **7** and **8**, find the perimeter of each polygon.

7. Rectangle

15 m

3 m

8. Equilateral triangle

4 yd

*For another example, see Set A on page 388.

Find the perimeter of the pool that has a rectangle shape.

Remember: Opposite sides of a rectangle are the same length.

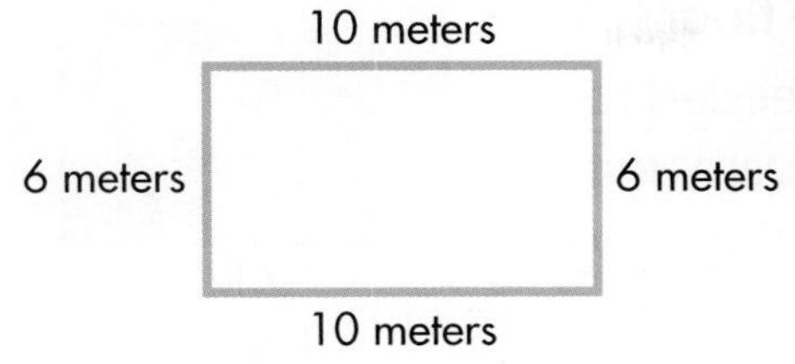

$10 + 6 + 10 + 6 = 32$

The perimeter of this pool is 32 meters.

Find the perimeter of the pool that has a square shape.

Remember: All four sides of a square are the same length.

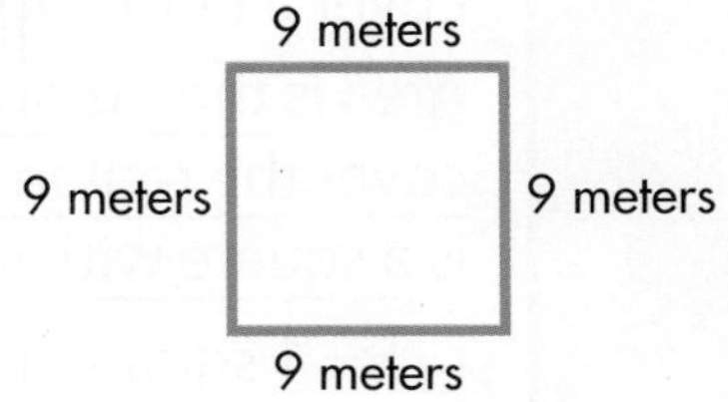

$9 + 9 + 9 + 9 = 36$

The perimeter of this pool is 36 meters.

TAKS Problem Solving

9. **Writing to Explain** Cora uses ribbons to make three different sizes of bows. How much more ribbon does it take to make 2 large bows than 2 small bows? Explain how you found your answer.

Data

Size of Bow	Length of Ribbon
Small	27 in.
Medium	36 in.
Large	49 in.

10. The base of Philip Johnson's Glass House in New Canaan, Connecticut, is a rectangle. What is the perimeter of the base of the Glass House?

11. What is the perimeter of the cloth patch outlined below?

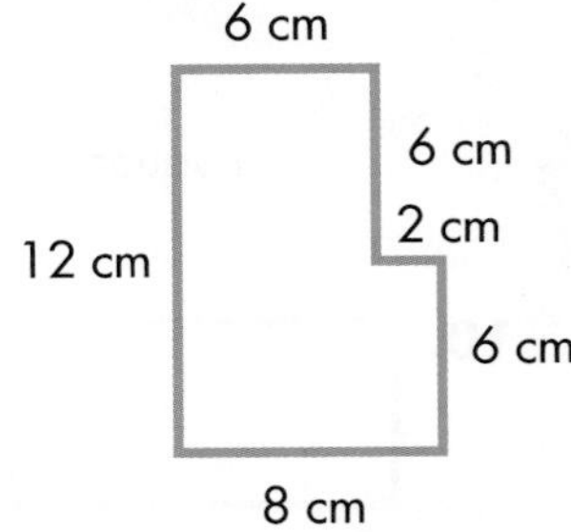

A 96 cm **C** 38 cm

B 40 cm **D** 32 cm

12. Ami's room is in the shape of a square. What is the perimeter of the room?

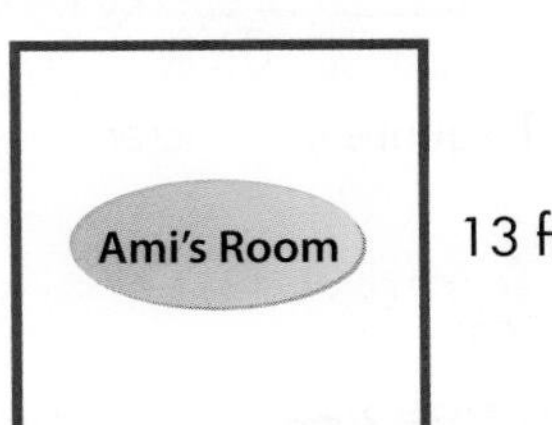

Lesson

17-3

TEKS 3.11C: Use concrete and pictorial models of square units to determine the area of two-dimensional surfaces.

Understanding Area

Hands-On
tiles

How do you find area?

Raj needs to know how many tiles to buy to cover a floor. What is the area of the floor?

Area is the number of square units needed to cover the region inside a figure. A square unit is a square with sides that are each 1 unit long.

☐ = 1 square unit

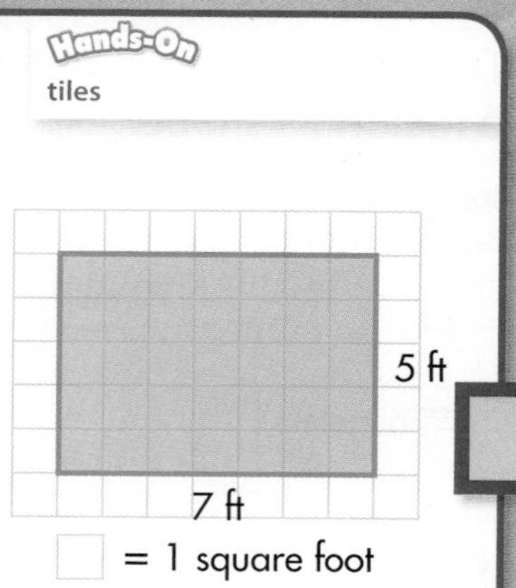

Guided Practice*

Do you know HOW?

In **1** and **2**, find the area of each figure. Use tiles or draw a picture on grid paper to help.

1. **2.**

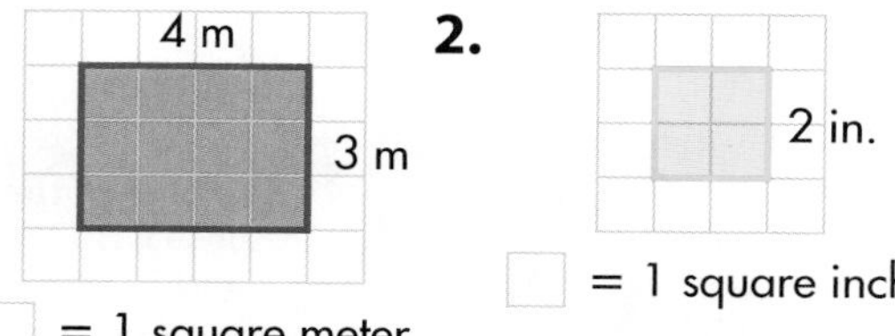

Do you UNDERSTAND?

3. Use the example above. Explain how finding area is different from finding the perimeter of a figure.

4. The lid of Mella's jewelry box is a rectangle 3 inches wide. The area is 15 square inches. Use tiles or grid paper to model the lid.

Independent Practice

In **5–10**, find the area of each figure. Use tiles or draw a picture on grid paper.

5.

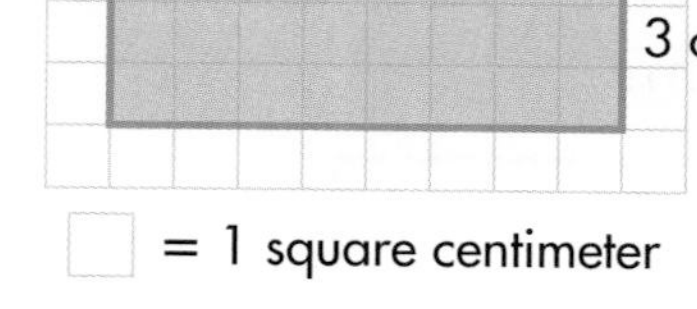

6.

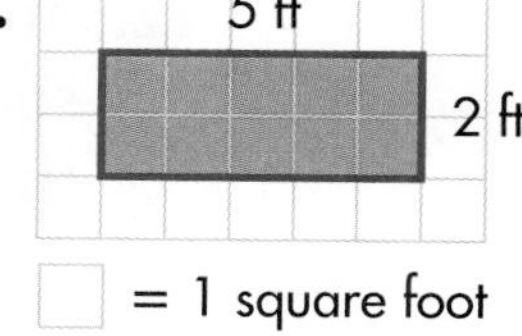

7.

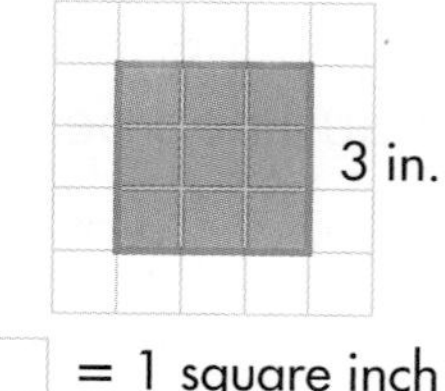

8.

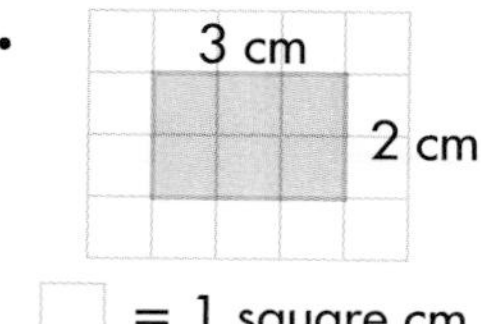

9.

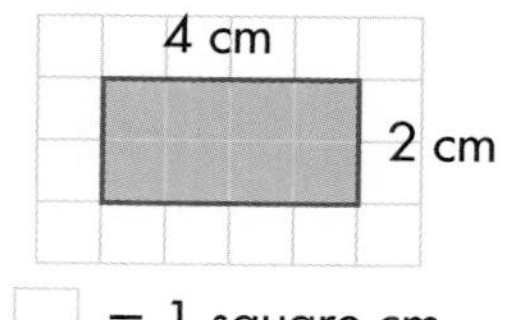

10.

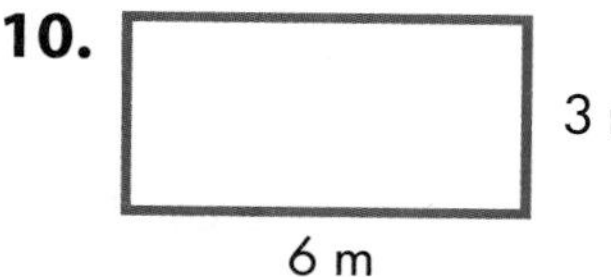

DIGITAL Animated Glossary, eTools **www.pearsonsuccessnet.com**

*For another example, see Set B on page 388.

Count the square units.

There are 35 square units inside the figure.

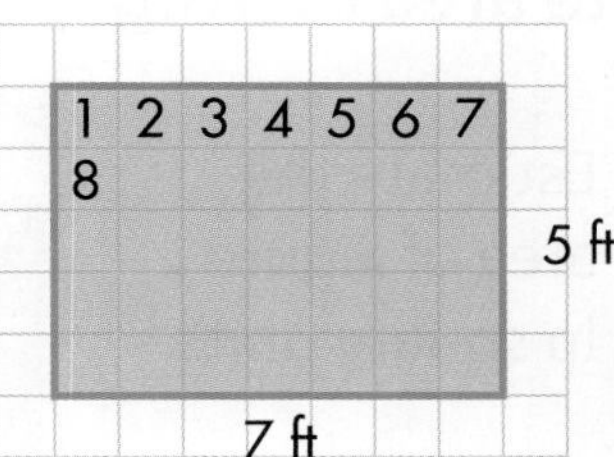

The lengths are given in feet. The area of the floor is 35 square feet.

Another Way

When you find the area of a rectangle or square, you can think of the grid squares as an array.

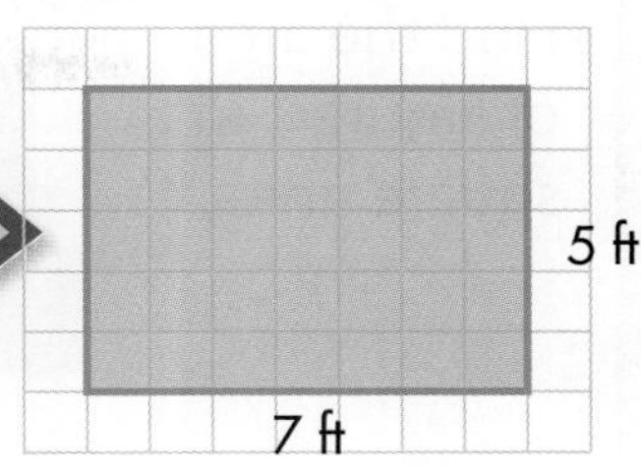

There are 5 rows with 7 squares in each row.

$5 \times 7 = 35$

The area of the floor is 35 square feet.

TAKS Problem Solving

11. The Acton State Historic Site is the smallest state park in Texas. What is the area of the Acton State Historic Site?

4 yd

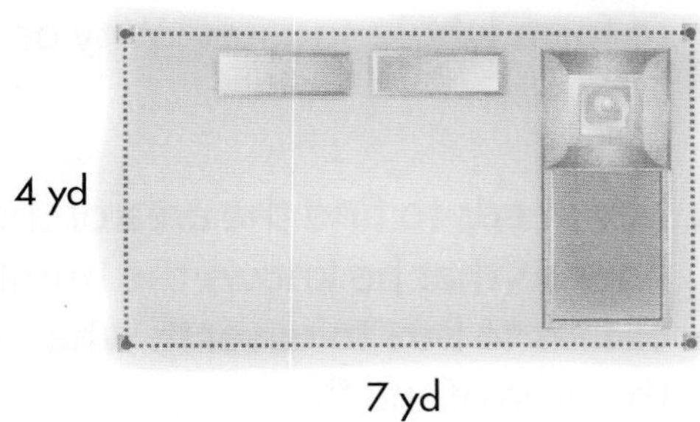

7 yd

12. Use grid paper. Draw two different figures, each with an area of 24 square units. Find the perimeter of each figure.

13. **Writing to Explain** Tamiya cut a 12-inch piece of string into 3 equal parts. She also cut a 24-inch piece of ribbon into 8 equal parts. Which was longer, a piece of the string or a piece of the ribbon? Explain how you decided.

14. What is the area of the picture Abe made with square tiles?

A 20 square inches

B 21 square inches

C 24 square inches

D 30 square inches

□ = 1 square inch

Lesson

17-4

TEKS 3.11C: Use concrete and pictorial models of square units to determine the area of two-dimensional surfaces.

Estimating and Measuring Area

How do you find and estimate area of irregular shapes?

Find the area of Figure 1 in square units.

Figure 1

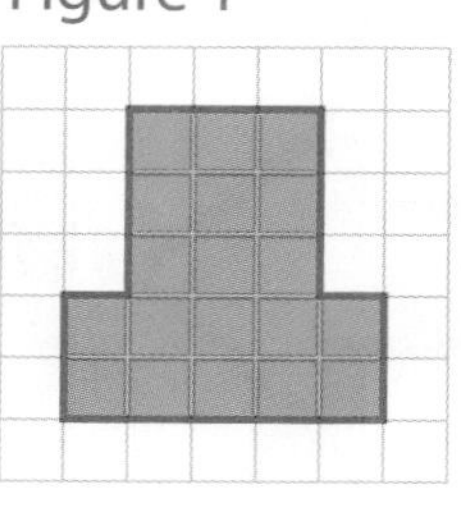

Estimate the area of Figure 2 in square units.

Figure 2

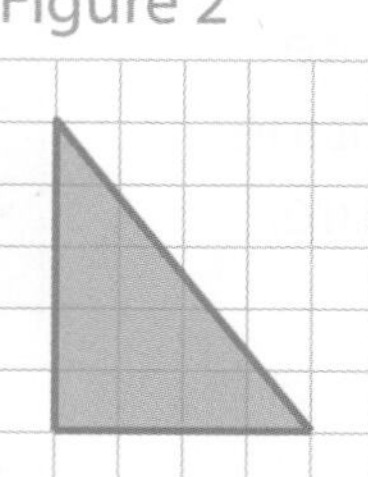

Guided Practice*

Do you know HOW?

1. Find the area in square units.

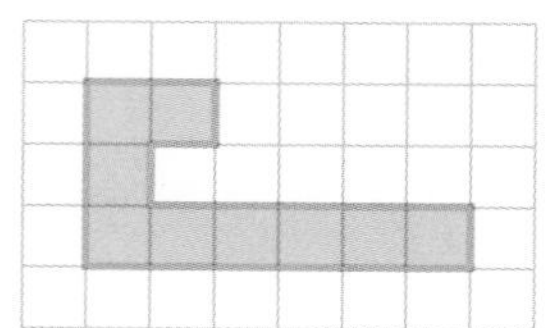

2. Estimate the area in square units.

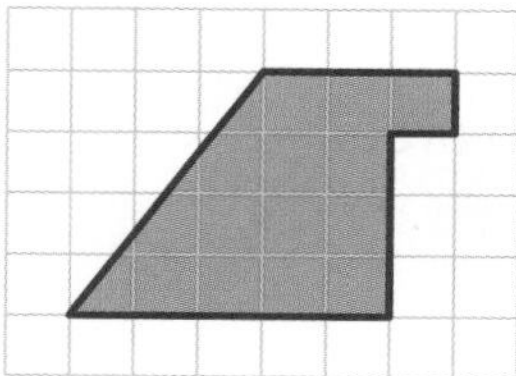

Do you UNDERSTAND?

3. Will partial squares always combine to form whole squares? Why or why not?

4. Kev needs to find the area of the floor so that he knows the number of tiles to buy to cover it. What is the area of the floor?

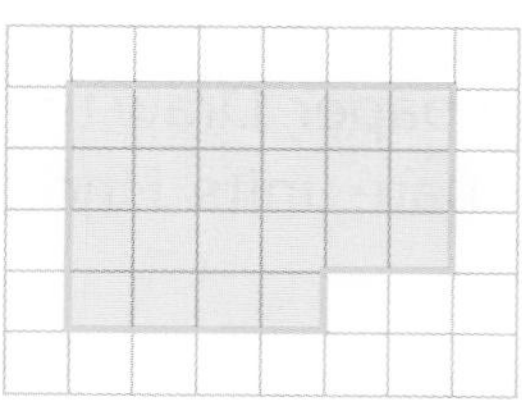

Independent Practice

In **5–7**, find each area in square units.

5.

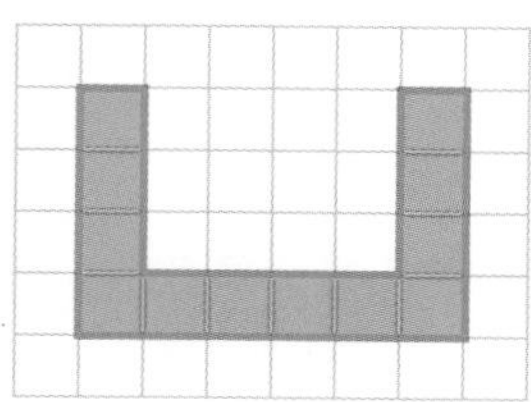

6.

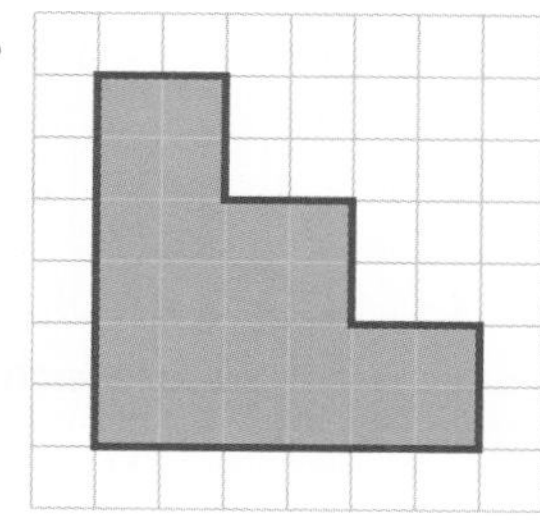

7.

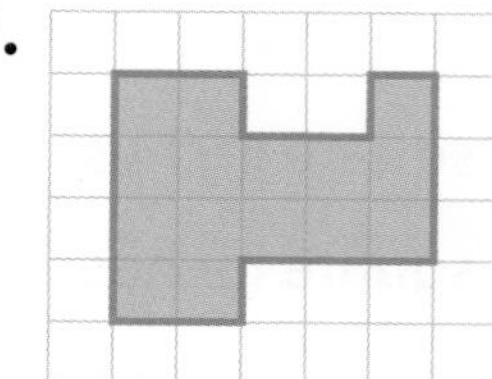

For another example, see Set C on page 389.

To find the area of Figure 1, count the squares.

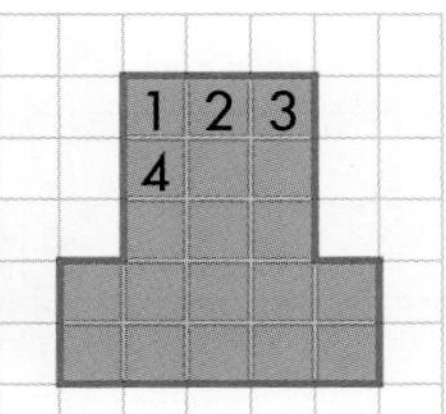

There are 19 square units inside Figure 1.

The area of Figure 1 is 19 square units.

To estimate the area of Figure 2, count whole squares first.

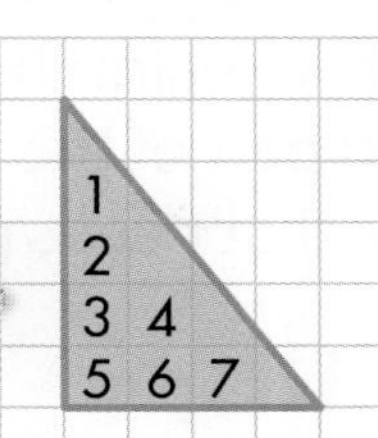

There are 7 whole squares.

Combine partial squares to make whole squares.

The partial squares make up about 3 whole squares.

$7 + 3 = 10$

The area of Figure 2 is about 10 square units.

In **8–10**, estimate each area in square units.

8.

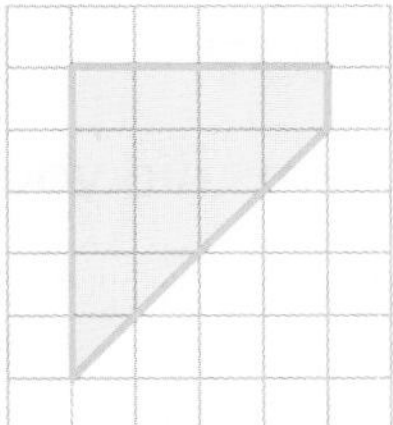

9.

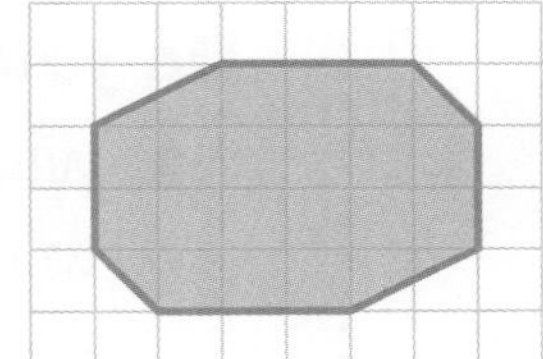

10.

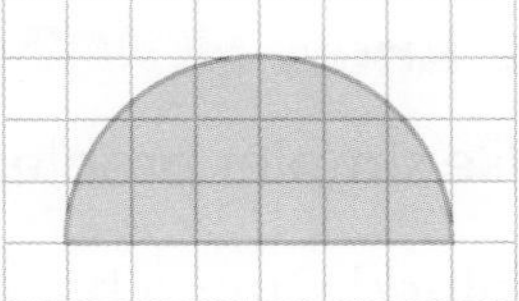

TAKS Problem Solving

11. Chen will use tiles to make a picture. He needs to estimate the area of the picture so that he buys enough tiles. Estimate the area of Chen's picture.

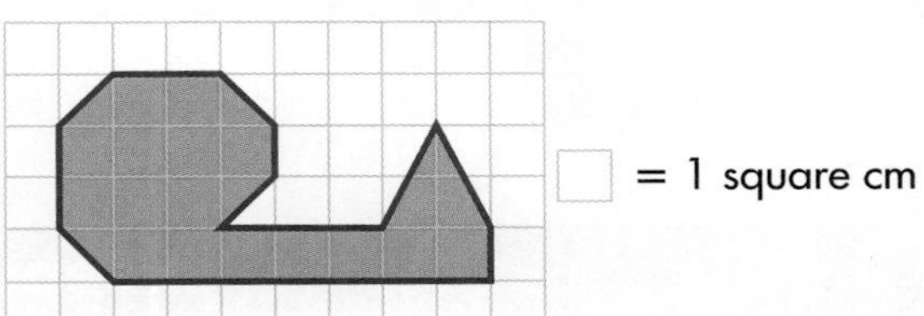

12. Suni put blue tiles on a wall. What is the area of the part of the wall with blue tiles?

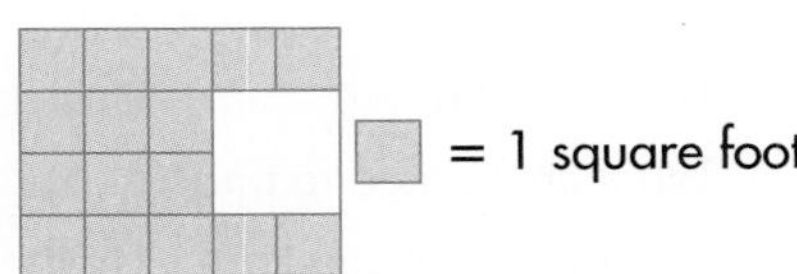

A 4 square feet **C** 16 square feet

B 12 square feet **D** 20 square feet

13. Writing to Explain Joe says the area of this chessboard is between 1 and 2 square inches. Do you agree? Explain.

Each side of this chessboard is $1\frac{1}{4}$ inches long.

scale: ☐ = 1 sq. in.

14. Reasonableness Bobby estimated that the sum of $138 and $241 is about $480. Is his estimate reasonable? Explain.

Lesson
17-5

TEKS 3.14C: Select or develop an appropriate problem-solving plan or strategy, including drawing a picture, looking for a pattern, systematic guessing and checking, acting it out, making a table, working a simpler problem, or working backwards to solve a problem.

Problem Solving

Solve a Simpler Problem

Janet wants to paint the door to her room. The shaded part of the figure shows the part of the door that needs paint.

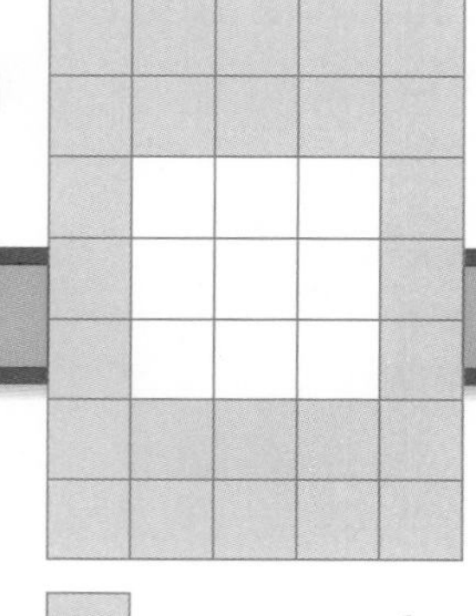

What is the area of the part of the door that needs paint?

Guided Practice*

Do you know HOW?

Solve. Use simpler problems.

1. Lil glued square beads on the shaded part of the frame. What is the area of the part she decorated?

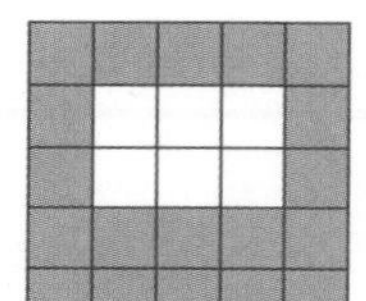

= 1 square inch

Do you UNDERSTAND?

2. What simpler problems did you use to solve Problem 1?

3. **Write a Problem** Write a real-world problem that you can solve by solving simpler problems. You may draw a picture to help.

Independent Practice

4. Solve. Use simpler problems.

   Reg wants to put tiles on a wall. The shaded part of the figure shows the part that needs tiles. What is the area of the shaded part?

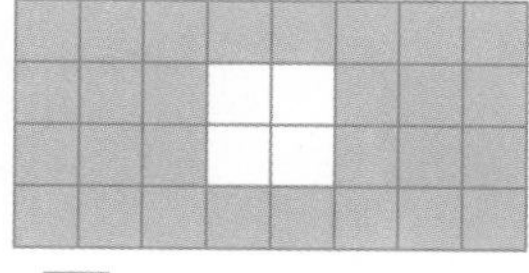

= 1 square foot

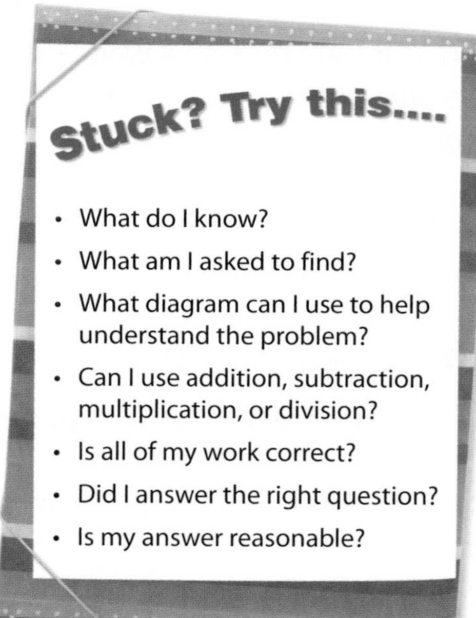

*For another example, see Set D on page 389.

Plan

I can solve simpler problems.

I can find the area of a rectangle and then the area of a square.

Then I can subtract to find the area of the shaded part.

Solve

Area of the whole rectangle
7 rows with 5 squares in each row
$7 \times 5 = 35$

Area of the square
3 rows with 3 squares in each row
$3 \times 3 = 9$

Subtract
$35 - 9 = 26$

The area of the part of the door that needs paint is 26 square feet.

5. Jim wants to tile the floor. The shaded part of the figure shows the part of the floor that needs tiles. What is the area of the shaded part?

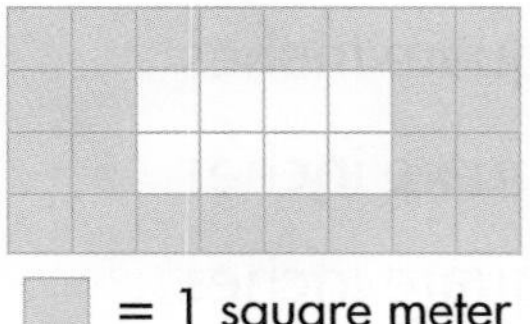

= 1 square meter

6. Dan wants to paint the floor of a pool. The shaded part of the figure shows the part of the floor that needs paint. What is the area of the shaded part?

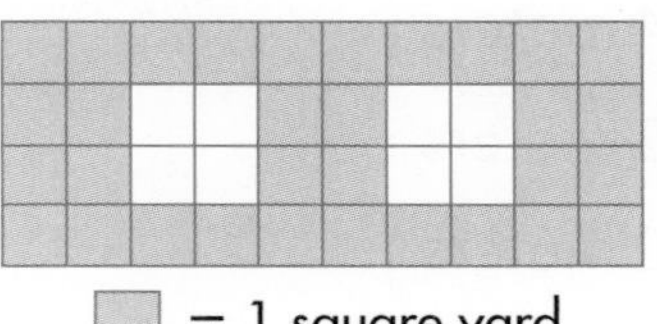

= 1 square yard

7. Macy drew two designs. How much greater is the area of the yellow figure than the area of the green figure?

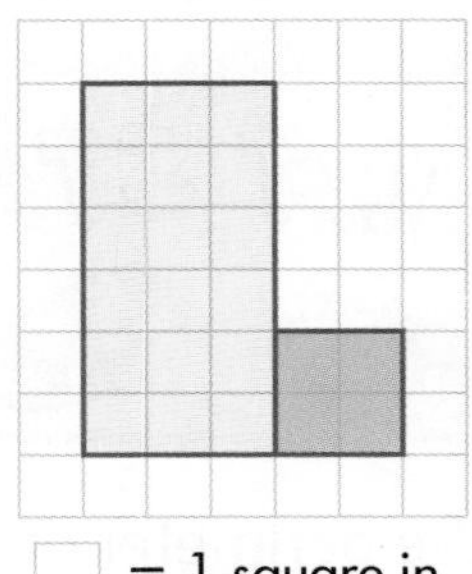

= 1 square in.

8. Mr. Eli grows vegetables in different patches on his farm. What is the total area of the corn and bean patches?

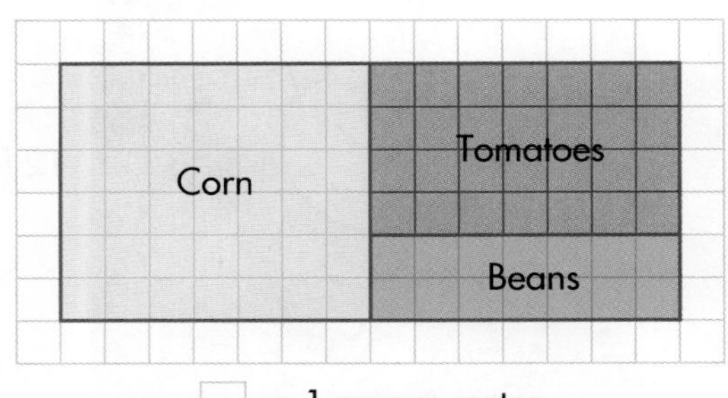

= 1 square meter

9. Neva built these figures using toothpicks. If she continues the pattern, how many toothpicks in all will she use for the 4th figure? the 5th figure?

1. A drawing of the rose garden in the park is shown. What is the perimeter of the rose garden? (17-1)

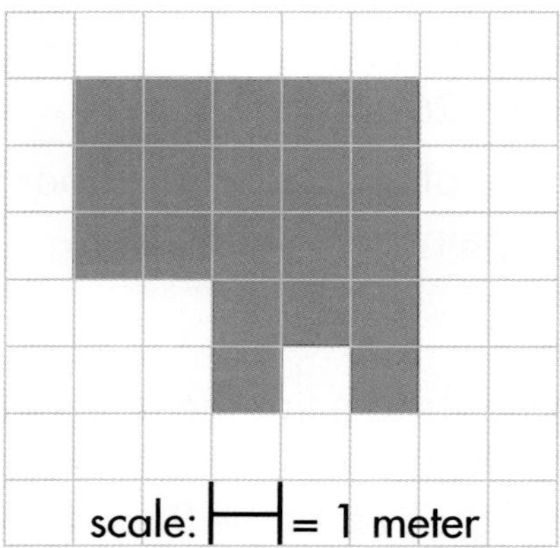

A 26 meters

B 24 meters

C 22 meters

D 20 meters

2. The patio in Marta's backyard is in the shape of a square. What is the perimeter of the patio? (17-2)

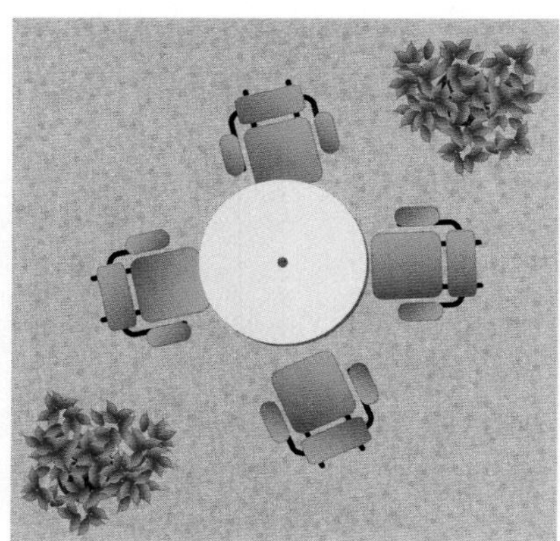

F 144 feet

G 48 feet

H 36 feet

J 24 feet

3. Which is the best estimate of the area of the shape shown below? (17-4)

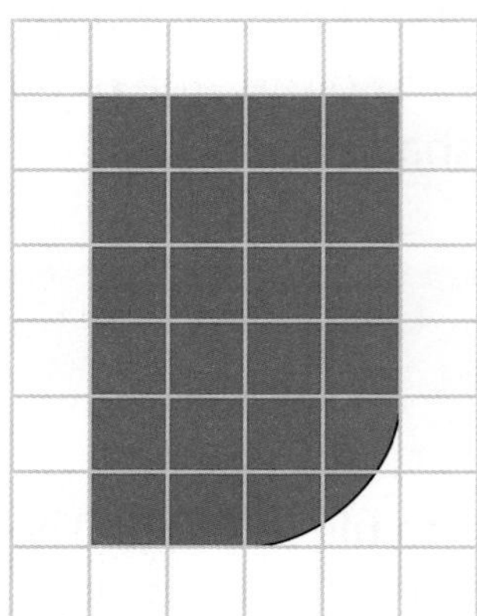

scale: □ = 1 square in.

A 12 square inches

B 14 square inches

C 16 square inches

D 23 square inches

4. Cecil earned the patch below during Art Awareness Week at school. Use a ruler to measure the perimeter of the patch in centimeters. (17-2)

What is the perimeter of the patch to the nearest centimeter?

F 13 centimeters

G 17 centimeters

H 20 centimeters

J 21 centimeters

5. Mrs. Gomez made a quilt for her daughter's doll. What is the area of the doll's quilt? (17-3)

= 1 square inch

A 50 square inches

B 45 square inches

C 40 square inches

D 30 square inches

6. Janie wants to make a border to go around the outside edge of the two tables she pushed together. The tables are shown below. What is the perimeter of the tables? (17-1)

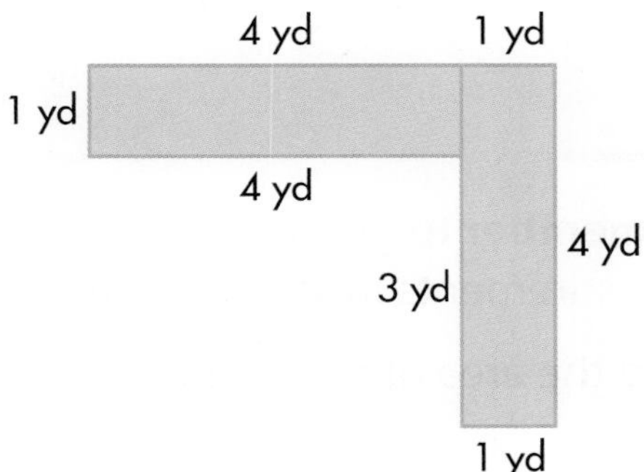

F 18 yards

G 15 yards

H 14 yards

J 12 yards

7. What is the area of the small bandage shown below? (17-3)

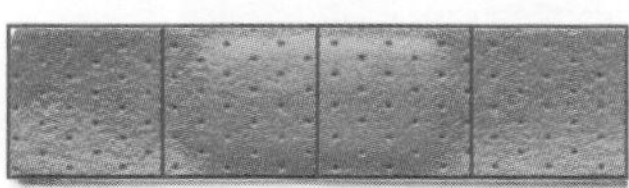

A 16 square centimeters

B 10 square centimeters

C 5 square centimeters

D 4 square centimeters

8. A diagram of a town is shown below. Each square measures 1 square mile. What is the area of the town? (17-4)

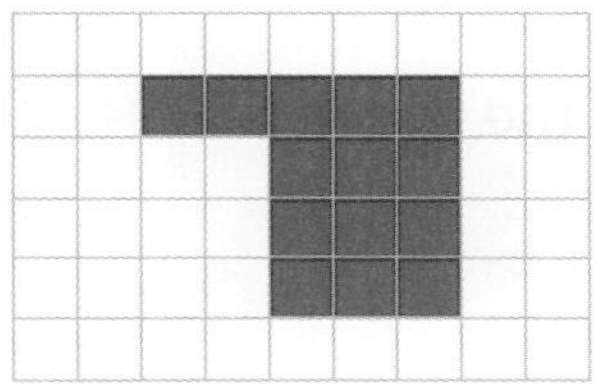

= 1 square mile

F 18 square miles

G 17 square miles

H 15 square miles

J 14 square miles

9. **Griddable Response** A pool area is drawn below. How many square yards of green tiles are around the pool? (17-5)

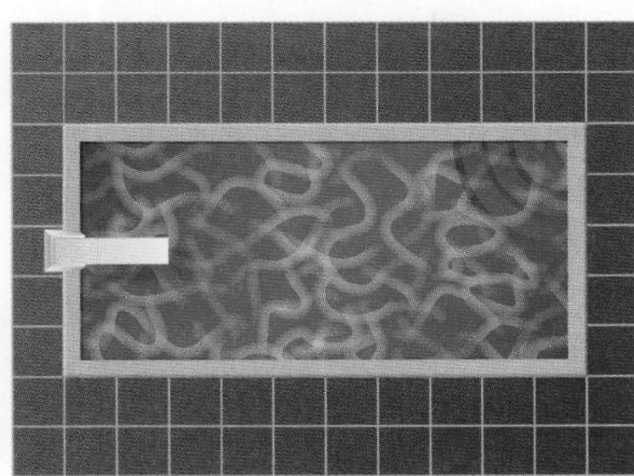

Reteaching

Set A, pages 376–379

What is the perimeter of the figure below?

Add the lengths of the sides to find the perimeter.

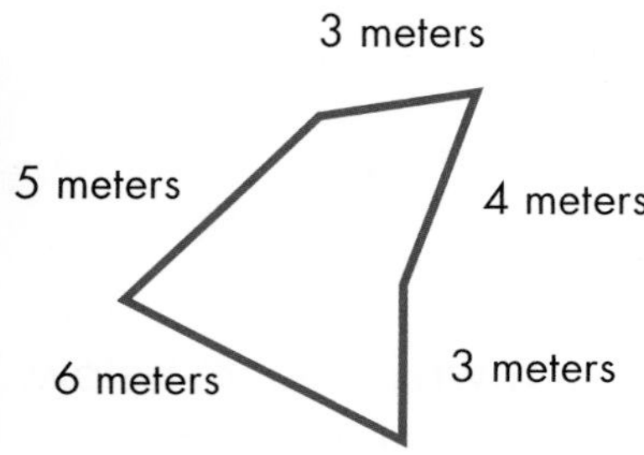

$3 + 4 + 3 + 6 + 5 = 21$ meters

The perimeter of the figure is 21 meters.

Remember the side on which you began adding so that you know where to stop.

Find the perimeter.

1. 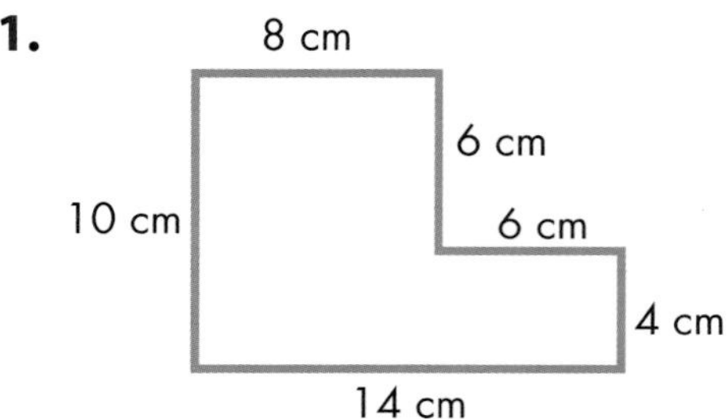

2. 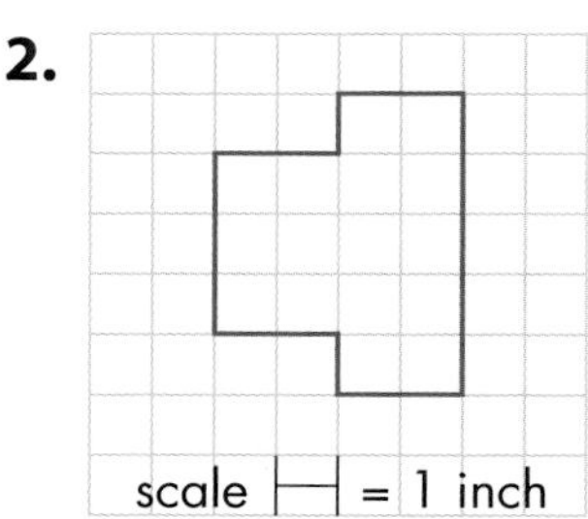

3. 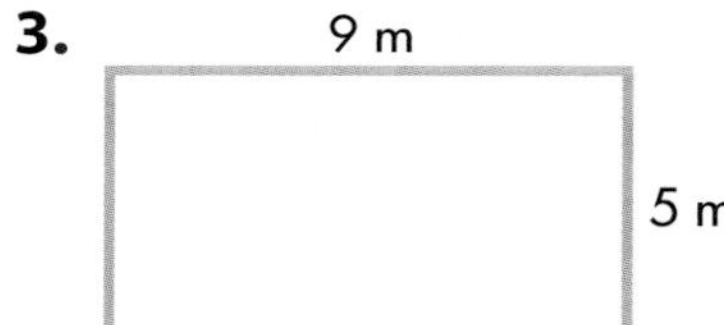

Set B, pages 380–381

What is the area of the rectangle?

For a rectangle or square, think of an array.
□ = 1 square meter

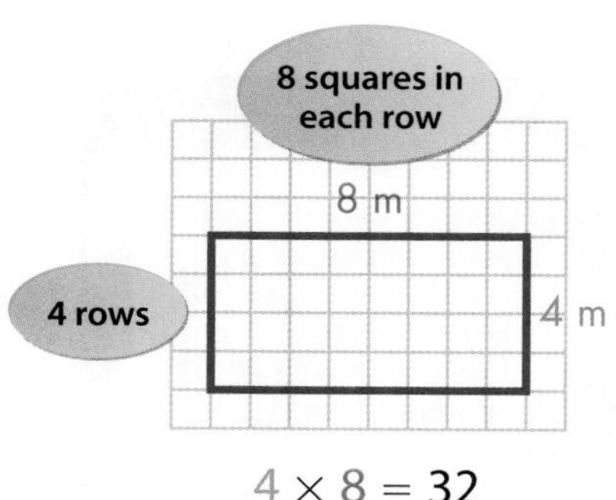

$4 \times 8 = 32$

The area of the rectangle is 32 square meters.

Remember to give area measurements in square units.

Find the area of each figure.

1. 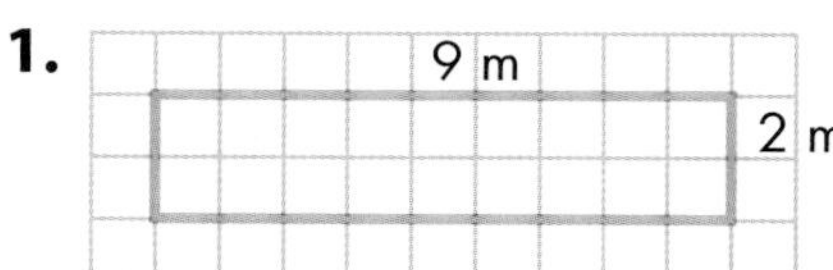

2. 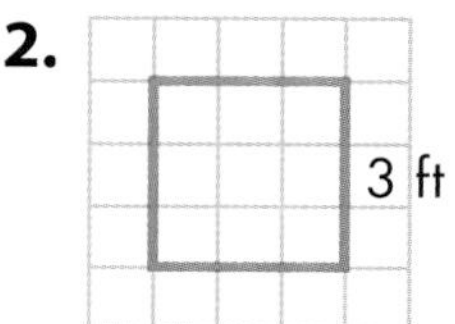

Set C, pages 382–383

Estimate the area of the irregular shape.

Count whole squares.

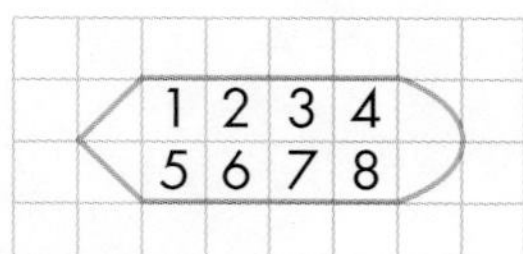

There are 8 whole squares.

Combine partial squares to make whole squares.

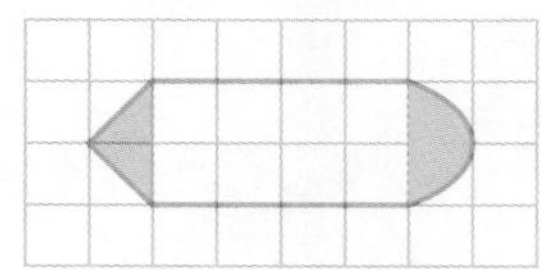

The partial squares make up about 2 whole squares.

$8 + 2 = 10$

The area of the shape is about 10 sq units.

Remember to give area measurements in square units.

1. Find the area of this figure.

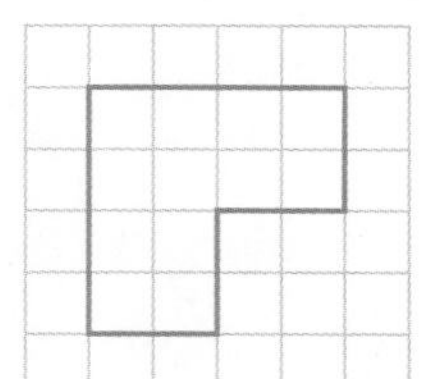

2. Estimate the area of this figure.

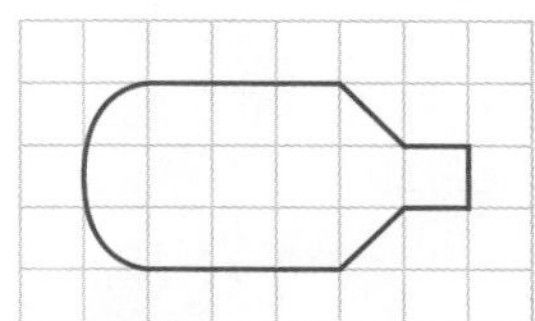

Set D, pages 384–385

What is the area of the shaded part of the rectangle?

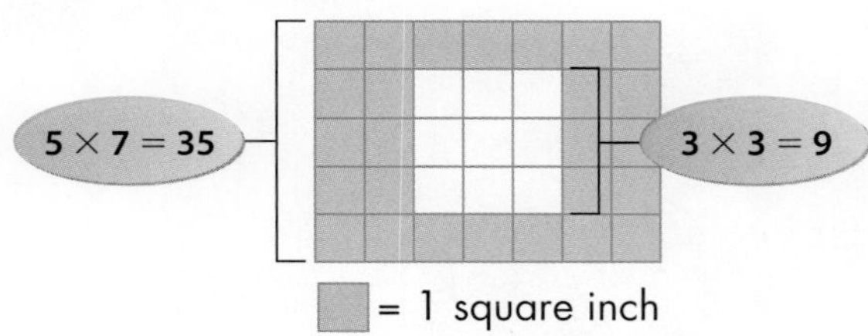

Use simpler problems.
Find the area of the whole rectangle.
Find the area of the square.
Subtract: $35 - 9 = 26$

The area of the shaded part of the rectangle is 26 square inches.

Remember to check your solution. Make sure your solution fits the information given in the problem.

1. Solve. Use simpler problems.

   Walt wants to put tiles on a wall. The shaded part of the figure is the part that needs tiles. What is the area of the shaded part?

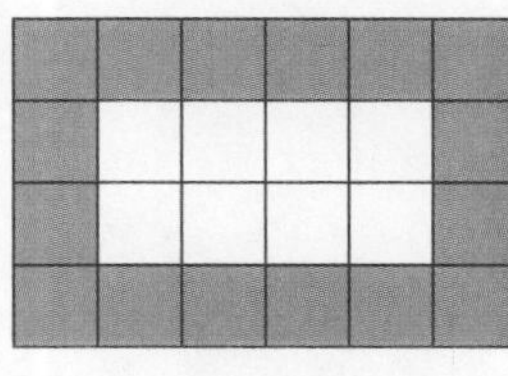

Topic 18

Volume, Capacity, Weight, and Mass

1 The sandgrouse soaks up water in its fluffy feathers and carries it many miles to its chicks. About how much water can a sandgrouse carry in its feathers? You will find out in Lesson 18-4.

2 This kind of hat is sometimes called a 10-gallon hat. Does it really hold ten gallons? You will find out in Lesson 18-2.

3 Do you know how many grains of sand equal 1 gram? You will find out in Lesson 18-5.

4 Owen, a baby hippo, and Mzee, a giant tortoise, met after a tsunami. When they first met, how much more did Mzee weigh than Owen? You will find out in Lesson 18-3.

Review What You Know!

Vocabulary

Choose the best term from the box.

- cubes
- feet
- pounds
- quarts

1. You can measure weight in ___?___.

2. You can measure a liquid in ___?___.

3. You can measure length in ___?___.

Compare Measurements

Choose the greater amount.

4. 3 inches or 3 feet

5. 20 quarts or 2 quarts

6. 6 pounds or 60 pounds

Add

Find each sum.

7. $2 + 6 + 4$

8. $10 + 10 + 5$

9. $3 + 7 + 3$

10. $15 + 15 + 15$

Arrays

Writing to Explain Use the array for **11** and **12**. Write an answer for each question.

11. How can you find the number of dots in the array?

●●●
●●●
●●●
●●●

12. Suppose there were 6 dots in each row. How could you find the number of dots in the array?

Lesson

18-1

TEKS 3.11F: Use concrete models that approximate cubic units to determine the volume of a given container or other three-dimensional geometric figure.

Volume

Hands-On
unit cubes

How can you measure the space inside a solid figure?

What is the volume of the box?

The volume of a figure is the number of cubic units needed to fill it.

A cubic unit is a cube with edges that are 1 unit long.

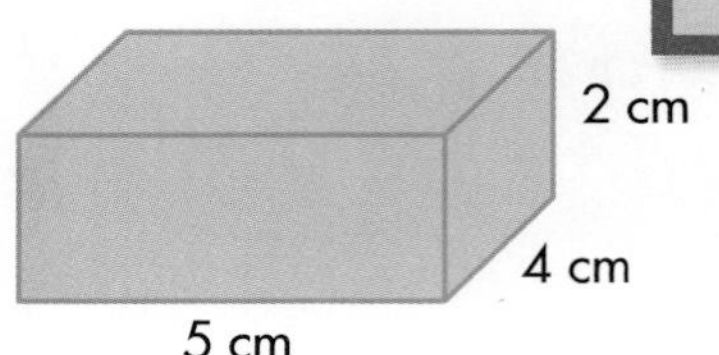

Another Example **How can you measure the volume of other kinds of figures?**

How can you find the volume of this figure?

Count all the cubes.

The figure has 2 rows of cubes.
There are 8 cubes in the back row.
There are 2 more cubes in the front row.
8 cubes + 2 cubes = 10 cubes

So the volume is 10 cubic units.

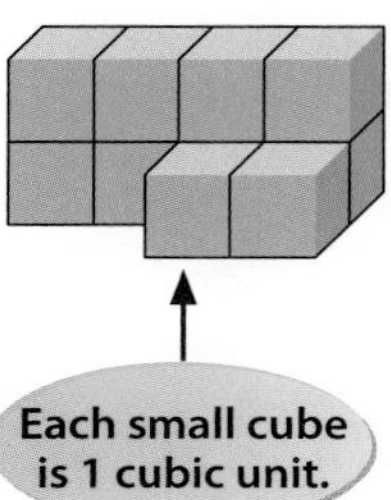

Each small cube is 1 cubic unit.

Explain It

1. Describe how to find the volume of the figure below.

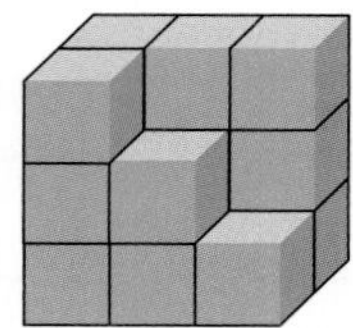

For **2** and **3**, use the figures at the right.

2. How are these two figures the same? How are they different?

3. Find the volume of each of the two figures.

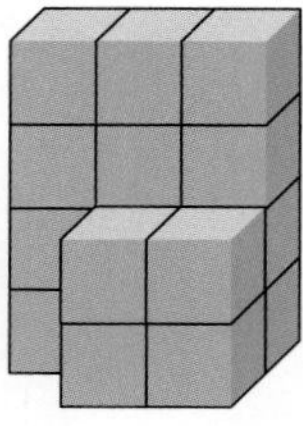

Step 1

Make a model of the box using cubes.

The box is measured in centimeters.

The volume will be in cubic centimeters.

Step 2

Count all the cubes in 1 layer.

There are 20 cubes in each layer.
There are 2 layers.
20 cubes + 20 cubes = 40 cubes

Since there are 40 cubes, the volume is 40 cubic centimeters.

Guided Practice*

Do you know HOW?

Find the volume of each figure in cubic units.

1. 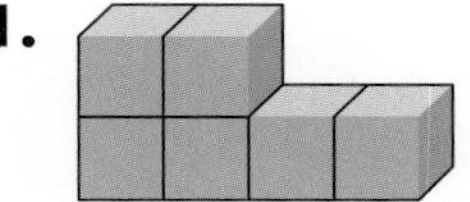

2. 

3. 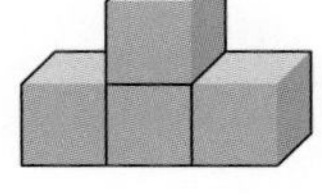

4. 

Do you UNDERSTAND?

5. How do you know the volume of the box above is 40 cubic centimeters and not 40 cubic meters?

6. Pedro has a box that is 4 inches long, 4 inches wide, and 2 inches tall. A model of the box is shown below. What is the volume of the box?

 *Each cube is one cubic inch.*

Independent Practice

For **7–9**, find the volume of each figure in cubic units.

7. 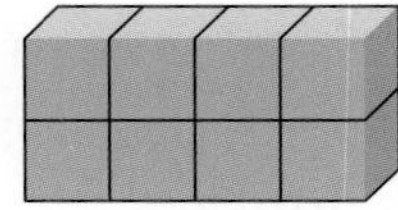

8. 

9. 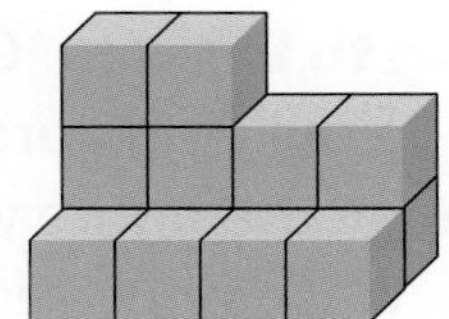

For another example, see Set A on page 408.

Independent Practice

For **10–12**, find the volume of each figure in cubic units.

10. 

11. 

12. 

TAKS Problem Solving

13. Estimation Use the cubes shown at the right to estimate the volume of the rectangular prism.

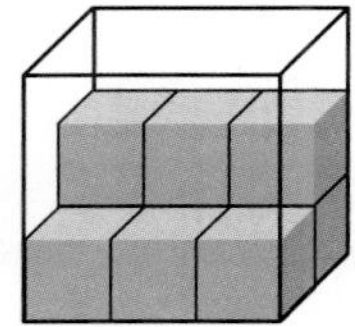

14. Derek made a rectangular prism with 4 layers of cubes. He put 5 cubes in each layer. What is the volume of the rectangular prism?

15. Draw or describe two different solid figures, each with a volume of 16 cubic units.

16. Reasoning One rectangular prism has 3 cubes in each of 7 layers. Another rectangular prism has 7 cubes in each of 3 layers. Which prism has the greater volume?

17. Dana has a jewelry box that looks like the model at the right. What is the volume of the jewelry box?

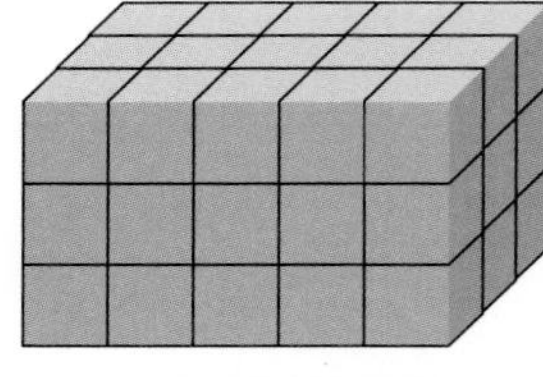

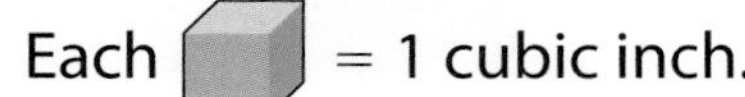

A 25 cubic inches

B 34 cubic inches

C 39 cubic inches

D 45 cubic inches

18. Writing to Explain Carmen used cubes to build a figure. She said the volume of the figure was 15 square inches. Was she correct? Explain why or why not.

19. Tessa drinks 9 cups of water each day. In one week, how many cups of water does Tessa drink?

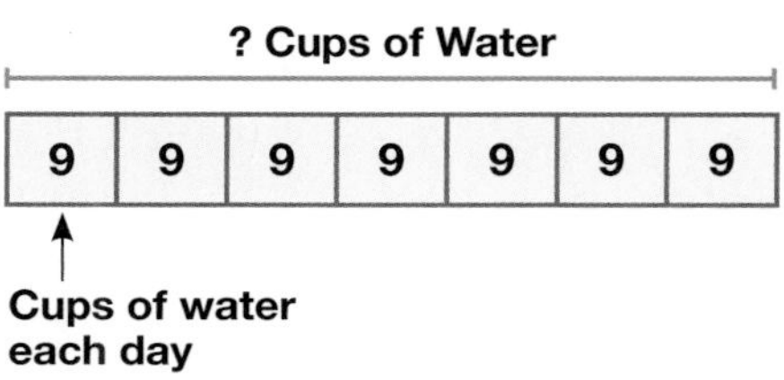

Perimeter and Area

Use e tools

Geometry Drawing

Draw a polygon with an area of 8 square units. Find the perimeter.

Step 1 Go to the Geometry Drawing eTool. Select the Geoboard workspace. Then click on the polygon drawing tool. Click on one point in the workspace. Drag the mouse to a second point 4 units down and click again. Drag the mouse to a point 2 units to the right and click. Drag the mouse 4 units up and click. Finally, drag the mouse 2 units left and click on point A.

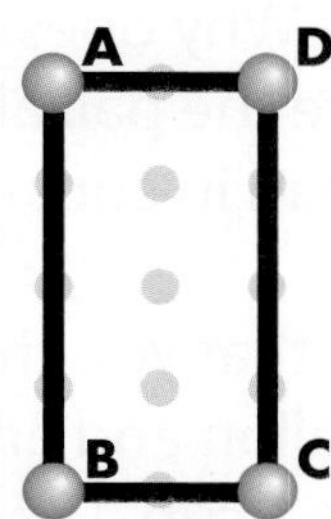

Step 2 Click on the area measurement tool icon and then on the rectangle you just drew. In the lower right corner, under Measurements, the area will appear. Make sure it is 8.00 square units. The area is 8 square units.

Step 3 Click on the perimeter measurement tool icon and then on the rectangle you just drew. In the lower right corner, under Measurements, the perimeter will appear. Make sure it is 12.00 units. The perimeter is 12 units.

Practice

1. Draw two other polygons with an area of 8 square units. Find the perimeter of each.

2. Use the broom icon to clear the workspace. Draw two polygons with an area of 9 square units. Find the perimeter of each.

Lesson

18-2

TEKS 3.11E: Identify concrete models that approximate standard units for capacity and use them to measure capacity.

Customary Units of Capacity

What customary units describe how much a container holds?

The capacity of a container is the volume of a container measured in liquid units. What is the capacity of this pail?

Guided Practice*

Do you know HOW?

For **1** and **2**, choose the better estimate for each.

1.

1 c or 1 qt

2.

3 pt or 3 gal

Do you UNDERSTAND?

3. Number Sense Why does it make sense to measure the pail above in gallons rather than in cups?

4. Find a container that you think holds about 1 gallon and another that holds about 1 cup. Then use measuring containers to see how well you estimated each capacity.

Independent Practice

For **5–12**, choose the better estimate for each.

5.

1 pt or 1 gal

6.

1 c or 1 pt

7.

1 c or 1 pt

8.

2 pt or 2 qt

9. kitchen sink

22 c or 22 qt

10. water glass

1 c or 1 qt

11. baby bottle

1 qt or 1 c

12. tea kettle

3 qt or 3 c

*For another example, see Set B on page 408.

Step 1

Cups, pints, quarts, and gallons are customary units of capacity.

Choose an appropriate unit and estimate.

The cup, pint, and quart are too small. So use gallons.

The pail looks like it will hold more than 1 gallon.

Units of Capacity
1 pint = 2 cups
1 quart = 2 pints
1 gallon = 4 quarts

Step 2

Measure the capacity of the pail.

Count how many times you can fill a gallon container and empty it into the pail.

The pail holds about 2 gallons.

Choose the better unit to measure the capacity of each.

13. teacup
pt or c

14. swimming pool
pt or gal

15. water bottle
pt or gal

16. pitcher of juice
c or qt

17. Writing to Explain Can containers with different shapes have the same capacity? Why or why not?

18. Look at the cowboy hat at the right. It is called a ten-gallon hat!

a Can this hat really hold 10 gallons? How do you know?

b Can this hat hold 1 gallon? How do you know?

19. Which measurement best describes the capacity of a bathtub?

A 50 cups

B 50 quarts

C 50 gallons

D 50 pints

20. Which of the objects below holds about 1 pint?

F can of soup

G punch bowl

H gas tank

J pool

21. Jeanne made 5 pitchers of lemonade. Each pitcher served 12 customers at her lemonade stand. If Jeanne had 1 pitcher of lemonade left, how many customers did Jeanne serve?

Lesson

18-3

TEKS 3.11D: Identify concrete models that approximate standard units of weight/mass and use them to measure weight/mass.

Units of Weight

What customary units describe how heavy something is?

The weight of an object is a measure of how heavy the object is. What is the weight of this apple?

1 ounce (oz)

1 pound (lb)

about 1 ton (T)

Guided Practice*

Do you know HOW?

For **1** and **2**, choose the better estimate for each.

1.

1 oz or 1 lb

2.

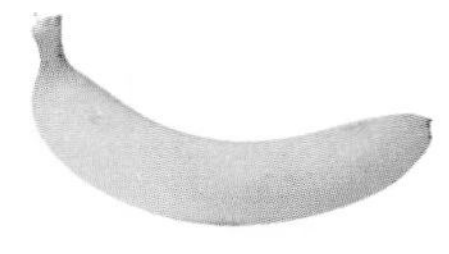

6 oz or 6 lb

Do you UNDERSTAND?

3. Number Sense If you buy a bag of 6 apples, what unit would you use for its weight? Explain.

4. Find an object that you think weighs about 1 pound and another that weighs about 1 ounce. Then weigh the objects to see how well you estimated.

Independent Practice

For **5–12**, choose the better estimate for each.

5.

10 oz or 10 lb

6.

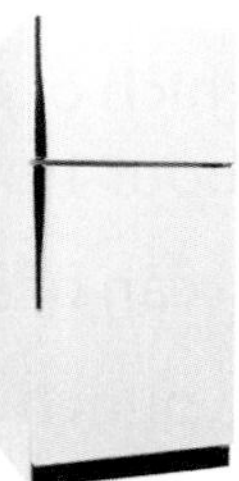

300 lb or 300 T

7.

200 lb or 2 T

8.

2 oz or 2 lb

9. cracker

1 oz or 1 lb

10. television set

30 oz or 30 lb

11. baseball hat

5 oz or 5 lb

12. elephant

30 lb or 3T

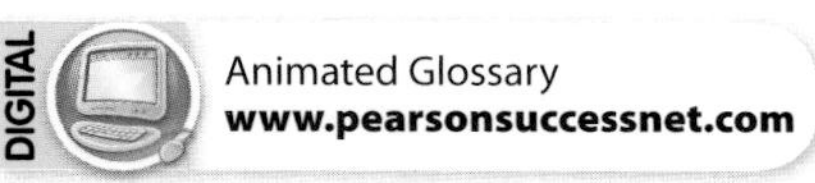

*For another example, see Set C on page 408.

Step 1

Ounces, pounds, and tons are units of weight.

Choose a unit and estimate.

The units pound and ton are too big. Use ounces.

Units of Weight
16 ounces = 1 pound
2,000 pounds = 1 ton

The apple weighs less than 1 pound but more than 1 ounce.

Step 2

Weigh the apple.

Three stacks of three 1-ounce weights balance with the apple.

The apple weighs about 9 ounces.

For **13–16**, choose the better unit to measure the weight of each.

13. student desk
lb or T

14. lemon
oz or lb

15. bicycle
oz or lb

16. truck
oz or T

TAKS Problem Solving

17. How much does the orange weigh?

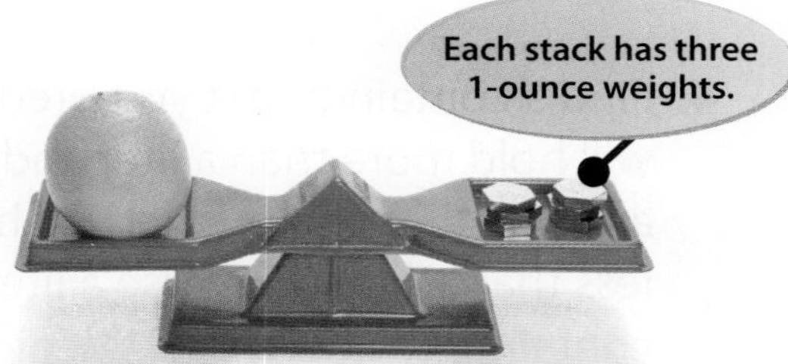

18. When would you use this scale instead of a pan balance?

19. **Number Sense** Which weighs more—a pound of rocks or a pound of feathers? Explain your thinking.

20. **Writing to Explain** Do small objects always weigh less than large objects? Use examples to explain your thinking.

21. When Owen and Mzee first met, Owen weighed 600 pounds. Mzee weighed 661 pounds. How much more did Mzee weigh than Owen when they first met?

Mzee
661 pounds

Owen
600 pounds

22. Which animal weighs about 1 ton?

A squirrel
B giraffe
C wolf
D monkey

Lesson
18-4

TEKS 3.11E: Identify concrete models that approximate standard units for capacity and use them to measure capacity.

Metric Units of Capacity

What metric units describe how much a container holds?

Two metric units of capacity are milliliters and liters. What is the capacity of this pail?

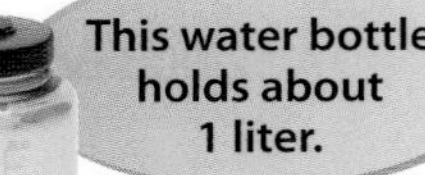

A milliliter is about 20 drops from this eyedropper.

Milliliter (mL)

This water bottle holds about 1 liter.

Liter (L)

Guided Practice*

Do you know HOW?

Choose the better estimate for each.

1. 
250 mL or 2 L

2. 
5 mL or 1 L

Do you UNDERSTAND?

3. **Writing to Explain** Suppose the capacity of the pail above is given in milliliters. Is this number greater or less than the number of liters? Explain.

4. Find a container that you predict will hold more than a liter and another that you predict will hold less than a liter. Then use a liter container to check your predictions.

Independent Practice

In **5–12**, choose the better estimate for each.

5. 
40 mL or 40 L

6. 
15 mL or 1 L

7. 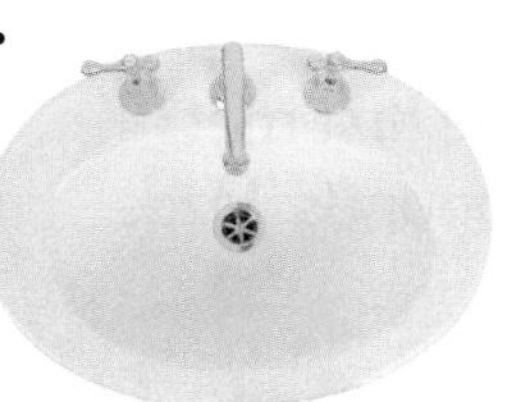
14 mL or 14 L

8. 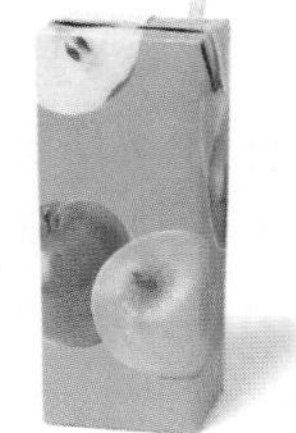
250 mL or 250 L

9. teacup
15 L or 150 mL

10. bathtub
115 mL or 115 L

11. bottle cap
3 mL or 3 L

12. teapot
1 L or 10 L

*For another example, see Set D on page 409.

Step 1

Choose an appropriate unit and estimate.

Units of Capacity
1,000 milliliters = 1 liter

A milliliter is too small. So use liters.

The pail will hold several liters.

Step 2

Measure the capacity.

Count how many times you can fill a liter container and empty it into the pail.

The pail holds about 8 liters.

In **13–16**, choose the unit you would use to measure the capacity of each.

13. soup can

mL or L

14. water pitcher

mL or L

15. swimming pool

ml or L

16. baby bottle

mL or L

TAKS Problem Solving

Estimation For **17–20**, is the capacity of each container more than a liter or less than a liter?

17. large pot

18. glass of juice

19. washing machine

20. mug

21. Reasoning Which cooler holds more ice? Explain your thinking.

Cooler B
Volume: 350 cubic centimeters

Cooler A
Volume: 250 cubic centimeters

22. Which measurement best describes the capacity of a can of paint?

A 4 mL

B 4 L

C 40 L

D 40 mL

23. Number Sense A sandgrouse can soak up water in its fluffy feathers. It can carry the water many miles to its chicks. Does a sandgrouse carry 20 milliliters of water or 2 liters of water?

Lesson

18-5

TEKS 3.11D: Identify concrete models that approximate standard units of weight/mass and use them to measure weight/mass.

Units of Mass

What metric units describe mass?

Mass is a measure of the amount of matter in an object. Grams and kilograms are two metric units of mass. What is the mass of this apple?

Guided Practice*

Do you know HOW?

Choose the better estimate for each.

1. 

5 g or 5 kg

2. 

40 g or 4 kg

Do you UNDERSTAND?

3. **Writing to Explain** There are 10 weights on the pan balance above. Why isn't the mass of the apple 10 grams?

4. Find an object that has a mass more than a kilogram and another that has a mass less than a kilogram. Then use a pan balance to see if you are correct.

Independent Practice

For **5–12**, choose the better estimate for each.

5. 

100 g or 10 kg

6. 

15 g or 15 kg

7. 

4 g or 400 g

8. 

400 g or 4 kg

9. bicycle

2 kg or 12 kg

10. feather

1 g or 1 kg

11. horse

5 kg or 550 kg

12. penny

3 g or 300 g

*For another example, see Set E on page 409.

Step 1

Choose a unit and estimate.

Units of Mass
1,000 grams = 1 kilogram

The unit kilogram is too big. Use grams.

The mass of the apple is less than 1 kilogram but more than 1 gram.

Step 2

Measure the mass of the apple.

Two 100-gram weights, six 10-gram weights, and two 1-gram weights balance with the apple.

The apple has a mass of 262 grams.

TAKS Problem Solving

For **13–17**, choose the best tool to measure each.

13. the capacity of a glass

14. the temperature of water

15. the length of a box

16. the weight of a pear

17. the length of time you sleep

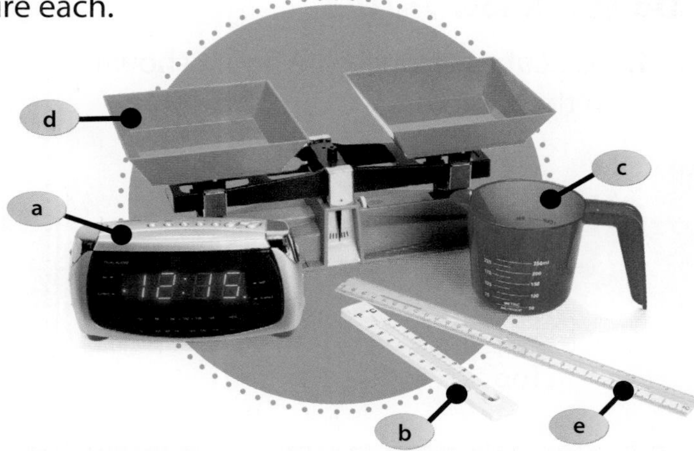

18. What is the mass of the orange?

Two 100-gram weights, four 10-gram weights, and two 1-gram weights balance with the orange.

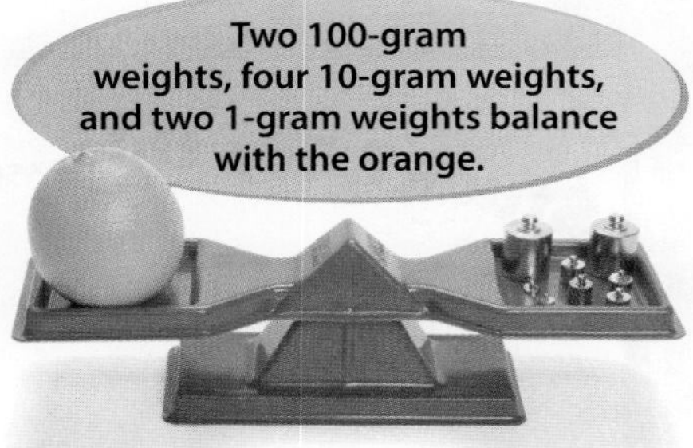

19. Correct the mistakes in the shopping list below.

Shopping List
2 L of apples
3 kg of milk
5 cm of flour

20. A bag holds 500 grams of sand. About how many grains of sand are in the bag?

There are about 1,000 grains of sand in 1 gram.

21. Which measurement best describes the mass of a rabbit?

A 2 grams

B 2 kilograms

C 2 liters

D 2 meters

Lesson

18-6

TEKS 3.14C: Select or develop an appropriate problem-solving plan or strategy including… acting it out…to solve a problem.
Also TEKS 3.14D

Problem Solving

Act It Out and Use Reasoning

Hands-On
cubes

You can use different views of a figure to tell what the figure looks like.

Janet built this figure out of cubes. Then she colored the faces she could see.

Guided Practice*

Do you know HOW?

1. Use cubes to build the figure shown in these pictures.

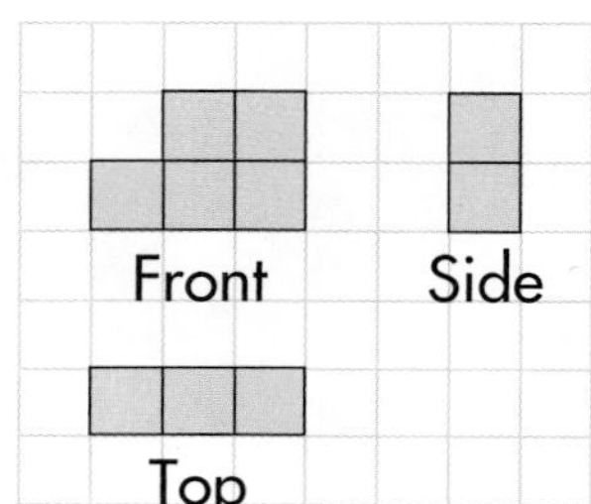

Do you UNDERSTAND?

2. **Writing to Explain** Would a drawing showing the right side of Janet's figure be the same as the drawing showing the left side?

3. Add one more block any place you wish to Janet's figure. Then make drawings to show how each view would change.

Independent Practice

Use grid paper. Draw the front, side, and top views of the figures shown below.

4. 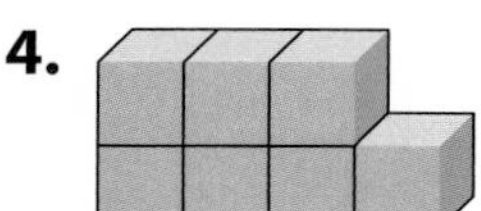

5. 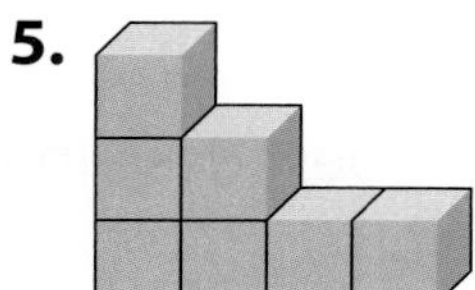

- What do I know?
- What am I asked to find?
- What diagram can I use to help understand the problem?
- Can I use addition, subtraction, multiplication, or division?
- Is all of my work correct?
- Did I answer the right question?
- Is my answer reasonable?

*For another example, see Set F on page 409.

Here are 3 different views of the figure Janet built.

Front

Front View

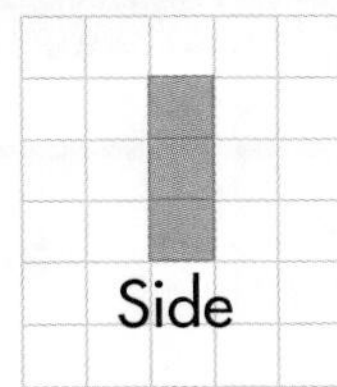

Left Side View

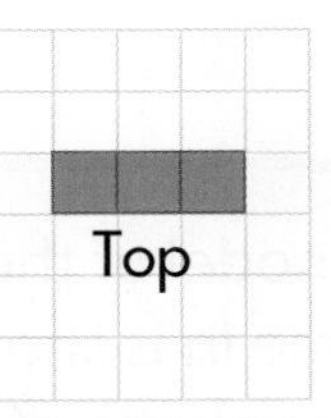

Top View

Use the drawings to help you build the same figure. You will need 8 cubes.

6. Use cubes to build the figure shown in these pictures.

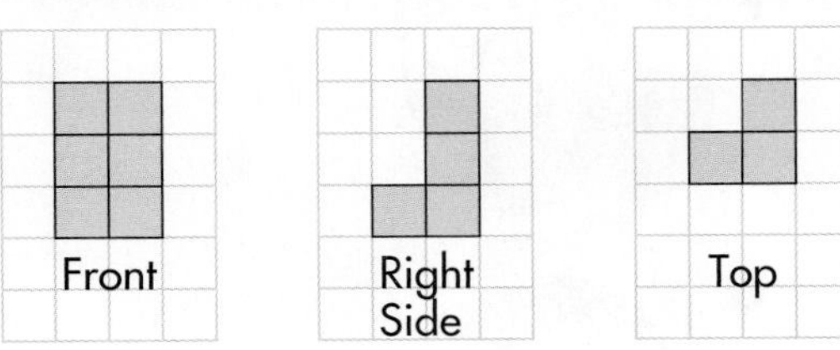

In **7** and **8**, use the figure shown below.

7. Use grid paper. Draw the front, right side, and top view of the figure.

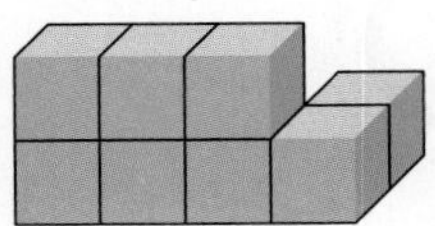

8. What is the volume of the figure?

9. Which drawing shows the front view of this figure?

A 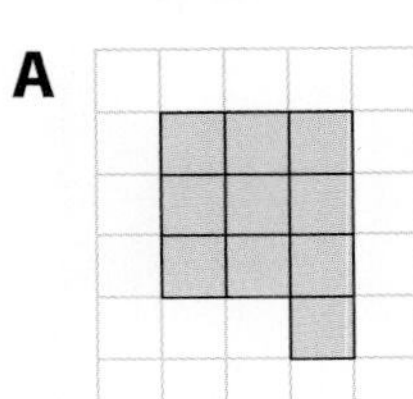

B 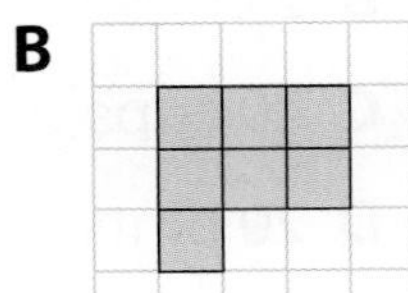

C 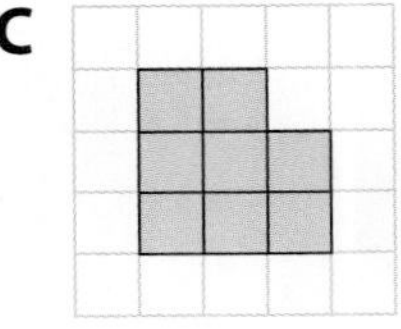

D 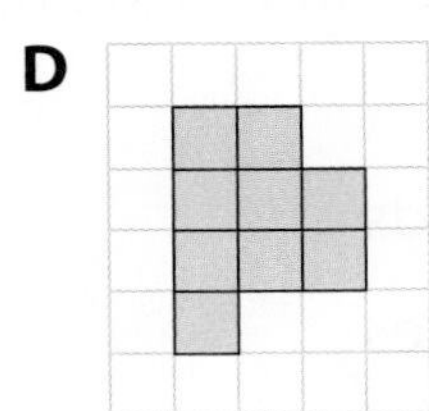

DIGITAL eTools **www.pearsonsuccessnet.com**

Topic 18

TAKS Test Prep

1. A model of the box that a toy came in is shown below. What is the volume of the box? (18-1)

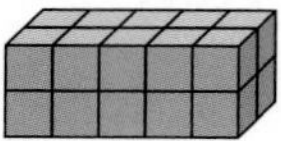

A 15 cubic units

B 16 cubic units

C 20 cubic units

D 24 cubic units

2. Which is the best estimate of the weight of an adult American bison, also called the American buffalo? (18-3)

F 1 ton

G 1 pound

H 10 pounds

J 10 ounces

3. Which of these units would best measure the capacity of a swimming pool? (18-2)

A Cups

B Gallons

C Pints

D Quarts

4. The weight of a pear is best measured in which unit? (18-3)

F Tons

G Pounds

H Ounces

J Cups

5. Which of the following would you measure in milliliters? (18-4)

A Capacity of a bathtub

B Capacity of an aquarium

C Capacity of a coffee pot

D Capacity of an eyedropper

6. Which of the following weighs closest to 1 pound? (18-3)

F

G

H

J

7. Which of the following best describes the capacity of a water balloon? (18-2)

A 2 quarts

B 2 cups

C 20 cups

D 20 pints

8. Which of the following best describes the mass of an orange? (18-5)

F 20 kilograms

G 200 kilograms

H 20 grams

J 200 grams

9. Which of the following best describes the capacity of a bottle of syrup? (18-4)

A 709 pints

B 709 liters

C 709 cups

D 709 milliliters

10. Which unit would best measure the mass of a mouse? (18-5)

F Liters

G Kilograms

H Grams

J Milliliters

11. Which unit would best measure the height of the world's heaviest land animal, pictured below? (18-3)

A Inches

B Tons

C Pounds

D Ounces

12. Which drawing shows the front view of this figure? (18-6)

F 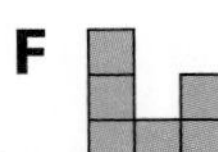

G 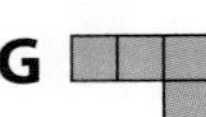

H 

J 

13. Which container would best be measured in cups? (18-2)

A Gasoline tank

B Sink

C Soup bowl

D Bucket

14. What is the volume of this figure? (18-1)

F 24 cubic units

G 18 cubic units

H 14 cubic units

J 8 cubic units

15. **Griddable Response** What is the number of cubic units in the volume of the figure shown below? (18-1)

Set A, pages 392–394

What is the volume of the figure?

← Each small cube is 1 cubic unit.

Count the cubes in each floor. Then add.

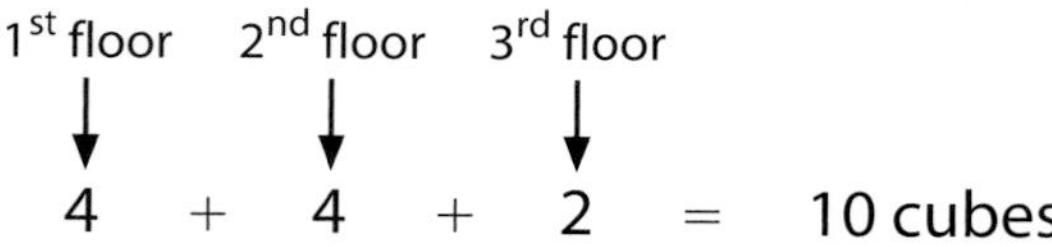

1st floor — 2nd floor — 3rd floor

4 + 4 + 2 = 10 cubes

So, the volume is 10 cubic units.

Remember to count all the cubes, even the ones you can't see.

Find the volume of each figure. Write your answers in cubic units.

1. 

2. 

Set B, pages 396–397

What is the capacity of this teapot?

Choose an appropriate unit and estimate.

Gallon and quart are too big. The teapot holds more than 1 but fewer than 2 pints.

If you estimate using cups, the teapot looks like it holds about 3 cups.

Remember to use the examples of a cup, pint, quart, and gallon to help you estimate.

1. 

1 c or 1 qt

2. 

30 pt or 30 gal

Set C, pages 398–399

What is the weight of a tennis ball?

Choose a unit and estimate.

A tennis ball does not weigh as much as a ton or even a pound, so estimate using ounces.

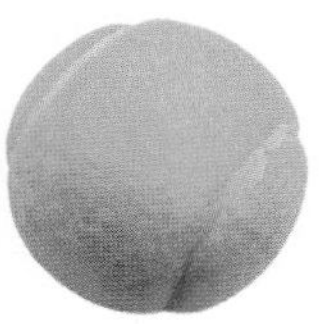

The tennis ball weighs about as much as 4 small cubes of cheese, or about 4 ounces.

Remember to use the examples of an ounce, pound, and ton to help you estimate.

Choose the better estimate.

1.  8 oz or 8 lb

2. 20 lb or 20 T

Set D, pages 400–401

What is the capacity of this pitcher?

Choose an appropriate unit and estimate.

A milliliter is too small, so estimate using liters.

It looks like the pitcher will hold about 2 liters.

Remember that more than one unit can be used to measure the capacity of a container.

Choose the better estimate.

1.

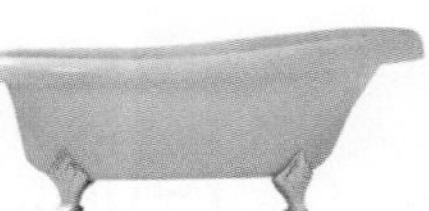

150 mL or 150 L

2.

5 mL or 5 L

Set E, pages 402–403

What is the mass of this bar of soap?

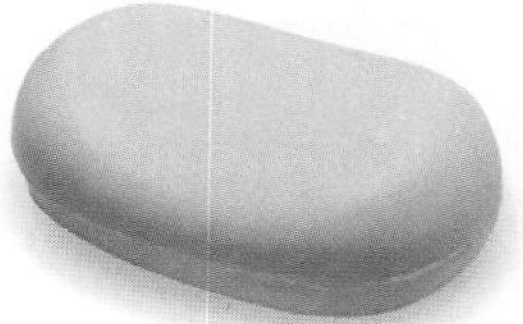

Choose a unit and estimate.

A kilogram is too much, so estimate using grams.

The bar of soap has about the same mass as 100 grapes, or about 100 grams.

Remember to use the examples of a gram and kilogram to help you estimate.

Choose the better estimate.

1.

15 g or 15 kg

2.

2 g or 2 kg

Set F, pages 404–405

Les built this figure with cubes. How can you draw the front, side, and top view of the figure?

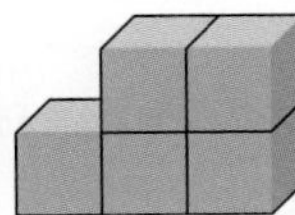

Turn the front of the figure to face you.

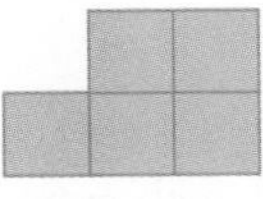

Front View

Then turn the figure to the side.

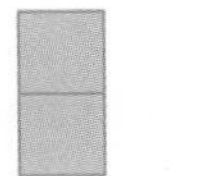

Side View

Then look at the figure from above.

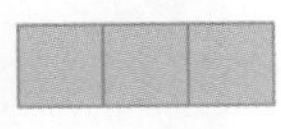

Top View

Remember to check your solution.

Use grid paper. Draw the front, side, and top view of each figure.

1.

2.

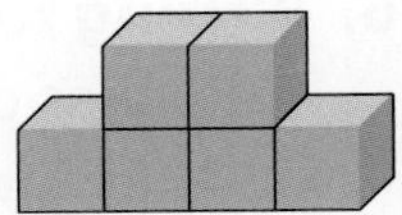

Topics 1–18

Spiral Review

Number and Operations

1. Which number is between 4,977 and 6,927?

4,977		6,927

A 6,928 **C** 4,968

B 6,899 **D** 4,892

2. Sue has 2 red cubes and 3 blue cubes. What fraction of the cubes are blue?

F one-third **H** three-fifths

G two-fifths **J** three-halves

3. Trish eats 5 cups of cereal every week. Which number sentence shows how many weeks it will take Trish to eat 15 cups of cereal?

A $15 \div 5 = 3$ **C** $15 + 5 = 20$

B $15 \times 5 = 75$ **D** $15 - 5 = 10$

4. Write a number sentence that is in the same fact family as $42 \div 6 = 7$.

5. Tal placed cubes from 3 boxes onto 7 tables, with 36 cubes on each table. What was the total number of cubes Tal placed onto tables?

6. **Writing to Explain** Mr. Lum drove 178 miles on Monday and 249 miles on Tuesday. Explain how to regroup to find how far he drove in all.

Geometry and Measurement

7. All of the sides of this figure are the same length. What is the perimeter of the figure?

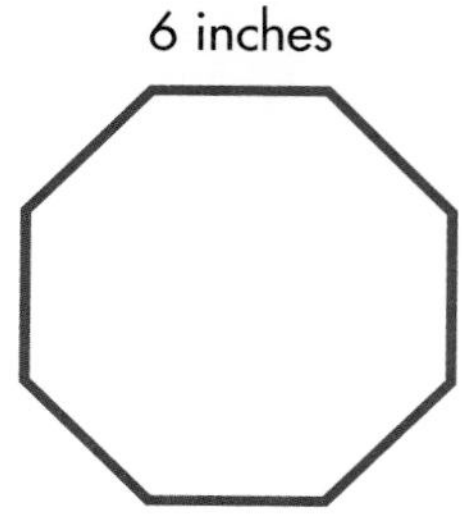

F 12 in. **H** 48 in.

G 36 in. **J** 54 in.

8. Bea is covering part of a wall with square tiles, as shown below.

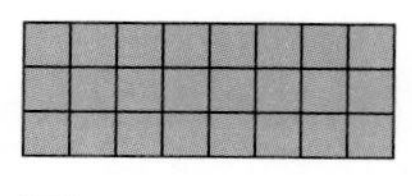

= 1 square inch

What is the area that the tiles are covering?

A 8 square inches

B 18 square inches

C 21 square inches

D 24 square inches

9. Write a measurement in customary units that could be the capacity of a pitcher of water.

10. **Writing to Explain** Explain how you can use cubes to measure the volume of this figure.

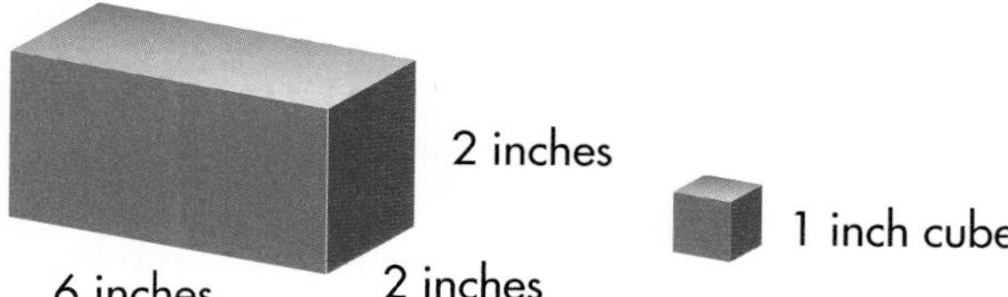

Probability and Statistics

11. Al has a bag that contains 3 blue, 2 green, 5 red, and 2 yellow cards. If he picks a card from the bag without looking, what color is he most likely to pick?

F Blue **H** Red

G Green **J** Yellow

12. Evan drew 13 tally marks to show how many cars passed by his home in 15 minutes. Which shows his tally marks?

A 𝍸𝍸|||

B 𝍸𝍸𝍸|||

C 𝍸𝍸𝍸𝍸|||

D 𝍸𝍸𝍸𝍸𝍸|||

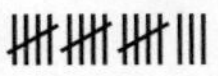

13. Meg made the graph below. How many people voted for grape juice?

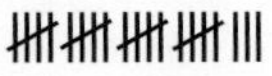

Favorite Juice

Apple	
Grape	
Orange	

Each ▯ = 2 votes.

F 60 **H** 11

G 12 **J** 6

14. Writing to Explain Write about one event that is certain to happen today. Explain why you chose this event.

Algebraic Thinking

15. What number is missing in the pattern below?

91	84	77	70	

A 74 **C** 64

B 67 **D** 63

16. What number is missing in the pattern below?

7, 13, 19, ▢, 31

F 20 **H** 25

G 23 **J** 30

17. The table shows how many hats Dina made each day.

Day	1	2	3	4
Number of Hats Made	2	5	8	11

If the pattern continues, how many hats will she make on the sixth day?

A 17 **C** 14

B 16 **D** 13

18. Copy and complete. Write <, >, or =.

$4 \times 34 \bigcirc 4 \times 39$

19. Copy and complete the number sentence.

$9 \times (2 \times 4) = \square \times 8$

20. Writing to Explain Sara and her sister Vy each want to save $24. Sara will save $4 each week. Vy will save $3 each week. Who will take more weeks to save $24? Explain.

Topic 19

Time and Temperature

1 What is the year-round temperature in Sonora Caverns in Texas? You will find out in Lesson 19-3.

2 How quickly does a Venus flytrap close after catching its next meal? You will find out in Lesson 19-4.

3

How long does the Hubble Telescope take to orbit Earth? You will find out in Lesson 19-2.

Review What You Know!

Vocabulary

Choose the best term from the box.

- hour
- o'clock
- minute
- thermometer

1. Luz read the time. She saw that the time was nine __?__.
2. It takes about one __?__ for Anita to tie her shoelaces.
3. Corey will read the __?__ to tell his friend in another state how warm it is.

Time

Write each time.

4. 

5. 

Temperature

Write whether each temperature is hot or cold.

6. 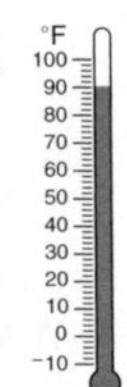

7. 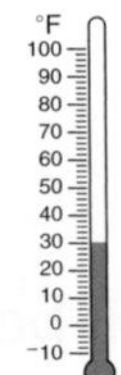

8. **Writing to Explain** Draw a clock face. Draw the hour hand on the 8 and the minute hand on the 12. Write the time. Explain how to read the time on a clock.

Lesson

19-1

TEKS 3.12B: Tell and write time shown on analog and digital clocks.

Time to the Half Hour and Quarter Hour

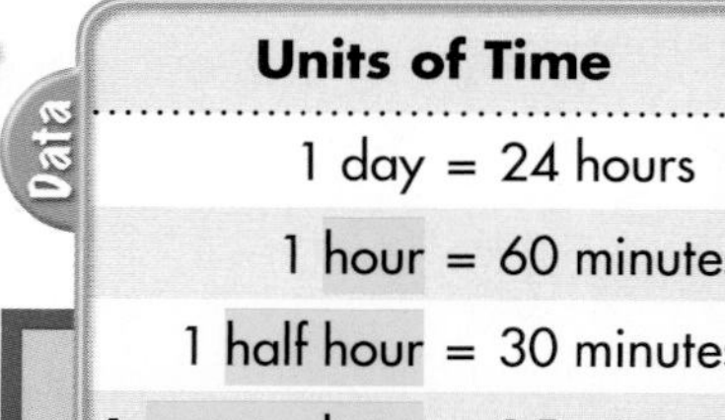

Units of Time		
1 day	=	24 hours
1 hour	=	60 minutes
1 half hour	=	30 minutes
1 quarter hour	=	15 minutes
1 minute	=	60 seconds

How do you tell time to the nearest half hour or quarter hour?

The clocks show the time that the bus arrives at school and the time it leaves.

Bus Arrives

Bus Leaves

Another Example **How do you decide whether the time is A.M. or P.M.?**

The hours of the day between midnight and noon are A.M. hours. The hours between noon and midnight are P.M. hours.

Would the time the bus arrives at school more likely be 8:30 A.M. or 8:30 P.M.?

8:30 P.M. is in the evening. The bus probably would not arrive for school in the evening. 8:30 A.M. is in the morning.

The bus would more likely arrive at school at 8:30 A.M.

Would the time the bus leaves school more likely be 2:45 A.M. or 2:45 P.M.?

2:45 A.M. is in the middle of the night. The bus probably would not be leaving school at that time. 2:45 P.M. is in the afternoon.

The bus would more likely leave school at 2:45 P.M.

Explain It

1. Why might it be important to use A.M. or P.M. when you give a time?
2. Would you be more likely to leave your home to go to school at 8:15 A.M. or 8:15 P.M.?
3. Would you be more likely to eat lunch at 12:30 A.M. or 12:30 P.M.?

Tell the time the bus arrives.

Write 8:30 in three other ways.

When the minute hand is on the 6, you can say the time is "half past" the hour.

The bus arrives at *eight thirty*, or *half past eight*, or *30 minutes past eight*.

Tell the time the bus leaves.

Write 2:45 in three other ways.

When the minute hand is on the 9, you can say the time is "15 minutes to" or "quarter to" the hour.

The bus leaves at *two forty-five*, or *15 minutes to three*, or *quarter to three*.

Guided Practice*

Do you know HOW?

In **1** and **2**, write the time shown on each clock in two ways.

1. 

2. 

Do you UNDERSTAND?

3. In the example above, why do you think the fraction word "quarter" is used for the time when the minute hand is on the 9?

4. The clock shows the time that Etta's skating lesson starts. What time does it start? Give the time in 3 ways.

Independent Practice

In **5–7**, write the time shown on each clock in two ways.

5. 

6. 

7. 

DIGITAL Animated Glossary **www.pearsonsuccessnet.com**

For another example, see Set A on page 426.

Independent Practice

In **8–10**, write the time shown on each clock in two ways.

8. 

9. 

10. 

TAKS Problem Solving

11. The clocks below show the time that the Flying Horse Carousel in Rhode Island opens and closes. What time does the carousel open? What time does it close?

Opens 

Closes 

12. **Writing to Explain** Mr. Boyd gave his students a math test at 10:45. Explain why this time is most likely an A.M. time.

For **13–16**, use the table at the right.

13. **Estimation** Whose bowling score was about 20 points less than Beth's?

14. Whose bowling score was 15 points more than Cal's?

15. What is the order of the friends' names from greatest to least score?

Data

Bowling Scores

Name	Score
Cal	63
Beth	78
Rusty	59
Pang	82

16. **Algebra** Write a number sentence that compares the total of Cal's and Beth's scores with the total of Rusty's and Pang's scores.

17. Ronaldo delivers a newspaper to the Hong family between 7:00 A.M. and 8:00 A.M. each day. Which clock shows a time between 7:00 A.M. and 8:00 A.M.?

A 

B 

C 

D 

Telling Time

Use eTools

Time

Write the time shown on each clock in two ways.

Step 1 Go to the Time eTool. Move the minute hand on the clock until it shows the same time as the first clock above. The digital clock shows 6:45, so that is the time on the first clock. You can also write the time as quarter to seven.

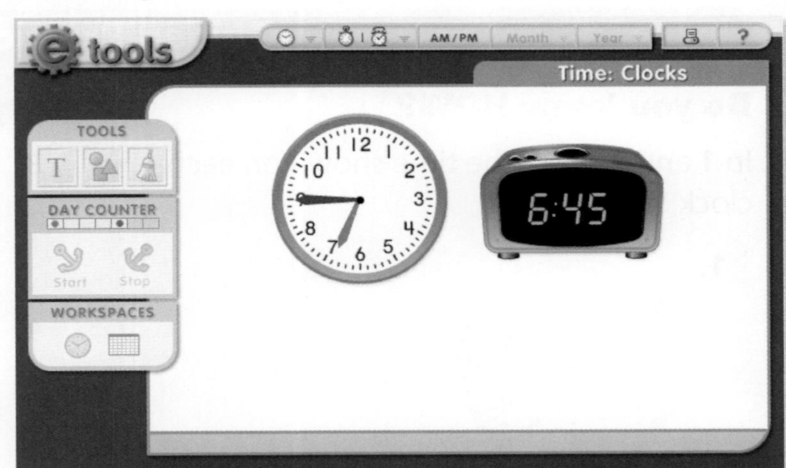

Step 2 Move the minute hand on the clock until it shows the time on the second clock above. The digital clock shows 1:15, so that is the time on the second clock. You can also write the time as quarter after one.

Practice

Write the time shown on each clock in two ways.

1. 
2. 
3. 
4. 
5. 
6. 

Lesson

19-2

TEKS 3.12B: Tell and write time shown on analog and digital clocks.

Time to the Minute

How do you tell time to the nearest minute?

The clock shows the time a train is scheduled to arrive at Pinewood Station. What time is the train scheduled to arrive? Give the time in digital form and in two other ways.

Guided Practice*

Do you know HOW?

In **1** and **2**, write the time shown on each clock in two ways.

1.

2.

Do you UNDERSTAND?

3. Reasoning In the example above, why is 42 minutes past 12 the same as 18 minutes to 1? Explain.

4. The clock below shows the time that an airplane landed. Write the time in two ways.

Independent Practice

In **5–7**, write the time shown on each clock in two ways.

5.

6.

7.

*For another example, see Set B on page 426.

Step 1

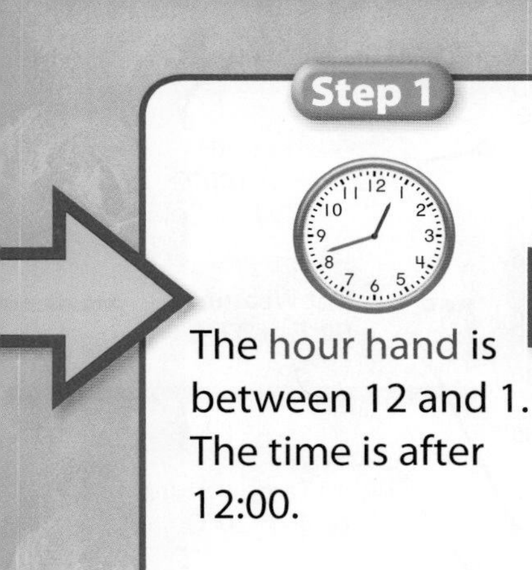

The hour hand is between 12 and 1. The time is after 12:00.

Step 2

In 5 minutes, the minute hand moves from one number to the next.

Count by 5s from the 12 to the 8: 40 minutes

Step 3

In 1 minute, the minute hand moves from one mark to the next. After counting by 5s, count two minutes more.

The digital time is 12:42.
It is 42 minutes past 12 or 18 minutes to 1.

TAKS Problem Solving

8. Toya's family went to see a movie. The clock shows the time that the movie ended. Write the digital time.

9. The Hubble Space Telescope has been moving in its orbit for 1 hour. In 37 more minutes it will complete an orbit. How many minutes does it take the Hubble Space Telescope to complete 1 orbit?

10. **Geometry** Enzo drew a picture of a figure he will paint. Estimate the area of the figure.

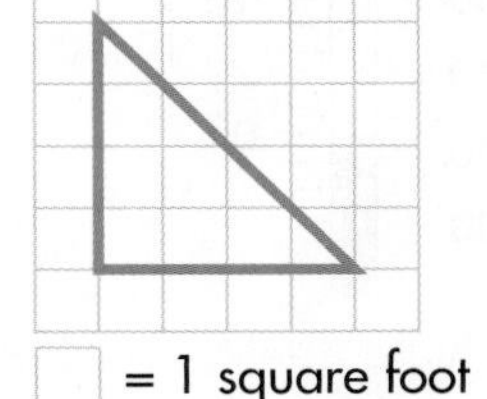

11. **Writing to Explain** Which figure has a greater area, a square showing a side length of 4 feet or the figure Enzo drew? Explain how you found your answer.

12. Ross walks his dog between 3:15 P.M. and 4:00 P.M. Which clock shows a time between 3:15 P.M. and 4:00 P.M.?

A

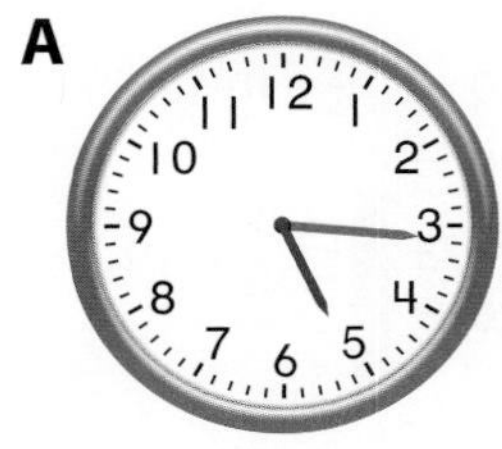

B

C

D

Lesson
19-3

TEKS 3.12A: Use a thermometer to measure temperature.

Temperature

How are temperatures measured?

A thermometer measures temperature in degrees Fahrenheit (°F) or degrees Celsius (°C). Fahrenheit and Celsius are different scales used to measure temperature.

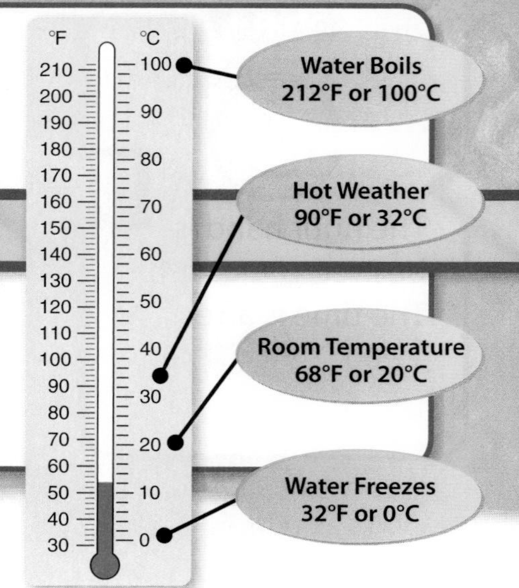

Guided Practice*

Do you know HOW?

In **1** and **2**, write each temperature in °F and in °C.

1.

2.

Do you UNDERSTAND?

3. Look at the thermometer above. Would you swim outside if the temperature was 28°C? Explain.

4. Writing to Explain Which is the better temperature to go bicycling outside, 15°F or 50°F? Explain.

5. Mateo needs to wear a coat to go outside today. The thermometer shows the temperature. What is the temperature in degrees Fahrenheit?

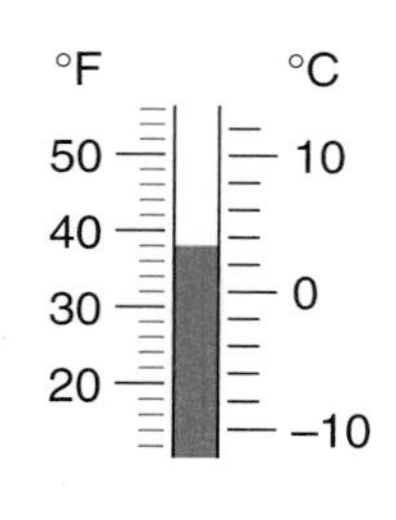

Independent Practice

In **6–8**, write each temperature in °F and °C.

6.

7.

8.

*For another example, see Set C on page 427.

Rita will wear a jacket outside today. What is the temperature outside, shown on the thermometer?

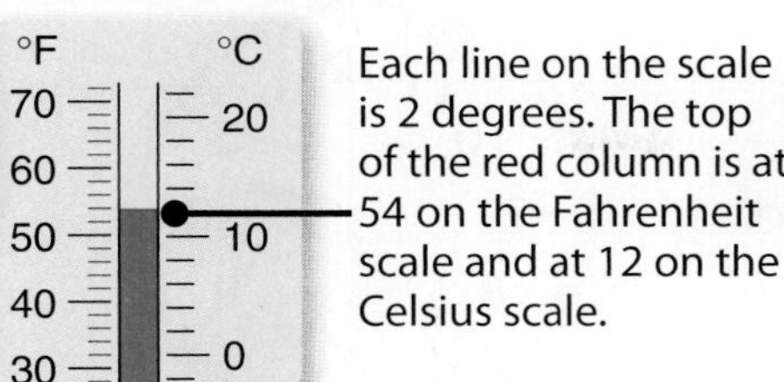

The temperature is 54°F or 12°C.

Dave will wear a T-shirt outside today. What is the temperature outside, shown on the thermometer?

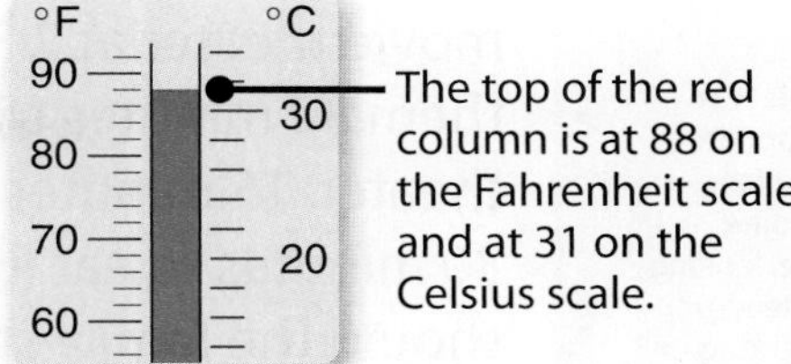

The temperature is 88°F or 31°C.

TAKS Problem Solving

9. The temperature in Cascade Caverns is always the same. The thermometer shows that temperature. What is the temperature in degrees Fahrenheit?

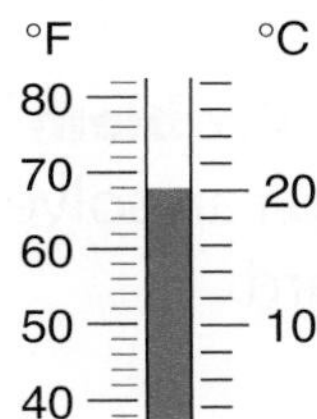

10. **Algebra** The year-round temperature in Carlsbad Caverns in New Mexico is 56°F. Copy and complete the number sentence to compare the temperature in Carlsbad Caverns with the temperature in Cascade Caverns.

56 ◯ ▢

11. **Reasonableness** Roy says that a scarf and a hat together cost about the same as 2 blankets. Is his estimate reasonable? Explain.

12. **Algebra** What did Jorge buy at the sale if $(3 \times \$19) + \$23$ stands for the total cost?

Winter Sale	
Blanket	$19
Hat	$12
Scarf	$18
Shovel	$23

13. The temperature in Sonora Caverns is always about 70°F. Which thermometer shows this temperature?

A

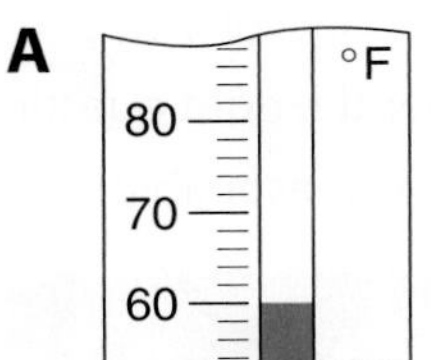

B

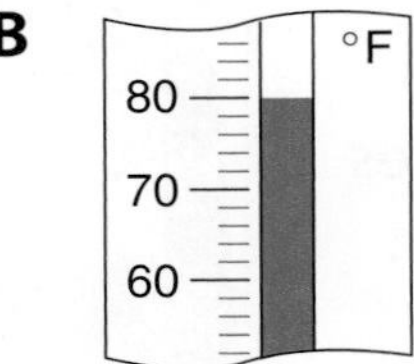

C

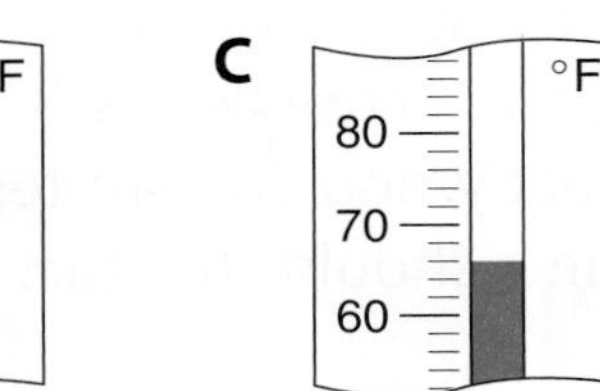

D

°F
80
70
60

Lesson

19-4

TEKS 3.14C: Select or develop an appropriate problem-solving plan or strategy, including drawing a picture, looking for a pattern, systematic guessing and checking, acting it out, making a table, working a simpler problem, or working backwards to solve a problem.

Problem Solving

Work Backward

Eric's family wants to arrive at the movie theater at 2:30 P.M. It takes them 30 minutes to travel to the theater, 15 minutes to get ready, and 30 minutes to eat lunch. What time should the family start eating lunch?

Arrive at Theater

Guided Practice*

Do you know HOW?

Solve the problem by drawing a picture and working backward.

1. The swim meet starts at 10:15 A.M. It takes Abby 15 minutes to walk to the pool. On her way, she needs 15 minutes to shop. It takes her 30 minutes to get ready. What time should Abby start getting ready?

Do you UNDERSTAND?

2. In the example above, why do the arrows in the Solve step move to the left?

3. **Write a Problem** Write a problem that you can solve by working backward.

Independent Practice

In **4** and **5**, solve the problem by drawing a picture and working backward.

4. Emilio read the thermometer one evening. The temperature was 56°F. This temperature was 9°F less than the temperature that afternoon. The afternoon temperature was 7°F greater than the temperature in the morning. What was the temperature in the morning?

5. Jana's dentist appointment is at 4:30 P.M. It takes Jana 20 minutes to walk to the dentist's office, 20 minutes to get ready, and 30 minutes to clean her room. What time should she start cleaning her room?

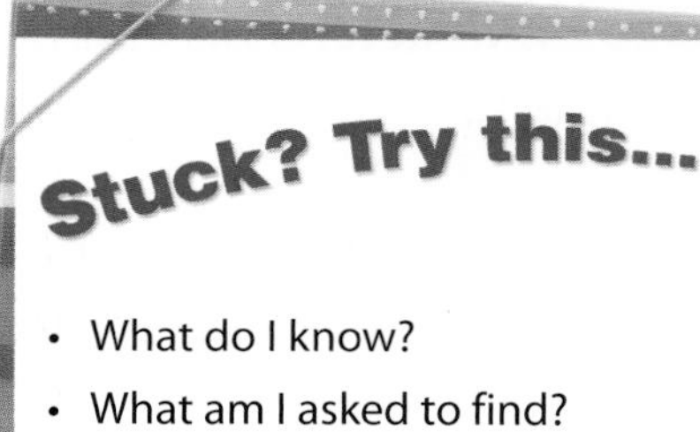

Stuck? Try this....

- What do I know?
- What am I asked to find?
- What diagram can I use to help understand the problem?
- Can I use addition, subtraction, multiplication, or division?
- Is all of my work correct?
- Did I answer the right question?
- Is my answer reasonable?

*For another example, see Set D on page 427.

Read and Understand

What do I know? Arrive 2:30 P.M., 30 minutes to travel, 15 minutes to get ready, 30 minutes to eat lunch

What am I being asked to find? The time the family should start eating lunch

Plan and Solve

Draw a picture to show each change.

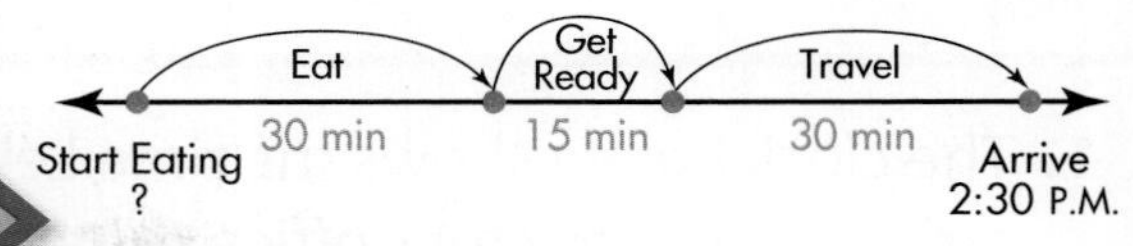

Work backward from the end.

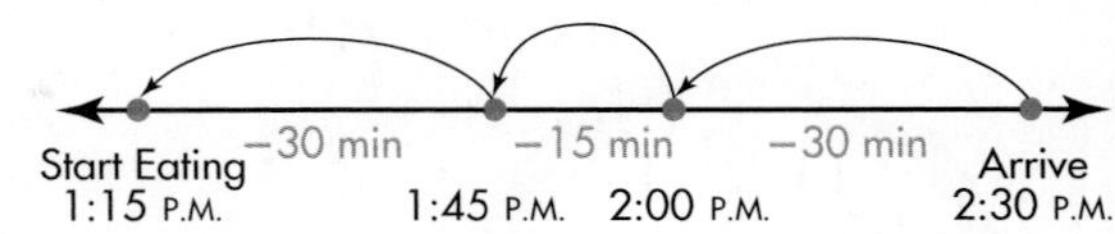

Eric's family should start eating lunch at 1:15 P.M.

6. Kent read the thermometer this evening. The temperature was 65°F. This temperature was 15°F less than the temperature in the afternoon. The afternoon temperature was 14°F greater than the temperature in the morning. What was the temperature in the morning?

7. Corinna read the thermometer at 7:00 P.M. The temperature was 16°C. This temperature was 9°C less than the temperature at 2:00 P.M. The temperature at 2:00 P.M. was 10°C higher than the temperature at 8:00 A.M. What was the temperature at 8:00 A.M.?

8. Wan-li drew these polygons. What is the same in all three polygons?

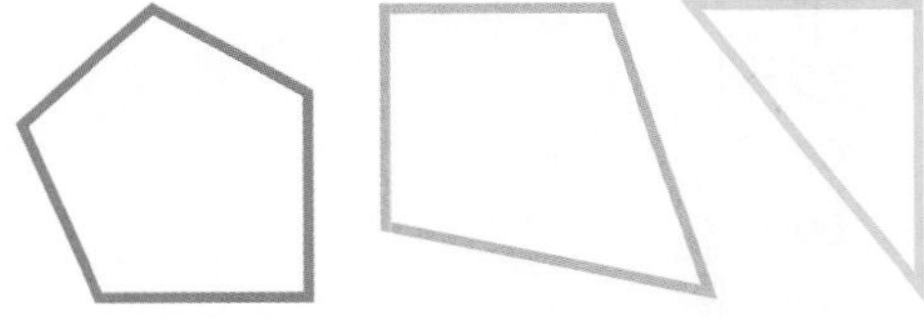

9. School starts at 8:15 A.M. It takes Shane 15 minutes to walk to school, 20 minutes to eat, 15 minutes to walk his dog, and 15 minutes to get ready. What time should he get up?

10. A scientist recorded the data shown in the table. About how long does it take a Venus flytrap to close after an insect or spider lands on it?

A Less than 1 second

B More than 1 second

C More than 1 minute

D More than 2 minutes

Data

Time Prey Landed	Time Flytrap Closed
2:07	$\frac{1}{2}$ second after 2:07
2:49	$\frac{3}{4}$ second after 2:49
2:53	$\frac{1}{2}$ second after 2:53

TAKS Test Prep

1. The clock below shows the time Levi arrived at the doctor's office. What time did he arrive? (19-2)

A 3:42

B 3:37

C 3:35

D 2:37

2. What is one way to write the time shown on the clock? (19-1)

F Quarter to 1

G 15 past 1

H Quarter past 2

J Quarter to 2

3. Avi got to school at 8:05 A.M. She was on the bus 15 minutes, stood at the bus stop for 10 minutes, and took 40 minutes to get ready after she got up. What time did Avi get up? (19-4)

A 9:10 A.M.

B 7:05 A.M.

C 7:00 A.M.

D 6:55 A.M.

4. The temperature outside on Mikal's birthday was 54°F. Which thermometer shows this temperature? (19-3)

F
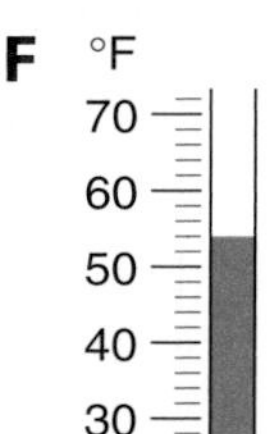

G
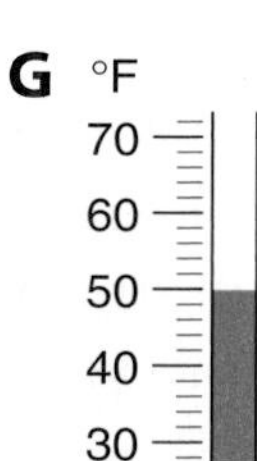

H
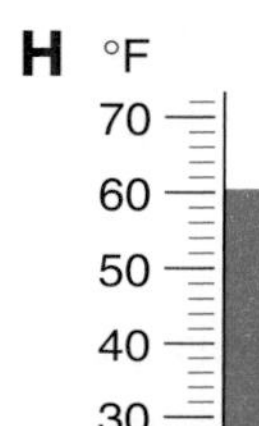

J
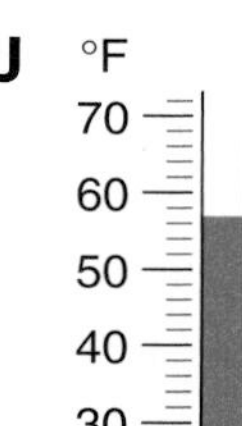

5. Which of the following is a time that Jose would be asleep during the night? (19-1)

A 3:15 P.M.

B 11:45 P.M.

C 10:45 A.M.

D 12:30 P.M.

6. What temperature in °F is shown? (19-3)

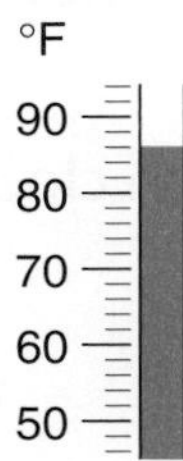

F 88°F

G 86°F

H 84°F

J 83°F

7. The 3rd grade play began at the time shown on the clock.

What time did the play begin? (19-1)

A 3:40

B 6:15

C 6:35

D 7:15

8. Olivia left her house at 6:30 to go to the movies. Which is another way to write 6:30? (19-1)

F quarter to 6

G quarter past 6

H half past 6

J quarter to 7

9. Rachael gets ready for bed between 8:45 P.M. and 9:30 P.M. Which clock shows a time between 8:45 P.M. and 9:30 P.M.? (19-2)

A

B

C

D

10. **Griddable Response** The 3:00 P.M. temperature was 93°F. This was 8° warmer than the temperature at noon. The noon temperature was 13° warmer than the 9:00 A.M. temperature. What was the 9:00 A.M. temperature in °F? (19-4)

Reteaching

Set A, pages 414–416

The clocks show the time that a movie starts. What time does the movie start? Write the time in at least 3 ways.

When the minute hand is on the 9, you can say "15 minutes to" the hour. You can also say "a quarter to" the hour.

The movie starts at four forty-five, or 15 minutes to five, or a quarter to five.

Remember to find where the hour hand points and where the minute hand points to tell the time.

Write the time shown on each clock in two ways.

1. 

2. 

Set B, pages 418–419

What is the time to the nearest minute?

The hour hand is between 10 and 11. The time is after 10:00.

Count by 5s from the 12 to the 5.
5, 10, 15, 20, 25 minutes.

After counting by 5s, count the marks by 1.
5, 10, 15, 20, 25, 26, 27 minutes.

The digital time is 10:27.
It is 27 minutes past 10 or 33 minutes to 11.

Remember that for minutes, count numbers on the clock by 5s, then count marks by 1.

Write the time shown on each clock in two ways.

1. 

2. 

Set C, pages 420–421

Rona wears a light shirt to go outside today. The thermometer shows the temperature outside. What is the temperature?

Each line on the scale is 2 degrees.

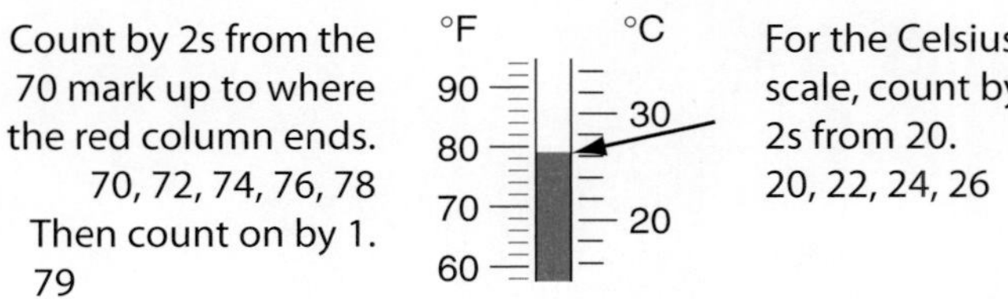

The temperature is 79°F and also 26°C.

Remember that each line on the scale on these thermometers is 2 degrees.

Write each temperature in °F and °C.

1. 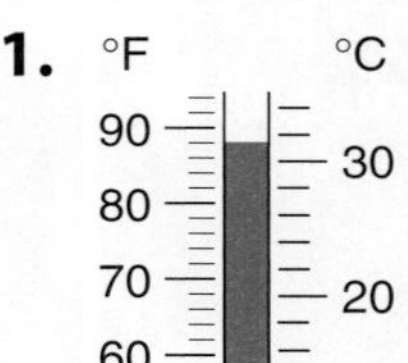

2. 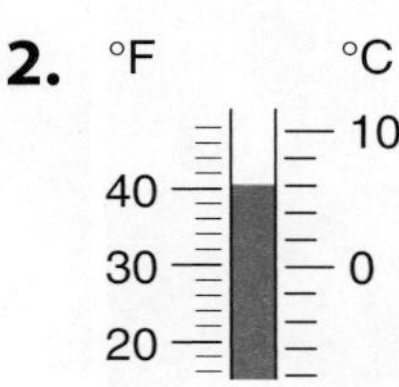

Set D, pages 422–423

Jay needs to arrive at soccer practice at 10:00 A.M. It takes him 30 minutes to walk to the field. It takes him 10 minutes to walk his dog and 10 minutes to get ready. What time should Jay start getting ready?

Draw a picture to show each change.

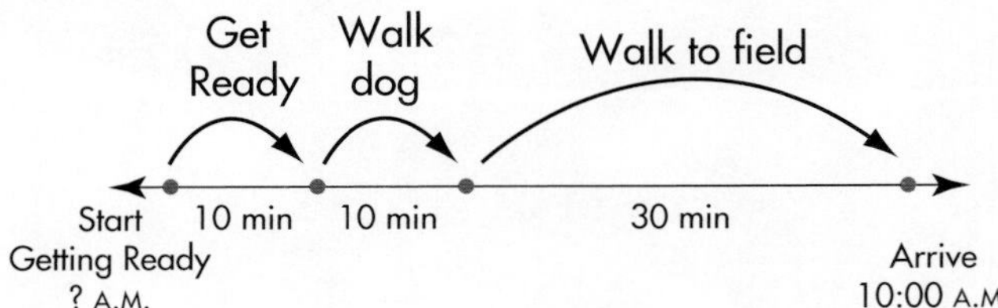

Work backward from the end using the opposite of each change.

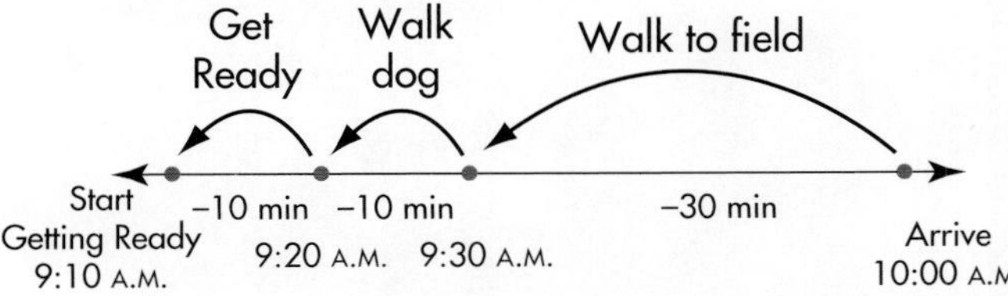

Jay should start getting ready at 9:10 A.M.

Remember to check your solution by working forward.

Solve each problem by drawing a picture and working backward.

1. Hal needs to meet Lou at 1:00 P.M. It takes him 10 minutes to walk to Lou's house, 10 minutes to get ready, and 20 minutes to eat lunch. What time should he start eating lunch?

2. Leeza's skating lesson is at 5:30 P.M. It takes her 15 minutes to walk to the skating rink, 15 minutes to get ready, and 30 minutes to do her homework. What time should she start doing her homework?

Topic 20

Data, Graphs, and Probability

1 How fast can a peregrine falcon fly? You will find out in Lesson 20-4.

2 Does Kyle Field have more seats than other college football stadiums in Texas? You will find out in Lesson 20-2.

3

If you put each of the letters in this sign in a bag and took one without looking, which letter are you most likely to get? You will find out in Lesson 20-5.

4

How many gold, silver, and bronze medals were won by the United States in the 2006 Winter Olympic Games? You will find out in Lesson 20-1.

Review What You Know!

Vocabulary

Choose the best term from the box.

- data
- less likely
- more likely
- tally

1. A graph can be used to compare _?_.
2. Elisa is at a library. It is _?_ that she will look at a book than eat lunch.
3. The time is 4 A.M. It is _?_ that you are playing soccer than sleeping.

Order Numbers

Write in order from least to greatest.

4. 56, 47, 93, 39, 10
5. 20, 43, 23, 19, 22
6. 24, 14, 54, 34, 4
7. 65, 33, 56, 87, 34

Skip Counting

Find the next two numbers in each pattern. Write the rule for the pattern.

8. 5, 10, 15, 20, ▢, ▢
9. 2, 4, 6, 8, ▢, ▢
10. 10, 20, 30, 40, ▢, ▢
11. 4, 8, 12, 16, ▢, ▢

Comparing

12. **Writing to Explain** Explain how to use place value to compare 326 and 345.

Lesson

20-1

TEKS 3.13A: Collect, organize, record, and display data in pictographs and bar graphs where each picture or cell might represent more than one piece of data.

Organizing Data

How can you collect and organize data?

A survey asked students, "What is your favorite after-school sport?"

Information you collect is called data. To take a survey, collect data by asking many people the same question.

Favorite After-School Sport		
Swimming	Swimming	Soccer
Softball	Soccer	Swimming
Softball	Softball	Softball
Soccer	Swimming	Softball
Softball	Soccer	Softball
Soccer	Softball	Soccer

Guided Practice*

Do you know HOW?

In **1–2**, use the survey data below.

Favorite Color			
Blue	Red	Blue	Blue
Red	Yellow	Red	Green
Blue	Red	Red	Red
Red	Red	Red	Blue

1. Make a tally chart for the data.

2. How many more students chose red than blue as their favorite color?

Do you UNDERSTAND?

In **3–5**, use the tally chart above.

3. What does the chart show?

4. How many students in all answered the survey?

5. Later, six more students answered the survey. Here are their answers.

Softball	Soccer	Softball
Swimming	Softball	Soccer

Make a new tally chart that includes their answers.

Independent Practice

For **6–9**, use the survey data at the right.

6. Make a tally chart for the data.

7. How many people answered the survey?

8. Which kinds of pet were the favorite of the same number of people?

9. Which pet was chosen most often?

Favorite Kind of Pet			
Cat	Cat	Dog	Hamster
Fish	Bird	Dog	Dog
Dog	Bird	Hamster	Bird
Dog	Cat	Bird	Fish
Cat	Dog	Dog	Cat
Bird	Cat	Dog	Dog

*For another example, see Set A on page 448.

Step 1

A tally chart is one way to record data. A tally mark is a mark used to record data on a tally chart.

Title the tally chart.
Label the columns.

Favorite After-School Sport

Sport	Tally	Number

Step 2

Make a tally mark for each answer given.

Favorite After-School Sport

Sport	Tally	Number
Soccer	𝍸 I	
Softball	𝍸 III	
Swimming	IIII	

Step 3

Count the tally marks. Record the number.

Favorite After-School Sport

Sport	Tally	Number
Soccer	𝍸 I	6
Softball	𝍸 III	8
Swimming	IIII	4

TAKS Problem Solving

For **10** and **11**, use the tally chart at the right.

Favorite Sport to Watch

Sport	Tally	Number
Football	𝍸 𝍸 I	
Baseball	𝍸 𝍸 𝍸 II	
Hockey		8
Basketball		15

10. Copy and complete the chart.

11. Write the sports in order from most to least favorite.

12. **Number Sense** What number is shown by 𝍸 𝍸 𝍸 𝍸 𝍸?

13. Make a tally chart to show how many times the letters *a*, *e*, *i*, *o*, and *u* are used in this exercise.

14. **Writing to Explain** How would you make a tally chart to show what kind of pizza your classmates like most?

15. **Reasoning** Dennis is 2 inches taller than Mica and 1 inch shorter than Rosa. Is Rosa shorter than Mica or taller than Mica? How much shorter or taller?

16. In the 2006 Winter Olympic Games, the United States won 9 gold medals, 9 silver medals, and 7 bronze medals. Which tally chart shows these results?

A

U.S. Medals

Medal	Tally
Gold	𝍸 III
Silver	𝍸 III
Bronze	𝍸 I

B

U.S. Medals

Medal	Tally
Gold	𝍸 IIII
Silver	𝍸 IIII
Bronze	𝍸 II

C

U.S. Medals

Medal	Tally
Gold	𝍸 𝍸 I
Silver	𝍸 𝍸 I
Bronze	𝍸 III

D

U.S. Medals

Medal	Tally
Gold	𝍸 𝍸 II
Silver	𝍸 𝍸 II
Bronze	𝍸 𝍸

Lesson
20-2

TEKS 3.13B: Interpret information from pictographs and bar graphs.

Reading Pictographs and Bar Graphs

How can you read graphs?

A pictograph uses pictures or symbols to show data.

Number of Hockey Teams in Each League

League	
East Falls	X X X /
North Falls	X X /
South Falls	X X
West Falls	X X X X X /

Each X = 2 teams. Each / = 1 team.

The key explains what each picture represents.

Another Example How can you read a bar graph?

A bar graph uses bars to compare information. This bar graph shows the number of goals scored by different players on a hockey team.

The scale shows the units used.

On this graph, every other grid line is labeled: 0, 2, 4, and so on. But each grid line represents one unit. For example, the line halfway between 4 and 6 represents 5 goals.

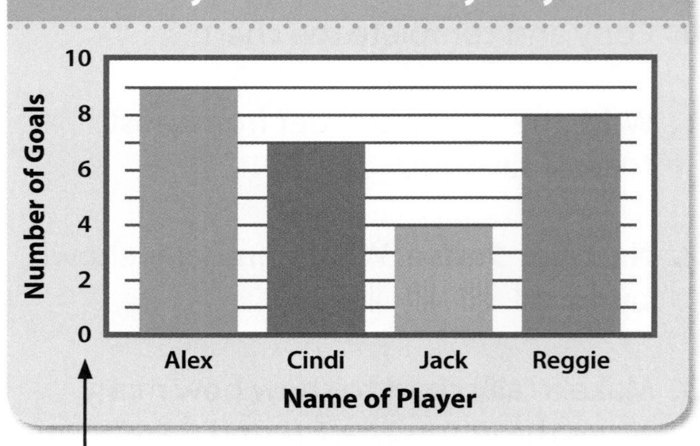

scale

How many goals did Cindi score?

Find Cindi's name. Use the scale to find how high the bar reaches. Cindi scored 7 goals.

Who scored the fewest goals? Which bar is shortest?

The bar for Jack is shortest. He scored the fewest goals.

Explain It

1. Explain how to find how many more goals Alex scored than Cindi.
2. Who scored 8 goals?
3. How many goals in all did Alex and Reggie score?

How many teams are in the East Falls League?

Use the key.

Each (two crossed sticks) represents 2 teams.

Each (one stick) represents 1 team.

There are 3 (two crossed sticks) and 1 (one stick).

$2 + 2 + 2 + 1 = 7$

There are 7 teams in the East Falls League.

How many more teams does the East Falls League have than the South Falls League?

Compare the two rows.

East Falls League

3 more teams

South Falls League

The East Falls League has 3 more teams than the South Falls League.

Guided Practice*

Do you know HOW?

1. Which hockey league in the pictograph above has 5 teams?

2. Which league has the most teams? How many teams are in that league?

Do you UNDERSTAND?

In **3** and **4**, use the pictograph above.

3. Explain how to find which league has the fewest teams.

4. How many teams in all are in the North Falls and West Falls Leagues?

Independent Practice

In **5–7**, use the pictograph at the right.

5. Which area has lights on for the most hours in a week?

6. Which area of the Tri-Town Sports Center has lights on for 50 hours each week?

7. In one week, how many more hours are lights on in the exercise room than in the swimming pool?

Tri-Town Sports Center
Number of Hours Lights Are on Each Week

Exercise Room	7 whole bulbs, 1 half bulb
Locker Room	9 whole bulbs
Swimming Pool	5 whole bulbs, 1 half bulb
Tennis Court	5 whole bulbs

Each (bulb) = 10 hours. Each (half bulb) = 5 hours.

DIGITAL Animated Glossary **www.pearsonsuccessnet.com**

For another example, see Set B on page 448.

TAKS Problem Solving

In **8–12**, use the bar graph at the right.

8. How fast can a jack rabbit run?

9. Which animal has the greatest top running speed?

10. Which animal has a top running speed of 50 miles per hour?

11. How much greater is the top running speed of a coyote than that of a grizzly bear?

12. Which animals have the same top running speed?

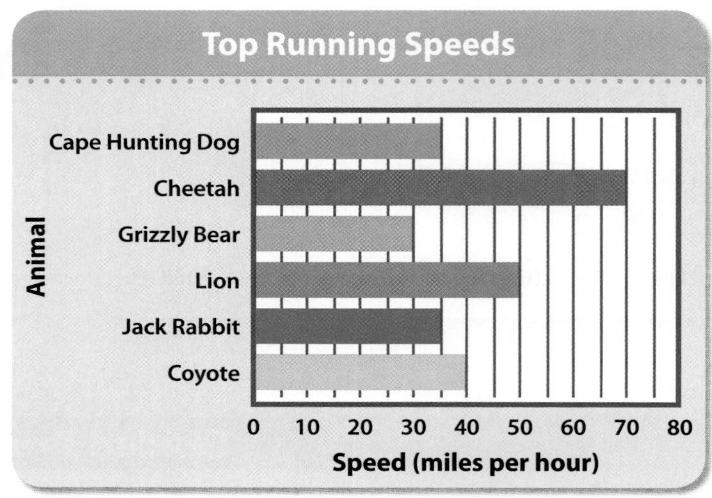

In **13–15**, use the pictograph.

13. To the nearest 10,000, how many seats are in Rice Stadium?

14. **Estimation** Which two stadiums have about the same number of seats?

15. **Writing to Explain** Maria says Floyd Casey Stadium has about 5,000 seats. Is she correct? Explain.

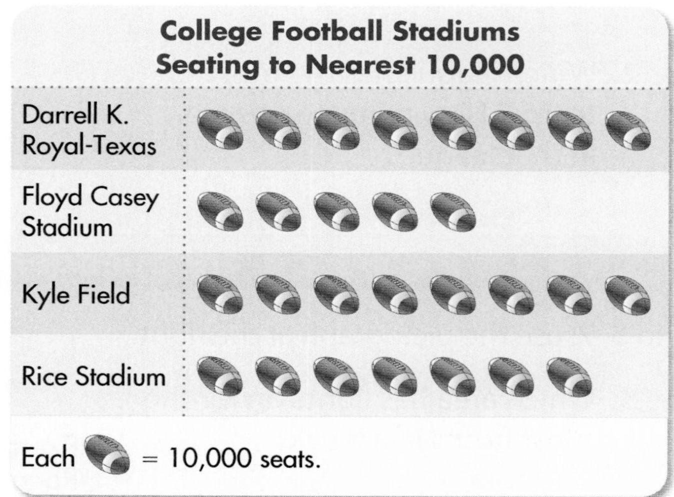

In **16** and **17**, use the bar graph.

16. How many more soccer balls than basketballs are in the gym closet?

A 8 **C** 4

B 5 **D** 3

17. How many balls in all are in the gym closet?

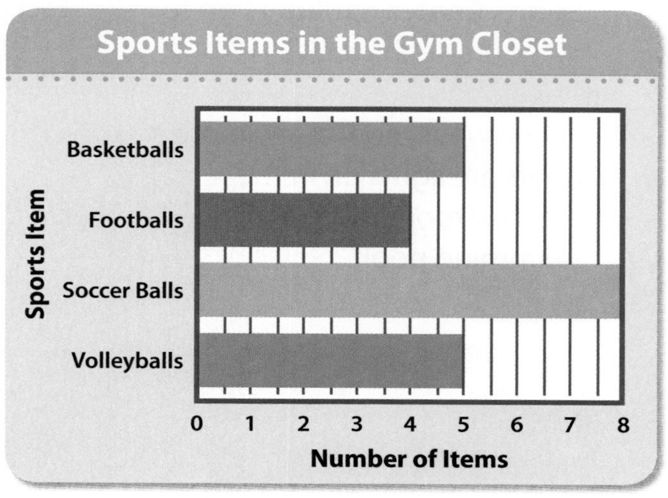

Mixed Problem Solving

The government where you live uses money from the taxes that people pay to provide different kinds of services. The bar graph at the right shows how much money different departments in Park Town receive. Use the graph to answer the questions.

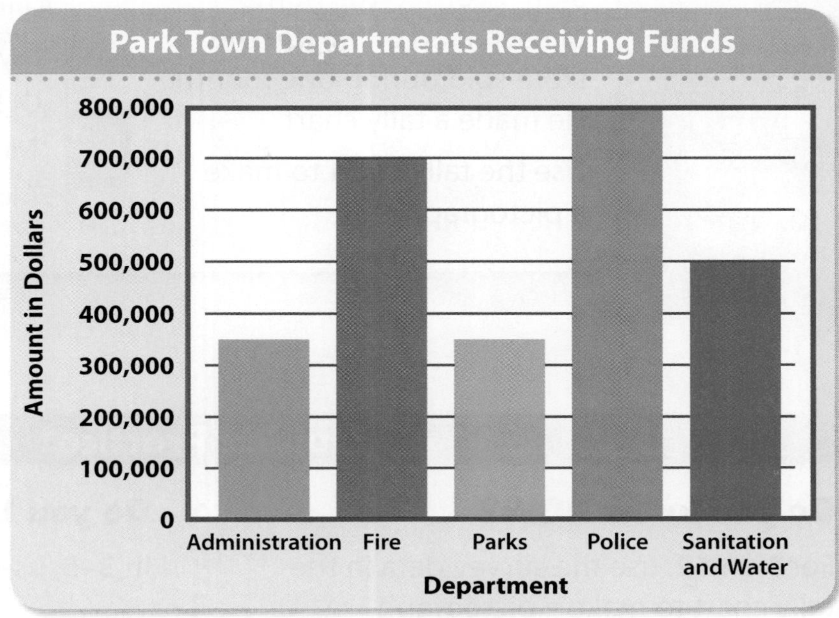

1. Which service in Park Town will receive the most funds?

2. Which two departments will get the same amount?

3. About how much money will the Parks Department and the Sanitation and Water Department receive in all?

4. How much more will the Police Department receive than the Fire Department?

5. Use the table below that shows how the Police Department money is used.

Data

Police Department

Expenses	Amount
Cars	$42,000
Computers	$14,000
Police Equipment	$88,000
Salaries	$643,000
Station Expenses	$13,000

Which expenses are less than $50,000?

6. **Strategy Focus** Solve. Use the strategy Write a Number Sentence.

The representatives voted on a state budget plan. Each representative has 1 vote. There were 86 votes for the plan and 34 votes against the plan. How many representatives voted in all?

Lesson
20-3

TEKS 3.13A: Collect, organize, record, and display data in pictographs and bar graphs where each picture or cell might represent more than one piece of data.

Making Pictographs

How do you make a pictograph?

Sam recorded the number of each kind of bicycle the store sold during one month. He made a tally chart.

Use the tally chart to make a pictograph.

Kind of Bicycle	Tally	Number
Boy's	卌 卌	10
Girl's	卌 卌 卌 卌	20
Training	卌 卌 卌	15
Tricycle	卌 卌	10

Guided Practice*

Do you know HOW?

For **1** and **2**, use the survey data in the tally chart to make a pictograph.

Which is your favorite school lunch?		
Lunch	**Tally**	**Number**
Taco	||	2
Pizza	卌 |||	8
Salad	|||	3
Sandwich	卌 |	6

1. What is the title? What is the symbol for the key? How many votes will each symbol stand for?

2. List the lunch choices. Draw the symbols to complete the graph.

Do you UNDERSTAND?

In **3–5**, use the pictograph above.

3. Explain the symbols that were used for the number of training bicycles that were sold.

4. How many symbols would be used for the training bicycles sold if the key was △ = 5 bicycles?

5. Suppose 25 mountain bicycles were also sold. Draw symbols to show a row in the graph for mountain bicycles.

Independent Practice

Goals Each Kickball Team Has Scored		
Team Name	**Tally**	**Number**
Cubs	卌 卌	10
Hawks	卌 卌 卌 卌	20
Lions	卌 卌 卌 卌 卌 卌	30
Roadrunners	卌 卌 卌	15

For **6** and **7**, use the chart.

6. Make a pictograph to show the data.

7. Explain how you decided the number of symbols to draw to show the goals for the Roadrunners.

*For another example, see Set B on page 448.

Write a title for the pictograph.

The title is Kinds of Bicycles Sold.

Choose a symbol for the key. Decide what each symbol and half-symbol will represent.

Each △ means 10 bicycles.

Each ◿ means 5 bicycles.

Set up the graph and list the kinds of bicycles. Decide how many symbols you need for each number sold. Draw the symbols.

Kinds of Bicycles Sold	
Boy's	△
Girl's	△ △
Training	△ ◿
Tricycle	△

Each △ = 10 bicycles.
Each ◿ = 5 bicycles.

TAKS Problem Solving

Ed made a tally chart of the items he picked from the plants in his garden.

8. Make a pictograph to show the data in Ed's chart. Write a title and the key.

9. How many green peppers and red peppers did Ed pick in all?

Data

Vegetables from Garden		
Kind	**Tally**	**Number of Items**
Green Pepper	||||	4
Red Pepper	||	2
Tomato	~~||||~~	5

10. Geometry Ed's garden has a square shape. Each side is 9 feet long. What is the area of Ed's garden?

In **11** and **12**, suppose you are going to make a pictograph to show Simon's Book Shop data.

11. Choose a symbol to stand for 5 books sold. Draw the row for fiction books sold.

12. Reasoning Why is 5 a good number to use in the key?

Data

Simon's Book Shop	
Kind of Book	**Number Sold**
Fiction	25
Nonfiction	40
Poetry	20
Dictionary	15

Plants Sold at Garden Shop	
April	🌱 🌱 🌱 🌱 🌱
May	🌱 🌱 🌱 🌱 🌱 🌱
June	

Each 🌱 = 5 plants

13. Marisol is making a pictograph to show plant sales. There were 35 plants sold in June. How many symbols should Marisol draw for June?

A 5 **B** 7 **C** 11 **D** 35

Lesson
20-4

TEKS 3.13A: Collect, organize, record, and display data in pictographs and bar graphs where each picture or cell might represent more than one piece of data.

Making Bar Graphs

Hands-On
grid paper

How do you make a bar graph?

Greg made a table to show the amount of money he saved each month.

Use the data in the table to make a bar graph on grid paper. A bar graph can make it easy to compare data.

Data

Month	Amount Saved
January	$25
February	$50
March	$65
April	$40

Guided Practice*

Do you know HOW?

Use the chart to make a bar graph.

Data

Class	Tally	Number of People Signed Up
Chess	𝍸		6
Guitar	𝍸 𝍸	10
Painting	𝍸 ||	7
Writing	𝍸 ||||	9

1. Write a title. Choose the scale. What does each grid line represent?

2. Set up the graph with the scale, each class, and labels. Draw each bar.

Do you UNDERSTAND?

In **3–5**, use the bar graph above.

3. In the bar graph above, explain why the bar for January ends between 20 and 30.

4. In which month did Greg save the most money?

5. Suppose Greg saved $35 in May. Between which grid lines would the bar for May end?

Independent Practice

In **6** and **7**, use the chart.

Data

Favorite Store for Clothes		
Store	**Tally**	**Number of Votes**
Deal Mart	𝍸 𝍸 𝍸	15
Jane's	𝍸 𝍸 𝍸 𝍸 𝍸 𝍸	30
Parker's	𝍸 𝍸 𝍸 𝍸	20
Trends	𝍸	5

6. Make a bar graph to show the data.

7. Explain how to use the bar graph to find the store that received the most votes.

*For another example, see Set C on page 449.

Write a title.

The title of this bar graph is Amount Greg Saved Each Month.

Choose the scale. Decide how many units each grid line will represent.

Each grid line will represent $10.

Set up the graph with the scale, each month listed in the table, and labels. Draw a bar for each month.

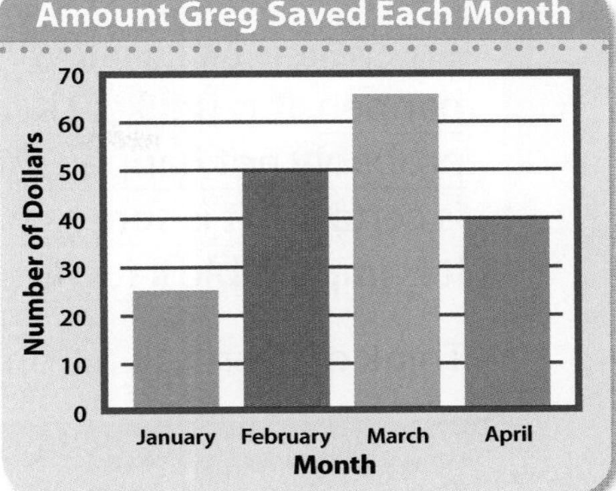

TAKS Problem Solving

For **8** and **9**, use the table at the right.

8. Make a bar graph. Write a title. Choose the scale. Draw bars that go across.

Data

Which kind of movie is your favorite?

Kind of Movie	Adventure	Cartoon	Comedy	Science Fiction
Number of Votes	16	8	10	7

9. **Number Sense** Which two kinds of movies received about the same number of votes?

10. **Strategy Focus** Solve. Use the strategy Draw a Picture.

Each movie ticket costs $8. What is the total cost of tickets for a family of 6 people?

In **11** and **12**, suppose you are going to make a bar graph to show the data in the table.

11. **Writing to Explain** What scale would you choose? Explain.

12. Which would be the longest bar?

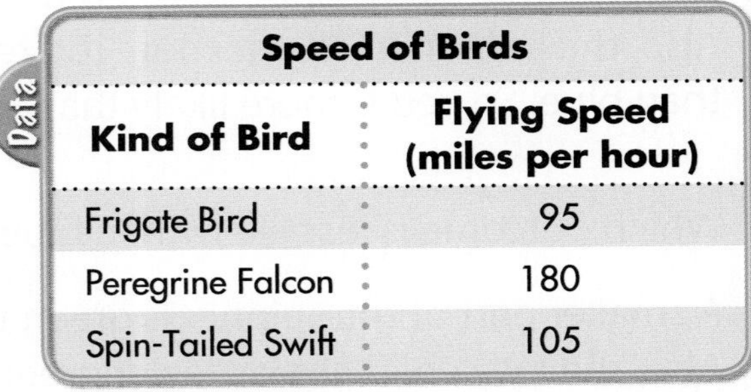

Data

Speed of Birds

Kind of Bird	Flying Speed (miles per hour)
Frigate Bird	95
Peregrine Falcon	180
Spin-Tailed Swift	105

13. Luz made the graph to show how many friends wore each color of shoe. Which information does Luz need to complete the graph?

A How many friends wore black shoes

B The color of shoes with the longest bar

C The color of shoes worn by exactly 8 friends

D The color of shoes worn by exactly 7 friends

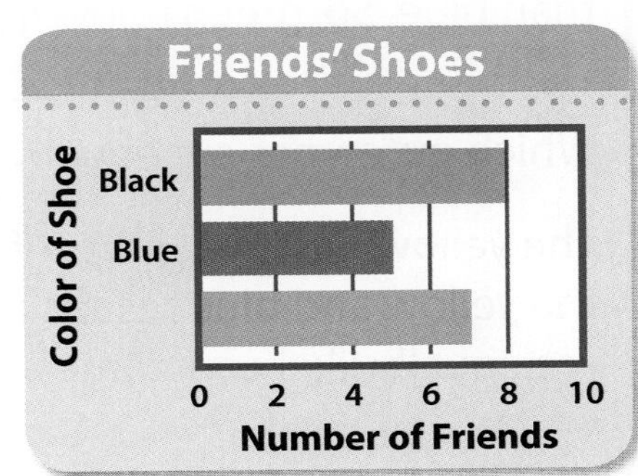

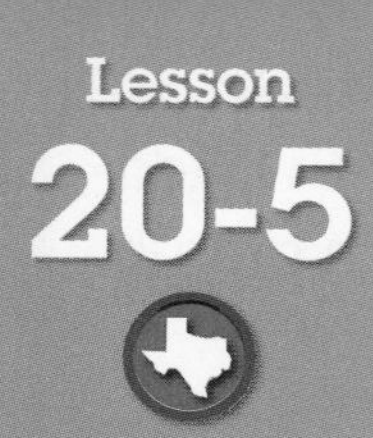

Lesson
20-5

TEKS 3.13C: Use data to describe events as more likely than, less likely than, or equally likely as.

How Likely?

Will an event happen?

An event is likely if it will probably happen. It is unlikely if it will probably not happen. An event is certain if it is sure to happen. It is impossible if it will never happen.

Think of events in a tropical rainforest.

Certain event: seeing green plants

Impossible event: seeing a polar bear

Likely event: seeing colorful birds

Unlikely event: seeing dry soil

Other Examples

How can you compare chances?

Outcomes with the same chance of happening are equally likely.

Sometimes you compare two outcomes.
The outcome with a greater chance of happening is more likely.
The outcome with the lesser chance of happening is less likely.

The tally chart shows the results of 48 spins of the spinner above.

Which outcome is more likely than blue?

A bigger part of the spinner is red than blue. Also, the tally chart shows more red results than blue. So, red is more likely than blue.

Data

Spin Results

Outcome	Tally	Number
Red	𝍸 𝍸 𝍸 ||||	19
Yellow	𝍸 𝍸 |||	13
Green	𝍸	5
Blue	𝍸 𝍸 |	11

Which outcome is less likely than blue?

A smaller part of the spinner is green than blue. Also, the tally chart shows fewer green results than blue. So, green is less likely than blue.

Which outcomes are equally likely?

The yellow and blue parts of the spinner are the same size. Also, the yellow and blue results are nearly equal. So, yellow and blue are equally likely outcomes.

A possible result of a game or experiment is called an outcome.

What are the outcomes of spinning this spinner?

When you spin the spinner, the outcome might be blue, red, yellow, green, or a line.

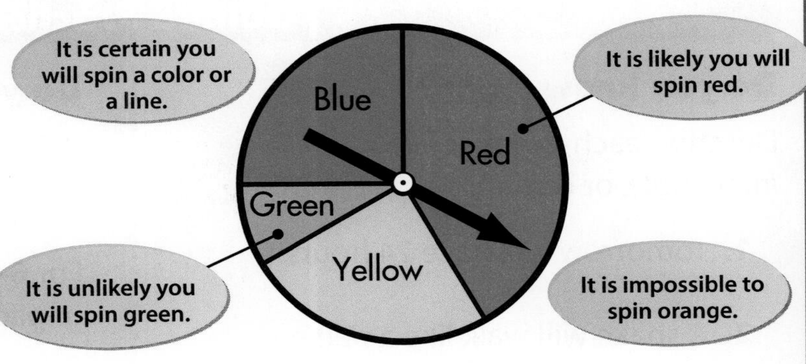

Another Example

Look at the spinner at the right. Which tally chart shows the most likely results of 25 spins?

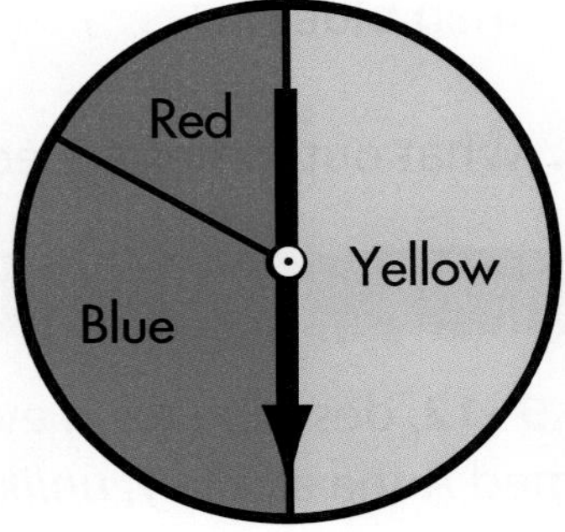

A

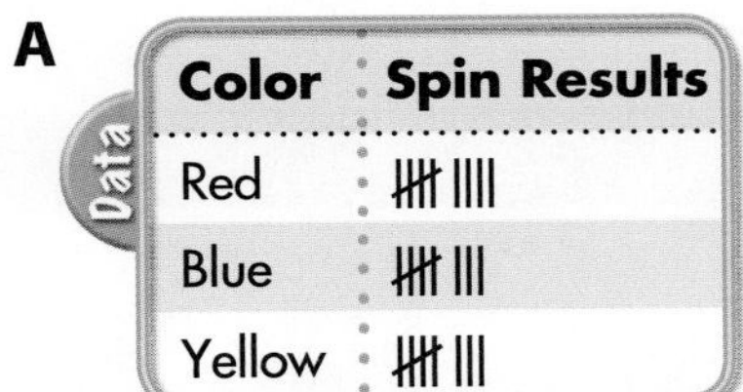

Color	Spin Results
Red	𝍸 ||||
Blue	𝍸 |||
Yellow	𝍸 |||

C

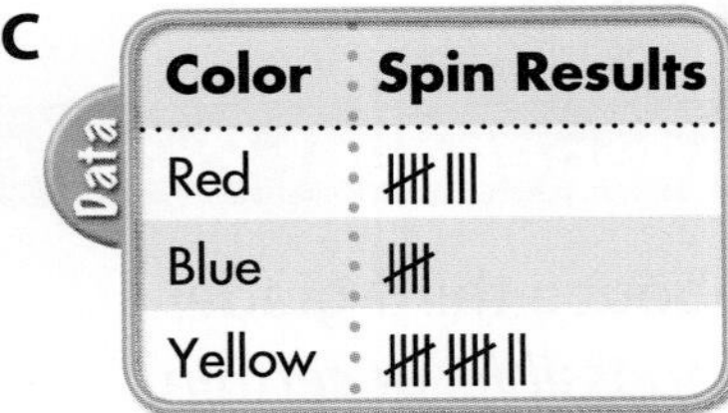

Color	Spin Results
Red	𝍸 |||
Blue	𝍸
Yellow	𝍸 𝍸 ||

B

Color	Spin Results
Red	𝍸
Blue	𝍸 ||||
Yellow	𝍸 𝍸 |

D

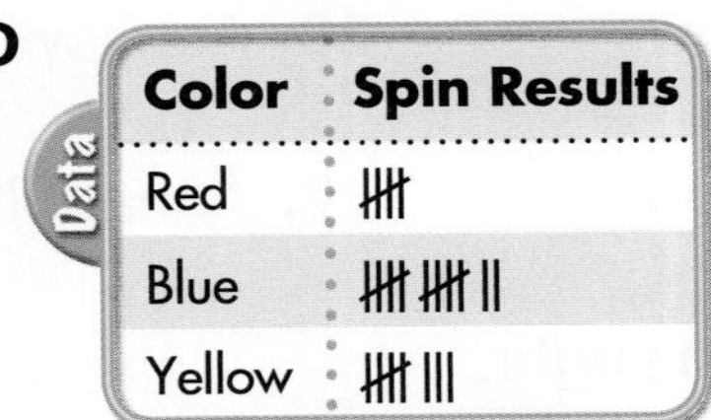

Color	Spin Results
Red	𝍸
Blue	𝍸 𝍸 ||
Yellow	𝍸 |||

Red is the smallest part of the spinner, so red should have the fewest tally marks. So, **A** and **C** are not good choices.

Look at choices **B** and **D**. The yellow part of the spinner is bigger than the blue part, so yellow should have more tally marks than blue. So, **D** is not a good choice.

Choice **B** shows the most likely results of 25 spins.

Explain It

1. Suppose a tally chart shows spin results. How can you tell if one part of the spinner is much larger than the others?

Guided Practice*

Do you know HOW?

Describe each event as *likely*, *unlikely*, *impossible*, or *certain*.

1. Tomorrow will have 24 hours.

2. A snake will walk like a person.

There are 6 white counters, 12 black counters, 2 red counters, and 6 blue counters in a bag. You take one counter from the bag without looking.

3. What outcome is more likely than blue?

4. What outcomes are equally likely?

Do you UNDERSTAND?

5. What is the difference between a certain event and a likely event?

For **6–8**, use the spinner at the top of page 441.

6. Which outcome is less likely than yellow?

7. Is purple a more likely or less likely outcome than blue?

8. Which outcome is more likely than yellow?

Independent Practice

For **9–12**, describe each event about a third-grader named Anna as *likely*, *unlikely*, *impossible*, or *certain*.

9. Anna will need food to grow.

10. Anna will grow to be 100 feet tall.

11. Anna will travel to the moon.

12. Anna will watch television tonight.

For **13–17**, use the spinner at the right.

13. What outcome is less likely than yellow?

14. What outcomes are equally likely?

15. What outcome is most likely?

16. Name an outcome that is certain.

17. Name an outcome that is impossible.

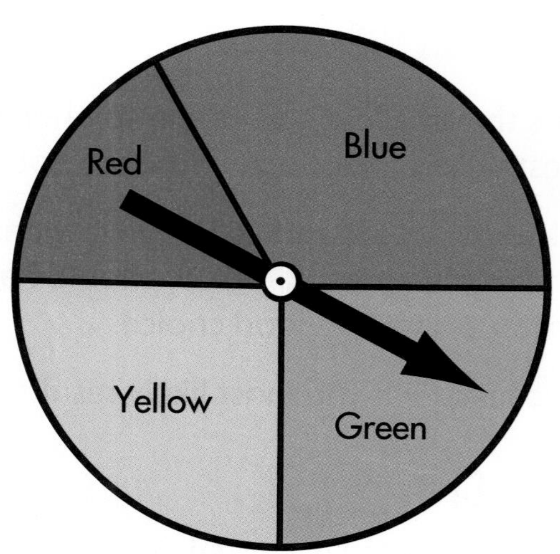

*For another example, see Set D on page 449.

TAKS Problem Solving

18. Suppose that each of the letters in the word *GRILL* is placed in a bag. You draw one letter from the bag without looking. What outcome is more likely than the others?

19. Writing to Explain How can you tell by looking at a spinner that one outcome is more likely than another outcome?

20. There are 4 medium boxes inside a large box. Inside each medium box, there are 3 small boxes. How many boxes are there in all?

21. Look at the spinner at the right. Which tally chart shows the most likely results of 30 spins?

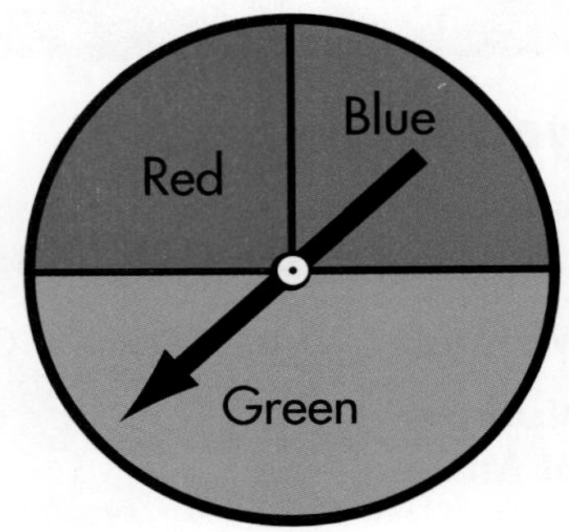

A

Color	Spin Results
Red	卌 IIII
Blue	卌 II
Green	卌 卌 IIII

C

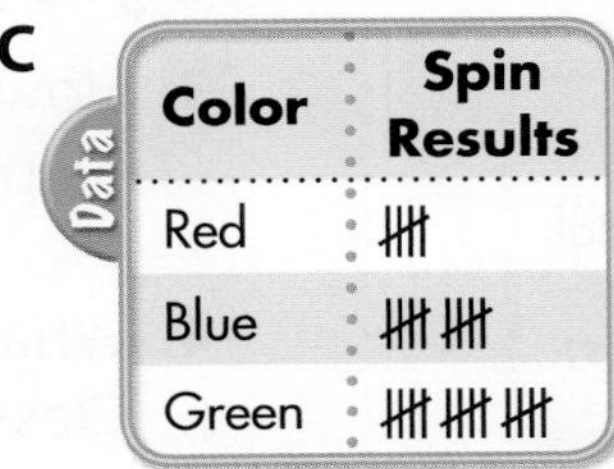

Color	Spin Results
Red	卌
Blue	卌 卌
Green	卌 卌 卌

B

Color	Spin Results
Red	卌 卌
Blue	卌 卌
Green	卌 卌

D

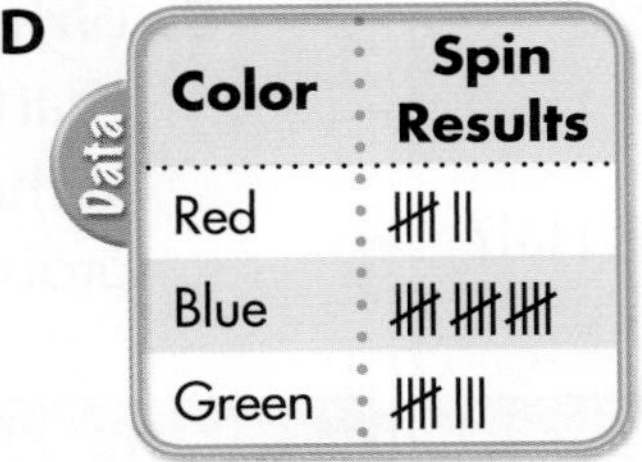

Color	Spin Results
Red	卌 II
Blue	卌 卌 卌
Green	卌 III

In **22** and **23**, use the table that shows the number of paper clips of each color in a box. Suppose Mary takes 1 paper clip out of the box without looking.

Paper Clip Colors

Color	Number in Box
Green	27
Red	38
Yellow	21
Blue	27

22. Which colors does she have an equally likely chance of taking?

F Green and red

G Red and blue

H Green and blue

J Red and yellow

23. Which of the four colors is she least likely to choose?

Lesson
20-6

TEKS 3.14C: Select or develop an appropriate problem-solving strategy including drawing a picture, looking for a pattern, systematic guessing and checking, acting it out, making a table, working a simpler problem, and working backwards to solve a problem.

Problem Solving

Use Tables and Graphs to Draw Conclusions

The tally chart shows data about the favorite hobbies of two Grade 3 classes. Compare the hobbies of the two classes.

Data

Favorite Hobbies

	Class A		Class B	
Hobby	**Tally**	**Number**	**Tally**	**Number**
Model Building	|||	3	~~||||~~	5
Drawing	~~||||~~ ~~||||~~ ||	12	~~||||~~ ||	7
Rock Collecting	||||	4	||||	4
Reading	~~||||~~		6	~~||||~~ ||||	9

Guided Practice*

Do you know HOW?

Data

Bicycle Club Miles

Member	Victor	Rosita	Gary	Hal
Number of Miles	20	35	30	20

1. Which club member rode exactly 10 miles more than Hal?

2. Who rode the same distance as Hal?

Do you UNDERSTAND?

3. How do the bars on a bar graph help you to compare data?

4. What is the favorite hobby of Class A? of Class B?

5. **Write a Problem** Use the tally charts or graphs above or the table at the left to write a comparison problem. Then solve the problem.

Independent Practice

For **6** and **7**, use the pictograph.

T-Shirt Sales

	Store A	Store B
Blue	[shirt] [shirt] [half shirt]	[shirt]
Red	[shirt] [shirt]	[shirt] [shirt] [half shirt]
Green	[half shirt]	[half shirt]

Each [shirt] = 10 T-shirts. Each [half shirt] = 5 T-shirts.

6. What color was sold most often at each store? equally at both stores?

7. Where was blue sold more often?

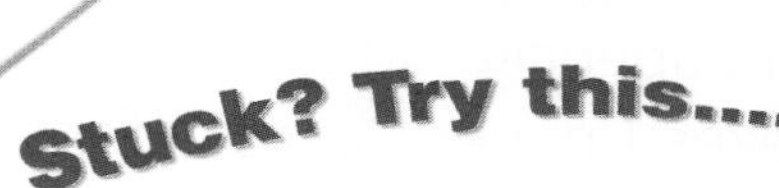

- What do I know?
- What am I asked to find?
- What diagram can I use to help understand the problem?
- Can I use addition, subtraction, multiplication, or division?
- Is all of my work correct?
- Did I answer the right question?
- Is my answer reasonable?

*For another example, see Set C on page 449.

Plan

Make a bar graph for each class.

Favorite Hobbies of Class A

Hobby: Model Building, Drawing, Rock Collecting, Reading

0 2 4 6 8 10 12 14

Number of Students

Favorite Hobbies of Class B

Hobby: Model Building, Drawing, Rock Collecting, Reading

0 2 4 6 8 10 12 14

Number of Students

Solve

Now read the graphs and make comparisons.

- More students in Class B like model building than in Class A.
- The same number of students in each class like rock collecting.

For **8–10**, use the bar graph at the right.

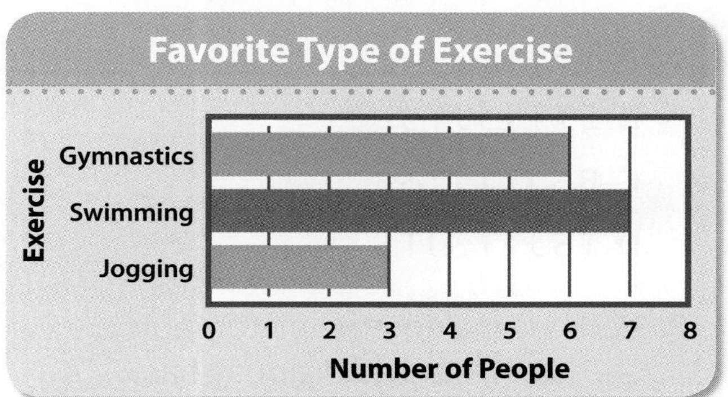

8. How many people in all voted for their favorite type of exercise?

9. How many more people voted for gymnastics than for jogging?

10. **Write a Problem** Write and solve a word problem different from Exercises 8 and 9.

For **11–13**, use the tally chart.

Data

Books Read by Reading Club Members

Member	Number of Books Read
Daryl	卌 卌 卌 |||
Alice	卌 卌 卌 |
Sandra	卌 |||
Helmer	卌 卌 ||||

11. Make a graph to show the data. Choose a pictograph or a bar graph.

12. Who read exactly ten more books than Sandra?

13. Write the members in order from most to fewest books read.

14. **Strategy Focus** Solve. Use the strategy Make a Table.

At the farmer's market, Matt gives 2 free apples for every 6 apples you buy. If you buy 24 apples, how many free apples will you get?

15. **Write to Explain** What kinds of comparisons can you make when you look at a bar graph or a pictograph?

1. Trudy took a survey and made the tally chart shown. Which set of data matches the tally chart? (20-1)

First Initials

Initial	Tally
J	||
S	|||
T	||||

A T S J T T S J

B S T T J S J T S

C B S J T T J T S

D T S J T T S J T S

2. Pedro is making the pictograph shown. He knows Uruguay has 50 people for each square mile.

People for Each Square Mile

Chad	🚶 🚶
United States	🚶 🚶 🚶 🚶 🚶 🚶 🚶 🚶
Uruguay	

Each 🚶 = 10 people

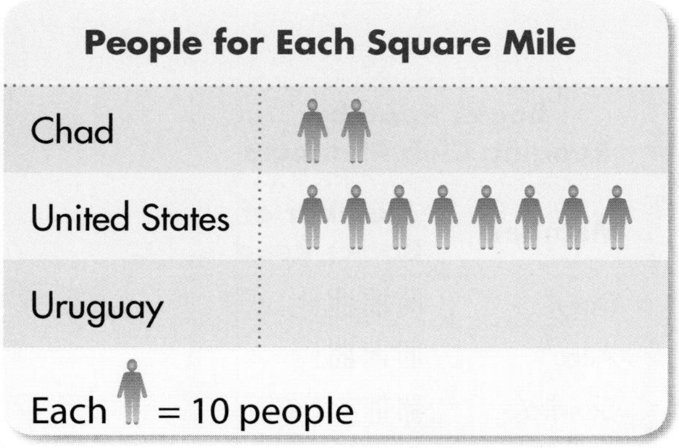

How many symbols should Pedro draw for Uruguay? (20-3)

F 5

G 10

H 25

J 50

Use the tally chart below for **3–5**. Suppose you are making a bar graph to show this data.

Favorite Planet

Planet	Tally
Mars	卌 |||
Saturn	卌 |
Venus	卌 ||||
Jupiter	||||

3. How many bars will you draw on the graph? (20-4)

A 3

B 4

C 2

D 5

4. Which planet will have the tallest bar on the graph? (20-4)

F Mars

G Saturn

H Venus

J Jupiter

5. Suppose each tally mark stands for 1 vote on a paper ballot. If you pick 1 ballot without looking, which planet are you least likely to pick? (20-5)

A Jupiter

B Venus

C Saturn

D Mars

6. Which statement is true about the data in the graphs? (20-6)

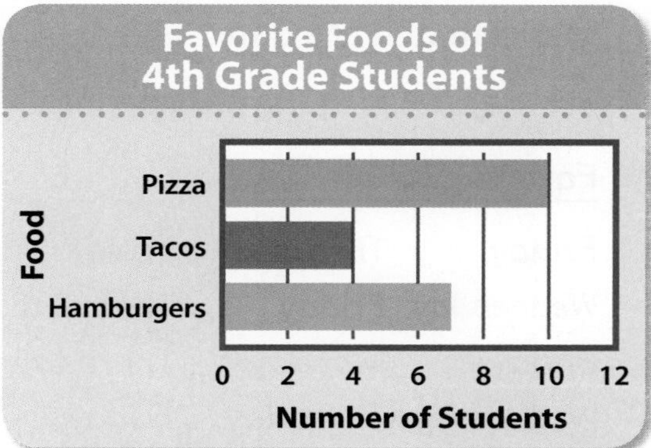

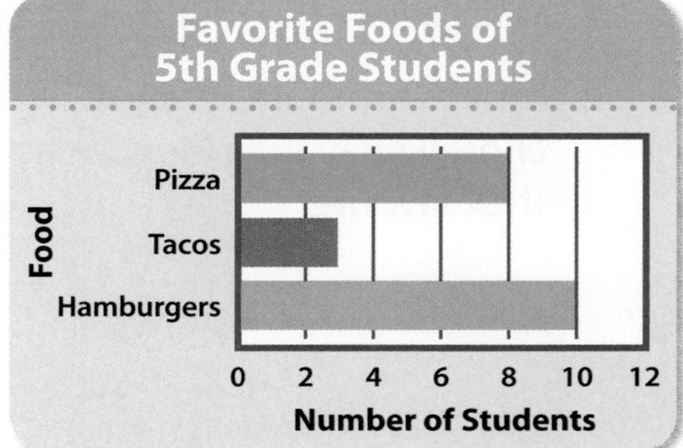

F Pizza is the favorite in both grades.

G The same number of students in both grades like tacos.

H More students in grade 4 than in grade 5 like hamburgers.

J More students in grade 4 than in grade 5 like pizza.

7. At the fair, the fish pond has 15 red fish, 9 blue fish, 10 yellow fish, and 5 orange fish. If Tammy hooks a fish without looking, what color fish is she most likely to get? (20-5)

A Blue

B Orange

C Red

D Yellow

8. Each member of Mrs. Lin's class voted on paper for the city they would most like to visit. There were 6 votes for Orlando, 8 for Dallas, 6 for New York, and 4 for Chicago. If Mrs. Lin picks a paper vote without looking, which two cities is she equally likely to pick? (20-5)

F Dallas and Chicago

G Orlando and New York

H Dallas and New York

J Orlando and Dallas

Ms Ortiz had her students take a survey of their favorite national park. The results are shown in the pictograph below. Use the graph for **9** and **10**.

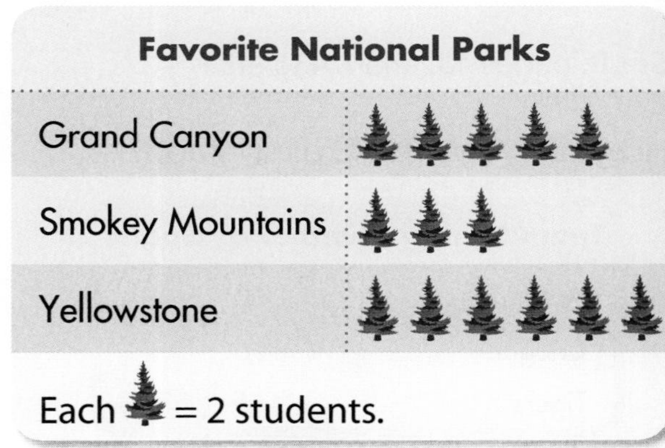

9. Griddable Response How many students chose Yellowstone as their favorite national park? (20-2)

10. Griddable Response How many students in all gave their answer to the survey question? (20-2)

Reteaching

Set A, pages 430–431

What is the favorite season of these students?

Favorite Season

Summer	Spring	Fall	Summer
Spring	Summer	Winter	Fall
Summer	Spring	Winter	Summer

Make a tally chart.

Choose a title and label the columns.

Favorite Season		
Season	Tally	Number
Fall	||	2
Spring	|||	3
Summer	𝍸	5
Winter	||	2

Make a tally mark for each answer students gave.

Count the tally marks and record the number. Summer received the most votes.

Remember to check your work. Make sure your tally marks match the data.

For **1** and **2**, use the survey data.

Favorite School Day

Friday	Tuesday	Friday
Wednesday	Friday	Thursday
Friday	Monday	Thursday
Wednesday	Thursday	Friday

1. Make a tally chart for the data.
2. How many more students chose Friday than Monday as their favorite?

Set B, pages 432–434, 436–437

How can you make a pictograph?

Team Name	Number of Goals
Aces	10
Cougars	15
Tigers	5

Study the numbers in the data. Choose a key.

Each ◇ represents 10 goals. Each ◁ represents 5 goals.

Team Name	Number of Goals
Aces	◇
Cougars	◇ ◁
Tigers	◁

Remember that if a symbol stands for more than 1 item, half of that symbol stands for half as many items.

Use the table below.

Which color do you like best?	
Color	Number of Votes
Blue	20
Green	10
Red	15
Yellow	5

1. Choose a key and make a pictograph to show the data.

Set C, pages 438–439, 444–445

How can you make a bar graph to help you draw conclusions?

Data

Month	Amount Saved
January	$20
February	$35
March	$30
April	$15

Use the data to choose a scale.

Choose 10 for the scale. Amounts with a 5 in the ones place will be halfway between 2 grid lines.

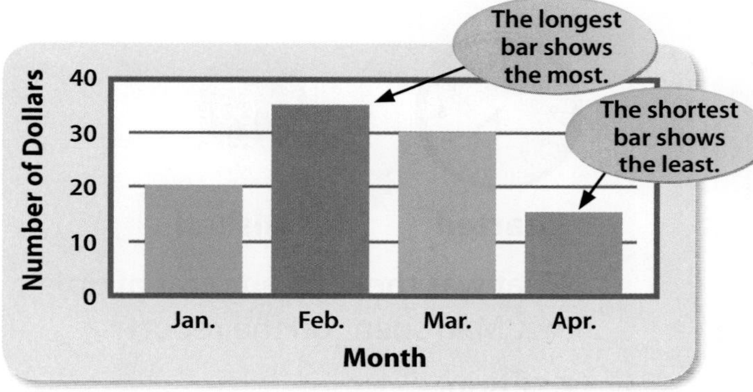

Remember that you can draw conclusions by comparing the length of the bars.

Use the table below.

Data

Pennies Saved		
Day	**Tally**	**Number**
Monday	𝍸𝍸𝍸𝍸𝍸	25
Tuesday	𝍸𝍸𝍸𝍸	20
Wednesday	𝍸𝍸𝍸	15
Thursday	𝍸𝍸	10

1. Choose a scale and make a bar graph to show the data.
2. Explain how the bar graph shows the day the fewest pennies were saved.
3. Suppose the bar for Friday is as long as the bar for Tuesday. What conclusion can you draw about how many pennies were saved on Friday?

Set D, pages 440–443

When you spin this spinner, what outcome is likely? unlikely? impossible? certain?

It is likely you will spin 1.

It is unlikely you will spin 3.

It is impossible to spin 5.

It is certain you will spin a number or a line.

Remember that you are deciding what will probably happen.

For **1** and **2**, use this spinner.

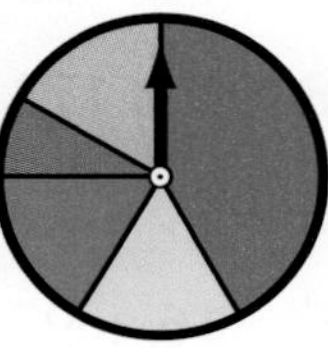

1. What outcome is likely?
2. What outcome is unlikely?

Topics 1–20

Spiral Review

Number and Operations

1. Which is the word form of 260,417?

   A Two hundred sixty thousand, six hundred, four seventeen

   B Twenty-six thousand, four hundred seventeen

   C Two hundred sixty thousand, four hundred seventy

   D Two hundred sixty thousand, four hundred seventeen

2. At 12:00, 115 people arrived at the fair. At 1:00, 207 more people arrived. At 2:00, 138 more people arrived. Which describes how many people arrived from 12:00 to 2:00?

   F $115 + 207 = \square$

   G $115 + 138 = \square$

   H $115 + 207 + 138 = \square$

   J $115 + 200 + 138 = \square$

3. Of the 316 letters Jack mailed, 95 were going to Midtown and 173 were going to Riverton. The rest were going to another state. Which number sentence shows one way to find the number of letters going to another state?

   A $316 - 95 - 173 = \square$

   B $95 \times 173 - 316 = \square$

   C $95 \times 173 \div 316 = \square$

   D $316 + 95 \div 173 = \square$

4. **Writing to Explain** Wilma has cut 2 oranges into 8 slices each. She and 3 friends eat 7 slices. Explain how to find how many slices are left.

Geometry and Measurement

5. How many faces does a cube have?

   F 4 **G** 6 **H** 8 **J** 12

6. Cal read the thermometer outside his window. What was the temperature?

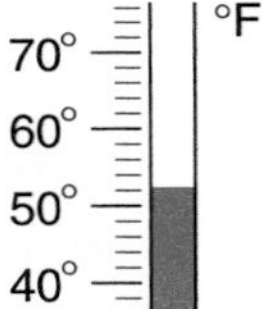

   A 54°F **C** 51°F

   B 52°F **D** 50°F

7. Mari wrote a report in one afternoon. The clocks show the time she started and finished.

Started

Finished

   What was the total amount of time that Mari spent on the report?

   F 1 hour

   G 1 hour 30 minutes

   H 2 hours

   J 2 hours 30 minutes

8. What is the area of the shaded part of the figure?

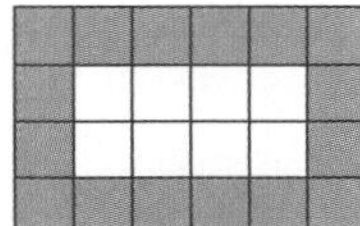

=1 square foot

9. **Writing to Explain** Explain why 1 gallon is not a good estimate for the capacity of a juice box. About how much is the capacity?

Topics 1–20

Spiral Review

Probability and Statistics

For **10** and **11**, use Ed's bar graph below.

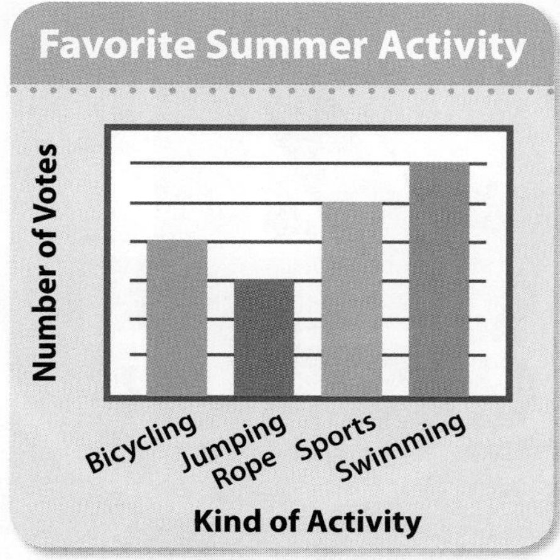

10. What should Ed do to finish the graph?

A Draw a bar for bicycling.

B Draw a bar for swimming.

C Label the bar that shows 15.

D Write numbers on the scale.

11. Which activity got the most votes?

F Bicycling **H** Sports

G Jumping rope **J** Swimming

12. Ina is making a pictograph titled "Visitors to the Art Show." She knows Week 3 had 50 visitors. How many symbols should she draw for Week 3 if each symbol stands for 10 visitors?

13. Writing to Explain Draw a spinner that fits these spin results: Blue 𝍸; Red 𝍸𝍸𝍸. Explain how you decided which part should be larger.

Algebraic Thinking

14. Carmen counted the corners on triangles in groups of 3. Which lists numbers she could have named?

A 3, 6, 18, 29 **C** 6, 9, 12, 15

B 3, 12, 24, 35 **D** 12, 18, 21, 26

15. The chart shows how many chairs there are for each number of tables.

Number of Tables	1	2	3	4
Number of Chairs	4	8	12	16

Which describes the pattern?

F Multiply the number of tables by 4.

G Multiply the number of tables by 2.

H Add 4 to the number of tables.

J Add 3 to the number of tables.

16. Copy and complete. Write $<$, $>$, or $=$.
$27 \times 3 \bigcirc 21 \div 3$

17. Copy and complete. Write the number that makes the number sentence true.
$12 \times 7 = \square \times 12$

18. Writing to Explain Ned and Sal spent the same amount. Ned bought two ties for $3 each. Then he bought a hat. Sal bought a hat for $6 and two ties for $3 each. How much was Ned's hat? Explain.

Step Up to Grade 4

Step-Up Lesson 1

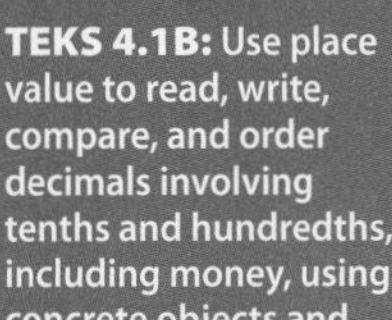

TEKS 4.1B: Use place value to read, write, compare, and order decimals involving tenths and hundredths, including money, using concrete objects and pictorial models.

Decimal Place Value

What are some ways to represent decimals?

A squirrel can weigh 1.64 pounds. There are different ways to represent 1.64.

Guided Practice

Do you know HOW?

For **1** and **2**, write the expanded form for each number.

1. 4.52 **2.** 2.39

In **3** and **4**, draw and shade a grid for each number. Then, write the word form for each number.

3. 2.07 **4.** 1.63

Do you UNDERSTAND?

5. In Exercise 1, what digit is in the tenths place? in the hundredths place?

6. Near the end of a basketball game, there are 5.81 seconds left on the clock. How would the referee say this number?

When you read a number or write a number in word form, replace the decimal point with the word and.

Independent Practice

In **7** through **9**, write the decimal for each shaded part.

7. 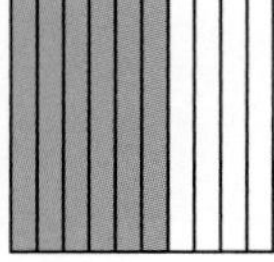

8. 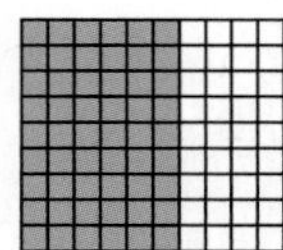

9. 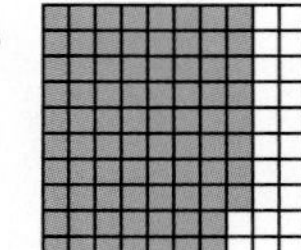

In **10** through **12**, write the number in standard form.

10. eight and twenty-nine hundredths **11.** 9 + 0.4 + 0.08 **12.** 3 + 0.01

One Way

Use a decimal model.

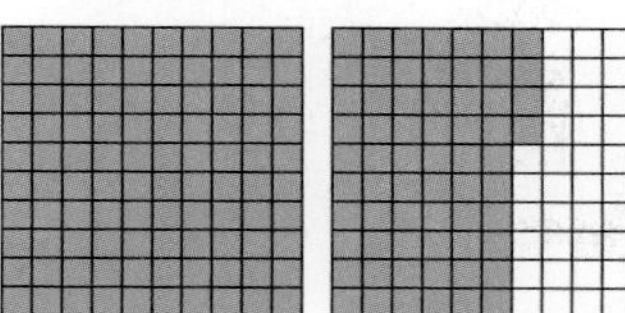

Expanded form: 1 + 0.6 + 0.04
Standard form: 1.64
Word form: one and sixty-four hundredths

Another Way

Use a place-value model.

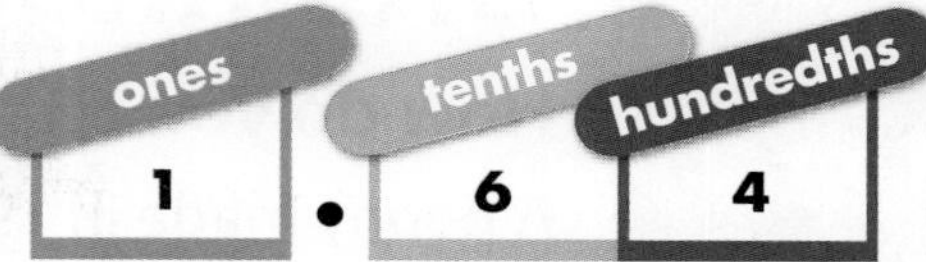

Expanded form: 1 + 0.6 + 0.04
Standard form: 1.64
Word form: one and sixty-four hundredths

In **13** through **17**, write the number in word form and give the value of the red digit for each number.

13. 3.21 **14.** 7.58 **15.** 41.89 **16.** 8.03 **17.** 17.45

In **18** through **22**, write each number in expanded form.

18. 6.74 **19.** 17.99 **20.** 4.05 **21.** 0.23 **22.** 45.1

TAKS Problem Solving

23. Reasoning Write a number that has a 3 in the tens place and a 7 in the hundredths place.

24. Mrs. Frank has 7 gallons of gas in her car. Her car can hold 15 gallons in its gas tank. Will Mrs. Frank need more or less than 10 gallons to fill her tank?

25. Luz wrote this amount:
Three dollars and four cents.

a What is the decimal word form for this amount?

b What is the decimal number?

26. Number Sense Write three numbers between 6.1 and 6.2.

Use hundredths grids or money to help.

27. Writing to Explain Use the decimal model below to explain why 0.07 is less than 0.1.

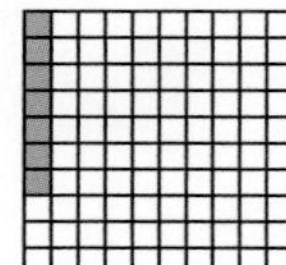

28. What is the value of the 8 in 29.83?

A eight hundredths

B eight tenths

C eighty-three hundredths

D eight

TEKS 4.1B Use place value to read, write, compare, and order decimals involving tenths and hundredths, including money, using concrete objects and pictorial models.

Comparing and Ordering Decimals

How do you compare decimals?

A penny made in 1982 weighs about 0.11 ounces. A penny made in 2006 weighs about 0.09 ounces. Which penny weighs more, a 1982 penny or a 2006 penny?

Another Example How do you order decimals?

Patrick has a 1982 penny, a 2006 penny, and a dime in his pocket. Order the weights of the coins from least to greatest.

First compare the tenths place.

$0.\underline{1}1$

$0.\underline{0}9$

$0.\underline{1}0$

The least number is 0.09 because it has 0 in the tenths place.

Compare the remaining numbers. First compare the tenths. Both decimals have a 1 in the tenths place.

$0.\underline{1}0$

$0.\underline{1}1$

Compare the hundredths place.

$0.1\underline{0}$

$0.1\underline{1}$

$1 > 0$, so 0.11 is the greatest decimal.

The order from least to greatest is 0.09, 0.10, 0.11.

Explain It

1. Order the numbers above from greatest to least.

2. Which place did you use to compare 0.10 and 0.11?

One Way

Use hundredths grids.

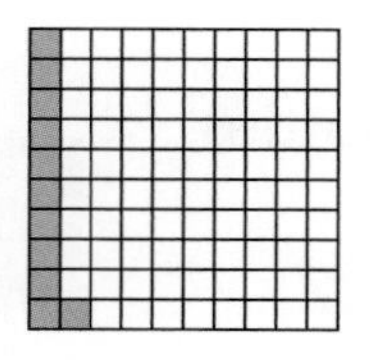

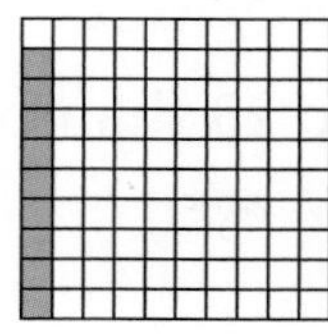

11 hundredths > **9 hundredths**

0.11 > 0.09

Another Way

Use place value.

Start at the left. Look for the first place where the digits are different.

0.11 0.09

1 tenth > **0 tenths**

0.11 > 0.09

A penny made in 1982 weighs more than a penny made in 2006.

Guided Practice

Do you know HOW?

In **1** and **2**, write >, <, or = for each ◯. Use grids to help.

1. 0.3 ◯ 0.23 **2.** 0.96 ◯ 1.02

In **3** and **4**, order the numbers from least to greatest.

3. 0.91 0.85 0.9 **4.** 2.1 2.11 2.01

Do you UNDERSTAND?

5. Maria told Patrick that her quarter weighs less than what a nickel weighs because 0.2 has less digits than 0.18. How can Patrick show Maria that 0.2 is greater than 0.18?

Independent Practice

For **6** through **9**, compare. Write >, <, or = for each. Use grids to help.

6. 0.07 ◯ 0.7 **7.** 0.42 ◯ 0.37 **8.** 6.01 ◯ 5.99 **9.** 4.1 ◯ 4.10

For **10** through **12**, order the numbers from least to greatest.

10. 5.3, 5.32, 5.23 **11.** 0.13, 0.14, 0.32 **12.** 0.84, 3.64, 1.74

13. **Number Sense** A bag of 250 nickels weighs 2.75 pounds. A bag of 100 half dollars weighs 2.5 pounds. Which bag weighs more?

14. **Writing to Explain** Evan said the numbers 8.57, 8.56, 7.23, and 7.32 were in order from greatest to least. Is he correct?

Step-Up Lesson 3

TEKS 4.4A: Model factors and products using arrays and area models.

Breaking Apart Arrays

Hands-On place-value blocks

How can you use arrays to find products?

A display has 4 rows. Each row can hold 23 shampoo bottles. Each bottle is on sale for $6. How many shampoo bottles can the display hold?

Choose an Operation Multiply to find the total for an array.

Guided Practice

Do you know HOW?

In **1** through **6**, use place-value blocks to build an array. Find the partial products and the product.

1. $3 \times 21 = \square$

2. $2 \times 13 = \square$

3. $6 \times 25 = \square$

4. $4 \times 22 = \square$

5. $2 \times 29 = \square$

6. $3 \times 17 = \square$

Do you UNDERSTAND?

7. In the example above, what are the two number sentences that give the partial products?

8. In the example at the top, what would you pay to buy one row of these shampoo bottles?

Independent Practice

Leveled Practice In **9** through **21**, use place-value blocks or draw a picture to show each array. Find the partial products and the product.

You can draw lines to show tens and Xs to show ones. This picture shows 2×28.

______ ______ XXXXXXXX
______ ______ XXXXXXXX

9. $2 \times 24 = \square$ Find the partial products: $2 \times 20 = \square$ $2 \times 4 = \square$
Add the partial products to find the product: $2 \times 24 = \square$

10. $2 \times 33 = \square$

11. $4 \times 27 = \square$

12. $5 \times 23 = \square$

13. $5 \times 19 = \square$

14. $7 \times 17 = \square$

15. $3 \times 26 = \square$

16. $5 \times 25 = \square$

17. $3 \times 22 = \square$

18. $3 \times 14 = \square$

19. $2 \times 28 = \square$

20. $4 \times 23 = \square$

21. $6 \times 19 = \square$

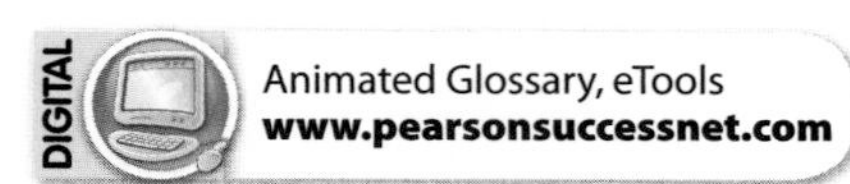

Build an array for 4×23.
Break it into tens and ones. Find how many in each part.

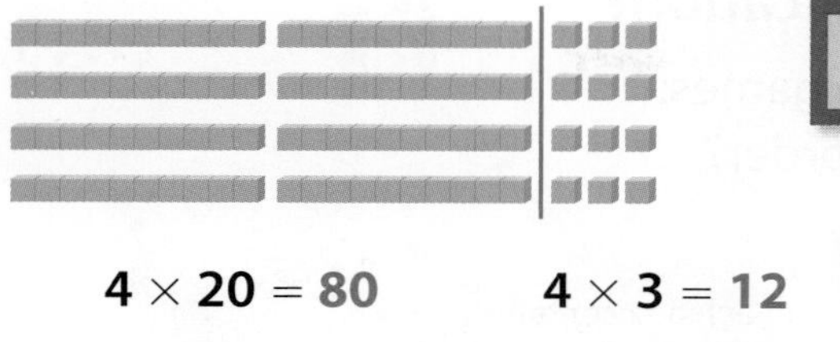

$4 \times 20 = 80$ $4 \times 3 = 12$

Add each part to get the product.

$4 \times 20 = 80$ $4 \times 3 = 12$

$80 + 12 = \mathbf{92}$

80 and **12** are called partial products because they are parts of the product.

The display can hold 92 bottles.

TAKS Problem Solving

22. **Algebra** Look for patterns in the table. Copy and complete.

x	▒	2	3	4	▒	6
y	20	40	?	80	100	▒

23. **Geometry** How many 1-foot by 1-foot tiles does it take to cover a rectangular floor that measures 7 tiles on one side and 25 tiles on the other side?

Tip *Draw an array.*

24. Paul's gymnastic scores for his first three events are shown in the table below. He needs a total of 32 points to qualify for the state meet.

a If his total score was 33 points, what was his score on the Horse routine?

b The total time (in seconds) for his routine on the Bars was 13 times the points he earned. What was the total time for the Bars routine?

Data

Paul's Gymnastics Scores	
Vault	8
Bars	8
Floor	7
Horse	▒
Total	▒

25. Each cabin on the London Eye Ferris Wheel can hold up to 25 passengers. How many passengers can 6 cabins hold?

A 150 passengers

B 175 passengers

C 200 passengers

D 225 passengers

Each cabin can hold up to 25 people.

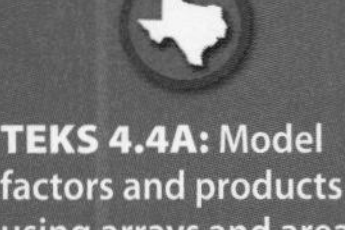

TEKS 4.4A: Model factors and products using arrays and area models.

Hands-On
place-value blocks

How can you record multiplication?

A store ordered 2 boxes of video games. How many games did the store order?

Choose an Operation Multiply to join equal groups.

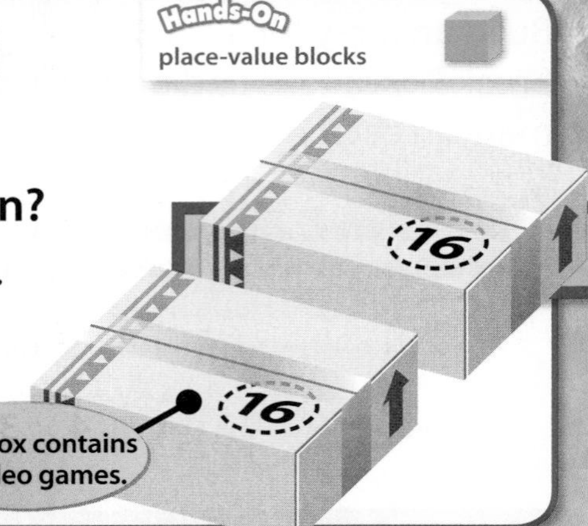

Another Example How do you record multiplication when the product has three digits?

Gene played his new video game 23 times each day for 5 days. How many times did he play his video game in 5 days?

A 18

B 28

C 115

D 145

Choose an Operation Since 5 equal groups of 23 are being joined, you will multiply. Find 5×23.

What You Show

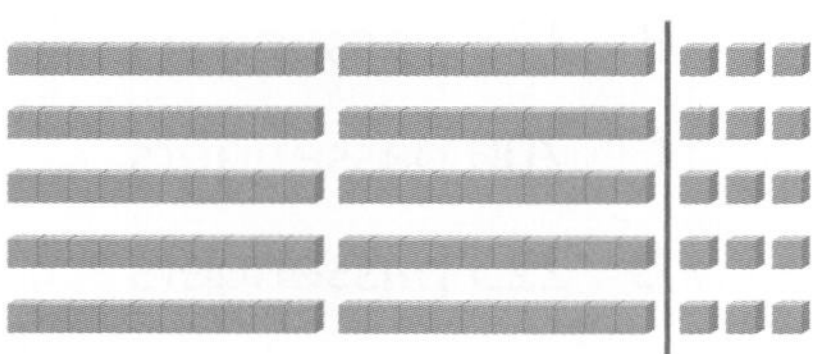

What You Write

$$\begin{array}{r} 23 \\ \times \quad 5 \\ \hline 15 \\ +\ 100 \\ \hline 115 \end{array}$$

Gene played his video game 115 times in 5 days.
The correct choice is **C**.

Explain It

1. Explain how the partial products, 15 and 100, were found in the work above.

2. **Reasonableness** How can an estimate help you eliminate choices above?

What You Show

Build an array to show 2×16.

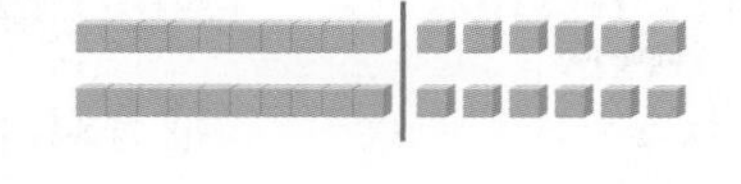

$2 \times 10 = 20$ $2 \times 6 = 12$

$20 + 12 = 32$

What You Write

Here is one way to record multiplication.

$$\begin{array}{r} 16 \\ \times \quad 2 \\ \hline 12 \\ + \ 20 \\ \hline 32 \end{array}$$

← Partial Products (12 and 20)

The store ordered 32 games.

Guided Practice

Do you know HOW?

In **1** and **2**, use place-value blocks or draw pictures to build an array for each. Copy and complete the calculation.

1. $2 \times 32 = \square$

$$\begin{array}{r} 32 \\ \times \quad 2 \\ \hline \square \\ + \ \square\square \\ \hline \square\square \end{array}$$

2. $3 \times 16 = \square$

$$\begin{array}{r} 16 \\ \times \quad 3 \\ \hline \square\square \\ + \ \square\square \\ \hline \square\square \end{array}$$

Do you UNDERSTAND?

Use the array and the calculation shown for Problem 3.

$$\begin{array}{r} 14 \\ \times \quad 3 \\ \hline 12 \\ + \ 30 \\ \hline 42 \end{array}$$

3. What calculation was used to give the partial product 12? 30? What is the product of 3×14?

Independent Practice

Leveled Practice In **4** through **8**, copy and complete the calculation. Draw a picture to help.

4. $\begin{array}{r} 24 \\ \times \quad 5 \\ \hline \square\square \\ + \ \square\square\square \\ \hline \square\square\square \end{array}$

5. $\begin{array}{r} 18 \\ \times \quad 4 \\ \hline \square\square \\ + \ \square\square \\ \hline \square\square \end{array}$

6. $\begin{array}{r} 17 \\ \times \quad 2 \\ \hline \square\square \\ + \ \square\square \\ \hline \square\square \end{array}$

7. $\begin{array}{r} 21 \\ \times \quad 6 \\ \hline \square \\ + \ \square\square\square \\ \hline \square\square\square \end{array}$

8. $\begin{array}{r} 28 \\ \times \quad 3 \\ \hline \square\square \\ + \ \square\square \\ \hline \square\square \end{array}$

9. Large tables have 8 chairs and small tables have 4 chairs. How many students can sit at 4 large tables and 6 small tables if each seat is filled?

10. The length of a side of a square is 12 inches. What is the perimeter of the square?

DIGITAL eTools **www.pearsonsuccessnet.com**

Step-Up Lesson 5

TEKS 4.4D: Use multiplication to solve problems (no more than two digits times two digits without technology).

Multiplying 2-Digit by 1-Digit Numbers

What is a common way to record multiplication?

How many T-shirts with the saying, *and your point is...* are in 3 boxes?

Choose an Operation Multiply to join equal groups.

Saying on T-shirt	Number of T-shirts per Box
Trust Me	30 T-shirts
and your point is...	26 T-shirts
I'm the princess that's why	24 T-shirts
Because I said so	12 T-shirts

Another Example Does the common way to record multiplication work for larger products?

Mrs. Stockton ordered 8 boxes of T-shirts with the saying, *I'm the princess that's why.* How many of the T-shirts did she order?

Choose an Operation Since you are joining 8 groups of 24, you will multiply. Find 8×24.

Step 1 Multiply the ones. Regroup if necessary.

$$\begin{array}{r} {}^{3} \\ 24 \\ \times \quad 8 \\ \hline 2 \end{array}$$

$8 \times 4 = 32$ ones
Regroup 32 ones as 3 tens 2 ones

Step 2 Multiply the tens. Add any extra tens.

$$\begin{array}{r} {}^{3} \\ 24 \\ \times \quad 8 \\ \hline 192 \end{array}$$

8×2 tens $= 16$ tens
16 tens $+$ 3 tens $= 19$ tens or 1 hundred 9 tens

Mrs. Stockton ordered 192 T-shirts.

Explain It

1. **Reasonableness** How can you use estimation to decide if 192 is a reasonable answer?
2. In the example above, 8×2 or 8×20? Explain.

Remember, one way to multiply is to find partial products.

$$\begin{array}{r} 26 \\ \times \quad 3 \\ \hline 18 \\ +\ 60 \\ \hline 78 \end{array}$$

18 and 60 ← Partial Products

A shortcut for the partial products method is shown at the right.

Step 1

Multiply the ones. Regroup if necessary.

$$\begin{array}{r} \scriptstyle 1 \\ 26 \\ \times \quad 3 \\ \hline 8 \end{array}$$

Step 2

Multiply the tens. Add any extra tens.

$$\begin{array}{r} \scriptstyle 1 \\ 26 \\ \times \quad 3 \\ \hline 78 \end{array}$$

There are 78 T-shirts in 3 boxes.

Guided Practice

Do you know HOW?

Find each product. Estimate to check reasonableness.

1. $\begin{array}{r} 17 \\ \times \quad 5 \\ \hline \end{array}$

2. $\begin{array}{r} 24 \\ \times \quad 3 \\ \hline \end{array}$

3. 7×34

4. 4×45

Do you UNDERSTAND?

5. Explain how you would estimate the answer in Exercise 3.

6. Carrie bought 8 boxes of T-shirts with the saying *Because I said so.* How many T-shirts did Carrie buy?

Independent Practice

Find each product. Estimate to check reasonableness.

7. $\begin{array}{r} 13 \\ \times \quad 6 \\ \hline \end{array}$

8. $\begin{array}{r} 16 \\ \times \quad 7 \\ \hline \end{array}$

9. $\begin{array}{r} 74 \\ \times \quad 5 \\ \hline \end{array}$

10. $\begin{array}{r} 39 \\ \times \quad 8 \\ \hline \end{array}$

11. 4×21

12. 3×52

13. 2×69

14. 9×42

For **15** and **16**, use the table to the right.

15. What is the average length fingernails will grow in one year?

16. How much longer will hair grow than fingernails in one month? in 6 months?

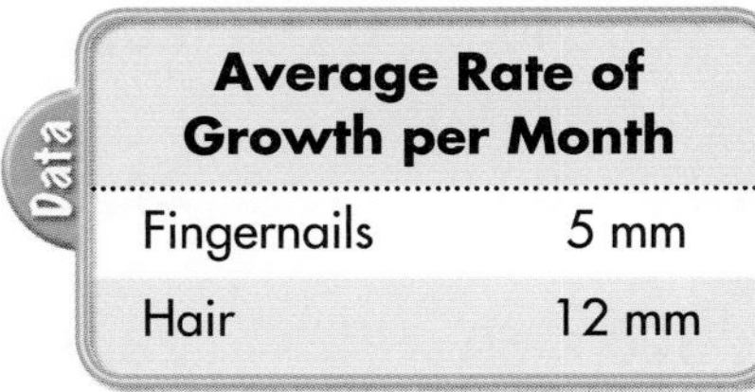

Data

Average Rate of Growth per Month	
Fingernails	5 mm
Hair	12 mm

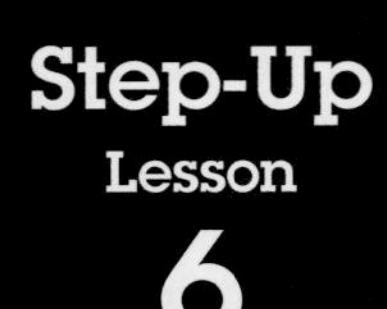

TEKS 4.6B: Use patterns to multiply by 10 and 100. Also **TEKS 4.4D:** Use multiplication to solve problems.

Using Mental Math to Multiply 2-Digit Numbers

How can you multiply by multiples of 10 and 100?

How many adults under 65 visit the Sunny Day Amusement Park in 10 days? How many children visit the park in 100 days? How many adults 65 and over visit the park in 200 days?

Guided Practice

Do you know HOW?

In **1** through **8**, use basic facts and patterns to find the product.

1. 60 × 100 **2.** 10 × 1,000

3. 100 × 25 **4.** 60× 400

5. 40 × 40 **6.** 20 × 100

7. 200 × 50 **8.** 50 × 600

Do you UNDERSTAND?

9. When you multiply 60 × 500, how many zeros are in the product?

10. In cold weather, fewer people go to Sunny Day Amusement Park. November has 30 days. If the park sells 300 tickets each day in November, how many would they sell for the whole month?

Independent Practice

For **11** through **34**, multiply using mental math.

11. 20 × 10	**12.** 100 × 30	**13.** 60 × 10	**14.** 70 × 40
15. 30 × 1,000	**16.** 80 × 900	**17.** 20 × 20	**18.** 30 × 500
19. 90 × 40	**20.** 20 × 50	**21.** 400 × 40	**22.** 10 × 90
23. 70 × 80	**24.** 30 × 800	**25.** 80 × 500	**26.** 300 × 70
27. 500 × 60	**28.** 90 × 300	**29.** 40 × 25	**30.** 30 × 200
31. 400 × 10	**32.** 800 × 20	**33.** 500 × 40	**34.** 90 × 600

Adults under 65 in 10 Days

To multiply 400 × 10, use a pattern.

$4 \times 10 = 40$

$40 \times 10 = 400$

$400 \times 10 = 4{,}000$

4,000 adults under 65 visit the park in 10 days.

Children in 100 Days

The number of zeros in the product is the total number of zeros in both factors.

$800 \times 100 = 80{,}000$

2 zeros 2 zeros 4 zeros

80,000 children visit the park in 100 days.

Adults 65 and over in 200 Days

If the product of a basic fact ends in zero, include that zero in the count.

$5 \times 2 = 10$

$50 \times 200 = 10{,}000$

10,000 adults 65 and over visit the park in 200 days.

TAKS Problem Solving

For **35** and **36**, use the table at the right.

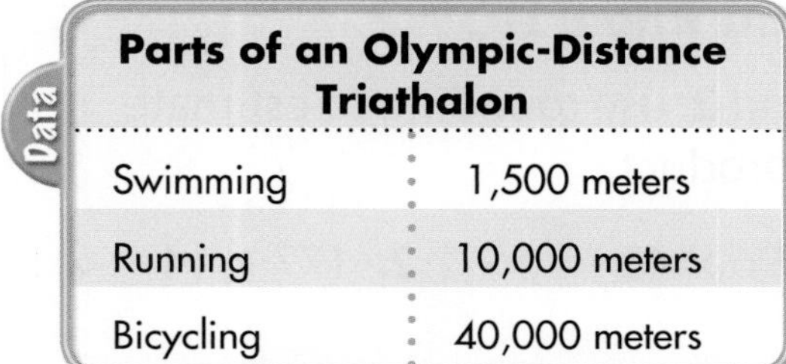

Parts of an Olympic-Distance Triathalon	
Swimming	1,500 meters
Running	10,000 meters
Bicycling	40,000 meters

35. What is the total distance traveled in one triathalon?

36. Susan has completed 10 triathalons. How far did she run in the races?

37. **Writing to Explain** Explain why the product of 50 and 600 has four zeros when 50 has one zero and 600 has two zeros.

38. Lindsey had 4 coins and two dollar bills to buy a snack at school. She paid $1.30 for her snack. She had exactly one dollar left. How did Lindsey pay for her snack?

39. For every 30 minutes of television air time, about 8 of the minutes are given to TV commercials. If 60 minutes of television is aired, how many minutes of commercials will be played?

A 8 minutes

B 16 minutes

C 38 minutes

D 60 minutes

40. The weatherman said that last year the city recorded a total of 89 rainy days. How many days did it NOT rain last year? (Hint: There are 365 days in one year.)

TEKS 4.5B: Use strategies including rounding and compatible numbers to estimate solutions to multiplication and division problems.

Estimating Products

What are some ways to estimate?

In 1991, NASA launched the Upper Atmosphere Research Satellite (UARS). It orbits Earth about 105 times each week. There are 52 weeks in one year.

About how many orbits does it make in one year?

Guided Practice

Do you know HOW?

In **1** and **2**, use rounding to estimate each product.

1. 196 × 43 **2.** 177 × 14

In **3** and **4**, use compatible numbers to estimate each product.

3. 390 × 26 **4.** 15 × 23

Do you UNDERSTAND?

5. **Writing to Explain** In the example above, why are the estimates not the same?

6. About how many times does UARS orbit Earth in 4 weeks?

Independent Practice

For **7** through **30**, use rounding or compatible numbers to estimate each product.

You can round just one number or round both to make compatible numbers.

7. 33 × 81 **8.** 63 × 85 **9.** 32 × 47 **10.** 62 × 59

11. 41 × 704 **12.** 51 × 19 **13.** 26 × 43 **14.** 62 × 204

15. 63 × 20 **16.** 19 × 73 **17.** 12 × 91 **18.** 21 × 29

19. 69 × 52 **20.** 27 × 42 **21.** 347 × 19 **22.** 6 × 109

23. 604 × 42 **24.** 83 × 52 **25.** 69 × 69 **26.** 98 × 38

27. 216 × 19 **28.** 77 × 18 **29.** 55 × 68 **30.** 6 × 85

One Way

Use **rounding** to estimate the number of orbits in one year.

52×105

Round 105 to 100.

$52 \times 100 = 5{,}200$

UARS orbits Earth about 5,200 times each year.

Another Way

Use **compatible numbers** to estimate the number of orbits in one year.

Compatible numbers are easy to multiply.

52×105

Change 52 to 55.

Change 105 to 100.

$55 \times 100 = 5{,}500$

UARS orbits Earth about 5,500 times each year.

TAKS Problem Solving

31. A long-haul truck driver made 43 trips last year. If her average trip was 975 miles, about how far did she drive in all?

32. In one mission, an American astronaut spent more than 236 hours in space. About how many minutes did he spend in space?

There are 60 minutes in 1 hour.

33. Estimate to decide which has a greater product, 48×32 or 42×42. Explain.

34. The Mars Orbiter circles the planet Mars every 25 hours. About how many hours does it take to make 115 orbits?

35. Use the diagram below. In 1858, two ships connected a telegraph cable across the Atlantic Ocean for the first time. One ship laid out 1,010 miles of cable. The other ship laid out 1,016 miles of cable. Estimate the total length of cable used.

36. Think About the Process About 57 baseballs are used in a professional baseball game. What is the best way to estimate how many baseballs are used in a season of 162 games?

A 6×100

B 60×160

C $60 \times 1{,}000$

D 200×200

1,010 miles

1,016 miles

TEKS 4.4A: Model factors and products using arrays and area models.

Arrays and an Expanded Algorithm

Hands-On
grid paper, colored pencils

How can you multiply using an array?

There are 13 bobble-head dogs in each row of the carnival booth. There are 24 equal rows. How many dogs are there?

Choose an Operation
Multiply to join equal groups.

13 dogs per row

Another Example What is another way to show the partial products?

There are 37 rows with 26 seats set up at the ring at the dog show. How many seats are there?

Estimate $40 \times 25 = 1{,}000$

Step 1 Draw a table. Separate each factor into tens and ones. $(30 + 7) \times (20 + 6)$

	30	7
20		
6		

Step 2 Multiply to find the partial products.

	30	7
20	600	140
6	180	42

Step 3 Add the partial products to find the total.

$$\begin{array}{r} 42 \\ 180 \\ 140 \\ +\ 600 \\ \hline 962 \end{array}$$

$26 \times 37 = 962$
There are 962 seats at the dog show ring.

Explain It

1. How is breaking apart the problem 37×26 like solving four simpler problems?
2. **Reasonableness** Explain why the answer 962 is reasonable.

Step 1

Find 24×13.

Draw an array for 24×13.

Add each part of the array to find the product.

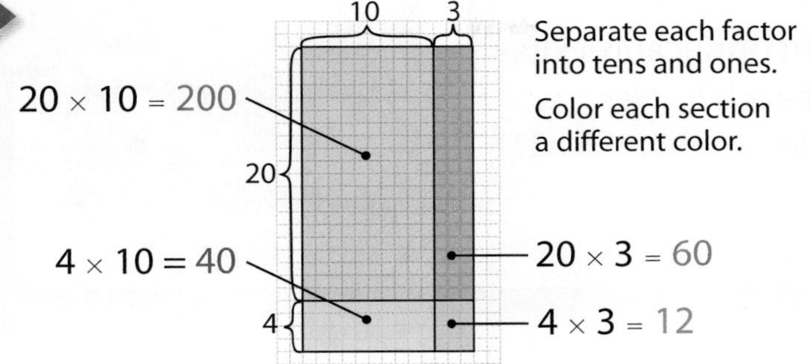

Step 2

Find the number of squares in each rectangle.

$$\begin{array}{r} 12 \\ 40 \\ 60 \\ +\ 200 \\ \hline 312 \end{array}$$

partial products

In the booth there are 312 bobble-head dogs.

Guided Practice

Do you know HOW?

In **1** and **2**, copy and complete the calculation by finding the partial products.

1. 26×17

	20	6
10		
7		

2. $\begin{array}{r} 14 \\ \times\ 18 \\ \hline \end{array}$

Do you UNDERSTAND?

3. In the example at the top, what four simpler multiplication problems were used to find 24×13?

4. At the dog show, the first 2 rows are reserved. How many people can sit in the remaining 35 rows?

Independent Practice

In **5** through **12**, copy and find the partial products. Then find the total.

5. 35×18

	30	5
10		
8		

6. 23×12

	20	3
10		
2		

7. 48×21

	40	8
20		
1		

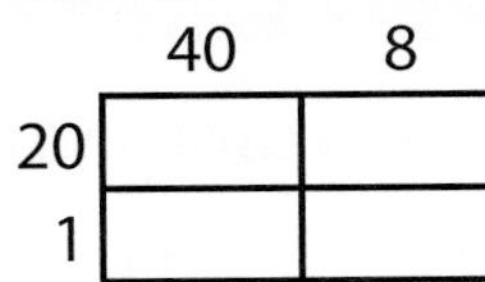

8. $\begin{array}{r} 17 \\ \times\ 11 \\ \hline \end{array}$ **9.** $\begin{array}{r} 22 \\ \times\ 31 \\ \hline \end{array}$ **10.** $\begin{array}{r} 34 \\ \times\ 12 \\ \hline \end{array}$ **11.** $\begin{array}{r} 25 \\ \times\ 14 \\ \hline \end{array}$ **12.** $\begin{array}{r} 42 \\ \times\ 13 \\ \hline \end{array}$

13. Writing to Explain Why is the product of 16×43 equal to the sum of 10×43 and 6×43?

14. The flagpole in front of City Hall in Luis' town is 30 feet tall. How many inches tall is the flagpole?

DIGITAL eTools **www.pearsonsuccessnet.com**

Step-Up Lesson 9

TEKS 4.4D: Use multiplication to solve problems (no more than two digits times two digits without technology).

Multiplying 2-Digit Numbers and Multiples of Ten

How can you find the product?

Mr. Jeffrey buys 20 rock identification kits for his science classes. If each kit has 28 rocks, how many rocks are there in all?

Choose an Operation
Multiply to find the number of rocks.

Guided Practice

Do you know HOW?

In **1** through **6**, multiply to find each product.

1. $\begin{array}{r} 16 \\ \times\ 20 \\ \hline 0 \end{array}$

2. $\begin{array}{r} 21 \\ \times\ 30 \\ \hline 0 \end{array}$

3. 35 × 30

4. 41 × 20

5. 27 × 50

6. 72 × 40

Do you UNDERSTAND?

7. Writing to Explain Why is there a zero in the ones place when you multiply by 20 in the example above?

8. What simpler multiplication problem can you solve to find 38 × 70?

9. Each year, Mr. Jeffrey's school orders 100 rock kits. How many rocks are in all of the kits?

Independent Practice

Leveled Practice In **10** through **30**, multiply to find each product.

10. $\begin{array}{r} 23 \\ \times\ 10 \\ \hline 0 \end{array}$

11. $\begin{array}{r} 14 \\ \times\ 30 \\ \hline 0 \end{array}$

12. $\begin{array}{r} 33 \\ \times\ 50 \\ \hline 0 \end{array}$

13. $\begin{array}{r} 71 \\ \times\ 20 \\ \hline 0 \end{array}$

14. $\begin{array}{r} 62 \\ \times\ 40 \\ \hline 0 \end{array}$

15. 19 × 10

16. 20 × 52

17. 31 × 30

18. 40 × 18

19. 24 × 80

20. 23 × 50

21. 40 × 72

22. 85 × 30

23. 78 × 40

24. 21 × 60

25. 14 × 50

26. 70 × 23

One Way

Find 20×28.

Break 28 into tens and ones: $28 = 20 + 8$.

Use a grid to find the partial products.

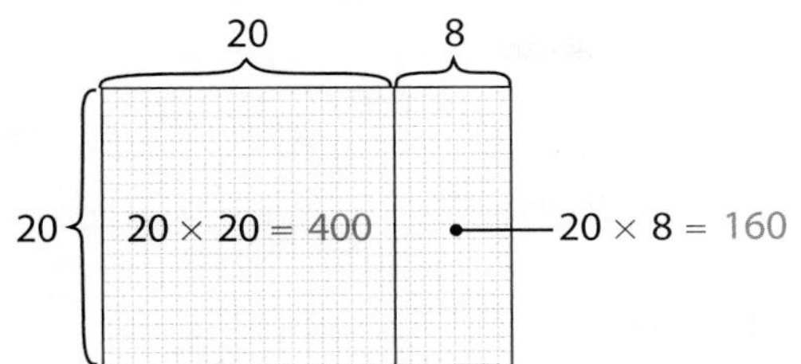

Add the partial products to find the total.

$400 + 160 = 560$

Another Way

Find 20×28.

Multiply 2 tens $\times$ 28.

$$\begin{array}{r} {}^{1} \\ 28 \\ \times\ 20 \\ \hline 560 \end{array}$$

Record a 0 in the ones place of the answer. This shows how many ones are in the answer.

There are 560 rocks in all.

TAKS Problem Solving

27. **Number Sense** Ian's class raised frogs from tadpoles. The class has 31 students, and each raised 8 tadpoles. All but 8 of the tadpoles grew to be frogs. Write a number sentence to show how many frogs the class has.

28. How many fossil kits with 10 samples each have the same number of fossils as 30 fossil kits with 8 samples each?

A 18 fossil kits
B 24 fossil kits
C 80 fossil kits
D 240 fossil kits

29. A ride on the Pike's Peak Cog Railway takes 75 minutes. If the train's average speed is 100 feet per minute how long is the Pike's Peak Cog Railway?

30. In the United States, students spend about 900 hours per year in school. How many hours would a student spend in 6 years of school?

31. A roller coaster runs rides 20 times an hour and reaches speeds of 70 miles per hour. If each ride takes 8 rows of 4 people, how many people ride each hour?

A 32 people
B 90 people
C 640 people
D 2,240 people

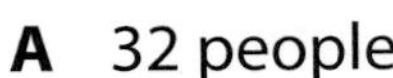

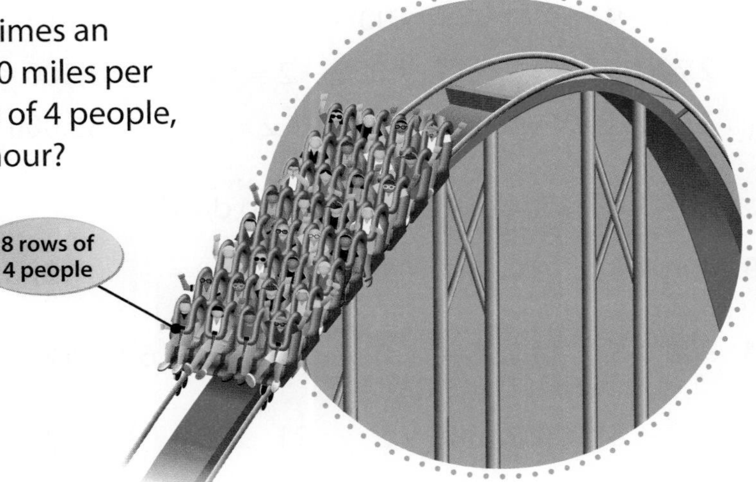

Step-Up Lesson 10

TEKS 4.4E: Use division to solve problems (no more than one-digit divisors and three-digit dividends without technology).

Mental Math

How can you use patterns to help you divide mentally?

Mr. Díaz ordered a supply of 320 pastels. He needs to divide them equally among four art classes. How many pastels does each class get?

320 pastels in all

Choose an Operation

Division is used to make equal groups.

Guided Practice

Do you know HOW?

In **1** and **2**, use patterns to find each quotient.

1. 42 ÷ 7 = ▢
420 ÷ 7 = ▢
4,200 ÷ 7 = ▢
42,000 ÷ 7 = ▢

2. 64 ÷ 8 = ▢
640 ÷ 8 = ▢
6,400 ÷ 8 = ▢
64,000 ÷ 8 = ▢

Do you UNDERSTAND?

3. How is dividing 320 by 4 like dividing 32 by 4?

4. José orders 240 binders and divides them equally among the 4 classes. How many binders will each class get? What basic fact did you use?

Independent Practice

Leveled Practice In **5** through **8**, use patterns to find each quotient.

5. 27 ÷ 9 = ▢
270 ÷ 9 = ▢
2,700 ÷ 9 = ▢
27,000 ÷ 9 = ▢

6. 10 ÷ 2 = ▢
100 ÷ 2 = ▢
1,000 ÷ 2 = ▢
10,000 ÷ 2 = ▢

7. 35 ÷ 5 = ▢
350 ÷ 5 = ▢
3,500 ÷ 5 = ▢
35,000 ÷ 5 = ▢

8. 24 ÷ 8 = ▢
240 ÷ 8 = ▢
2,400 ÷ 8 = ▢
24,000 ÷ 8 = ▢

For **9** through **23**, use mental math to divide.

9. 400 ÷ 5
10. 360 ÷ 4
11. 360 ÷ 9
12. 160 ÷ 4
13. 140 ÷ 2
14. 900 ÷ 3
15. 560 ÷ 8
16. 360 ÷ 6
17. 150 ÷ 3
18. 210 ÷ 7
19. 480 ÷ 8
20. 500 ÷ 5
21. 280 ÷ 7
22. 630 ÷ 9
23. 540 ÷ 6

Find $320 \div 4$.

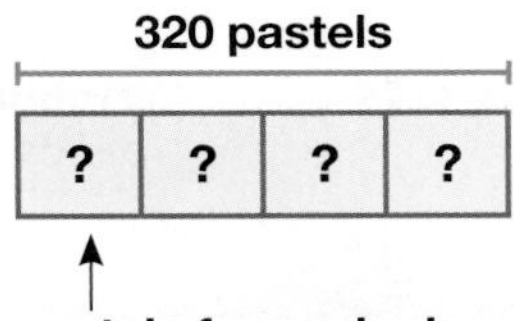

The basic fact is $32 \div 4 = 8$.

32 tens $\div$ 4 = 8 tens or 80.
$320 \div 4 = 80$

Each class will get 80 pastels.

Mr. Díaz wants to divide 400 erasers among 8 classes. How many erasers will each class get? Find $400 \div 8$.

The basic fact is $40 \div 8$.

40 tens $\div$ 8 = 5 tens or 50.
$400 \div 8 = 50$

Each class will get 50 erasers.

TAKS Problem Solving

24. Number Sense Matt used a basic fact to help solve $480 \div 6$. What basic fact did Matt use?

25. There are 52 weeks in 1 year. How many years are equivalent to 520 weeks?

26. At the North American Solar Challenge, teams use up to 1,000 solar cells to design and build solar cars for a race. If there are 720 solar cells in rows of 9, how many solar cells are in each row?

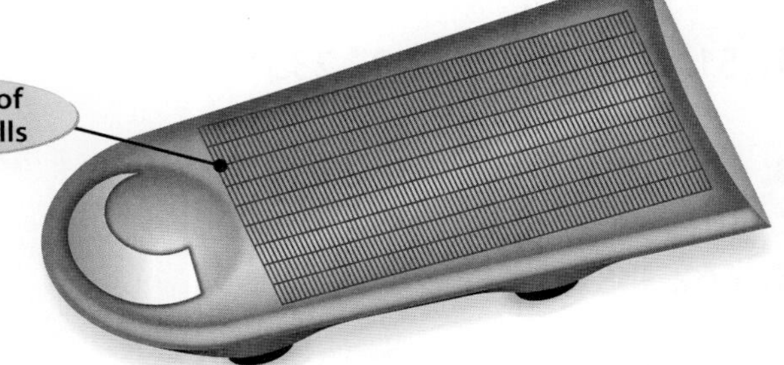

27. A bakery produced 37 loaves of bread an hour. How many loaves were produced in 4 hours?

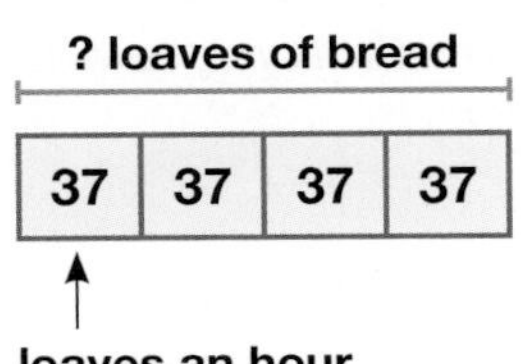

28. On Friday night, 350 people attended a play. The seating was arranged in 7 equal rows. How many people sat in each row? How do you know?

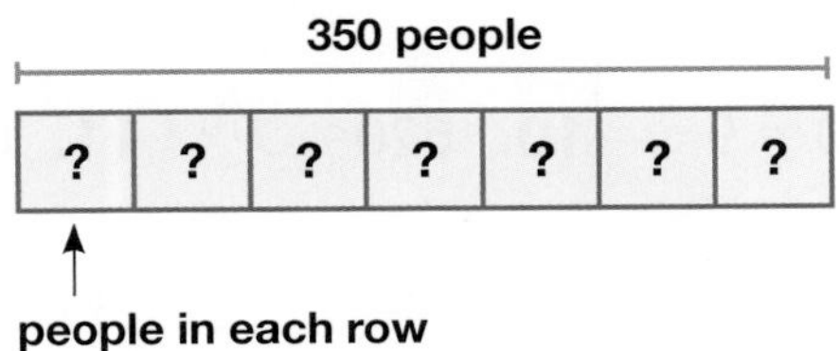

29. Each row of seats in a stadium has 45 chairs. If the first 2 rows are completely filled, how many people are in the first 2 rows?

A 47 people
B 80 people
C 90 people
D 810 people

30. Writing to Explain If you know that $30 \div 6 = 5$, how does that fact help you find $300 \div 6$?

TEKS 4.5B: Use strategies including rounding and compatible numbers to estimate solutions to multiplication and division problems.

Estimating Quotients

When and how do you estimate quotients to solve problems?

Max wants to make 9 rubber-band balls. He bought a jar of 700 rubber bands. About how many rubber bands can he use for each ball?

700 rubber bands

Guided Practice

Do you know HOW?

In **1** through **6**, estimate each quotient. Use rounding or compatible numbers.

1. 51 ÷ 5 **2.** 235 ÷ 8

3. 485 ÷ 6 **4.** 192 ÷ 5

5. 662 ÷ 8 **6.** 89 ÷ 3

Do you UNDERSTAND?

7. Writing to Explain In Exercise 4, to what number should you adjust 192? Why?

8. Reasonableness Max decides to use the 700 rubber bands to make 8 balls. Is it reasonable to say that each ball would contain about 90 rubber bands?

Independent Practice

Leveled Practice In **9** through **28**, estimate the quotient.

First round to the nearest ten. Then try multiples of ten that are near the rounded number.

9. 530 ÷ 9 **10.** 620 ÷ 7 **11.** 159 ÷ 5 **12.** 232 ÷ 6 **13.** 119 ÷ 3

14. 403 ÷ 8 **15.** 652 ÷ 6 **16.** 599 ÷ 9 **17.** 400 ÷ 6 **18.** 326 ÷ 4

19. 637 ÷ 6 **20.** 197 ÷ 2 **21.** 747 ÷ 8 **22.** 256 ÷ 9 **23.** 283 ÷ 4

24. 552 ÷ 7 **25.** 438 ÷ 5 **26.** 173 ÷ 4 **27.** 625 ÷ 3 **28.** 821 ÷ 3

One Way

Use compatible numbers.

What number close to 700 is easily divided by 9?

Try multiples of ten near 700.

710 is not easily divided by 9.

720 is 72 tens and can be divided by 9.

$720 \div 9 = 80$

A good estimate is 80 rubber bands for each ball.

Another Way

Use multiplication.

9 times what number is about 700?

$9 \times 8 = 72$,
so $9 \times 80 = 720$.

$700 \div 9$ is about 80.

TAKS Problem Solving

Use the chart at the right for **29** and **30**.

29. Lia sold her mugs in 6 weeks. About how many did she sell each week?

30. Bob sold his mugs in 7 weeks. About how many did he sell each week?

31. **Number Sense** Marcos is asked to give two different estimates for $600 \div 8$. Name two numbers that are compatible with 8 that he could use to replace 600.

32. **Writing to Explain** Copy and complete by filling in the circle with $>$ or $<$. Without dividing, explain how you know which quotient is greater.

$930 \div 4$ ◯ $762 \div 4$

33. The International Space Station takes 644 minutes to orbit Earth 7 times. About how long does each orbit take?

A 80 minutes

B 90 minutes

C 95 minutes

D 100 minutes

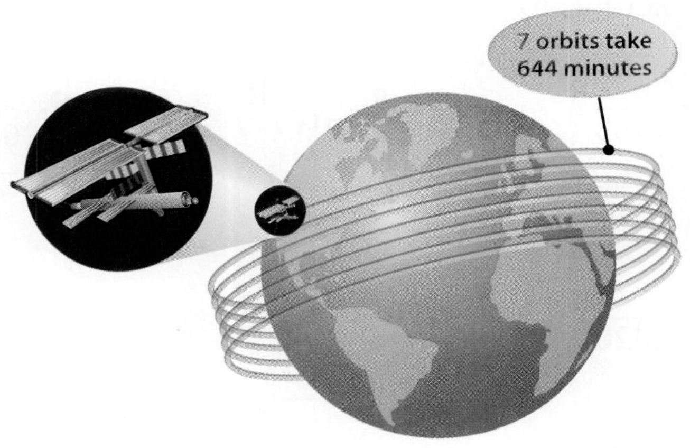

Step-Up Lesson 12

TEKS 4.4E: Use division to solve problems (no more than one-digit divisors and three-digit dividends without technology).

Dividing with Remainders

Hands-On: counters

What happens when some are left?

Maria has 20 pepper plants to place in 3 rows. She has to plant the same number in each row. How many plants will go in each row? How many are left over?

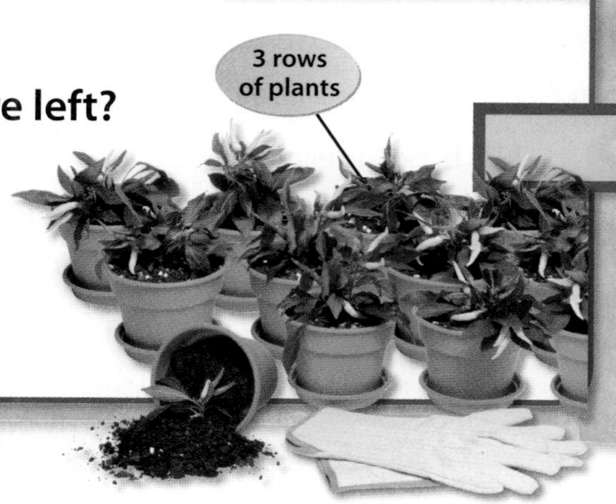

Guided Practice

Do you know HOW?

In **1** through **4**, use counters or draw pictures. Tell how many items are in each group and how many are left over.

1. 36 pens
5 groups

2. 48 cars
7 boxes

3. 23 marbles
4 bags

4. 40 balls
6 bins

Do you UNDERSTAND?

5. Writing to Explain When you divide a number by 6 what remainders are possible?

6. Tia is planting her garden with 15 plants. She wants them planted in equal groups of 4. How many groups of 4 can she make? How many plants will she have left over?

Independent Practice

Leveled Practice In **7** through **14**, copy and then complete the calculations. Use counters or pictures to help.

The remainder should always be less than the divisor.

7. $8\overline{)33}$ R

8. $3\overline{)17}$ R

9. $6\overline{)51}$ R

10. $5\overline{)48}$ R

11. $6\overline{)26}$ R

12. $7\overline{)67}$ R

13. $9\overline{)77}$ R

14. $4\overline{)30}$ R

Animated Glosssary, eTools
www.pearsonsuccessnet.com

Divide 20 counters among 3 rows.

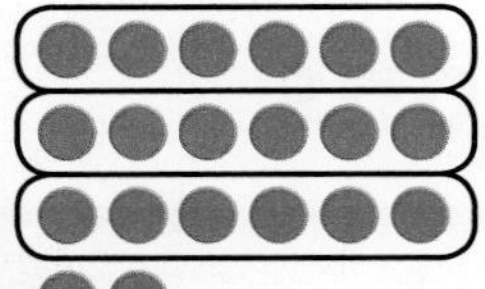

$3 \times 6 = 18$ counters

The part that is left after dividing is called the remainder.

There are 2 counters left over. This is not enough for another row, so the remainder is 2.

Check your answer.

$$\begin{array}{r} 6 \text{ R}2 \\ 3\overline{)20} \\ -18 \\ \hline 2 \end{array}$$

Divide: 3 groups of 6 in 20
Multiply: $3 \times 6 = 18$
Subtract: $20 - 18 = 2$
Compare: $2 < 3$

$3 \times 6 = 18$, and $18 + 2 = 20$

Maria can plant 6 plants in each row. She will have 2 plants left over.

In **15** through **29**, divide. You may use counters or pictures to help.

15. $3\overline{)17}$ **16.** $7\overline{)41}$ **17.** $9\overline{)82}$ **18.** $8\overline{)62}$ **19.** $7\overline{)37}$

20. $6\overline{)45}$ **21.** $4\overline{)22}$ **22.** $6\overline{)28}$ **23.** $4\overline{)33}$ **24.** $8\overline{)75}$

25. $9\overline{)59}$ **26.** $6\overline{)34}$ **27.** $7\overline{)50}$ **28.** $5\overline{)23}$ **29.** $8\overline{)63}$

TAKS Problem Solving

30. Algebra If $38 \div 8 = n$ R6, what is the value of n?

31. How many pieces are left if 9 friends equally share 100 puzzle pieces?

32. Write a division sentence with a quotient of 6 and remainder of 2.

33. Number Sense When you divide by 6, can the remainder be 8?

34. Reasonableness Carl's teacher took 27 photos on their class trip. She wants to arrange them on the wall in 4 equal rows. Carl said if she does this, she will have 7 photos left over. Is this reasonable?

35. Reasoning Carly is thinking of a number between 269 and 281. It is an even number but the digit in the tens place is odd. What is the number?

36. **Think About the Process** Chase helped Mrs. Martin pack 58 books in 7 boxes. Each box held 8 books. Which expression is best used to find how many books he had left?

A $58 - 9$ **C** $58 - 7$

B $58 \div 9$ **D** $58 \div 7$

37. At the school concert there were 640 people seated in 8 rows. If there were no empty seats, how many people were in each row?

F 648 people **H** 80 people

G 90 people **J** 70 people

Step-Up Lesson 13

TEKS 4.2C: Compare and order fractions using concrete objects and pictorial models.

Using Models to Compare and Order Fractions

Hands-On fraction strips

How can you use fraction strips to compare and order fractions?

The table shows the amount of time three students spent practicing guitar each day. Who spent more time practicing—Jack or Lynn? Who spent less time practicing—Chase or Jack?

Data

Guitar Practice	
Jack	$\frac{3}{4}$ hour
Chase	$\frac{2}{3}$ hour
Lynn	$\frac{1}{4}$ hour

Another Example How can you use fraction strips to order fractions?

Use the table above. Which choice below shows the amount of time the students practiced in order from least to greatest?

A $\frac{3}{4}$ h, $\frac{2}{3}$ h, $\frac{1}{4}$ h

B $\frac{2}{3}$ h, $\frac{3}{4}$ h, $\frac{1}{4}$ h

C $\frac{1}{4}$ h, $\frac{3}{4}$ h, $\frac{2}{3}$ h

D $\frac{1}{4}$ h, $\frac{2}{3}$ h, $\frac{3}{4}$ h

You can use fraction strips to order the fractions.

$\frac{1}{4} < \frac{2}{3} < \frac{3}{4}$

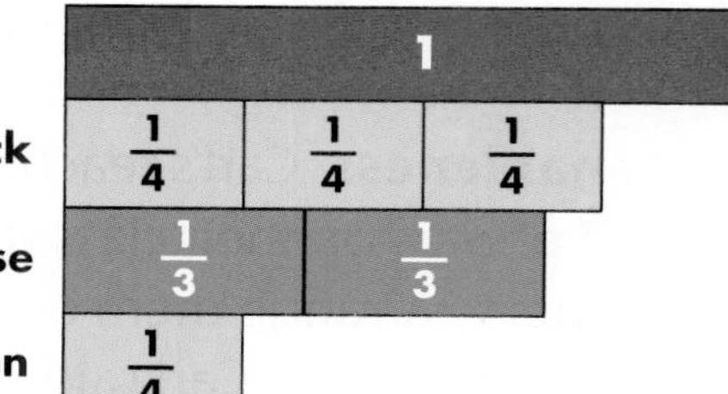

So, the order of the practice times from least to greatest is $\frac{1}{4}$ h, $\frac{2}{3}$ h, $\frac{3}{4}$ h.

The correct choice is **D**.

Explain It

1. Look at the fraction strips for $\frac{3}{4}$, $\frac{2}{3}$, and $\frac{1}{4}$. Which of the fractions are greater than $\frac{1}{2}$? Explain how you found your answer.

2. Look at the fraction strips for $\frac{1}{4}$, $\frac{5}{6}$, and $\frac{5}{12}$. Which of the fractions are less than $\frac{1}{2}$? Explain how you found your answer.

Who practiced more—Jack or Lynn? Compare $\frac{3}{4}$ and $\frac{1}{4}$.

You can use fraction strips to compare.

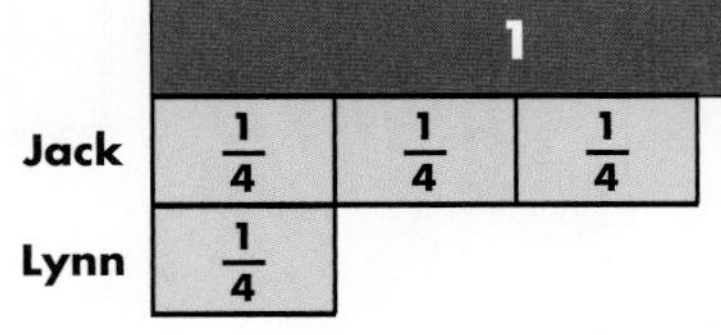

$\frac{3}{4} > \frac{1}{4}$

Jack spent more time practicing than Lynn.

Who practiced less—Chase or Jack? Compare $\frac{2}{3}$ and $\frac{3}{4}$.

You can use fraction strips to compare.

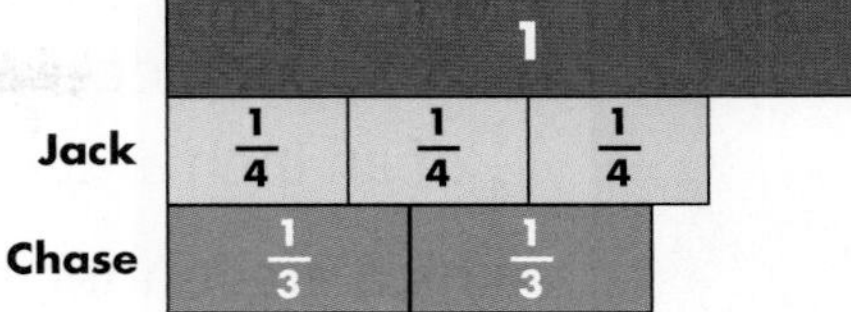

$\frac{2}{3} < \frac{3}{4}$

Chase spent less time practicing than Jack.

Guided Practice

Do you know HOW?

For **1**, order the numbers from least to greatest. Use fraction strips or drawings to help.

1. $\frac{1}{3}, \frac{3}{4}, \frac{1}{6}$

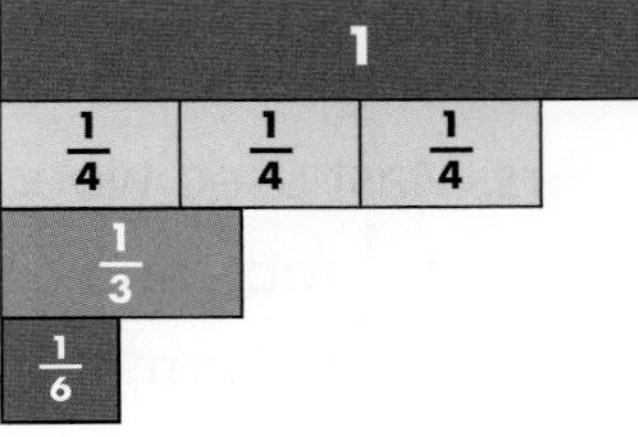

Do you UNDERSTAND?

2. Who practiced more—Chase or Lynn?

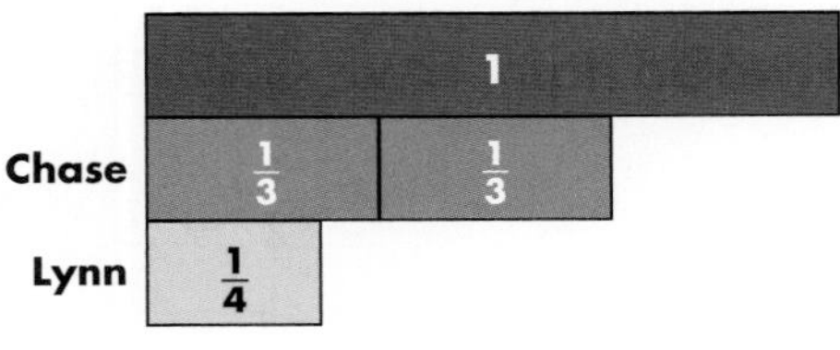

Independent Practice

For **3** through **5**, order the numbers from least to greatest. Use fraction strips or drawings to help.

3. $\frac{5}{8}, \frac{3}{4}, \frac{1}{2}$

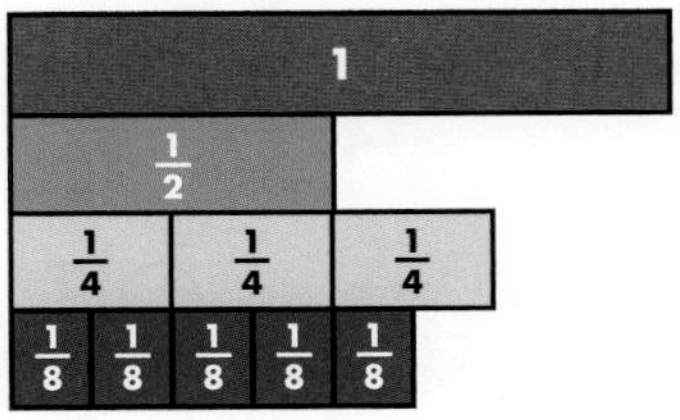

4. $\frac{1}{3}, \frac{3}{12}, \frac{3}{6}$

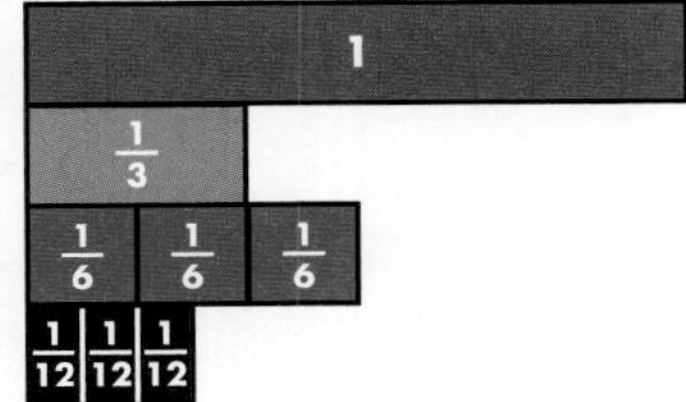

5. $\frac{3}{4}, \frac{3}{8}, \frac{1}{2}$

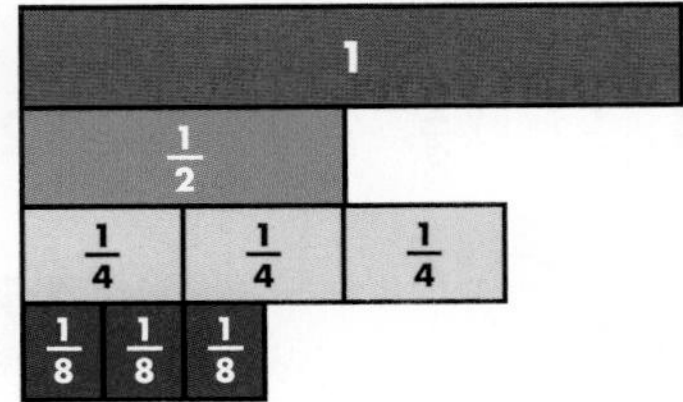

6. Three students practiced piano for $\frac{5}{12}$ hour, $\frac{1}{3}$ hour, and $\frac{3}{8}$ hour. Write these amounts of time in order from least to greatest.

7. Reasoning How do you know that $\frac{3}{8}$ is greater than $\frac{3}{10}$?

Step-Up Lesson 14

TEKS 4.2C: Compare and order fractions using concrete objects and pictorial models.

Comparing Fractions

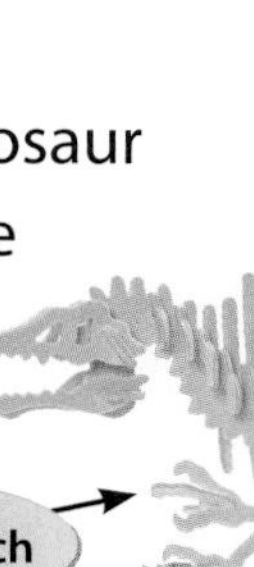

How can you compare fractions?

Isabella's father is building a model dinosaur with spare pieces of wood that measure $\frac{1}{4}$ of an inch and $\frac{5}{8}$ of an inch. Which are longer, the $\frac{1}{4}$ inch pieces or the $\frac{5}{8}$ inch pieces?

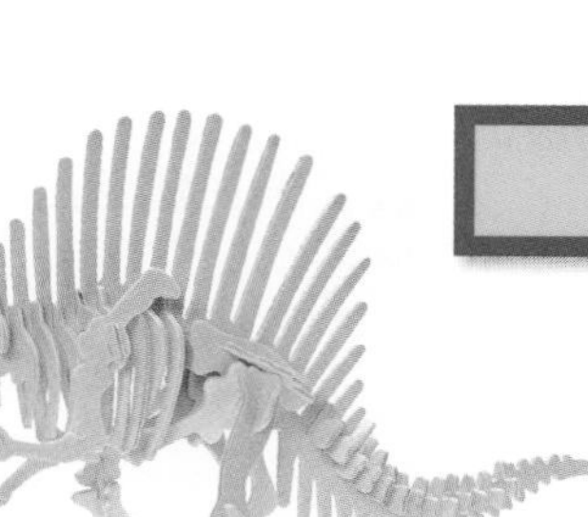

Guided Practice

Do you know HOW?

Compare. Write >, <, or = for each ◯. Use fraction strips or drawings to help.

1. $\frac{4}{8}$ ◯ $\frac{1}{2}$
2. $\frac{5}{6}$ ◯ $\frac{2}{3}$
3. $\frac{3}{5}$ ◯ $\frac{1}{5}$
4. $\frac{1}{2}$ ◯ $\frac{4}{5}$

Do you UNDERSTAND?

5. Mary says that $\frac{1}{8}$ is greater than $\frac{1}{4}$ because 8 is greater than 4. Is she right? Explain your answer.
6. Mrs. Mast used wood measuring $\frac{2}{5}$ foot, $\frac{1}{3}$ foot, and $\frac{3}{7}$ foot to build a birdhouse. Compare these lengths of wood.

Independent Practice

For **7** through **38**, compare, and then write >, <, or = for each ◯. Use fraction strips or benchmark fractions to help.

7. $\frac{2}{6}$ ◯ $\frac{3}{6}$
8. $\frac{3}{10}$ ◯ $\frac{7}{8}$
9. $\frac{6}{12}$ ◯ $\frac{1}{2}$
10. $\frac{7}{8}$ ◯ $\frac{3}{4}$
11. $\frac{1}{3}$ ◯ $\frac{2}{8}$
12. $\frac{5}{6}$ ◯ $\frac{7}{8}$
13. $\frac{7}{12}$ ◯ $\frac{3}{4}$
14. $\frac{2}{3}$ ◯ $\frac{5}{12}$
15. $\frac{3}{8}$ ◯ $\frac{2}{3}$
16. $\frac{3}{4}$ ◯ $\frac{1}{8}$
17. $\frac{2}{3}$ ◯ $\frac{1}{4}$
18. $\frac{1}{12}$ ◯ $\frac{1}{10}$
19. $\frac{1}{5}$ ◯ $\frac{2}{10}$
20. $\frac{7}{12}$ ◯ $\frac{6}{12}$
21. $\frac{5}{12}$ ◯ $\frac{4}{5}$
22. $\frac{2}{6}$ ◯ $\frac{3}{12}$
23. $\frac{8}{10}$ ◯ $\frac{3}{4}$
24. $\frac{4}{8}$ ◯ $\frac{11}{12}$
25. $\frac{5}{6}$ ◯ $\frac{10}{12}$
26. $\frac{7}{8}$ ◯ $\frac{1}{6}$

Use benchmark fractions.

Compare $\frac{1}{4}$ and $\frac{5}{8}$.

You can use fraction strips to compare both fractions to $\frac{1}{2}$.

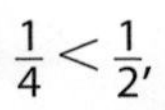

$\frac{1}{4} < \frac{1}{2}$,

$\frac{5}{8} > \frac{1}{2}$,

So, $\frac{1}{4} < \frac{5}{8}$

The $\frac{5}{8}$ inch pieces are longer.

Compare $\frac{1}{4}$ and $\frac{3}{4}$.

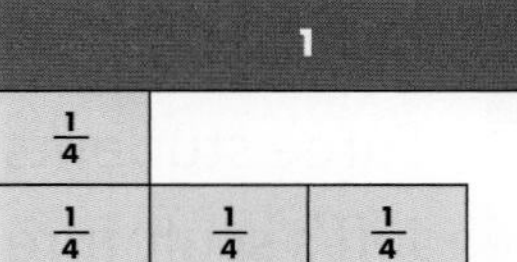

When the two fractions have the same denominators, you compare the numerators.

$$3 > 1$$

So, $\frac{3}{4} > \frac{1}{4}$.

27. $\frac{2}{8} \bigcirc \frac{5}{8}$ **28.** $\frac{2}{4} \bigcirc \frac{4}{8}$ **29.** $\frac{9}{12} \bigcirc \frac{1}{2}$ **30.** $\frac{1}{3} \bigcirc \frac{4}{9}$

31. $\frac{6}{8} \bigcirc \frac{8}{10}$ **32.** $\frac{3}{5} \bigcirc \frac{3}{6}$ **33.** $\frac{2}{12} \bigcirc \frac{2}{10}$ **34.** $\frac{5}{6} \bigcirc \frac{4}{5}$

35. $\frac{3}{3} \bigcirc \frac{1}{1}$ **36.** $\frac{3}{4} \bigcirc \frac{9}{12}$ **37.** $\frac{7}{8} \bigcirc \frac{3}{5}$ **38.** $\frac{1}{4} \bigcirc \frac{2}{8}$

TAKS Problem Solving

39. Number Sense Janet drew the picture at the right to show that $\frac{3}{8}$ is greater than $\frac{3}{4}$. What was Felicia's mistake?

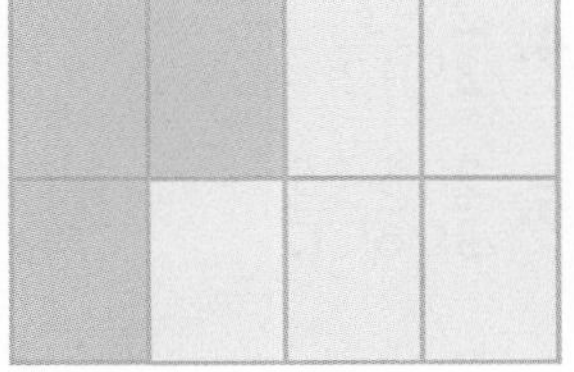

40. Writing to Explain Why can you compare two fractions with the same denominator by only comparing the numerators?

41. What can you conclude about $\frac{3}{4}$ and $\frac{12}{16}$ if you know that $\frac{3}{4} = \frac{6}{8}$ and that $\frac{6}{8} = \frac{12}{16}$?

42. Reasoning Which is longer, $\frac{1}{2}$ foot or $\frac{1}{2}$ yard? Explain.

43. If $34 \times 20 = 680$ then $34 \times 200 = \square$

44. A melon was divided into 10 equal slices. Juan ate three slices. Bob and Sandy ate the remaining slices. What fraction of the melon did Bob and Sandy eat?

A $\frac{1}{5}$ **B** $\frac{3}{10}$ **C** $\frac{7}{10}$ **D** $\frac{13}{10}$

45. Ted is setting up for a dinner party. He has 5 tables each seating 6 guests and another table seating the left over 3 guests. How many people are coming to Ted's dinner party?

TEKS 4.2C: Compare and order fractions using concrete objects and pictorial models.

Ordering Fractions

Hands-On
fraction strips

How can you order fractions?

Three students made sculptures for a school project. Jeff's sculpture is $\frac{9}{12}$ foot tall, Scott's sculpture is $\frac{1}{3}$ foot tall, and Kristen's sculpture is $\frac{3}{6}$ foot tall. List the heights of the sculptures in order from least to greatest.

$\frac{9}{12}$ foot tall

Guided Practice

Do you know HOW?

For **1** through **6**, order the fractions from least to greatest. Use fraction strips or drawings to help.

1. $\frac{5}{8}, \frac{1}{4}, \frac{3}{8}$

2. $\frac{5}{6}, \frac{1}{3}, \frac{1}{6}$

3. $\frac{1}{2}, \frac{7}{8}, \frac{3}{4}$

4. $\frac{2}{3}, \frac{3}{12}, \frac{3}{4}$

5. $\frac{7}{9}, \frac{2}{3}, \frac{4}{9}$

6. $\frac{2}{3}, \frac{5}{6}, \frac{5}{12}$

Do you UNDERSTAND?

7. What denominator would you use to find equivalent fractions when comparing $\frac{2}{3}, \frac{2}{4}, \frac{2}{12}$?

8. Three other students made sculptures with these heights: $\frac{2}{3}$ foot, $\frac{5}{6}$ foot, and $\frac{2}{12}$ foot. Write these heights in order from least to greatest.

Independent Practice

For **9** through **20**, find equivalent fractions with a common denominator and order from least to greatest. Use drawings or fraction strips to help.

9. $\frac{1}{3}, \frac{1}{5}, \frac{1}{2}$

10. $\frac{2}{5}, \frac{2}{8}, \frac{2}{12}$

11. $\frac{5}{12}, \frac{2}{3}, \frac{1}{4}$

12. $\frac{2}{3}, \frac{5}{6}, \frac{7}{12}$

13. $\frac{5}{6}, \frac{3}{4}, \frac{8}{12}$

14. $\frac{1}{2}, \frac{3}{5}, \frac{2}{10}$

15. $\frac{3}{5}, \frac{4}{10}, \frac{1}{2}$

16. $\frac{8}{12}, \frac{1}{2}, \frac{3}{4}$

17. $\frac{2}{4}, \frac{3}{12}, \frac{2}{3}$

18. $\frac{6}{8}, \frac{1}{2}, \frac{3}{8}$

19. $\frac{10}{12}, \frac{1}{2}, \frac{3}{4}$

20. $\frac{2}{5}, \frac{3}{10}, \frac{3}{5}$

Step 1

Find equivalent fractions with a common denominator.

$\frac{3}{6} = \frac{6}{12}$

$\frac{1}{3} = \frac{4}{12}$

Step 2

Compare the numerators.

$\frac{4}{12} < \frac{6}{12} < \frac{9}{12}$ Order the fractions from least to greatest.

So, $\frac{1}{3} < \frac{3}{6} < \frac{9}{12}$.

The heights of the sculptures in order from least to greatest are $\frac{1}{3}$ foot, $\frac{3}{6}$ foot, $\frac{9}{12}$ foot.

TAKS Problem Solving

21. Writing to Explain Sandy's sculpture is taller than Jason's. Becca's sculpture is taller than Sandy's sculpture. If Sandy's sculpture is $\frac{2}{3}$ foot tall, how tall could Jason's and Becca's sculptures be?

22. Estimation The fraction $\frac{3}{4}$ is $\frac{1}{4}$ less than 1 whole. Without finding equivalent fractions, order the fractions $\frac{7}{8}$, $\frac{3}{4}$, and $\frac{5}{6}$ from least to greatest.

23. The table at the right shows the number of pages four students read. Which lists the number of pages in order from greatest to least?

A 96, 64, 69, 25 **C** 64, 25, 69, 96

B 25, 64, 69, 96 **D** 96, 69, 64, 25

Data

Students	Number of Pages
Francine	25
Ty	69
Greg	96
Vicki	64

24. Algebra Find the missing numbers in the pattern below.

___, 24, 32, ___, ___, 56, ___

25. Cathy asked Julie to name 3 fractions between 0 and 1. Julie said $\frac{5}{12}$, $\frac{1}{4}$, and $\frac{2}{6}$. Order Julie's fractions from least to greatest.

26. Annika had 6 necklaces. Sydney had 2 times as many. How many necklaces did Sydney have?

27. Each student in third grade had the same book to read. James read $\frac{3}{4}$ of the book, and Tony read $\frac{3}{5}$ of the book. Who read more?

TEKS 4.9B: Use translations, reflections, and rotations to verify that two shapes are congruent.

Congruent Figures

Hands-On
grid paper

When are figures congruent?

Figures that are the same size and shape are congruent.

You can use tracing paper and translations, reflections, and rotations to test if two figures are congruent.

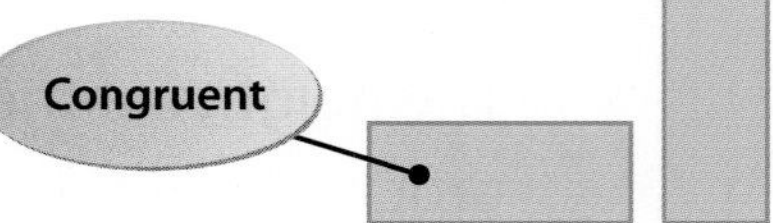

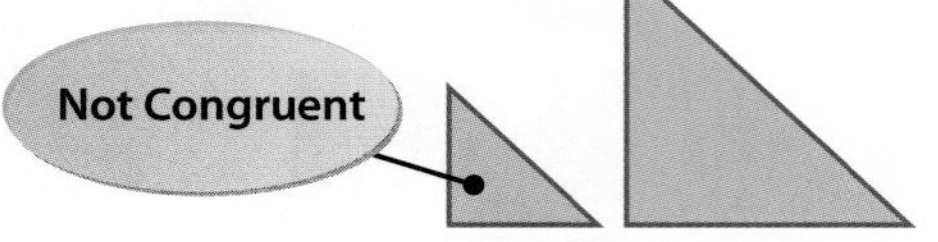

Guided Practice

Do you know HOW?

For **1** through **4**, tell if the figures in each pair are congruent.

1. 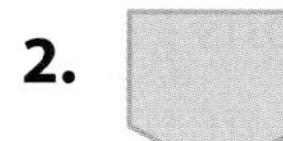

2. 

3. 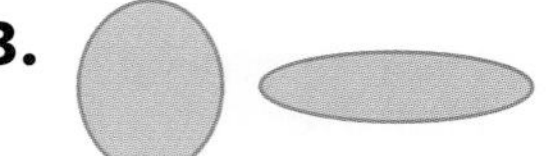

4. 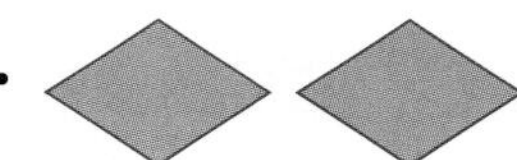

Do you UNDERSTAND?

5. If one of the house shapes above is rotated $\frac{1}{4}$ turn, will the two shapes still be congruent?

6. **Writing to Explain** Can a circle and a square ever be congruent? Why or why not?

Independent Practice

For **7** through **15**, tell if the figures in each pair are congruent.

7. 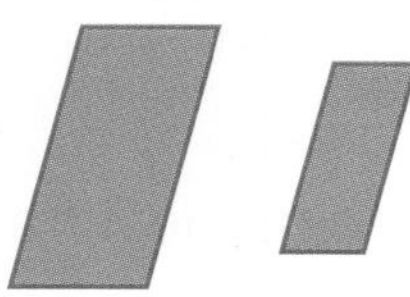

8. 

9. 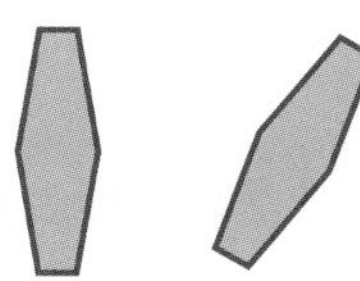

10. 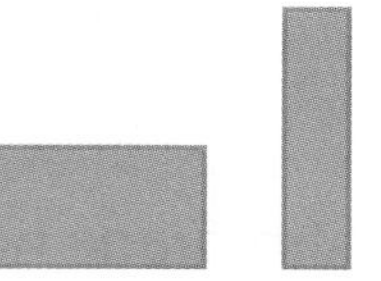

11. 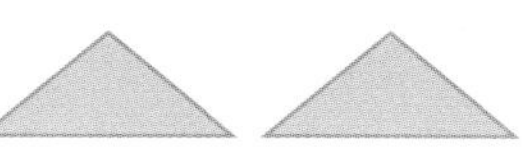

12. 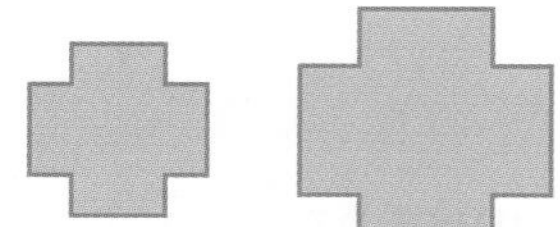

13. 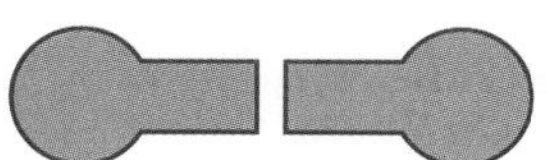

14. 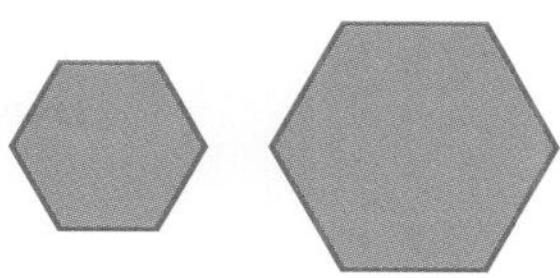

15. 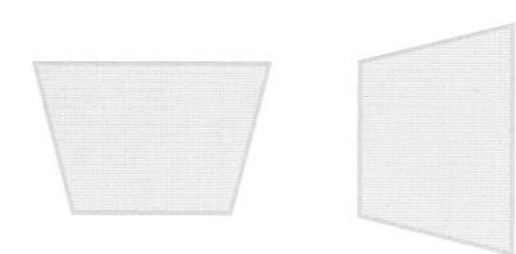

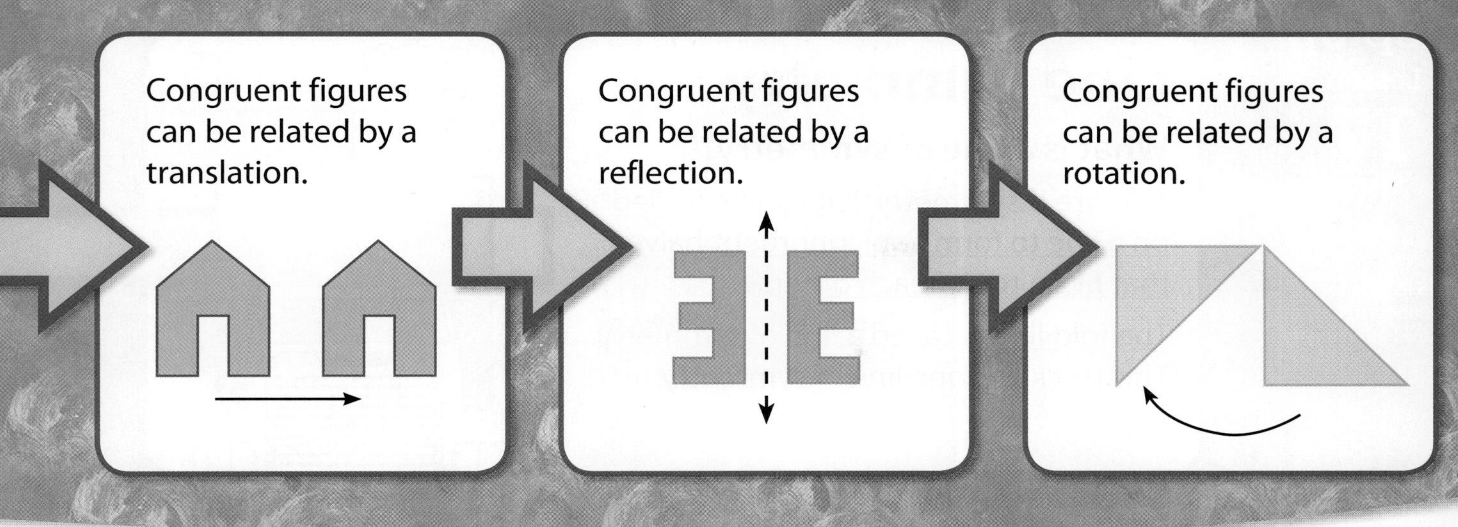

TAKS Problem Solving

For **16** and **17**, describe everything that is the same and everything that is different about each pair of figures. Then tell if the figures are congruent.

16.

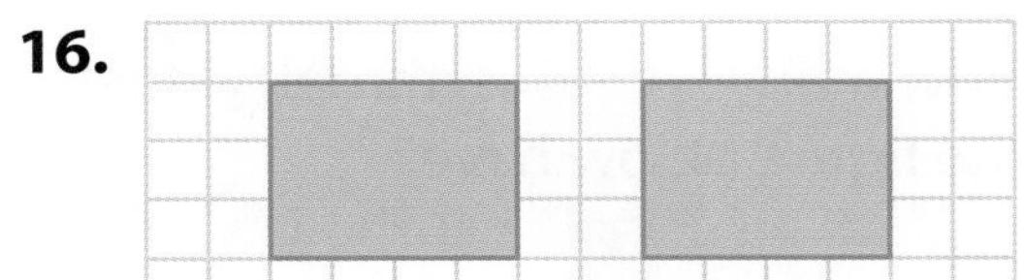

17.

18. Draw one line segment to connect the opposite corners of a rectangle. What polygons have you created? Are these polygons congruent?

19. On a bus ride, Kelsey counted 24 taxis and 12 buses. How many buses and taxis did she count in all?

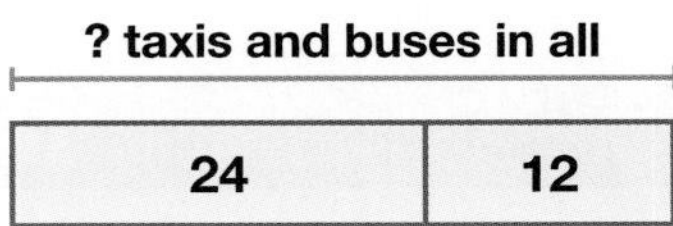

20. Reasoning Use the diagram below. Eliza wrote a message on paper and held it up to a mirror. What does the message say?

THIS IS A REFLECTION.

21. Terrence travels 25 minutes to get to work each day, but it takes him 40 minutes to get home. What is his travel time in hours and minutes?

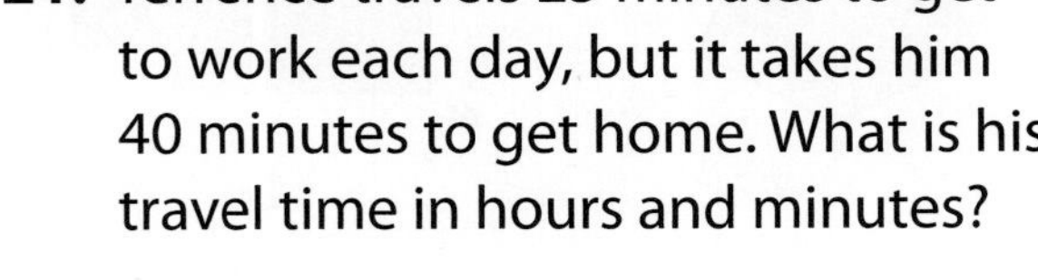

22. How many days are in 26 weeks?

A 33 days
B 142 days
C 182 days
D 365 days

DIGITAL Animated Glossary, eTools **www.pearsonsuccessnet.com**

Step-Up Lesson 17

TEKS 4.9C: Use reflections to verify that a shape has symmetry.

Line Symmetry

Hands-On
grid paper

What is a line of symmetry?

A figure is symmetric if it can be folded on a line to form two congruent halves that fit on top of each other.

The fold line is called a line of symmetry. This truck has one line of symmetry.

Guided Practice

Do you know HOW?

For **1** and **2**, tell if each line is a line of symmetry.

1. 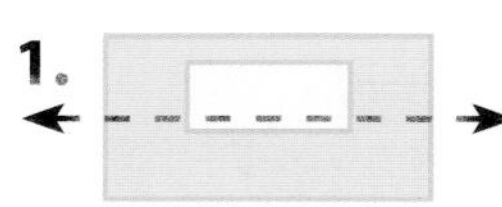

2. 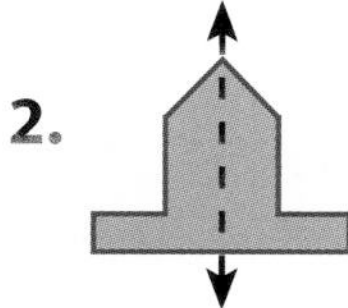

For **3** and **4**, tell how many lines of symmetry each figure has.

3. 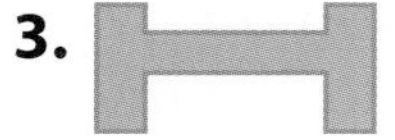

4. 

Do you UNDERSTAND?

5. Do some figures have no lines of symmetry?

6. How many lines of symmetry does the figure below have?

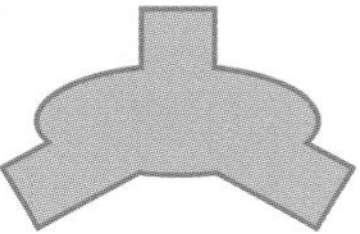

7. Writing to Explain How many lines of symmetry does a bicycle tire have?

Independent Practice

For **8** through **11**, tell if each line is a line of symmetry.

8. 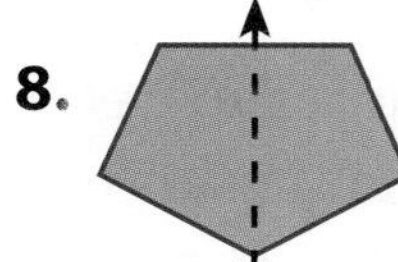

9. 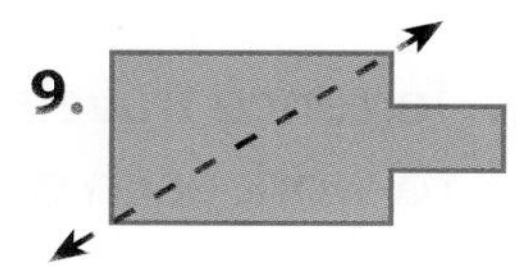

10. 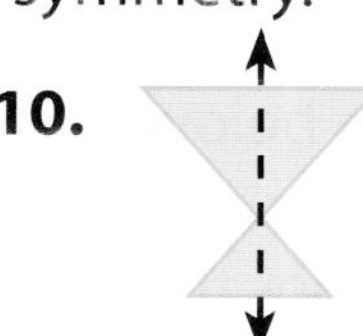

11. 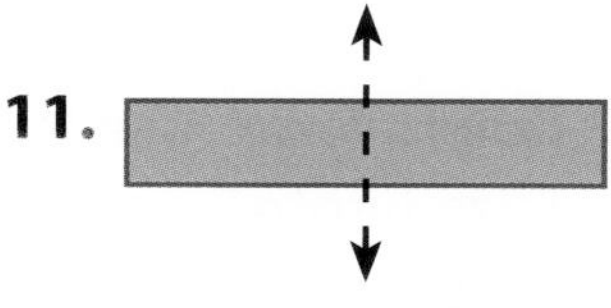

For **12** through **15**, tell how many lines of symmetry each figure has.

12. 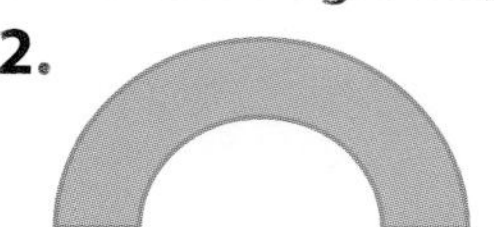

13. 

14. 

15. 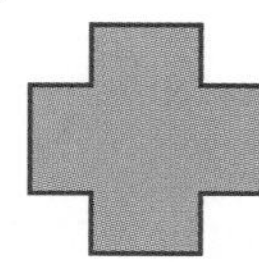

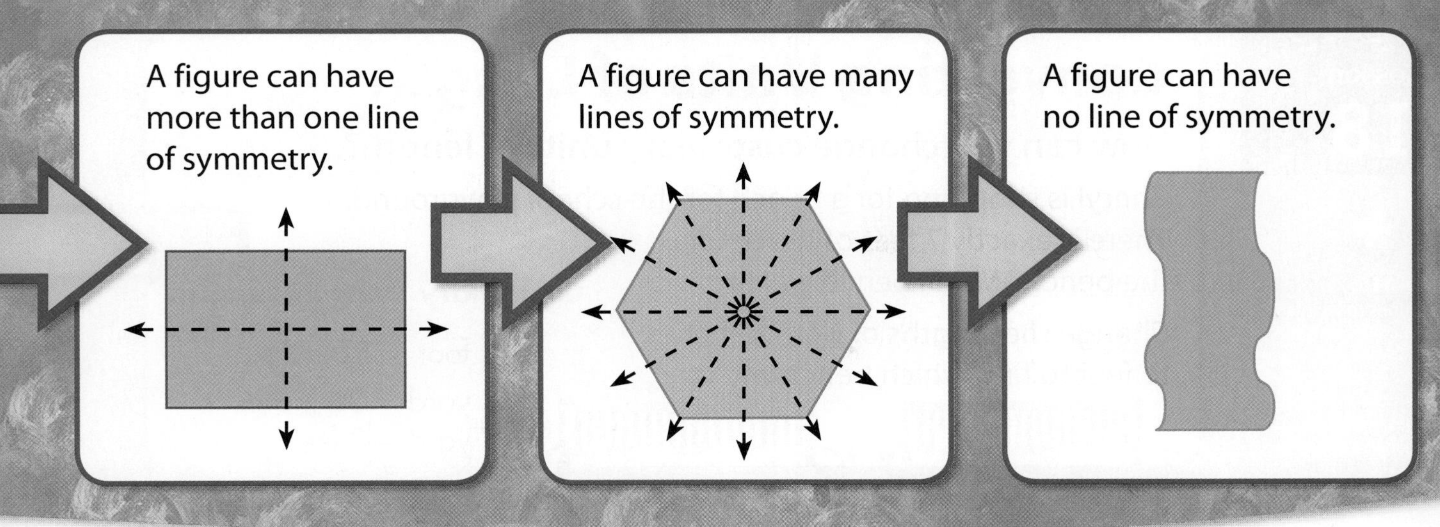

For **16** through **23**, trace each figure and draw lines of symmetry if you can.

16. 

17. 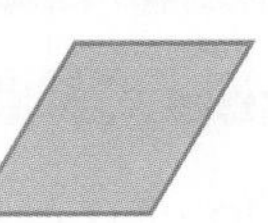

18. 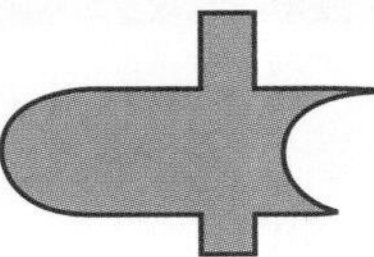

19. 

20. 

21. 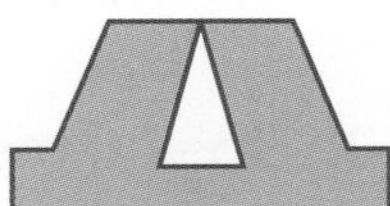

22. 

23. 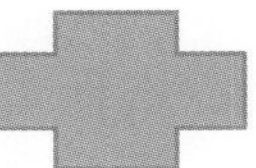

TAKS Problem Solving

24. How many lines of symmetry does the capital letter H have?

25. How many lines of symmetry does the capital letter J have?

26. **Reasoning** Maria drew a figure and said that it had an infinite number of lines of symmetry. What figure did she draw?

27. Draw a quadrilateral that does not have a line of symmetry.

28. The Alamo is a key symbol of Texas independence. Use the picture at the right to describe where the line of symmetry is.

29. Draw a triangle that has at least one line of symmetry.

30. How many lines of symmetry does a square have?

A None

B 2 lines

C 4 lines

D 6 lines

DIGITAL Animated Glossary, eTools **www.pearsonsuccessnet.com**

Step-Up Lesson 18

TEKS 4.11B: Perform simple conversions between different units of length, between different units of capacity, and between different units of weight within the customary measurement system.

Converting Units of Length

How can you change customary units of length?

Cheryl is shopping for a bench for the school playground. There is exactly 7 feet of space for the bench. Which bench will fit?

Change the lengths of both benches to feet to find which bench will fit.

Customary Units of Length
1 foot = 12 inches
1 yard = 36 inches 1 yard = 3 feet
1 mile = 5,280 feet 1 mile = 1,760 yards

Guided Practice

Do you know HOW?

For **1** through **8**, find each missing number.

1. 3 yd = ▢ ft **2.** 2 mi = ▢ ft

3. 36 ft = ▢ yd **4.** 72 in. = ▢ yd

5. 2 mi = ▢ yd **6.** 6 yd = ▢ in.

7. 60 in. = ▢ ft **8.** 9 yd = ▢ ft

Do you UNDERSTAND?

9. Do you multiply or divide to convert from feet to yards?

10. Do you multiply or divide to change feet to inches?

11. **Writing to Explain** The student council finds another bench that is 86 inches. Will this bench fit?

Independent Practice

Leveled Practice For **12** through **27**, find each missing number.

12. 12 ft = ▢ yd
12 ÷ 3 = ▢ yd

13. 48 in. = ▢ ft
48 ÷ 12 = ▢ ft

14. 36 in. = ▢ yd
36 ÷ 36 = ▢ yd

15. 3 mi = ▢ ft
3 × 5,280 = ▢ ft

16. 10 ft = ▢ in.
10 × 12 = ▢ in.

17. 6 yd = ▢ ft
6 × 3 = ▢ ft

18. 24 in. = ▢ ft
24 ÷ 12= ▢ ft

19. 3 mi = ▢ yd
3 × 1,760 = ▢ yd

20. 33 ft = ▢ yd **21.** 90 yd = ▢ ft **22.** 36 in. = ▢ ft **23.** 18 yd = ▢ ft

24. 1 mi = ▢ yd **25.** 72 in. = ▢ ft **26.** 12 in. = ▢ ft **27.** 10,560 ft = ▢ mi

To change smaller units to larger ones, divide.

82 inches = ▢ feet

12 inches = 1 foot. So, divide 82 inches by 12.

$$12\overline{)82} = 6 \text{ R}10$$
$$-72$$
$$10$$

82 inches = 6 feet 10 inches

Since this is less than 7 feet, this bench will fit.

To change larger units to smaller ones, multiply.

2 yards = ▢ feet

1 yard = 3 feet. So, multiply 2 yards by 3.

$2 \times 3 = 6$

2 yards = 6 feet

Since 6 feet is less than 7 feet, this bench will also fit.

TAKS Problem Solving

28. A super-stretch limousine is 20 feet long. A pickup truck is 228 inches long. Which is longer?

29. **Geometry** If one side of a square measures 6 inches long, what is the area of the square?

30. **Reasonableness** A newspaper reports that a giraffe's height is 180 inches, or 15 yards. What mistake was made?

31. A marathon is about 26 miles long. How many yards is this?

A 4,576 yd **C** 45,760 yd

B 13,728 yd **D** 137,280 yd

32. The longest tail feathers of any bird are those of the Argus Pheasant. The feathers measure 5 feet 7 inches in length. How many inches long are these feathers?

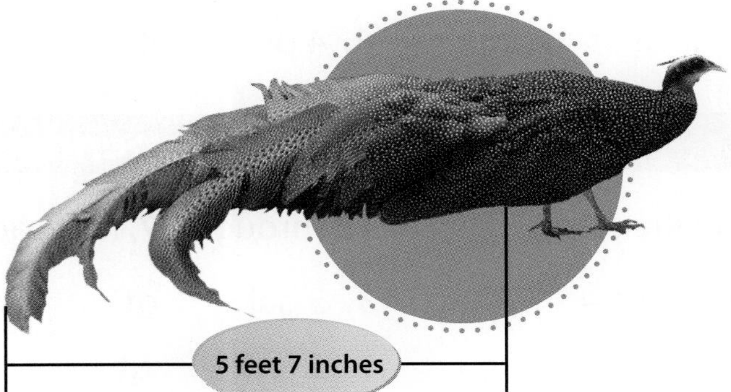

Use the information and the table at the right for **33** through **35**.

Data

Type of Bird	Width of Cage
Finch	18 inches
Parakeet	24 inches
Macaw	36 inches

33. Will 3 macaw cages fit side by side in the birdhouse if it is 10 feet wide?

34. Will 5 parakeet cages fit side by side in the birdhouse if it is 3 yards wide?

35. Suppose that 4 macaw cages fit side by side in a birdhouse. Will 8 finch cages fit in this same space?

Step-Up Lesson 19

TEKS 4.11B: Perform simple conversions between different units of length, between different units of capacity, and between different units of weight within the customary measurement system.

Converting Units of Capacity

How can you change customary units of capacity?

Alicia has 7 one-pint bottles of water. How many quarts of water does Alicia have?

How many one-cup glasses can she fill?

1 tablespoon (tbsp) = 3 teaspoons (tsp)
1 fluid ounce (fl oz) = 2 tablespoons
1 cup = 8 fluid ounces
1 pint = 2 cups
1 quart = 2 pints
1 gallon = 4 quarts

Guided Practice

Do you know HOW?

For **1** through **8**, find each missing number.

1. 12 qt = ☐ gal **2.** 2 c = ☐ fl oz

3. 7 gal= ☐ qt **4.** 5 pt = ☐ c

5. 32 fl oz = ☐ c **6.** 4 tbsp = ☐ tsp

7. 16 qt = ☐ gal **8.** 4 pt = ☐ qt

Do you UNDERSTAND?

9. Do you multiply or divide to convert fluid ounces to cups?

10. **Writing to Explain** In the second example above, why do you multiply?

11. Tom has 2 quarts of water. How many pints is this?

Independent Practice

Leveled Practice For **12** through **27**, find each missing number.

12. 6 pt = ☐ c
$6 \times 2 =$ ☐ c

13. 5 gal = ☐ qt
$5 \times 4 =$ ☐ qt

14. 32 fl oz = ☐ c
$32 \div 8 =$ ☐ c

15. 9 tsp = ☐ tbsp
$9 \div 3 =$ ☐ tbsp

16. 24 qt = ☐ gal
$24 \div 4 =$ ☐ gal

17. 12 pt = ☐ qt
$12 \div 2 =$ ☐ qt

18. 12 c = ☐ fl oz
$12 \times 8 =$ ☐ fl oz

19. 30 qt = ☐ pt
$30 \times 2 =$ ☐ pt

20. 18 qt = ☐ pt **21.** 80 fl oz = ☐ c **22.** 16 pt = ☐ qt **23.** 15 c = ☐ fl oz

24. 8 tbsp = ☐ tsp **25.** 20 c = ☐ pt **26.** 20 gal = ☐ qt **27.** 48 fl oz = ☐ c

To change smaller units to larger ones, divide.

7 pints = ▢ quarts

2 pints = 1 quart. So, divide 7 pints by 2.

$$\begin{array}{r} 3\text{ R}1 \\ 2\overline{)7} \\ -\underline{6} \\ 1 \end{array}$$

Alicia has 3 quarts and 1 pint of water.

To change larger units to smaller units, multiply.

7 pints = ▢ cups

1 pint = 2 cups. So, Multiply 7 pints by 2.

pt		pt		pt		pt		pt		pt		pt	
c	c	c	c	c	c	c	c	c	c	c	c	c	c

$7 \times 2 = 14$ cups

Alicia can fill 14 one-cup glasses.

TAKS Problem Solving

28. Craig is making a soup that calls for 8 cups of water. Can he mix the soup in a 1-quart pot? Explain.

qt				qt			
pt		pt		pt		pt	
c	c	c	c	c	c	c	c

29. Every day more than 17,000,000 gallons of water flow through the Trevi Fountain. How many quarts of water is this?

A 68 qt **C** 68,000 qt

B 6,800 qt **D** 68,000,000 qt

30. Geometry What is the perimeter of a rectangle that is 6 inches long and 2 inches wide?

6 inches

2 inches

31. Number Sense Without using a calendar, find the date three weeks after May 5th.

32. Writing to Explain A recipe calls for 3 quarts of milk. How many pints is this?

33. Writing to Explain Which unit of measure would you use to measure the length of a pencil?

34. Clint poured 11 cups of punch. Lisa poured 5 pints of punch. Ryan poured 3 quarts of punch. Who poured the most punch?

Step-Up Lesson 20

TEKS 4.11B: Perform simple conversions between different units of length, between different units of capacity, and between different units of weight within the customary measurement system.

Converting Units of Weight

How can you change units of weight?

A fruit company is shipping 30,000 pounds of peaches across the country. Each box in the shipment weighs 20 pounds.

How many tons of peaches are being shipped? How many ounces of peaches are in each box?

1 pound (lb) = 16 ounces (oz)

1 ton (T) = 2,000 pounds

Guided Practice

Do you know HOW?

For **1** through **8**, find each missing number.

1. 2 T = ☐ lb

2. 64 oz = ☐ lb

3. 48 oz = ☐ lb

4. 16,000 lb = ☐ T

5. 1,000 lb = ☐ oz

6. 7 lb = ☐ oz

7. 6,000 lb = ☐ T

8. 16 oz = ☐ lb

Do you UNDERSTAND?

9. Do you multiply or divide to convert from pounds to ounces?

10. Writing to Explain In the first example above, why do you divide?

11. The average peach weighs 8 ounces. If a small box holds 20 peaches, about how many pounds of peaches are in a small box?

Independent Practice

Leveled Practice For **12** through **27**, find each missing number.

12. 15 T = ☐ lb
15 × 2,000 = ☐ T

13. 5 lb = ☐ oz
5 × 16 = ☐ oz

14. 64 oz = ☐ lb
64 ÷ 16 = ☐ lb

15. 22,000 lb = ☐ T
22,000 ÷ 2,000 = ☐ T

16. 20 lb = ☐ oz
20 × 16 = ☐ T

17. 6 lb = ☐ oz
6 × 16 = ☐ oz

18. 32 oz = ☐ lb
32 ÷ 16 = ☐ lb

19. 24 T= ☐ lb
24 × 2,000 = ☐ lb

20. 6 T = ☐ lb

21. 160 oz = ☐ lb

22. 16 oz = ☐ lb

23. 10,000 lb = ☐ T

24. 3 lb = ☐ oz

25. 1 T = ☐ lb

26. 11 lb = ☐ oz

27. 60,000 lb = ☐ T

To change smaller units to larger ones, divide.

30,000 pounds = ▢ tons

2,000 pounds = 1 ton
Divide 30,000 pounds by 2,000.

Think $30 \div 2 = 15$
So, $30{,}000 \div 2{,}000 = 15$.

The shipment weighs 15 tons.

To change larger units to smaller ones, multiply.

20 pounds = ▢ ounces

1 pound = 16 ounces
Multiply 20 pounds by 16.

$20 \times 16 = 320$ ounces

There are 320 ounces of peaches in each box.

TAKS Problem Solving

28. Suppose there are 50 penguins in a colony, and each penguin eats 12 pounds of krill and 18 pounds of squid each day. How much food does the colony eat each day?

29. Mrs. Hanley uses a bowling ball that weighs 12 pounds. How many ounces does the bowling ball weigh?

A 120 oz **C** 172 oz

B 144 oz **D** 192 oz

Use the table at the right for **30** through **32**.

The weight of objects on other planets and the Moon is different than it is on Earth.

Approximate Weight of a 3rd-Grader

Earth	Jupiter	Venus	Moon
85 lb	215 lb	77 lb	14 lb

30. What is the approximate weight in ounces of a third grader on the Moon?

31. What is the approximate weight in ounces of a third grader on Venus?

32. **Writing to Explain** Would an adult weigh more on Earth or on Venus? Explain your reasoning.

33. Mateo bought 3 pounds of apples and 2 pounds of pears for a fruit salad. How many ounces of each did he purchase?

34. This air tanker fights fires using lake water. It refills its tanks by skimming the surface of a lake. If the plane can scoop up 4,000 pounds of water, how many tons of water can it carry?

Glossary

A.M. Time between midnight and noon.

acute angle An angle that measures less than a right angle.

acute triangle A triangle with three acute angles.

addends Numbers added together to give a sum.

Example: 2 + 7 = 9

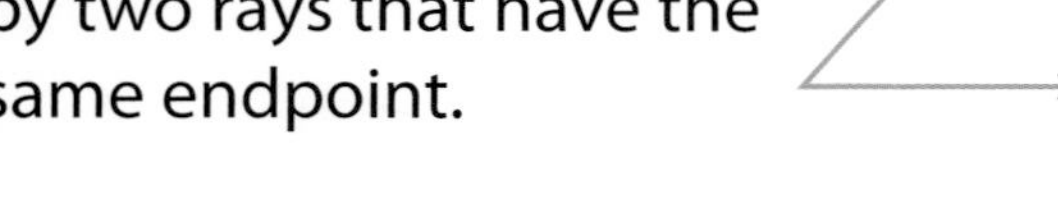

angle A figure formed by two rays that have the same endpoint.

area The number of square units needed to cover a region.

array A way of displaying objects in rows and columns.

Associative (Grouping) Property of Addition The grouping of addends can be changed and the sum will be the same.

Associative (Grouping) Property of Multiplication The grouping of factors can be changed and the product will be the same.

bar graph A graph using bars to show data.

capacity The volume of a container measured in liquid units.

centimeter (cm) A metric unit of length.

certain event An event that is sure to happen.

Commutative (Order) Property of Addition Numbers can be added in any order and the sum will be the same.

Commutative (Order) Property of Multiplication Numbers can be multiplied in any order and the product will be the same.

compare To decide if one number is greater than or less than another number.

compatible numbers Numbers that are easy to add, subtract, multiply or divide mentally.

cone A solid figure with a circle as its base and a curved surface that meets at a point.

congruent figures Figures that have the same shape and size.

corner Where 3 or more edges meet in a solid figure.

cube A solid figure with six faces that are congruent squares.

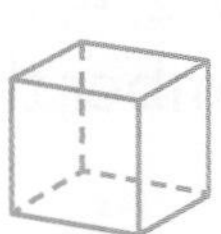

cubic unit A cube with edges 1 unit long, used to measure volume.

cup A customary unit of capacity.

cylinder A solid figure with two congruent circles as bases.

D

data Pieces of collected information.

decimal A number with one or more digits to the right of the decimal point.

decimal point A dot used to separate dollars from cents and ones from tenths in a number.

decimeter (dm) A metric unit of length. 1 decimeter equals 10 centimeters.

degree Celsius (°C) A metric unit of temperature.

degree Fahrenheit (°F) A customary unit of temperature.

denominator The number below the fraction bar in a fraction, the total number of equal parts in all.

difference The answer when subtracting two numbers.

digits The symbols 0, 1, 2, 3, 4, 5, 6, 7, 8, and 9 used to write numbers.

dividend The number to be divided.
Example: $63 \div 9 = 7$
(arrow pointing to 63: Dividend)

divisible Can be divided by another number without leaving a remainder.
Example: 10 is divisible by 2.

division An operation that tells how many equal groups there are or how many are in each group.

divisor The number by which another number is divided.
Example: $63 \div 9 = 7$
(arrow pointing to 9: Divisor)

dollar sign ($) A symbol used to indicate money.

E

edge A line segment where two faces of a solid figure meet.

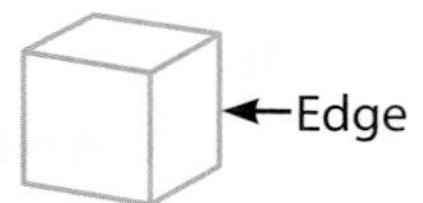

elapsed time Total amount of time that passes from the beginning time to the ending time.

equally likely outcomes Outcomes that have the same chance of happening.

equilateral triangle A triangle with all sides the same length.

equivalent fractions Fractions that name the same part of a whole, same part of a set, or same location on a number line.

estimate To give an approximate number or answer.

even number A whole number that has 0, 2, 4, 6, or 8 in the ones place; A number that is a multiple of 2.

expanded form A number written as the sum of the values of its digits.
Example: $2{,}476 = 2{,}000 + 400 + 70 + 6$

face A flat surface of a solid that does not roll.

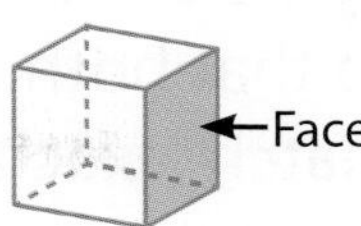

fact family A group of related facts using the same numbers.

factors Numbers that are multiplied together to give a product.
Example: $7 \times 3 = 21$
Factor Factor

foot (ft) A customary unit of length. 1 foot equals 12 inches.

fraction A symbol, such as $\frac{2}{8}$, $\frac{5}{1}$, or $\frac{5}{5}$, used to name a part of a whole, a part of a set, or a location on a number line.

gallon (gal) A customary unit of capacity. 1 gallon equals 4 quarts.

gram (g) A metric unit of mass, the amount of matter in an object.

half hour A unit of time equal to 30 minutes.

hexagon A polygon with 6 sides.

hour A unit of time equal to 60 minutes.

hundredth One of 100 equal parts of a whole.

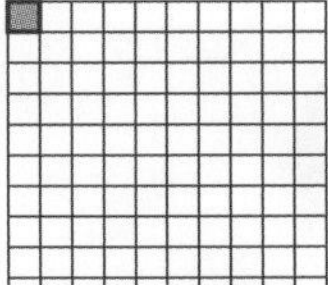

I

Identity (One) Property of Multiplication The product of any number and 1 is that number.

Identity (Zero) Property of Addition The sum of any number and zero is that same number.

impossible event An event that will never happen.

inch (in.) A customary unit of length.

inequality A number sentence that uses $<$ (less than) or $>$ (greater than).

intersecting lines Lines that cross at one point.

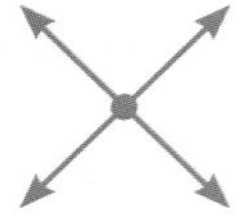

isosceles triangle A triangle with at least two sides the same length.

K

key Explanation of what each symbol represents in a pictograph.

kilogram (kg) A metric unit of mass, the amount of matter in an object. 1 kilogram equals 1,000 grams.

kilometer (km) A metric unit of length. 1 kilometer equals 1,000 meters.

L

likely event An event that will probably happen.

line A straight path of points that is endless in both directions.

line of symmetry A line on which a figure can be folded so that both parts match exactly.

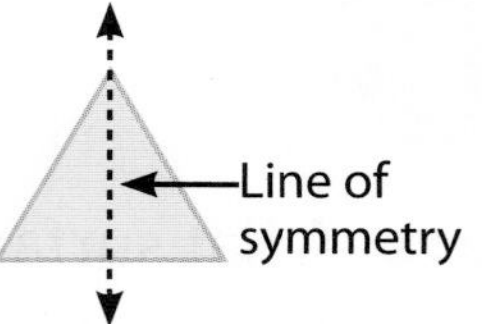

line segment A part of a line that has two endpoints.

liter (L) A metric unit of capacity. 1 liter equals 1,000 milliliters.

M

meter (m) A metric unit of length. 1 meter equals 100 centimeters.

mile (mi) A customary unit of length. 1 mile equals 5,280 feet.

milliliter (mL) A metric unit of capacity. 1,000 milliliters equals 1 liter.

millimeter (mm) A metric unit of length. 1,000 millimeters equals 1 meter.

minute A unit of time equal to 60 seconds.

mixed number A number with a whole number part and a fraction part.
Example: $2\frac{3}{4}$

month One of the twelve parts into which a year is divided.

multiple The product of the number and any other whole number.
Example: 0, 4, 8, 12, and 16 are multiples of 4.

multiplication An operation that gives the total number when you put together equal groups.

number line A line that shows numbers in order using a scale.
Example: 0 1 2 3 4

numerator The number above the fraction bar in a fraction.

numerical expression An expression that contains numbers and at least one operation. A numerical expression is also called a number expression.

obtuse angle An angle that measures more than a right angle.

obtuse triangle A triangle with one obtuse angle.

octagon A polygon with 8 sides.

odd number A whole number that has 1, 3, 5, 7, or 9 in the ones place; A number not divisible by 2.

order To arrange numbers from least to greatest or from greatest to least.

ounce (oz) A customary unit of weight.

outcome A possible result of a game or experiment.

P.M. Time between noon and midnight.

parallel lines Lines that never intersect.

parallelogram A quadrilateral in which opposite sides are parallel.

pentagon A polygon with 5 sides.

perimeter The distance around a figure.

period A group of three digits in a number, separated by a comma.

perpendicular lines Two lines that intersect to form right angles.

pictograph A graph using pictures or symbols to show data.

pint (pt) A customary unit of capacity. 1 pint equals 2 cups.

place value The value given to the place a digit has in a number. *Example:* In 3,946, the place value of the digit 9 is *hundreds.*

point An exact position often marked by a dot.

polygon A closed figure made up of straight line segments.

possible event An event that might or might not happen.

pound (lb) A customary unit of weight. 1 pound equals 16 ounces.

probability The chance an event will happen.

product The answer to a multiplication problem.

pyramid A solid figure whose base is a polygon and whose faces are triangles with a common point.

Q

quadrilateral A polygon with 4 sides.

quart (qt) A customary unit of capacity. 1 quart equals 2 pints.

quarter hour A unit of time equal to 15 minutes

quotient The answer to a division problem.

R

ray A part of a line that has one endpoint and continues endlessly in one direction.

rectangle A quadrilateral with four right angles.

rectangular prism A solid figure with faces that are rectangles.

reflection The change in the position of a figure that is the result of picking it up and turning it over.
Example:

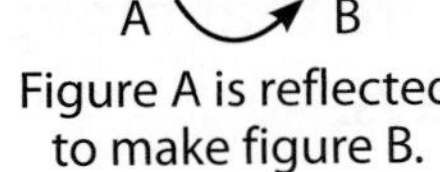

Figure A is reflected to make figure B.

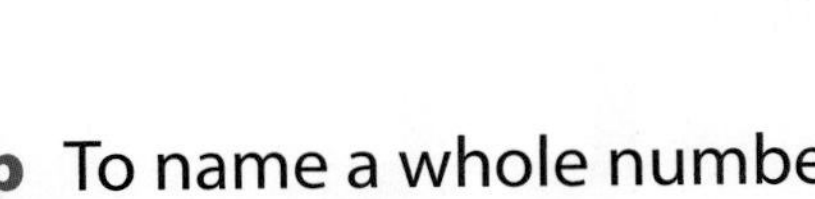

regroup To name a whole number in a different way.
Example: 28 = 1 ten 18 ones.

remainder The number that is left over after dividing.
Example: 31 ÷ 7 = 4R3

Remainder

rhombus A quadrilateral with opposite sides parallel and all sides the same length.

right angle An angle that forms a square corner.

right triangle A triangle with one right angle.

rotation The change in the position of a figure that moves it around a point.
Example:

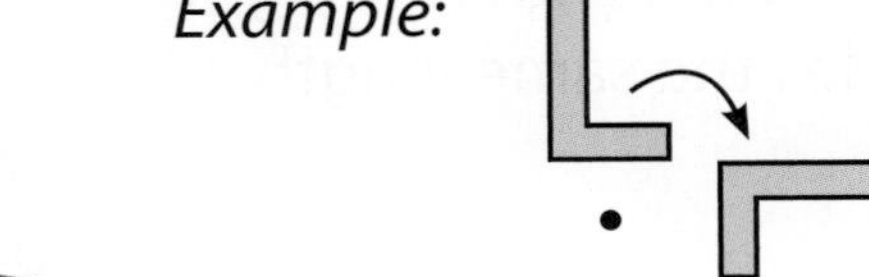

rounding Replacing a number with a number that tells about how much or how many to the nearest ten, hundred, thousand, and so on.
Example: 42 rounded to the nearest 10 is 40.

S

scale The numbers that show the units used on a graph.

scalene triangle A triangle with no sides the same length.

second A unit of time. 60 seconds equal 1 minute.

side A line segment forming part of a polygon.

solid figure A figure that has length, width, and height.

sphere A solid figure in the shape of a ball.

square A quadrilateral with four right angles and all sides the same length.

square unit A square with sides 1 unit long, used to measure area.

standard form A way to write a number showing only its digits.
Example: 3,845

sum The answer when adding two or more addends.
Example: 7 + 9 = 16
↑ Sum

survey Collecting information by asking a number of people the same question and recording their answers.

symmetric figure A figure that has at least one line of symmetry.

symmetry A figure has symmetry if it can be folded along a line so that both parts match exactly.

tally chart A chart on which data is recorded.

tally mark A mark used to record data on a tally chart.
Example: 𝍸 = 5

tenth One out of 10 equal parts of a whole.

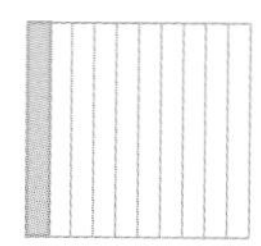

thermometer A device used to measure temperature.

translation The change in the position of a figure that moves it up, down, or sideways.
Example:

trapezoid A quadrilateral with only one pair of parallel sides.

triangle A polygon with 3 sides.

twice Two times a number.

unit fraction A fraction with a numerator of 1.
Example: $\frac{1}{2}$

unlikely event An event that probably won't happen.

vertex (plural, vertices) The point where two rays meet to form an angle. The points where the sides of a polygon meet. The points where 3 or more edges meet in a solid figure that does not roll. The pointed part of a cone.

volume The number of cubic units needed to fill a solid figure.

week A unit of time equal to 7 days.

word form A number written in words.
Example: 9,325 = nine thousand, three hundred twenty-five

yard (yd) A customary unit of length. 1 yard equals 3 feet or 36 inches.

year A unit of time equal to 365 days, or 52 weeks, or 12 months.

Zero Property of Multiplication The product of any number and zero is zero.

Cover

Luciana Navarro Powell

Illustrations

Dick Gage 8, 10, 14, 34, 55, 60, 164, 360, 416; Joe LeMonnier 8, 14, 223, 241-242, 256; Neil Stewart 58, 100, 140, 148, 164, 353, 358, 361-363, 366, 386; Leslie Kell 82, 96, 125, 138-139, 158, 161-162, 184, 192, 209-210, 225, 243, 255, 309, 327, 339, 345, 354, 368, 377, 381, 387

Photographs

Every effort has been made to secure permission and provide appropriate credit for photographic material. The publisher deeply regrets any omission and pledges to correct errors called to its attention in subsequent editions.

Unless otherwise acknowledged, all photographs are the property of Scott Foresman, a division of Pearson Education.

Photo locators denoted as follows: Top (T), Center (C), Bottom (B), Left (L), Right (R), Background (Bkgd).

Front Matter:

xvi ©Bob Mitchell/Corbis

2 (C) ©David R. Frazier Photolibrary, Inc./ Alamy, (TR) Roy Beusker/©Weijers Domino Productions b.v.; 3 (TL) ©Steve Bly/Alamy, (BL) ©Simon Belcher/Alamy; 6 Dave King/©DK Images; 12 (TR) ©Purestock/Alamy Images, (BR) Peter Wilson/©DK Images, (CR) ©Brad Perks Lightscapes/Alamy, (BC) Getty Images; 15 (CR) Jerry Young/©DK Images, (R) ©WizData, Inc./Alamy, (L) Dave King/©DK Images, (CL) ©Kennan Ward/Corbis; 19 ©John Van Hasselt/Corbis; 26 (TR) ©Ken Usami/ Getty Images, (BL) ©Bruce Coleman Inc./ Alamy Images, (BR) ©Christian Kober/Alamy Images; 27 ©Westend61/Alamy Images; 31 ©Wyman Meinzer; 34 (C) Getty Images, (L) ©IT Stock Free/Jupiter Images; 38 (BR) ©Westend61/Alamy Images, (CR) ©Kathleen Murtagh; 40 ©Royalty-Free/Corbis; 44 ©ImageDJ/Index Open; 50 Jupiter Images; 52 (C) ©Ron Watts/Corbis, (TR) ©Denny Ellis/Alamy; 53 ©Kristin Siebeneicher/AP Images; 62 (TR, CR) ©imagebroker/Alamy, (C) Frank Greenaway/©DK Images; 70 (L) ©Joe Tucciarone/Photo Researchers, Inc., (B) Bedrock Studios/©DK Images, (CR) ©Bo Zaunders/Corbis; 71 (TL) Getty Images, (B) Frans Lanting Photography; 76 Getty Images; 79 ©David Wootton/Alamy Images; 92 (B) ©David R. Frazier Photolibrary, Inc./Alamy Images, (CR) ©blickwinkel/fotototo/Alamy Images, (TR) Getty Images; 93 (TL) ©Wyman Meinzer, (B) ©Miodrag Nejkovic/Alamy Images; 102 ©David R. Frazier Photolibrary, Inc./Alamy Images; 114 ©Kevin Schafer/ zefa/Corbis; 115 ©Jill Stephenson/Alamy; 123 Golden Dollar Obverse ©1999 United States Mint. All Rights Reserved. Used with permission.; 134 (TR) Getty Images, (BR) Jupiter Images; 136 (L) ©Joe McBride/Aurora/ Getty Images, (CR) ©Hulton Archive/Getty Images; 137 (TL) ©Geoff Dann/Dorling Kindersley/Getty Images, (BL) ©London Express/Getty Images; 151 (CR) ©Photos Select/Index Open, (CR) ©ImageDJ/Index Open; 153 Getty Images; 156 (TL) ©Geoff du Feu/Alamy, (B) ©Les Chatfield, (TL) ©D. Robert & Lorri Franz/Corbis; 157 (BL) NASA/JPL-Caltech/M. Kelley (Univ. of Minnesota)/NASA, (TL) ©J. Rockey Haley; 180 (T) ©Bill Rambow/Mid-Atlantic Air Museum, (BL) ©Stephen Street/Alamy Images, (BR) ©Douglas Faulkner/Alamy Images; 181 (TL) ©Mike Hill/Alamy Images, (BL) ©Jim Cummins/Corbis; 194 ©Alain Dragesco-Joffe/ Animals Animals/Earth Scenes; 196 ©Bill Romerhaus/Index Open; 204 (B) NASA, (TR) Getty Images; 205 (TL) ©Rubberball/Getty Images, (BL) ©Greg Vaughn/Alamy Images; 212 Getty Images; 228 (CR) ©Archivberlin Fotoagentur GmbH/Alamy Images, (C) ©Juniors Bildarchiv/Alamy Images; 236 (TR) ©Allen Matheson/Photohome, (B) ©Photowood Inc./Corbis, (CC) Getty Images; 237 (TL) ©Lester V. Bergman/Corbis, (BL) Dream Maker Software; 243 ©Allen Matheson/Photohome; 245 ©Lester V. Bergman/Corbis; 260 (TR) ©Directphoto/ Alamy, (CL) ©Kike Calvo/VWPICS/Alamy Images, (B) ©Panoramic Images/Getty Images; 261 Digital Vision; 265 ©Directphoto/ Alamy; 266 Jupiter Images; 270 ©Alissa Crandall/Corbis; 286 ©Jamal Saidi/Corbis; 287 (TC) ©WildPictures/Alamy Images, (TL) ©Ed Reschke/Peter Arnold/Alamy Images, (B) ©Danita Delimont/Alamy Images; 296 (TR) ©James Robinson/Animals Animals/ Earth Scenes, (TR) ©John T. Fowler/Alamy Images, (TC) ©David M. Dennis/Animals Animals/Earth Scenes; 304 (TL) ©Desmond Boylan/Reuters Media, (B) ©Baron Wolman/ Getty Images; 305 (TC) ©Alan Weintraub/ Alamy Images, (B) ©Andy King/Orange Dot Productions; 306 (BL) Jupiter Images, (BR) ©photolibrary/Index Open; 307 (BL) ©Vstock/Index Open, (BC) ©photolibrary/ Index Open; 308 Getty Images; 313 (TR, C, BR) Getty Images, (CR) Jupiter Images; 315 ©Baron Wolman/Getty Images; 319 ©Alan Weintraub/Alamy Images; 323 ©Andy King/Orange Dot Productions; 332 (B, TR) Getty Images, (CL) ©Bettmann/Corbis; 341 ©Photos Select/Index Open; 348 (B) ©Creatas/Jupiter Images, (TL) Digital Vision; 349 (TL) ©Mary Evans Picture Library/Alamy Images, (BL) ©Wolfgang Pölzer/Alamy Images; 351 Jupiter Images; 354 (CL) ©photolibrary/Index Open, (CL) Corbis, (BL) Getty Images; 355 (TR) Jupiter Images, (CL, CR) ©Photos Select/Index Open, (B) ©Mistral Images/Index Open; 357 Getty Images; 358 ©Grady Harrison/Alamy Images; 360 (T) ©Creatas, (CL) Digital Vision, (BL) Hemera Technologies, (BR) ©Foodcollection/Getty Images, (CL) ©photolibrary/Index Open; 361 (CL) ©Jim Lane/Alamy Images, (CR) ©Michele Westmorland/Corbis, (R) Jupiter Images, (BL, C) Getty Images; 364 ©PCL/Alamy Images; 369 (L) Getty Images, (R) Corbis; 370 (TR) Stockdisc, (CR) ©Photos Select/Index Open; 372 ©Ablestock/Index Open; 374 (CL, TR) ©Jeff Saward/Labyrinthos Picture Library, (BR) ©Richard Schulman/Corbis, (BL) Photo courtesy of Pleasant Time Industries; 375 ©Ken Kuhl; 379 ©W. Blaine Pennington Photo; 390 (TR) ©Ingrid van den Berg/AGE Fotostock, (CC) ©Gary Cralle/Getty Images; 391 (BL) ©Gary Roberts/Rex USA, (TL) Getty Images; 396 (CR) ©Image Source Limited, (BL) ©Comstock Inc., (BC) G. Huntington, (BR) Jupiter Images; 397 ©Simple Stock Shots; 398 (TR) ©Royalty-Free/Corbis, (BL, CL, R) Getty Images, (BR) ©D. Hurst/Alamy, (L) Jupiter Images, (TR) ©Mark Duffy/Alamy; 399 ©AP Images; 400 (CL) ©photolibrary/Index Open, (BR) ©Simple Stock Shots; 401 (BC) Hemera Technologies, (BR) ©Juergen & Christine Sohns/Animals Animals/Earth Scenes; 402 (CR) Stockdisc, (BL) Jupiter Images, (BC) Getty Images; 406 (C) Getty Images, (B) Corbis, (T) ©Vstock/Index Open; 407 Jupiter Images; 408 (CR) Stockdisc, (BR) ©Royalty-Free/Corbis, (CR) ©Photos Select/Index Open, (BL) Jupiter Images; 409 (TC) ©MIXA/Getty Images, (CL) Getty Images, (CR) ©photolibrary/Index Open, (CR) ©Hot Ideas/Index Open; 412 (TR) ©Rainer Hackenberg/Corbis, (B) ©Thinkstock/ Jupiter Images, (CL) ©David Maitland/ Getty Images; 413 NASA Image Exchange; 421 (T, CR) Getty Images, (BR) Jupiter Images; 428 (CR) ©Ronald Martinez/Getty Images, (L) ©Eric Hosking/Corbis; 429 (BL) ©Adam Pretty/Getty Images, (TL) ©Ingram Publishing/Jupiter Images; 440 ©Timothy Laman/National Geographic/Getty Images; 443 ©Ingram Publishing/Jupiter Images; 454 ©VStock/Index Open; 459 ©Steve Vidler/ SuperStock; 466 GSFC/NASA; 487 ©Dean Fox/SuperStock; 488 Jupiter Images; 489 ©Dr. John Corder; 491 ©Royalty-Free/Corbis; 493 (L) ©Royalty-Free/Corbis, (LC) Getty Images, (B) Courtesy of Air Tractor, Inc., (CR) Digital Vision, (R) Jupiter Images

Index

Scott Foresman · Addison Wesley

enVisionMATH™

Texas

Scott Foresman • Addison Wesley

enVisionMATH™

Texas